Spencer Dayton.

THE
History of Barbour County,

West Virginia,

From its Earliest Exploration and Settlement to the Present Time.

ILLUSTRATED.

BY

HU MAXWELL.

Southern Historical Press, Inc.
Greenville, South Carolina

This volume was reproduced
from a personal copy located in
the Publishers private library

All rights reserved. No part of this publication may be reproduced,
stored in a retrieval system, transmitted in any form, posted
on the web in any form or by any means without the
prior written permission of the publisher.

Please direct all correspondence and book orders to:
SOUTHERN HISTORICAL PRESS, Inc.
1071 Park West Blvd.
Greenville, SC 29611

Published Morganton, WV 1899
New Material Copyright 2025:
   Southern Historical Press, Inc
ISBN #978-1-63914-647-5
Printed in the United States of America

INTRODUCTION.

This book is divided into three parts. Part First treats of the State in general; Part Second of the county in particular; and Part Third of biography. The territory now embraced in Barbour County formed a part of Virginia from the first settlement about 1607 till 1863, when it became a portion of West Virginia. During that period it was, in succession, in Essex County, in Spotsylvania, Orange, Augusta, West Augusta, Monongalia, Harrison, Randolph and Barbour. It became a separate county in 1843. The territory east of the Valley River was taken from Randolph, that west was taken from Harrison and Lewis. This book was written in the spring and summer of 1899, and the material (much of it collected long before) was gathered from every available source. Many persons in the county encouraged and assisted the effort; many did not. The county officials, and especially the clerks of the courts, Richard E. Talbott and Granville E. Taft, helped in every way possible. Many others in professional or private life contributed to the success of the work. Where so many did much, it seems partial to single out a few for particular mention; yet justice would not be done if the names of Spencer Dayton, Joshua S. Corder, Lewis Wilson and John Hopkins Woods were omitted. Valuable information, relating to the beginning of the Civil War within Barbour County, was furnished by Colonel George A. Porterfield, of Charlestown, West Virginia. Lists of Confederate soldiers from Barbour were furnished by Benjamin Holly Woodford, of this county, and by George W. Printz, of Randolph. Data concerning agricultural matters were contributed by the Farmers' Institute. In the collection of biographical and miscellaneous notes, special credit is due to A. F. Hawkins, of Philippi, and Winfield S. Lang, of Meadowville. For the names of others who assisted in the most substantial way to make the History of Barbour County a success, the reader is referred to the list of subscribers published in this book.

There are three thousand families in Barbour, no member of which took interest in or contributed toward the success of this book. Each one of them probably has a reason for not doing so, which, to himself, is satisfactory. So let them rest. History passes them in silence. Yet, in the criticisms of this enterprise, as of all enterprises, it will be found that those who encouraged it least and contributed nothing to its success, will be first to find fault and the loudest in proclaiming it.

Philippi, W. Va., Nov. 1, 1899.

TABLE OF CONTENTS.

———:o:———

Part First.

	PAGE.
Chapter I. Explorations West of Blue Ridge	19
Chapter II. Indians and Moundbuilders	25
Chapter III. The French and Indian War	29
Chapter IV. The Dunmore War	39
Chapter V. West Virginia in the Revolution	47
Chapter VI. Subdivisions and Boundaries	57
Chapter VII. The Newspapers of West Virginia	66
Chapter VIII. Geography, Geology and Climate	71
Chapter IX. Among Old Laws	83
Chapter X. Constitutional History	89
Chapter XI. John Brown's Raid	105
Chapter XII. The Ordinance of Secession	109
Chapter XIII. The Reorganized Government	113
Chapter XIV. Formation of West Virginia	120
Chapter XV. Organizing for War	126
Chapter XVI. Progress of the War	138
Chapter XVII. Chronology of the War	147

Part Second.

Chapter XVIII. Settlements and Indian Troubles	175
Chapter XIX. Notes from the Records	198
Chapter XX. The Civil War in Barbour	247
Chapter XXI. Miscellanies	276

Part Third.

Chapter XXII. Family History	335

ILLUSTRATIONS.

―――:o:―――

Maps and Diagrams.

Map of Hampshire County in 1755....................................61
Map of Augusta County in 1772....................................172
Map of the District of West Augusta...............................175
Map of Washington's Canal Route..................................177
Map Showing Indian Trails...179
Map of Randolph County in 1787..................................199
Map of Philippi and Vicinity.......................................252
Map of Flatwood and Vicinity.....................................298

Autographs.

Autographs of Early Randolph County Justices....................200
Autographs of Early Randolph County Sheriffs....................201
Autographs of Barbour County Circuit Clerks.....................230
Autographs of Barbour County Clerks.............................230
Autographs of Randolph County Circuit Clerks....................230
Autographs of Circuit Judges.....................................231
Autographs of Barbour County Sheriffs...........................232
Autographs of Presidents of Boards of Supervisors................235

Residences, Etc.

Residence of Melville Peck..175
Residence of A. G. Dayton..195
Residence of Samuel V. Woods....................................212
Residence of J. Hop. Woods......................................233
Mansfield Flouring Mill..262
Dyer & Switzer's Store..262
Residence of Granville E. Taft....................................273
Residence of J. E. Hall..292
A Farm Scene..323
Peel Tree Postoffice...343
The Dickenson Monument..383
Residence of Ai Cleavenger.......................................383
Residence of G. H. Hamrick......................................390
Residence of Sylvanus Talbott....................................433
A. W. Woodford's Farm...505
Residence of Dr. E. D. Talbot....................................512

ILLUSTRATIONS.

Historical Buildings and Places.

Fort Henry Attacked by British and Indians 54
First Courthouse in West Virginia................................88
Site of the Files Cabin 181
First Courthouse in Randolph County...............................181
Grave of the Connollys...181
Philippi...182
The Horseshoe Fort 189
The Minear Fort..190
Scene of the Murder of John Minear 191
Bridge at Philippi 202
Barbour County Courthouse 202
Talbott Hill 259
Battlefield of Rich Mountain 265
Nobusiness Hill..276
The Philippi Bridge 277
Simeon Harris' Old Chimney 310
Brushy Fork Iron Furnace 317
First Courthouse in Harrison County 394
Second Courthouse in Randolph County............................394
Westfall's Fort 394
Lewis Wilson's Mill...508
Wilson Homestead 511

Geological Diagrams, Etc.

The Erosion of Laurel Hill (4 cuts)................................292
Rock Column in Randolph County 296
Rock Column in Barbour County 296
Depths of Erosion 297
Prehistoric Valley at Flatwood....................................300
Rock Section at Brushy Fork 318
Mechanism of Artesian Wells.....................................319
The Philippi Artesian Well.......................................319
An Ideal Oil-Bearing Anticline 320
Elk City Gas Well 344
Wells Falls..344
Beech Glen Falls 364
Hanging Rock...433

Portraits.

Allen, Lewis	89
Arnett, U. N.	89
Atkinson, J. H.	89
Bowman, Stuart H.	282
Bartlett, Elder J. N.	332
Bartlett, B. B.	332
Barnes, G. W.	333
Bibey, R. M.	345
Bradford, T. A.	384
Brock, Mr. and Mrs. J. F.	384
Bartlett, W. J.	423
Bowman, Capt. A. C.	433
Bowman, L. C.	433
Barbe, Rev. S.	459
Bartlett, P. F.	488
Bartlett, E. M.	488
Byrnside, J. M.	89
Bassell, John	89
Bee, Isaiah	89
Byrne, B. W.	89
Brown, Wm. G.	89
Butcher, B. H.	89
Coonts, Adam	335
Coonts, Adam T.	333
Coffman, James	333
Campbell, Geo. A.	345
Corder, Elder, J. S.	353
Chrislip, A. G.	464
Campbell, Alexan'r	89
Criswell, Hanson	89
Cushing, Alonzo	89
Calfee, James	89
Crim, J. N. B.	89
Core, W. G. H.	89
Cunningham, A. J.	89
Digman, J. D.	332
Davis, J. A.	333
Dyer, Mr. and Mrs. E. R.	364
Dayton, A. G.	373
Dennisson, J. M.	433
Dadisman, Ira L.	459
Dayton, Spencer Fronticepiece	
Dickinson, H. M.	89
Davenport, Geo. O.	89
Elliott, Rev. J. B.	344
Elliott, Guy C.	344
Fitzwater, Jesse	332
Foreman, Naylor	459
Faulkner, C. J.	89
Fitzhugh, Nicholas	89
Ferguson, C. W.	89
Ferrell, Thomas	89
Gainer, Sylvia A.	332
Gall, Mr. & Mrs. J. J.	332
Gall, R. B.	332
George, W. T.	364
Goode, John	459
Graham, Grant	459
Gall, D. W.	464
Gawthrop, J. W.	488
Gallaher, J. W.	89
Galligan, Barney	89
Gall, Mrs. G. W.	512
Gall, Bessie	512
Gall, Enda C.	512
Haymond, Luther	283
Hall, J. E.	292
Harris, John, sr.	332
Harris, Mr. & Mrs. H. C.	332
Hoff, Henson L.	333
Harris, Geo. A.	345
Holsberry, Dr. F. S.	345
Holsberry, L. V.	397
Hulderman, W. T.	364
Hoff, Dr. & Mrs. M. M.	433
Hamrick, G. H.	459
Hathaway, J. P.	459
Hawkins, A. F.	459
Hawkins, A. S.	459
Haymond, A. F.	89
Hoge, John Blair	89
Haynes, Wm.	89
Hall, Septimus	89
Holt, Homer A.	89
Harding, J. F.	89
Hagans, J. M.	89
Ice, Mr. and Mrs. Daniel	345
Isner, J. B. and family	384
Ice, Judge Wm. T.	404
Jackson, R. E.	332
Jones, A. W.	332
Jenkins, Capt. W. K.	333
Johnson, I. V.	364
Jenkins, H. M.	459
Jones, Rev. J. L. B.	438
Jackson, James M.	89
Johnson, D. D.	89
Johnson, Okey	89
Jackson, Blackwell	89
Kittle, George M.	345
Kelley, Columbus	423
Kittle, W. B.	464
Knight, E. B.	89
Kantner, Charles	89
Lang, W. S.	344
Lang, J. L.	344
Lantz, Mr. and Mrs. Willis	343
Lang, Lieut. Col. D. B.	413
Lough, M. C.	423
Leonard, D. H.	89
Lurty, B. H.	89
Mason, Rev. J. L.	332
Montgomery, Mrs. Susan	333
Moore, Mr. and Mrs. S. A.	344
Miller, Jacob	344
McLean, C. L.	364
McLean, E. P.	364
Morrall, Mr. & Mrs. L. D.	453
McKinney, Delbert	488
Murphy, Dr. & Mrs. F. B.	488
Miller, W. W.	89
Martin, B. F.	89
Mathews, H. M.	89
Maslin, Thomas	89
Moffitt, G. H.	89
McCleary, A. W.	89

PORTRAITS.

Morgan, W. A.	89	
Monroe, Alex	89	
McCreery, Wm.	89	
O'Neal, S. L.	292	
Osburn, Logan	89	
Phillips, Miss May	232	
Phillips, J. M.	232	
Pitts, W. A.	233	
Pepper, Mrs. S. D.	333	
Price, Samuel	89	
Pendleton, W. K.	89	
Pawnell, A. J.	89	
Pipes, J. M.	89	
Price, Wm.	89	
Pate, Wm. D.	89	
Pearce, J. T.	89	
Park, T. R.	89	
Pugh, D. A.	89	
Porterfield, Col. Geo. A.	253	
Price, H. H.	332	
Poling, Isaac	345	
Poling, Mrs. Rachel	344	
Phillips, J. C.	432	
Poling, Rev. Cyrus	459	
Ryan, H. H.	332	
Reed, Miss Ida L.	333	
Robinson, L. D. and family	343	
Robinson, Wm.	459	
Reger, J. T.	470	
Rohrbaugh, B. B.	470	
Rohrbough, A. F.	470	
Robinson, Mr. and Mrs. J. W.	488	
Reed, S. F.	503	
Roberts, D. A.	89	
Robinson, J. A.	89	
Randolph, J. F.	89	
Semmelman, C. A.	332	

Strawderman, Samuel	333	
Shank, Mr. and Mrs. J. W.	333	
Switzer, Charles L.	332	
Stewart, Mr. and Mrs. J. E.	345	
Stipe, Geo. E.	364	
Strickler, Isaac H.	383	
Sturm, Mr. and Mrs. David	383	
Shomo, C. W.	433	
Switzer, P. A.	459	
Smith, Mrs. Melissa	459	
Strickler, A. D. W.	459	
Shaw, D. W.	497	
Stalnaker, W. W.	488	
Shaw, John C.	488	
Shaw, Joseph C.	488	
Smith, Fountain	89	
Snyder, Joseph	89	
Strickler, J. P.	89	
Staton, M. A.	89	
Stump, Lemuel	89	
Teter, Joseph	442	
Talbott, S. S.	459	
Talbott, R. E.	464	
Talbott, W. W.	479	
Talbott, Mrs. W. W.	479	
Talbott, L. W.	479	
Talbott, Mary F.	479	
Talbott, A. I.	479	
Talbott, Virginia B.	479	
Talbott, S. L.	479	
Talbott, R. D.	479	
Talbott, Floyd	479	
Talbott, Rosa M.	479	
Talbott, E. D.	479	
Talbott, F. L.	479	
Talbott, W. T.	479	
Talbott, R. M.	488	
Travers, W. H.	89	
Thornburg, Thos.	89	

Thayer, A. H.	89
Thompson, J. J.	89
Talbot, Dr. and Mrs. E. D.	512
Talbot, D. C.	512
Talbot, M. C.	512
Utterback, G. W.	333
Woods, Samuel V.	223
Woods, Judge Samuel	243
Woods, J. Hop	509
Wentz, W. H.	303
Wilson, Lewis	312
Woodford, A. W.	323
Woodford, D. R.	332
Willoughby, J. C.	332
Wilson, A. C.	344
Ware, J. B.	384
Ware, J. K.	432
Wolverton, Alba	458
Woodford, J. F.	485
Woodford, B. H.	485
Woodford, Jacob	488
Wheat, J. S.	89
Wilson, Benjamin	89
Willey, W. T.	89
Waggener, C. B.	89
Ward, Evermont	89
Warth, J. A.	89
Wetzel, D. J.	89
Yowell, Franklin	333
Yowell, James	333
Young, Miss Clara	322
Zinn, A. J.	332
Zinn, Sylvanus	345
Zinn, W. D.	459
Zirkle, J. H.	470
Zinn, D. W.	488
Zirkle, C. I.	503

LIST OF SUBSCRIBERS.

Arnett, W. S.

Bailey, R. M.
Barbe, Rev. S.
Barnes, George W.
Bartlett, Mrs. Rebecca.
Bartlett, H. C.
Bartlett, B. B.
Bartlett, Elder J. N.
Bartlett, Miss Bertha.
Bennett, C. S.
Blue, Fred O.
Boehm, E. W.
Bolton, N. B.
Bolton, W. T.
Bolyard, James.
Bowman, Captain A.C.
Bowman, L. C.
Boyles, Barnet.
Boyles, Daniel.
Boyles, Charles.
Boyles, J. I.
Brooks, S. L.
Brock, John F.
Bradford, Alex S.
Brock, James P.
Burgess, Rev. J. M.
Burner, R. B.

Campbell, George.
Carder, Reuben B.
Carder, J. M.
Carlin, J. G.
Cleavenger, James W.
Cleavenger, Ai.
Cleavenger, C. W.
Cleavenger, James K.
Chrislip, A. G.
Corder, Elder Joshua S.
Corder, W. A.
Corder, W. B.
Corder, Coney E.
Cole, John R.
Coffman, James.
Compton, E. H.
Coonts, Isaac J.

Coonts, Adam T.
Coonts, Frederick M.
Cox, William A.
Crim, J. N. B.
Cross, Elder J. B.

Dadisman, C. G.
Dadisman, Ira L.
Daugherty, Henry C.
Davis, John A.
Dayton, A. G. (3 copies)
Dennisson, J. M.
Dickenson, G. W.
Digman, J. D.
Durrett, F. B.
Dyer, E. R.

Ekis, J. H.
Elbon, W. A.
Elliott, L. C.
Elliott, J. B.
Elliott, Guy C.

Felton, Samuel D.
Felton, James H.
Felton, Capt. John C.
Foreman, Naylor.

Gall, D. W. (4 copies.)
Gall, John J., jr.
Gall, John J.
Gall, Andrew J.
Gainer, John W.
Gawthrop, J. W.
George, W. T.
Goode, John M.
Graham, Grant.

Hall, J. E.
Hamilton, A.
Haller, George E.
Hamrick, J. N.
Hamrick, D. P.
Harris, H. C.
Harris, George A.
Harbaugh, Mrs. J. E.

Haskins, Ryland G.
Hawkins, A. F. (3 cop.)
Hathaway, J. P.
Heatherly, L. E.
Hewitt, John F.
Hoff, Dr. M. M.
Hoff, O. P.
Hoff, Mrs. Emily.
Hoffman, John D.
Holsberry, J. K.
Holsberry, L. V.
Holsberry, J. D.
Hovey, J. M. R.
Howell, John.
Howell, G. T.
Holden, Floyd T.
Hulderman, W. T.
Hymes, G. S.

Ice, Hon. W. T.
Ice, Martin
Isner, James B.

Jackson, R. E.
Jenning, L. A.
Jenkins, Capt. W. K.
Jenkins, H. M.
Johnson, J. L.
Johnson, R. M.
Johnson, Levi,
Johnson, Hon. I. V.
Jones, Rev. J. L. B.
Jones, Albert W.

Kelley, Columbus
Kelley, J. L. B.

Kinsman, Mrs. O. D.
Kittle, George M.
Kittle, W. B.
Knapp, J. H.
Knight, E. L.

Lang, W. S.
Lantz, W. H.
Lantz, Willis

LIST OF SUBSCRIBERS.

Law, T. A.
Lough, Myron C.

Main, Mrs. S. J.
Mann, John C.
Mason, Rev. J. F.
Marks, O. T.
Mason, T. B.
Martin, I. D.
Means, J. E.
McCutcheon, R. A.
McCutcheon, H. K.
McLean, Jacnb
McKinney, Delbert
Miller, A. K.
Miller, John H.
Montgomery, Mrs. Susan
Moore, S. A.
Moore, Jethro
Murphy, T. J.
Murphy, Dr. F. B.

O'Neal, S. L.
Owen, F. J.

Parks, Noah S.
Payne, Charles E.
Peck, Melville
Pepper, S. D.
Phillips, Washington.
Phillips, F. C.
Phillips, Mrs. Virginia
Phillips, Granville
Phillips, J. M.
Phillips, Miss May
Pitts, W. A.
Poling, Aldine S.
Poling, I. C.
Poling, Rev. Cyrus, (3 copies)
Poling, R. D.
Poling, I. M.
Poling, C. H.
Poling, Laura A.
Poling, Mrs. Rachel H.
Poling, Wade
Poling, L. S.
Poling, J. S.
Porterfield, Col. G. A.
Price, W. G. W.

Proudfoot, D. M.
Proudfoot, J. R.

Racer, M. D.
Reed, Stuart F.
Reed, Milton D.
Reger, John T.
Right, G. M.
Riley, M. D.
Robinson, J. W.
Robinson, L. D.
Robinson, Ira
Rohrbough, B. B.
Rohrbough, C. L.
Rohrbough, Amos F.
Rosenberger, H. C.
Ryan, H. H.

Sammelman, S. L.
See, Rev. C. S. M.
Shaw, John C.
Shaw, D. W.
Shank, John W.
Shomo, C. W.
Shroyer, J. W.
Simon, Andrew
Simon, A. D.
Snodgrass, C. W.
Smith, Eskar T.
Strader, Aaron
Stalnaker, G. J.
Stalnaker, W. W. (2 copies)
Stalnaker, W. P.
Stipe, Charles R.
Sturm, David
Sturm, Jacob W.
Stewart, J. Ed.
Strawderman, F. A.
Strickler, A. D. W.
Strawderman, A. W.
Switzer, P. A.
Switzer, C. K.

Talbott, Columbus
Talbott, S. S.
Talbott, R. E. (4 copies)
Talbott, R. M.
Talbott, S. H.
Talbott, J. W.
Talbott, W. W.

Talbot, M. C.
Taft, Granville E.
Teter, C. F.
Teter, G. B.
Teter, Mrs. Dorrinda
Teter, Thomas B.
Thacker, J. S.
Thompson, J. L.
Thompson, Mrs. A. J.
Trimble, Henry

Umback, Mrs. Augusta
Utterback, George W.

Ware, J. B.
Ware, J. K.
Walter, Lewis
Ward, D. B.
Watring, F. M.
Winans, Simon
Wilson, John
Wilson, J. G.
Williamson, Mrs.
Wentz, W. H.
Wince, Jasper
Willoghby, J. C.
Wolverton, Alba
Woodford, A. W.
Woodford, Mrs. C. A.
Woodford, John F.
Woodford, J. M.
Woodford, B. H.
Woodford, I. C.
Woodford, D. R.
Woodford, Mrs. B.
Woods, J. Hop
Woods, Samuel V.

Young, Miss Clara
Yowell, W. C.

Zinn, John A.
Zinn, W. D.
Zinn, S. W.
Zinn, A. J.
Zinn, D. W.
Zirkle, C. I.
Zirkle, John H.

INDEX.

Part First.

Alleghany Mountain a barrier to emigration, 21, the King forbids settlements beyond, 22, geology of, 72, battle of, 141.

Averell, Gen. W. W., ordered to West Virginia, 158, advises the fortification of mountain fastnesses, 159, in battle at Rocky Gap, 160, at Droop Mountain, 161, on the Salem Raid, 162, 163, on the Dublin Raid, 165, defeats McCausland at Moorefield, 167.

Batte, Captain Henry, 19

Bald Eagle, murder of, 42

Bill of Rights, The, 89, 93, 96

Bingamon, seven Indians Killed by, 34

Blair, Jacob B., 121

Boreman, Arthur I., 118, elected governor, 124

Bouquet, Gen., at Brushy Run, 37, conquers the Indians, 38

Botetourt County formed, 61

Braddock, Gen., campaign, 32

Brodhead, Gen., expedition of against Coshocton 54

British posts in the northwest, refusal to surrender, 55, flag shot down at Wheeling, 55, 92

Brady, Samuel, 92.

Brown, John, raid of, 105, proclaims freedom to slaves, 107, execution of, 108, W. G., labor for admission of West Virginia, 122, Bailey, killed at Fetterman, 147.

Bushwhackers, 138.

B. & O. Railroad, its importance in the Civil War, 144, its destruction advocated and attempted by the Confederates, 147

Battles and Skirmishes in West Virginia during the Civil War:

Glover's Gap, Philippi, St. George, near Keyser, Righter's, Patterson Creek, Hannahsville, Falling Water, Harper's Ferry, Middle Fork Bridge, Glenville, Belington, Rich Mountain 148

Corrick's Ford, Romney, Barboursville, Scarry Creek, in Tucker County, Piggott's Mill, Cross Lanes, Blue Creek, near Hawk's Nest, Cheat Mountain, Elkwater, Princeton, Hanging Rocks, Mechanicsburg Gap, Romney.... 149

High Log Cabin Run, Greenbrier River, Bolivar Heights, on New River, on the Kanawha. Wire Bridge, Romney, near Gauley Bridge, Cotton Hill, Guyandotte, Laurel Creek, McCoy's Mill, South Branch, near Little Capon, Camp, Alleghany, Meadow Bluff, Sutton, in Webster County, Bath...... 150

Huntersville, Sir John's Run, Slanesville, Big Capon Bridge, Blue's Gap, in Logan County, Springfield, Blue Stone, Moorefield, Bloomery Gap, Patterson Creek Bridge, Martinsburg, Boothville, in Webster County....... 151

In Webster County, Grassy Lick, Princeton, Camp Creek, Wardensville, in Clay and Roane Counties, Wolf Creek, Witheville Cross Roads, Lewisburg, near Franklin, near Wardensville, Shaver's Fork,

INDEX.

Muddy Creek, Baker's Tavern, in Wyoming County............152

Summersville, near Hayne's Ferry, Pack's Ferry, in Wyoming County, St. George, near Corrick's Ford, Buckhannon, Weston, Glenville, Fayetteville, Charleston......153

Point Pleasant, Buffalo, Standing Stone, Glenville, near Shepardstown, Blue's Gap, Little Capon Bridge, Pawpaw, Big Birch, Hedgeville, near Petersburg, near Kanawha Falls, St. George, South Fork, in Greenbrier County, Shepardstown....................154

Sinking Creek, Moorefield, Darkesville, near Bunker Hill, near Wardensville, Charlestown, near Moorefield, in Pocahontas County, near Smithfield, near Romney.155

Greenspring, Hurricane Bridge, Point Pleasant, Mud River, near Burlington, Going's Ford, Johnstown, Beverly, Greenland Gap.156

Terra Alta, Rowlesburg, Morgantown, Fairmont, Bridgeport...157

Lewisburg, Jane Lew, Cairo, Summersville, Fayetteville.......158

Bunker Hill, Martinsburg, Romney, St. George, Long Creek, Beverly, Huttonsville, near Harper's Ferry, Falling Water, near Charlestown, North Mountain, near Martinsburg, Cold Spring Gap 159

In Hardy County, near Glenville, near Huntersville, Rocky Gap, in Braxton County, Cedar Creek, Petersburg Gap, near Moorefield, Smithfield, Seneca Road, Greenbrier Bridge, Cheat River.....160

Summit Point, Bulltown, Salt Lick Bridge, Hedgeville, Charlestown, Cackleyville, Hillsboro, Droop Mountain, Little Sewell Mountain, Muddy Creek, Second Creek, Burlington...........161

Averell's Raids..............162

Big Sewell, Marlin Bottom, Lewisburg 163

Hurricane Bridge, near Meadow Bluff, Petersburg, Springfield, Medley, Red House..........164

Kabletown, Sinks of Gandy, Marlin Bottom, Dublin Raid, Bulltown, Piedmont 165

Princeton, Halltown, Cheat Mountain, Lost River Gap, near Charlestown, Panther Gap, near Moorefield, near Kabletown, near Petersburg, Springfield, Sweet Sulphur Springs, Leetown, Darkestown, Martinsburg, North River Mills, South Branch Bridge...166

North Branch Bridge, Harper's Ferry, Sir John's Run, Big Capon Bridge, Romney, Bunker Hill, Martinsburg, near Shepardstown, Green Spring, Keyser, near Moorefield, Summit Point, Welch's Spring, Charlestown, Halltown 167

Bunker Hill, near Berryville, in Upshur County, Martinsburg, Weston, Buckhannon, Coal River, near Petersburg, Winfield, Bevly, Greenspring, Buffalo Shoals, Moorefield, Keyser 168

Beverly, Petersburg, South Fork, Patterson Creek, near Charlestown.......................169

Camp Charlotte, 45

Campbell Alexander, 91, 92

Cambrian Rocks, oldest in West Virginia, 74

Carlile, John S., 95, 115, 116, elected to United States Senate, 119; strives to defeat the New State, 120 to 124

Carnifex Ferry, 143

Celeron, Captain, explores the Ohio River, 30

Clarke, Gen. George R., invasion of Illinois by, 53

Climate, West Virginia's, 71, 78

INDEX.

Coal, how formed, 75, 76

Constitutions, history of, 89; that of 1776, 90; that of 1830, 91; West Virginia's delegates to, 91; that of 1852, delegates to, 94; that of 1872, delegates to, 101; vote upon, 120

Connolley, John, 41; warns settlers of danger, 42

Constables, fees of, 87

Coroners, duties of, 87

Cornstalk, 43; at Point Pleasant, 44; makes peace, 45; assassinated, 50

Corrick's Ford, battle of, 136

Cox, Gen. G. D., in Kanawha Valley, 142

Counties, original in Virginia, 60; formation of and areas of in West Virginia, 65; vote of for Constitution of 1830, 94

Cranmer, G. L., 118

Dayton, Spencer, 114, 117

Decker, Thomas, plants a colony at Morgantown, 22

Delegates, Constitutional Convention of 1830, 91; to that of 1851, 94; to first West Virginia Constitutional Convention, 99; to that of 1872, 101; to the Secession Convention, 110; to first Wheeling Convention, 114, 116; to the second Wheeling Convention, 117

Devonian rocks, 75

Dinwiddie, Governor, sends messenger to the French, 30

Doddridge, Philip, 91, 91

Donnelley's fort attacked by Indians 49, 52

Drouths, 79

Ducking stool, 86

Duncan, E. S., 91

Dunmore's War, 39; his greed for land, 40; resisted by Pennsylvania, 41; orders out the militia, 42; invades Ohio, 43

Eckerly, Thomas, fails to plant a colony, 22

Elkwater, skirmish at, 140

Elliott, Matthew, leads Indians against Wheeling, 49

Fairfax, Lord, 20, surveys the Potomac, 59

Fairfax, Stone, 59, 60

Faulkner, Charles J., report of on the Potomac River, 60

Floyd, Gov., resists Maryland's claims, 60

Fertilizers, 81

Ferries, 88

Foreman, Captain William, killed, 52

Forbes, Gen., leads army against Duquesne, 35

Fort Duquesne, built by French, 30, expedition against under Braddock, 32, Washington urges destruction of, 34, its capture, 35.

Fort Leybert, massacre of 33

Fort Sigonier, besieged by Pontiac, 37

Fort Pitt, repulses Pontiac, 37

Fort Randolph, 45, attacked, 52

Fort Gower, meeting at, 47

Fort Henry, attacked, 49, siege of, 51

Fort McIntosh, 53

Fort Laurens, 53

French and Indian War, 29, closed, 35

Fry, Col. Joshua, marches to the West, 30

Garnett, Gen. R. S. 127, meets disappointments in West Virginia, 128, fortifies Laurel Hill, 134, retreats and is killed 136.

Geology and Geography of West Virginia, 71.

Girty, Simon, 41, 46, on a peaceful mission, 49, not at the siege of Wheeling 51, joins the Indians, 52, James Girty 52.

Gibson, Col. John, wrote "Logan's speech," 46, commandant of Fort Laurens, 53.

Gist, Christopher, makes explorations, 21, companion of Washington, 30.

Governor, the first election of 97.

Greenbrier River, The, land grant on 21, settlements on deserted, 37, soldiers in the Dunmore War, 43, settlers build a road to the Kanawha, 49, battle at, 141.

INDEX. 13

Hamilton, Henry, 50, sent in chains to Richmond, 53.
Hampshire County, settlement of 21, invaded by Indians, 33.
Harmar, Gen. defeat of, 56.
Harpers Ferry, 106, arsenal at is seized by Confederates, 112.

Imboden, Gen. John D., St. George raids, 153, 154, great raid, 155 to 158.
Irreducible school fund 101.
Indians in West Virginia, 25, their origin unknown 26, their numbers small, 27, trails, 28, General Amherst's opinion of, 37, disregard Bouquet's treaty, 42, their soldierly qualities underestimated, 43, custom of taking prisoners 49, Moravians massacred 54.

Kanawha Valley campaign 141.
Kelley, Gen. B. F., leads Federal troops from Wheeling 130, captures Philippi, 132.
Kentucky, invasion of by Indians and British, 54.
Killbuck, burns Fort Seybert, 33.

Land, modes of acquiring it 23, Virginia's vast domain, 58.
Laurel Hill, fortified by Confederates, 134.
Laws, early in Virginia, 83, against swearing and stealing, 84, against tattling, 85.
Lewis, Captain Joshua, fights Indians in Hampshire County, 23, Gen. Andrew, marches to the Ohio, 34, in the Dunmore War, 43, at Point Pleasant, 44.
Lee, Gen. R. E., appointed commander of Virginia's forces, 126, sends guns into West Virginia, 127, prepares to attack Grafton, 139, defeated at Elkwater, 140.
Letcher, Governor John, 97, calls out the militia, 127, publishes proclamation at Huttonsville, 148.
Libel, law of 100.
Limestones, how formed, 74.
Logan, the Mingo, 45.

Loring, Major A., at Huntersville, 139, delays the campaign, 140.

Mason, Captain Samuel, ambuscade of, 51.
Mason & Dixon's Line, 58.
Mass Meetings, to oppose secession, 114.
Mayo, William, explores the North Branch, 20.
Monongahela River, first settlement on, 22.
Moundbuilders, The, 26.
Morris, Gen. T. A., attacks Confederates at Laurel Hill and Corrick's Ford, 136.
McCullough, Major Samuel, 52.
McCausland, Gen. John, sent to the Kanawha Valley, 127.
McClellan, Gen. Geo. B., campaign of, in West Virginia, 132.

New River, 19, visited by Christopher Gist, 21.
Neally's Fort, attacked by Indians, 33.
Newspapers, history of in West Virginia, 66.

Ogle, Capt. James, ambuscaded, 51.

Pegram, Colonel John, defeated at Rich Mountain, 135.
Philippi, militia company at, 127, fight at, 131.
Pierpont, F. H., 99, 117, elected governor, 118, 124, Benjamin F. Butler's criticism of, 125.
Pillory, 86.
Porterfield, Colonel George A., is ordered to Grafton, 127, burns railroad bridges, 130, retreats from Philippi, superceded by General Garnett, 132.
Polsley, Daniel, 99, 119.
Pontiac War, 35, the chief's designs, 36, price on his head, 37, help refused by the French, 38.
Point Pleasant, battle of, 43, prominent men who took part in, 44.
Pratt, Captain, attacks Wheeling, 54.
Printing presses, 69.

Press, freedom of, 90, 100.
Preachers, not eligible to the Legislature, 93.
Property qualification a basis for suffrage, 92, 95.
Public Schools, Virginia's poor showing, 93, 94, West Virginia's provision for them, 101.

Quebec Act, The, nullified by Governor Dunmore, 41, 45, not recognized by our government, 57.

Rainfall, West Virginia's share, 79.
Randolph County, first settlement in, 22.
Red Eagle, 45, assassinated, 51.
Rice's fort attacked, 55.
Roberts, General B. S., superseded, 158.
Robertson, James, 43.
Reynolds, General, succeeds McClellan in West Virginia, 138.
Rosecrans, General, in Kanawha Valley, 142, defeats General Floyd at Carnifex Ferry, 143.
Roberts, Captain Christian, killed, 148.

Sevier, Valentine, 43
See, Adam, 91
Sesession, convention called, 98, the ordinance 109, convention assembled 110, measure carried through by storm, 111, 112, the vote 117.
Shelby, Evan, 44; Isaac 44
Sheriff's fees, 86
Shawnees, 43
Silurian rocks, formation in West Virginia, 74
Snows, depth of, in West Virginia, 79
Soils, of what composed, 80, 81
South Branch explored, 20
Spotswood, Governor, 20
Smith, Captain Jeremiah fights Indians in Hampshire County, 33
St. Clair, General, defeat of, 56
Summers, Lewis, 91, G. W. opposes secession, 111
Swearengen, Colonel Andrew, 52

Taft, N. H., 117.
Tory, uprising of, on the Monongahela, 48, on the South Branch, 49
Tyler, Colonel E. B., defeated at Cross Lanes, 142

Vandalia, proposed province of, 21, 40, 109.
Virginia, failure of its trans-alleghany colonization scheme, 22; its reorganized government, 113, 118
Washington, George, surveys for Lord Fairfax, 20, mission to the Ohio, 30, defeats Jumonville 30, is defeated at the Great Meadows, 31, marches with Braddock, 32, at Braddock's defeat, 33, is appointed commander of Virginia's forces, 34, captures Fort Duquesne, 35
Ward, Ensign, expedition to the Ohio, 30
Watauga troops in West Virginia, 43
Waley, J. K., 121
Wayne, General Anthony, defeats the Indians, 56
West Augusta, district of, 61, 62
Whipping Post, 86.
Wetzel, Lewis, 92
Willey, W. T., 94, 96, 99, in sesession convention, 111, 116, elected to United States Senate, 119, urges the admission of West Virginia, 121
Wolves, bounty on scalps of, 87.
Wheeling, attacked by Indians, 49, siege of, 51, third siege of, 54, convention at, 98, 114, second convention, 117.
West Virginia, first exploration of, 19, settlers diven out by soldiers, 22, colonies in, 23, 60, population of in 1790, 65, five Indian Wars in, 29, its fate in the balance, 35, ten years of peace, 39, Indians no right in, 42, in the Revolution, 47, troops from the State join Washington at Boston, 48, its boundaries, 57 to 60, newspapers of, 66, its geography, geology and climate, 71, its central plateau, 77, its rainfall, 79, soils, 80, loyalty to the Union, 97, its first constitutional convention,

99, votes against secession, 112, how created, 113, secession nullified, 114, the vote for a new State, 119, formation of, 120, admission into Union, 122, influence of A. W. Campbell, 123, President Lincoln's views, 123, slavery in, 124, first State officers elected, 124, commencement of Civil War in, 126, arms received from Massachusetts, 129, captains of State troops, 170.

Zane, Ebenezer, 92.

Part Second.

The portion of the county's history which is derived chiefly from records forms Part Second of this book. It contains many thousand names, and to index it fully would be almost equivalent to reprinting it For that reason it is deemed best to give, in place of an index, an outline of what each chapter contains.

Chapter XVIII. Settlements and Indian Troubles. Trails, 178—Colonization of Randolph County, 180— of Upshur County, 185— of Tucker County, 186— The numerous murders by Indians, the founding of settlements, the building of forts and the names and sketches of early settlers are given between pages 175 and 199.

Chapter XIX. Notes from the Records. Boundaries of Barbour, 198- The first Court, 200— The Courthouse, 205— Early Court proceedings, 207— The Circuit Court, 211— Last Wills and Testaments, 212— First Deed Book, 215— Early Marriage Licenses, 215— Election Returns, 221— List of Lawyers, 225— Constables, 227— Justices of the Peace, 228—Clerks and Judges, 230— Prosecuting Attorneys, Sheriffs and County Surveyors, 231- Assessors and School Commissioners, 232— School Superintendents, Supervisors and County Commissioners, 235— Early Prices of Farm Stock, 236.

Chapter XX. The Civil War in Barbour County. Candidacy of Samuel Woods and Thomas A. Bradford for the Richmond Convention, 237— "States Rights" Meetings on Hacker's Creek and Stewart's Run, 239— Meeting in Philippi, 240—Spencer Dayton's Stand for the Union, 240— Secession Advocated by the *Jeffersonian*, 241—The "Shoeshop Convention," 245—Confederates Occupy Philippi, 246—The "Barbour Greys" and "Captain Jenkins'" Cavalry, 247—Captain Hill's Company, 248—Grafton Occupied by Colonel Porterfield, 249—Colonel Porterfield's Account of the Fight at Philippi, 250—Captain Dilworth's Attempt to Cut General McClellan off, 255—Confederates Retreat from Philippi, 256—Colonel Kelley Wounded, 257—Escape of Captain Jenkins' Cavalry, 258—General Garnett in Barbour, 259—His Plans for Attacking the Railroad, 260—General Morris at Belington, 262—Battle of Rich Mountain, 265—Retreat and Death of Garnett, 266—Internal Affairs during the War, 266—Spencer Dayton's Resolution in Court, 267—Sheriff Trahern Kidnapped, 267—The Imboden Raid, 268—Major Lang's Expedition, 269—General Mulligan in Barbour,

270—Spencer Dayton Saves the Records, 270—Federal Soldiers from Barbour, 271—Captain Haller's Home Guards, 272.

Chapter XXI. Miscellanies. This chapter, beginning on page 276 and ending on page 329, is made up of incidents, topics, events and occurrences of all kinds, including Public and Private Improvements, names and locations of early settlers, the county's Geology, Geography and Mineral Resources, Secret Orders, Churches and Towns. It may be regarded as the Industrial and Social History of the County.

Part Third.

Chapter XXII. Biography. The sketches in this Chapter are arranged Alphabetically and need no Index. The chapter begins on page 335 and ends on page 517

PART FIRST
State History

CHAPTER I.

―:o:―

EXPLORATIONS WEST OF BLUE RIDGE.

It is impossible to say when and where the first white man set foot on the soil of what is now West Virginia. In all probability no record was ever made of the first visit. It is well known that adventurers always push into new countries in advance of organized exploring parties; and it is likely that such was the case with West Virginia when it was only an unnamed wilderness. Probably the Indians who waged war with the early colonists of Virginia carried prisoners into this region on their hunting excursions. Sixty-five years were required for the colonists of Virginia to become superficially acquainted with the country as far west as the Blue Ridge, which, until June, 1670, was the extreme limit of explorations in that direction. The distance from Jamestown, the first colony, to the base of the Blue Ridge, was two hundred miles. Nearly three-quarters of a century was required to push the outposts of civilization two hundred miles, and that, too, across a country favorable for exploration, and with little danger from Indians during most of the time. In later years the outposts of civilization moved westward at an average yearly rate of seventeen miles. The people of Virginia were not satisfied to allow the Blue Ridge to remain the boundary between the known and unknown countries; and in 1670, sixty-three years after the first settlement in the State, the Governor of Virginia sent out an exploring party under Captain Henry Batte, with instructions to cross the mountains of the west, seek for silver and gold, and try to discover a river flowing into the Pacific Ocean. Early in June of that year, 1670, the explorers forced the heights of the Blue Ridge which they found steep and rocky, and descended into the valley west of that range. They discovered a river flowing due north. The observations and measurements made by these explorers perhaps satisfied the royal Governor who sent them out; but their accuracy may be questioned. They reported that the river which they had discovered was four hundred and fifty yards wide; its banks in most places one thousand yards high. Beyond the river they said they could see towering mountains destitute of trees, and crowned by white cliffs, hidden much of the time in mist, but occasionally clearing sufficiently to give a glimpse of their ruggedness. They expressed the opinion that those unexplored mountains might contain silver and gold. They made no attempt to cross the river, but set out on their return. From their account of the broad river and its banks thousands of feet high, one might suppose that they had discovered the Canyon of the Colorado; but it was only New River, the principle tributary of the Kanawha. The next year, 1671, the Governor of Virginia sent explorers to continue the work, and they remained a considerable time in the valley of New River. If they penetrated as far as the present territory of West Virginia, which is uncertain, they probably crossed the line into what is now Monroe or Mercer Counties.

Forty-five years later, 1716, Governor Spotswood, of Virginia, led an exploring party over the Blue Ridge, across the Shenandoah River and to the base of the Alleghany Mountains. Daring hunters and adventurers no doubt were by that time acquainted with the geography of the eastern part of the State. Be that as it may, the actual settlement of the counties of Jefferson, Berkeley, Morgan, Hampshire and Hardy was now at hand. The gap in the Blue Ridge at Harper's Ferry, made by the Potomac breaking through that range, was soon discovered, and through that rocky gateway the early settlers found a path into the Valley of Virginia, whence some of them ascended the Shenandoah to Winchester and above, and others continued up the Potomac, occupying Jefferson County and in succession the counties above; and before many years there were settlements on the South Branch of the Potomac. It is known that the South Branch was explored within less than nine years after Governor Spotswood's expedition, and within less than thirteen years there were settlers in that county.

Lord Fairfax claimed the territory in what is now the Eastern Panhandle of West Virginia. But his boundary lines had never been run. The grant called for a line drawn from the head of the Potomac to the head of the Rappahannock. Several years passed before it could be ascertained where the fountains of those streams were. An exploring party under William Mayo traced the Potomac to its source in the year 1736, and on December 14 of that year ascertained and marked the spot where the rainfall divides, part flowing into the Potomac and part into Cheat River on the west. This spot was selected as the corner of Lord Fairfax's land; and on October 17, 1746, a stone was planted there to mark the spot and has ever since been called the Fairfax Stone. It stands at the corner of two states, Maryland and West Virginia, and of four counties, Garrett, Preston, Tucker and Grant. It is about half a mile north of the station of Fairfax, on the West Virginia Central and Pittsburg Railroad, at an elevation of three thousand two hundred and sixteen feet above sea level.

George Washington spent the summers of three years surveying the estate of Lord Fairfax, partly in West Virginia. He began work in 1748, when he was sixteen, and persecuted it with ability and industry. There were other surveyors employed in the work as well as he. By means of this occupation he became acquainted with the fertility and resources of the new country, and he afterwards became a large land-holder in West Virginia, one of his holdings lying as far west as the Kanawha. His knowledge of the country no doubt had something to do with the organization of the Ohio Company in 1749, which was granted 500,000 acres between the Monongahela and the Kanawha. Lawrence Washington, a half brother of George Washington, was a member of the Ohio Company. The granting of land in this western country no doubt had its weight in hastening the French and Indian War of 1755, by which England acquired possession of the Ohio Valley. The war would have come sooner or later, and England would have secured the Ohio Valley in the end, and it would have passed ultimately to the United States; but the events were hastened by Lord Fairfax's sending the youthful Washington to survey his lands near the Potomac. While engaged in this work, Washington frequently met small parties of friendly Indians. The presence of these natives was not a rare thing in the South Branch country. Trees are still pointed out as the corners or lines of surveys made by Washington.

EXPLORATIONS WEST OF THE BLUE RIDGE.

About this time the lands on the Greenbrier River were attracting attention. A large grant was made to the Greenbrier Company; and in 1749 and 1750 John Lewis surveyed this region, and settlements grew up in a short time. The land was no better than the more easily accessible land east of the Alleghany Mountains; but the spirit of adventure which has always been characteristic of the American people, led the daring pioneers into the wilderness west of the mountains, and from that time the outposts of settlements moved down the Greenbrier and the Kanawha, and in twenty-two years had reached the Ohio River. The frontiersmen of Greenbrier were always foremost in repelling Indian attacks and in carrying the war into the enemy's country.

The eastern counties grew in population. Prior to the outbreak of the French and Indian War in 1755, there were settlements all along the Potomac River, not only in Jefferson, Berkeley and Hampshire, but also in Hardy, Grant and Pendleton Counties. It is, of course, understood that those counties, as now named, were not in existence at that time.

The Alleghany Mountains served as a barrier for awhile to keep back the tide of emigration from the part of the State lying west of that range; but when peace was restored after the French and Indian War the western valleys soon had their settlements. Explorations had made the country fairly well known prior to that time as far west as the Ohio. Immense tracts of land had been granted in that wilderness, and surveyors had been sent to mark the lines. About the time of the survey of the Greenbrier country, the Ohio Company sent Christopher Gist to explore its lands already granted and to examine West Virginia, Ohio and Kentucky for choice locations in view of obtaining future grants. Mr. Gist, a noted character of his time, and a companion of Washington a few years later, performed his task well, and returned with a report satisfactory to his employers. He visited Ohio and Kentucky, and on his return passed up the Kanawha and New Rivers in 1751, and climbed to the summit of the ledge of rocks now known as Hawk's Nest, or Marshall's Pillar, overhanging the New River, and from its summit had a view of the mountains and inhospitable country.

In speaking of the exploration and settlement of West Virginia, it is worthy of note that the Ohio River was explored by the French in 1749; but they attempted no settlement within the borders of this State.

Had Virginia allowed religious freedom, a large colony would have been planted on the Ohio Company's lands, between the Monongahela and the Kanawha, about 1750, and this would probably have changed the early history of that part of West Virginia. A colony in that territory would have had its influence in the subsequent wars with the Indians. And when we consider how little was lacking to form a new state, or province, west of the Alleghanies about 1772, to be called Vandalia, it can be understood what the result might have been had the Ohio Company succeeded in its scheme of colonization. Its plan was to plant a colony of two hundred German families on its land. The settlers were to come from eastern Pennsylvania. All arrangements between the company and the Germans were satisfactory, but when the hardy Germans learned that they would be in the province of Virginia, and that they must become members of the English Church or suffer persecution in the form of extra taxes laid on dissenters by the Episcopacy of Virginia, they would not go, and the Ohio Company's colonization scheme failed.

Another effort to colonize the lands west of the Alleghanies, and from which much might have come, also failed. This attempt was made by Virginia. In 1752 the House of Burgesses offered Protestant settlers west of the Alleghanies, in Augusta county, ten years' exemption from taxes; and the offer was subsequently increased to fifteen years' exemption. The war with the French and Indians put a stop to all colonization projects. Virginia had enough to do taking care of her settlements along the western border without increasing the task by advancing the frontier seventy-five miles westward. The first settlement, if the occupation by three white men may be called a settlement, on the Monongahela was made about 1752. Thomas Eckerly and two brothers, from eastern Pennsylvania, took up their home there to escape military duty, they being opposed to war. They wished to live in peace remote from civilized man, but two of them fell victims to the Indians while the third was absent. Prior to 1753 two families had built houses on the headwaters of the Monongahela, in what is now Randolph County. The Indians murdered or drove them out in 1753. The next settlement was by a small colony near Morgantown under the leadership of Thomas Decker. This was in 1758, while the French and Indian War was at its height. The colony was exterminated by Indians.

In 1763, October 7, a proclamation was issued by the King of England forbidding settlers from taking up land or occupying it west of the Alleghanies until the country had been bought from the Indians. It is not known what caused this sudden desire for justice on the part of the king, since nearly half the land west of the Alleghanies, in this State, had already been granted to companies or individuals; and, since the Indians did not occupy the land and there was no tribe within reach of it with any right to claim it, either by occupation, conquest or discovery. Governor Fauquier, of Virginia, issued three proclamations warning settlers west of the mountains to withdraw from the lands. No attention was paid to the proclamations. The Governors of Virginia and Pennsylvania were ordered, 1765, to remove the settlers by force. In 1766 and the next year soldiers from Fort Pitt, now Pittsburg, were sent into West Virginia to dispossess the settlers. It is not probable that the soldiers were over-zealous in carrying out the commands, for the injustice and nonsense of such orders must have been apparent to the dullest soldier in the West. Such settlers as were driven away returned, and affairs went on as usual. Finally Pennsyvania bought the Indian lands within its borders; but Virginia, after that date, never paid the Indians for any lands in West Virginia. The foregoing order was the first one forbidding settlements in West Virginia north of the Kanawha and west of the Alleghanies. Another order was issued ten years later. Both were barren of results. The second will be spoken of more at length in the account of the incorporation of part of Ohio in the Province of Quebec.

Settlements along the Ohio, above and below Wheeling, were not made until six or seven years after the close of the French and Indian War. About 1769 and 1770 the Wetzels and Zanes took up land in that vicinity, and others followed. Within a few years Wheeling and the territory above and below, formed the most prosperous community west of the Alleghanies. That part of the State suffered from Indians who came from Ohio, but the attacks of the savages could not break up the settlements, and in 1790, five years before the close of the Indian war, Ohio County had more than five thousand inhabitants, and Monongalia had nearly as many.

During the Revolutionary War parts of the interior of the State were

EXPLORATIONS WEST OF THE BLUE RIDGE. 23

occupied by white men. Harrison County, in the vicinity of Clarksburg and further west, was a flourishing community four or five years before the Revolution. Settlers pushed up the West Fork of the Monongahela, and the site of Weston, in Lewis County, was occupied soon after. Long before that time frontiersmen had their cabins on the Tygart Valley River as far south as the site of Beverly, in Randolph County. The first settlement in Wood County, near Parkersburg, was made 1773, and the next year the site of St. George, in Tucker County, was occupied by a stockade and a few houses. Monroe County, in the southeastern part of the state, was reclaimed from the wilderness fifteen years before the Revolution, and Tyler county's first settlement dates back to the year 1776. Pocahontas was occupied at a date as early as any county west of the Alleghanies, there being white settlers in 1749, but not many. Settlements along the Kanawha were pushed westward and reached the Ohio River before 1776.

The population of West Virginia at the close of the Revolution is not known. Perhaps an estimate of thirty-five thousand would not be far out of the way. In 1790 the population of the territory now forming West Virginia was 55,873; in 1800 it was 78,592, a gain of nearly forty per cent. in ten years. In 1810 the population was 105,469, a gain of thirty-five per cent. in the decade. The population in 1820 was 136,768, a gain of nearly twenty-three per cent. In 1830 there were 176,924, a gain in ten years of over twenty-two per cent. In 1840 the population was 224,537, a gain of more than twenty-one per cent. The population in 1850 was 302,313, a gain in the decade of more than twenty-five per cent. In 1860 the population was 376,388, a gain of more than twenty-two per cent. In 1870 the population was 442,014, a gain in ten years of nearly fifteen per cent. In 1880 the population of the State was 618,457, a gain of twenty-six per cent. In 1890 the population of the State was 762,794, a gain of more than twenty-three per cent. in ten years.

Land was abundant and cheap in the early days of West Virginia settlements, and the State was generous in granting land to settlers and to companies. There was none of the formality required, which has since been insisted upon. Pioneers usually located on such vacant lands as suited them, and they attended to securing a title afterwards. What is usually called the "tomahawk right" was no right in law at all; but the persons who had such supposed rights were usually given deeds for what they claimed. This process consisted in deadening a few trees near a spring or brook, and cutting the claimant's name in the bark of trees. This done, he claimed the adjacent land, and his right was usually respected by the frontier people, but there was very naturally a limit to his pretensions. He must not claim too much; and it was considered in his favor if he made some improvements, such as planting corn, within a reasonable time. The law of Virginia gave such settler a title to 400 acres, and a pre-emption to 1,000 more adjoining, if he built a log cabin on the claim and raised a crop of corn. Commissioners were appointed from time to time, some as early as 1779, who visited different settlements and gave certificates to those who furnished satisfactory proof that they had complied with the law. These certificates were sent to Richmond, and if no protest or contest was filed in six months, the settler was given a deed to the land. It can thus be seen that a tomahawk right could easily be merged into a settler's right. He could clear a little land, build his hut, and he usually obtained the land. The good locations were the first taken, and the poorer land was left until somebody wanted it. The surveys were usually made in the crudest manner, often without accuracy and without ascertaining whether they overlapped some earlier claim or not. The foundation was laid for many future law suits, some of which may still be on the court dockets of this State. It is said that there are places in West Virginia where land titles are five deep. Some of them are old colonial grants, stretching perhaps across two or three counties. Others are grants made after Virginia became a member of the United States. Then follow sales made subsequently by parties having or claiming a right in the land. The laws of West Virginia are such that a settlement of most of these claims is not difficult where the metes and bounds are not in dispute.

After the Revolution Virginia sold its public land usually in the following manner: A man would buy a warrant, for say ten thousand acres, and was given a certificate authorizing him to locate the land wherever he could find it. He could select part of it here, another part there, or he could sell his warrant, or part of it, to some one else, and the purchaser could locate the land. Land warrants were often sold half dozen times. There were persons who grew wealthy buying warrants for large tracts, from fifty thousand to one hundred thousand acres, and selling their warrants to different parties at an advanced price. Nearly all the land in West Virginia west of the Alleghanies, if the title is traced back, will be found to have been obtained originally on these land warrants. The most of the land east of the Alleghanies was originally granted by the King of England to companies or individuals. This title is called a "Crown Grant." There are also a few "Crown Grants" west of the Alleghanies, but the most of the land west of the mountains belonged to the State of Virginia at the close of the Revolution. None of it ever belonged to the United States.

CHAPTER II.

―:o:―

INDIANS AND MOUNDBUILDERS.

Indians enter largely into the early history of the State, and few of the early settlements were exempt from their visitations. Yet, at the time West Virginia first became known to white men, there was not an Indian settlement, village or camp of any considerable consequence within its borders. There were villages in the vicinity of Pittsburg, and thence northward to Lake Erie and westward into Ohio; but West Virginia was vacant; it belonged to no tribe and was claimed by none with shadow of title. There were at times, and perhaps at nearly all times, a wigwam here or there within the borders, but it belonged to temporary sojourners, hunters or fishermen, who expected to remain only a short time. So far as West Virginia is concerned, the Indians were not dispossessed of it by the white man, and they were never justified in waging war for any wrong done them within this State. The white race simply took land which they found vacant, and dispossessed nobody.

There was a time when West Virginia was occupied by Indians, and they were driven out or exterminated; but it was not done by the white race, but by other tribes of Indians, who, when they had completed the work of destruction and desolation, did not choose to settle on the land they had made their own by conquest. This war of extermination was waged between the years 1656 and 1672, as nearly as the date could be ascertained by the early historians, who were mostly missionaries among the tribes further north and west. The conquerors were the Mohawks, a fierce and powerful tribe whose place of residence was in western New York, but whose warlike excursions were carried into Massachusetts, Virginia, Pennsylvania, West Virginia, and even further south. They obtained firearms from the Dutch colonies on the Hudson, and having learned how to use them, they became a nation of conquerors. The only part of their conquests which comes within the scope of this inquiry was their invasion of West Virginia. A tribe of Indians, believed to be the Hurons, at that time occupied the country from the forks of the Ohio southward along the Monongahela and its tributaries, on the Little Kanawha, on the Great Kanawha and to the Kentucky line. During the sixteen years between 1656 and 1672 the Mohawks overran the country and left it a solitude, extending their conquest to the Guyandotte River. There was scarcely a Huron left to tell the tale in all this State. Genghis Kahn, the Tartar, did not exterminate more completely than did those Mohawks. If there were any Huron refugees who escaped they never returned to their old homes to take up their residence again.

There is abundant evidence all over the State that Indians in considerable numbers once made their home here. Graveyards tell of those who

CHAPTER II.

―――:o:―――

INDIANS AND MOUNDBUILDERS.

Indians enter largely into the early history of the State, and few of the early settlements were exempt from their visitations. Yet, at the time West Virginia first became known to white men, there was not an Indian settlement, village or camp of any considerable consequence within its borders. There were villages in the vicinity of Pittsburg, and thence northward to Lake Erie and westward into Ohio; but West Virginia was vacant; it belonged to no tribe and was claimed by none with shadow of title. There were at times, and perhaps at nearly all times, a wigwam here or there within the borders, but it belonged to temporary sojourners, hunters or fishermen, who expected to remain only a short time. So far as West Virginia is concerned, the Indians were not dispossessed of it by the white man, and they were never justified in waging war for any wrong done them within this State. The white race simply took land which they found vacant, and dispossessed nobody.

There was a time when West Virginia was occupied by Indians, and they were driven out or exterminated; but it was not done by the white race, but by other tribes of Indians, who, when they had completed the work of destruction and desolation, did not choose to settle on the land they had made their own by conquest. This war of extermination was waged between the years 1656 and 1672, as nearly as the date could be ascertained by the early historians, who were mostly missionaries among the tribes further north and west. The conquerors were the Mohawks, a fierce and powerful tribe whose place of residence was in western New York, but whose warlike excursions were carried into Massachusetts, Virginia, Pennsylvania, West Virginia, and even further south. They obtained firearms from the Dutch colonies on the Hudson, and having learned how to use them, they became a nation of conquerors. The only part of their conquests which comes within the scope of this inquiry was their invasion of West Virginia. A tribe of Indians, believed to be the Hurons, at that time occupied the country from the forks of the Ohio southward along the Monongahela and its tributaries, on the Little Kanawha, on the Great Kanawha and to the Kentucky line. During the sixteen years between 1656 and 1672 the Mohawks overran the country and left it a solitude, extending their conquest to the Guyandotte River. There was scarcely a Huron left to tell the tale in all this State. Genghis Kahn, the Tartar, did not exterminate more completely than did those Mohawks. If there were any Huron refugees who escaped they never returned to their old homes to take up their residence again.

There is abundant evidence all over the State that Indians in considerable numbers once made their home here. Graveyards tell of those who

was occupied by man long before the dawn of history in the old world or the new. Stone hatchets and other implements of war or the chase, now found buried in the gravel left by ice sheets which covered the Ohio and the Upper Mississippi Valleys show that men were there at a time which, at the lowest estimate, was thousands of years before the date given in chronology for the creation of Adam. America had people who were no doubt coeval with the prehistoric savages who fought tigers and hyenas in the caves of England and France. It is, therefore, an idle waste of time to seek in recorded history for clews to the origin of America's first people. It would be as profitable to inquire whether the oak tree originated in the old world or the new.

The number of Indians inhabiting a given territory was surprisingly small. They could hardly be said to occupy the land. They had settlements here and there. Of the number of Hurons in the limits of this State before the Mohawk invasion, there is no record and no estimate Probably not more than the present number of inhabitants in the State capital, Charleston. This will appear reasonable when it is stated that, according to the missionary census, in 1640, the total number of Indians in the territory east of the Mississippi, north of the Gulf of Mexico and south of the St. Lawrence river, was less than one-fourth of the present population of the State of West Virginia. The total number is placed at 180,000. Nearly all the Indians who were concerned in the border wars in West Virginia lived in Ohio. There were many villages in that State, and it was densely populated in comparison with some of the others; yet there were not, perhaps, fifteen thousand Indians in Ohio, and they could not put three thousand warriors in the field. The army which General Forbes led against Fort Duquesne (Pittsburg) in 1758 was probably larger than could have been mustered by the Indians of Ohio, Indiana and Illinois combined, and the number did not exceed six thousand. The Indians were able to harrass the frontier of West Virginia for a quarter of a century by prowling about in small bands and striking the defenseless. Had they organized an army and fought pitched battle they would have been subdued in a few months.

While the Indians roamed over the whole country, hunting and fishing, they yet had paths which they followed when going on long journeys. Those paths were not made with tools, but were simply the result of walking upon them for generations. They nearly always followed the best grades to be found, and modern road-makers have profited by the skill of savages in selecting the most practicable routes. Those paths led long distances, and in one general direction, unvarying from beginning to end, showing that they were not made at haphazzard, but with design. Thus, crossing West Virginia, the Catawba warpath led from New York to Georgia. It entered West Virginia from Fayette County, Pennsylvania, crossed Cheat River at the mouth of Grassy Run, passed in a direction south by southwest through the State, and reached the headwaters of the Holsten River in Virginia, and thence continued through North Carolina, South Carolina and it is said reached Georgia. The path was well defined when the country was first settled, but at the present time few traces of it remain. It was never an Indian thoroughfare after white men had planted settlements in West Virginia, for the reason that the Indian tribes of Pennsylvania and New York had enough war on hand to keep them busy without making long excursions to the south. It is not recorded that any Indian ever came over this trail to attack the frontiers of West Virginia. The early settlements in Pennsylvania to the north of us cut off incursions from that quarter. A second path, called by the early settlers Warrior Branch, was a branch of the Catawba path. That is, they formed one path southward from New York to southern Pennsylvania, where they separated, and the Warrior Branch crossed Cheat River at McFarland's, took a southwesterly direction through the State and entered southern Ohio and passed into Kentucky. Neither was this trail much used in attacking the early settlements in this State. It is highly probable that both this and the Catawba path were followed by the Mohawks in their wars against the Hurons in West Virginia, but there is no positive proof that such was the case. Indian villages were always on or near large trails, and by following these and their branches the invaders would be led directly to the homes of the native tribe which they were bent on exterminating.

There were other trails in the State, some of them apparently very old, as if they had been used for many generations. There was one, sometimes called the Eastern Path, which came from Ohio, crossed the northern part of West Virginia, through Preston and Monongalia Counties, and continued eastward to the South Branch of the Potomac. This path was made long before the Ohio Indians had any occasion to wage war upon white settlers, but it was used in their attacks upon the frontiers. Over it the Indians traveled who harrassed the settlements on the South Branch; and later, those on the Monongahela and Cheat Rivers. The settlers whose homes happened to lie near this trail were in constant danger of attack. During the Indian wars, after 1776, it was the custom for scouts to watch some of the leading trails near the crossing of the Ohio, and when a party of Indians were advancing to outrun them and report the danger in time for the settlers to take refuge in forts. Many massacres were averted in this way. There was a trail leading from the Ohio River up the Little Kanawha, to and across the Alleghanies, passing through Randolph County.

The arms and ammunition with which the Indians fought the pioneers of this State were obtained from white traders; or, as from 1776 to 1783 or later, were often supplied by British agents. The worst depredations which West Virginia suffered from the Indians were committed with arms and ammunition obtained from the British in Canada. This was during the Revolutionary War, when the British made allies of the Indians and urged them to harrass the western frontiers, while the British regular army fought the Colonial army in the eastern States.

CHAPTER III.

―――:o:―――

THE FRENCH AND INDIAN WAR.

For the first twenty-five years after settlements were commenced in the present territory of West Virginia there was immunity from Indian depredations There was no occasion for trouble. No tribe occupied the South Branch Valley when the first colony was made; and the outposts of the white man could have been pushed across the State until the Ohio River was reached without taking lands claimed or occupied by Indians, except, perhaps, in the case of two or three very small camps; and this most likely would have been done without conflict with the Indians, had not Europeans stirred up those unfortunate children of the forest and sent them against the colonists. This was done by two European nations, first by France, and afterwards by England. There were five Indian wars waged against West Virginia; the War of 1775 and Pontiac's War of 1763, the Dunmore War of 1774 and the Revolutionary War of 1776, and the war which broke out about 1790 and ended in 1795. In the war beginning in 1755 the French incited and assisted the Indians against the English settlements along the whole western border. In the Revolutionary War the British took the place of the French as allies of the Indians, and armed the savages and sent them against the settlers.

It is proper that the causes bringing about the French and Indian War be briefly recited. No State was more deeply concerned than West Virginia. Had the plan which was outlined by the French been successfully executed, West Virginia would have been French instead of English, and the settlements by the Virginians would not have been carried west of the Alleghany Mountains. The coast of America, from Maine to Georgia, was colonized by English. The French colonized Canada and Louisiana. About the middle of the eighteenth century the design, which was probably formed long before, of connecting Canada and Louisiana by a chain of forts and settlements, began to be put into execution by the King of France. The cordon was to descend the Alleghany River from Lake Erie to the Ohio, down that stream to the Mississippi and thence to New Orleans. The purpose was to confine the English to the strip of country between the Alleghanies and the Atlantic Ocean, which would include New England, the greater part of New York, New Jersey, Delaware, Eastern Pennsylvania, the greater part of Maryland, seven eastern counties of West Virginia, Virginia, North Carolina, South Carolina and Georgia. The French hoped to hold everything west of the Alleghany Mountains. The immediate territory to be secured was the Ohio Valley. Missionaries of the Catholic Church were the first explorers, not only of the Ohio, but of the Mississippi Valley, almost to the head springs of that river. The French took formal possession of both banks of the Ohio in the summer of 1749, when an expedition under Captain Celeron descended that stream and claimed the country in the name of France.

The determination of the Virginians to plant settlements in the Ohio Valley was speedily observed by the French, who set to work to counteract the movement. They began the erection of a fort on one of the upper tributaries of the Alleghany River, and no one doubted that they intended to move south as rapidly as they could erect their cordon of forts. Governor Dinwiddie, of Virginia, decided to send a messenger to the French, who already were in the Ohio Valley, to ask for what purpose they were there, and to inform them that the territory belonged to England. It was a mere diplomatic formality not expected to do any good. This was in the autumn of 1753, and George Washington, then twenty-one years of age, was commissioned to bear the dispatch to the French commander on the Alleghany River. Washington left Williamsburg, Virginia, November 14, to travel nearly six hundred miles through a wilderness in the dead of winter. When he reached the settlement on the Monongahela where Christopher Gist and twelve families had planted a colony, Mr. Gist accompanied him as a guide. The message was delivered to the French commandant, and the reply having been written, Washington and Gist set out upon their return, on foot. The boast of the French that they would build a fort the next summer on the present site of Pittsburg seemed likely to be carried out. Washington counted two hundred canoes at the French fort on the Alleghany River, and he rightly conjectured that a descent of that stream was contemplated. After many dangers and hardships, Washington reached Williamsburg and delivered to Governor Dinwiddie the reply of the French commandant.

It was now evident that the French intended to resist by force all attempts by the English to colonize the Ohio Valley, and were resolved to meet force with force. Governor Dinwiddie called the Assembly together, and troops were sent into the Ohio Valley. Early in April, 1754, Ensign Ward, with a small detachment, reached the forks of the Ohio, where Pittsburg now stands, and commenced the erection of a fort. Here began the conflict which raged for several years along the border. The French soon appeared in the Alleghany with one thousand men and eighteen cannon and gave the English one hour in which to leave. Resistance was out of the question, and Ward retreated. The French built a fort which they called Duquesne, in honor of the Governor of Canada.

The English were not disposed to submit tamely. Virginia and Pennsylvania took steps to recover the site at the forks of the Ohio, and to build a fort there. Troops were raised and placed in command of Colonel Fry, while Washington was made lieutenant colonel. The instructions from Governor Dinwiddie were explicit, and directed that all persons, not the subjects of Great Britain, who should attempt to take possession of the Ohio River or any of its tributaries, be killed, destroyed or seized as prisoners. When the troops under Washington reached the Great Meadows, near the present site of Brownsville, Pennsylvania, it was learned that a party of about fifty French were prowling in the vicinity, and had announced their purpose of attacking the first English they should meet. Washington, at the head of fifty men, left the camp and went in search of the French, came upon their camp early in the morning, fought them a few minutes, killed ten, including the commander, Jumonville, and took twenty-two prisoners, with the loss of one killed and two or three wounded. The wounded Frenchmen were tomahawked by Indians who accompanied Washington. The prisoners were sent to Williamsburg, and, at the same time, an urgent appeal for more troops was made. It was correctly surmised that as soon as news of the fight reached Fort Duquesne, a large force of French would be sent out to attack the English. Re-enforcements were raised in Virginia and were advanced as far as Winchester; but, with the exception of an independent company from South Carolina, under Captain Mackay, no re-enforcements reached the Great Meadows where the whole force under Colonel Fry amounted to less than four hundred men.

The Indians had been friendly with the settlers on the western border up to this time; but the French having supplied them bountifully with presents, induced them to take up arms against the English, and henceforward the colonists were obliged to fight both the French and the Indians. Of the two, the Indians were the more troublesome. They had a deep-seated hatred for the English, who had dispossessed the tribes east of the Alleghanies of their land, and were now invading the territory west of that range. But it is difficult to see wherein they hoped to better their condition by assisting the French to gain possession of the country; for the French were as greedy for land as were the English. However, the majority of the natives could not reason far enough to see that point; and without much investigation they took up arms in aid of the French.

After the brush with Jumonville's party, it was expected that the French in strong force would march from Fort Duquesne to drive back the English. Washington built Fort Necessity about fifty miles west of Cumberland, Maryland, and prepared for a fight. News was brought to him that large re-enforcements from Canada had reached Fort Duquesne; and within a few days he was told that the French were on the road to meet him. Expected re-enforcements from Virginia had not arrived, and Washington, who had advanced a few miles toward the Ohio, fell back to Fort Necessity. There, on the third of July, 1754, was fought a long and obstinate battle. Many Indians were with the French. Washington offered battle in open ground, but the offer was declined, and the English withdrew within the entrenchments. The enemy fought from behind trees, and some climbed to the top of trees in order to get aim at those in the trenches. The French were in superior force and better armed than the English. A rain dampened the ammunition and rendered many of the guns of the English useless. Washington surrendered upon honorable terms, which permitted his soldiers to retain their arms and baggage, but not the artillery. The capitulation occurred July 4, 1754, just twenty-two years before the signing of the Declaration of Independence. The French and Indians numbered seven hundred men. Their loss in killed was three or four. The loss of the English was thirty.

When Washington's defeated army retreated from the Ohio Valley, the French were in full possession, and no attempt was made that year to renew the war in that quarter; but the purpose on the part of the English of driving the French out was not abandoned. It was now understood that nothing less than a general war could settle the question, and both sides prepared for it. It was with some surprise, in January, 1755, that a proposition was received from France that the portion of the Ohio Valley between that river and the Alleghanies be abandoned by both the French and the English. The latter, believing that the opportunity had arrived for driving a good bargain, demanded that the French destroy all their forts as far as the Wabash, raze Niagara and Crown Point, surrender the Peninsula of Nova Scotia, and a strip of land sixty miles wide along the Bay of Fundy and the Atlantic, and leave the intermediate country as far as the St. Lawrence a neutral desert. France rejected this proposition, and understanding the designs of the English, sent three thousand men to Canada. General Braddock was already on his way to America with two regiments; yet no war had been declared between England and France. The former announced that it would act only on the defensive, and the latter affirmed its desire for peace.

When General Braddock arrived in America he prepared four expeditions against the French, yet still insisting that he was acting only on the defensive. One was against Nova Scotia, one against Niagara, one against Crown Point, and the fourth against the Ohio Valley, to be led by Braddock in person. This last is the only one that immediately concerns West Virginia, and it will be spoken of somewhat at length.

Much was expected of Braddock's campaign. He promised that he would be beyond the Alleghanies by the end of April; and after taking Fort Duquesne, which he calculated would not detain him above three days, he would invade Canada by ascending the Alleghany River. He expressed no concern from attacks by Indians, and showed contempt for American soldiers who were in his own ranks. He expected his British regulars to win the battles. Never had a general gone into the field with so little comprehension of what he was undertaking. He paid for it with his life. He set out upon his march from Alexandria, in Virginia, and in twenty-seven days reached Cumberland with about two thousand men, some of them Virginians. Here Washington joined him as one of his aids. From Cumberland to Fort Duquesne the distance was one hundred and thirty miles. The army could not march five miles a day. Everything went wrong. Wagons broke down, horses and cattle died, Indians harrassed the flanks. On June 19, 1755, the army was divided, and a little more than half of it pushed forward in hope of capturing Fort Duquense before the arrival of re-enforcements from Canada. The progress was yet slow, altogether the heaviest baggage had been left with the rear division. Not until July 8 was the Monongahela reached. This river was forded, and marching on its southern bank, Braddock decided to strike terror to the hearts of his enemies by a parade. He drew his men up in line and spent an hour marching to and fro, believing that the French were watching his every movement from the bluff beyond the river. He wished to impress them with his power. The distance to Fort Duquesne was less than twelve miles. He recrossed the river at noon. This was July 9. The troops pushed forward toward the fort, and while cutting a road through the woods, were assailed by French and Indians in ambush. The attack was as unexpected as it was violent. It is not necessary to enter fully into details of the battle which was disastrous in the extreme. The regular soldiers were panic stricken. They could do nothing against a concealed foe which numbered eight hundred and sixty-seven, of which only two hundred and thirty were French. About the only fighting on the side of the English was done by the Virginians under Washington. They prevented the slaughter of the whole army. Of the three companies of the Virginians, scarcely thirty remained alive. The battle continued two hours. Of the eighty-six officers in the army, twenty-six were killed, and thirty-seven were wounded. One-half of the army was killed or wounded. Washington had two horses killed under him and four bullets

THE FRENCH AND INDIAN WAR. 33

passed through his coat; yet he was not wounded. The regulars, when they had wasted their ammunition in useless firing, broke and ran like sheep, leaving everything to the enemy. The total loss of the English was seven hundred and fourteen killed and wounded. Braddock had five horses shot under him, and was finally mortally wounded and carried from the field.

The battle was over. The English were flying toward Cumberland, throwing away whatever impeded their retreat. The dead and wounded were abandoned on the field. Braddock was borne along in the rout, conscious that his wound was mortal. He spoke but a few times. Once he said: "Who would have thought it!" and again: "We shall know better how to deal with them another time." He no doubt was thinking of his refusal to take Washington's advice as to guarding against ambuscades. Braddock died, and was buried in the night about a mile west of Fort Necessity. Washington read the funeral service at the grave.

When the fugitives reached the division of the army under Dunbar, which had been left behind and was coming up, the greatest confusion prevailed. General Dunbar destroyed military stores to the value of half a million dollars. In his terror he destroyed all he had, and when he recovered his senses he was obliged to send to Cumberland for provisions to keep his men alive until he could reach that place. He did not cease to retreat until he reached Philadelphia, where he went into winter quarters. The news of the defeat spread rapidly, and the frontier from New York to North Carolina prepared for defense, for it was well known that the French, now flushed with victory, would arm the Indians and send them against the exposed settlements. Even before the defeat of Braddock a taste of Indian warfare was given many outposts. After the repulse of the army there was no protection for the frontiers of Virginia except such as the settlers themselves could provide. One of the first settlements to receive a visit from the savages was in Hampshire County. Braddock's defeated army had scarcely withdrawn before the Indians appeared near the site of Romney and fired at some of the men near the fort, and the fire was returned. One man was wounded, and the Indians, about ten in number, were driven off. Early the next spring a party of fifty Indians, under the leadership of a Frenchman, again invaded the settlements on the Potomac, and Captain Jeremiah Smith, with twenty men, went in pursuit of them. A fight occurred near the source of the Capon, and the Frenchman and five of his savages were killed. Smith lost two men. The Indians fled. A few days later a second party of Indians made their way into the country, and were defeated by Captain Joshua Lewis, with eighteen men. The Indians separated into small parties and continued their depredations for some time, appearing in the vicinity of the Evans fort, two miles from Martinsburg; and later they made an attack on Neally's fort, and in that vicinity committed several murders. A Shawnee chief named Killbuck, whose home was probably in Ohio, invaded what is now Grant and Hardy Counties in the spring of 1756, at the head of sixty or seventy savages. He killed several settlers and made his escape. He appeared again two years later in Pendleton County, where he attacked and captured Fort Seybert, twelve miles west of the present town of Franklin, and put to death more than twenty persons who had taken refuge in the fort. The place no doubt could have made a successful resistance had not the inmates trusted to the promise of safety made by the Indians, who thus were admitted into the fort, and at once massacred the settlers. In 1758 the Indians again invaded Hampshire County and killed a settler near Forks of Capon. This same year eight Indians came into the country on the South Branch of the Potomac, near the town of Petersburg, and attacked the cabin of a man named Bingaman. They had forced their way into the house at night, and being at too close quarters for shooting, Bingaman clubbed his rifle and beat seven of them to death. The eighth made his escape. In 1759 the Indians committed depredations on the Monongahela River near Morgantown.

The settlement on the Roanoke River in Virginia, between the Blue Ridge and the Alleghany Mountains, was the theatre of much bloodshed in 1756 by Indians from Ohio who made their way, most probably, up the Kanawha and New River, over the Alleghanies. An expedition against them was organized in the fall of 1756, under Andrew Lewis, who eighteen years later, commanded the Virginians at the battle of Point Pleasant. Not much good came of the expedition which marched, with great hardship, through that part of West Virginia south of the Kanawha, crossed a corner of Kentucky to the Ohio River, where an order came for the troops not to cross the Ohio nor invade the country north of that river. They returned in dead of winter, and suffered extremely from hunger and cold. This is notable from the fact that it was the first military expedition by an English-speaking race to reach the Ohio River south of Pittsburg.

During the three years following Braddock's defeat the frontier was exposed to incessant danger. Virginia appointed George Washington commander-in-chief of all forces raised or to be raised in that State. He traveled along the frontier of his State, inspecting the forts and trying to bring order out of chaos. His picture of the distress of the people and the horrors of the Indian warfare is summed up in these words, addressed to the Governor of Virginia: "The supplicating tears of the women, and the moving petitions of the men, melt me with such deadly sorrow that I solemnly declare, if I know my own mind, I would offer myself a willing sacrifice to the butchering enemy, provided that would contribute to the people's ease." He found no adequate means of defense. Indians butchered the people and fled. Pursuit was nearly always in vain. Washington insisted at all times that the only radical remedy for Indian depredation was the capture of Fort Duquesne. So long as that rallying point remained the Indians would be armed and would harrass the frontiers. But, in case the reduction of Fort Duquesne could not be undertaken, Washington recommended the erection of a chain of twenty-two forts along the frontier, to be garrisoned by two thousand soldiers.

In 1756 and again in 1757 propositions were laid before the Government of Virginia, and also before the commander-in-chief of the British forces in America, by Washington for the destruction of Fort Duquesne. But in neither of these years was his proposition acted upon. However, the British were waging a successful war against the French in Canada, and by this were indirectly contributing to the conquest of the Ohio Valley. In 1758 all was in readiness for striking a blow at Fort Duquesne with the earnest hope that it would be captured and that rallying point for savages ultimately destroyed. The settlements in the eastern part of West Virginia were nearly broken up. Only two frontier forts west of Winchester held out, exclusive of military posts. Both were in Hampshire County, one at Romney, the other on Capon. The savages swarmed over the Blue Ridge and spread destruction in the Valley of Virginia.

THE FRENCH AND INDIAN WAR.   35

General Joseph Forbes was given command of the army destined for the expedition against Fort Duquesne. This was early in 1758. He had twelve hundred Highlanders; two thousand seven hundred Pennsylvanians; nineteen hundred Virginians, and enough others to bring the total to about six thousand men. Washington was leader of the Virginians. Without him, General Forbes never would have seen the Ohio. The old General was sick, and his progress was so slow that but for the efforts of Washington in pushing forward, the army could not have reached Duquesne that year. A new road was constructed from Cumberland, intended as a permanent highway to the West. When the main army had advanced about half the distance from Cumberland to Fort Duquesne, Major Grant with eight hundred Highlanders and Virginians, went forward to reconnoitre. Intelligence had been received that the garrison numbered only eight hundred, of whom three hundred were Indians. But a re-inforcement of four hundred men from Illinois had arrived unknown to Major Grant, and he was attacked and defeated with heavy loss within a short distance of the Fort. Nearly three hundred of his men were killed or wounded, and Major Grant was taken prisoner.

On November 5, 1758, General Forbes arrived at Hannastown and decided to advance no further that year; but seven days later it was learned that the garrison of Fort Duquesne was in no condition for resistance. Washington and twenty-five hundred men were sent forward to attack it. General Forbes, with six thousand men, had spent fifty days in opening fifty miles of road, and fifty miles remained to be opened. Washington's men, in five days from the advance from Hannastown, were within seventeen miles of the Ohio. On November 25 the fort was reached. The French gave it up without a fight, set fire to it and fled down the Ohio.

The power of the French in the Ohio Valley was broken. When the despairing garrison applied the match which blew up the magazine of Fort Duquesne, they razed their last stronghold in the Valley of the West. The war was not over; the Indians remained hostile, but the danger that the country west of the Alleghanies would fall into the hands of France had passed. Civilization, progress and religious liberty were safe. The gateway to the great West was secured to the English race, and from that day there was no pause until the western border of the United States was washed by the waters of the Pacific. West Virginia's fate hung in the balance until Fort Duquesne fell. The way was then cleared for colonization, which speedily followed. Had the territory fallen into the hands of France, the character of the inhabitants would have been different, and the whole future history of that part of the country would have been changed. A fort was at once erected on the site of that destroyed by the French, and in honor of William Pitt was named Fort Pitt. The city of Pittsburg has grown up around the site. The territory now embraced in West Virginia was not at once freed from Indian attacks, but the danger was greatly lessened after the rendezvous of Fort Duquesne was broken up. The subsequent occurrences of the French and Indian War, and Pontiac's War, as they affected West Virginia, remain to be given.

The French and Indian War closed in 1761, but the Pontiac War soon followed. The French had lost Canada and the Ohio Valley and the English had secured whatever real or imaginary right the French ever had in the country. But the Indians rebelled against the English, who had speedily taken possession of the territory acquired from France. There is no evidence that the French gave assistance to the Indians in this war; but much proof that more than one effort was made by the French to restrain the savages. Nor is the charge that the French supplied the Indians with ammunition well founded. The savages bought their ammunition from traders, and these traders were French, English and American. In November, 1760, Rogers, an English officer, sailed over Lake Erie to occupy French posts further west. While sailing on the Lake he was waited upon by Pontiac, who may be regarded as the ablest Indian encountered by the English in America. He was a Delaware captive who had been adopted by the Ottawas, and became their chief. He hailed Rogers and informed him that the country belonged neither to the French nor English, but to the Indians, and told him to go back. This Rogers refused to do, and Pontiac set to work forming a confederacy of all the Indians between Canada on the north, Tennessee on the south, the Mississippi on the west and the Alleghanies on the east. His object was to expell the English from the country west of the Alleghany mountains.

The superiority of Pontiac as an organizer was seen, not so much in his success in forming a confederacy as in keeping it secret. He struck in a moment, and the blow fell almost simultaneously from Illinois to the frontier of Virginia. In almost every case the forts were taken by surprise. Detroit, Fort Pitt and Fort Ligonier were almost the only survivors of the fearful onset of the savages. Detroit had warning from an Indian girl who betrayed the plans of the savages; and when Pontiac, with hundreds of his warriors, appeared in person and attempted to take the Fort by surprise, he found the English ready for him. He besieged the post nearly a year. The siege began May 9, 1763, and the rapidity with which blows were struck over a wide expanse of country shows how thorough were his arrangements, and how well the secret had been kept. Fort Sandusky, near Lake Erie, was surprised and captured May 16, seven days after Detroit was besieged. Nine days later the Fort at the mouth of St. Joseph's was taken; two days later Fort Miami, on the Maumee river, fell, also taken by surprise. On June 1 Fort Ouatamon in Indiana, was surprised and captured. Machilimackinac, far north in Michigan, fell also. This was on June 2. Venango in Pennsylvania, near Lake Erie, was captured, and not one of the garrison escaped to tell the tale. Fort Le Boeuf, in the same part of the country, fell June 18. On June 22 Presque Isle, now Erie, Pennsylvania, shared the fate of the rest. On June 21 Fort Ligonier was attacked and the siege was prosecuted with vigor, but the place held out. It was situated on the road between Fort Pitt and Cumberland. On June 22 the savages appeared before the walls of Fort Pitt, but were unable to take the place by surprise, although it was in poor condition for defense. The fortifications had never been finished, and a flood had opened three sides. The commandant raised a rampart of logs round the Fort and prepared to fight till the last. The garrison numbered three hundred and thirty men. More than two hundred women and children from the frontiers had taken refuge there.

Despairing of taking the Fort by force, the savages tried treachery, and asked for a parley. When it was granted, the chief told the commandant of the Fort that resistance was useless; that all the forts in the North and West had been taken, and that a large Indian army was on its march to Fort Pitt, which must fall: But, said the chief, if the English would abandon the Fort and retire east of the Alleghanies, they would be permitted to depart in peace, provided they would set out at once. The reply given by

THE FRENCH AND INDIAN WAR.

the commandant was, that he intended to stay where he was, and that he had provisions and ammunition sufficient to enable him to hold out against all the savages in the woods for three years, and that English armies were at that moment on their march to exterminate the Indians. This answer apparently discouraged the savages, and they did not push the siege vigorously. But in July the attack was renewed with great fury. The savages made numerous efforts to set the Fort on fire by discharging burning arrows against it; but they did not succeed. They made holes in the river bank and from that hiding place kept up an incessant fire, but the Fort was too strong for them. On the last day of July, 1763, the Indians raised the siege and disappeared. It was soon learned what had caused them to depart so suddenly. General Bouquet was at that time marching to the relief of Fort Pitt, with five hundred men and a large train of supplies. The Indians had gone to meet him and give battle. As Bouquet marched west from Cumberland he found the settlements broken up, the houses burned, the grain unharvested, and desolation on every hand, showing how relentless the savages had been in their determination to break up the settlements west of the Alleghanies.

On August 2, 1763, General Bouquet arrived at Fort Ligonier, which had been besieged, but the Indians had departed. He left part of his stores there, and hastened forward toward Fort Pitt. On August 5 the Indians who had been besieging Fort Pitt attacked the troops at Bushy Run. A desperate battle ensued. The troops kept the Indians off by using the bayonet, but the loss was heavy. The next day the fight was resumed, the Indians completely surrounding the English. The battle was brought to a close by Bouquet's stratagem. He set an ambuscade and then feigned retreat. The Indians fell into the trap and were routed. Bouquet had lost one-fourth of his men in killed and wounded; and so many of his pack horses had been killed that he was obliged to destroy a large part of his stores because he could not move them. After a march of four days the army reached Fort Pitt.

The effect of this sudden and disastrous war was wide-spread. The settlers fled for protection from the frontiers to the forts and towns. The settlements on the Greenbrier were deserted. The colonists hurried east of the Alleghanies. Indians prowled through all the settled portions of West Virginia, extending their raids to the South Branch of the Potomac. More than five hundred families from the frontiers took refuge at Winchester. Amherst, commander-in-chief of the British forces in America, was enraged when he learned of the destruction wrought by the Indians. He offered a reward of five hundred dollars to any person who would kill Pontiac, and he caused the offer of the reward to be proclaimed at Detroit. "As to accommodation with these savages," said he, "I will have none until they have felt our just revenge." He urged every measure which could assist in the destruction of the savages. He classed the Indians as "the vilest race of beings that ever infested the earth, and whose riddance from it must be esteemed a meritorious act for the good of mankind." He declared them not only unfit for allies, but unworthy of being respected as enemies. He sent orders to the officers on the frontiers to take no prisoners, but kill all who could be caught.

Bouquet's force was not large enough to enable him to invade the Indian country in Ohio at that time; but he collected about two thousand men, and the next summer carried the war into the enemy's country, and struck directly at the Indian towns, assured that by no other means could the savages be brought to terms. The army had not advanced far west of Pittsburg when the tribes of Ohio became aware of the invasion and resorted to various devices to retard its advance and thwart its purposes. But General Bouquet proceeded rapidly, and with such caution and in such force, that no attack was made on him by the Indians. The alarm among them was great. They foresaw the destruction of their towns; and when all other resources had failed, they sent a delegation to Bouquet to ask for peace. He signified his willingness to negotiate peace on condition that the Indians surrender all white prisoners in their hands. He did not halt however in his advance to wait for a reply The Indians saw that the terms must be accepted and be complied with without delay if they would save their towns. The army was now within striking distance. The terms were therefore accepted, and more than two hundred prisoners, a large number of whom were women and children, were given up. Other prisoners remained with the Indians in remote places, but the most of them were sent to Fort Pitt the next spring, according to promise. Thus closed Pontiac's War.

An agency had been at work for some time to bring about peace, but unknown to the English. It was the French, and without their co-operation and assistance it is probable the Indians would not have consented to the peace. DeNeyon, the French officer at Fort Chartres, wrote a letter to Pontiac advising him to make peace with the English, as the war between the French and English was over and there was no use of further bloodshed. This letter reached Pontiac in November while he was conducting the siege of Detroit, and its contents becoming known to his Indian allies, greatly discouraged them; for it seems that up to that time they believed they were helping the French and that the French would soon appear in force and fight as of old. When the Indians discovered that no help from France was to be expected, they became willing to make peace with Bouquet, and for ten years the western frontiers enjoyed immunity from war.

CHAPTER IV.

———:0:———

THE DUNMORE WAR.

The progress of the settlement of West Virginia from 1764 to 1774 has been noticed elsewhere in this volume. There were ten years of peace; but in the year 1774 war with the Indians broke out again. Peace was restored before the close of the year. The trouble of 1774 is usually known as Dunmore's War, so called from Lord Dunmore who was at that time Governor of Virginia, and who took personal charge of a portion of the army operating against the Indians. There has been much controversy as to the origin or cause of hostilities, and the matter has never been settled satisfactorily to all. It has been charged that emissaries of Great Britain incited the Indians to take up arms, and that Dunmore was one of the moving spirits in this disgraceful conspiracy against the colony of Virginia. It is further charged that Dunmore hoped to see the army under General Andrew Lewis defeated and destroyed at Point Pleasant, and that Dunmore's failure to form a junction with the army under Lewis according to agreement, was intentional, premeditated and in the hope that the southern division of the army would be crushed.

This is a charge so serious that no historian has a right to put it forward without strong evidence for its support—much stronger evidence than has yet been brought to light. The charge may be neither wholly true nor wholly false. There is not a little evidence against Dunmore in this campaign, especially when taken in connection with the state of feeling entertained by Great Britain against the American colonies at that time. In order to present this matter somewhat clearly, yet eliminating many minor details, it is necessary to speak of Great Britain's efforts to annoy and intimidate the colonies, as early as 1774, and of the spirit in which these annoyances were received by the Americans.

Many people, both in America and England, saw, in 1774, that a revolution was at hand. The Thirteen Colonies were arriving very near the formation of a confederacy whose avowed purpose was resistance to Great Britain. Massachusetts had raised ninety thousand dollars to buy powder and arms; Connecticut provided for military stores and had proposed to issue seventy thousand dollars in paper money. In fact, preparations for war with England were going steadily forward, although hostilities had not begun. Great Britain was getting ready to meet the rebellious colonies, either by strategy or force, or both. Overtures had been made by the Americans to the Canadians to join them in a common struggle for liberty. Canada belonged to Great Britain, having been taken by conquest from France in the French and Indian War. Great Britain's first move was regarding Canada; not only to prevent that country from joining the Americans, but to use Canada as a menace and a weapon against them. England's plan was deeply laid. It was largely the work of Thurlow and Wedderburn. The Canadians were to be granted full religious liberty and a large share of political liberty in order to gain their friendship. They were mostly Catholics, and with them England, on account of her trouble with her Thirteen Colonies, took the first step in Catholic emancipation. Having won the Canadians to her side, Great Britain intended to set up a separate empire there, and expected to use this Canadian empire as a constant threat against the colonies. It was thought that the colonists would cling to England through fear of Canada.

The plan having been matured, its execution was at once attempted. The first step was the emancipation of the Canadian Catholics. The next step was the passage of the Quebec Act, by which the Province of Quebec was extended southward to take in western Pennsylvania and all the country belonging to England north and west of the Ohio River. The King of England had already forbidden the planting of settlements between the Ohio River and the Alleghany Mountains in West Virginia; so the Quebec Act was intended to shut the English colonies out of the West and confine them east of the Alleghany Mountains. Had this plan been carried into execution as intended, it would have curtailed the colonies, at least Pennsylvania and Virginia, and prevented their growth westward. The country beyond the Ohio would have become Canadian in its laws and people, and Great Britain would have had two empires in America, one Catholic and the other Protestant; or, at least, one composed of the Thirteen Colonies and the other of Canada extended southward and westward, and it was intended that these empires should restrain, check and threaten each other, thus holding both loyal to and dependent upon Great Britain.

Some time before the passage of the Quebec Act a movement was on foot to establish a new province called Vandalia, west of the Alleghanies, including the greater part of West Virginia and a portion of Kentucky. Benjamin Franklin and George Washington were interested in it. The capital was to be at the mouth of the Kanawha. The province was never formed. Great Britain was not inclined to create states west of the mountains at a time when efforts were being made to confine the settlements east of that range. To have had West Virginia and a portion of Kentucky neutral ground, and vacant, between the empire of Canada and the empire of the Thirteen Colonies would have pleased the authors of the Quebec Act. But acts of Parliament and proclamations by the King had little effect on the pioneers who pushed into the wilderness of the West to find new homes.

Before proceeding to a narration of the events of the Dunmore War, it is not out of place to inquire concerning Governor Dunmore, and whether, from his past acts and general character, he would be likely to conspire with the British and the Indians to destroy the western settlements of Virginia. Whether the British were capable of an act so savage and unjust as inciting savages to harrass the western frontier of their own colonies is not a matter for controversy. It is a fact that they did do it during the Revolutionary War. Whether they had adopted this policy so early as 1774, and whether Governor Dunmore was a party to the scheme, is not so certain. Therefore let us ask, who was Dunmore? He was a needy, rapacious Scotch earl, of the House of Murray, who came to America to amass a fortune and who at once set about the accomplishment of his object, with little regard for the rights of others or the laws of the country. He was Governor of New York a short time; and, although poor when he came, he was the

THE DUNMORE WAR.   41

owner of fifty thousand acres of land when he left, and was preparing to decide, in his own court, in his own favor, a large and unfounded claim which he had preferred against the Lieutenant Governor. When he assumed the office of Governor of Virginia his greed for land and money knew no bounds. He recognized no law which did not suit his purpose. He paid no attention to positive instructions from the crown, which forbade him to meddle with lands in the west. These lands were known to be beyond the borders of Virginia, as fixed by the treaties of Fort Stanwix and Lochaber, and therefore were not in his jurisdiction. He had soon acquired two large tracts in southern Illinois, and also held lands where Louisville, Kentucky, now stands, and in Kentucky opposite Cincinnati. Nor did his greed for wealth and power stop with appropriating wild lands to his own use; but, without any warrant in law, and in violation of all justice, he extended the boundaries of Virginia northward to include much of western Pennsylvania, Pittsburg in particular; and he made that the county seat of Augusta County. and moved the court from Staunton to that place. He even changed the name Fort Pitt to Fort Dunmore. He appointed forty-two justices of the peace. Another appointment of his, as lieutenant of militia, was Simon Girty, afterwards notorious and infamous as a deserter and a leader of Indians in their war against the frontiers. He appointed John Connolly, a physician and adventurer, commandant of Fort Pitt and its dependencies, which were supposed to include all the western country. Connolly was a willing tool of Dunmore in many a questionable transaction. Court was held at Fort Pitt until the spring of 1776. The name of Pittsburg first occurs in the court records on August 20, 1776. When Connolly received his appointment he issued a proclamation setting forth his authority. The Pennsylvanians resisted Dunmore's usurpation, and arrested Connolly. The Virginia authorities arrested some of the Pennsylvania officers, and there was confusion, almost anarchy, so long as Dunmore was Governor.

Dunmore had trouble elsewhere. His domineering conduct, and his support of some of Great Britain's oppressive measures, caused him to be hated by the Virginians, and led to armed resistance. Thereupon he threatened to make Virginia a solitude, using these words: "I do enjoin the magistrates and all loyal subjects to repair to my assistance, or I shall consider the whole country in rebellion, and myself at liberty to annoy it by every possible means, and I shall not hesitate at reducing houses to ashes and spreading devastation wherever I can reach. With a small body of troops and arms, I could raise such a force from among Indians, negroes and other persons as would soon reduce the refractory people of the colony to obedience." The patriots of Virginia finally rose in arms and drove Governor Dunmore from the country. Some of these events occurred after the Dunmore War, but they serve to show what kind of a man the Governor was.

Perhaps the strongest argument against the claim that Dunmore was in league with Indians, backed by Great Britain, to push back the frontier of Virginia to the Alleghanies, is the fact that Dunmore at that time was reaching out for lands, for himself, in Illinois, Kentucky and Ohio; and his land-grabbing would have been cut off in that quarter had the plan of limiting Virginia to the Alleghanies been successful. He could not have carried out his schemes of acquiring possessions in the West had the Quebec Act been sustained. Dunmore did more to nullify the Quebec Act than any one else. He exerted every energy to extend and maintain the Virginia frontier as far west as possible. By this he opposed and circumvented the efforts of Great Britain to shut Virginia off from the West. He and the government at home did not work together, nor agree on the frontier policy; and in the absence of direct proof sustaining the charge that he was in conspiracy with the British government and the Indians to assail the western frontier, the doubt as to his guilt on the charge must remain in his favor.

From the time of the treaty made by General Bouquet with the Indians, 1764, to the year 1773, there was peace on the frontiers. War did not break out in 1773, but murders were committed by Indians which excited the frontier settlements, and were the first in a series which led to war. The Indians did not comply with the terms of the treaty with General Bouquet. They had agreed to give up all prisoners. It was subsequently ascertained that they had not done so. Some captives were still held in bondage. But this in itself did not lead to the war of 1774. The frontiers, since Bouquet's treaty, had been pushed to the Ohio River, in West Virginia, and into Kentucky. Although Indians had no right by occupation to either West Virginia or Kentucky, and although they had given up by treaty any right which they claimed, they yet looked with anger upon the planting of settlements in those countries. The first act of hostility was committed in 1773, not in West Virginia, but further south. A party of emigrants, under the leadership of a son of Daniel Boone, were on their way to Kentucky when they were set upon and several were killed, including young Boone. There can be no doubt that this attack was made to prevent or hinder the colonization of Kentucky. Soon after this, a white man killed an Indian at a horse race. This is said to have been the first Indian blood shed on the frontier of Virginia by a white man after Pontiac's War. In February 1774 the Indians killed six white men and two negroes; and in the same month, on the Ohio, they seized a trading canoe, killed the men in charge and carried the goods to the Shawnee towns. Then the white men began to kill also. In March, on the Ohio, a fight occurred between settlers and Indians, in which one was killed on each side, and five canoes were taken from the Indians. John Connolly wrote from Pittsburg on April 21, to the people of Wheeling to be on their guard, as the Indians were preparing for war. On April 26, two Indians were killed on the Ohio. On April 30, nine Indians were killed on the same river near Steubenville. On May 1, another Indian was killed. About the same time an old Indian named Bald Eagle was killed on the Monongahela River; and an Indian camp on the Little Kanawha, in the present county of Braxton, was broken up, and the natives were killed. This was believed to have been done by settlers on the West Fork, in the present County of Lewis. They were induced to take that course by intelligence from the Kanawha River that a family named Stroud, residing near the mouth of the Gauley River had been murdered, and the tracks of the Indians led toward the Indian camp on the Little Kanawha. When this camp was visited by the party of white men from the West Fork, they discovered clothing and other articles belonging to the Stroud family. Thereupon the Indians were destroyed. A party of white men with Governor Dunmore's permission destroyed an Indian village on the Muskingum River. The frontiers were alarmed. Forts were built in which the inhabitants could find shelter from attacks. Expresses were sent to Williamsburg entreating assistance. The Virginia Assembly in May discussed the dangers from Indians on the frontier, and intimated that the militia should be called out. Governor Dunmore ordered out the militia of the frontier counties. He then proceeded in person to Pittsburg, partly to look after his lands, and partly to take charge of the campaign against the Indians. The Delawares and Six Nations renewed their treaty of peace in September, but the Shawnees, the most powerful and warlike tribe in Ohio, did not. This tribe had been sullen and unfriendly at Bouquet's treaty, and had remained sour ever since. Nearly all the captives yet in the hands of the Indians were held by this fierce tribe, which defied the white man and despised treaties. These savages were ruled by Cornstalk, an able and no doubt a good man, opposed to war, but when carried into it by the headstrong rashness of his tribe, none fought more bravely than he. The Shawnees were the chief fighters on the Indian side in the Dunmore war, and they were the chief sufferers.

After arranging his business at Pittsburg, Governor Dunmore descended the Ohio River with twelve hundred men. Daniel Morgan, with a company from the Valley of Virginia, was with him. A second army was being organized in the southwestern part of Virginia, and Dunmore's instructions were that this army, after marching down the Great Kanawha, should join him on the Ohio where he promised to wait. The Governor failed to keep his promise, but crossed into Ohio and marched against the Shawnee towns which he found deserted. He built a fort and sat down to wait.

In the meantime the army was collecting which was to descend the Kanawha. General Andrew Lewis was commander. The pioneers on the Greenbrier and New River formed a not inconsiderable part of the army which rendezvoused on the site of Lewisburg in Greenbrier County, In this army were fifty men from the Watauga, among whom were Evan Shelby, James Robertson and Valentine Sevier, names famous in history. Perhaps an army composed of better fighting material than that assembled for the march to Ohio, never took the field anywhere. The distance from Lewisburg to the mouth of the Great Kanawha was about one hundred and sixty miles. At that time there was not so much as a trail, if an old Indian path, hard to find, is excepted. At the mouth of Elk River the army made canoes and embarking in them, proceeded to Point Pleasant, the mouth of the Kanawha, which they reached October 6, 1774. Prior to that date Simon Girty arrived at Point Pleasant with dispatches from Dunmore, who was then at the mouth of the Little Kanawha with his army. The dispatches ordered Lewis to proceed to the mouth of the Hockhocking. When Girty reached Point Pleasant, Lewis had not arrived, and the dispatches were deposited in a hollow tree in a conspicuous place where they would be seen. Girty returned to Dunmore's army, which marched to the Hockhocking. Another messenger was sent to Point Pleasant. Scouts passed between the two armies, and on October 13 Dunmore ordered Lewis to proceed to the Pickaway towns in Ohio. But, in the mean time the battle of Point Pleasant had been fought. On October 10 the Indian army under Cornstalk arrived, about one thousand in number. The Virginians were encamped on the narrow point of land formed by the meeting of the Kanawha and Ohio. The Indians crossed the Ohio the evening before, or during the night, and went into camp on the West Virginia side, and about two miles from the Virginians. They were discovered at daybreak, October 10, by two young men who were hunting. The Indians fired and killed one of them; the other escaped and carried the news to the army.

This was the first intelligence the Virginians had that the Indians had come down from their towns in Ohio to give battle. By what means the savages had received information of the advance of the army in time to collect their forces and meet it before the Ohio River was crossed, has never been ascertained; but it is probable that Indian scouts had watched the progress of General Lewis from the time he took up his march from Greenbrier. Cornstalk laid well his plans for the destruction of the Virginian army at Point Pleasant. He formed his line across the neck of land, from the Ohio to the Kanawha, and enclosed the Virginians between his line and the two rivers. He posted detachments on the farther banks of the Ohio and the Kanawha to cut off General Lewis should he attempt to retreat across either river. Cornstalk meant not only to defeat the army but to destroy it. The Virginians numbered eleven hundred.

When the news of the advance of the Indian army reached General Lewis, he prepared for battle, and sent three hundred men to the front to meet the enemy. The fight began at sunrise. Both armies were soon engaged over a line a mile long. Both fought from behind trees, logs and whatever would offer protection. The lines were always near each other; sometimes twenty yards, sometimes less; occasionally near enough to use the tomahawk. The battle was remarkable for its obstinacy. It raged six hours, almost hand to hand. Then the Indians fell back a short distance and took up a strong position, and all efforts to dislodge them by attacks in front failed. Cornstalk was along his whole line, and above the din of battle his powerful voice could be heard: "Be strong! Be strong!" The loss was heavy among the Virginians, and perhaps nearly as heavy among the Indians. Late in the afternoon General Lewis discovered a way to attack the Indians in flank. A small stream with high banks empties into the Kanawha at that point, and he sent a detachment up this stream, the movement being concealed from the Indians, and when an advantageous point was reached, the soldiers emerged and attacked the Indians. Taken by surprise, the savages retreated. This movement decided the day in favor of the Virginians. The Indians fled a short distance up the Ohio and crossed to the western side, the most of them on logs and rude rafts, probably the same on which they had crossed the stream before the battle. The Virginians lost sixty men killed and ninety-six wounded. The loss of the Indians was not ascertained. They left thirty-three dead on the field, and were seen to throw others into the Ohio River. All their wounded were carried off.

The battle of Point Pleasant was the most stubbornly contested of all frontier battles with the Indians; but it was by no means the bloodiest. Several others could be named in which the loss of life was much greater; notably Braddock's defeat, and the defeat of General St. Clair. The battle of Point Pleasant was also remarkable from the number of men who took part in it who afterwards became noted. Among them may be mentioned Isaac Shelby, the first Governor of Kentucky; William Campbell, the hero of King's Mountain, and who died on the battlefield of Eutaw Springs; Colonel John Steel, afterward Governor of Mississippi; George Mathews, afterward Governor of Georgia; Colonel William Fleming, Governor of Virginia, and many others. Nearly all the men who were in that battle and afterward returned to their homes, were subsequently soldiers of the American army in the war for independence.

The Indians possessed soldierly qualities which have generally been underestimated. On the battlefield they were brave and confident. In their pitched battles with American soldiers on the frontiers they were nearly always out-numbered, and yet they were defeated with difficulty. With a smaller force they defeated Braddock; a smaller force fought Bouquet and almost defeated him. St. Clair's disastrous rout was caused by an inferior force of Indians. After many defeats from Indians in the Northwest, they were whipped only when General Wayne attacked them with three men to their one. The loss of the Indians was nearly always smaller than that of the force opposing them; sometimes, as in the case of Braddock's and of St. Clair's defeats, not more than one-tenth as great. The Indians selected their ground for a fight with cunning judgment, unsurpassed by any people. They never fought after they began to loose heavily, but immediately retreated. This was the only policy possible for them. They had few men, and if they lost heavily, the loss was irreparable.

The day following the battle, Colonel Christian arrived with three hundred soldiers from Fincastle. Fort Randolph was built at Point Pleasant; and after leaving a garrison there, General Lewis crossed the Ohio October 17, and marched nearly a hundred miles to the Scioto River to join Governor Dunmore. Before he arrived at Fort Charlotte, where Dunmore was, he received a message from the Governor, ordering him to stop, and giving as a reason that he was about to negotiate a treaty with the Indians. General Lewis and his men refused at first to obey this order. They had no love for Dunmore, and they did not regard him as a friend of Virginia. Not until a second express arrived did General Lewis obey.

After the fight at Point Pleasant, Cornstalk, Logan and Red Eagle, the three principal chiefs who had taken part in the battle, retreated to their towns with their tribesmen. Seeing that pursuit was swift and vigorous, Cornstalk called a council and asked what should be done. No one had any advice to offer. He then proposed to kill the old men, women and children; and the warriors then should go out to meet the invaders and fight till every Indian had met his death on the field of battle. No reply was made to this proposition. Thereupon Cornstalk said that since his men would not fight, he would go and make peace; and he did so. Thus ended the war. Governor Dunmore had led an army of Virginians into Ohio, and assumed and exercised authority there, thus setting aside and nullifying the Act of Parliament which extended the jurisdiction of Quebec to the Ohio River.

The treaty was made at Camp Charlotte. The Indian Logan, Chief of the Mingoes, as is generally stated, but there seems to be no evidence that he was a chief at all, refused to attend the conference with Dunmore, but sent a speech which has become famous because of the controversy which it has occasioned. The speech, which nearly every school boy knows by heart, is as follows:

"I appeal to any white man to say, if ever he entered Logan's cabin hungry, and he gave him not meat, if ever he came cold and naked, and he clothed him not. During the course of the last long and bloody war, Logan remained idle in his cabin, an advocate of peace. Such was my love for the whites that my countrymen pointed as they passed, and said, Logan is the friend of white men.' I had even thought to have lived with you, but for the injuries of one man, Colonel Cresap, who last spring in cold blood and unprovoked, murdered all the relatives of Logan, not even sparing my women and children. There runs not a drop of my blood in the veins of any living creature. This called upon me for vengeance. I have sought it. I have killed many. I have fully glutted my vengeance. For my country I rejoice at the beams of peace. But do not harbor the thought that mine is the joy of fear. Logan never felt fear. He will not turn on his heel to save his life. Who is there to mourn for Logan? Not one."

The charge has been made that this speech was a forgery, written by Thomas Jefferson. Others have charged that it was changed and interpolated after it was delivered. The part referring to Cresap, in particular, has been pointed out as an interpolation, because it is now known, and was then known, that Cresap (Captain Michael Cresap was meant) did not murder Logan's relatives. The facts in regard to the speech are these: Logan did not make the speech in person, and he did not write it, and he did not dictate it to any person who wrote it; but the speech, substantially as we now have it, read at the conference at Camp Charlotte. Logan would not attend the conference. Simon Girty, who was employed as interpreter, but who could neither read nor write, was sent by Lord Dunmore from Camp Charlotte to hunt for Logan, and found him in his camp, which seems to have been a few miles distant. Logan would not go to the conference, and Girty returned without him. As he approached the circle where the conference was in progress, Captain John Gibson walked out to meet him. He and Girty conversed a few minutes, and Gibson entered his tent alone, and in a few minutes came out with a piece of clean paper on which, in his own hand, was written the now famous Logan speech. It is probable that in the conversation between Logan and Girty, the former had made use of sentiments similar to those in the speech, and Girty repeated them as nearly as he remembered them, to Gibson, and Gibson, who was a good scholar, put the speech in classic English. At the most, the sentiment only, not the words, were Logan's.

CHAPTER V.

—:0:—

WEST VIRGINIA IN THE REVOLUTION.

The territory of the present State of West Virginia was not invaded by a British army, except one company of forty, during the war for American independence. Its remote position made it safe from attack from the east; but this very remoteness rendered it doubly liable to invasion from the west where Great Britain had made allies of the Indians, and had armed and supplied them, and had sent them against the frontiers from Canada to Georgia, with full license to kill man, woman and child. No part of America suffered more from the savages than West Virginia. Great Britain's purpose in employing Indians on the frontiers was to harrass the remote country, and not only keep at home all the inhabitants for defense of their settlements, but also to make it necessary that soldiers be sent to the West who otherwise might be employed in opposing the British near the sea coast. Notwithstanding West Virginia's exposed frontier on the west, it sent many soldiers to the Continental Army. West Virginians were on almost every battlefield of the Revolution. The portion of the State east of the Alleghanies, now forming Jefferson, Berkeley, Morgan, Hampshire, Hardy, Grant, Mineral and Pendleton counties, was not invaded by Indians during the Revolution, and from this region large numbers of soldiers joined the armies under Washington, Gates, Greene and other patriots.

As early as November 5, 1774, an important meeting was held by West Virginians in which they clearly indicated under which banner they would be found fighting, if Great Britain persisted in her course of oppression. This was the first meeting of the kind west of the Alleghanies, and few similar meetings had then been held anywhere. It occurred during the return of Dunmore's Army from Ohio, twenty-five days after the battle of Point Pleasant. The soldiers had heard of the danger of war with England; and, although they were under the command of Dunmore, a royal Governor, they were not afraid to let the country know that neither a royal Governor nor any one else could swerve them from their duty as patriots and lovers of liberty. The meeting was held at Fort Gower, north of the Ohio River. The soldiers passed resolutions which had the right ring. They recited that they were willing and able to bear all hardships of the woods; to get along for weeks without bread or salt, if necessary; to sleep in the open air; to dress in skins if nothing else could be had; to march further in a day than any other men in the world; to use the rifle with skill and with bravery. They affirmed their zeal in the cause of right, and promised continued allegiance to the King of England, provided he would reign over them as a brave and free people. "But," they continued, "as attachment to the real interests and just rights of America outweigh every other consideration, we resolve that we will exert every power within us for the defence of American liberty, when regularly called forth by the unanimous voice of our countrymen." It was such spirit as this, manifested on every occasion during the Revolution, which prompted Washington in the darkest year of the war to exclaim that if driven from every point east of the Blue Ridge, he would retire west of the mountains and there raise the standard of liberty and bid defiance to the armies of Great Britain.

At two meetings held May 16, 1775, one at Fort Pitt, the other at Hannastown, several West Virginians were present and took part in the proceedings. Resolutions were passed by which the people west of the mountains pledged their support to the Continental Congress, and expressed their purpose of resisting the tyranny of the mother country. In 1775 a number of men from the Valley of the Monongahela joined Washington's army before Boston. The number of soldiers who went forward from the eastern part of the State was large.

There were a few persons in West Virginia who adhered to the cause of England; and who from time to time gave trouble to the patriots; but the promptness with which their attempted risings were crushed is proof that traitors were in a hopeless minority. The patriots considered them as enemies and dealt harshly with them. There were two attempted uprisings in West Virginia, one in the Monongahela Valley, which the inhabitants of that region were able to suppress; the other uprising was on the South Branch of the Potomac, in what is now Hardy and Grant Counties, and troops were sent from the Shenandoah Valley to put it down. In the Monongahela Valley several of the tories were arrested and sent to Richmond. It is recorded that the leader was drowned in Cheat River while crossing under guard on his way to Richmond. Two men of the Morgan family were his guard. The boat upset while crossing the river. It was the general impression of the citizens of the community that the upsetting was not accidental. The guards did not like to take the long journey to Richmond while their homes and the homes of their neighbors were exposed to attacks from Indians. The tory uprising on the South Branch was much more serious. The first indication of trouble was given by their refusal to pay their taxes, or to furnish their quota of men for the militia. Complaint was made by the Sheriff of Hampshire county, and Colonel Vanmeter with thirty men was sent to enforce the collection of taxes. The tories armed themselves, to the number of fifty, for resistance, and placed themselves under the leadership of John Brake, a German, whose house was above Petersburg, in what is now Grant County. These enemies of their country had made his place their rendezvous. They met the militia from Hampshire, but no fight took place. Apparently each side was afraid to begin. There was a parley in which Colonel Vanmeter pointed out to the tories the consequence which must follow, if they persisted in their present course. He advised them to disperse, go to their homes and conduct themselves as law-abiding citizens. He left them and marched home.

The disloyal elements grew in strength and insolence. They imagined that the authorities were afraid and would not again interfere with them. They organized a company, elected John Claypole their captain, and prepared to march off and join the British forces. General Morgan was at that time at his home in Frederick County, and he collected militia to the number of four hundred, crossed the mountain and fell on the tories in such dead earnest that they lost all their enthusiasm for the cause of Great Britain. Claypole was taken prisoner, and William Baker, who refused to surrender, was shot, but not killed. Later a man named Mace was killed. Brake was overawed; and after two days spent in the neighborhood, the militia, under General Morgan, returned home. The tories were crushed. A number of them were so ashamed of what they had done that they joined the American army and fought as patriots till the close of the war, thus endeavoring to redeem their lost reputations.

The contrast between the conduct of the tories on the South Branch and the patriotic devotion of the people on the Greenbrier is marked. Money was so scarce that the Greenbrier settlers could not pay their taxes, although willing to do so. They fell delinquent four years in succession and to the amount of thirty thousand dollars. They were willing to perform labor if arrangements could be made to do it. Virginia agreed to the proposition, and the people of Greenbrier built a road from Lewisburg to the Kanawha River in payment of their taxes.

The chief incidents in West Virginia's history during the Revolutionary War were connected with the Indian troubles. The State was invaded four times by forces large enough to be called armies; and the incursions by smaller parties were so numerous that the mere mention of them would form a list of murders, ambuscades and personal encounters of tedious and monotonous length. The first invasion occurred in 1777 when Fort Henry, now Wheeling, was attacked; the second, 1778, when Fort Randolph, now Point Pleasant, was besieged for one week, the Indians moving as far east as Greenbrier County, where Donnolly's fort was attacked; the third invasion was in August, 1781, when Fort Henry was again attacked by 250 Indians under the leadership of Matthew Elliott. The fourth invasion occurred in September, 1782, when Wheeling was again attacked. The multitude of incursions by Indians must be passed over briefly. The custom of the savages was to make their way into a settlement and either lie in wait along paths and shoot those who attempted to pass or break into houses and murder the inmates or take them prisoner, and then make off hastily for the Ohio River. Once across that stream, pursuit was not probable.

The custom of the Indians in taking prisoners, and their great exertion to accomplish that purpose, is a difficult thing to explain. Prisoners were of little or no use to them. They did not make slaves of them. If they sometimes received money as ransom for captives the hope of ransom money seems seldom or never to have prompted them to carry prisoners to their towns. They sometimes showed a liking, if not affection, for captives adopted into their tribes and families; but this kindly feeling was shallow and treacherous, and Indians would not hesitate to burn at the stake a captive who had been treated as one of their family for months if they should take it into their heads that revenge for injuries received from others called for a sacrifice. The Indians followed no rule or precedent as to which of their captives they would kill and which carry to their towns. They sometimes killed children and spared adults, and sometimes the reverse.

When the Revolutionary War began the English and the Americans strove to obtain the good will of the western Indians. The Americans sent Simon Girty and James Wood on a peaceful mission to the Ohio tribes in July, 1775. On February 22 of that year Simon Girty had taken the oath of allegiance to the King of England, but when war commenced he took sides with the Americans. In July, 1775, Congress created three Indian departments, that embracing the portions of West Virginia and Pennsylvania west of the Alleghanies, to be known as the Middle Department. Commissioners were appointed to establish and maintain friendly relations with the Indians. In October of that year delegates from several of the Ohio tribes visited Pittsburg, which, since September before, had been occupied by Captain John Neville and a garrison of one hundred Americans. The Indian delegates made a treaty and agreed to remain neutral during the trouble between the colonies and Great Britain.

The British were less humane. Instead of urging the savages to remain neutral, as the Americans had done, they excited the tribes to take up the hatchet against the Americans. The subsequent horrors of the Indian warfare along the frontier are chargeable to the British, who resorted to "every means which God and nature had placed in their power" to annoy the Americans. The most industrious of British agents in stirring up the Indians was Henry Hamilton, who in April, 1775, was appointed Lieutenant-Governor and Indian agent, with headquarters at Detroit. His salary was one thousand dollars a year. He reached his destination November 9, 1775. The Indians flocked to him and importuned him for permission and assistance to attack the settlements. But Hamilton had not yet received instructions from his government, authorizing him to employ Indians, and he did not send them to war at that time. In June, 1776, George Morgan, Indian agent for the Middle Department, held a conference with some of the Ohio tribes and succeeded in keeping them away from Detroit at that time. The suggestion that Indians be employed against the Americans came from Governor Hamilton late in 1776. The proposition was eagerly accepted; and on March 26, 1777, Lord George Germain gave the fatal order that Hamilton assemble all the Indians possible and send them against the frontiers, under the leadership of proper persons who could restrain them. This order was received by Governor Hamilton in June 1777, and before August 1 he had sent out fifteen marauding parties aggregating 289 Indians.

The year 1777 is called in border history the "bloody year of the three sevens." The British sent against the frontiers every Indian who could be prevailed upon to go. Few settlements from New York to Florida escaped. In this State the most harm was done on the Monongahela and along the Ohio in the vicinity of Wheeling. Monongalia County was visited twice by the savages that year, and a number of persons were killed. A party of twenty invaded what is now Randolph county, killed a number of settlers, took several prisoners and made their escape. It was on November 10 of this year that Cornstalk, the Shawnee chief, was assassinated at Point Pleasant by militiamen who assembled there from Greenbrier and elsewhere for the purpose of marching against the Indian towns. Earlier in the year Cornstalk had come to Fort Randolph, at Point Pleasant, on a visit, and also to inform the commandant of the fort that the British were inciting the Indians to war, and that his own tribe, the Shawnees, would likely be swept along with the current, in spite of his efforts to keep them at home. Under these circumstances the commandant of the fort thought it best to detain Cornstalk as a hostage to insure the neutrality of his tribe. It does not seem that the venerable Chief was unwilling to remain. He wanted peace. Some time after that his son came to see him, and crossed the Ohio, after making his presence known by hallooing from the other side. The next day two of the militiamen crossed the Ohio to hunt and one was killed by an Indian. The other gave the alarm, and the militiamen crossed the river and brought in the body of the dead man. The soldiers believed that the Indian who had committed the deed had come the day before with Cornstalk's son, and had lain concealed until an opportunity occurred to kill a man. The soldiers were enraged, and started up the river bank toward the cabin where Cornstalk resided, announcing that they would kill the Indians. There were with Cornstalk his son and another Indian, Red Eagle. A sister of Cornstalk, known as the Granadier Squaw, had lived at the fort some time as interpreter. She hastened to the cabin and urged her brother to make his escape. He might have done so, but refused, and admonished his son to die like a man. The soldiers arrived at that time and fired. All three Indians were killed. The leaders of the men who did it were afterwards given the semblance of a trial in Virginia, and were acquitted.

It is the opinion of those acquainted with border history that the murder of Cornstalk brought more suffering upon the West Virginia frontier than any other event of that time. Had he lived, he would perhaps have been able to hold the Shawnees in check. Without the co-operation of that bloodthirsty tribe the border war of the succeeding years would have been different. Four years later Colonel Crawford, who had been taken prisoner, was put to death with extreme torture in revenge for the murder of Cornstalk, as some of the Indians claimed.

Fort Henry was besieged September 1, 1777, by two hundred Indians. General Hand, of Fort Pitt, had been informed that the Indians were preparing for an attack in large numbers upon some point of the frontier, and the settlements between Pittsburg and Point Pleasant were placed on their guard. Scouts were sent out to discover the advance of the Indians in time to give the alarm. But the scouts discovered no Indians. It is now known that the savages had advanced in small parties, avoiding trails, and had united near Wheeling, crossed the Ohio a short distance below that place, and on the night of the last day of August approached Fort Henry, and setting ambuscades near it, waited for daylight. Fort Henry was made of logs set on end in the ground, in the manner of pickets, and about seventeen feet high. There were port holes through which to fire. The garrison consisted of less than forty men, the majority of whom lived in Wheeling and the immediate vicinity. Early in the morning of September 1 the Indians decoyed Captain Samuel Mason with fourteen men into the field some distance from the fort, and killed all but three. Captain Mason alone reached the fort, and two of his men succeeded in hiding, and finally escaped. When the Indians attacked Mason's men, the firing was heard at the fort, together with the yells of the savages. Captain Joseph Ogle with twelve men sallied out to assist Mason. He was surrounded and nine of his men were killed. There were only about a dozen men remaining in the fort to resist the attack of four hundred Indians, flushed with victory. There were perhaps one hundred women and children in the stockade.

In a short time the Indians advanced against the fort, with drum and fife, and the British flag waving over them. It is not known who was leader. He was a white man, or at least there was a white man among them who seemed to be leader. Many old frontier histories, as well as the testimony of those who were present, united in the assertion that the Indians at this siege were led by Simon Girty. It is strange that this mistake could have been made, for it was a mistake. Simon Girty was not there. He was at that time, and for nearly five months afterwards, near Fort Pitt. The commander of the Indian army posted himself in the window of a house within hearing of the fort, and read the proclamation of Governor Hamilton, of Detroit, offering Great Britain's protection in case of surrender, but massacre in case of resistance. Colonel Shepherd, commandant of the fort, replied that the garrison would not surrender. The leader was insisting upon the impossibility of holding out, when his words were cut short by a shot fired at him from the fort. He was not struck. The Indians began the assault with a rush for the fort gate. They tried to break it open; and failing in this, they endeavored to push the posts of the stockade down. They could make no impression on the wall. The fire of the garrison was deadly, and the savages recoiled. They charged again and again, some times trying to break down the walls with battering rams, attempting to set them on fire; and then sending their best marksmen to pick off the garrison by shooting through the port holes. In course of time the deadly aim of those in the fort taught the savages a wholesome caution. Women fought as well as men. The siege continued two nights and two days, but all attempts of the Indians to burn the fort or break into it were unavailing. They killed many of the cattle about the settlement, partly for food partly from wantonness. They burned nearly all the houses and barns in Wheeling. The savages were preparing for another assault when Colonel Andrew Swearengen, with fourteen men, landed near the fort and gained an entrance. Shortly afterwards Major Samuel McColloch, at the head of forty men, arrived, and after a severe fight, all reached the fort except McColloch, who was cut off, but made his escape. The Indians now despaired of success, and raised the siege. No person in the fort was killed. The loss of the Indians was estimated at forty or fifty.

In September of this year, 1777, Captain William Foreman, of Hampshire County, with about twenty men of that county, who had gone to Wheeling to assist in fighting the savages, was ambushed and killed at Grave Creek, below Wheeling, by Indians supposed to have been a portion of those who had besieged Fort Henry.

On March 28, 1778, Simon Girty ran away from Pittsburg in company with Alexander McKee, Robert Surphitt, Matthew Elliott, —— Higgins and two negroes belonging to McKee. It is misleading to call Girty a deserter, as he was not in the military service. He had formerly been an interpreter in pay, but he was discharged for unbecoming behavior. He had two brothers, James and George, who also joined the British and did service among the Indians; and one brother who remained true to the Americans. Simon Girty reached Detroit in June, 1778, after a loitering journey through the Indian country, during which he busied himself stirring up mischief. He was employed by the British as interpreter at two dollars a day, and was sent by Hamilton to work among the Ohio Indians. His influence for evil was great, and his character shows few redeeming traits.

The year 1778 was one of intense excitement on the frontier. An Indian force of about two hundred attacked Fort Randolph, at the mouth of the Kanawha, in May, and besieged the place one week. The savages made several attempts to carry it by storm. But they were unsuccessful. They then moved off, up the Kanawha, in the direction of Greenbrier. Two soldiers from Fort Randolph eluded the savages, overtook them within twenty miles of the Greenbrier settlement, passed them that night, and alarmed the people just in time for them to flee to the blockhouses. Donnally's fort stood within two miles of the present village of Frankfort, in Greenbrier County. Twenty men, with their families, took shelter there.

At Lewisburg, ten miles distant, perhaps one hundred men had assembled, with their families. The Indians apparently knew which was the weaker fort, and accordingly proceeded against Donnally's, upon which they made an attack at daybreak. One of the men had gone out for kindling wood and had left the gate open. The Indians killed this man and made a rush for the fort and crowded into the yard. While some crawled under the floor, hoping to gain an entrance by that means, others climbed to the roof. Still others began hewing the door, which had been hurriedly closed. All the men in the fort were asleep except one white man and a negro slave. As the savages were forcing open the door, the foremost was killed with a tomahawk by the white man, and the negro discharged a musket loaded with heavy shot into the faces of the Indians. The men in the fort were awakened and fired through the port holes. Seventeen savages were killed in the yard. The others fell back, and contented themselves with firing at longer range. In the afternoon sixty-six men arrived from Lewisburg, and the Indians were forced to raise the siege. Their expedition to Greenbrier had been a more signal failure than the attempt on Fort Randolph.

The country along the Monongahela was invaded three times in the year 1778, and once the following year. Few settlements within one hundred miles of the Ohio River escaped. In 1780 Greenbrier was again paid a visit by the savages; and in this year their raids extended eastward into Randolph County, and to Cheat River, in Tucker County, to the very base of the Alleghany Mountains. The Monongahela Valley, as usual, did not escape, and ten settlers were killed.

In this year General George Roger Clark, with a small but excellent army, invaded Illinois to break up the British influence there. He left Captain Helm in charge of Vincennes, Indiana. No sooner had Governor Hamilton heard of the success of Clark than he set out from Detroit to reestablish the British prestige. He took with him thirty-five British regulars, forty-four irregulars, seventy militia and sixty Indians. He picked other Indians up on the way, and reached Vincennes December 17. Captain Helm surrendered. Hamilton then dismissed the Indians, ordering them to re-assemble the next spring with large reenforcements. His designs were ambitious, embracing conquests no less extensive than the driving of the Americans out of Illinois, Indiana, Kentucky, West Virginia, and the capture of Pittsburg. But General Clark destroyed all of these high hopes. Marching in the dead of winter he captured Vincennes, February 25, 1779, after a severe fight, and released nearly one hundred white prisoners, chastised the Indians, captured stores worth fifty thousand dollars, cleared the whole country of British from the Mississippi to Detroit; and, most important of all, captured Governor Hamilton himself, and sent him in chains to Richmond. This victory secured to the United States the country as far as the Mississippi; and it greatly dampened the ardor of the Indians. They saw for the first time that the British were not able to protect them.

Fort McIntosh was built in 1778 on the north bank of the Ohio, below the mouth of Beaver, and the headquarters of the army were moved from Pittsburg to that place, October 8, 1778. In the same year Fort Laurens was built on the west bank of the Tuscarawas, below the mouth of Sandy Creek, and Colonel John Gibson was placed in command with 150 men. On March 22, 1779, Captain Bird, a British officer from Detroit, and Simon Girty, with 120 Indians and seven or eight British soldiers, besieged the fort and remained before it nearly a month, but failed to take it, although they killed a number of soldiers.

In April, 1781, General Brodhead, with 150 regulars and 150 militia, crossed the Ohio at Wheeling and led an expedition against the Delawares at Coshocton. He killed or captured thirty Indians and destroyed a few towns. He suffered little loss. In 1782 occurred the massacre of the Moravian Indians in Ohio. They lived under the care of missionaries, and claimed to be at peace with all men. But articles of clothing were discovered among them which were recognized as belonging to white settlers who had been murdered in West Virginia. This confirmed the suspicion that the Moravian Indians, if they did not take part in raids against the settlements, had a good understanding with Indians who were engaged in raiding They were therefore put to death. The act was barbarous and inexcusable.

The third and last siege of Wheeling occurred in September 1782. The British planned an attack on Wheeling in July of that year, just after Crawford's defeat which had greatly encouraged the Indians. They had scarcely ended the torture of prisoners who had fallen into their hands, including Colonel Crawford, when they clamored to be led against the settlements. The British were only too willing to assist them; and in July a number of British soldiers and 300 Indians, under command of a white man named Caldwell, moved toward Wheeling. Simon and George Girty were in this force. Before the army had fairly set out, news came that General Clark was invading the Indian country. The army on the march to Wheeling halted. At the same time a rumor was spread that General Irvine was marching toward Canada from Pittsburg. Re-inforcements for Canada were asked for, and 1400 Indians assembled. Subsequently it was learned that the reports of invasions were unfounded, and the Indian army dispersed. Caldwell with George and Simon Girty and 300 Indians invaded Kentucky and attacked Bryant's station August 14, 1782. The British and Indians did not give up the proposed expedition against Wheeling, and Capt. Pratt with 40 British regulars and 238 Indians marched against the place and attacked it September 11. James Girty was with this expedition but had no command. Simon Girty was never present at any attack on Wheeling.

There were fewer than twenty men in Fort Henry at Wheeling when the Indians appeared. The commandant, Captain Boggs, had gone to warn the neighboring settlements of danger. The whole attacking force marched under the British flag. Just before the attack commenced, a boat, in charge of a man named Sullivan, arrived from Pittsburg, loaded with cannon balls for the garrison at Louisville, Kentucky. Mr. Sullivan and his party seeing the danger, tied the boat and made their way to the fort and assisted in the defense. The besiegers demanded an immediate surrender, which was not complied with. The attack was delayed till night. The experience gained by the Indians in the war had taught them that little is gained by a wild rush against the walls of a stockade. No doubt Captain Pratt advised them also what course to pursue. When night came they made their assault. More than twenty times did they pile hemp against the walls of the fort and attempt to set the structure on fire. But the hemp was damp and burned slowly. No harm was done. Colonel Zane's cabin stood near the stockade. His house had been burned at the siege in 1777; and when the Indians again appeared he resolved to defend his building. He remained in the cabin with two or three others, among them a negro slave. That night an Indian crawled up with a chunk of fire to burn

THE LAST BATTLE OF THE REVOLUTION, SEPTEMBER 11, 1782.

This picture is made (by special permission) from the remarkable historical painting by Joseph A. Faris. A force of British and Indians attacked enry (Wheeling, W. Va.) and was repulsed. The flag which was shot down by a rifleman during the attack was the last flag carried in battle by a force on United States soil during the Revolution.

the house, but a shot from the negro's gun crippled him and he gave up his incendiary project. Attempts were made to break down the gates, but they did not succeed. A small cannon mounted on one of the bastions was occasionally discharged among the savages, much to their discomfiture. On one occasion when a number of Indians had gathered in a loft of one of the nearest cabins and were dancing and yelling in defiance of the garrison, the cannon was turned on them, and a solid shot cutting one of the joists, precipitated the savages to the floor beneath and put a stop to their revelry.

The Indians captured the boat with the cannon balls, and decided to use them. They procured a hollow log, plugged one end, and wrapped it with chains stolen from a neighboring blacksmith shop. They loaded the piece with powder and ball, and fired it at the fort. Pieces of the wooden cannon flew in all directions, killing and maiming several Indians, but did not harm the fort. The savages were discouraged, and when a force of seventy men, under Captain Boggs, approached, the Indians fled. They did not, however, leave the country at once, but made an attack on Rice's fort, where they lost four warriors and accomplished nothing.

The siege of Fort Henry is remarkable from the fact that the flag under which the army marched to the attack, and which was shot down during the fight, was the last British flag to float over an army in battle, during the Revolution, within the limits of the United States. West Virginia was never again invaded by a large Indian force, but small parties continued to make incursions till 1795. The war with England closed by a treaty of peace in 1783. In July of that year DePeyster, Governor at Detroit, called the Indians together, told them that the war between America and Great Britain was at an end, and dismissed them. After that date the Indians fought on their own account, although the British still held posts in the Northwest, under the excuse that the Americans had not complied with the terms of the treaty of peace. It was believed, and not without evidence, that the savages were still encouraged by the British, if not directly supplied with arms, to wage war against the frontiers. In the autumn of 1783 there was a large gathering of Indians at Sandusky, where they were harangued by Sir John Johnson, the British Superintendent of Indian affairs. Simon Girty was present and was using his influence for evil. Johnson urged the Indians to further resistance.

In February, 1783, while the English Parliament was discussing the American treaty, about to be ratified, Lord North, who opposed peace on the proposed terms, insisted that the Americans should be shut away from the Great Lakes; the forts in that vicinity should be held, and Canada should be extended to the Ohio River. He declared that the Indian allies of Great Britain ought to be cared for, and that their independence ought to be guaranteed by Great Britain. In the autumn of that year, 1783, when the order was given for the evacuation of New York by the British, Lord North, on the petition of merchants and fur traders of Canada, withheld the order for the evacuation of the posts about the lakes. On August 8 of that year Baron Steuben, who had been sent for that purpose by the Americans, demanded of Governor Haldimand of Canada, that British forces be withdrawn from the posts in the Northwest. Governor Haldimand replied that he had received no instructions on that subject, and he would not surrender the posts. The British, in 1785, claimed that they continued to hold the posts in Ohio, Indiana and beyond because some of the states, and especially Virginia, had not yet opened their courts to British creditors for the collection of debts against Americans incurred before the war. Thus the British continued to occupy posts clearly within the United States, much to the irritation of the American people. The Indians were restless, and the belief was general, and was well founded, that the British were encouraging them to hostility. They became insolent, and invaded the settlements in West Virginia and Kentucky, and in 1790 the United States declared war upon them and took vigorous measures to bring them to terms. General Harmar invaded the country north of the Ohio at the head of a strong force in 1790. He suffered his army to be divided and defeated. The next year General St. Clair led an army into the Indian country, and met with one of the most disastrous defeats in the annals of Indian warfare. He lost nearly eight hundred men in one battle. General Wayne now took charge of the campaign in the Indian country. When he began to invade the northern part Ohio, the British about Lake Erie moved south and built a fort on the Maumee River, opposite Perrysville, Ohio. This was in the summer of 1794. The object in building the fort was clearly to encourage the Indians and to insult the Americans. On August 20, 1794, General Wayne found the Indians within two miles of the British fort, prepared for battle. He made an attack on the savages, routed them in a few minutes and drove them. They were crushed and there was no more fight in them for fifteen years.

General Wayne was a Revolutionary soldier, and had little love for the British. The sight of their fort on American soil filled him with impatience to attack it; but he did not wish to do so without a pretext. He hoped to provoke the garrison to attack him, to give him an excuse to destroy the fort. He therefore camped his army after the battle within half a mile of the fort. The commandant sent a message to him saying: "The commandant of the British fort is surprised to see an American army advanced so far into this country," and "why has the army had the assurance to camp under the very mouths of His Majesty's cannon?" General Wayne answered that the battle which had just taken place might well inform the British what the American army was doing in that country, and added: "Had the flying savages taken shelter under the walls of the fort, His Majesty's cannon should not have protected them." Two days later General Wayne destroyed everything to within one hundred yards of the fort, and laid waste the Indian fields of corn, pumpkins and beans for miles around. The country was highly cultivated, there being thousands of acres in corn and vegetables. Finding that his efforts thus far had failed to provoke an attack by the garrison, General Wayne led his soldiers to within pistol shot of the walls, in hope of bringing a shot from his inveterate enemies. But the only reply General Wayne received was a flag of truce with another message, which stated that "the British commandant is much aggrieved at seeing His Majesty's colors insulted." Wayne then burned all the houses and destroyed all the property to the very walls of the fort. This campaign ended the depredation of the Indians in West Virginia.

CHAPTER VI.

SUBDIVISIONS AND BOUNDARIES.

West Virginia's boundaries coincide, in part, with the boundaries of five other States, Ohio, Pennsylvania, Maryland, Virginia and Kentucky. Some of these lines are associated with events of historical interest, and for a number of years were subjects of controversy, not always friendly. It is understood, of course, that all the boundary lines of the territory now embraced in West Virginia, except the line between this State and Virginia, were agreed to and settled before West Virginia became a seperate State. That is, the lines between this State and Pennsylvania, Maryland, Kentucky and Ohio were all settled more than one hundred years ago. To speak briefly of each, the line separating West Virginia from Ohio may be taken first.

At the time the Articles of Confederation were under discussion in Congress, 1778, Virginia's territory extended westward to the Mississippi River. The government of the United States never recognized the Quebec Act, which was passed by the English Parliament before the Revolutionary War, and which extended the province of Quebec south to the Ohio River. Consequently, after the Declaration of Independence was signed, Virginia's claim to that territory was not disputed by the other colonies; but when the time came for agreeing to the Articles of Confederation which bound the states together in one common country, objection was raised to Virginia's extensive territory, which was nearly as large as all the other states together. The fear was expressed that Virginia would become so powerful and wealthy, on account of its extent, that it would possess and exercise an influence in the affairs of government too great for the well-being of the other states.

Maryland appears to have been the first state to take a decided stand that Virginia should cede its territory north and west of the Ohio to the general government. It was urged in justification of this course that the territory had been conquered from the British and the Indians by the blood and treasure of the whole country, and that it was right that the vacant lands should be appropriated to the use of the citizens of the whole country. Maryland took this stand June 22, 1778. Virginia refused to consent to the ceding of her western territory; and from that time till February 2, 1781, Maryland refused to agree to the Articles of Confederation. On November 2, 1778, New Jersey formally filed an objection to Virginia's large territory; but the New Jersey delegates finally signed the Articles of Confederation, expressing at the same time the conviction that justice would in time remove the inequality in territories as far as possible. On February 22, 1779, the delegates from Delaware signed, but also remonstrated, and presented resolutions setting forth that the United States Congress ought to have power to fix the western limits of any state claiming territory to the Mississippi or beyond. On May 21, 1779, the delegates from Maryland laid before Congress instructions received by them from the General Assembly of Maryland. The point aimed at in these instructions was that those states having almost boundless western territory had it in their power to sell lands at a very low price, thus filling their treasuries with money, thereby lessening taxation; and at the same time the cheap lands and the low taxes would draw away from adjoining states many of the best inhabitants. Congress was, therefore, asked to use its influence with those states having extensive territory, to the end that they would not place their lands on the market until the close of the Revolutionary War. Virginia was not mentioned by name, but it was well known that reference was made to that State. Congress passed, October 30, 1779, a resolution requesting Virginia not to open a land office till the close of the war. On March 7, 1780, the delegates from New York announced that State ready to give up its western territory; and this was formally done on March 1, 1781. New York having thus opened the way, other states followed the example and ceded to the United States their western territories or claims as follows: Virginia, March 1, 1784; Massachusetts, April 19, 1785; Connecticut, September 14, 1786; South Carolina, August 9, 1787; North Carolina, February 25, 1790; Georgia, April 24, 1802.

Within less than two months after Virginia ceded her northwest territory to the United States, Congress passed an ordinance for the government of the territory. The deed of cession was made by Thomas Jefferson, Arthur Lee, Samuel Hardy and James Monroe, delegates in Congress from Virginia. The boundary line between Virginia and the territory ceded to the general government was the northwest bank of the Ohio River at low water. The islands in the stream belonged to Virginia. When West Virginia became a separate State, the boundary remained unchanged.

The line between West Virginia and Kentucky remains the same as that formerly separating Virginia from Kentucky. The General Assembly of Virginia, December 18, 1789, passed an act authorizing a convention to be held in the District of Kentucky to consider whether it was expedient to form that district into a separate State. The convention decided to form a State, and Kentucky was admitted into the Union in 1792. Commissioners were appointed to adjust the boundary line between Virginia and Kentucky, and agreed that the line separating the two states should remain the same as that formerly separating Virginia from the District of Kentucky. The line is as follows so far as West Virginia and Kentucky are contiguous: Beginning at the northwestern point of McDowell County, thence down Big Sandy River to its confluence with the Ohio.

The line dividing the northern limits of West Virginia from the southern limits of Pennsylvania was for many years a matter of dispute. Maryland and Pennsylvania had nearly a century of bickering concerning the matter before Virginia took it up in earnest. It is not necessary at this time to give the details of the controversy. A few facts will suffice. Pennsylvania and Maryland having contended for a long time over their common boundary line, two eminent astronomers, Charles Mason and Jeremiah Dixon of England, were employed to mark a line five degrees west from the Delaware River at a point where it is crossed by the parallel of north latitude 39 degrees, 43 minutes, 26 seconds. They commenced work in the latter part of 1763, and completed it in the latter part of 1767. This line,

SUBDIVISIONS AND BOUNDARIES.

called Mason and Dixon's line, was accepted as the boundary between Pennsylvania and Maryland, and the controversy was at an end. But beyond the west line of Maryland, where Virginia's and Pennsylvania's posessions came in contact, a dispute arose, almost leading to open hostilities between the people of the two states. Virginia wanted Pittsburg, and boldly and stubbornly set up a claim to territory, at least as far north as the fortieth degree of latitude. This would have given Virginia part of Fayette and Greene Counties, Pennsylvania. On the other hand, Pennsylvania claimed the country south to the thirty-ninth degree, which would have extended its jurisdiction over the present territory of West Virginia included in the counties of Monongalia, Preston, Marion, Taylor, parts of Tucker, Barbour, Upshur, Lewis, Harrison, Wetzel and Randolph. The territory in dispute was about four times as large as the State of Rhode Island. It was finally settled by a compromise. It was agreed that the Mason and Dixon's line be extended west five degrees from the Delaware River. The commissioners appointed to adjust the boundary were Dr. James Madison and Robert Andrews on the part of Virginia, and David Ritenhouse, John Ewing and George Bryan on the part of Pennsylvania. They met at Baltimore in 1779 and agreed upon a line. The next year the agreement was ratified, by Virginia in June and Pennsylvania in September. A line was then run due north from the western end of Mason and Dixon's line, till it reached the Ohio River. This completed the boundary lines between Virginia and Pennsylvania; and West Virginia's territory is bounded by the same lines.

The fixing of the boundary between Virginia and Maryland was long a subject of controversy. It began in the early years of the colony, long before the Revolutionary War, and has continued, it may be said, till the present day, for occasionally the agitation is revived. West Virginia inherited most of the subject of dispute when it set up a separate government. The controversy began so early in the history of the country, when the geography of what is now West Virginia was so imperfectly understood, that boundaries were stated in general terms; following certain rivers; and in after time these general terms were differently understood. Nearly two hundred years ago the Potomac River was designated as the dividing line between lands granted in Maryland and lands granted in Virginia; but at that time the upper tributaries of that river had never been explored, and as no one knew what was the main stream and what were tributary streams, Lord Fairfax had the stream explored, and the explorers decided that the main river had its source at a point where the Fairfax Stone was planted, the present corner of Tucker, Preston and Grant Counties, in West Virginia. It also was claimed as the southwest corner of Maryland. It has so remained to this day, but not without much controversy on the part of Maryland.

The claim was set up by Maryland, in 1830, that the stream known as the South Branch of the Potomac is the main Potomac River, and that all territory north of that stream and south of Pennsylvania, belonged to Maryland. A line drawn due north from the source of the South Branch to the Pennsylvania line was to be the western boundary of Maryland. Had that State succeeded in establishing its claim and extending its jurisdiction, the following territory would have been transferred to Maryland: Part of Highland County, Virginia; portions of Randolph, Tucker, Preston, Pendleton, Hardy, Grant, Hampshire and all of Mineral Counties, West Virginia. The claim of Maryland was resisted, and Governor Floyd, of Virginia, appointed Charles J. Faulkner, of Martinsburg, to investigate the whole matter, and ascertain, if possible, which was the main Potomac, and to consult all available early authorities on the subject. Mr. Faulkner filed his report November 6, 1832, and in this report he showed that the South Branch was not the main Potomac, and that the line as fixed by Lord Fairfax's surveyors remained the true and proper boundary between Virginia and Maryland. The line due north from the Fairfax Stone to the Pennsylvania line remains the boundary in that quarter between West Virginia and Maryland, but the latter State is still disputing it.

When West Virginia separated from Virginia and took steps to set up a government for itself, it was at one time proposed to call the State Kanawha; and its eastern boundary was indicated so as to exclude some of the best counties now in the State. The counties to be excluded were Mercer, Greenbrier, Monroe, Pocahontas, Pendleton, Hardy, then including Grant; Hampshire, then including Mineral; Morgan, Berkeley and Jefferson. It was provided that any adjoining county of Virginia on the east might become a part of the State of West Virginia whenever a majority of the people of the county expressed a willingness to enter the new State. But, before the State was admitted the boundary line was changed and was fixed as it now is found.

As is well known, the territory which now forms West Virginia was a portion of Virginia from the first exploration of the country until separated from the State during the Civil War, in 1863. For a quarter of a century after the first settlement was planted in Virginia there were no counties; but as the country began to be explored, and when the original settlement at Jamestown grew, and others were made, it was deemed expedient to divide the State into counties, although the entire population at that time was scarcely enough for one respectable county. Accordingly, Virginia was divided into eight counties in 1634. The western limits were not clearly defined, except that Virginia claimed the land from the Atlantic to the Pacific, and it was no doubt intended that the counties on the west should embrace all her territory in that direction. The country beyond the Blue Ridge was unexplored, and only the vaguest ideas existed concerning it. There was a prevailing belief that beyond the Blue Ridge the country sloped to the Pacific, and that a river would be found with its source in the Blue Ridge and its mouth in that ocean.

The eastern portion of West Virginia, along the Potomac and its tributaries in 1735, was no longer an unbroken wilderness, but settlements existed in several places. In 1738 it was urged that there were people enough in the territory to warrant the formation of a new county. Accordingly, that portion of Orange west of the Blue Ridge was formed into two counties, Augusta and Frederick. Thus Orange County no longer embraced any portion of the territory now in this State. Frederick County embraced the lower, or northern part of the Shenandoah Valley, with Winchester as the county seat, and Augusta the Southern, or Upper Valley, with Staunton as the seat of justice. Augusta then included almost all of West Virginia and extended to the Mississippi River, including Ohio, Kentucky, Michigan, Indiana and Illinois. From its territory all the counties of West Virginia, except Jefferson, Berkeley and part of Morgan, have been formed, and its subdivision into counties will be the subject of this chapter. No part of West Virginia retains the name of Augusta, but the county still exists in

SUBDIVISIONS AND BOUNDARIES. 61

Virginia, part of the original county of that name, and its county seat is the same as at first—Staunton.

In 1769 Botetourt county was formed from Augusta and included the territory now embraced in McDowell, Wyoming, Mercer, Monroe, Raleigh and portions of Greenbrier, Boone and Logan. No county in West Virginia now has the name Botetourt. It is thus seen that no one of the first counties in the territory of West Virginia retains any name in it. Essex, Spotsylvania, Orange, Augusta and Botetourt, each in its turn, embraced large parts of the State, but all the territory remaining under the original names is found in old Virginia, where the names are preserved. The District of West Augusta was a peculiar division of West Virginia's present

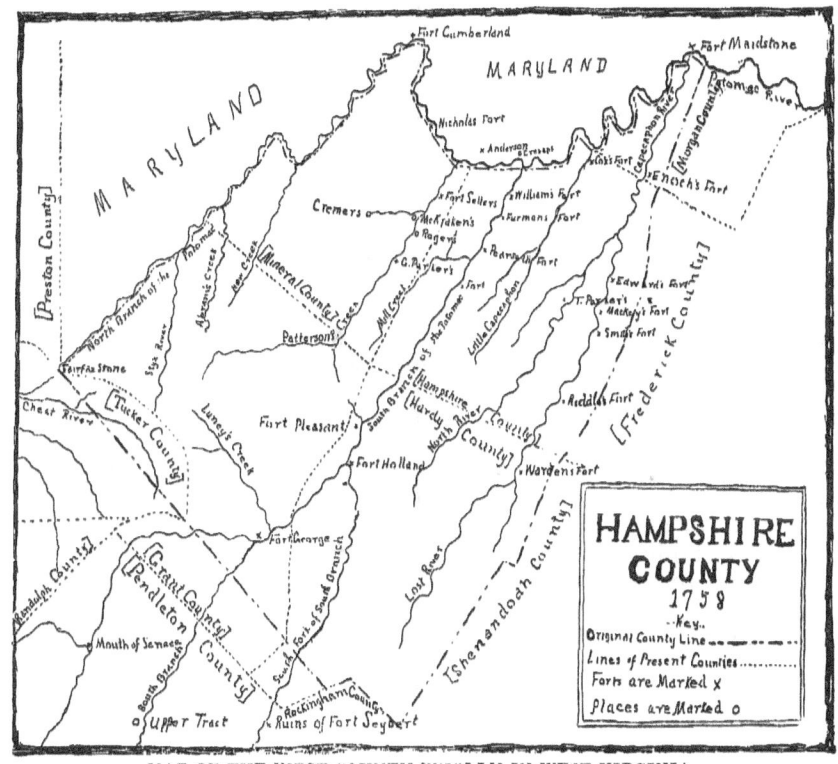

MAP OF THE FIRST COUNTY WHOLLY IN WEST VIRGINIA.

territory. It was not a county. Its boundary lines as laid down in the Act of Assembly in 1776, failed to meet—that is, one side of the District was open and without a boundary. Yet counties were formed from West Augusta as if it were a county and subject to division. From it Monongalia was taken, yet part of Monongalia was never in the District of West Augusta. The confusion was due to the ignorance of the geography of the region at that time. The boundary lines, from a mathematical standpoint, enclosed nothing, or, at any rate, it is uncertain what they enclosed. The act of 1776, declaring the line between Augusta County and the District of West Augusta reads as follows:

"Beginning on the Alleghany Mountain between the heads of the Potomac, Cheat and Greenbrier Rivers, thence along the ridge of mountains which divides the waters of

Cheat from those of Greenbrier, and that branch of the Monongahela called Tygart's Valley River to the Monongahela River, thence up the said river and the west fork thereof to Bingeman's Creek, on the northwest side of the said west fork, thence up the said creek to the head thereof, thence in a direct course to the head of the Middle Island Creek, a branch of the Ohio, including all the waters of said creek in the aforesaid District of West Augusta. All that territory lying to the northward of the aforesaid boundary, and to the westward of the states of Pennsylvania and Maryland, shall be deemed, and is hereby declared to be in the District of West Augusta."

The territory so laid off would include of the present counties of West Virginia a narrow strip through the center of Randolph, east of Cheat Mountain, one fourth of Tucker, the western half of Preston, nearly all of Marion, and Monongalia, Wetzel, Marshall, Ohio, Brooke and Hancock, part of Tyler and Pleasants, a small corner of Doddridge, and an indefinite part of the present State of Pennsylvania. The eastern parts of Tucker, Randolph and Preston, outside the boundaries of West Augusta, were subsequently included in Monongalia County, under the apparent presumption that they had belonged to West Augusta.

Following is a list of the counties of West Virginia, with the date of formation, area and from whom named:

HAMPSHIRE, 630 square miles; formed 1754 from Augusta; named for Hampshire, England; settled about 1730.

BERKELEY, 820 square miles; formed 1772 from Frederick; named for Governor Berkeley, of Virginia; settled about 1730.

MONONGALIA, 360 square miles; formed 1776 from West Augusta; named for the river; settled 1758.

OHIO, 120 miles; formed 1776 from West Augusta; settled 1770; named for the river.

GREENBRIER, 1000 miles; formed 1777 from Botetourt; settled 1750; named for briers growing on the river bank.

HARRISON, 450 miles; formed 1784 from Monongalia; settled 1770; named for Benjamin Harrison, Governor of Virginia.

HARDY, 700 miles; formed from Hampshire 1785; settled 1740; named for Samuel Hardy, of Virginia.

RANDOLPH, 1080 miles; formed 1786 from Harrison; settled 1753; named for Edmund Randolph.

PENDLETON, 650 miles; formed 1787 from Augusta, Hardy and Rockingham; settled 1750; named for Edmund Pendleton.

KANAWHA, 980 miles; formed 1789 from Greenbrier and Montgomery; settled 1774; named for the river.

BROOKE, 80 miles; formed from Ohio 1796; settled about 1772; named for Robert Brooke, Governor of Virginia.

WOOD, 375 miles; formed from Harrison 1798; settled about 1773; named for James Wood, Governor of Virginia.

MONROE, 460 miles; formed 1799 from Greenbrier; settled about 1760; named for James Monroe.

JEFFERSON, 250 miles; formed 1801 from Berkeley; settled about 1730; named for Thomas Jefferson.

MASON, 430 miles; formed 1804 from Kanawha; settled about 1774; named for George Mason, of Virginia.

CABELL, 300 miles; formed from Kanawha 1809; settled about 1790; named for William H. Cabell, Governor of Virginia.

TYLER, 300 miles; formed from Ohio 1814; settled about 1776; named for John Tyler.

SUBDIVISIONS AND BOUNDARIES. 63

LEWIS, 400 miles; formed from Harrison 1816; settled about 1780; named for Colonel Charles Lewis.

NICHOLAS, 720 miles; formed 1818 from Kanawha, Greenbrier and Randolph; named for W. C. Nicholas, Governor of Virginia.

PRESTON, 650 miles; formed 1818 from Monongalia; settled about 1760; named for James P. Preston, Governor of Virginia.

MORGAN, 300 miles; formed 1820 from Hampshire and Berkeley; settled about 1730; named for Daniel Morgan.

POCAHONTAS, 820 miles; formed 1821 from Bath, Pendleton and Randolph; settled 1749; named for Pocahontas, an Indian girl.

LOGAN, 400 miles, formed from Kanawha, Giles, Cabell and Tazwell, 1824; named for Logan, an Indian.

JACKSON, 400 miles; formed 1831 from Kanawha, Wood and Mason; settled about 1796; named for Andrew Jackson.

FAYETTE, 750 miles; formed from Logan, Kanawha, Greenbrier and Nicholas 1831; named for Lafayette.

MARSHALL, 240 miles; formed 1835 from Ohio; settled about 1769; named for Chief Justice Marshall.

BRAXTON, 620 miles; formed 1836 from Kanawha, Lewis and Nicholas; settled about 1794; named for Carter Braxton.

MERCER, 400 miles; formed 1837 from Giles and Tazwell; named for General Hugh Mercer.

MARION, 300 miles; formed 1842 from Harrison and Monongalia; named for General Marion.

WAYNE, 440 miles; formed 1841 from Cabell; named for General Anthony Wayne.

TAYLOR, 150 miles; formed 1844 from Harrison, Barbour and Marion; named for John Taylor.

DODDRIDGE, 300 miles; formed 1845 from Harrison, Tyler, Ritchie and Lewis; named for Philip Doddridge.

GILMER, 360 miles; formed 1845 from Kanawha and Lewis; named for Thomas W. Gilmer of Virginia.

WETZEL, 440 miles; formed 1846 from Tyler; named for Lewis Wetzel.

BOONE, 500 miles; formed 1847 from Kanawha, Cabell and Logan; named for Daniel Boone.

PUTNAM, 320 miles; formed 1848 from Kanawha, Cabell and Mason; named for Israel Putnam.

BARBOUR, 360 miles; formed 1843 from Harrison, Lewis and Randolph; named for James Barbour, governor of Virginia.

RITCHIE, 400 miles; formed 1844 from Harrison, Lewis and Wood; named for Thomas Ritchie of Virginia.

WIRT, 290 miles; formed 1848 from Wood and Jackson; settled about 1796; named for William Wirt.

HANCOCK, 100 miles; formed 1848 from Brooke; settled about 1776; named for John Hancock.

RALEIGH, 680 miles; formed 1850 from Fayette; named for Sir Walter Raleigh.

WYOMING, 660 miles; formed 1850 from Logan; an Indian name.

PLEASANTS, 150 miles; formed 1851 from Wood, Tyler and Ritchie; named for James Pleasants, governor of Virginia.

UPSHUR, 350 miles; formed 1851 from Randolph, Barbour and Lewis; settled about 1767; named for Judge A. P. Upshur.

SUBDIVISIONS AND BOUNDARIES.

CALHOUN, 260 miles; formed 1856 from Gilmer; named for J. C. Calhoun.

ROANE, 350 miles; formed 1856 from Kanawha, Jackson and Gilmer; settled about 1791; named for Judge Roane of Virginia.

TUCKER, 340 miles; formed 1856 from Randolph; settled about 1774; named for Judge St. George Tucker.

CLAY, 390 miles; formed 1858 from Braxton and Nicholas; named for Henry Clay.

MCDOWELL, 860 miles; formed 1858 from Tazwell; named for James McDowell, governor of Virginia.

WEBSTER, 450 miles; formed 1860 from Randolph, Nicholas and Braxton; named for Daniel Webster.

MINERAL, 300 miles; formed 1866 from Hampshire; named for its coal.

GRANT, 620 miles; formed 1866 from Hardy; named for General U. S. Grant; settled about 1740.

LINCOLN, 460 miles; formed 1867 from Kanawha, Cabell, Boone and Putnam; settled about 1799; named for Abraham Lincoln.

SUMMERS, 400 miles; formed 1871 from Monroe, Mercer, Greenbrier and Fayette; named for Lewis and George W. Summers.

MINGO, about 400 miles; formed 1895 from Logan; named for Logan the Mingo.

SUBDIVISIONS AND BOUNDARIES. 65

POPULATION OF THE COUNTIES OF WEST VIRGINIA EACH TEN YEARS FROM 1790 TO 1890, BOTH INCLUSIVE.

	1790	1800	1810	1820	1830	1840	1850	1860	1870	1880	1890
Hampshire	7346	8348	9784	10889	11279	12245	14036	13913	7613	10336	11419
Berkeley	19713	22006	11479	11211	10518	19972	11771	12525	14900	17380	18702
Monongalia	4768	8540	12793	11060	14056	17368	12357	13048	13547	14985	15705
Ohio	5212	4740	8175	9182	15584	13357	18006	22422	28831	37457	41557
Greenbrier	6015	4345	5914	7041	9006	8695	10022	12211	11417	15060	18034
Harrison	2080	4848	9958	10932	14722	17669	11728	13790	16714	20181	21919
Hardy	7336	6627	5525	5700	6798	7622	9543	9864	5518	6794	7567
Randolph	951	1826	2854	3357	5000	6208	5243	4990	5563	8102	11633
Pendleton	2452	3962	4239	4846	6271	6940	5797	6164	6455	8022	8711
Kanawha		3239	3666	6399	9326	13567	15353	16151	22349	32466	42756
Brooke		4706	5843	6631	7041	7948	5054	5494	5464	6013	6660
Wood		1217	3036	5860	6429	7923	9450	11046	19000	25006	28612
Monroe		4188	5444	6580	7798	8422	10204	10757	11124	11501	12429
Jefferson			11851	13087	12927	14082	15357	14535	13219	15005	15553
Mason			1991	4868	6534	6777	7539	9173	15978	22296	22863
Cabell			2717	4789	5884	8163	6299	8020	6429	13744	23528
Tyler				2314	4104	6954	5498	6517	7832	11073	11962
Lewis				4247	6241	8151	10031	7999	10175	13269	15895
Nicholas				1853	3346	2255	3963	4627	4458	7223	9307
Preston				3422	5144	6866	11708	13312	14555	19091	20335
Morgan				2500	2694	4253	3557	3732	4315	5777	6774
Pocahontas					2542	2922	3598	3958	4069	5591	6814
Logan					3680	4309	3620	4938	5124	7329	11101
Jackson						4890	6544	8306	10300	16312	19021
Fayette						3924	3955	5997	6647	11560	20542
Marshall						6937	10138	12937	14941	18840	20735
Braxton						2575	4212	4992	6480	9787	13928
Mercer						2233	4222	6819	7064	7467	16002
Marion							10552	12722	12107	17198	20721
Wayne							4760	6747	7852	14739	18652
Taylor							5357	8463	9367	11455	12147
Doddridge							2750	5203	7076	10552	12183
Gilmer							3475	3759	4338	7108	9746
Wetzel							4282	6703	8559	13896	16841
Boone							3237	4840	4553	5824	6885
Putnam							5335	6301	7794	11375	14342
Barbour							9005	8958	10312	11870	12702
Ritchie							3902	6847	9055	13474	16621
Wirt							3353	3751	4804	7104	9411
Hancock							4050	4445	4363	4882	6414
Raleigh							1765	3367	3673	7367	9597
Wyoming							1645	2861	3171	4322	6247
Pleasants								2945	3012	6256	7539
Upshur								7292	8023	10249	12714
Calhoun								2502	2930	6072	8155
Roane								5381	7232	12184	15303
Tucker								1428	1907	3151	6459
Clay								1787	2196	3460	4659
McDowell								1535	1952	3074	7300
Webster								1555	1730	3207	4783
Mineral									6332	8630	12085
Grant									4467	5542	6802
Lincoln									5053	8739	11246
Summers										9033	13117
Mingo											

5

CHAPTER VII.

―――:o:―――

THE NEWSPAPERS OF WEST VIRGINIA.

Newspaper history commenced in the territory now forming West Virginia nearly one hundred years ago; that is, in 1803. The beginning was small, but ambitious; and although the first journal to make its appearance in the State, ceased to pay its visits to the pioneers generations ago; yet, from that small beginning has grown a press which will rank with that of any State in the Union, if population and other conditions are taken into account. West Virginia has no large city, and consequently has no paper of metropolitan pretensions, but its press fulfills every requirement of its people; faithfully represents every business interest; maintains every honorable political principle; upholds morality; encourages education, and has its strength in the good will of the people. This chapter can do little more than present an outline of the growth of journalism in this State, together with facts and figures relating to the subject.

The first paper published in West Virginia was the Monongalia Gazette, at Morgantown in 1803. The Farmer's Register, printed at Charlestown, Jefferson County, was the next. These were the only papers in the State in 1810. The oldest paper still being published in West Virginia is the Virginia Free Press, printed at Charlestown. It was founded in 1821. The Monongalia Gazette was perhaps an up-to-date journal in its day; but it would be unsatisfactory at the present time. It was in four page form, each page sixteen inches long and ten inches wide. There were four columns to the page. Its editors were Campbell and Briton; its subscription rate was six cents a copy, or two dollars a year. It was impossible that a weekly paper so small could efficiently cover the news, even though the news of that day was far below the standard set for the present time. Yet, had such a paper been edited in accordance with modern ideas, it could have exerted a much wider influence than it did exert. No other paper was near enough to make inroads upon its field of circulation and influence; and it might have had the whole region to itself. But it did not expand, as might have been expected; on the contrary, within three years it reduced its size about one-half. More space in it was given to foreign news than to the happenings of County, State and Nation. Before the days of railroads, steamboats and telegraphing, it may readily be understood that the events recorded from foreign countries were so stale at the date of their publication in the backwoods paper that they almost deserved classification as ancient history. The domestic news, particularly that relating to distant states, was usually several weeks old before it found place in the Gazette. County occurrences, and happenings in the neighboring counties, were given little attention. Many a valuable scrap of local history might have been permanently preserved in that pioneer journal; but the county historian looks through the crumpled and yellow files in vain. But, on the other hand, he encounters numerous mentions of Napoleon's movements; the Emperor of Russia's undertakings, and England's achievements; all of which would have been valuable as history were it not that Guizot, Rambaud and Knight have given us the same things in better style; so that it is labor thrown away to search for them in the circumscribed columns of a pioneer paper printed on the forest-covered banks of the Monongahela. Joseph Campbell, one of the editors and proprietors of the Gazette, had learned the printing trade in Philadelphia. It is not known at what date the paper suspended publication. It was customary in early times, as well as at the present day, to incorporate two or more papers into one, drop the name of one and continue the publication. The Gazette may thus have passed quietly out of its individual existence.

Monongalia County fostered the first newspaper west of the Alleghanies in the State, and it also has had perhaps as many papers as any county of West Virginia. The full list, from the first till the present time, numbers between thirty and forty. The list compiled by Samuel T. Wiley, the historian of Monongalia, shows that the County had thirty-one papers prior to 1880. Nearly all of these suspended after brief careers. It would be difficult to compile a list of all the papers established in this State from the earliest times till the present. It would perhaps be impossible to do so, for some of them died in their infancy, and a copy cannot now be found. There were, no doubt, many whose very names are not now remembered. It would not be an extravagant estimate to place the total number of papers published in this State, both those still in existence and those which are dead, at five hundred. It would be a surprise to many persons to learn how ephemeral is the average newspaper. It comes and goes. It has its beginning, its prosperity, its adversity, its death. Another follows in its path. Few can be called relatively permanent. There are now more than one hundred newspapers published in West Virginia. Only nine of these were in existence in 1863, when the State was admitted into the Union. These nine are the Wheeling Intelligencer, Wheeling Register, Clarksburg Telegram, Charlestown Free Press, Charlestown Spirit of Jefferson, Shepherdstown Register, Barbour County Jeffersonian, Wellsburg Herald and Point Pleasant Register. Of the papers in existence in this State in 1870 only sixteen have come down to the present day. The cause of the early death of so many papers which begin life in such earnest hope is that the field is full. Two newspapers try to exist where there is room for only one. It does not require an evolutionist to foretell the result. Both must starve or one must quit. If one quits there is always another anxious to push in and try its luck.

West Virginia's experience does not differ from experience elsewhere. Journalism in country towns is much the same the country over. In cities the business is more stable, because conducted on business principles. Men with experience and business training accustom themselves to look before they leap. The inexperienced man who is ambitious to crowd some one else out of the newspaper business in the interior towns is too prone to leap first and do his looking afterwards. There is no scarcity of good newspaper men outside the cities, and West Virginia has its share, but at the same time there are too many persons who feel themselves called upon to enter the arena, although unprepared for the fray, and who cannot hold their own in competition with men of training in the profession. To the efforts and failures of these latter persons is due the ephemeral character of the lives of newspapers, taken as a whole. Country journalism comes to be looked upon as a changing, evanescent, uncertain thing, always respectable; only moderately and occasionally successful; inaugurated in hope; full of promise as the rainbow is full of gold; sometimes materializing into things excellent; now and then falling like Lucifer, but always to hope again. There is something sublime in the rural journalist's faith in his ability to push forward. Though failures have been many, country journalism has builded greater than it knew. West Virginia's development and the rural press have gone hand in hand. Every railroad pushing into the wilderness has carried the civilizing editor and his outfit. He goes with an unfaltering belief in printer's ink and confidence in its conquering power. He is ready to do and suffer all things. The mining town and the latest county seat; the lumber center and the oil belt; the manufacturing village and the railroad terminus; these are the fields in which he casts his lot. Here he sets up his press; he issues his paper; he booms the town; he records the births, marriages and deaths with a monotonous faithfulness; he expresses his opinion freely and generously. In return he expects the town and the surrounding country to support his enterprise as liberally as he has given his time, talent and energy in advancing the interests of the town. Sometimes his expectations are realized; sometimes not. If not, perhaps he packs his worldly assets and sets out for another town, richer in experience but poorer in cash. There are men in West Virginia who have founded a number of newspapers, usually selling out after a year or two in order to found another journal.

This is the class of editors who blaze the way into the woods. They bear the same relation to the journalism which follows as the "tomahawk right" bore in early days to the plantations and estates which succeeded them. After the adventurous and restless journalist has passed on, then comes the newspaper man who calculates before he invests. He does not come in a hurry. He is not afraid some one will get ahead of him. He does not locate before he has carefully surveyed the field, and has satisfied himself that the town and the surrounding country are able to support such a journal as he proposes establishing. His aim is to merit and receive the patronage of the people. This becomes the solid, substantial paper, and its editor wields a permanent influence for good. Such papers and such editors are found all over West Virginia.

Journalism among businesses is like poetry among the fine arts—the most easily dabbled in but the most difficult to succeed in. It may not appear to the casual observer that the newspaper business is nearly always unsuccessful, or at least, that nearly all the papers which come into existence meet untimely death in the very blossom of their youth. An examination of the history of newspapers in nearly any town a half century old will show that ten have failed where one has succeeded. The history of journalism in Monongalia County, already alluded to, differs little from the history of the papers in any county of equal age and population.

In 1851, when Horace Greeley was asked by a Parliamentary Committee from England "at what amount of population of a town in America do they first begin the publication of a weekly newspaper?" he replied that every county will have one, and a county of twenty thousand population usually has two weekly papers; and when a town has fifteen thousand people it usually has a daily paper. This rule does not state the case in West Virginia today. The average would probably show one newspaper for each six thousand people. In the small counties the average is sometimes as low as one paper to two thousand people, and not one-fourth of these people subscribe for a paper. It is not difficult to see that the field can be easily over-supplied; and among newspapers there must be a survival of the fittest.

The early journals published in this State, as well as those published elsewhere at that time, say seventy or eighty years ago, were very different in appearance from those of today. The paper on which the printing was done was rough, rugged and discolored, harsh to the touch, and of a quality inferior to wrapping paper of the present time. Some of them advertised that they would take clean rags at four cents a pound in payment of subscriptions. At that time paper was made from rags. It is now mostly made from wood. The publishers no doubt shipped the rags to the paper mills and received credit on their paper accounts. Some of these early journals clung to the old style of punctuation and capitalization; and some, to judge by their appearance, followed no style at all, but were as outlandish as possible, particularly in the use of capital letters. They capitalized all nouns, and as many other words as they could, being limited, apparently, only by the number of capital letters in their type cases.

As late as 1835 all the printing presses in the United States were run by hand power. On the earliest press the pressure necessary was obtained by means of a screw. Fifty papers an hour was fast work. The substitution of the lever for the screw increased the capacity of the press five fold. This arrangement reached its greatest development in the Washington Hand Press, patented in 1829 by Samuel Rust. This press is still the stand-by in many small offices. The printing done with it is usually good; but the speed is slow, and two hundred and fifty impressions an hour is a high average. Printers call this press "The Man-Killer," because its operation requires so much physical exertion.

The early newspapers in backwoods towns attempted to pull neck and neck with the city journals. They tried to give the news from all over the world; and the result was, they let the home news go. They were long in learning that a small paper's field should be small, and that the readers of a local paper expect that paper to contain the local news. Persons who desired national and foreign news subscribed for metropolitan papers. This was the case years ago the same as now. In course of time the lesson was learned; the local papers betook themselves to their own particular fields, with the result that the home paper has become a power at home. The growth of journalism has a tendency to restrict the influence of individual great papers to smaller and smaller geographical limits. All round the outer borders of their areas of circulation other papers are taking possession of their territory and limiting them. No daily paper now has a general and large circulation farther away from the place of publication than can be reached in a few hours. This is not so much the case with small papers. When once firmly established they can hold their small circulation and local influence much more securely than large circulation and large influence can be held by metropolitan papers. The trouble with the country papers is that the most of them die before they can establish themselves.

Some of the earliest statesmen feared danger from what they termed a newspaper aristocracy, formed by the concentration of the influence of the press about a comparatively few journals advantageously located in commercial centers. This danger is feared no more. The power of the press has been infinitesimally divided; among the metropolitan papers first; then among those in the smaller cities; lastly, among those in the smaller towns, until all fear of concentration is a thing of the past. The fundamental law of evolution, which rules the influence of the press as it rules the destinies of nations, or the growth and decline of commerce and political power, renders it impossible that any aggregate of newspapers, acting in concert, can long wield undisputed influence over wide areas. They must divide into smaller aggregate, and subdivide again, each smaller aggregate exercising its peculiar power in its own appropriated sphere and not trespassing upon the domains of others. The lowest subdivision is the country paper; and so secure is it from the inroads of the city journals that it can hold its ground as securely as the metropolitan journal can hold its field against the paper of the interior.

CHAPTER VIII.
―:o:―
GEOGRAPHY, GEOLOGY AND CLIMATE.

In this chapter will be presented facts concerning West Virginia's geography, climate, soil and geology. Its geography relates to the surface of the State as it exists now; its geology takes into account not only the present surface, but all changes which have affected the surface in the past, together with as much of the interior as may be known and understood. The climate, like geography, deals chiefly with present conditions; but the records of geology sometimes give us glimpses of climates which prevailed ages ago. The soil of a State, if properly studied, is found to depend upon geography, geology and climatology. The limits prescribed for this chapter render impossible any extended treatise; an outline must suffice.

Reference to the question of geology naturally comes first, as it is older than our present geography or climate. We are told that there was a time when the heat of the earth was so great that all substances within it or upon its surface were in a molten state. It was a white-hot globe made of all the inorganic substances with which we are acquainted. The iron, silver, gold, rock, and all else were liquid. The earth was then larger than it is now, and the days and nights were longer. After ages of great length had passed the surface cooled and a crust or shell was formed on the still very hot globe. This was the first appearance of "rock," as we understand the word now. The surface of the earth was no doubt very rough, but without high mountains. The crust was not thick enough to support high mountains, and all underneath of it was still melted. Probably for thousands of years after the first solid crust made its appearance there was no rain, although the air was more filled with moisture then than now. The rocks were so hot that a drop of water, upon touching them, was instantly turned to steam. But they gradually cooled, and rains fell. Up to this point in the earth's history we are guided solely by inductions from the teachings of astronomy, assisted to some extent by well-known facts of chemistry. Any description of our world at that time must be speculative, and as applicable to one part as to another. No human eye ever saw and recognized as such one square foot of the original crust of the earth in the form in which it cooled from the molten state. Rains, winds, frosts and fire have broken up and worn away some parts, and with the sand and sediment thus formed, buried the other parts. But that it was exceedingly hot is not doubted; and there is not wanting evidence that only the outer crust has yet reached a tolerable degree of coolness, while all the interior surpasses the most intense furnace heat. Upheavals and depressions affecting large areas, so often met with in the study of geology, are supposed to be due to the settling down of the solid crust in one place and the consequent upheaval in another. Could a railroad train run thirty minutes, at an ordinary speed, toward the center of the earth, it would probably reach a temperature that would melt iron. And it may be stated, parenthetically, could the same train run at the same speed for the same time away from the center of the earth, it would reach a temperature so cold that the hottest day would show a thermometer one hundred degrees below zero. So narrow is the sphere of our existence—below us is fire; above us "the measureless cold of space."

When we look out upon our quiet valleys, the Kanawha, the Potomac, the Monongahela, or contemplate our mountains, rugged and near, or robed in distant blue, rising and rolling, range beyond range, peak above peak; cliffs overhanging gorges and ravines; meadows, uplands, glades beyond; with brooks and rivers; the landscape fringed with flowers or clothed with forests, we are too apt to pause before fancy has had time to call up that strange and wonderful panorama of distant ages when the waves of the sea swept over all, or when only broken and angular rocks thrust their shoulders through the foam of the ocean as it broke against the nearly submerged ledges where since have risen the highest peaks of the Alleghanies and the Blue Ridge. Here where we now live have been strange scenes. Here have been beauty, awfulness and sublimity, and also destruction. There was a long age with no winter. Gigantic ferns and rare palms, enormous in size, and with delicate leaves and tendrils, flourished over wide areas and vanished. And there was a time when for ages there was no summer. But we know of this age of cold from records elsewhere, for its record in West Virginia has been blotted out. Landscapes have disappeared. Fertile valleys and undulating hills, with soil deep and fruitful, have been washed away, leaving only a rocky skeleton, and in many places even this has been ground to powder and carried away or buried under sands and drift from other regions.

An outline of some of the changes which have affected the little spot in the earth's surface now occupied by West Virginia will be presented, not by any means complete, but sufficient to convey an idea of the agencies which enter into the workings of geology. It is intended for the young into whose hands this book will come, not for those whose maturer years and greater opportunities have already made them acquainted with this sublime chapter in the book of creation.

When the crust of the earth had cooled sufficiently rains washed down the higher portions, and the sands and sediment thus collected were spread over the lower parts. This sand, when it had become hardened, formed the first layers of rock, called strata. Some of these very ancient formations exist yet and have been seen, but whether they are the oldest of the layer rocks no man knows. Some of the ancient layers of great thickness, after being deposited at the sea bottoms, were heated from the interior of the earth and were melted. In these cases the stratified appearance has usually disappeared, and they are called metamorphic rocks. Some geologists regard most granite as a rock of this kind.

As the earth cooled more and more it shrank in size, and the surface was shriveled and wrinkled in folds, large and small. The larger of these wrinkles were mountains. Seas occupied the low places, and the first brooks and rivers began to appear, threading their way wherever the best channels could be found. Rains, probably frost also, attacked the higher

GEOGRAPHY, GEOLOGY AND CLIMATE.

ridges and rocky slopes, almost destitute of soil, and the washings were carried to the seas, forming other layers of rocks on the bottoms, and thus the accumulation went on, varying in rate at times, but never changing the general plan of rock-building from that day to the present. All rock, or very nearly all, in West Virginia were formed at the bottom of the ocean, of sand, mud and gravel, or of shells, or a mixture of all, the ingredients of which were cemented together with silica, iron, lime, or other mineral substance held in solution in water. They have been raised up from the water, and now form dry land, and have been cut and carved into valleys, ridges, gorges and the various inequalities seen within our State. These rocks are sometimes visible, forming cliffs and the bottoms and banks of streams and the tops of peaks and barren mountains; but for the greater part of West Virginia the underlying rocks are hidden by soil. This soil, however, at the deepest, is only a few feet thick, and were it all swept off we should have visible all over the State a vast and complicated system of ledges and bowlders, carved and cut to conform to every height and depression now marking the surface. The aggregate thickness of these layers, as they have been seen and measured in this State, is no less than four miles. In other words, sand and shells four miles deep (and perhaps more) were in past time spread out on the bottom of a sea which then covered West Virginia, and after being hardened into rock, were raised up and then cut into valleys and other inequalities as we see them today. The rockbuilding was not all done during one uninterrupted period, nor was there only one upheaval. West Virginia, or a portion of it, has been several times under and above the sea. The coast line has swep back and forth across it again and again. We read this history from the rocks themselves. The skilled geologist can determine, from an examination of the fossil shells and plants in a stratum, the period of the earth's history when the stratum was formed. He can determine the old and the youngest in a series of strata. Yet, not from fossils alone may this be determined. The position of the layers with regard to one another is often a sure guide in discovering the oldest and youngest. The sands having been spread out in layers, one above the other, it follows that those on top are not so old as those below, except in cases, unusual in this State, where strata have been folded so sharply that they have been broken and turned over. Thus the older rocks may lie above the newer.

Unmeasured as are the ages recorded in the mountains and cliffs of West Virginia, yet the most ancient of our ledges are young in comparison with those of other parts of the world, or even of neighboring provinces. North of us is a series of rocks, the Laurentian of Canada, more than five miles thick, formed, like ours, of the slow accumulation of sand. Yet that series was finished and was probably partly worn away before the first grain of sand or the first shell, of which we have any record, found a resting place on the bottom of the Cambrian sea, which covered West Virginia. If the inconceivable lapse of years required for accumulating shell and sand four miles deep in the sea bottom, where we now live, amazes us, what must we say of that vaster period reaching back into the cycles of the infant world, all of which were past and gone before the foundations of our mountains were laid! Nor have we reached the beginning yet. No man knows whether the Laurentian rocks are oldest of the layers, and if they are, still back of them stretches that dim and nebulous time, unrecorded, uncharted, penetrated only by the light of astronomy, when the unstratified rocks were taking form, from whose disintegrated material all subsequent formations have been built.

Let us begin with the Cambrian age, as geologists call it. Within the limits of our State we have little, if any, record of anything older. Were a map made of eastern United States during that early period it would show a mass of land west of us, covering the Middle States, Ohio, Indiana, Illinois and beyond. Another mass of land would lie east of us, occupying the Atlantic Coastal Plain, from New England to South Carolina, and extending to an unknown distance eastward, where the Atlantic Ocean now is. Between these two bodies of land spread a narrow arm of the sea, from the Gulf of St. Lawrence to Alabama. West Virginia was at the bottom of that sea, whose eastern coast line is believed to have occupied nearly the position, and to have followed the general direction, of what is now the Blue Ridge. Sand washed from this land east of us was spread upon the bottom of the sea and now forms the lowest layers of rocks met with in West Virginia, the foundations of our mountains. But this rock is so deep that it is seen only in a few places where it has been brought up by folds of the strata, and where rivers have cut deep. For the most part of the State these Cambrian rocks lie buried, under subsequent formations, thousands of feet deep.

There were mountains of considerable magnitude in that land east of the sea. The country west of the sea must have been low. During the immense time, before the next great change, the eastern mountains were worn down and carried, as sand and mud, into the sea. The Silurian age followed, and as it drew near, the region began to sink. The sea which had covered the greater part of West Virginia, or at least the eastern part of it, began to overflow the country both east and west. The waters spread westward beyond the present Mississippi. The land to the eastward had become low and not much sediment was now coming from that direction. The washings from the rounded hills were probably accumulating as a deep soil in the low plains and widening valleys. Over a large part of West Virginia, during the Silurian age, thick beds of limestone were formed of shells, mixed with more or less sediment. Shell-fish lived and died in the ocean, and when dead their skeletons sank to the bottom. It is thus seen that the origin of limestone differs from that of sandstone in this, that the former is a product of water, while the material for sandstone is washed into water from land.

The character of rocks usually tells how far from land they were formed, and if sandstone, what kind of country furnished the material. The coarsest sandstones were deposited near shore, back of which the country was usually high and steep. Fine-grained sandstones, or shales, were probably laid down along flat shores, above which the land had little elevation. Or they may have been deposited from fine sediment which drifted a considerable distance from land. If limestone is pure, it is proof that little sediment from the land reached it while being formed. The limestone deposited over a considerable part of West Virginia during the closing of the Cambrian and the beginning of the Silurian age forms beds from three thousand to four thousand feet thick. During the long period required for the accumulation of this mass of shells, the land to the east remained comparatively flat or continued slowly to sink. We know this, because there is not much sediment mixed with the limestone, and this would not be the case had large quantities been poured into the sea from the land.

GEOGRAPHY, GEOLOGY AND CLIMATE. 75

Another great change was at hand. The land area east of us began to rise, and the surface became steep. What perhaps had been for a long time low, rounding hills, and wide, flat valleys, with a deep accumulation of soil, was raised and tilted; and the stronger and more rapid current of the streams, and the rush of the rain water down the more abrupt slopes, sluiced off the soil into the sea. The beds of limestone were covered two thousand feet deep beneath sand and mud, the spoils from a country which must have been fertile and productive. The land was worn down. Ages on ages passed, and the work of grinding went on; the rains fell; the winds blew; the floods came; the frost of winter and the heat of summer followed each other through years surpassing record. Near the close of the Silurian time the shore of the continent to the east rose and sank. The vertical movements were perhaps small; they may have been just enough to submerge the coastal plain, then raise it above water, repeating the operation two or more times. The record of this is in the alternating coarse and fine sediments and sand composing the rocks formed during that time. At the close of the Silurian period the continent east of us was worn down again and had become low. The sea covering West Virginia had been cut off from the Gulf of St. Lawrence by an upheaval in the State of New York. The uplift of the land seems to have been much greater during this time north of us than south. The Devonian age followed, which was a great rock-builder in the North. The aggregate thickness of the Devonian rocks in Pennsylvania is no less than nine thousand feet. From there to southward it thins out, like a long, sloping wedge, until it disappears in Alabama, after thinning to twenty-five feet in southern Tennessee. In some parts of West Virginia the Devonian rocks are seven thousand feet thick. The sediments of which these strata were made were usually fine-grained, forming shales and medium sandstones, with some limestones here and there. The long, dreary Devonian age at last drew to a close, and an epoch, strange and imperfectly understood, dawned upon the earth. It was during this age that the long summer prevailed; the winterless climate over the northern hemisphere; the era of wonderful vegetation; the time of plant-growth such as was perhaps never on earth before, nor will be again. It is known as the Carboniferous age.

During that period our coal was formed. The rocks deposited on the sea bottom in the Carboniferous age range in thickness from two thousand to eight thousand feet in different parts of West Virginia. During this time there is evidence of the breaking up and re-distribution of a vast gravel bar which had lain somewhere out of reach of the waves since earlier ages. This bar, or this aggregation whether a bar or not, was made up of quartz pebbles, varying in size from a grain of sand to a cocoanut, all worn and polished as if rolled and fretted on a beach or in turbulent mountain streams for centuries. By some means the sea obtained possession of them and they were spread out in layers, in some places 800 feet thick, and were cemented together, forming coarse, hard rocks. We see them along the summits of the Alleghanies, and the outlaying spurs and ridges, from the southern borders of our State, to the Pennsylvania line, and beyond. The formation is called conglomerate; and the popular names are "Bean Rock," "Millstone Grit," etc. A heavy stratum of this stone forms the floor of the coal measures. The pebbles probably represent the most indestructible remnant of mountains, once seamed with quartz veins, but degraded and obliterated before the middle of the Carboniferous era, perhaps long before.

The quartz, on account of its hardness, resisted the grinding process which pulverized the adjacent rock, and remained as pebbles, in bars and beds, until some great change swept them into the sea. Their quantity was enormous. The rocks composed of them now cover thousands of square miles.

As the Carboniferous age progressed the sea which had covered the greater part of West Virginia since Cambrian time, was nearing its last days. It had come down from the Cambrian to the Silurian, from the Silurian to the Devonian, from the Devonian to the Carboniferous, but it came down through the ages no further. From that area where the waves had rolled for a million years they were about to recede. With the passing of the sea, rose the land, which has since been crossed by ranges of the Alleghany, Blue Ridge, Laurel Ridge, and all their spurs and hills. From the middle of the Carboniferous epoch to its close was a period of disturbance over the whole area under consideration. The bottom of the sea was lifted up, became dry land, and sank again. It seemed that a mighty effort was being made by the land to throw back the water which had so long held dominion. It was a protracted, powerful struggle, in which first the land and then the water gained the mastery. Back and forth for hundreds of miles swept and receded the sea. Years, centuries, millennials, the struggle continued, but finally the land prevailed, was lifted up and the waves retreated westward and southward to the Gulf of Mexico, and West Virginia was dry land, and it has remained such to this day.

Beds of coal, unlike layers of rock, are made above water, or at its immediate surface. While the oscillation between sea and land was going on, during the Carboniferous age, West Virginia's coal fields were being formed. Coal is made of wood and plants of various kind, which grew with a phenomenal luxuriance during a long period of summer that reigned over the northern half of the earth. Each bed of coal represents a swamp, large or small, in which plants grew, fell and were buried for centuries. The whole country in which coal was forming was probably low and it was occasionally submerged for a few thousand years. During the submergence sand and mud settled over it and hardened into rock. Then the land was lifted up again, and the material for another bed of coal was accumulated. Every alternation of coal and rock marks an elevation and subsidence of the land—the coal formed on land, the rock under water. This was the period when the sea was advancing and receding across West Virginia, as the Carboniferous age was drawing to a close.

Other ages of geology succeeeded the Carboniferous; but little record of them remains in West Virginia. The land here was above the sea; no sediment could be deposited to form rocks, and of course there was little on which a permanent record could be written. The strata underlying the greater part of our State grew thicker and deeper from the Cambrian age to the Carboniferous; then the sea receded, and from that time to the present the layers of rock have been undergoing the wear and tear of the elements, and the aggregate has been growing thinner. The strata have been folded, upraised by subterranean force and cut through by rivers. In some places the Carboniferous rocks have not yet been worn away; in other places the river gorges have reached the bottom of the Devonian rocks; in still other localities the great Silurian layers have been cut through; and in a few places the cutting has gone down deep into the Cambrian rocks. The Glacial age, the empire of "steadfast, inconceivable cold," which followed the warm period in which coal was formed, did not write its history in West Virginia as indelibly as in some other parts of our country. The great morains and bowlders so conspicuous in other localities are not found with us. No doubt the cold here was intense; perhaps there were glaciers among the high lands; but the evidence has been well-nigh obliterated.

Land seems to have been lifted up in two ways, one a vertical movement which elevated large areas and formed plateaus, but not mountains; the other, a horizontal movement which caused folds in the strata, and these folds, if large enough, are ranges of mountains. In West Virginia we have both acting in the same area. Independently of the mountains, West Virginia has a rounding form, sloping gradually upward from three directions. Imagine the mountain ranges sheared off until no irregular elevations exist in the State. The resulting figure would show West Virginia's surface as it would be presented to us if no strata had been folded to make mountain ranges. This is the shape given by the vertical upheaval since the Carboniferous age, uninfluenced by the horizontal thrust of strata. The figure would show a great swell in the surface, the highest portion at the interlocking sources of the Greenbrier, the Elk, the Potomac, the east fork of the Monongahela, and Cheat. From that highest point the surface slopes in every direction, as shown by the course of the rivers. There is a long, curved arm of the plateau, thrust out toward the southwest, reaching around through Pocahontas, Greenbrier, Monroe and McDowell Counties, and overlapping into the State of Virginia. The New River, from the highlands of North Carolina, cuts through this plateau to join the Kanawha on the western side. The highest part of this rounded area is perhaps three thousand feet above sea level, not counting the mountains which stand upon the plateau, for, in order to make the matter plain, we have supposed all the mountains sheared off level with the surface of the plateau.

Having now rendered it clear that portions of West Virginia would be high if there were not a mountain in the State, let us proceed to consider how the mountains were formed and why nearly all the highest summits are clustered in three or four counties. We have already observed that ranges of mountains, such as ours, were formed by the folding of layers of rocks. This is apparent to any one who has seen one of our mountains cut through from top to bottom, such as the New Creek Mountain at Greenland Gap, in Grant County. Place several layers of thick cloth on a table, push the ends toward each other. The middle of the cloth will rise in folds. In like manner were our mountains formed. The layers of rock were pushed horizontally, one force acting from the southeast, the other from the northwest. Rivers and rains have carved and cut them, changing their original features somewhat; but their chief characteristics remain. The first upheaval, which was vertical, raised the West Virginia plateau, as we believe; the next upheaval, which was caused by horizontal thrust, folded the layers of rocks and made mountain ranges. From this view it is not difficult to account for so many high peaks in one small area. The mountain ranges cross the plateau, running up one slope, across the summit, and down the opposite slope. These ranges are from one thousand to nearly two thousand feet high, measuring from the general level of the country on which they stand. But that general level is itself, in the highest part about three thousand feet above the sea. So a mountain, in itself one thousand feet in elevation, may stand upon a plateau three times that high, and thus its summit will be four thousand feet above the sea.

GEOGRAPHY, GEOLOGY AND CLIMATE.

The highest peaks in the State are where the ranges of mountains cross the highest part of the plateau. There are many other mountains in the State which, when measured from base to summit, are as high as those just mentioned, but they do not have the advantage of resting their bases on ground so elevated, consequently their summits are not so far above sea level. To express it briefly, by a homely comparison, a five-foot man on three-foot stilts is higher than a six-foot man on the ground; a one thousand-foot mountain on a three thousand-foot plateau is higher than a two thousand-foot mountain near the sea level.

Exact measurements showing the elevation of West Virginia in various parts of its area, when studied in connection with a map of the State, show clearly that the area rises in altitude from all sides, culminating in the nest of peaks clustered around the sources of the Potomac, the Kanawha and Monongahela. The highest point in the State is Spruce Mountain, in Pendleton County, 4,860 feet above sea level; the lowest point is the bed of the Potomac at Harper's Ferry, 260 feet above the sea; the vertical range is 4,600 feet. The Ohio, at the mouth of Big Sandy, on the boundary between West Virginia and Kentucky, is 500 feet; the mouth of Cheat, at the Pennsylvania line, is 775. The general level of Pocahontas County is about 3,000 above the sea. The bed of Greenbrier River where it enters Pocahontas is 3,300 feet in elevation. Where Shaver's Fork of Cheat River leaves Pocahontas its bed is 3,700 feet. A few of the highest peaks in Pocahontas, Pendleton, Randolph and Tucker Counties are: Spruce Knob, Pendleton County, 4,860 feet above sea level; Bald Knob, Pocahontas County, 4,800; Spruce Knob, Pocahontas County, 4,730; High Knob, Randolph County, 4,710; Mace Knob, Pocahontas County, 4,700; Barton Knob, Randolph County, 4,600; Bear Mountain, Pocahontas County, 4,600; Elleber Ridge. Pocahontas County, 4,600; Watering Pond Knob, Pocahontas County, 4,600; Panther Knob, Pendleton County, 4,500; Weiss Knob, Tucker County, 4,490; Green Knob, Randolph County, 4,485; Brier Patch Mountain, Randolph County, 4,480; Yokum's Knob, Randolph County, 4,330; Pointy Knob, Tucker County, 4,286; Hutton's Knob, Randolph County, 4,260.

We do not know whether the vertical upheaval which raised the plateau, or the horizontal compression which elevated the mountains, has yet ceased. We know that the work of destruction is not resting. Whether the uplift is still acting with sufficient force to make our mountains higher, or whether the elements are chiseling down rocks and lowering our whole surface, we cannot say. But this we can say, if the teachings of geology may be taken as warrant for the statement, every mountain, every hill, every cliff, rock, upland, even the valleys, and the whole vast underlying skeleton of rocks must ultimately pass away and disappear beneath the sea. Rain and frost, wind and the unseen chemical forces, will at last complete the work of destruction. Every rock will be worn to sand, and the sand will go out with the currents of our rivers, until the rivers no longer have currents, and the sea will flow in to cover the desolation. The sea once covered a level world; the world will again be level, and again will the sea cover it.

There is greater diversity of climate in West Virginia than in almost any other area of the United States of equal size. The climate east of the Alleghanies is different from that west of the range; while that in the high plateau region is different from both. The State's topography is responsible for this, as might be expected from a vertical range of more than four thousand feet, with a portion of the land set to catch the west wind, and a portion to the east, and still other parts to catch every wind that blows. Generally speaking, the country east of the Alleghanies has the warmer and dryer climate. In the mountain regions the summers are never very hot, and the winters are always very cold. The thermometer sometimes falls thirty degrees below zero near the summit of the Alleghanies, while the highest summer temperature is seldom above ninety degrees, but the record shows ninety-six. The depth of snow varies with the locality and the altitude. Records of snow six and seven feet deep near the summits of the highest mountains have been made. At an elevation of fifteen hundred feet above the sea there was snow forty-two inches deep in 1856 along the mountains and valleys west of the Alleghanies. In 1831, at an elevation of less than one thousand feet, snow accumulated three feet deep between the mountains and the Ohio River. Tradition tells of a snow in the northwestern part of the State in 1780 which was still deeper; but exact measurements were not recorded. The summers of 1838 and 1854 were almost rainless west of the mountains. In the same region in 1834 snow fell four inches deep on the fifteenth of May; and on June 5, 1859, a frost killed almost every green thing in the central and northern part of the State.

The average annual rainfall for the State of West Virginia, including melted snow, is about forty-seven inches. During some years the rainfall is three or four times as great as in other years. The precipitation is greater west of the Alleghanies than east, and greatest near the summit of these mountains, on the western side. Our rains and snows come from two general directions, from the west-southwest and from the east. Local storms may come from any direction. Eastern storms are usually confined to the region east of the Alleghanies. The clouds which bring rains from that quarter come from the Atlantic Ocean. The high country following the summits of the Appalachian range from Canada almost to the Gulf of Mexico is the dividing line between the two systems of rains and winds which visit West Virginia. Storms from the Atlantic move up the gentle slope from the coast to the base of the mountains, precipitating their moisture in the form of rain or snow as they come. They strike the abrupt eastern face of the Alleghanies, expending their force and giving out the remainder of their moisture there, seldom crossing to the west side. The Blue Ridge is not high enough to interfere seriously with the passage of clouds across their summits; but the Alleghanies are usually a barrier, especially for eastern storms. As the clouds break against their sides there are sometimes terrific rains below, while very little and perhaps none falls on the summit. On such an occasion an observer on one of the Alleghany peaks can look down upon the storm and can witness the play of lightning and hear the thunder beneath him. Winds which cross high mountains seldom deposit much rain or snow on the leeward side.

Whence, then, does the western part of our State receive its rains? Not from the Atlantic, because the winds which bring rain for the country west of the Alleghanies blow towards that ocean, not from it. No matter in what part of the world rain or snow falls, it was derived from vapor taken up by the sun from some sea or ocean. An insignificant portion of the world's rainfall is taken up as vapor from land. From what sea, then, do the winds blow which bring the rain that falls against the western slopes of the mountains and waters the country to the Ohio river and beyond?

Take the back track of the winds and follow them to their starting point and that will settle the question. They come from a direction a little west of southwest. That course will lead to the Pacific Ocean west of Mexico. Go on in the same direction two thousand or three thousand miles, and reach the equator. Then turn at right angles and go southeast some thousand miles further and reach that wide domain of the Pacific which stretches from South America to Australia. There, most probably, would be found the starting point of the winds which bring us rain. The evidence to substantiate this statement is too elaborate and complex to be given here; suffice it that the great wind systems of the world, with their circuits, currents and counter-currents, have been traced and charted until they are almost as well known as are the rivers of the world.* Not only is the great distance from which our rains come an astonishing theme for contemplation, but the immense quantity transported is more amazing—a sheet of water nearly four feet thick and covering an area of twenty thousand square miles, lifted by the sun's rays every year from the South Pacific, carried through the air ten thousand miles and sprinkled with a bountiful profusion upon our mountains, hills, vales, meadows and gardens to make them pleasing and fruitful.

The soil of a country is usually understood to be the covering of the solid rock. It is very thin in comparison with the thickness of the subjacent rock, not often more than four or five feet and frequently less. This is not the place for a chemical discussion of soils; but a few plain facts may be given. What is soil? Of what is it made? In the first place, leaving chemical questions out, soil is simply pulverized rock, mixed with vegetable or animal remains. The rocky ledges underlying a country, become disintegrated near the surface; they decompose; the sand and dust accumulate, washing into the low places and leaving the high points more or less bare, and a soil of sufficient depth is formed to support vegetation. A soil in which little or no vegetable humus is intermixed, is poor, and it produces little growth. Sand alone, no matter how finely pulverized is not capable of supporting vegetation, except a few peculiar species or varieties. This is why hillsides are so often nearly bare. The soil is deep enough, but it is poor. The state of being poor is nothing more than a lack of humus, or decaying vegetation. Those poor hillside soils either never had humus in them, or it has been washed out. A soil tolerable fertile is sometimes made miserably poor by being burned over each year when the leaves fall. The supply of vegetable matter which would have gone to furnish what the soil needed, is thus burned and destroyed; and in course of time that which was already in the soil is consumed or washed out, and instead of a fertile woodland, there is a blasted, lifeless tract. Examples of this are too often met with in West Virginia.

Excessive tillage of land exhausts it, because it takes out the organic matter and puts nothing back. It does not exhaust the disintegrated rock —the sand, the clay, the dust; but it takes out the vital part, the mold of vegetation. Fertilizers are used to restore the fertility of exhausted land. That process is misleading, in many cases. Too often the fertilizing material is a stimulant rather than a food to the land. It often adds no element of fertility, but, by a chemical process, compels the soil to give up all the remaining humus; and when the vegetable matter is all gone from the soil, all the fertilizers of that kind in the world would not cause the land to pro-

---

*See Maury's Physical Geography of the Sea.

GEOGRAPHY, GEOLOGY AND CLIMATE.

duce a crop. The intelligent farmer does not need be told this. His experience has taught him the truth of it. No land is so completely sterile as that which, through excessive use of fertilizers, has been compelled to part with its vegetable matter. Something cannot be created from nothing. If a soil has no plant food in it, and a fertilizer contains no plant food, the mixing of the two will not produce plant life.

A crop of clover, of buckwheat, of rye, or any other crop, plowed under, fertilizes land because it adds vegetable matter to the soil. Then if the soil is stubborn about yielding up its fertility, a treatment of the proper fertilizing agent will compel it to do so. Bottom lands along the rivers and creeks are usually more fertile than lands on the hills because rains leach the uplands and wash the decaying leaves and the humus down upon the lowlands. The soil along the river bottoms is often many feet deep, and fertile all the way down. This is because the washings from the hills have been accumulating there for ages faster than the vegetation which annually drew from it could exhaust the supply. It sometimes happens that the surface of a deep soil is exhausted by long cultivation; and that a sub-soil plow, which goes deeper than usual, turns up a new fertile soil which had lain beyond the reach of plant roots for ages. Occasionally a flood which covers bottom lands leaves a deposit of mud which is full of humus. This enriches the land where it lodges, but the mountain districts from which it was carried were robbed of that much fertility.

Disintegrated rock of all kinds cannot be made fertile by the usual addition of vegetable humus. Certain chemical conditions must be complied with. Limestone generally forms good soil because it contains elements which enter into plants. Strata of rock, as we now see them, were once beds of sand and sediment. They hardened and became stone. Sandstone is formed of accumulations of sand; shale is made from beds of clay or mud; limestone was once an aggregation of shells and skeletons of large and small living creatures. When these rocks are broken up, disintegrated and become soils, they return to that state in which they were before they became rock. The limestone becomes shells and bones, but of course pulverized, mixed and changed; sandstone becomes sand again; shale becomes mud and clay as it originally was. This gives a key to the cause of some soils being better than others. A clay bank is not easily fertilized; but a bed of black mud usually possesses elements on which plants can feed. So, if the disintegrating shale was originally sterile clay, it will make a poor soil; but if it was originally a fertile mud, the resulting soil will be good. If the disintegrating sandstone was once a pure quartz sand, the soils will likely be poor, but if it was something better, the soil will be better. The fertility of limestone soil is mainly due to the animal matter in the rock. It should always be borne in mind, however, that the difference of soils is dependent not so much upon their chemical composition as upon the physical arrangements of their particles.

Plants do not feed exclusively upon the soil. As a matter of fact, a large part of the material which enters into the construction of the stems and leaves of some plants is derived from the air. Some plants prosper without touching the soil. A species of Chinese lily flourishes in a bowl of water with a few small rocks in the bottom. On the other hand there are plants that will wither in a few minutes if taken from the ground. This shows that some plants extract more material from the soil than other. It is a common saying that buckwheat rapidly exhausts land.

Some lands are more affected by drought than others, when both receive the same rainfall. This may be due to the character of the underlying rocks, although usually due to a different cause. If the soil is shallow and the subjacent rocks lie oblique and on edge, they are liable to carry the water away rapidly by receiving it into their openings and crevices, thus draining the soil. But if the subjacent rocks lie horizontally, water which sinks through the soil is prevented from escaping, and is held as in a tub, and is fed gradually upward through the soil by capilliary attraction. This land will remain moist a long time. But the more usual reason that one soil dries more rapidly than another, is that one is loose and the other compact. The compact soil dries quickest. The smaller the interspaces between the ultimate particles which make up the soil, the more rapidly water raises from the wet subsoil by capilliary attraction, and the supply is soon exhausted. The more compact the soil the smaller the spaces between the particles. In loose ground the interspaces are larger, the water rises slowly or not at all, and the dampness remains longer beneath the surface. In the western countries where the summers are hot and rainless, the farmers irrigate their land, thoroughly soaking it from a neighboring canal. If they shut the water off and leave the land alone, in a few days it is baked, parched, hard and as dry as a bone. But the farmer does not do this. As soon as the water is turned off, he plows and harrows the land making the surface as loose as possible. The result is, the immediate top becomes dry, but a few inches below the surface the soil remains moist for weeks. The water cannot escape through the porous surface. The same rule applies everywhere. If two cornfields lie side by side, especially in a dry season, and one is carefully tilled and the surface kept loose, while the other is not, the difference in the crops will show that in one case the moisture in the soil was prevented from escaping and was fed to the corn roots, while in the other case it rose to the surface and was blown away by the wind, leaving the corn to die of thirst.

CHAPTER IX.

―:o:―

AMONG OLD LAWS.

"Yet I doubt not through the ages one increasing purpose runs,
And the thoughts of men are widened with the process of the suns."
—Tennyson.

The settlement of the territory now embraced in West Virginia commenced about 1730, and before the close of the eighteenth century there were cabins or colonies in the valleys of all the principal rivers of the State. The first settlers were governed by the laws in force in Virginia from the earliest occupation of our territory until 1863. A proper consideration of the history of our State requires that mention be made of some of the old laws. They should be studied to show the progress of society during the past century. There are persons who speak of the "good old times" as though everything were better than now, and who speak of the people of a hundred years ago as if they were greater, purer, nobler than the men of today, and as if, when they died, wisdom died with them. The historian knows that this belief is erroneous. Not only are there men now living who are as upright, wise and patriotic as any who ever lived, but society, in all its branches and departments, has grown better. Only the pessimist refuses to see that the human race is climbing to a higher level, and not retrograding.

To bring this truth nearer home to the people, let a retrospective view of the customs and laws prevailing here a century ago be taken. That the people of Virginia tolerated barbarous laws long after the close of the Revolutionary War is proof that the laws were not obnoxious to a majority of the people, otherwise they would have changed them. Before proceeding to a statement of the Acts of the Virginia Legislature, let it be remembered that at that time Washington was President of the United States and the great men of Virginia, at the close of the last century and the beginning of this, were in their prime. They were responsible for the bad laws as well as for the good; if not directly, at least indirectly, for they were looked upon as leaders. Patrick Henry, who had exclaimed, "give me liberty or give me death," was yet living and practicing law; John Randolph, of Roanoke, was entering his career of greatness; James Monroe, soon to be President of the United States, was a leader in Virginia; George Mason, the author of the Bill of Rights, had not yet lost his influence; James Madison, also to be President of the United States, was a leader among the Virginians; William Wirt, one of Virginia's greatest lawyers, was in his prime; Edmund Randolph, Governor of Virginia, was in politics; John Marshall, the famous Chief Justice, was practicing in the courts; Thomas Jefferson, the author of the Declaration of Independence, was in the height of power;

and the list might be extended much further. Yet, with all of these truly great men in power in Virginia, the Legislature of that State passed such laws as will be found below:

On December 26, 1792, an Act was passed for the purpose of suppressing vice, and provided that for swearing, cursing or being drunk the fine should be eighty-three cents for each offense, and if not paid, the offender should have ten lashes on the bare back. For working on Sunday the fine was one dollar and sixty-seven cents. For stealing a hogshead or cask of tobacco found lying by the public highway, the punishment was death.

On December 19, 1792, an Act was passed by the Virginia Legislature providing that any person found guilty of forgery must be put to death; and the same punishment was provided for those who erased, defaced or changed the inspector's stamp on flour or hemp. No less severe was the punishment for those who stole land warrants. But for the man who made, passed or had in his possession counterfeit money, knowing it to be such, the penalty of death was not enough. He was not only to be put to death, but was forbidden the attendance of a minister, and must go to execution "in the blossom of his sin." The design of the law-makers evidently was to add to his punishment not only in this life, but, if possible, send him to eternal punishment after death. It is not in the province or power of the writers of history to ascertain whether the Virginia Assembly ever succeeded in killing a man and sending him to eternal torment in the lake of fire and brimstone because he had a counterfeit dime in his pocket, but the probability is that the powers of the law-makers ceased when they had hanged their man, and a more just and righteous tribunal then took charge of his case.

It is evident that the early Virginia law-makers laid great stress on the idea of clergy to attend the condemned man. If they wished to inflict extreme punishment they put on the finishing touches by denying the privilege of clergy. On November 27, 1789, an Act was passed by the Legislature segregating crimes into two classes, one of which was designated as "clergyable," and the other as "unclergyable." It was provided that the unclergyable crimes were murder in the first degree, burglary, arson, the burning of a Court-House or prison, the burning of a clerk's office, feloneously stealing from the church or meeting-house, robbing a house in presence of its occupants, breaking into and robbing a dwelling house by day, after having put its owner in fear. For all these offences the penalty was death. A provision was made in some cases for clergy; but, lest the convicted man's punishment might not thereby be too much lightened, it was stipulated that he must have his hand burned before he was hanged. The same law further provided that, although a man's crime might not be unclergyable, yet if he received the benefit of clergy, and it was subsequently ascertained that he had formerly committed an unclergyable offense, he must then be put to death without further benefit of clergy. In this law it was expressly provided that there should be no mitigation of punishment in case of women.

By an Act of December 26, 1792, it was provided that the man who apprehended a runaway servant and put him in jail was to receive one dollar and forty-seven cents, and mileage, to be paid by the owner. This law was, no doubt, intended to apply chiefly to slaves rather than to white servants. If the runaway remained two months in jail unclaimed, the sheriff must advertise him in the *Virginia Gazette*, and after putting an iron collar on his neck, marked with the letter "F," hire him out, and from his wages pay the costs. After one year, if still unclaimed, he was to be sold. The money, after the charges were paid, was to be given to the former owner if he ever proved his claim, and if he did not do so, it belonged to the State.

The law-makers believed in discouraging gossip and tattling. A law passed by the Virginia Legislature, December 27, 1792, was in the following language: "Whereas, many idle and busy-headed people do forge and divulge false rumors and reports, be it resolved by the General Assembly, that what person or persons soever shall forge or divulge any such false report, tending to the trouble of the country, he shall be by the next Justice of the Peace sent for and bound over to the next County Court, where, if he produce not his author, he shall be fined forty dollars or less if the court sees fit to lessen it, and besides give bond for his good behavior, if it appear to the court that he did maliciously publish or invent it."

There was a studied effort on the part of the Legislators to discourage hog-stealing. It is not apparent why it should be a worse crime to steal a hog than to steal a cow; or why the purloining of a pig should outrank in criminality the taking of a calf; or why it should be a greater offense to appropriate a neighbor's shoat than his sheep. But the early law-makers in Virginia seem to have so considered it and they provided a law for the special benefit of the hog thief. This law, passed by the Legislature December 8, 1792, declared that "any person, not a slave, who shall steal a hog, shoat or pig," should receive thirty-five lashes on the bare back; or if he preferred to do so, he might escape the lashing by paying a fine of thirty dollars; but whether he paid the fine or submitted to the stripes, he still must pay eight dollars to the owner for each hog stolen by him. This much of the law is comparatively mild, but it was for the first offense only. As the thief advanced in crime the law's severity increased. For the second offense in hog-stealing the law provided that the person convicted, if not a slave, should stand two hours in a pillory, on a public court day, at the Court-House, and have both ears nailed to the pillory, and at the end of two hours. should have his ears cut loose from the nails. It was expressly provided that no exception should be made in the case of women. If the hog thief still persisted in his unlawful business and transgressed the law a third time, he was effectually cured of his desire for other people's hogs by being put to death.

The slave had a still more severe punishment for stealing hogs. For the first offense he received "thirty-nine lashes on the bare back, well laid on, at the public whipping-post." For the second offense he was nailed by the ears to a post, and after two hours of torture, had his ears cut off. For the third offense he was put to death. The law provided that if a negro or Indian were put on the stand as a witness against a person accused of stealing hogs, and did not tell the truth, he should be whipped, nailed to a post, his ears cut, and if he still testified falsely, he paid the penalty with his life. It is not provided how the court shall be led to the knowledge whether or not the witness had told the truth. It appears that the judge was presumed to be infallible in separating false from true testimony in trials for hog-stealing. After a hog had been stolen and killed, the relentless law still followed it to try to discover if some one else might not be punished. If a person bought, or received into his possession, a hog from which the ears had been removed, he was adjudged guilty of hog-stealing, unless he could prove that the hog was his own property. There was also a law forbidding any one from purchasing pork of Indians unless the ears went with the pork. There would be some inconvenience in retailing pork under this restriction, as it would require a skillful butcher to so cut up a hog that each ham, shoulder, side and the sausage should retain the ears.

If stealing hogs was a crime almost too heinous to be adequately punished in this world, horse-stealing was so much worse that the law-makers of Virginia would not undertake to provide a law to reach the case. They, therefore, enacted a law, December 10, 1792, that the convicted horse-thief must be put to death; and, in order that he should certainly reach eternal punishment beyond death, he was forbidden to have spiritual advice. The language of the law is that the horse thief shall be "utterly excluded."

An Act of unnecessary severity was passed December 22, 1792, against negroes who should undertake to cure the sick. It is reasonable and right that the law should carefully guard the people against harm from those who ignorantly practice medicine; but to us of the present day it appears that a less savage law would have answered the purpose. It was provided that any negro who prepared, exhibited, or administered medicine should be put to death without benefit of clergy. It was provided, however, that a negro might, with the knowledge and consent of his master, have medicine in his possession.

The law of Virginia required every county to provide a Court-House, Jail, Pillory, Whipping Post, Stocks and a Ducking Stool. But the Ducking Stool might be dispensed with if the County Court saw fit to do so. The Whipping Post was the last of these relics of barbarism to be removed. So far as can be ascertained the last public and legalized burning of a convicted man in West Virginia occurred in July, 1828, in the old Court-House in Hampshire County. A negro slave, named Simon, the property of David Collins, was tried on a charge of assault. The record does not show that he had a jury. The court found him guilty and ordered the Sheriff to burn him on the hand and give him one hundred lashes, chain him, and keep him on "coarse and low diet." The minutes of the court state that the Sheriff "immediately burned him in the hand in the presence of the court," and gave him then and there twenty-five lashes. The remaining seventy-five were reserved for future days.

It is but justice to the law-makers of Virginia, and the people at that time, to state that nearly all of those severe laws came from England, or were enacted in the colony of Virginia many years before the Revolutionary War. Some of them date back to the time of Cromwell, or even earlier. Although the people of Virginia took the lead in the movement for greater liberty, both mental and physical, they could not all at once cut loose from the wrecks of past tyranny. They advanced rapidly along some lines, but slowly along others. They found those old laws on the statute books, and re-enacted them, and suffered them to exist for a generation or more. But we should not believe that such men as Patrick Henry, Edmund Randolph, Thomas Jefferson, George Washington and the other statesmen and patriots of that time believed that a man should be nailed to a post for stealing a pig, or that the crime of stealing a hymn book from a church should be punished with death without benefit of clergy.

A law passed near the close of the last century, and still in force in 1819, provided Sheriff's fees on a number of items, among which were the following: For making an arrest, sixty-three cents; for pillorying a criminal, fifty- wo cents; for putting a criminal in the stocks, twenty-one cents; for ducking a criminal in pursuance of an order of court, forty-two cents; for putting a criminal in prison, forty-two cents; for hanging a criminal, five dollars and twenty-five cents; for whipping a servant, by order of court, to be paid by the master and repaid to him by the servant, forty-two cents; for whipping a free person, by order of court, to be paid by the person who received the whipping, forty-two cents; for whipping a slave, by order of court, to be paid by the county, forty-two cents; for selling a servant at public outcry, forty-two cents; for keeping and providing for a debtor in jail, each day, twenty-one cents.

It was more expensive to be whipped or pilloried by the Sheriff than by a Constable, although there is no evidence that the Sheriff did the work any more effectively. Since the person who received the punishment usually paid the fees of the officer who performed the service, it is probable that such person preferred being whipped or nailed to a post by a Constable, because it was less expensive. Some of the Constable's fees are shown below: For putting a condemned man in the stocks, twenty-one cents; for whipping a servant, twenty-one cents; for whipping a slave, to be paid by the master, twenty-one cents; for removing a person likely to become a charge on the county, per mile, four cents.

Within the past century several important changes have taken place in the laws under which West Virginia has been governed. An Act of Assembly, passed November 29, 1792, provided that in cases where a person is suspected of having committed a murder, and the Coroner's jury recommend that he be held for trial, and he eludes arrest, the Coroner must seize his house and property and hold them until he surrenders himself or is arrested. Where a defendant was found guilty the costs of the prosecution was collected by sale of his property, if he had any property; but he might pay cost and thus save his property. No Constable, miller, surveyor of roads or hotel-keeper was eligible to serve on a grand jury. A law passed January 16, 1801, provided a fine of five dollars as a penalty for killing deer between January 1 and August 1 of each year. A law enacted January 26, 1814, provided that sheep-killing dogs should be killed. If the owner prevented the execution of the law upon the dog he was subject to a fine of two dollars for each day in which he saved the life of the dog. The bounty on wolves was made six dollars for each scalp, by a law passed February 9, 1819. But the bounty was not always the same, nor was it uniform throughout the counties of Virginia. Each county could fix the bounty within its jurisdiction. A law of January 16, 1802, provided a fine of thirty dollars for setting the woods on fire; and a law of January 4, 1805, punished by a fine of ten dollars the catching of fish in a seine between May 15 and August 15.

There was a severe law passed by the Virginia Legislature February 22, 1819, for the benefit of tavern-keepers. It provided a fine of thirty dollars for each offense, to be levied against any person not a licensed tavern-keeper, who should take pay from a traveler for entertainment given. Not only was this law in force in and near towns, but also within eight hundred yards of any public road. There was a law enacted by the Assembly of Virginia December 24, 1796, which was intended to favor the poor people. It is in marked contrast with many of the laws of that time, for they were generally not made to benefit the poor. The law had for its object the aiding of persons of small means in reaching justice through the courts. A man who had no money had it in his power to prosecute a suit against a rich man. He could select the court in which to have his case tried; the court furnished him an attorney free; he was charged nothing for his subpœnas and other writs; and he was not charged with costs in case he lost his suit. A law similar to that is still in force in West Virginia.

In 1792 an Act was passed by the Virginia Legislature establishing ferries across the principal streams of the State, and fixing the rate of toll. The State was in the ferry business strictly for the money in it. The law provided that no person should operate a private ferry for profit where he would take patronage from a public ferry. The penalty for so doing seems unnecessarily severe. The person who undertook to turn a few dimes into his own pocket by carrying travelers across a river, where those travelers might go by public ferry, was fined twenty dollars for each offense, half of it to go to the nearest public ferryman and the other half to the person who gave the information; and in case the public ferryman gave the information, the entire fine went into his pocket. It will readily be surmised that the public ferryman maintained a sharp lookout for private boats which should be so presumptuous as to dare enter into competition for a portion of the carrying trade, and it is equally probable that competition with public service soon became unpopular, when a man might receive five cents for carrying a traveler across a river and to be fined twenty dollars for it.

Messengers and other persons on business for the State were not required to pay toll, and they must be carried across immediately, at any hour of the day or night. But, as a precaution against being imposed upon by persons falsely claiming to be in the service of the State, the ferryman was authorized to demand proof, which the applicant was obliged to furnish. This proof consisted of a letter, on the back of which must be written "public service," and must be signed by some officer, either in the civil or military service of the State. Inasmuch as the punishment for forgery at that time was death, it is improbable that any person would present forged documents to the ferryman in order to save a few cents toll. The men who kept the ferries enjoyed some immunities and privileges denied to the masses. They were exempt from work on the public roads. They were not required to pay county taxes, but whether this privilege was extended only to poll tax, or whether it applied also to personal property and real estate, is not clear from the reading of the regulations governing the business. They were exempt from military service due the State, and they were excused from holding the office of Constable.

FIRST COURT-HOUSE IN WEST VIRGINIA,
Hampshire County.

MEMBERS OF THE CONSTITUTIONAL CONVENTION OF 1872.

1 Samuel Price, 2 Wm. K. Pendleton, 3 James S. Wheat, 4 Charles J. Faulkner 5 Samuel Woods, 6 Nicholas Fitzhugh, 7 James M. Jackson, 8 William H. Travers, 9 A. F. Haymond, 10 Benjamin Wilson, 11 James D. Armstrong, 12 A. J. Pawnell, 13 J. M. Byrnside, 14 D. D. Johnson, 15 W. T. Willey, 16 Logan Osborn, 17 Alexander Campbell, 18 W. W. Miller, 19 C. W. Ferguson, 20 E. B. Knight, 21 B. F. Martin, 22 Okey Johnson, 23 C. B. Waggener, 24 Evermont Ward, 25 H. M. Dickenson, 26 H. M. Mathews, 27 James M. Pipes, 28 Thomas Maslin, 29 John Blair Hoge, 30 John Bassel, 31 Thomas Thornburg, 32 William Haynes, 33 Isaiah Bee, 34 Lewis Allen, 35 John A. Warth, 36 G. H. Moffett, 37 U. N. Arnett, 38 Septimus Hall, 39 Wm. Price, 40 H. A. Holt, 41 D. D. T. Farnsworth, 42 J. F. Harding, 43 A. H. Thayer, 44 J. J. Thompson, 45 B. W. Byrne, 46 D. A. Roberts, 47 Fountain Smith, 48 Charles D. Boggs, 49 D. H. Leonard, 50 George O. Davenport, 51 William G. Brown, 52 John H. Atkinson, 53 Wm. D. Pate, 54 Blackwell Jackson, 55 A. W. McCleary, 56 Wm. A. Morgan, 57 Charles Kantner, 58 John T. Pearce, 59 Joseph Snyder, 60 Hanson Criswell, 61 J. P. Strickler, 62 J. M. Hagans, 63 Alonzo Cushing, 64 James Calfee, 65 M. A. Staton, 66 Thomas R. Park, 67 Alexander Monroe, 68 Lemuel Stump, 69 J. A. Robinson, 70 Thomas Ferrell, 71 J. N. B. Crim, 72 David A. Pugh, 73 J. F. Randolph, 74 J. W. Gallaher, 75 W. G. H. Core, 76 Wm. McCreery, 77 B. H. Lurty, 78 A. J. Cunningham, Sergeant-at-Arms, 79 B. H. Butcher, Clerk, 80 Barney Galligan, Assistant Clerk, 81 D. J. Wetzel, Door-keeper.

CHAPTER X.

―:o:―

CONSTITUTIONAL HISTORY.

The territory now embraced in the State of West Virginia has been governed under five State constitutions, three of Virginia's and two of West Virginia's. The first was adopted in 1776, the second in 1830, the third in 1851, the fourth in 1863, the fifth in 1872. The first constitution was passed by the Virginia Convention, June 29, 1776, five days before the signing of the Declaration of Independence. Virginia had taken the lead in declaring the United States independent and capable of self-government; and it also took the lead in preparing a system of government for itself. The constitution passed by its convention in 1776 was one of the first documents of the kind in the world, and absolutely the first in America. Its aim was lofty. It had in view greater liberty than men had ever before enjoyed. The document is a masterpiece of statesmanship, yet its terms are simple. It was the foundation on which nearly all the State constitutions have been based. It was in force nearly fifty years, and not until experience had shown wherein it was defective was there any disposition to change it or form a new constitution. Viewed now in the light of nearly a century and a quarter of progressive government, there are features seen in it which do not conform to the ideas of statesmen of today. But it was so much better, at the time of its adoption, than anything gone before that it was entirely satisfactory.

A Bill of Rights preceded the first constitution. On May 15, 1776, the Virginia Convention instructed its delegates in Congress to propose to that body to declare the United Colonies independent, and at the same time the Convention appointed a committee to prepare a Declaration of Rights and a plan of government for Virginia. On June 12 the Bill of Rights was passed. The document was written by George Mason, member of the committee. This state paper is of interest, not only as being one of the earliest of the kind in America, but because it contains inconsistencies which in after years clung to the laws of Virginia, carrying injustice with them, until West Virginia, when it became a State, refused to allow them to become part of the laws of the new Commonwealth. The chief of these inconsistencies is found in the just declaration at the outset of the Bill of Rights, "that all men are by nature equally free and independent;" and yet further on it paves the way for restricting the privilege of suffrage to those who own property, thereby declaring in terms, if not in words, that a poor man is not as free and independent as a rich man. Here was the beginning of the doctrine so long held in Virginia by its law-makers, that a man without property should not have a voice in the government. In after years this doctrine was combated by the people of the territory now forming West

Virginia. The inhabitants west of the Blue Ridge, and especially west of the Alleghanies, were the champions of universal suffrage, and they labored to attain that end, but with little success until they were able to set up a government for themselves, in which government men were placed above property. Further on in this chapter something more will be found on this subject.

The Bill of Rights declares that the freedom of the press is one of the chief bulwarks of liberty. This is in marked contrast with and a noticeable advance beyond the doctrine held by Sir William Berkeley, one of Virginia's royal governors, who solemnly declared, "I thank God we have not free schools or printing, and I hope we will not have these hundred years, for learning has brought disobedience and heresy and sects into the world, and printing has divulged them and libels against the government. God keep us from both." This solemn protest of Virginia's Governor was made nearly forty years after the founding of Harvard University in Massachusetts. It has been sometimes cited as an illustration of the difference between the Puritan civilization in Massachusetts and the Cavalier civilization of Virginia. But the comparison is unfair. It was no test of Virginia's civilization, for the Governor was carrying out instructions from England to suppress printing, and he did not consult the people of the colony whether they wanted printing presses or not. But when a printer, John Buckner by name, ten years after Governor Berkeley asked divine protection against schools and printing, ventured into Virginia with a press he was promptly brought before the Governor and was compelled to give bond that he would print nothing until the King of England gave consent.

In view of this experience it is not to be wondered at that the Virginians were prompt in declaring in their Bill of Rights that the press should be free. But they did not embrace that excellent opportunity to say a word in favor of schools. Nor could they, at one sweep, bring themselves to the broad doctrine that property does not round off and complete the man, but that "a man's a man for a' that," and capable, competent and trustworthy to take full part in the affairs of government. This Bill of Rights was brought into existence in the early part of the Revolutionary War, and at that very time the bold, patient, patriotic and poor backwoodsmen from the frontiers were in the American armies, fighting and dying in the cause of liberty and equal rights; and yet, by laws then being enacted, these same men were denied the right to take part in the management of the government which they were fighting to establish. It was for no other reason than that they were not assessed with enough property to give "sufficient evidence of permanent common interest with and attachment to the community." This notion had been brought from England, and had been fastened upon the colony of Virginia so firmly that it could not be shaken off when that State severed the political ties which bound it to the mother country. The idea clung to the constitution passed in 1776; to that of 1830; to that of 1851; but sentiment against the property qualification for suffrage constantly grew, and particularly among the people of Western Virginia, until it manifested itself in striking the obnoxious clause from the constitution when the State of West Virginia came into separate existence.

If the War of the Revolution did not teach the statesmen of Virginia that the poor man can be a patriot, and if the thirty-five or more years intervening between the adoption of the constitution of 1776 and the second war with England had not sufficed to do so, it might be supposed that the new

CONSTITUTIONAL HISTORY. 91

experience of the War of 1812 would have made the fact clear. But it did not convince the law-maker. Virginia was speedily invaded by the British after the declaration of war, and some of the most valuable property in the State was destroyed, and some of the best territory was overrun by the enemy. The city of Washington, just across the Potomac from Virginia, was captured and burned. An ex-President of the United States was compelled to hide in the woods to avoid capture by the enemy. In this critical time no soldiers fought more valiantly, none did more to drive back the invader, than the men from Western Virginia, where lived most of those who were classed too poor to take part in the affairs of government. It is said that sometimes half the men in a company of soldiers had never been permitted to vote because they did not own enough property.

The people of Western Virginia felt the injustice keenly. They never failed to respond promptly to a call when their services were needed in the field, but in time of peace they sought in a lawful and decent manner the redress of their grievances. They could not obtain this redress under the constitution then in force, and the War of 1812 had scarcely come to a close when the subject of a new constitution began to be spoken of. It was agitated long in vain. Nor was the restriction of suffrage the only wrong the people of Western Virginia endured, somewhat impatiently, but always with full respect for the laws then in force.

The eastern part of Virginia had the majority of inhabitants and the largest part of the property, and this gave that portion of the State the majority in the Assembly. This power was used with small respect for the rights of the people in the western part of the State. Internal improvements were made on a large scale in the east, but none were made west of the mountains, or very few. Men in the western counties had little encouragement to aspire to political distinction. The door was shut on them. The State offices were filled by men from the wealthy eastern districts. At length the agitation of the question of a new constitution ripened into results. The Assembly of Virginia in 1828 passed a bill submitting to a vote of the people whether they would have a constitutional convention called. At the election there were 38,542 votes cast, of which 21,896 were in favor of a constitutional convention. By far the heaviest vote favoring the convention was cast west of the Blue Ridge. The wealthy slave-owners of the lower counties wanted no change. The constitution had been framed to suit them, and they wanted nothing better. They feared that any change would give them something less suitable. Nevertheless, when the votes were counted and it was ascertained that a new constitution was inevitable, the representatives of the wealth of the State set to work to guard against any invasion of the privileges they had so long enjoyed.

The delegates from what is now West Virginia elected to this convention were: E. M. Wilson and Charles S. Morgan, of Monongalia County; William McCoy, of Pendleton County; Alexander Campbell and Philip Doddridge, of Brooke County; Andrew Beirne, of Monroe County; William Smith, of Greenbrier County; John Baxter, of Pocahontas; H. L. Opie and Thomas Griggs, of Jefferson; William Naylor and William Donaldson, of Hampshire; Philip Pendleton and Elisha Boyd, of Berkeley; E. S. Duncan, of Harrison; John Laidley, of Cabell; Lewis Summers, of Kanawha; Adam See, of Randolph. The leader of the western delegates in the convention was Philip Doddridge, who did all in his power to have the property qualification clause omitted from the new constitution.

The convention met at Richmond, October 5, 1829. From the very first meeting the western members were slighted. No western man was named in the selection of officers of the convention. It was seen at the outset that the property qualification for suffrage would not be given up by the eastern members without a struggle, and it was soon made plain that this qualification would have a majority. It was during the debates in this convention that Philip Doddridge, one of West Virginia's greatest men, came to the front in his full stature. His opponents were Randolph, Leigh, Upshur, Tazewell, Standard and others, who supported the doctrine that a voter should be a property-owner. One of Doddridge's colleagues was Alexander Campbell, the founder of the Church of the Disciples of Christ, sometimes known as the Christian Church, and again called, from its founder, the Campbellite Church. Here were two powerful intellects, Doddridge and Campbell, and they championed the cause of liberty in a form more advanced than was then allowed in Virginia. Doddridge himself had followed the plow, and he felt that the honest man does not need a certain number of acres before he can be trusted with the right of suffrage. He had served in the Virginia Legislature and knew from observation and experience the needs of the people in his part of the State. He was born on the bank of the Ohio River two years before the backwoodsmen of Virginia annulled the Quebec Act, passed by the Parliament of England, and he had grown to manhood in the dangers and vicissitudes of the frontiers. He was but five years old at the first siege of Fort Henry, and was ten years old at the second siege; and the shot which brought down the last British flag that floated above the soil of Virginia during the Revolutionary War was fired almost within hearing of his home. Among his neighbors were Lewis Wetzel, Ebenezer Zane, Samuel Brady and the men who fought to save the homes of the frontier settlers during the long and anxious years of Indian warfare. Although Doddridge died two years after this convention, while serving in Congress, he had done enough to give West Virginia reason for remembering him. The work of Campbell does not stand out in so conspicuous a manner in the proceedings of the convention, but his influence for good was great; and if the delegates from west of the mountains labored in vain for that time, the result was seen in later years.

The work of the convention was brought to a close in 1830, and a new constitution was given to the voters of the State for their approval or rejection. The western members had failed to strike out the distasteful property qualification. They had all voted against it except Doddridge, who was unable to attend that session on account of sickness, no doubt due to overwork. His vote, however, would have changed nothing, as the eastern members had a large majority and carried every measure they wanted. In the dissatisfaction consequent upon the failure of the western counties to secure what they considered justice began the movement for a new State. More than thirty years elapsed before the object was attained, and it was brought about by means and from causes which not the wisest statesman foresaw in 1830, yet the sentiment had been growing all the years. The old State of Virginia was never forgiven the offense and injury done the western district in the constitutional convention of 1829-1830. If the injustice was partly removed by the enlarged suffrage granted in the constitution adopted twenty years after, it was then too late for the atonement to be accepted as a blotting out of past wrongs; and in 1861 the people of West Virginia replied to the old State's long years of oppression and tyranny.

CONSTITUTIONAL HISTORY. 93

The constitution of 1830 adopted the Bill of Rights of 1776 without amendment or change. Then followed a long preamble reciting the wrongs under which Virginia suffered, prior to the Revolutionary War, before independence was secured. Under this constitution the Virginia House of Delegates consisted of one hundred and thirty-four members, of which twenty-six were chosen by the counties lying west of the Alleghenies; twenty-five by the counties between the Blue Ridge and the Alleghanies; forty-two by the counties between the Blue Ridge and tidewater, and thirty-six by the tidewater counties. The Senate consisted of thirty-two members, of which thirteen were from the counties west of the Blue Ridge. No priest or preacher was eligible to the Legislature. The right of suffrage was based on a property qualification. The ballot was forbidden and all voting was viva voce. Judges of the supreme court and of the superior courts were not elected by the people, but by the joint vote of the Senate and House of Delegates. The Attorney General was chosen in the same way. Sheriffs and Coroners were nominated by the county courts and appointed by the Governor. Justices of the Peace were appointed by the Governor and the Constables were appointed by the Justices. Clerks were appointed by the courts. The State Treasurer was elected by the joint vote of the Senate and House of Delegates. It is thus seen that the only State officers for which people could vote directly were Senators and members of the House of Delegates. Such an arrangement would be very unsatisfactory at the present day among people who have become accustomed to select their officers, almost without exception, from the highest to the lowest. The growth of the Republican principle of Government has been gradual. It was not all grasped at once; nor has it reached its fullest developement yet. The Bill of Rights and the first constitution of Virginia were a great step forward from the bad Government under England's Colonial system; but the gathered wisdom of more than a century has discovered and corrected many imperfections.

It is noticable that the constitution of 1830 contains no provisions for public schools. It may be stated generally that the early history of Virginia shows little development of the common school idea. The State which was satisfied for seventy-five years with suffrage denied the poor would not be likely to become famous for its zeal in the cause of popular education. The rich, who voted, could afford schools for their children; and the father who was poor could neither take part in the Government nor educate his children. Virginia was behind most of the old states in free schools. At the very time that Governor Berkeley thanked God that there were neither free schools nor printing presses in Virginia, Connecticut was devoting to education one fourth of its revenue from taxation. As late as 1857 Virginia with a population of nearly a million and a half, had only 41,608 children in common schools. When this is compared with other states, the contrast is striking. Massachusetts with a smaller population had five times as many children in the free schools; New Hampshire with one-fifth the population had twice as many; Illinois had nearly eight times as many, yet a smaller population; Ohio with a population a little larger had more than fourteen times as many children in public schools as Virginia. The following additional states in 1857 had more children attending common schools than Virginia had in proportion to their population: Maine, Vermont, Rhode Island, Connecticut, New York, Pennsylvania, New Jersey, Delaware, Indiana, Michigan, Iowa, Wisconsin, Missouri, Kentucky,

Maryland, Louisiana, Tennessee, North Carolina, Georgia, Alabama. The states with a smaller percentage of children in the common schools than Virginia's were South Carolina, California and Mississippi. For the remainder of the states, the statistics for that year were not compiled.

The showing is bad for Virginia. Although the lack of provision for popular education in the convention of 1830 does not appear to have caused opposition from the western members, yet the promptness with which the State of West Virginia provided for public schools as soon as it had a chance, is evidence that the sentiment west of the Alleghanies was strong in favor of popular education.

When the western delegates returned home after completing their labors in the convention of 1829–1830, they found that their constituents were much dissatisfied with the constitution. The chief thing contended for, less restriction on suffrage, had been refused, and the new constitution, while in some respects better than the old, retained the most objectionable feature of the old. At the election held early in 1830 for ratifying or rejecting the new constitution, 41,618 votes were cast, of which, 26,055 were for ratification and 15,563 against. The eastern part of the State voted strongly for ratification; the western part against it. Only two counties in what is now West Virginia gave a majority for it; and only one east of the Blue Ridge voted against it. The vote by counties in West Virginia was as follows: Berkeley, for 95, against 161; Brooke, the home of Doddridge and Campbell, for 0, against 371; Cabell, for 5, against 334; Greenbrier, for 34, against 464; Hampshire, for 241, against 211; Hardy, for 63, against 120; Harrison, for 8, against 1,112; Jefferson, for 243, against 53; Kanawha, for 42, against 266; Lewis, for 10, against 546; Logan, for 2, against 255; Mason, for 31, against 369; Monongalia, for 305, against 460; Monroe, for 19, against 451; Morgan, for 29, against 156; Nicholas, for 28, against 325; Ohio for 3, against 643; Pendleton, for 58, against 219; Pocahontas, for 9, against 288; Preston, for 121, against 357; Randolph, for 4, against 567; Tyler, for 5, against 299; Wood, for 28, against 410. Total, for 1,383, against 8,375.

Although the constitution of 1830 was unsatisfactory to the people of the western counties, and they had voted to reject it, it had been fastened upon them by the vote of the eastern counties. However, the matter was not to end there. In a Republican Government the way to reach a redress of grievances is to keep the proposed reform constantly before the people. If right, it will finally prevail. In all reform movements or questions, the right is nearly always in the minority at first; perhaps it is always so. The Western Virginians had been voted down, but they at once began to agitate the question of calling another constitutional convention. They kept at it for twenty years. Finally a Legislature was chosen which called an election on the subject of a constitutional convention. The majority of the Legislature was in favor of the convention, and in May, 1850, an election was held to choose delegates. Those elected from the country west of the Alleghanies, and from districts partly east and partly west of those mountains, were John Kenny, A. M. Newman, John Lionberger, George E. Deneale, G. B. Samuels, William Seymour, Giles Cook, Samuel C. Williams, Allen T. Caperton, Albert G. Pendleton, A. A. Chapman, Charles J. Faulkner, William Lucas, Dennis Murphy, Andrew Hunter, Thomas Sloan, James E. Stewart, Richard E. Byrd, Charles Blue, Jefferson T. Martin, Zachariah Jacob, John Knote, Thomas Gally, Benjamin H. Smith, William Smith,

CONSTITUTIONAL HISTORY.

Samuel Price, George W. Summers, Joseph Johnson, John F. Snodgrass. Gideon D. Camden, Peter G. Van Winkle, William G. Brown. Waitman T, Willey, Edward J. Armstrong, James Neeson, Samuel L. Hayes, Joseph Smith, John S. Carlile, Thomas Bland, Elisha W. McComas, Henry J. Fisher, and James H. Ferguson.

One of these delegates, Joseph Johnson, of Harrison County, was the only man up to that time ever chosen Governor from the district west of the Alleghanies; and in the three-quarters of a century since the adoption of Virginia's first constitution, no man from west of the Alleghanies had ever been sent to the United States Senate; and only one had been elected from the country west of the Blue Ridge. Eastern property had out-voted western men. Still the people west of the mountains sought their remedy in a new constitution, just as they had sought in vain nearly a generation before.

The constitutional convention met and organized for work. The delegates from the eastern part of the State at once showed their hand. They insisted from the start that there should be a property qualification for suffrage. This was the chief point against which the western people had been so long contending, and the members from west of the Alleghanies were there to resist such a provision in the new constitution and to fight it to the last. Lines were drawn upon this issue. The contending forces were at once arrayed for the fight. It was seen that the western members and the members who took sides with them were not in as hopeless a minority as they had been in the convention of 1830. Still they were not so strong as to assure victory, and the battle was to be long and hard-fought. If there was one man among the western members more conspicuous as a leader than the others, that man was Waitman T. Willey, of Monongalia County. An unswerving advocate of liberty in its widest interpretation, and with an uncompromising hatred of tyranny and oppression, he had prepared himself to fight in the front when the question of restriction of suffrage should come up. The eastern members forced the issue, and he met it. He denied that property is the true source of political power; but, rather, that the true source should be sought in wisdom, virtue, patriotism; and that wealth, while not bad in itself, frequently becomes a source of political weakness. The rights of persons are above the rights of property. Mr. Scott, a delegate from Fauquier County, declared that this movement by the western members was simply an effort to get their hands on the pocket books of the wealthy east. Mr. Willey repelled this impeachment of the integrity of the west. Other members in sympathy with the property qualification took up the cue and the assault upon the motives of the people of the west became severe and unjust. But the members from that part of the State defended the honor of its people with a vigor and a success which defeated the property qualification in the constitution.

It was not silenced however. It was put forward and carried in another form, by a proviso that members of the Assembly and Senate should be elected on an arbitrary basis until the year 1865, and at that time the question should be submitted to a vote of the people whether their delegates in the Legislature should be apportioned on what was called the "white basis" or the "mixed basis." The first provided that members of the Legislature should be apportioned according to the number of white inhabitants; the second, that they should be apportioned according to both property and inhabitants. The eastern members believed that in 1865 the vote of the State would favor the mixed basis, and thus the property qualification would again be in force, although not in exactly the same form as before.

The proceedings of the convention had not advanced far when it became apparent that a sentiment in that body was in favor of electing many or all of the County and State officers. The sentiment favoring electing judges was particularly strong. Prior to that time the judges in Virginia had been chosen by the Legislature or appointed by the Governor, who was a creature of the Legislature. The members from Western Virginia, under the leadership of Mr. Willey, were in favor of electing the judges. It was more in conformity with the principles of republican government that the power which selected the makers of laws should also select the interpreters of those laws, and also those whose duty it is to execute the laws. The power of the people was thus increased, and with increase of power there was an increase also in their responsibility. Both are wholesome stimulants for the citizens of a commonwealth who are rising to new ideas and higher principles. The constitution of 1850 is remarkable for the general advance embodied in it. The experience of nearly half a century has shown that many improvements could be made, but at the time it was adopted its landmarks were set on higher ground. But as yet the idea that the State is the greatest beneficiary from the education of the people, and that it is the duty of the State to provide free schools for this purpose, had not gained sufficient footing to secure so much as an expression in its favor in the constitution of 1850.

The work of the convention was completed, and at an election held for the purpose in 1852 it was ratified and became the foundation for State government in Virginia. The Bill of Rights, passed in 1776 and adopted without change as a preamble or introduction to the constitution of 1830, was amended in several particulars and prefixed to the constitution of 1850. The constitution of 1830 required voting by viva voce, without exception. That of 1850 made an exception in favor of deaf and dumb persons. But for all other persons the ballot was forbidden. The property qualification for suffrage was not placed in the constitution. Although a provision was made to foist a property clause on the State to take effect in 1865, the great and unexpected change made by the Civil War before the year 1865 rendered this provision of no force. The leading features of the "mixed basis" and "white basis," as contemplated by the constitution, were: In 1865 the people, by vote, were to decide whether the members of the State Senate and Lower House should be apportioned in accordance with the number of voters, without regard to property, or whether, in such apportionment, property should be represented. The former was called the white basis or suffrage basis; the latter mixed basis. Under the mixed basis the apportionment would be based on a ratio of the white inhabitants and of the amount of State taxes paid. Provision was made for the apportionment of Senators on one basis and members of the Lower House on the other, if the voters should so decide. The members of the convention from West Virginia did not like the mixed basis, but the clause making the provision for it went into the constitution in spite of them. They feared that the populous and wealthy eastern counties would out-vote the counties beyond the Alleghanies and fasten the mixed basis upon the whole State. But West Virginia had separated from the old State before 1865 and never voted on that measure. There was a clause which went so far as to provide that the members of the Senate might be apportioned solely on the basis of taxation, if the people so decided by vote.

Under the constitution free negroes were not permitted to reside in Virginia unless free at the time the constitution went into effect. Slaves thereafter manumitted forfeited their freedom by remaining twelve months in the State. Provision was made for enslaving them again.

For the first time in the history of the State the Governor was to be elected by the people. He had before been appointed by the Legislature. County officers, clerks, sheriff, prosecuting attorney and surveyor, were now to be elected by the people. The county court, composed of not less than three or more than five justices of the peace, held sessions monthly, and had enlarged jurisdiction. This arrangement was not consistent with the advance made in other branches of County and State government as provided for in the constitution. That county court was not satisfactory, and even after West Virginia became a State, it did not at first rid itself of the tribunal which had out-lived its usefulness. But after a number of years a satisfactory change was made by the new State. Under Virginia's constitution of 1850 the Auditor, Treasurer and Secretary were selected by the Legislature.

The first constitution of West Virginia was a growth rather than a creation by a body of men in one convention. The history of that constitution is a part of the history of the causes leading up to and the events attending the creation of a new State from the counties in the western part of Virginia, which had refused to follow the old State when it seceded from the Union. Elsewhere in this volume will be found a narrative of the acts by which the new State was formed. The present chapter will consider only those movements and events directly related to the first constitution.

The efforts of the Northern States to keep slavery from spreading to new territory, and the attempts of the South to introduce it into the West; the passage of laws by the Northern States by which they refused to deliver runaway slaves to their masters; decisions of courts in conflict with the wishes of one or the other of the great parties to the controversy; and other acts or doctrines favorable to one or the other, all entered into the presidential campaign of 1860 and gave that contest a bitterness unknown before or since in the history of American politics. For many years the South had been able to carry its points by the ballot-box or by statesmanship, but in 1860 the power was slipping away, and the North was in the ascendancy with its doctrines of no further extension of slavery. There were four candidates in the field, and the Republicans elected Abraham Lincoln. Had the Southern States accepted the result, acquiesced in the limitation of slavery within those States wherein it already had an undisputed foothold, the Civil War would not have occurred at that time, and perhaps never. Slavery would have continued years longer. But the rashness of the Southern States hastened the crisis, and in its result slavery was stamped out. South Carolina led the revolt by a resolution December 20, 1860, by which that State seceded from the Union. Other Southern States followed, formed "The Confederate States of America," and elected Jefferson Davis President.

Virginia, as a State, went with the South, but the people of the western part, when confronted with the momentous question, "Choose ye this day whom ye will serve," chose to remain citizens of the United States. Governor Letcher, of Virginia, called an extra session of the Legislature to meet January 7, 1861, to consider public affairs. The Legislature passed a bill calling a convenion of the people of Virginia, whose delegates were to be elected February 4, to meet in Richmond, February 13, 1861. A substitute for this bill, offered in the Lower House of the Legislature, providing that a vote of the people of the State should be taken on the question of calling the convention, was defeated. The convention was thus convened without the consent of the people, a thing which had never before been done in Virginia.

Delegates were chosen for Western Virginia. They were nearly all opposed to secession and worked to defeat it in the convention. Finding their efforts in vain, they returned home, some of them escaping many dangers and overcoming much difficulty on the way. The action of the Virginia Convention was kept secret for some time, while State troops and troops from other States were seizing United States arsenals and other government property in Virginia. But when the delegates returned to their homes in Western Virginia with the news that Virginia had joined the Southern Confederacy there was much excitement and a widespread determination among the people not to be transferred to the Confederacy. Meetings were held, delegates were chosen to a convention in Wheeling to meet June 11 for the purpose of re-organizing the government of Virginia.

Owing to the peculiar circumstances in which the State of Virginia was placed, part in and part out of the Southern Confederacy, the constitution of 1850 did not apply to the case, and certainly did not authorize the re-organization of the State Government in the manner in which it was about to be done. No constitution and no statute had ever been framed to meet such an emergency. The proceeding undertaken by the Wheeling convention was authorized by no written law, and so far as the statutes of the State contemplated such a condition, they forbade it. But, as the gold which sanctified the Temple was greater than the Temple, so men who make the law are greater than the law. The principle is dangerous when acted upon by bad men, but patriots may, in a crisis which admits of no delay, be a law unto themselves. The people of Western Virginia saw the storm, saw the only salvation, and with promptness they seized the helm and made for the harbor.

The constitution of Virginia did not apply. The Wheeling Convention passed an ordinance for the government of the re-organized State. This ordinance could scarcely be called a constitution, yet it was a good temporary substitute for one. It authorized the convention to appoint a Governor and Lieutenant Governor to serve until their successors were elected and qualified. They were to administer the existing laws of Virginia. The General Assembly was called to meet in Wheeling, where it was to provide for the election of a Governor and Lieutenant Governor. The capital of Virginia was thus changed from Richmond to Wheeling, so far as that convention could change it. The Senators and Assemblymen who had been chosen at the preceding election were to constitute the Legislature. A Council of Five was appointed by the convention to assist the Governor in the discharge of his duties. An allusion to the State Constitution, made in this ordinance, shows that the convention considered the Virginia Constitution of 1850 still in force, so far as it was applicable to the changed conditions. There was no general and immediate change of county and district officers provided for, but an oath was required of them that they would support the Constitution of the United States. Provision was made for removing from office such as refused to take the oath, and for appointing others in their stead.

Under and by virtue of this ordinance the convention elected Francis H. Pierpont Governor of Virginia, Daniel Polsley Lieutenant Governor, and James S. Wheat Attorney General. Provision having been made by the General Assembly which met in Wheeling for an election of delegates to frame a constitution for the State of West Virginia, provided a vote of the people should be in favor of a new State, and the election having shown that a new State was desired, the delegates to the Constitutional Convention assembled in Wheeling November 26, 1861. The purpose at first had not been to form a new State, but to re-organize and administer the government of Virginia. But the sentiment in favor of a new State was strong, and resulted in the assembling of a convention to frame a constitution. The list of delegates were, Gordon Batelle, Ohio County; Richard L. Brooks, Upshur; James H. Brown, Kanawha; John J. Brown, Preston; John Boggs, Pendleton; W. W. Brumfield, Wayne; E. H. Caldwell, Marshall; Thomas R. Carskadon, Hampshire; James S. Cassady, Fayette; H. D. Chapman, Roane; Richard M. Cooke, Mercer; Henry Dering, Monongalia; John A. Dille, Preston; Abijah Dolly, Hardy; D. W. Gibson, Pocahontas; S. F. Griffith, Mason; Stephen M. Hansley, Raleigh; Robert Hogar, Boone; Ephraim B. Hall, Marion; John Hall, Mason; Thomas W. Harrison, Harrison; Hiram Haymond, Marion; James Hervey, Brooke; J. P. Hoback, McDowell; Joseph Hubbs, Pleasants; Robert Irvine, Lewis; Daniel Lamb, Ohio; R. W. Lauck, Wetzel; E. S. Mahon, Jackson; A. W. Mann, Greenbrier; John R. McCutcheon, Nicholas; Dudley S. Montague, Putnam; Emmett J. O'Brien, Barbour; Granville Parker, Cabell; James W. Parsons, Tucker; J. W. Paxton, Ohio; David S. Pinnell, Upshur; Joseph S. Pomeroy, Hancock; John M. Powell, Harrison; Job Robinson, Calhoun; A. F. Ross, Ohio; Lewis Ruffner, Kanawha; Edward W. Ryan, Fayette; George W. Sheets, Hampshire; Josiah Simmons, Randolph; Harmon Sinsel, Taylor; Benjamin H. Smith, Logan; Abraham D. Soper, Tyler; Benjamin L. Stephenson, Clay; William E. Stevenson, Wood; Benjamin F. Stewart, Wirt; Chapman J. Stewart, Doddridge; G. F. Taylor, Braxton; M. Titchenell, Marion; Thomas H. Trainer, Marshall; Peter G. Van Winkle, Wood; William Walker, Wyoming; William W. Warder, Gilmer; Joseph S. Wheat, Morgan; Waitman T. Willey, Monongalia; A. J. Wilson, Ritchie; Samuel Young, Pocahontas.

There were two sessions of this convention, the first in the latter part of 1861, the second beginning February 12, 1863. The constitution was completed at the first session, as was supposed, but when the question of admitting the State into the Union was before Congress that body required a change of one section regarding slavery, and the convention was re-convened and made the necessary change.

When the convention assembled November 15, 1861, it set about its task. The first intention was to name the new State Kanawha, but there being objections to this, the name of Augusta was suggested; then Alleghany, Western Virginia, and finally the name West Virginia was chosen. Selecting a name for the new State was not the most difficult matter before the convention. Very soon the question of slavery came up. The sentiment against that institution was not strong enough to exclude it from the State. No doubt a majority of the people would have voted to exclude it, but there was a strong element not yet ready to dispense with slavery, and a division on that question was undesirable at that time. Accordingly, the constitution dismissed the slavery question with the provision that no slave should be brought into the State nor free negroes come into the State after the adoption of the constitution. Before the constitution was submitted to a vote of the people it was changed to provide for the emancipation of slaves.

The new constitution had a provision which was never contained in the constitutions of Virginia; it affirmed that West Virginia shall remain a member of the United States. When this constitution was framed it did not regard Hampshire, Hardy, Pendleton and Morgan as parts of the State, but provided that they might become parts of West Virginia if they voted in favor of adopting the constitution. They so voted and thus came into the State. The same provision was made in regard to Frederick County, but it chose to remain a portion of Virginia. It was declared that there should be freedom of the press and of speech, and the law of libel was given a liberal interpretation and was rendered powerless to curtail the freedom of the press. It was provided that in suits of libel the truth could be given in evidence, and if it appeared that the matter charged as libelous was true, and was published with good intentions, the judgement should be for the defendant in the suit. The days of viva voce voting were past. The constitution provided that all voting should be by ballot. The Legislature was required to meet every year.

A clause was inserted declaring that no person who had aided or abetted the Southern Confederacy should become citizens of the State unless such persons had subsequently volunteered in the army or the navy of the United States. This measure seems harsh when viewed from after years, when the passions kindled by the Civil War have cooled and the prejudice and hatred have become things of the past. It must be remembered that the constitution came into existence during the war. The better judgment of the people at a later day struck out that clause. But at the worst the measure was only one of retaliation, in remembrance of the tyranny recently shown within this State toward loyal citizens and office-holders by sympathizers of the Southern Confederacy. The overbearing spirit of the politicians of Richmond found its echo west of the Alleghanies. Horace Greeley had been deterred from delivering a lecture in Wheeling on the issues of the day, because his lecture contained references to the slavery question. In Ohio County, at that time, those who opposed slavery were in the majority, but not in power. There were not fifty slave-holders in the county. Horace Greeley was indicted in Harrison County because he had caused the *Tribune*, his newspaper, to be circulated there. The agent of the *Tribune* fled from the State to escape arrest. Postmasters, acting, as they claimed, under the laws of Virginia, refused to deliver to subscribers such papers as the New York *Tribune* and the New York *Christian Advocate*. A Baptist minister who had taught colored children in Sunday school was for that act ostracized and he left Wheeling. Newsdealers in Wheeling were afraid to keep on their shelves a statistical book written by a North Carolinian, because it treated of slavery in its economic aspect. Dealers were threatened with indictment if they handled the book. Cassius Clay, of Kentucky, was threatened with violence for coming to Wheeling to deliver a lecture which he had delivered in his own State. The newspapers of Richmond reproached Wheeling for permitting such a paper as the *Intelligencer* to be published there.

These instances of tyranny from Southern sympathizers are given, not so much for their value as simple history as to show the circumstances under which West Virginia's first constitution was made, and to give an insight into the partisan feeling which led to the insertion of the clause disfranchising those who took part against the United States. Those who upheld the Union had in the meantime come into power, and in turn had become the oppressors. Retaliation is never right as an abstract proposition and seldom best as a political measure. An act of injustice should not be made a precedent or an excuse for a wrong perpetrated upon the authors of the unjust act. Time has done its part in committing to oblivion the hatred and the wrong which grew out of the Civil War. Under West Virginia's present constitution no man has lesser or greater political powers because he wore the blue or the grey.

Representation in the State Senate and House of Delegates was in proportion to the number of people. The question of the "white basis" or the "mixed basis," as contained in the Virginia constitution of 1850, no longer troubled West Virginia. Suffrage was extended until the people elected their officers, State, County and District, including all judges.

The constitution provided for free schools, and authorized the setting apart of an irreduceable fund for that purpose. The fund is derived from the sale of delinquent lands; from grants and devises, the proceeds of estates of persons who die without will or heirs; money paid for exemption from military duty; such sums as the Legislature may appropriate, and from other sources. This is invested in United States or State securities, and the interest is annually appropriated to the support of the schools. The principal must not be expended.

The constitution was submitted to the people for ratification in April, 1863, and the vote in favor of it was 18,862, and against it 514. Jefferson and Berkeley Counties did not vote. They had not been represented in the convention which formed the constitution. With the close of the war Virginia claimed them and West Virginia claimed them. The matter was finally settled by the Supreme Court of the United States in 1870, in favor of West Virginia. It was at one time considered that the counties of Northampton and Accomack on the eastern shore of Virginia belonged to the new State of West Virginia, because they had sent delegates to the Wheeling Convention for the reorganization of the State government. It was once proposed that these two counties be traded to Maryland in exchange for the two western counties in that State which were to be added to West Virginia, but the trade was not consummated.

Under the constitution of 1863 the State of West Virginia was governed nine years, and there was general prosperity. But experience demonstrated that many of the provisions of the constitution were not perfect. Amendments and improvements were suggested from time to time, and there gradually grew up a strong sentiment in favor of a new constitution. On February 23, 1871, a call was issued for an election of delegates to a constitutional convention. The election was held in August of that year, and in January, 1872, the delegates met in Charleston and began the work. They completed it in a little less than three months.

The following delegates were elected by the various senatorial and assembly districts of the State: Brooke County, Alexander Campbell, William K. Pendleton; Boone, William D. Pate; Braxton, Homer A. Holt; Berkeley, Andrew W. McCleary, C. J. Faulkner, John Blair Hoge; Barbour, Samuel Woods, J. N. B. Crim; Clay, B. W. Byrne; Calhoun, Lemuel Stump; Cabell, Evermont Ward, Thomas Thornburg; Doddridge, Jeptha F. Randolph; Fayette, Hudson M. Dickinson; Greenbrier, Henry M. Mathews, Samuel Price; Harrison, Bejamin Wilson, Beverly H. Lurty, John Bassel; Hampshire, J. D. Armstrong, Alexander Monroe; Hardy, Thomas Maslin; Hancock, John H. Atkinson; Jefferson, William H. Travers, Logan Osburn, William A. Morgan; Jackson, Thomas R. Park; Kanawha, John A. Warth, Edward B. Knight, Nicholas Fitzhugh; Lewis, Mathew Edmiston, Blackwell Jackson; Logan, M. A. Staton; Morgan, Lewis Allen; Monongalia, Waitman T. Willey, Joseph Snider, J. Marshall Hagans; Marion, U. N. Arnett, Alpheus F. Haymond, Fountain Smith; Mason, Charles B. Waggener, Alonzo Cushing; Mercer, Isaiah Bee, James Calfee; Mineral, John A. Robinson, John T. Pearce; Monroe, James M. Byrnsides, William Haynes; Marshall, James M. Pipes, J. W. Gallaher, Hanson Criswell; Ohio, George O. Davenport, William W. Miller, A. J. Pawnell, James S. Wheat; Putnam, John J. Thompson; Pendleton, Charles D. Boggs; Pocahontas, George H. Moffett; Preston, William G. Brown, Charles Kantner; Pleasants, W. G. H. Care; Roane, Thomas Ferrell; Ritchie, Jacob P. Strickler; Randolph, J. F. Harding; Raleigh, William Price, William McCreery; Taylor, A. H. Thayer, Benjamin F. Martin; Tyler, Daniel D. Johnson, David S. Pugh; Upshur, D. D. T. Farnsworth; Wirt, D. A. Roberts, David H. Leonard; Wayne, Charles W. Ferguson; Wetzel, Septimus Hall; Wood, James M. Jackson, Okey Johnson.

The new constitution of West Virginia enters much more fully into the ways and means of government than any other constitution Virginia or West Virginia had known. It leaves less for the courts to interpret and decide than any of the former constitutions. The details are elaborately worked out, and the powers and duties of the three departments of State government, the Legislative, Judicial and Executive, are stated in so precise terms that there can be little ground for controversy as to what the constitution means. The terms of the State officers were increased to four years, and the Legislature's sessions were changed from yearly to once in two years. A marked change in the tone of the constitution regarding persons who took part in the Civil War against the government is noticeable. Not only is the clause in the former constitution disfranchising those who took part in the Rebellion not found in the new constitution, but in its stead is a clause which repudiates, in express terms, the sentiment on this subject in the former constitution. It is stated that "political tests requiring persons, as a pre-requisite to the enjoyment of their civil and political rights, to purge themselves, by their own oaths, of past alleged offenses, are repugnant to the principles of free government, and are cruel and oppressive." The ex-Confederates and those who sympathized with and assisted them in their war against the United States could have been as effectively restored to their rights by a simple clause to that effect as by the one employed, which passes judgment upon a part of the former constitution. The language on this subject in the new constitution may, therefore, be taken as the matured judgment and as an expression of the purer conception of justice by the people of West Virginia when the passions of the war had subsided, and when years had given time for reflection. It is provided, also, that no person who aided or participated in the Rebellion shall be liable to any proceedings, civil or criminal, for any act done by him in accordance with the rules of civilized warfare. It was provided in the constitution of Virginia that ministers and priests should not be eligible to seats in the Legislature. West Virginia's new constitution broke down the barrier against a worthy and law-abiding class of citizens. It is provided that "all men shall be free to profess, and, by argument, to maintain their opinions in matters of religion, and the same shall in no wise affect, diminish or enlarge their civil capacities."

A change was made in the matter of investing the State School Fund. The first constitution authorized its investment in United States or West Virginia State securities only. The new constitution provided that it might be invested in other solvent securities, provided United States or this State's securities cannot be had. The provision for courts did not meet general approval as left by the constitution, and this dissatisfaction at length led to an amendment which was voted upon October 12, 1880, and was ratified by a vote of 57,941 for, to 34,270 against. It provides that the Supreme Court of Appeals shall consist of four judges who shall hold office twelve years, and they and all other judges and justices in the State shall be elected by the people. There shall be thirteen circuit judges, and they must hold at least three terms of court in every county of the State each year. Their tenure of office is eight years. The county court was remodeled. It no longer consists of justices of the peace, nor is its power as large as formerly. It is composed of three commissioners whose term of office is six years. Four regular terms of court are held yearly. The powers and duties of the justices of the peace are clearly defined. No county shall have fewer than three justices nor more than twenty. Each county is divided into districts, not fewer than three nor more than ten in number. Each district has one justice, and if its population is more than twelve hundred it is entitled to two. They hold office four years.

There is a provision in the constitution that any county may change its county court if a majority of the electors vote to do so, after the forms laid down by law have been complied with. It is left to the people, in such a case, to decide what shall be the nature of the tribunal which takes the place of the court of commissioners.

The growth of the idea of liberty and civil government in a century, as expressed in the Bill of Rights and the Virginia Constitution of 1776, and as embodied in the subsequent constitutions of 1830, 1850, 1863 and 1872, shows that the most sanguine expectations of the statesmen of 1776 have been realized and surpassed in the present time. The right of suffrage has been extended beyond anything dreamed of a century ago, and it has been demonstrated that the people are capable of understanding and enjoying their enlarged liberty. The authors of Virginia's first constitution believed that it was unwise to entrust the masses with the powers of government. Therefore the chief part taken by the people in their own government was in the selection of their Legislature. All other State, County and District offices were filled by appointments or by elections by the Legislature. Limited as was the exercise of suffrage, it was still further restricted by a property qualification which disfranchised a large portion of the people. Yet this liberty was so great in comparison with that enjoyed while under England's colonial government that the people were satisfied for a long time. But finally they demanded enlarged rights and obtained them. When they at length realized that they governed themselves, and were not governed by others, they speedily advanced in the science of government. The property qualification was abolished. The doctrine that wealth is the true source of political power was relegated to the past. From that it was but a step for the people to exercise a right which they had long suffered others to hold—that of electing all their officers. At first they did not elect their own governor, and as late as 1850 they acquiesced, though somewhat reluctantly, in the doctrine that they could not be trusted to elect their own judges. But they have thrown all this aside now, and their officers are of their own selection; and no man, because he is poor, if capable of self-support, is denied an equal voice in government with that exercised by the most wealthy. Men, not wealth; intelligence, not force, are the true sources of our political power.

CHAPTER XI.

―:o:―

JOHN BROWN'S RAID.

The attempt of John Brown to free the slaves; his seizure of the United States Armory at Harper's Ferry; his capture, trial and execution, form a page in West Virginia's history in which the whole country, and in a lesser degree the whole civilized world, felt an interest at the time of its occurrence; and that interest will long continue. The seizure of the Government property at that place by an ordinary mob would have created a stir; but the incident would have lost its interest in a short time, and at a short distance from the scene of disturbance. But Brown's accomplices were no ordinary mob; and the purpose in view gave his attempt its great importance. In fact, much more importance was attached to the raid than it deserved. Viewed in the light of history, it is plain that Brown could not have freed many slaves, nor could he have caused any wide-spread uprising among them. The military resources of the Government, or even of the State of Virginia, were sufficient to stamp out in short order any attempted insurrection at that time. There were not enough people willing and ready to assist the attempt. There were too many willing and ready to put it down. Brown achieved about as much success as he could reasonably expect, and his attempt at emancipating slaves ran its logical course. But the extreme sensitiveness of the slave holders and their fears that abolitionists would incite an uprising, caused Brown's bold dash to be given an importance at the time far beyond what it deserved.

John Brown was a man of great courage; not easily excited; cool and calculating; not bloodthirsty, but willing to take the life of any one who stood between him and the accomplishment of his purpose. He has been very generally regarded as a fanatic, who had followed an idea until he became a monomaniac. It is difficult to prove this view of him to be incorrect; yet, without doubt, his fanaticism was of a superior and unusual kind. The dividing line between fanatics and the highest order of reformers, those who live before their time, who can see the light touching the peaks beyond the valleys and shadows in which other men are walking, is not always clearly marked. It is not for us to say to which class of men Brown belonged; and certainly it is not given us to set him among the blind fanatics. If he must be classified, we run less risk of error if we place him with those whose prophetic vision outstrips their physical strength; with the sentinel on the watch tower of Sier, of whom Isaiah speaks.

What he hoped to accomplish, and died in an attempt to accomplish, was brought about in less than five years from his death. If he failed to free the slaves, they were speedily freed by that sentiment of which he was an extreme representative. It cannot be said that Brown's efforts were the immediate, nor even the remote, cause which emancipated the black race in the United States; but beyond doubt the affair at Harper's Ferry had a powerful influence in two directions, either of which worked toward emancipation. The one influence operated in the North upon those who desired emancipation, stimulating them to renewed efforts; the other influence had its effect among the Southern slave owners, kindling their anger and their fear, and urging them to acts by which they hoped to strengthen their grip upon the institution of slavery, but which led them to war against the Government, and their hold on slavery was shaken loose forever. John Brown was born in Connecticut, went to Kansas with his family and took part in the contention in that state which occurred between the slave faction and those opposed to the spread of slavery. Brown affiliated with the latter and fought in more than one armed encounter. He was one of the boldest leaders, fearless in fight, stubborn in defense, and relentless in pursuit. He hated slavery with an inappeasable hatred. He belonged to the party in the North called Abolitionists, whose avowed object was to free the slaves. He was perhaps more radical than the majority of that radical party. They hoped to accomplish their purpose by creating a sentiment in its favor. Brown appears to have been impatient at this slow process. He believed in uniting force and argument, and he soon became the leader of that wing of the Ultra Abolitionists. On May 8, 1858, a secret meeting was held in Chatham, Canada, which was attended by delegates from different states, and from Canada. The object was to devise means of freeing the slaves. It is not known exactly what the proceedings of the meeting were, except that a constitution was outlined for the United States, or for such states as might be taken possession of. Brown was commander-in-chief; one of his companions named Kagi was secretary of war. Brown issued several military commissions.

Harper's Ferry was selected as the point for the uprising. It was to be seized and held as a place of rendezvous for slaves from Maryland and Virginia, and when a sufficient number had assembled there they were to march under arms across Maryland into Pennsylvania and there disperse. The negroes were to be armed with tomahawks and spears, they not being sufficiently acquainted with firearms to use them. It was believed that the slaves would eagerly grasp the opportunity to gain their freedom, and that the movement, begun at one point, would spread and grow until slavery was stamped out. Brown no doubt incorrectly estimated the sentiment in the North in favor of emancipation by force of arms. In company with his two sons, Watson and Oliver, Brown rented a farm near Sharpsburg, in Maryland, from Dr. Kennedy. This was within a few miles of Harper's Ferry, and was used as a gathering point for Brown's followers, and as a place of concealment for arms. Brown represented that his name was Anderson. He never had more than twenty-two men about the farm. From some source in the East, never certainly ascertained, arms were shipped to Brown, under the name of J. Smith & Son. The boxes were double, so that no one could suspect their contents. In this manner he received two hundred and ninety Sharp's rifles, two hundred Maynard revolvers and one thousand spears and tomahawks. Brown expected from two thousand to five thousand men, exclusive of slaves, to rise at his word and come to his assistance. In this he was mistaken. He knew that twenty-two men could not hold Harper's Ferry, and without doubt he calculated, and expected even to the last hour before capture, that his forces would rally to his assistance. When he found that they had not done so, he concluded that the blow had been struck too soon.

About ten o'clock on the night of October 16, 1859, with seventeen white men and five negroes, Brown proceeded to Harper's Ferry, overpowered the sentry on the bridge, seized the United States arsenal, in which were stored arms sufficient to equip an army, took several persons prisoner and confined them in the armory; visited during the night some of the farmers in the vicinity, took them prisoner and declared freedom to their slaves; cut the telegraph wires leading from Harper's Ferry; seized an eastbound train on the Baltimore and Ohio Railroad, but subsequently let it proceed, after announcing that no other train would be permitted to pass through Harper's Ferry.

The people in the town knew nothing of what was taking place until daybreak. At that time a negro porter at the railroad station was shot and killed because he refused to join the insurgents, and an employe at the armory was shot at when he refused to be taken prisoner. A merchant witnessed the shooting, and fired from his store at one of Brown's men. He missed, but was shot dead in return. When workmen belonging to the armory appeared at the hour for beginning their daily labors they were arrested and confined in one of the Government buildings as a prison. The village was now alarmed. The mayor of the town, Fontaine Beckham, and Captain George Turner, formerly of the United States Army, appeared on the scene, and were fired upon and killed. The wires, having been cut, news of the insurrection was slow in reaching the surrounding country; but during the forenoon telegrams were sent from the nearest offices. The excitement throughout the South was tremendous. The people there believed that a gigantic uprising of the slaves was at hand. The meagre information concerning the exact state of affairs at Harper's Ferry caused it to be greatly over estimated. At Washington the sensation amounted to a shock. General Robert E. Lee was ordered to the scene at once with one hundred marines.

Military companies began to arrive at Harper's Ferry from neighboring towns. The first upon the scene was Colonel Baylor's company from Charlestown. Shortly afterwards two companies arrived from Martinsburg. A desultory fire was kept up during the day, in which several persons were killed. An assault on one of the buildings held by Brown was successfully made by the militia. Four of the insurgents were killed and a fifth was made prisoner. Brown and the remainder of his men took refuge in the engine house at the armory, except four who fled and escaped to Pennsylvania. Two of them were subsequently captured. Two of Brown's men came out to hold a parley and were shot and taken prisoner. One was killed in revenge for the death of Mayor Beckham; the other was subsequently tried, convicted and hanged. About three o'clock in the afternoon of October 17, about twenty railroad men made a dash at the engine house, broke down the door and killed two of Brown's men. But they were repulsed with seven of their number wounded.

Before sunset there were more than one thousand men in Harper's Ferry under arms, having come in from the surrounding country; but no further assault was made on Brown's position that day for fear of killing the men whom he held prisoner in the building with him. That night R. E. Lee arrived from Washington with one hundred marines and two pieces of artillery. Lieutenant J. E. B. Stuart was with him. Early Tuesday morning, October 18, Stuart was sent to demand an unconditional surrender, promising only that Brown and his men should be protected from immediate violence, and should have a trial under the laws of the country. Brown refused to accept these terms, but demanded that he and his men be permitted to march out with their prisoners, cross the Potomac unpursued. They would then free their prisoners and would escape if they could; if not they would fight. Of course Stuart did not accept this offer. Preparations were made for an attack. The marines brought up a heavy ladder, and using it as a battering ram, broke open the door of the engine house and rushed in. Brown and his men fought till killed or overpowered. The first man who entered, named Quinn, was killed. Brown was stabbed twice with bayonets and then cut down by a sabre stroke. All of his men but two were killed or wounded. These were taken prisoner. Of the whole band of twenty-two, ten white men and three negroes were killed; three white men were wounded; two had made their escape; all the others were captured.

It was believed that Brown's injuries would prove fatal in a few hours, but he rallied. Within the next few days he was indicted for murder, and for treason against the United States. In his case the customary interval did not elapse between his indictment and his trial. He was captured October 18, and on October 26 his case was called for trial in the county court at Charlestown, in Jefferson County. Brown's attorney asked for a continuance on the ground that the defendant was physically unable to stand trial. The motion for a continuance was denied, and the trial proceeded. Brown reclined on a cot, being unable to sit. The trial was extremely short, considering the importance of the case. Within less than three days the jury had brought in a verdict of guilty, and Brown was sentenced to be hanged December 16. Executive clemency was sought. Under the law of Virginia at that time the Governor was forbidden to grant pardon to any one convicted of treason except with the consent of the Assembly. Governor Henry A. Wise notified the Assembly of Brown's application for pardon. That body passed a resolution, December 7, by which it refused to interfere in Brown's behalf, and he died on the scaffold at the appointed time. Six of his companions were executed, four on the same day with their leader, and two in the following March.

The remains of Brown were taken to North Elba, New York, where Wendell Phillips pronounced a eulogy. Perhaps Brown contributed more to the emancipation of slaves by his death than by his life.

CHAPTER XII.

―:o:―

THE ORDINANCE OF SECESSION.

Although West Virginia at the time was a part of Virginia, it refused to go with the majority of the people of that State in seceding from the United States and joining the Southern Confederacy. The circumstances attending that refusal constitute an important chapter in the history of West Virginia. Elsewhere in this book, in speaking of the constitution of this and the mother State, reference is made to the differences in sentiment and interests between the people west of the Alleghanies and those east of that range. The Ordinance of Secession was the rock upon which Virginia was broken in twain. It was the occasion of the west's separating from the east. The territory which ought to have been a separate State at the time Kentucky became one seized the opportunity of severing the political ties which had long bound it to the Old Dominion. After the war Virginia invited the new State to reunite with it, but a polite reply was sent that West Virginia preferred to retain its statehood. The sentiment in favor of separation did not spring up at once. It had been growing for three-quarters of a century. Before the close of the Revolutionary War the subject had attracted such attention that a report on the subject was made by a committee in Congress. But many years before that time a movement for a new State west of the Alleghanies had been inaugurated by George Washington, Benjamin Franklin and others, some of whom were interested in land on the Kanawha and elsewhere. The new State was to be named Vandalia, and the capital was to be at the mouth of the Great Kanawha. The movement for a new State really began there, and never afterwards slept; and finally, in 1863, it was accomplished, after no less than ninety-three years of agitation.

The Legislature of Virginia met in extra session January 7, 1861. The struggle had begun. The Confederates had not yet opened their batteries on Fort Sumpter, but the South had plainly spoken its defiance. The Southern Confederacy was forming. The elements of resistance were getting together. The storm of war was about to break upon the country. States further South had seceded or had decided to do so. Virginia had not yet decided. Its people were divided. The State hesitated. If it joined the Confederacy it would be the battle ground in the most gigantic war the world ever saw. It was the gateway by which the armies of the North would invade the South. Some affected to believe, perhaps some did believe, that there would be no war; that the South would not be invaded; that the North would not go beyond argument. But the people of better judgment foresaw the storm and they knew where it would break. The final result no man foresaw. Many hoped, many doubted, but at that time

THE ORDINANCE OF SECESSION.

no man saw what four years would bring forth. Thus Virginia hesitated long before she cast her fortunes with the States already organized to oppose the government. When she took the fatal step; when she fought as only the brave can fight; when she was crushed by weight rather than vanquished, she accepted the result and emerged from the smoke of battle still great; and like Carthage of old, her splendor seemed only the more conspicuous by the desolation which war had brought.

The Virginia Legislature called a convention to meet at Richmond February 13, 1861. The time was short, but the crisis was at hand. The flame was kindling. Meetings were being held in all the eastern part of the State, and the people were nearly unanimous in their demand that the State join the Confederacy. At least few opposed this demand, but at that time it is probable that one-half of the people of the State opposed secession. The eastern part was in favor of it. West of the Alleghany Mountains the case was different. The mass of the people did not at once grasp the situation. They knew the signs of the times were strange; that currents were drifting to a center; but that war was at hand of gigantic magnitude, and that the State of Virginia was "choosing that day whom she would serve," were not clearly understood at the outset. But, as the great truth dawned and as its lurid light became brighter, West Virginia was not slow in choosing whom she would serve. The people assembled in their towns and a number of meetings were held even before the convening of the special session of the Legislature, and there was but one sentiment expressed and that was loyalty to the government. Preston county held the first meeting, November 12, 1860; Harrison County followed the twenty-sixth of the same month; two days later the people of Monongalia assembled to discuss and take measures; a similar gathering took place in Taylor County, December 4, and another in Wheeling ten days later; and on the seventh of the January following there was a meeting in Mason County.

On January 21 the Virginia Legislature declared by resolution that, unless the differences between the two sections of the country could be reconciled, it was Virginia's duty to join the Confederacy. That resolution went side by side with the call for an election of delegates to the Richmond Convention, which was to "take measures." The election was held February 4, 1861, and nine days later the memorable convention assembled. Little time had been given for a campaign. Western Virginia sent men who were the peers of any from the eastern part of the State. The following delegates were chosen from the territory now forming West Virginia: Barbour County, Samuel Woods; Braxton and Nicholas, B. W. Byrne; Berkeley, Edmund Pendleton and Allen C. Hammond; Brooke, Campbell Tarr; Cabell, William McComas; Doddridge and Tyler, Chapman J. Stuart; Fayette and Raleigh, Henry L. Gillespie; Greenbrier, Samuel Price; Gilmer and Wirt, C. B. Conrad; Hampshire, David Pugh and Edmund M. Armstrong; Hancock, George M. Porter; Harrison, John S. Carlile and Benjamin Wilson; Hardy, Thomas Maslin; Jackson and Roane, Franklin P. Turner; Jefferson, Alfred M. Barbour and Logan Osburn; Kanawha, Spicer Patrick and George W. Summers; Lewis, Caleb Boggess; Logan, Boone and Wyoming, James Lawson; Marion, Ephraim B. Hall and Alpheus S. Haymond; Marshall, James Burley; Mason, James H. Crouch; Mercer, Napoleon B. French; Monongalia, Waitman T. Willey and Marshall M. Dent; Monroe, John Echols and Allen T. Caperton; Morgan, Johnson Orrick; Ohio, Chester D. Hubbard and Sherard Clemens; Pocahontas, Paul McNeil; Preston,

THE ORDINANCE OF SECESSION.   111

William G. Brown and James C. McGrew; Putnam, James W. Hoge; Ritchie, Cyrus Hall; Randolph and Tucker, J. N. Hughes; Taylor, John S. Burdette; Upshur, George W. Berlin; Wetzel, L. S. Hall; Wood, General John J. Jackson; Wayne, Burwell Spurlock.

When the convention met it was doubtful if a majority were in favor of Secession. At any rate the leaders in that movement, who had caused the convention to be called for that express purpose, appeared afraid to push the question to a vote, and from that day began the work which ultimately succeeded in winning over enough delegates, who at first were opposed to Secession, to carry the State into the Confederacy.

There were forty-six delegates from the counties now forming West Virginia. Nine of these voted for the Ordinance of Secession, seven were absent, one was excused, and twenty-nine voted against it. The principal leaders among the West Virginia delegates who opposed Secession were J. C. McGrew, of Preston County; George W. Summers, of Kanawha County; General John J. Jackson, of Wood County; Chester D. Hubbard, of Ohio County, and Waitman T. Willey, of Monongalia County. Willey was the leader of the leaders. He employed all the eloquence of which he was master, and all the reason and logic he could command to check the rush into what he clearly saw was disaster. No man of feeble courage could have taken the stand which he took in that convention. The agents from the States which had already seceded were in Richmond urging the people to Secession. The convention held out for a month against the clamor, and so fierce became the populace that delegates who opposed Secession were threatened with personal assault and were in danger of assassination. The peril and the pressure induced many delegates to go over to the Confederacy. But the majority held out against Secession. In the front was General John J. Jackson, one of West Virginia's most venerable citizens. He was of the material which never turns aside from danger. A cousin of Stonewall Jackson, he had seen active service in the field before Stonewall was born. He had fought the Seminoles in Florida, and had been a member of General Andrew Jackson's staff. He had been intrusted by the Government with important and dangerous duties before he was old enough to vote. He had traversed the wilderness on horseback and alone between Florida and Kentucky, performing in this manner a circuitous journey of three thousand miles, much of it among the camps and over the hunting grounds of treacherous Indians. Inured to dangers and accustomed to peril, he was not the man to flinch or give ground. He stood up for the Union; spoke for it; urged the convention to pause on the brink of the abyss before taking the leap. Another determined worker in the famous convention was Judge G. W. Summers, of Charleston. He was in the city of Washington attending a "Peace Conference" when he received news that the people of Kanawha County had elected him a delegate to the Richmond Convention. He hurried to Richmond and opposed with all his powers the Ordinance of Secession. A speech which he delivered against that measure has been pronounced the most powerful heard in the convention.

On March 2 Mr. Willey made a remarkable speech in the convention. He announced that his purpose was not to reply to the arguments of the disunionists, but to defend the right of free speech which Richmond, out of the halls of the convention and in, was trying to stifle by threats and derision. He warned the people that when free speech is silenced liberty is no longer a realty, but a mere mockery. He then took up the Secession question, although he had not intended to do so when he began speaking, and he presented in so forcible a manner the arguments against Secession that he made a profound impression upon the convention. During the whole of that month the Secessionists were unable to carry their measure through. But when Fort Sumpter was fired on, and when the President of the United States called for 75,000 volunteers, the Ordinance of Secession passed, April 17, 1861.

The next day, April 18, a number of delegates from Western Virginia declared that they would not abide by the action of the convention. Amid the roar of Richmond run mad, they began to consult among themselves what course to pursue. On April 20 several of the West Virginians met in a bed-room of the Powhatan hotel, and decided that nothing more could be done by them at Richmond to hinder or defeat the Secession movement. They agreed to return home and urge their constituents to vote against the Ordinance at the election set for May 24. They began to depart for their homes. Some had gotten safely out of Richmond and beyond the reach of the Confederates before it became known that the western delegates were leaving. Others were still in Richmond, and a plan was formed to keep them prisoners in the city—not in jail—but they were required to obtain passes from the Governor before leaving the city. It was correctly surmised that the haste shown by these delegates in taking their departure was due to their determination to stir up opposition to the Ordinance of Secession in the western part of the State. But when it was learned that most of the western delegates had already left Richmond it was deemed unwise to detain the few who yet remained, and they were permitted to depart, which they did without loss of time.

Before the people knew that an Ordinance of Secession had passed, the convention began to levy war upon the United States. Before the seal of secrecy had been removed from the proceedings of that body, large appropriations for military purposes had been made. Officers were appointed; troops were armed; forts and arsenals belonging to the Government had been seized. The arsenal at Harper's Ferry and that at Norfolk had fallen before attacks of Virginia troops before the people of that State knew that they were no longer regarded as citizens of the United States. The convention still in secret session, without the knowledge or consent of the people of Virginia, had annexed that State to the Southern Confederacy. It was all done with the presumption that the people of the State would sustain the Ordinance of Secession when they had learned of its existence and when they were given an opportunity to vote upon it. The election came May 24, 1861; and before that day there were thirty thousand soldiers in the State east of the Alleghanies, and troops had been pushed across the mountains into Western Virginia. The majority of votes cast in the State were in favor of ratifying the Ordinance of Secession; but West Virginia voted against it. Eastern Virginia was carried by storm. The excitement was intense. The cry was for war, if any attempt should be made to hinder Virginia's going into the Southern Confederacy. Many men whose sober judgment was opposed to Secesssion, were swept into it by their surroundings.

CHAPTER XIII.

―――:o:―――

THE RE-ORGANIZED GOVERNMENT.

The officers and visible government of Virginia abdicated when they joined the Southern Confederacy. The people reclaimed and resumed their sovereignty after it had been abdicated by their regularly constituted authorities. This right belongs to the people and can not be taken from them. A public servant is elected to keep and exercise this sovereignty in trust, but he can do no more. When he ceases doing this the sovereignty returns whence it came—to the people. When Virginia's public officials seceded from the United States and joined the Southern Confederacy they carried with them their individual persons and nothing more. The people of the State were deprived of none of the rights of self-government, but their government was left, for the time being, without officers to execute it and give it form. In brief, the people of Virginia had no government, but had a right to a government, and they proceeded to create one by choosing officers to take the place of those who had abdicated. This is all there was in the re-organization of the Government of Virginia, and it was done by citizens of the United States, proceeding under that clause in the Federal Constitution which declares: "The United States shall guarantee to every State in this Union a Republican form of government."

The Government of Virginia was re-organized; the State of West Virginia was created, and nothing was done in violation of the strictest letter and spirit of the United States Constitution. The steps were as follows, stated briefly here, but more in detail elsewhere in this book. The loyal people of Virginia reclaimed and resumed their sovereignty and re-organized their government. This government, through its Legislature, gave its consent for the creation of West Virginia from a part of Virginia's territory. Delegates elected by the people of the proposed new State prepared a constitution. The people of the proposed new State adopted this constitution. Congress admitted the State. The President issued a proclamation declaring West Virginia to be one of the United States. This State came into the Union in the same manner and by the same process and on the same terms as all other States. The details of the re-organization of the Virginia State Government will now be set forth more in detail.

When Virginia passed the Ordinance of Secession the territory now forming West Virginia refused to acquiesce in that measure. The vote on the Ordinance in West Virginia was about ten to one against it, or forty thousand against four thousand. In some of the counties there were more than twenty to one against Secession. The sentiment was very strong, and it soon took shape in the form of mass meetings, which were largely attended. When the delegates from West Virginia arrived home from the Richmond Convention and laid before their constituents the state of affairs there was an immediate movement having for its object the nullification of the Ordinance. Although the people of Western Virginia had long wanted a new State, and although a very general sentiment favored an immediate movement toward that end, yet a conservative course was pursued. Haste and rashness gave way to mature judgment, and the new State movement took a course strictly constitutional. The Virginia Government was first re-organized. That done, the Constitution of the United States provided a way for creating the new State, for when the re-organized government was recognized by the United States, and when a Legislature had been elected, that Legislature could give its consent to the formation of a new State from a portion of Virginia's territory, and the way was thereby provided for the accomplishment of the object.

On the day in which the Ordinance of Secession was passed, April 17, 1861, and before the people knew what had been done, a mass-meeting was held at Morgantown which adopted resolutions declaring that Western Virginia would remain in the Union. A division of the State was suggested in case the eastern part should vote to join the Confederacy. A meeting in Wetzel County, April 22, voiced the same sentiment, and similar meetings were held in Taylor, Wood, Jackson, Mason and elsewhere. But the movement took definite form at a mass-meeting of the citizens of Harrison County, held at Clarksburg, April 22, which was attended by twelve hundred men. Not only did this meeting protest against the course which was hurrying Virginia out of the Union, but a line of action was suggested for checking the Secession movement, at least in the western part of the State. A call was sent out for a general meeting, to be held in Wheeling, May 13. The counties of Western Virginia were asked to elect their wisest men to this convention. Its objects were stated in general terms to be the discussion of ways and means for providing for the State's best interests in the crisis which had arrived.

Twenty-five counties responded, and the delegates who assembled in Wheeling on May 13 were representatives of the people, men who were determined that the portion of Virginia west of the Alleghany Mountains should not take part in a war against the Union without the consent and against the will of the people of the affected territory. Hampshire and Berkeley Counties, east of the Alleghanies, sent delegates. Many of the men who attended the convention were the best known west of the Alleghanies, and in the subsequent history of West Virginia their names have become household words. The roll of the convention was as follows:

Barbour County—Spencer Dayton, E. H. Manafee, J. H. Shuttleworth.

Berkeley County—J. W. Dailey, A. R. McQuilkin, J. S. Bowers.

Brooke County—M. Walker, Bazael Wells, J. D. Nichols, Eli Green, John G. Jacob, Joseph Gist, Robert Nichols, Adam Kuhn, David Hervey, Campbell Tarr, Nathaniel Wells, J. R. Burgoine, James Archer, Jesse Edgington, R. L. Jones, James A. Campbell.

Doddridge County—S. S. Kinney, J. Cheverout, J. Smith, J. P. F. Randolph, J. A. Foley.

Hampshire County—George W. Broski, O. D. Downey, Dr. B. B. Shaw, George W. Sheetz, George W. Rizer.

Hancock County—Thomas Anderson, W. C. Murray, William B. Freeman, George M. Porter, W. L. Crawford, L. R. Smith, J. C. Crawford, B. J. Smith, J. L. Freeman, John Gardner, George Johnston, J. S. Porter,

THE RE-ORGANIZED GOVERNMENT. 115

James Stevenson, J. S. Pomeroy, R. Breneman, David Donahoo, D. S. Nicholson, Thayer Melvin, James H. Pugh, Ewing Turner, H. Farnsworth, James G. Marshall, Samuel Freeman, John Mahan, Joseph D. Allison, John H. Atkinson, Jonathan Allison, D. C. Pugh, A. Moore, William Brown, William Hewitt, David Jenkins.

Harrison County—W. P. Goff, B. F. Shuttleworth, William Duncan, L. Bowen, William E. Lyon, James Lynch, John S. Carlile, Thomas L. Moore, John J. Davis, S. S. Fleming, Felix S. Sturm.

Jackson County—G. L. Kennedy, J. V. Rowley, A. Flesher, C. M. Rice, D. Woodruff, George Leonard, J. F. Scott.

Lewis County—A. S. Withers, F. M. Chalfant, J. W. Hudson, P. M. Hale, J. Woofter, J. A. J. Lightburn, W. L. Grant.

Marshall County—Thomas Wilson, Lot Enix, John Wilson, G. Hubbs, John Ritchie, J. W. Boner, J. Alley, S. B. Stidger, Asa Browning, Samuel Wilson, J. McCondell, A. Bonar, D. Price, D. Roberts, G. W. Evans, Thos. Dowler, R. Alexander, E. Conner, John Withers, Charles Snediker, Joseph McCombs, Alexander Kemple, J. S. Riggs, Alfred Gaines, V. P. Gorby, Nathan Fish, A. Francis, William Phillips, S. Ingram, J. Garvin, Dr. Marshman, William Luke, William Baird, J. Winders, F. Clement, James Campbell, J. B. Hornbrook, John Parkinson, John H. Dickey, Thomas Morrissa, W. Alexander, John Laughlin, W. T. Head, J. S. Parriott, W. J. Purdy, H. C. Kemple, R. Swan, John Reynolds, J. Hornbrook, William McFarland, G. W. Evans, W. R. Kimmons, William Collins, R. C. Holliday, J. B. Morris, J. W. McCarriher, Joseph Turner, Hiram McMechen, E. H. Caldwell, James Garvin, L. Gardner, H. A. Francis, Thomas Dowler, John R. Morrow, William Wasson, N. Wilson, Thomas Morgan, S. Dorsey, R. B. Hunter.

Monongalia County—Waitman T. Willey, William Lazier, James Evans, Leroy Kramer. W. E. Hanaway, Elisha Coombs, H. Dering, George McNeeley, H. N. Mackey, E. D. Fogle, J. T. M. Laskey, J. T. Hess, C. H. Burgess, John Bly, William Price, A. Brown, J. R. Boughner, W. B. Shaw, P. L. Rice, Joseph Jolliff, William Anderson, E. P. St. Clair, P. T. Lashley, Marshall M. Dent, Isaac Scott, Jacob Miller, D. B. Dorsey, Daniel White, N. C. Vandervort, A. Derranet, Amos S. Bowlsby, Joseph Snyder, J. A. Wiley, John McCarl, A. Garrison. E. B. Taggart, E. P. Finch.

Marion County—F. H. Pierpont, Jesse Shaw, Jacob Streams, Aaron Hawkins, James C. Beatty, William Beatty, J. C. Beeson, R. R. Brown, J. Holman, Thomas H. Bains, Hiram Haymond, H. Merryfield, Joshua Carter, G. W. Jolliff, John Chisler, Thomas Hough.

Mason County—Lemuel Harpold, W. E. Wetzel, Wyatt Willis, John Goodley, Joseph McMachir, William Harper, William Harpold, Samuel Davis, Daniel Polsley. J. N. Jones, Samuel Yeager, R. C. M. Lovell, Major Brown, John Greer, A. Stevens, W. C. Starr, Stephen Comstock, J. M. Phelps, Charles B. Waggener, Asa Brigham, David Rossin, B. J. Rollins, D. C. Sayre, Charles Bumgardner, E. B. Davis, William Hopkins, A. A. Rogers, John O. Butler, Timothy Russell, John Hall.

Ohio County—J. C. Orr, L. S. Delaplain, J. R. Stifel, G. L. Cranmer, A. Bedillion, Alfred Caldwell, John McClure, Andrew Wilson, George Forbes, Jacob Berger, John C. Hoffman, A. J. Woods, T. H. Logan, James S. Wheat, George W. Norton, N. H. Garrison, James Paull, J. M. Bickel, Robert Crangle, George Bowers, John K. Botsford, L. D. Waitt, J. Hornbrook, S. Waterhouse, A. Handlan, J. W. Paxton, S. H. Woodward, C. D. Hubbard, Daniel Lamb, John Stiner, W. B. Curtis, A. F. Ross, A. B. Caldwell, J. R. Hubbard, E. Buchanon, John Pierson, T. Witham, E. McCaslin.

Pleasants County—Friend Cochran, James Williamson, Robert Parker, R. A. Cramer.

Preston County—R. C. Crooks, H. C. Hagans, W. H. King, James W. Brown, Summers McCrum, Charles Hooten, William P. Fortney, James A. Brown, G. H. Kidd, John Howard, D. A. Letzinger, W. B. Linn, W. J. Brown, Reuben Morris.

Ritchie County—D. Rexroad, J. P. Harris, N. Rexroad, A. S. Cole.

Roane County—Irwin C. Stump.

Taylor County—J. Means, J. M. Wilson, J. Kennedy, J. J. Warren, T. T. Monroe, G. R. Latham, B. Bailey, J. J. Allen, T. Cather, John S. Burdette.

Tyler County—Daniel Sweeney, V. Smith, W. B. Kerr, D. D. Johnson, J. C. Parker, William Pritchard, D. King, S. A. Hawkins, James M. Smith, J. H. Johnson, Isaac Davis.

Upshur County—C. P. Rohrbaugh, W. H. Williams.

Wayne County—C. Spurlock, F. Moore, W. W. Brumfield, W. H. Copley, Walter Queen.

Wirt County—E. T. Graham, Henry Newman, B. Ball.

Wetzel County—Elijah Morgan, T. E. Williams, Joseph Murphy, William Burrows, B. T. Bowers, J. R. Brown, J. M. Bell, Jacob Young, Reuben Martin, R. Reed, R. S. Sayres, W. D. Welker, George W. Bier, Thos. McQuown, John Alley, S. Stephens, R. W. Lauck, John McClaskey, Richard Cook, A. McEldowney, B. Vancamp.

Wood County—William Johnston, W. H. Baker, A. R. Dye, V. A. Dunbar, G. H. Ralston, S. M. Peterson, S. D. Compton, J. L. Padgett, George Loomis, George W. Henderson, E. Deem, N. H. Colston, A. Hinckley, Bennett Cook, S. S. Spencer, Thomas Leach, T. E. McPherson, Joseph Dagg, N. W. Warlow, Peter Riddle, John Paugh, S. L. A. Burche, J. J. Jackson, J. D. Ingram, A. Laughlin, J. C. Rathbone, W. Vroman, G. E. Smith, D. K. Baylor, M. Woods, Andrew Als, Jesse Burche, S. Ogden, Sardis Cole, P. Reed, John McKibben, W. Athey, C. Hunter, R. H. Burke, W. P. Davis, George Compton, C. M. Cole, Roger Tiffins, H. Rider, B. H. Bukey, John W. Moss, R. B. Smith, Arthur Drake, C. B. Smith, A. Mather, A. H. Hatcher, W. E. Stevenson, Jesse Murdock, J. Burche, J. Morrison, Henry Cole, J. G. Blackford, C. J. Neal, T. S. Conley, J. Barnett, M. P. Amiss, T. Hunter, J. J. Neal, Edward Hoit, N. B. Caswell, Peter Dils, W. F. Henry, A. C. McKinsey, Rufus Kinnard, J. J. Jackson, Jr.

The convention assembled to take whatever action might seem proper, but no definite plan had been decided upon further than that Western Virginia should protest against going into Secession with Virginia. The majority of the members looked forward to the formation of a new State as the ultimate and chief purpose of the convention. Time and care were necessary for the accomplishment of this object. But there were several, chief among whom was John S. Carlile, who boldly proclaimed that the time for forming a new State was at hand. There was a sharp division in the convention as to the best method of attaining that end. While Carlile led those who were for immediate action, Waitman T. Willey was among the foremost of those who insisted that the business must be conducted in a business-like way, first by re-organizing the Government of Virginia, and then obtaining the consent of the Legislature to divide the State. Mr. Carlile actually introduced a measure providing for a new State at once.

THE RE-ORGANIZED GOVERNMENT.   117

It met with much favor. But Mr. Willey and others pointed out that precipitate action would defeat the object in view, because Congress would never recognize the State so created. After much controversy there was a compromise reached, which was not difficult, where all parties aimed at the greatest good, and differed only as to the best means of attaining it.

At that time the Ordinance of Secession had not been voted upon. Virginia had already turned over to the Southern Confederacy all its military supplies, public property, troops and materials, stipulating that, in case the Ordinance of Secession should be defeated at the polls, the property should revert to the State. The Wheeling Convention took steps, pending the election, recommending that, in case Secession carried at the polls, a convention be held for the purpose of deciding what to do—whether to divide the State or simply re-organize the Government. This was the compromise measure which was satisfactory to both parties of the convention. Until the Ordinance of Secession had been ratified by the people Virginia was still, in law if not in fact, a member of the Federal Union, and any step was premature looking to a division of the State or a re-organization of its Government before the election. F. H. Pierpont, afterwards Governor, introduced the resolution which provided for another convention in case the Ordinance of Secession should be ratified at the polls. The resolution provided that the counties represented in the convention, and all other counties of Virginia disposed to act with them, appoint on June 4, 1861, delegates to a convention to meet June 11. This convention would then be prepared to proceed to business, whether that business should be the re-organization of the Government of Virginia or the dividing of the State, or both. Having finished its work, the convention adjourned. Had it rashly attempted to divide the State at that time the effort must have failed, and the bad effects of the failure, and the consequent confusion, would have been far-reaching. No man can tell whether such a failure would not have defeated for all time the creation of West Virginia from Virginia's territory.

The vote on the Ordinance of Secession took place May 23, 1861, and the people of eastern Virginia voted to go out of the Union, but the part now comprising West Virginia gave a large majority against seceding. Delegates to the Assembly of Virginia were elected at the same time. Great interest was now manifested west of the Alleghanies in the subject of a new State. Delegates to the second Wheeling Convention were elected June 4, and met June 11, 1861. The members of the first convention had been appointed by mass-meetings and otherwise, but those of the second convention had been chosen by the suffrage of the people. Thirty counties were represented as follows:

Barbour County—N. H. Taft, Spencer Dayton, John H. Shuttleworth.

Brooke County—W. H. Crothers, Joseph Gist, John D. Nichols, Campbell Tarr.

Cabell County—Albert Laidly was entered on the roll but did not serve.

Doddridge County—James A. Foley.

Gilmer County—Henry H. Withers.

Hancock County—George M. Porter, John H. Atkinson, William L. Crawford.

Harrison County—John J. Davis, Chapman J. Stewart, John C. Vance, John S. Carlile, Solomon S. Fleming, Lot Bowers, B. F. Shuttleworth.

Hardy County—John Michael.

Hampshire County—James Carskadon, Owen J. Downey, James J. Barracks, G. W. Broski, James H. Trout.
Jackson County—Daniel Frost, Andrew Flesher, James F. Scott.
Kanawha County—Lewis Ruffner, Greenbury Slack.
Lewis County—J. A. J. Lightburn, P. M. Hale.
Monongalia County—Joseph Snyder, Leroy Kramer, R. L. Berkshire, William Price, James Evans, D. B. Dorsey.
Marion County—James O. Watson, Richard Fast, Fontain Smith, Francis H. Pierpont, John S. Barnes, A. F. Ritchie.
Marshall County—C. H. Caldwell, Robert Morris, Remembrance Swan.
Mason County—Lewis Wetzel, Daniel Polsley, C. B. Waggener.
Ohio County—Andrew Wilson, Thomas H. Logan, Daniel Lamb, James W. Paxton, George Harrison, Chester D. Hubbard.
Pleasants County—James W. Willamson, C. W. Smith.
Preston County—William Zinn, Charles Hooten, William B. Crane, John Howard, Harrison Hagans, John J. Brown.
Ritchie County—William H. Douglass.
Randolph County—Samuel Crane.
Roane County—T. A. Roberts.
Tucker County—Solomon Parsons.
Taylor County—L. E. Davidson, John S. Burdette, Samuel B. Todd.
Tyler County—William I. Boreman, Daniel D. Johnson.
Upshur County—John Love, John L. Smith, D. D. T. Farnsworth.
Wayne County—William Ratcliff, William Copley, W. W. Brumfield.
Wetzel County—James G. West, Reuben Martin, James P. Ferrell.
Wirt County—James A. Williamson, Henry Newman, E. T. Graham.
Wood County—John W. Moss, Peter G. VanWinkle, Arthur I. Boreman.

James T. Close and H. S. Martin, of Alexandria, and John Hawxhurst and E. E. Mason, of Fairfax, were admitted as delegates, while William F. Mercer, of Loudoun, and Jonathan Roberts, of Fairfax, were rejected because of the insufficiency of their credentials. Arthur I. Boreman was elected president of the convention, G. L. Cranmer, secretary, and Thomas Hornbrook, sergeant-at-arms.

On June 13, two days after the meeting of the convention, a committee on Order of Business reported a declaration by the people of Virginia. This document set forth the acts of the Secessionists of Virginia, declared them hostile to the welfare of the people, done in violation of the constitution, and therefore null and void. It was further declared that all offices in Virginia, whether legislative, judicial or executive, under the government set up by the convention which passed the Ordinance of Secession, were vacant. The next day the convention began the work of re-organizing the State Government on the following lines: A Governor, Lieutenant Governor and Attorney General for the State of Virginia were to be appointed by the convention to hold office until their successors should be elected and qualified, and the Legislature was required to provide by law for the election of a Governor and Lieutenant Governor by the people. A Council of State, consisting of five members, was to be appointed to assist the Governor, their term of office to expire at the same time as that of the Governor. Delegates elected to the Legislature on May 23, 1861, and Senators entitled to seats under the laws then existing, and who would take the oath as required, were to constitute the re-organized Legislature, and were required

THE RE-ORGANIZED GOVERNMENT.

to meet in Wheeling on the first day of the following July. A test oath was required of all officers, whether State, County or Municipal.

On June 20 the convention proceeded to choose officers. Francis H. Pierpont was elected Governor of Virginia; Daniel Polsley was elected Lieutenant Governor; James Wheat was chosen Attorney General. The Governor's council consisted of Daniel Lamb, Peter G. VanWinkle, William Lazier, William A. Harrison and J. T. Paxton. The Legislature was required to elect an Auditor, Treasurer and Secretary of State as soon as possible. This closed the work of the convention, and it adjourned to meet August 6.

A new Government existed for Virginia. The Legislature which was to assemble in Wheeling in ten days could complete the work.

This Legislature of Virginia, consisting of thirty-one members, began its labors immediately upon organizing, July 1. A message from Governor Pierpont laid before that body the condition of affairs and indicated certain measures which ought to be carried out. On July 9 the Legislature elected L. A. Hagans, of Preston County, Secretary of Virginia; Samuel Crane, of Randolph County, Auditor; and Campbell Tarr, of Brooke County, Treasurer. Waitman T. Willey and John S. Carlile were elected to the United States Senate.

The convention which had adjourned June 20 met again August 6 and took up the work of dividing Virginia, whose government had been re-organized and was in working order. The people wanted a new State and the machinery for creating it was set in motion. On July 20 an ordinance was passed calling for an election to take the sense of the people on the question, and to elect members to a constitutional convention at the same time. In case the vote favored a new State, the men elected to the constitutional convention were to meet and frame a constitution. The convention adjourned August 2, 1861. Late in October the election was held, with the result that the vote stood about twenty-five to one in favor of a new State.

CHAPTER XIV.

―――:o:―――

FORMATION OF WEST VIRGINIA.

The Re-organized Government of Virginia made all things ready for the creation of the new commonwealth. The people of Western Virginia had waited long for the opportunity to divide the State. The tyranny of the more powerful eastern part had been borne half a century. When at last the war created the occasion, the people were not slow to profit by it, and to bring a new State into existence. The work began in earnest August 20, 1861, when the second Wheeling Convention called upon the people to vote on the question; and the labor was completed June 20, 1863, when the officers of the new State took charge of affairs. One year and ten months were required for the accomplishment of the work; and this chapter gives an outline of the proceedings relative to the new State during that time. It was at first proposed to call it Kanawha, but the name was changed in the constitutional convention at Wheeling on December 3, 1861, to West Virginia. On February 18, 1862, the constitutional convention adjourned, subject to the call of the chairman. In April of that year the people of the State voted upon the ratification of the constitution, and the vote in favor of ratification was 18,862, and against it, 514. Governor Pierpont issued a proclamation announcing the result, and at the same time called an extra session of the Virginia Legislature to meet in Wheeling May 6. That body met, and six days later passed an act by which it gave its consent to a division of the State of Virginia and the creation of a new State. This was done in order that the constitution might be complied with, for, before the State could be divided, the Legislature must give its consent. It yet remained for West Virginia to be admitted into the Union by an Act of Congress and by the President's proclamation. Had there been no opposition, and had there not been such press of other business this might have been accomplished in a few weeks. As it was there was a long contest in the Senate. The opposition did not come so much from outside the State as from the State itself. John S. Carlile, one of the Senators elected by the Legislature of the Re-organized Government of Virginia at Wheeling, was supposed to be friendly to the cause of the new State, but when he was put to the test it was found that he was strongly opposed to it, and he did all in his power to defeat the movement, and almost accomplished his purpose. The indignation in Western Virginia was great. The Legislature, in session at Wheeling, on December 12, 1862, by a resolution, requested Carlile to resign the seat he held in the Senate. He refused to do so. He had been one of the most active advocates of the movement for a new State while a member of the first Wheeling Convention, in May, 1861, and had been a leader in the new State movement before and after that date.

FORMATION OF WEST VIRGINIA.   121

Why he changed, and opposed the admission of West Virginia by Congress has never been satisfactorily explained.

One of the reasons given for his opposition, and one which he himself put forward, was that Congress attempted to amend the State constitution on the subject of slavery, and he opposed the admission of the State on that ground. He claimed that he would rather have no new State than have it saddled with a constitution, a portion of which its people had never ratified. But this could not have been the sole cause of Carlile's opposition. He tried to defeat the bill after the proposed objectionable amendment to the constitution had been satisfactorily arranged. He fought it in a determined manner till the last. He had hindered the work of getting the bill before Congress before any change in the State Constitution had been proposed.

The members in Congress from the Re-organized Government of Virginia were William G. Brown, Jacob B. Blair and K. V. Waley; in the Senate, John S. Carlile and Waitman T. Willey. In addition to these gentlemen, the Legislature appointed as commissioners to bring the matter before Congress, Ephraim B. Hall, of Marion County, Peter VanWinkle, of Wood County, John Hall, of Mason County, and Elbert H. Caldwell, of Marshall County. These commissioners reached Washington May 22, 1862. There were several other well-known West Virginians who also went to Washington on their own account to assist in securing the new State. Among them were Daniel Polsley, Lieutenant Governor of Virginia; Granville Parker and Harrison Hagans. There were members of Congress and Senators from other States who performed special service in the cause. The matter was laid before the United States Senate May 29, 1862, by Senator Willey, who presented the West Virginia Constitution recently ratified, and also the Act of the Legislature giving its consent to the creation of a new State within the jurisdiction of Virginia, and a memorial requesting the admission of the State. In presenting these documents, Senator Willey addressed the Senate and denied that the movement was simply to gratify revenge upon the mother State for seceding from the Union and joining the Southern Confederacy, but on the contrary, the people west of the Alleghanies had long wanted a new State, and had long suffered in consequence of Virginia's neglect, and of her unconcern for their welfare. Mr. Willey's address was favorably received, and the whole matter regarding the admission of West Virginia was laid before the Committee on Territories, of which Senator John S. Carlile was a member. It had not at that time been suspected that Carlile was hostile to the movement. He was expected to prepare the bill. He neglected to do so until nearly a month had passed and the session of Congress was drawing to a close. But it was not so much the delay that showed his hostility as the form of the bill. Had it been passed by Congress in the form proposed by Carlile the defeat of the new State measure must have been inevitable. No one acquainted with the circumstances and conditions had any doubt that the bill was prepared for the express purpose of defeating the wishes of the people by whom Mr. Carlile had been sent to the Senate. It included in West Virginia, in addition to the counties which had ratified the constitution, Alleghany, Augusta, Berkeley, Bath, Botetourt, Craig, Clark, Frederick, Highland, Jefferson, Page, Rockbridge, Rockingham, Shenandoah and Warren Counties. The hostility in most of those counties was very great. The bill provided that those counties, in conjunction with those west of the Alleghanies, should elect delegates to a constitutional convention and frame a constitution which should provide that all children born of slaves after 1863 should be free. This constitution was then to go back to the people of the several counties for ratification. Then, if the Virginia Legislature should pass an Act giving its consent to the creation of a new State from Virginia's territory, and the Governor of Virginia certify the same to the President of the United States, he might make proclamation of the fact, and West Virginia would become a State without further proceedings by Congress.

Senator Carlile knew that the counties he had added east of the Alleghanies were opposed to the new State on any terms, and that they would oppose it the more determinedly on account of the gradual emancipation clause in it. He knew that they would not appoint delegates to a constitutional convention, nor would they ratify the constitution should one be submitted to them. In short, they were strong enough in votes and sentiment to defeat the movement for a new State. All the work done for the creation of West Virginia would have been thrown away had this bill prevailed.

Three days later, June 26, the bill was called up, and Charles Sumner proposed an amendment regarding slavery. He would have no slavery at all. All indications were that the bill would defeat the measure for the new State, and preparations were made to begin the fight in a new quarter. Congressman Wm. G. Brown, of Preston County, proposed a new bill to be presented in the House of Representatives. But the contest went on. In July Senator Willey submitted an amendment, which was really a new bill. It omitted the counties east of the Alleghanies, and provided that all slaves under twenty-one years of age on July 4, 1863, should be free on arriving at that age. It now became apparent to Carlile that his bill was dead, and that West Virginia was likely to be admitted. As a last resort, he proposed a postponement till December, in order to gain time, but his motion was lost. Carlile then opposed the bill on the grounds that if passed it would impose upon the people of the new State a clause of the constitution not of their making and which they had not ratified. But this argument was deprived of its force by offering to submit the proposed amendment to the people of West Virginia for their approval. Fortunately the constitutional convention had adjourned subject to the call of the chair. The members were convened; they included the amendment in the constitution, and the people approved it. However, before this was done the bill took its course through Congress. It passed the Senate July 14, 1862, and was immediately sent to the Lower House. But Congress being about to adjourn, further consideration of the bill went over till the next session in December, 1862, and on the tenth of that month it was taken up in the House of Representatives and after a discussion continuing most of the day, it was passed by a vote of ninety-six to fifty-five.

The friends of the new State now felt that their efforts had been successful; but one more step was necessary, and the whole work might yet be rendered null and void. It depended on President Lincoln. He might veto the bill. He requested the opinion of his cabinet. Six of the cabinet officers complied, and three favored signing the bill and three advised the President to veto it. Mr. Lincoln took it under advisement. It was believed that he favored the bill, but there was much anxiety felt. Nearly two years before that time Mr. Lincoln, through one of his cabinet officers, had promised Governor Pierpont to do all he could, in a constitutional way, for the Re-organized Government of Virginia, and that promise was construed to mean that the new State would not be opposed by the President. Mr. Lincoln was evidently undecided for some time what course to pursue, for he afterwards said that a telegram received by him from A. W. Campbell, editor of the Wheeling *Intelligencer*, largely influenced him in deciding to sign the bill. On December 31, 1862, Congressman Jacob B. Blair called on the President to see if any action had been taken by the Executive. The bill had not yet been signed, but Mr. Lincoln asked Mr. Blair to come back the next day. Mr. Blair did so, and was given the bill admitting West Virginia into the Union. It was signed January 1, 1863.

On December 31, 1862, President Lincoln gave his own views on these questions in the following language:*

"The consent of the Legislature of Virginia is constitutionally necessary to the Bill for the Admission of West Virginia becoming a law. A body claiming to be such Legislature has given its consent. We cannot well deny that it is such, unless we do so upon the outside knowledge that the body was chosen at elections in which a majority of the qualified voters of Virginia did not participate. But it is a universal practice in the popular elections in all these States to give no legal consideration whatever to those who do not choose to vote, as against the effect of those who do choose to vote. Hence it is not the qualified voters, but the qualified voters who choose to vote, that constitute the political power of the State. Much less than to non-voters should any consideration be given to those who did not vote in this case, because it is also matter of outside knowledge that they were not merely neglectful of their rights under and duty to this Government, but were also engaged in open rebellion against it. Doubtless among these non-voters were some Union men whose voices were smothered by the more numerous Secessionists, but we know too little of their number to assign them any appreciable value.

"Can this Government stand if it indulges constitutional constructions by which men in open rebellion against it are to be accounted, man for man, the equals of those who maintain their loyalty to it? Are they to be accounted even better citizens, and more worthy of consideration, than those who merely neglect to vote? If so, their treason against the Constitution enhances their constitutional value. Without braving these absurd conclusions we cannot deny that the body which consents to the admission of West Virginia is the Legislature of Virginia. I do not think the plural form of the words 'Legislatures' and 'States' in the phrase of the constitution 'without the consent of the Legislatures of the States concerned' has any reference to the new State concerned. That plural form sprang from the contemplation of two or more old States contributing to form a new one. The idea that the new State was in danger of being admitted without its own consent was not provided against, because it was not thought of, as I conceive. It is said 'the Devil takes care of his own.' Much more should a good spirit—the spirit of the Constitution and the Union—take care of its own. I think it cannot do less and live.

"But is the admission of West Virginia into the Union expedient? This, in my general view, is more a question for Congress than for the Executive. Still I do not evade it. More than on anything else, it depends on whether the admission or rejection of the new State would, under all the circumstances, tend the more strongly to the restoration of the National authority throughout the Union. That which helps most in this direction is the most expedient at this time. Doubtless those in remaining Virginia would return to the Union, so to speak, less reluctantly without the division of the old State than with it, but I think we could not save as much in this quarter by rejecting the new State as we should lose by it in West Virginia. We can scarcely dispense with the aid of West Virginia in this struggle; much less can we afford to have her against us, in Congress and in the field. Her brave and good men regard her admission into the Union as a matter of life and death. They have been true to the Union under very severe trials. We have so acted as to justify their hopes, and we cannot fully retain their confidence and co-operation if we seem to break faith with them. In fact they could not do so much for us if they would. Again, the admission of the new State turns that much slave soil to free, and this is a certain and irrevocable encroachment upon the cause of the rebellion. The division of a State is dreaded as a precedent. But a measure made expedient by a war is no precedent in times of peace. It is said that the admission of West Virginia is secession. Well, if we call it by that name, there is still

---

* See "Works of Abraham Lincoln," by John Nicolay and John Hay, vol. 2, p. 285.

difference enough between secession against the constitution and secession in favor of the constitution. I believe the admission of West Virginia into the Union is expedient."

However, there was yet something to be done before West Virginia became a State. The bill passed by Congress and signed by President Lincoln went no further than to provide that the new State should become a member of the Union when a clause concerning slavery, contained in the bill, should be made a part of the constitution and be ratified by the people. The convention which had framed the State Constitution had adjourned to meet at the call of the chairman. The members came together on February 12, 1863. Two days later John S. Carlile, who had refused to resign his seat in the Senate when asked by the Virginia Legislature to do so, made another effort to defeat the will of the people whom he was sent to Congress to represent. He presented a supplementary bill in the Senate providing that President Lincoln's proclamation admitting West Virginia be withheld until certain counties of West Virginia had ratified by their votes the clause regarding slavery contained in the bill. Mr. Carlile believed that those counties would not ratify the constitution. But his bill was defeated in the Senate by a vote of 28 to 12.

The clause concerning slavery, as adopted by the constitutional convention on re-assembling at Wheeling, was in these words: "The children of slaves, born within the limits of this State after the fourth day of July, 1863, shall be free, and all slaves within the said State who shall, at the time aforesaid, be under the age of ten years, shall be free when they arrive at the age of twenty-one years; and all slaves over ten and under twenty-one years shall be free when they arrive at the age of twenty-five years; and no slave shall be permitted to come into the State for permanent residence therein." The people ratified the constitution at an election held for that purpose. The majority in favor of ratification was seventeen thousand.

President Lincoln issued his proclamation April 20, 1863, and sixty days thereafter, that is June 20, 1863, West Virginia was to become a State without further legislation. In the meantime, May 9, a State Convention assembled in Parkersburg to nominate officers. A Confederate force under General Jones advanced within forty miles of Parkersburg, and the convention hurried through with its labors and adjourned. It nominated Arthur I. Boreman, of Wood County, for Governor; Campbell Tarr, of Brooke County, for Treasurer; Samuel Crane, of Randolph County, for Auditor; Edgar J. Boyers, of Tyler County, for Secretary of State; A. B. Caldwell, of Ohio County, Attorney General; for Judges of the Supreme Court of Appeals, Ralph L. Berkshire, of Monongalia County; James H. Brown, of Kanawha County, and William A. Harrison, of Harrison County. These were all elected late in the month of May, and on June 20, 1863, took the oath of office and West Virginia was a State. Thus was fulfilled the prophecy of Daniel Webster in 1851 when he said that if Virginia took sides with a secession movement, the result would be the formation of a new State from Virginia's Transalleghany territory.

The creation of the new State of West Virginia did not put an end to the Re-organized Government of Virginia. The officers who had held their seat of government at Wheeling moved to Alexandria, and in 1865 moved to Richmond, where they held office until their successors were elected. Governor Pierpont filled the gubernatorial chair of Virginia about seven years.

In the summer of 1864 General Benjamin F. Butler, in command of Union forces in eastern Virginia, wrote to President Lincoln, complaining of the conduct of Governor Pierpont and the Secretary of State, intimating that they were not showing sufficient devotion to the Union cause. On August 9, 1864, Lincoln replied, and in the following language put a squelch on General Butler's meddling:

"I surely need not to assure you that I have no doubt of your loyalty and devoted patriotism, and I must tell you that I have no less confidence in those of Governor Pierpont and the Attorney General. The former—at first as the loyal Governor of all Virginia, including that which it now West Virginia, in organizing and furnishing troops, and in all other proper matters—was as earnest, honest and efficient to the extent of his means as any other loyal Governor. * * * * * * The Attorney General needs only to be known to be relieved from all question as to loyalty and thorough devotion to the national cause."*

---

* Works of Lincoln, vol. 2, p. 620.

CHAPTER XV.

―:o:―

ORGANIZING FOR WAR.

In a work of this sort it should not be expected that a full account of the Civil War, as it affected West Virginia, will be given. It must suffice to present only an outline of events as they occurred in that great struggle, nor is any pretence made that this outline shall be complete. The vote on the Ordinance of Secession showed that a large majority of the people in this State were opposed to a separation from the United States. This vote, while it could not have been much of a surprise to the politicians in the eastern part of Virginia, was a disappointment. It did not prevent Virginia, as a State, from joining the Southern Confederacy, but the result made it plain that Virginia was divided against itself, and that all the part west of the Alleghany Mountains, and much of that west of the Blue Ridge, would not take up arms against the general government in furtherance of the interests of the Southern Confederacy.

It therefore became necessary for Virginia, backed by the other Southern States, to conquer its own transmontane territory. The commencement of the war in what is now West Virginia was due to an invasion by troops in the service of the Southern Confederacy in an effort to hold the territory as a part of Virginia. It should not be understood, however, that there was no sympathy with the South in this State. As nearly as can be estimated the number who took sides with the South, in proportion to those who upheld the Union, was as one to six. The people generally were left to choose. Efforts were made at the same time to raise soldiers for the South and for the North, and those who did not want to go one way were at liberty to go the other. In the eastern part of the State considerable success was met in enlisting volunteers for the Confederacy, but in the western counties there were hardly any who went with the South. That the government at Richmond felt the disappointment keenly is evidenced by the efforts put forth to organize companies of volunteers, and the discouraging reports of the recruiting officers.

Robert E. Lee was appointed commander-in-chief of the military and naval forces of Virginia, April 23, 1861, and on the same day he wrote to Governor Letcher accepting the office. Six days later he wrote Major A. Loring, at Wheeling, urging him to muster into the service of the State all the volunteer companies in that vicinity, and to take command of them. Loring was asked to report what success attended his efforts. On the same day Lieutenant-Colonel John McCausland, at Richmond, received orders from General Lee to proceed at once to the Kanawha Valley and muster into service the volunteer companies in that quarter. General Lee named four companies already formed, two in Kanawha and two in Putnam Counties,

ORGANIZING FOR WAR.

and he expressed the belief that others would offer their services. McCausland was instructed to organize a company of artillery in the Kanawha Valley. On the next day, April 30, General Lee wrote to Major Boykin, at Weston, in Lewis County, ordering him to muster in the volunteer companies in that part of the State, and to ascertain how many volunteers could be raised in the vicinity of Parkersburg. General Lee stated in the letter that he had sent two hundred flint-lock muskets to Colonel Jackson (Stonewall) at Harper's Ferry, for the use of the volunteers about Weston. He said no better guns could be had at that time. The next day, May 1, Governor Letcher announced that arrangements had been made for calling out fifty thousand Virginia volunteers, to assemble at Norfolk, Richmond, Alexandria, Fredericksburg, Harper's Ferry, Grafton, Parkersburg, Kanawha and Moundsville. On May 4 General Lee ordered Colonel George A Porterfield to Grafton to take charge of the troops in that quarter, those already in service and those who were expected to volunteer. Colonel Porterfield was ordered, by authority of the Governor of Virginia, to call out the volunteers in the counties of Wood, Wirt, Roane, Calhoun, Gilmer, Ritchie, Pleasants and Doddridge, to rendezvous at Parkersburg; and in the counties of Braxton, Lewis, Harrison, Monongalia, Taylor, Barbour, Upshur, Tucker, Marion, Randolph and Preston, to rendezvous at Grafton. General Lee said he did not know how many men could be enlisted, but he supposed five regiments could be mustered into service in that part of the State.

In these orders sent out General Lee expressed a desire to be kept informed of the success attending the call for volunteers. Replies soon began to arrive at Richmond, and they were uniformly discouraging to General Lee. It was early apparent that the people of Western Virginia were not enthusiastic in taking up arms for the Southern Confederacy. Major Boykin wrote General Lee that the call for volunteers was not meeting with success. To this letter General Lee replied on May 11, and urged Major Boykin to persevere and call out the companies for such counties as were not so hostile to the South, and to concentrate them at Grafton. He stated that four hundred rifles had been forwarded from Staunton to Beverly, in Randolph County, where Major Goff would receive and hold them until further orders. Major Boykin requested that companies from other parts of the State be sent to Grafton to take the places of companies which had been counted upon to organize in that vicinity, but which had failed to materialize. To this suggestion General Lee replied that he did not consider it advisable to do so, as the presence of outside companies at Grafton would tend to irritate the people instead of conciliating them.

On May 16 Colonel Porterfield had arrived at Grafton and had taken a hasty survey of the situation, and his conclusion was that the cause of the Southern Confederacy in that vicinity was not promising. On that day he made a report to R. S. Garnett, at Richmond, Adjutant General of the Virginia army, and stated that the rifles ordered to Beverly from Staunton had not arrived, nor had they been heard from. It appears from this report that no volunteers had yet assembled at Grafton, but Colonel Porterfield said a company was organizing at Pruntytown, in Taylor County; one at Weston, under Captain Boggess; one at Philippi, another at Clarksburg, and still another at Fairmont. Only two of these companies had guns, flintlocks, and no ammunition. At that time all of those companies had been ordered to Grafton. Colonel Porterfield said, in a tone of discouragement, that those troops, almost destitute of guns and ammunition, were all he had to depend upon, and he considered the force very weak compared with the strength of those in that vicinity who were prepared to oppose him. He complained that he had found much diversity of opinion and "rebellion" among the people, who did not believe that the State was strong enough to contend against the Government. "I am, too, credibly informed," said he, "to entertain doubt that they have been and will be supplied with the means of resistance. * * * * Their efforts to intimidate have had their effect, both to dishearten one party and to encourage the other. Many good citizens have been dispirited, while traitors have seized the guns and ammunition of the State to be used against its authority. The force in this section will need the best rifles. * * * * There will not be the same use for the bayonet in these hills as elsewhere, and the movements should be of light infantry and rifle, although the bayonet, of course, would be desirable."

About this time, that is near the middle of May, 1861, General Lee ordered one thousand muskets sent to Beverly for the use of the volunteer companies organizing to the northward of that place. Colonel Heck was sent in charge of the guns, and General Lee instructed him to call out all the volunteers possible along the route from Staunton to Beverly. If the authorities at Richmond had learned by the middle of May that Western Virginia was not to be depended upon for filling with volunteers the ranks of the Southern armies, the truth was still more apparent six weeks later. By that time General Garnett had crossed the Alleghanies in person, and had brought a large force of Confederate troops with him and was entrenched at Laurel Hill and Rich Mountain, in Randolph County. It had been claimed that volunteers had not joined the Confederate standard because they were afraid to do so in the face of the stronger Union companies organizing in the vicinity, but that if a Confederate army were in the country to overawe the advocates of the Union cause then large numbers of recruits would organize to help the South. Thus Garnett marched over the Alleghanies and called for volunteers. The result was deeply mortifying to him as well as discouraging to the authorities at Richmond. On June 25, 1861, he wrote to General Lee, dating his letter at Laurel Hill. He complained that he could not find out what the movements of the Union forces were likely to be, and added that the Union men in that vicinity were much more active, numerous and zealous than the secessionists. He said it was like carrying on a campaign in a foreign country, as the people were nearly all against him, and never missed an opportunity to divulge his movements to McClellan, but would give him no information of what McClellan was doing. "My hope," he wrote to Lee, "of increasing my force in this region has so far been sadly disappointed. Only eight men have joined me here, and only fifteen at Colonel Heck's camp—not enough to make up my losses by discharges. The people are thoroughly imbued with an ignorant and bigoted Union sentiment."

If more time was required to ascertain the sentiment in the Kanawha Valley than had been necessary in the northern and eastern part of the State, it was nevertheless seen in due time that the Southern Confederacy's supporters ers in that quarter were in a hopeless minority. General Henry A. Wise, ex Governor of Virginia, had been sent into the Kanawha Valley early in 1861 to organize such forces as could be mustered for the Southern army. He was one of the most fiery leaders in the Southern Confederacy, and an able man, and of great influence. He had, perhaps, done more than any other

ORGANIZING FOR WAR.

man in Virginia to swing that State into the Southern Confederacy. He it was who, when the Ordinance of Secession was in the balance in the Richmond Convention, rose in the convention, drew a horse-pistol from his bosom, placed it upon the desk before him, and proceeded to make one of the most impassioned speeches heard in that tumultuous convention. The effect of his speech was tremendous, and Virginia wheeled into line with the other Confederate States. General Wise hurried to the field, and was soon in the thick of the fight in the Kanawha Valley. He failed to organize an army there, and in his disappointment and anger he wrote to General Lee, August 1, 1861, saying: "The Kanawha Valley is wholly disaffected and traitorous. It was gone from Charleston to Point Pleasant before I got there. Boone and Cabell are nearly as bad, and the state of things in Braxton, Nicholas and part of Greenbrier is awful. The militia are nothing for warlike uses here. They are worthless who are true, and there is no telling who is true. You cannot persuade these people that Virginia can or will reconquer the northwest, and they are submitting, subdued and debased." General Wise made an urgent request for more guns, ammunition and clothing.

While the Confederates were doing their utmost to organize and equip forces in Western Virginia, and were meeting discouragements and failure nearly everywhere, the people who upheld the Union were also at work, and success was the rule and failure almost unknown. As soon as the fact was realized that Virginia had joined the Southern Confederacy; had seized upon the government arsenals and other property within the State, and had commenced war upon the government, and was preparing to continue the hostilities, the people of Western Virginia, who had long suffered from the injustice and oppression of the eastern part of the State, began to prepare for war. They did not long halt between two opinions, but at once espoused the cause of the United States. Companies were organized everywhere. The spirit with which the cause of the Union was upheld was one of the most discouraging features of the situation, as viewed by the Confederates who were vainly trying to raise troops in this part of the State. The people in the Kanawha Valley who told General Wise that they did not believe Virginia could re-conquer Western Virginia had reasons for their conclusions. The people along the Ohio, the Kanawha, the Monongahela; in the interior, among the mountains, were everywhere drilling and arming.

There was some delay and disappointment in securing arms for the Union troops as they were organized in West Virginia. Early in the war, while there was yet hope entertained by some that the trouble could be adjusted without much fighting, there was hesitation on the part of the Government about sending guns into Virginia to arm one class of the people. Consequently some of the first arms received in Western Virginia did not come directly from the Government arsenals, but were sent from Massachusetts. As early as May 7, 1861, a shipment of two thousand stands of arms was made from the Watervleit arsenal, New York, to the northern Panhandle of West Virginia, above Wheeling. These guns armed some of the first soldiers from West Virginia that took the field. An effort had been made to obtain arms from Pittsburg, but it was unsuccessful. Campbell Tarr, of Brooke County, and others, went to Washington as a committee, and it was through their efforts that the guns were obtained. The government officials were very cautious at that time lest they should do something without express warranty in law. But Edwin M. Stanton advised that the guns be sent, promising that he would find the law for it afterwards. Governor Pierpont had written to President Lincoln for help, and the reply had been that all help that could be given under the constitution would be furnished.

The Civil War opened in West Virginia by a conflict between the Confederate forces in the State and the Federal forces sent against them. The first Union troops to advance came from Wheeling and beyond the Ohio River. Colonel Benjamin F. Kelley organized a force at Wheeling, and was instructed to obey orders from General McClellan, then at Cincinnati.

The first order from McClellan to Kelley was that he should fortify the hills about Wheeling. This was on May 26, 1861. This appears to have been thought necessary as a precaution against an advance on the part of the Confederates, but McClellan did not know how weak they were in West Virginia at that time. Colonel Porterfield could not get together men and ammunition enough to encourage him to hold Grafton, much less to advance to the Ohio River. It is true that on the day that Virginia passed the Ordinance of Secession Governor Letcher made an effort to hold Wheeling, but it signally failed. He wrote to Mayor Sweeney, of that city, to seize the postoffice, the custom house, and all government property in that city, hold them in the name of the State of Virginia. Mayor Sweeney replied: "I have seized upon the custom house, the postoffice and all public buildings and documents, in the name of Abraham Lincoln, President of the United States, whose property they are."

Colonel Kelley, when he received the order to fortify the hills about Wheeling, replied that he did not believe such a step was necessary, but that the proper thing to do was to advance to Grafton and drive the Confederates out of the country. McClellan accepted the suggestion, and ordered Kelley to move to Grafton with the force under his orders. These troops had enlisted at Wheeling and had been drilled for service. They were armed with guns sent from Massachusetts. They carried their ammunition in their pockets, as they had not yet been fully equipped with the accoutrements of war. They were full of enthusiasm, and were much gratified when the orders came for an advance. The agent of the Baltimore and Ohio Railroad at Wheeling refused to furnish cars for the troops, giving as his reason that the railroad would remain neutral. Colonel Kelley announced that if the cars were not ready by four o'clock next morning he would seize them by force, and take military possession of the railroad. The cars were ready at four the next morning.* While Kelley's troops were setting out from Wheeling an independent movement was in progress at Morgantown to drive the Confederates out of Grafton. A number of companies had been organized on the Monongahela, and they assembled at Morgantown, where they were joined by three companies from Pennsylvania, and were about to set out for Grafton on their own responsibility, when they learned that Colonel Kelley had already advanced from Wheeling, and that the Confederates had retreated. Colonel Porterfield learned of the advance from Wheeling and saw that he would be attacked before his looked-for reinforcements and arms could arrive. The poorly-equipped force under his command were unable to successfully resist an attack, and he prepared to retreat southward. He ordered two railroad bridges burned,

---

* "Loyal West Virginia," by T. F. Lang.

ORGANIZING FOR WAR.

between Fairmont and Mannington, hoping thereby to delay the arrival of the Wheeling troops.

At daybreak on May 27 Colonel Kelley's troops left Wheeling on board the cars for Grafton. When they reached Mannington they stopped long enough to rebuild the burnt bridges, which delayed them only a short time. While there Kelley received a telegram from McClellan informing him that troops from Ohio and Indiana were on their way to his assistance. When the Wheeling troops reached Grafton the town had been deserted by the Confederates, who had retreated to Philippi, about twenty-five miles south of Grafton. Colonel Kelley at once planned pursuit. On June 1 a considerable number of soldiers from Ohio and Indiana had arrived. Colonel R. H. Milroy, Colonel Irvine and General Thomas A. Morris were in command of the troops from beyond the Ohio. They were the van of General McClellan's advance into West Virginia. When General Morris arrived at Grafton he assumed command of all the forces in that vicinity. Colonel Kelley's plan of pursuit of Colonel Porterfield was laid before General Morris and was approved by him, and preparations were immediately commenced for carrying it into execution. It appears that Colonel Porterfield did not expect pursuit. He had established his camp at Philippi and was waiting for reinforcements and supplies, which failed to arrive. Since assuming command of the Confederate forces in West Virginia he had met one diappointment after another. His force at Philippi was stated at the time to number two thousand, but it was little more than half so large. General Morris and Colonel Kelley prepared to attack him with three thousand men, advancing at night by two routes to fall upon him by surprise.

Colonel Kelley was to march about six miles east from Grafton on the morning of June 2, and from that point march across the mountains during the afternoon and night, and so regulate his movements as to reach Philippi at four o'clock the next morning. Colonel Dumont, who had charge of the other column, was ordered to repair to Webster, a small town on the Parkersburg branch of the Baltimore and Ohio Railroad, four miles west from Grafton, and to march from that point toward Philippi, to appear before the town exactly at four o'clock on the morning of June 3. Colonel Kelley's task was the more difficult, for he followed roads that were very poor. General Morris suspected that spies in and about Grafton would discover the movement and would carry the news to Colonel Porterfield at Philippi, and that he would hurriedly retreat, either toward Beverly or eastward to St. George, on Cheat River. Colonel Kelley was therefore ordered, in case he received positive intelligence that Porterfield had retreated eastward, to follow as fast as possible and endeavor to intercept him; at the same time he was to notify Colonel Dumont of the retreat and of the movement to intercept the Confederates.

Colonel Kelley left Grafton in the early morning. It was generally supposed he was on his way to Harper's Ferry. Colonel Dumont's column left Grafton after dark on the evening of June 2. The march that night was through rain and in pitch darkness. This delayed Dumont's division, and it seemed that it would not be able to reach Philippi by the appointed time, but the men marched the last five miles in an hour and a quarter, and so well was everything managed that Kelley's and Dumont's forces arrived before Philippi within fifteen minutes of each other. The Confederates had not learned of the advance and were off their guard. The pickets fired a few shots and fled. The Union artillery opened on the camp and the utmost confusion prevailed. Colonel Porterfield ordered a retreat, and succeeded in saving the most of his men, but lost a considerable portion of the small supply of arms he had. He abandoned his camp and stores. This action was called the "Philippi Races," because of the haste with which the Confederates fled and the Union forces pursued. Colonel Kelley, while leading the pursuit, was shot through the breast and was supposed to be mortally wounded, but he subsequently recovered and took an active part in the war until its close.

General McClellan, who had not yet crossed the Ohio, was much encouraged by this victory, small as it appears in comparison with the momentous events later in the war. The Union people of West Virginia were also much encouraged, and the Confederates were correspondingly depressed.

Colonel Porterfield's cup of disappointment was full when, five days after his retreat from Philippi, he learned that he had been superseded by General Robert S. Garnett, who was on his way from Richmond to assume command of the Confederate forces in West Virginia. Colonel Porterfield had retreated to Huttonsville, in Randolph County, above Beverly, and there turned his command over to his successor. A court of inquiry was held to examine Colonel Porterfield's conduct. He was censured by the Richmond people who had sent him into West Virginia, had neglected him, had failed to supply him with arms or the adequate means of defense, and when he suffered defeat, they threw the blame on him when the most of it belonged to themselves. Little more than one month elapsed from that time before the Confederate authorities had occasion to understand more fully the situation beyond the Alleghanies; and the general who took Colonel Porterfields place, with seven or eight times his force of men and arms, conducted a far more disastrous retreat, and was killed while bringing off his broken troops from a lost battle.

Previous to General McClellan's coming into West Virginia he issued a proclamation to the people, in which he stated the purpose of his coming, and why troops were about to be sent across the Ohio river. This proclamation was written in Cincinnati, May 26, 1861, and sent by telegraph to Wheeling and Parkersburg, there to be printed and circulated. The people were told that the army was about to cross the Ohio as friends to all who were loyal to the Government of the United States; to prevent the destruction of property by the rebels; to preserve order, to co-operate with loyal Virginians in their efforts to free the State from the Confederates, and to punish all attempts at insurrection among slaves, should they rise against their masters. This last statement was no doubt meant to allay the fears of many that as soon as a Union army was upon the soil there would be a slave insurrection, which, of all things, was most dreaded by those who lived among slaves. On the same day General McClellan issued an address to his soldiers, informing them that they were about to cross the Ohio, and acquainting them with the duties to be performed. He told them they were to act in concert with the loyal Virginians in putting down the rebellion. He enjoined the strictest discipline and warned them against interfering with the rights or property of the loyal Virginians. He called on them to show mercy to those captured in arms, for many of them were misguided. He stated that, when the Confederates had been driven from northwestern Virginia, the loyal people of that part of the State would be able to organize and arm, and would be competent to take care of themselves, and then the

ORGANIZING FOR WAR.

services of the troops from Ohio and Indiana would be no longer needed, and they could return to their homes. He little understood what the next four years would bring forth.

Three weeks had not elapsed after Colonel Porterfield retreated from Philippi before General McClellan saw that something more was necessary before Western Virginia would be pacified. The Confederates had been largely reinforced at Huttonsville, and had advanced northward within twelve miles of Philippi and had fortified their camp. Philippi was at that time occupied by General Morris, and a collision between his forces and those of the Confederates was likely to occur at any time. General McClellan thought it advisable to be nearer the scene of operations, and on June 22, 1861, he crossed the Ohio with his staff and proceeded to Grafton, where he established his headquarters. He had at this time about twenty thousand soldiers in West Virginia, stationed from Wheeling to Grafton, from Parkersburg to the same place, and in the country round about.

Colonel Porterfield was relieved of his command by General Garnett, June 14, 1861, and the military affairs of northwestern Virginia were looked after by Garnett in person. The Richmond Government and the Southern Confederacy had no intention of abandoning the country beyond the Alleghanies. On the contrary, it was resolved to hold it at all hazards; but subsequent events showed that the Confederates either greatly underestimated the strength of McClellan's army or greatly overestimated the strength of their own forces sent against him. Otherwise Garnett, with a force of only six thousand, would not have been pushed forward against the lines of an army of twenty thousand, and that, too, in a position so remote that Garnett was practically isolated from all assistance. Reinforcements numbering about two thousand men were on the way from Staunton to Beverly at the time of Garnett's defeat, but had these troops reached him in time to be of service, he would still have had not half as large a force as that of McClellan opposed to him. Military men have severely criticised General Lee for what they regard as a blunder in thus sending an army to almost certain destruction, with little hope of performing any service to the Confederacy.

Had the Confederates been able to hold the Baltimore and Ohio Railroad, the disaster attending General Garnett's campaign would probably not have occurred. With that road in their hands, they could have thrown soldiers and supplies into Grafton and Clarksburg within ten hours from Harper's Ferry. They would thus have had quick communication with their base of supplies and an open way to fall back when compelled to do so. But they did not hold the Baltimore and Ohio Road, and their only practicable route into Western Virginia, north of the Kanawha, was by wagon roads across the Alleghanies, by way of the Valley of Virginia. This was a long and difficult route by which to transport supplies for an army; and in case that army was compelled to retreat, the line of retreat was liable to be cut by the enemy, as it actually was in the case of Garnett.

On July 1, 1861, General Garnett had about four thousand five hundred men. The most of them were from Eastern Virginia and the States further south. A considerable part of them were Georgians who had recently been stationed at Pensacola, Florida. Reinforcements were constantly arriving over the Alleghanies, and by July 10 he had six thousand men. He moved northward and westward from Beverly and fortified two points on Laurel Hill, one named Camp Rich Mountain, six miles west of Beverly, the other fifteen miles north by west, near Belington, in Barbour County. These positions were naturally strong, and their strength was increased by fortifications of logs and stones. They were only a few miles from the outposts of McClellan's army. Had the Confederate positions been attacked only from the front it is probably that they could have held out a considerable time. But there was little in the way of flank movements, and when McClellan made his attack, it was by flanking. General Garnett was not a novice in the field. He had seen service in the Mexican War; had taken part in many of the hardest battles; had fought Indians three years on the Pacific Coast, and at the outbreak of the Civil War he was traveling in Europe. He hastened home; resigned his position in the United States Army and joined the Confederate Army, and was almost immediately sent into West Virginia to be sacrificed.

While the Confederates were fortifying their positions in Randolph and Barbour Counties, the Union forces were not idle. On June 22 General McClellan crossed the Ohio River at Parkersburg. The next day at Grafton he issued two proclamations, one to the citizens of West Virginia, the other to his soldiers. To the citizens he gave assurance again that he came as a friend, to uphold the laws, to protect the law-abiding, and to punish those in rebellion against the Government. In the proclamation to his soldiers he told them that he had entered West Virginia to bring peace to the peaceable and the sword to the rebellious who were in arms, but mercy to disarmed rebels. He began to concentrate his forces for an attack on Garnett. He moved his headquarters to Buckhannon on July 2, to be near the center of operations. Clarksburg was his base of supplies, and he constructed a telegraph line as he advanced, one of the first, if not the very first, military telegraph lines in America. From Buckhannon he could move in any desired direction by good roads. He had fortified posts at Webster, Clarksburg, Parkersburg and Grafton. Eight days later he had moved his headquarters to Middle Fork, between Buckhannon and Beverly, and in the meantime his forces had made a general advance. He was now within sight of the Confederate fortifications on Rich Mountain. General Morris, who was leading the advance against Laurel Hill, was also within sight of the Confederates. There had already been some skirmishing, and all believed that the time was near when a battle would be fought. Colonel John Pegram, with thirteen hundred Confederates, was in command at Rich Mountain; and at Laurel Hill General Garnett, with between four thousand and five thousand men, was in command. There were about six hundred more Confederates at various points within a few miles.

After examining the ground McClellan decided to make the first attack on the Rich Mountain works, but in order to divert attention from his real purpose, he ordered General Morris, who was in front of General Garnett's position, to bombard the Confederates at Laurel Hill. Accordingly shells were thrown in the direction of the Confederate works, some of which exploded within the lines, but doing little damage. On the afternoon of July 10 General McClellan prepared to attack Pegram at Rich Mountain, but upon examination of the approaches he saw that an attack in front would probably be unsuccessful. The Confederate works were located one and a half miles west of the summit of Rich Mountain, where the Staunton and Parkersburg pike crosses. When the Union forces reached the open country at Roaring Creek, a short distance west of the Confederate position,

Colonel Pegram planned an attack upon them, but upon mature reflection, abondoned it. There was a path leading from Roaring Creek across Rich Mountain to Beverly, north of the Confederate position, and Colonel Pegram guarded this path with troops under Colonel Scott, but he did not know that another path led across the mountain south of his position, by which McClellan could flank him. This path was left unguarded, and it was instrumental in Pegram's defeat. General Rosecrans, who was in charge of one wing of the forces in front of the Confederate position, met a young man named David Hart, whose father lived one and a half miles in the rear of the Confederate fortifications, and he said he could pilot a force, by an obscure road, round the southern end of the Confederate lines and reach his father's farm, on the summit of the mountain, from which an attack on Colonel Pegram in the rear could be made. The young man was taken to General McClellan and consented to act as a guide. Thereupon General McClellan changed his plan from attacking in front to an attack in the rear. He moved a portion of his forces to the western base of Rich Mountain, ready to support the attack when made, and he then dispatched General Rosecrans, under the guidance of young Hart, by the circuitous route, to the rear of the Confederates. Rosecrans reached his destination and sent a messenger to inform General McClellan of the fact, and that all was in readiness for the attack. This messenger was captured by the Confederates, and Pegram learned of the new danger which threatened him, while McClellan was left in doubt whether his troops had been able to reach the point for which they had started. Had it not been for this perhaps the fighting would have resulted in the capture of the Confederates.

Colonel Pegram, finding that he was to be attacked from the rear, sent three hundred and fifty men to the point of danger, at the top of the mountain, and built the best breastworks possible in the short time at his disposal. When Rosecrans advanced to the attack he was stubbornly resisted, and the fight continued two or three hours, and neither side could gain any advantage. Pegram was sending up reinforcements to the mountain when the Union forces made a charge and swept the Confederates from the field. Colonel Pegram collected several companies and prepared to renew the fight. It was now late in the afternoon of July 11. The men were panic-stricken, but they moved forward, and were led around the mountain within musket range of the Union forces that had remained on the battle ground. But the Confederates became alarmed and fled without making an attack. Their forces were scattered over the mountain, and night was coming on. Colonel Pegram saw that all was lost, and determined to make his way to Garnett's army, if possible, about fifteen miles distant, through the woods. He commenced collecting his men and sending them forward. It was after midnight when he left the camp and set forward with the last remnants of his men in an effort to reach the Confederate forces on Laurel Hill. The loss of the Confederates in the battle had been about forty-five killed and about twenty wounded. All their baggage and artillery fell into the hands of the Union army. Sixty-three Confederates were captured. Rosecrans lost twelve killed and forty-nine wounded.

The retreat from Rich Mountain was disastrous. The Confederates were eighteen hours in groping their way twelve miles through the woods in the direction of Garnett's camp. Near sunset on July 12 they reached the Tygart River, three miles from the Laurel Hill camp, and there learned from the citizens that Garnett had already retreated and that the Union forces were in pursuit. There seemed only one possible avenue of escape open for Pegram's force. That was a miserable road leading across the mountains into Pendleton County. Few persons lived near the road, and the outlook was that the men would starve to death if they attempted to make their way through. They were already starving. Accordingly, Colonel Pegram that night sent a flag of truce to Beverly, offering to surrender, and at the same time stating that his men were starving. Early the next morning General McClellan sent several wagon loads of bread to them, and met them on their way to Beverly. The number of prisoners surrendered was thirty officers and five hundred and twenty-five men. The remainder of the force at Rich Mountain had been killed, wounded, captured and scattered. Colonel Scott, who had been holding the path leading over the mountain north of the Confederate position, learned of the defeat of Pegram and he made good his retreat over the Alleghanies by way of Huttonsville.

It now remains to be told how General Garnett fared. The fact that he had posted the greater part of his army on Laurel Hill is proof that he expected the principal attack to be made on that place. He was for a time deceived by the bombardment directed against him, but he was undeceived when he learned that Colonel Pegram had been defeated, and that General McClellan had thrown troops across Rich Mountain and had successfully turned the flank of the Confederate position. All that was left for Garnett was to withdraw his army while there was yet time. His line of retreat was the pike from Beverly to Staunton, and the Union forces were pushing forward to occupy that and to cut him off in that direction. On the afternoon of July 12, 1861, Garnett retreated, hastening to reach Beverly in advance of the Union forces. On the way he met fugitives from Pegram's army and was told by them that McClellan had already reached Beverly, and that the road in that direction was closed. Thereupon Garnett turned eastward into Tucker County, over a very rough road. General Morris pursued the retreating Confederates over the mountain to Cheat River, skirmishing on the way. General Garnett remained in the rear directing his skirmishers, and on July 14, at Corrick's Ford, where Parsons, the county seat of Tucker County, has since been located, he found that he could no longer avoid giving battle. With a few hundred men he opened fire on the advance of the pursuing army and checked the pursuit. But in bringing off his skirmishers from behind a pile of driftwood, Garnett was killed and his men were seized with panic and fled, leaving his body on the field, with a score or more of dead.

When it was found that the Confederates were retreating eastward Federal troops from Grafton, Rowlesburg and other points on the Baltimore and Ohio Railroad were ordered to cut off the retreat at St. George, in Tucker County. But the troops could not be concentrated in time, and the concentration was made at Oakland, in Maryland, with the expectation of intercepting the retreating Confederates at Red House, eight miles west of Oakland.

Up to the time of the fight at Corrick's Ford the retreat had been orderly, but after that it became a rout. The roads were narrow and rough, and the excessive rains had rendered them almost impassible. Wagons and stores were abandoned, and when Horse Shoe Run, a long and narrow defile leading to the Red House, in Maryland, was reached information was received that Union troops from Rowlesburg and Oakland were at the Red House, cutting off retreat in that direction. The artillery was sent to the front. A portion of the cavalry was piloted by a mountaineer along a narrow path across the Backbone and Alleghany Mountains. The main body continued its retreat to the Red House, and pursued its way unmolested across the Alleghanies to Monterey. Two regiments marching in haste to reinforce Garnett at Laurel Hill had reached Monterey when news of Garnett's retreat was received. The regiments halted there, and as Garnett's stragglers came in they were re-organized.

The Union army made no pursuit beyond Corrick's Ford, except that detachments followed to the Red House to pick up the stores abandoned by the Confederates. Garnett's body fell into the hands of the Union forces and was prepared for burial and sent to Richmond. It was carried in a canoe to Rowlesburg, on the Baltimore and Ohio Railroad, thirty miles below, on Cheat River, in charge of Whitelaw Reid, who had taken part in the battle at Corrick's Ford. Reid was acting in the double capacity of correspondent for the *Cincinnati Gazette* and an aid on the staff of General Morris. When Rowlesburg was reached Garnett's body was sent by express to Governor Letcher, at Richmond.

This closed the campaign in that part of West Virginia for 1861. The Confederates had failed to hold the country. On July 22 General McClellan was transferred to Washington to take charge of military operations there. In comparison with the greater battles and more extensive campaign later in the war, the affairs in West Virginia were small. But they were of great importance at the time. Had the result been different, had the Confederates held their ground at Grafton, Philippi, Rich Mountain and Laurel Hill, and had the Union forces been driven out of the State, across the Ohio, the outcome would have changed the history of the war, but probably not the result.

CHAPTER XVI.

─:o:─

PROGRESS OF THE WAR.

After Garnett's retreat in July, 1861, there were few Confederates in West Virginia, west of the Alleghanies, except in the Kanawha Valley. But the Government at Richmond and the Confederate Government were not inclined to give up so easily the part of Virginia west of the mountains, and in a short time preparations were made to send an army from the east to re-conquer the territory beyond the Alleghanies. A large part of the army with which McClellan had defeated Garnett had been sent to other fields; the terms of enlistment of many of the soldiers had expired. When the Confederates re-crossed the mountains late in the summer of 1861 they were opposed by less than ten thousand Federals stationed in that mountainous part of West Virginia about the sources of the Greenbrier, the Tygart Valley River, Cheat, and near the source of the Potomac. In that elevated and rugged region a remarkable campaign was made. It was not remarkable because of hard fighting, for there was no pitched battle; but because in this campaign the Confederates were checked in their purpose of re-conquering the ground lost by Garnett and of extending their conquest north and west. This campaign has also an historical interest because it was General Lee's first work in the field after he had been assigned the command of Virginia's land and sea forces. The outcome of the campaign was not what might be expected of a great and calculating general as Lee was. Although he had a larger army than his opponents in the field, and had at least as good ground, and although he was able to hold his own at every skirmish, yet, as the campaign progressed he constantly fell back. In September he fought at Elkwater and Cheat Mountain, in Randolph County; in October he fought at Greenbrier river, having fallen back from his first position. In December he had fallen back to the summit of the Alleghanies, and fought a battle there. It should be stated, however, that General Lee, although in command of the army, took part in person only in the skirmishing in Randolph County. The importance of this campaign entitles it to mention somewhat more in detail.

General Reynolds succeeded General McClellan in command of this part of West Virginia. He advanced from Beverly to Huttonsville, a few miles above, and remained in peaceful possession of the country two months after Garnett's retreat, except that his scouting parties were constantly annoyed by Confederate irregulars, or guerrillas, usually called bushwhackers. Their mode of attack was, to lie concealed on the summits of cliffs, overhanging the roads or in thickets on the hillsides, and fire upon the Union soldiers passing below. They were justly dreaded by the Union troops. These bushwhackers were usually citizens of that district who had taken to the woods after their well-known southern sympathies had rendered it unsafe or unpleasant to remain at home while the country was occupied by the Union armies. They were excellent marksmen, minutely acquainted with all the ins and outs of the mountains and woods; and, from their manner of attack and flight, it was seldom that they were captured or killed. They hid about the outposts of the Union armies; picked off sentinels; wayland scouts; ambushed small detachments, and fled to their mountain fastnesses where pursuit was out of the question. A war is considered severe in loss of life in which each soldier, taken as an average, kills one soldier on the other side, even though the war is prolonged for years. Yet, these bushwhackers often killed a dozen or more each, before being themselves killed. It can be readily understood why small detachments dreaded bushwhackers more than Confederate troops in pitched battle. Nor did the bushwhackers confine their attacks to small parties. They often fired into the ranks of armies on the march with deadly effect. While in the mountains of West Virginia General Averell's cavalry often suffered severely from these hidden guerrillas who fired and vanished. The bushwhacking was not always done by Confederates. Union soldiers or sympathizers resorted to it also at times.

General Reynolds, with headquarters at Beverly, spent the summer of 1861 in strengthening his position, and in attempting to clear the country of guerrillas. Early in September he received information that large numbers of Confederates were crossing the Alleghanies. General Loring established himself at Huntersville, in Pocahontas County, with 8500 men. He it was who had tried in vain to raise recruits in West Virginia for the Confederacy, even attempting to gain a foothold in Wheeling before McClellan's army crossed the Ohio River. He had gone to Richmond, and early in September had returned with an army. General H. R. Jackson was in command of another Confederate force of 6000 at Greenbrier River where the pike from Beverly to Staunton crosses that stream, in Pocahontas County. General Robert E. Lee was sent by the Government at Richmond to take command of both these armies, and he lost no time in doing so. No order sending General Lee into West Virginia has ever been found among the records of the Confederate Government. It was probably a verbal order, or he may have gone without any order. He concentrated his force at Big Spring, on Valley Mountain, and prepared to march north to the Baltimore and Ohio Road at Grafton. His design was nothing less than to drive the Union army out of northwestern Virginia. When the matter is viewed in the light of subsequent history, it is to be wondered at that General Lee did not succeed in his purpose. He had 14500 men, and only 9000 were opposed to him. Had he defeated General Reynolds; driven his army back; occupied Grafton, Clarksburg and other towns, it can be readily seen that the seat of war might have been changed to West Virginia. The United States Government would have sent an army to oppose Lee; and the Confederate Government would have pushed strong reinforcements across the mountains; and some of the great battles of the war might have been fought on the Monongahela river. The campaign in the fall of 1861, about the head waters of the principle rivers of West Virginia, therefore, derives its chief interest, not from battles, but from the accomplishment of a great purpose—the driving back of the Confederates—without a pitched battle. Virginia, as a State, made no determined effort after that to hold Western Virginia. By that time the campaign in the Kanawha Valley was drawing to a close and theConfederates were retiring. Consequently, Virginia's and the Southern Confederacy's efforts west of the Alleghanies in this State were defeated in the fall of 1861.

General Reynolds sent a regiment to Elkwater, and soon afterwards occupied Cheat Mountain. This point was the highest camp occupied by soldiers during the war. The celebrated "Battle Above the Clouds," on Lookout Mountain, was not one-half so high. The whole region, including parts of Pocahontas, Pendleton and Randolph Counties, has an elevation above three thousand feet, while the summits of the knobs and ridges rise to heights of more than four thousand, and some nearly five thousand feet. General Reynolds fortified his two advanced positions, Elkwater and Cheat Mountain. They were seven miles apart, connected by only a bridle path, but a circuitous wagon road, eighteen miles long, led from one to the other, passing around in the direction of Huttonsville. No sooner had the United States troops established themselves at Elkwater and Cheat Mountain than General Lee advanced, and skirmishing began. The Confederates threw a force between Elkwater and Cheat Mountain, and posted another force on the road in the direction of Huttonsville. They were attacked, and for three days there was skirmishing, but no general engagement. On September 13 Colonel John A. Washington, in the Confederate service, was killed near Elkwater. He was a relative of President Washington, and also a relative General R. E. Lee, whose family and the Washingtons were closely connected. General Lee sent a flag of truce and asked for the body. It was sent to the Confederate lines on September 14. That day the Confederates concentrated ten miles from Elkwater, and the next day again advanced, this time threatening Cheat Mountain, but their attack was unsuccessful. In this series of skirmishes the Union forces had lost nine killed, fifteen wounded and about sixty prisoners. The result was a defeat for the Confederates, who were thwarted in their design of penetrating northward and westward. The failure of the Confederates to bring on a battle was due to their different detachments not acting in concert. It was Lee's plan to attack both positions at the same time. He sent detachments against Elkwater and Cheat Mountain. The sound of cannon attacking one position was to be the signal for attacking the other. The troops marched in rain and mud, along paths and in the woods, and when they found themselves in front of the Federal position, the detachment which was to have begun the attack failed to do so. The other detachment waited in vain for the signal, and then retreated. General Lee was much hurt by the failure of his plan.*

General Loring's army of 8,500, which was camped at Huntersville, in Pocahontas County, was sent to that place for a particular purpose. He was to sweep round toward the west, then march north toward Weston and Clarksburg, strike the Baltimore and Ohio Railroad, and by threatening or cutting off General Reynolds' line of communication with his base of supplies, compel him to fall back. This plan was General Lee's. He left its execution to General Loring, who moved slowly, halted often, camped long, hesitated frequently, and consumed much valuable time. His men became sick. Rains made progress difficult, and he did not seem in a hurry to get along. General Lee waited but Loring still failed to march. He was an older officer than Lee, and although Lee had a right to order him forward,

---

* See H. A. White's Life of Robert E. Lee.

PROGRESS OF THE WAR.   141

he refrained from doing so for fear of wounding Loring's feelings. The time for executing the movement passed, and the flank movement, which probably would have succeeded, was given up.

The Confederates were not yet willing to abandon West Virginia. They fell back to the Greenbrier River, thirteen miles from the Union camp, on Cheat Mountain, and fortified their position. They were commanded by General H. R. Jackson, and their number was believed to be about nine thousand. On October 3, 1861, General Reynolds advanced at the head of five thousand troops. During the first part of the engagement the Union forces were successful, driving the Confederates nearly a mile, but here several batteries of artillery were encountered, and reinforcements arriving to the support of the Confederates, the battle was renewed and General Reynolds was forced to fall back, with a loss of nine killed and thirty-five wounded. On December 10 General Reynolds was transferred to other fields, and the command of the Union forces in the Cheat Mountain district was given to General R. H. Milroy. Within three days after he assumed command he moved forward to attack the Confederate camp on the summit of the Alleghanies. The Confederates had gone into winter quarters there; and as the weather was severe, and as the Union forces appeared satisfied to hold what they had without attempting any additional conquests in midwinter, the Confederates were not expecting an attack. However, on December 13, 1861, General Milroy moved forward and assaulted their position. The fighting was severe for several hours, and finally resulted in the retreat of the Union forces. The Confederates made no attempt to follow. General Milroy marched to Huntersville, in Pocahontas county, and went into winter quarters. The Rebels remained on the summit of the Alleghanies till spring and then went over the mountains, out of West Virginia, thus ending the attempt to re-conquer northwestern Virginia.

It now remains to be seen what success attended the efforts of the Confederates to gain control of the Kanawha Valley. Their campaign in West Virginia for the year 1861 was divided into two parts, in the northwest and in the Kanawha Valley. General Henry A. Wise was ordered to the Kanawha June 6, two days before General Garnett was ordered to take command of the troops which had been driven south from Grafton. Colonel Tompkins was already on the Kanawha in charge of Confederate forces. The authorities at Richmond at that time believed that a General, with the nucleus of an army in the Kanawha Valley, could raise all the troops necessary among the people there. On April 29 General Lee had ordered Major John McCausland to the Kanawha to organize companies for the Confederacy. Only five hundred flint-lock muskets could be had at that time to arm the troops in that quarter. General Lee suggested that the valley could be held by posting the force below Charleston. Very poor success attended the efforts at raising volunteers, and the arms found in the district were insufficient to equip the men. Supplies were sent as soon as possible from Virginia.

When General Wise arrived and had collected all his forces he had 8,000 men, of whom 2,000 were militia from Raleigh, Fayette and Mercer Counties. With these he was expected to occupy the Kanawha Valley, and resist invasion should Union forces attempt to penetrate that part of the State. General John B. Floyd, who had been Secretary of War under President Buchanan, was guarding the railroad leading from Richmond into Tennessee, and was posted south of the present limits of West Virginia, but within supporting distance of General Wise. In case a Union army invaded the Kanawha Valley it was expected that General Floyd would unite his forces with those of General Wise, and that they would act in concert if not in conjunction. General Floyd was the older officer, and in case their forces were consolidated he would be the commander in-chief. But General Floyd and General Wise were enemies. Their hatred for the Yankees was less than their hatred for each other. They were both Virginia politicians, and they had crossed each other's paths too often in the past to be reconciled now. General Lee tried in vain to induce them to work in harmony. They both fought the Union troops bravely, but never in concert. When Wise was in front of General Cox, General Floyd was elsewhere. When Floyd was pitted in battle against General Rosecrans, General Wise was absent. Thus the Union troops beat these quarreling Virginia Brigadier Generals in detail, as will be seen in the following narrative of the campaign during the summer and fall of 1861 in the Kanawha Valley.

When Generals Wise and Floyd were sent to their districts in the West it was announced in their camps that they would march to Clarksburg, Parkersburg and Wheeling. This would have brought them in conflict with General McClellan's army. On July 2 McClellan put troops in motion against the Confederates in the Kanawha Valley. On that date he appointed General J. D. Cox to the command of regiments from Kentucky and Ohio, and ordered him to cross the Ohio at Gallipolis and take possession of Point Pleasant, at the mouth of the Kanawha. On July 23 General Rosecrans succeeded McClellan in command of the Department of Ohio. Rosecrans pushed the preparation for a vigorous campaign, which had already been commenced. He styled the troops under General Cox the Brigade of Kanawha. On July 17, in Putnam County, a fight occurred between detachments of Union and Confederate forces, in which the latter appeared for the time victorious, but soon retreated eastward. From that time until September 10 there was constant skirmishing between the armies, the advantage being sometimes on one side, sometimes on the other; but the Union forces constantly advanced and the Confederates fell back. On August 1 General Wise was in Greenbrier County, and in a report made to General Lee on that date, he says he fell back not a moment too soon. He complained that his militia were worthless as soldiers, and urged General Lee to send him guns and other arms, and clothing and shoes, as his men were ragged and barefooted. On August 20 General Rosecrans was at Clarksburg preparing to go in person to lead reinforcements into the Kanawha. He issued a proclamation to the people of West Virginia, calling on them to obey the laws, maintain order and co-operate with the military in its efforts to drive the armed Confederates from the State.

Prior to that time Colonel E. B. Tyler, with a Federal force, had advanced to the Gauley River, and on August 13 he took up a position at Cross Lanes. He thus covered Carnifex Ferry. General Cox was at that time on the Gauley River, twenty miles lower down, near the mouth of that stream, nearly forty miles above Charleston. General Floyd advanced, and on August 26 crossed the Gauley at Carnifex Ferry with 2,500 men, and fell upon Colonel Tyler at Cross Lanes with such suddenness that the Union troops were routed, with fifteen killed and fifty wounded. The latter fell into the hands of the Confederates, who took fifty other prisoners also. The remainder of Tyler's force made its retreat to Charleston, and General Floyd fortified the position just gained and prepared to hold it. On Sep-

PROGRESS OF THE WAR.

tember 3 General Wise made an attack on General Cox at Gauley Bridge, near the mouth of the river, twenty miles below Carnifex Ferry. The attack failed. The Confederates were beaten and were vigorously pursued. Had Wise held Gauley Bridge, Floyd already being in possession of Carnifex Ferry, they would have been in positions to dispute the further advance of the Union forces up the Kanawha Valley.

General Rosecrans left Clarksburg September 3, with re-inforcements, and after a march of seven days reached Carnifex Ferry, and that same evening began an attack upon the Confederates under General Floyd, who were entrenched on top of a mountain on the west bank of the Gauley River, in Nicholas County. General Floyd had about 4000 men and sixteen cannon, and his position was so well protected by woods, that assault, with chance of success, was considered exceedingly difficult. He had fortified this naturally strong position, and felt confident that it could not be captured by any force the Union general could bring against him. The fight began late in the afternoon, General Rosecrans having marched seventeen miles that day. It was not his purpose to bring on a general engagement that afternoon, and he directed his forces to advance cautiously and find where the enemy lay; for the position of the Confederates was not yet known. While thus advancing a camp was found in the woods, from which the Confederates had evidently fled in haste. Military stores and private property were scattered in confusion. From this fact it was supposed that the enemy was in retreat, and the Union troops pushed on through thickets and over ridges. Presently they discovered that they had been mistaken. They were fired upon by the Confederate army in line of battle. From that hour until darkness put a stop to the fighting, the battle continued. The Union troops had not been able to carry any of the Rebel works; and General Rosecrans withdrew his men for the night, prepared to renew the battle next morning. But during the night General Floyd retreated. He had grown doubtful of his ability to hold out if the attack was resumed with the same impetuosity as on the preceding evening. But he was more fearful that the Union troops would cut off his retreat if he remained. So, while it was yet time, he withdrew in the direction of Lewisburg, in Greenbrier County, destroying the bridge over the Gauley, and also the ferry across that stream. General Rosecrans was unable to pursue because he could not cross the river. It is a powerful, turbulent stream, and at this place flows several miles down a deep gorge, filled with rocks and cataracts. Among spoils which fell into the hands of the victors was General Floyd's hospital, in which were fifty wounded Union soldiers who had been captured when Colonel Tyler was driven from this same place on August 26. General Rosecrans lost seventeen killed and one hundred and forty-one wounded. The Confederate loss was never ascertained.

After a rest of a few days the Union army advanced to Big Sewell Mountain. The weather was wet, and the roads became so muddy that it was almost impossible to haul supplies over them. For this reason it was deemed advisable to fall back. On October 5 General Rosecrans began to withdraw his forces to Gauley Bridge, and in the course of two weeks had transferred his command to that place, where he had water communication with his base of supplies.

On November 10 another action was fought between General Floyd and General Rosecrans, in which the Confederates were defeated. This virtually closed the campaign for the year 1861 in that quarter, and resulted in the occupation of all the lower Kanawha Valley and the greater part of the upper valley. The Confederates were finally driven out, and never again obtained a foothold in that part of the State, although large bodies were at times in the Valley of the Kanawha, and occasionally remained a considerable time.

The Confederate Government, and the State of Virginia as a member of that Government, had an object in view when they sent their forces into West Virginia at the commencement of the Civil War. Virginia as a State was interested in retaining the territory between the Alleghany Mountains and the Ohio River and did not believe she could do so without force and arms, because her long neglect and oppression had alienated the western counties. Virginia correctly judged that they would seize the first opportunity and organize a separate State. To prevent them from doing so, and to retain that large part of her domain lying west of the Alleghanies, were the chief motives which prompted Virginia, as a State, to invade the western part of her own territory, even before open war was acknowledged to exist between the Southern Confederacy and the United States Government. The purpose which prompted the Southern Confederacy to push troops across the Alleghanies in such haste was to obtain possession of the country to the borders of Ohio and Pennsylvania, and to fortify the frontiers against invasion from the north and west. It was well understood at the headquarters of the Southern Confederacy that the thousands of soldiers already mustering beyond the Ohio River, and the tens of thousands who would no doubt soon take the field in the same quarter, would speedily cross the Ohio, unless prevented. The bold move which the South undertook was to make the borders of Ohio and Pennsylvania the battle ground. The southern leaders did not at that time appreciate the magnitude of the war which was at hand. If they had understood it, and had had a military man in the place of Jefferson Davis, it is probable that the battle ground would have been different from what it was. Consequently, to rightly understand the early movements of the Confederates in West Virginia, it is necessary to consider that their purpose was to hold the country to the Ohio river. Their effort was weak, to be sure, but that was partly due to their miscalculation as to the assistance they would receive from the people of West Virginia. If they could have organized an army of forty thousand West Virginians and reinforced them with as many more men from the South, it can be readily seen that McClellan could not have crossed the Ohio as he did. But the scheme failed. The West Virginians not only would not enlist in the Confederate army, but they enlisted in the opposing force; and when Garnett made his report from Laurel Hill he told General Lee that, for all the help he received from the people, he might as well carry on a campaign in a foreign country. From that time it was regarded by the Confederates as the enemy's country; and when, later in the war, Jones, Jackson, Imboden and others made raids into West Virginia they acted toward persons and property in the same way as when raids were made in Ohio and Pennsylvania.

The Baltimore and Ohio Railroad, crossing West Virginia from Harper's Ferry to Wheeling, and from Grafton to Parkersburg, was considered of the utmost importance by both the North and the South. It was so near the boundary between what was regarded as the Southern Confederacy and the North that during the early part of the war neither the one side nor the other felt sure of holding it. The management of the road was in sympathy with the North, but an effort was made to so manage the property as not to give cause for hostility on the part of the South. At one time the trains were run in accordance with a time table prepared by Stonewall Jackson, even as far as Locust Point.* It was a part of the Confederate scheme in West Virginia to obtain possession and control, in a friendly way if possible, of the Baltimore and Ohio Railroad. The possession of it would not only help the Confederacy in a direct way, but it would cripple the Federal Government and help the South in an indirect way. Within six days after General Lee was appointed Commander-in-Chief of the Virginia armies he instructed Major Loring, at Wheeling, to direct his military operations for the protection of the terminus of the Baltimore and Ohio Railroad on the Ohio River, and also to protect the road elsewhere. Major Boykin was ordered to give protection to the road in the vicinity of Grafton. General Lee insisted that the peaceful business of the road must not be interfered with. The branch to Parkersburg was also to be protected. Major Boykin was told to "hold the road for the benefit of Maryland and Virginia." He was advised to obtain the co-operation of the officers of the road and afford them every assistance. When Colonel Porterfield was ordered to Grafton, on May 4, 1861, among the duties marked out for him by General Lee was the holding of the Baltimore and Ohio Railroad, and to prevent its being used to the injury of Virginia.

No one has ever supposed that the Southern Confederacy wanted the Baltimore and Ohio Road protected because of any desire to befriend that company. The leaders of the Confederacy knew that the officers of the road were not friendly to secession. As soon as Western Virginia had slipped out of the grasp of the Confederacy, and when the railroad could no longer help the South to realize its ambition of fortifying the banks of the Ohio, the Confederacy threw off the mask and came out in open hostility. George Deas, Inspector General of the Confederate Army, urged that the railroad be destroyed, bridges burned along the line, and the tunnels west of the Alleghanies blown up so that no troops could be carried east from the Ohio River to the Potomac. This advice was partly carried out by a raid from Romney on June 19, 1861, after Colonel Porterfield had retreated from Grafton and had been driven from Philippi. But the damage to the road was not great and repairs were speedily made. Governor Letcher, of Virginia, had recommended to the Legislature a short time before, that the Baltimore and Ohio Road ought to be destroyed. He said: "The Baltimore and Ohio Railroad has been a positive nuisance to this State, from the opening of the war till the present time. And unless the management shall hereafter be in friendly hands, and the government under which it exists be a part of our Confederacy, it must be abated. If it should be permanently destroyed we must assure our people of some other communication with the seaboard."† From that time till the close of the war the Confederacy inflicted every damage possible upon the road, and in many instances the damage was enormous.

When General Garnett established himself in Randolph and Barbour Counties, in June, 1861, he made an elaborate plan of attack on the Baltimore and Ohio Railroad. He intended to take possession of Evansville, in Preston County, and using that as a base, destroy east and west. The high

---

* See the History of the War, by General John D. Imboden.
† Records of the Rebellion.

trestles along the face of Laurel Hill, west of Rowlesburg, and the bridge across Cheat River at Rowlesburg, and the long tunnel at Tunnelton were selected for the first and principal destruction. General Garnett had the road from Rowlesburg up Cheat River to St. George surveyed with a view to widening and improving it, thereby making of it a military road by which he could advance or fall back, in case the road from Beverly to Evansville should be threatened. General Imboden twice made dashes over the Alleghanies at the head of Cheat River and struck for the Rowlesburg trestles, but each time fell back when he reached St. George. In the spring of 1863, when the great raid into West Virginia was made under Jones, Imboden and Jackson, every possible damage was done the Baltimore and Ohio Road, but again the Rowlesburg trestles escaped, although the Confederates approached within two miles of them.

It is proper to state here that an effort was made, after fighting had commenced, to win the West Virginians over to the cause of the South by promising them larger privileges than they had ever before enjoyed. On June 14, 1861, Governor Letcher issued a proclamation, which was published at Huttonsville, in Randolph County, and addressed to the people of Northwestern Virginia. In this proclamation he promised them that the injustice from unequal taxation of which they had complained in the past, should exist no longer. He said that the eastern part of the State had expressed a willingness to relinquish exemptions from taxation, which it had been enjoying, and was willing to share all the burdens of government. The Governor promised that in state affairs, the majority should rule; and he called upon the people beyond the Alleghanies, in the name of past friendship and of historic memories, to espouse the cause of the Southern Confederacy. It is needless to state that this proclamation fell flat. The people of Western Virginia would have hailed with delight a prospect of redress of grievances, had it come earlier. But its coming was so long delayed that they doubted both the sincerity of those who made the promise and their ability to fulfill. Twenty thousand soldiers had already crossed the Ohio, and had penetrated more than half way from the river to the Alleghanies, and they had been joined by thousands of Virginians. It was a poor time for Governor Letcher to appeal to past memories or to promise justice in the future which had been denied in the past. Coming as the promise did at that time, it looked like a death-bed repentance. The Southern Confederacy had postponed fortifying the bank of the Ohio until too late; and Virginia had held out the olive branch to her neglected and long-suffering people beyond the mountains when it was too late. They had already cast their lot with the North; and already a powerful army had crossed the Ohio to their assistance. Virginia's day of dominion west of the Alleghanies was nearing its close; and the Southern Confederacy's hope of empire there was already doomed.

CHAPTER XVII.

―:o:―

CHRONOLOGY OF THE WAR.*

In this chapter will be given an outline of the progress of the Civil War on the soil of West Virginia or immediately affecting the State. As there were more than three hundred battles and skirmishes within the limits of the State, and numerous scouts, raids and campaigns, it will be possible in the brief space of one chapter to give little more than the date of each, with a word of explanation or description. In former chapters the history of the opening of the war and accounts of the leading campaigns have been given. It yet remains to present in their chronological sequence the events of greater or lesser importance which constitute the State's war record.

1861.

April 17. The Ordinance of Secession was adopted by the Virginia Convention at Richmond.

April 18. Harper's Ferry was abandoned by the Federal troops. Lieutenant Roger Jones, the commandant, learning that more than two thousand Virginia troops were advancing to attack him, set fire to the United States armory and machine shops and retreated into Pennsylvania. Fifteen minutes after he left Harper's Ferry the Virginia forces arrived.

April 23. General Robert E. Lee assigned to the command of Virginia's land and naval forces.

April 27. Colonel T. J. Jackson assigned to the command of the Virginia forces at Harper's Ferry.

May 1. Governor Letcher calls out the Virginia militia.

May 3. Additional forces called for by the Governor of Virginia. The call was disregarded by nearly all the counties west of the Alleghanies.

May 4. Colonel George A. Porterfield assigned to the command of all the Confederate forces in Northwestern Virginia.

May 10. General Robert E. Lee assigned to the command of the forces of the Confederate States serving in Virginia.

May 13. General George B. McClellan assigned to the command of the Department of the Ohio, embracing West Virginia.

May 14. The Confederates at Harper's Ferry seized a train of cars.

May 15. General Joseph E. Johnston assigned to the command of Confederate troops near Harper's Ferry.

May 22. Bailey Brown was killed by a Confederate picket at Fetter-

---

* This chapter is compiled chiefly from the Records of the Rebellion, published by the United States War Department. A few of the items are from the West Virginia Adjutant General's Reports for 1865 and 1866, and a small number from other sources. The reports of officers, both Federal and Confederate, have been consulted in arriving at conclusions as to numbers engaged, the losses and the victory or defeat of forces.

man, Taylor County. Brown was the first enlisted man of the United States volunteer service killed in the war.

May 26. Federal forces from beyond the Ohio and those about Wheeling began to move against Grafton where Confederates, under Colonel Porterfield, had established themselves.

May 27. Captain Christian Roberts was killed by Federals under Lieutenant West, in a skirmish at Glover's Gap, between Wheeling and Fairmont. Captain Roberts was the first armed Confederate soldier killed in the war.

May 30. Grafton was occupied by Federal forces, the Confederates having retreated to Philippi.

June 3. Fight at Philippi and retreat of the Confederates into Randolph County.

June 6. Ex-Governor Henry A. Wise was sent to the Kanawha Valley to collect troops for the Confederacy.

June 8. General R. S. Garnett superseded Colonel Porterfield in command of Confederate forces in West Virginia.

June 10. A Federal force was sent from Rowlesburg to St. George, in Tucker County, capturing a lieutenant and two Confederate flags.

June 14. Governor Letcher, of Virginia, published at Huttonsville, Randolph County, a proclamation to the people west of the Alleghanies, urging them to stand by Virginia in its Secession, and promising them, if they would do so, that the wrongs of which they had so long complained should exist no more, and that the western counties should no longer be domineered over by the powerful eastern counties.

June 19. Skirmish near Keyser. Confederates under Colonel John C. Vaughn advanced from Romney and burned Bridge No. 21 on the Baltimore and Ohio Railroad, and defeated the Cumberland Home Guards, capturing two small cannon.

June 23. Skirmish between Federals and Confederates at Righter's.

June 26. Skirmish on Patterson Creek, Hampshire County, in which Richard Ashby was killed by thirteen Federals under Corporal David Hays.

June 29. Skirmish at Hannahsville, in Tucker County, in which Lieutenant Robert McChesney was killed by Federals under Captain Miller.

July 2. Fight at Falling Waters, near Martinsburg. Colonel John C. Starkweather defeated Stonewall Jackson. This was Jackson's first skirmish in the Civil War.

July 4. Skirmish at Harper's Ferry. Federals under Lietenant Galbraith were fired upon from opposite bank of the river. The Federals fell back with a loss of 4.

July 6. The forces under McClellan which were advancing upon Rich Mountain encountered Confederate outposts at Middle Fork Bridge, eighteen miles west of Beverly. The Federals fell back.

July 7. The Federals drove the Confederates from Middle Fork Bridge.

July 7. Skirmish at Glennville, Gilmer County.

July 8. Skirmish at Belington, Barbour County. General Morris with the left wing of McClellan's army attempted to dislodge the Confederates from the woods in the rear of the village, and was repulsed, losing 2 killed and 3 wounded.

July 11. Battle of Rich Mountain. The Confederates under Colonel Pegram were defeated by General Rosecrans.

July 12. General Garnett, with 4,585 Confederates, retreated from Laurel Hill through Tucker County, pursued by General Morris with 3,000 men.

July 12. Beverly was occupied by McClellan's forces, and a Confederate force, under Colonel Scott, retreated over Cheat Mountain toward Staunton.

July 13. Colonel Pegram surrendered six miles from Beverly to McClellan's army.

July 13. Battle of Corrick's Ford, in Tucker County. Garnett was killed and his army routed by Federals under General Morris.

July 13. General Lew Wallace with a Federal force advanced from Keyser and captured Romney.

July 15. Harper's Ferry was evacuated by the Confederates.

July 16. Skirmish at Barboursville, Cabell County. The Confederates were defeated.

July 17. Scarry Creek skirmish. Colonel Patton, with 1200 Confederates, defeated an equal number of Federals under Colonel Norton.

July 20. General W. W. Loring was placed in command of the Confederate forces in Northwestern Virginia.

August 1. General R. E. Lee was sent to take command of Confederate forces in West Virginia.

August 11. General John B. Floyd took command of Confederate troops in the Kanawha Valley.

August 13. A Federal force was sent from Grafton into Tucker County, capturing 15 prisoners, 90 guns, 150 horses and cattle and 15000 rounds of ammunition.

August 25. The Confederates were defeated in a skirmish at Piggot's Mill.

August 26. Fight at Cross Lanes, near Summerville. While the Federals were eating breakfast they were attacked and defeated by General Floyd.

September 1. Skirmish at Blue Creek.

September 2. Skirmish near Hawk's Nest in Fayette County. General Wise with 1,250 men attacked the Federals of equal force, but was repulsed.

September 10. Battle of Carnifex Ferry.

September 12. Skirmish at Cheat Mountain Pass, near Huttonsville. The Confederates under General Lee were repulsed in their attempt to fall upon the rear of the Federals.

September 13. Fight on Cheat Mountain. The Confederates were defeated. General Lee was foiled in his attempt on Elk Water.

September 14. Second skirmish at Elk Water. The Confederates were again unsuccessful.

September 15. The Confederates again were foiled in their attempt to advance to the summit of Cheat Mountain.

September 16. Skirmish at Princeton, Mercer County.

September 24. Skirmish at Hanging Rocks, in Hampshire County. The Federals were defeated.

September 24. Skirmish at Mechanicsburg Gap, Hampshire County. The Federals were defeated.

September 25. Colonel Cantwell defeated the Confederates under Colonel Angus McDonald and captured Romney, but was afterwards forced to retreat.

September 27. Captain Isaiah Hall was defeated by Confederate guerrillas at High Log Cabin Run, Wirt County.

October 3. Fight at Greenbrier River. The Federals were repulsed after severe fighting, but the Confederates fell back to the summit of the Alleghanies.

October 16. Skirmish near Bolivar Heights. About 500 Confederates under Turner Ashby attacked 600 Federals under Colonel John W. Geary. The Confederates were defeated.

October 19. There was skirmishing on New River, with various results.

October 23. Skirmishing on the Gauley between detachments of Federals and Confederates.

October 23. Colonel J. N. Clarkson, with a raiding force of Confederates, unsuccessfully attacked a steamer on the Kanawha.

October 26. Colonel Alexander Monroe, with 27 Hampshire County militia, attacked and defeated a large Federal force at Wire Bridge, on South Branch of the Potomac.

October 26. General Kelley with 3,000 Federals defeated Colonel McDonald's militia and captured Romney.

November 1. Commencement of a series of skirmishes for three days, near Gauley Bridge.

November 10. Skirmishes at Blake's Farm and Cotton Hill, with attendant movements, occupying two days.

November 10. Fight at Guyandotte. J. C. Wheeler, with 150 recruits, was surprised and cut to pieces by Confederate raiders under J. N. Clarkson. Among the Union prisoners was Uriah Payne, of Ohio, who was the first to plant the United States flag on the walls of Monterey, Mexico. Troops soon crossed to Guyandotte from Ohio and the Rebels retreated. A portion of the town was burned by the Federals.

November 12. Skirmish on Laurel Creek.

November 14. Skirmish near McCoy's Mill.

November 30. A detachment of Union troops was attacked by guerrillas on the South Branch, above Romney. The Federals retreated, with three wounded and a loss of six horses.

November 30. Skirmish near the mouth of Little Capon, in Morgan County. Captain Dyche defeated the Rebels.

December 13. Battle at Camp Alleghany. The Federals were defeated with a loss of 137 in killed and wounded.

December 15. Major E. B. Andrews set out on an expedition of six days to Meadow Bluff; defeated the Confederate skirmishers and captured a large amount of property.

December 28. Union forces occupied the county seat of Raleigh.

December 29. Sutton, Braxton County, was captured by 135 Rebels. The Union troops under Captain Rawland retreated to Weston. The Confederates burned a portion of the town.

December 30. Expedition into Webster County by 400 Union troops under Captain Anisansel. He pursued the Confederates who had burned Sutton; overtook them at Glades; defeated them; killed 22 and burned 29 houses believed to belong to Rebel bushwhackers.

1862.

January 3. Fight at Bath, in Morgan county, continuing two days. The Confederates under Stonewall Jackson victorious.

CHRONOLOGY OF THE WAR. 151

January 3. Major George Webster, with 700 Union troops, marched from Huttonsville to Huntersville, in Pocahontas County, drove out 250 Confederates, captured and destroyed military stores worth $30,000. These were the first Federals in Huntersville.

January 4. Skirmish at Sir John's Run, Morgan County. The fight continued late into the night. The Federals retreated.

January 4. Skirmish at Slanesville, Hampshire County. A squad of Union troops under Captain Sauls was ambushed and routed. Captain Sauls was wounded and taken prisoner. The Confederates were under Captain Isaac Kuykendall.

January 5. On or about January 5 the village of Frenchburg, six miles from Romney, was burned by order of General Lander on the charge that the people harbored Rebel bushwhackers.

January 5. Big Capon Bridge, on the Baltimore and Ohio Railroad, was destroyed by Confederates under Stonewall Jackson.

January 7. Fight at Blue's Gap, Hampshire County, in which the Confederates were defeated and lost two cannon—the same guns captured at Bridge No. 21 by the Confederates, June 19, 1861.

January 10. The Federal troops evacuated Romney.

January 11. Romney occupied by troops under Stonewall Jackson.

January 14. The seat of Logan County was burned by Union troops under Colonel E. Siber.

January 31. Confederates evacuated Romney by order of the Secretary of War of the Confederate States.

January 31. Stonewall Jackson, indignant at the interference with his plans by the Secretary of War, in recalling troops from Romney, tendered his resignation. He was persuaded by Governor Letcher, General Johnston and others to recall it.

February 2. Confederates at Springfield, Hampshire County, were defeated by General Lander.

February 8. Skirmish at the mouth of Blue Stone. Colonel William E. Peters, with 225 Confederates, was attacked by an equal force. The Federals retreated.

February 12. Fight at Moorefield, in which the Confederates retreated.

February 14. Confederates driven from Bloomery Gap, in Morgan County.

February 16. The Union troops were defeated at Bloomery Gap and compelled to retreat.

February 26. The Patterson Creek Bridge, in Mineral County, was burned by Rebel guerrillas.

March 3. Skirmish at Martinsburg.

April 12. Raid from Fairmont to Boothville by Captain J. H. Showalter, who was ordered by General Kelley to capture or kill John Righter, John Anderson, David Barker, Brice Welsh, John Lewis, John Knight and Washington Smith, who were agents sent by Governor Letcher into northwestern Virginia to raise recruits for the Confederacy. Captain Showalter killed three men of Righter's company.

April 17. Defeat of the Webster County guerrillas, known as Dare Devils, by Major E. B. Andrews, who marched from Summerville to Addison with 200 Federals. There were several skirmishes between April 17 and April 21. Several houses belonging to the guerrillas were burned.

April 18. An expedition was sent by General Schenck to clear the North Fork and Senaca in Pendleton County of Rebel bushwhackers.

April 18. Colonel T. M. Harris skirmished with Rebel bushwhackers in Webster County, killing 5 and burning 5 houses.

April 23. Skirmish at Grassy Lick, in Hampshire County. Confederate bushwhackers under Captain Umbaugh, who held a commission from Governor Letcher, concealed themselves in the house of Peter Poling and fired upon Colonel S. W. Downey's scouting party, killing three. Troops were sent from Romney and Moorefield and burned the house, after mortally wounding its owner.

May 1. Lieutenant Fitzhugh with 200 Federals was attacked near Princeton, Mercer County, and fought thirteen hours while retreating 23 miles, losing 1 killed, 12 wounded.

May 1. Skirmish at Camp Creek on Blue Stone River. Lieutenant Bottsford was attacked by 300 Rebels and lost 1 killed and 20 wounded. The Confederates were repulsed with 6 killed.

May 7. Skirmish near Wardensville, Hardy County. Troops under Colonel S. W. Downey attacked Captain Umbaugh a Rebel guerrilla, killing him and 4 of his men, wounding 4 and capturing 12. The fight occurred at the house of John T. Wilson.

May 8. Major B. F. Skinner led a scouting party through Roane and Clay counties from May 8 to May 21, skirmishing with Rebel guerrillas.

May 10. Federal scouts were decoyed into a house near Franklin, Pendleton County, and were set upon by bushwhackers and defeated with one killed. Two days later re-enforcements arrived, killed the owner of the house, and burned the building.

May 15. Fight at Wolf Creek, near New River, between Captain E. Schache and a squad of Confederates. The latter were defeated with 6 killed, 2 wounded and 6 prisoners.

May 16. The Confederates captured Princeton, Mercer County.

May 16. Skirmish at Wytheville Cross Roads. The Federals were attacked and defeated.

May 17. Federals captured Princeton with 15 prisoners.

May 23. Battle of Lewisburg, Greenbrier County. General Heth with 3000 Confederates attacked the forces of Colonel George Crook, 1300. The Confederates were stampeded and fled in panic, losing 4 cannon, 200 stands of arms, 100 prisoners, 38 killed, 66 wounded. The Union loss was 13 killed 53 wounded.

May 26. Skirmish near Franklin, Pendleton County.

May 29. Fight near Wardensville. Confederates were attacked and defeated with 2 killed, by Colonel Downey.

May 30. A Federal force under Colonel George R. Latham attacked guerrillas on Shaver Fork of Cheat River, defeating them, killing 4 and wounding several.

June 8. Major John J. Hoffman attacked and defeated a squad of Confederate Cavalry at Muddy Creek, near Blue Sulphur Springs, killing 3.

June 24. At Baker's Tavern, Hardy County, Capt. Chas. Farnsworth was fired upon by Rebel bushwhackers. He burned several houses in the vicinity as a warning to the people not to harbor bushwhackers.

June 24, Colonel J. D. Hines started upon a three days scout through Wyoming County. He defeated and dispersed Confederate guerrillas known as Flat Top Copperheads.

CHRONOLOGY OF THE WAR. 153

July 25. Lieutenant J. W. Miller, at Summerville, was attacked at daybreak by 200 Confederate cavalry and nearly all his men were captured.

August 2. A scouting party of Federals under Captain I. Stough left Meadow Bluff for the Greenbrier river. On August 4, near Haynes Ferry, he was defeated by the Confederates, losing 2 wounded. The Rebels had 5 killed.

August 5. Federals under Lieutenant Wintzer invaded Wyoming County. In a fight at the county seat he was defeated with a loss of 19 missing.

August 6. Rebels attacked Pack's Ferry, near the mouth of Blue Stone, and were driven off by Major Comly. The Confederates, 900 in number, were commanded by Colonel G. C. Wharton.

August 7. Rebel cavalry was defeated in a skirmish at Horse Pen Creek.

August 14. General John D. Imboden, with 300 Confederates, set out from Franklin, Pendleton County, on a raid to Rowlesburg to destroy the railroad bridge across Cheat River. His advance was discovered and he did not venture beyond St. George, in Tucker County, where he robbed the postoffice and set out on his retreat.

August 18. Skirmish near Corrick's Ford, in Tucker County, between Federal scouts and Confederates under Captain George Imboden.

August 22. The Confederate General, A. J. Jenkins, with 550 men, set out from Salt Sulphur Springs, in Monroe county, on an extensive raid. He passed through Greenbrier and Pocahontas Counties into Randolph, through Upshur, Lewis, Gilmer, Roane, Jackson, crossed the Ohio, and returned through the Kanawha Valley, marching 500 miles, capturing 300 prisoners and destroying the public records in many counties.

August 30. The Confederates under General Jenkins captured Buckhannon after the small Federal garrison fled. He secured and destroyed large quantities of military stores, including 5,000 stands of arms. He had intended to attack Beverly, but feared his force was too small. He crossed Rich Mountain to the head of the Buckhannon River, traveling 30 miles through an almost pathless forest and fell on Buckhannon by surprise.

August 31. Weston, in Lewis County, was captured by Confederates under General Jenkins.

September 1. General Jenkins captured Glenville, Gilmer County, the Federal garrison retreating after firing once.

September 2. Colonel J. C. Rathbone, with a Federal force stationed at Spencer, Roane County, surrendered to General Jenkins without a fight.

September 3. At Ripley, in Jackson County, General Jenkins captured $5,525 belonging to the United States Government. The Union soldiers stationed at the town retreated as the Confederates approached.

September 11. General W. W. Loring, with a strong force of Confederates, having invaded the Kanawha Valley, attacked the Federal troops under General J. A. J. Lightburn at Fayetteville and routed them. This was the beginning of an extensive Confederate raid which swept the Union troops out of the Kanawha Valley. Military stores to the value of a million dollars fell into the hands of the Rebels, who destroyed what they could not carry away.

September 13. General Lightburn, in his retreat down the Kanawha Valley, was overtaken at Charleston by General Loring and was compelled to abandon large stores in his flight to the Ohio.

CHRONOLOGY OF THE WAR.

September 15. General Loring, at Charleston, issued a proclamation to the people of the Kanawha Valley and neighboring parts of the State, informing them that the armies of the Confederacy had set them free from the danger and oppression of Federal bayonets, and he called on them to rise and maintain their freedom, and support the Government which had brought about their emancipation.

September 20. General Jenkins' forces, having re-crossed the Ohio River into the Kanawha Valley, skirmished with Federals at Point Pleasant.

September 27. Skirmish at Buffalo, twenty miles above Point Pleasant. Colonel John A. Turley attacked and defeated the Confederates, a portion of the force under Jenkins.

September 28. Skirmish at Standing Stone.

September 30. Fight at Glenville. Fifty Federals attacked and defeated 65 Confederate cavalry.

October 1. Fight near Shepherdstown between Federals under General Pleasanton and Confederates under Colonel W. H. F. Lee. Both sides claimed the victory.

October 2. Federals under Captain W. H. Boyd attacked and destroyed General Imboden's camp at Blue's Gap, in Hampshire County.

October 4. Confederates were captured at Blues' Gap.

October 4. General Imboden attacked and defeated the Federal Guard at Little Capon Bridge, in Morgan County and destroyed the bridge.

October 4. The Federal guard at Pawpaw, Morgan County, was captured by Imboden.

October 6. Skirmish at Big Birch.

October 16. General Loring was superseded by General John Echols as commander of Confederate forces in West Virginia.

October 20. Skirmish at Hedgeville.

October 29. Fight near Petersburg, Grant County, between Federals under Lieutenant Quirk and Rebel cattle raiders who were endeavoring to drive stock out of the South Branch Valley. The raiders were defeated, and lost 170 cattle.

October 31. Skirmish near Kanawha Falls.

November 9. St. George, Tucker County, was captured by Imboden together with the garrison of 31 Federals under Captain William Hall. Imboden had set out, November 9, from South Fork, in Pendleton county, to destroy the railroad bridge at Rowlesburg, but learning that troops from Beverly were moving in his rear, he retreated, passing up Glade Fork of Cheat River, through a dense and pathless wilderness. He reached South Fork November 14. He had 310 men, and carried howitzers on mules.

November 9. Skirmish on South Fork. General Kelley moved from Keyser and destroyed Imboden's camp, which he had left in charge of Lieutenant R. L. Doyle while Imboden was absent on his raid toward Rowlesburg.

November 9. Captain G. W. Gilmore with a Federal force invaded Greenbrier County, capturing a wagon train and 9 men. He returned November 11.

November 24. A force of 75 Federals under Captain Cogswell marched from Sharpsburg to Shepherdstown and captured Burke's guerrillas, killing Burke.

November 26, An expedition moved forward under W. H. Powell

CHRONOLOGY OF THE WAR. 155

from Summerville to Cold Knob, and with only 20 men defeated the Confederates at Sinking Creek and took 500 prisoners.

December 3. Confederates at Moorefield were defeated with loss of 12 by Lieut H. A. Myers with 100 men.

December 11. Lieutenant R. C. Pendergrast with 27 men defeated a detachment of Confederates at Darkesville, Berkeley County.

December 12. In a skirmish near Bunker Hill, Berkeley County, a squad of Federals captured 12 of Ashby's cavalry.

December 22. General Imboden attacked a supply train near Wardensville, Hardy County, capturing it. He lost six men. The Federals lost 20.

December 25. Sixty Confederates under Captain Boyle were defeated by Lieutenant Vermilyea, with 40 men, at Charlestown.

1863.

January 3. Fight near Moorefield. Federals under Colonel James Washburn were attacked by General William E. Jones. A second Union force, under Colonel James Mulligan, advanced from Petersburg, attacked the Confederates in the rear and defeated them.

January 3. Petersburg, Grant County, was occupied by Confederates after it was evacuated by the Federals, who burned military stores to the value of $20,000, which they could not move.

January 5. A supply train belonging to General Milroy's army was attacked and partly destroyed by Confederates under Captain John H. McNeill, four miles from Moorefield.

January 20. General Lee wrote to Imboden, outlining a policy of war for West Virginia and urged him to carry it out. Among other things, the municipal officers of the Re-organized Government of Virginia, called by Lee "the Pierpont government," were to be captured whenever possible; and Imboden was instructed to "render the position of sheriff as dangerous a position as possible."

January 22. Skirmish in Pocahontas County between Federals under Major H. C. Flesher and Confederates under Colonel Fontaine. Success was equally divided.

February 5. Scout by 70 Federals under Major John McMahan from Camp Piatt through Wyoming County. The men were out three days and nearly froze to death.

February 10. Captain C. T. Ewing left Beverly with a Union force of 135 for a two days' scout through Pocahontas County. He captured 13 prisoners, 15 horses and 135 cattle.

February 12. Skirmish near Smithfield, Jefferson County. A Union scouting party was attacked by Captain R. W. Baylor's cavalry, and lost six men, killed, wounded and captured. Federal reinforcements came up and retook the prisoners and captured Lieutenant George Baylor and several men.

February 12. Major John McMahan set out for a four days' scout from Camp Piatt through Boone, Logan and Wyoming Counties. He captured four prisoners.

February 16. Confederate guerrillas captured a wagon train and guard near Romney.

March 2. General John D. Imboden wrote General Lee, outlining his plan for invading West Virginia. The formidable raids under Imboden and Jones in April and May, 1863, were planned by Imboden, and the first mention of the plan to Lee seems to have been in the letter to that General on March 2. There was a three-fold object in view. First, it was designed to destroy as much of the Baltimore and Ohio Railroad as possible, and Imboden believed he could destroy nearly all of it. Second, he expected to enlist "several thousand" recruits in West Virginia. Third, he wanted to establish Confederate authority in as much of the northwest as possible and retain it long enough to enable the people to take part in the Virginia State election in May. No hint is found in the letter that the Confederates would be able to establish themselves permanently west of the Alleghanies. Except the partial destruction of the railroad and the carrying away of several thousand horses and cattle, the great raid was a failure so far as benefit to the Confederacy was concerned.

March 7. Skirmish at Green Spring Run, in Hampshire County.

March 28. Confederates were defeated at Hurricane Bridge, near the Kanawha, by Captain J. W. Johnson.

March 30. Skirmish at Point Pleasant. Captain Carter, with a Union force of 60 men, was attacked by Confederates and besieged several hours in the Court-House. The Rebels retreated when Federal reinforcements appeared upon the opposite bank of the Ohio.

April 5. Skirmish at Mud River. Captain Dove attacked and defeated Confederates under Captain P. M. Carpenter.

April 6. Lieutenant Speer, with five wagons and 11 men, was captured near Burlington, Mineral County, by Confederates under McNeill.

April 7. Federals under Captain Moore attacked the Confederates at Going's Ford, near Moorefield, defeated them and retook the wagons lost by Lieutenant Speer the day before.

April 11. Colonel G. R. Latham moved from Beverly toward Franklin, Pendleton County, and occupied the town without opposition. He returned to Beverly after an absence of seven days.

April 18. Fight in Harrison County. Colonel N. Wilkinson with a squad of Union troops captured Major Thomas D. Armstrong at Johnstown and scattered his forces on the head of Hacker's Creek.

April 20. Imboden set forward with 3000 men on his great raid. General W. E. Jones was sent through Hardy County to Oakland, Maryland, thence to move westward, destroying the railroad, while Imboden advanced through Randolph County toward Grafton, expecting to form a junction near that place with Jones, whence they would move west. The plan was generally carried out.

April 21. General Jones with 1300 men set forward on the great raid.

April 24. Beverly was captured by Imboden. Colonel Latham with 900 Federals retreated to Philippi, in Barbour County, over roads almost impassable for mud which in places was up to the saddle skirts. Imboden was unable to follow with artillery, but pursued with cavalry. General Roberts in command of the Union forces in the northwestern part of the State, called in all his outlying garrisons and retreated to Clarksburg. Colonel James Mulligan marched from Grafton with a Federal force and fought Imboden's troops in Barbour County, but hearing that General Jones was threatening Grafton, Mulligan fell back to defend that point. Imboden moved slowly toward Buckhannon over roads so bad that in one day he could advance only two miles.

April 25. Fight at Greenland Gap in Grant County. Captain Martin Wallace with less than 100 Federals held the pass five hours against the

Rebel army, and surrendered only when driven into a church and the building set on fire.

April 26. General Jones attacked and captured Cranberry Summit, now Terra Alta, in Preston County.

April 26. The Confederates attacked Rowlesburg for the purpose of destroying the railroad bridge and trestles. The town was defended by Major J. H. Showalter and 252 Union troops. General Jones did not lead the attack in person but remained at the bridge five miles above Rowlesburg where the Northwestern Pike crosses, for the purpose of burning the structure as soon as the town was taken. But his attacking parties were repulsed, and he abandoned the attack and marched to Evansville, in Preston County, not knowing that the Federal garrison of Rowlesburg was in full retreat toward Pennsylvania. Thus the town escaped capture, although defenseless; and the great trestles, for the destruction of which General Lee had planned so carefully, and the tunnel at Tunnelton, then the largest in the world, were saved; and the blow which would have paralyzed the Baltimore and Ohio Railroad for months, was not struck.

April 27. The suspension bridge across Cheat River at Albrightsville, three miles from Kingwood, was cut down by the Confederates. The cables were severed with an axe.

April 27. Bridges and trestles on the Baltimore and Ohio Railroad near Independence, Preston County, were burned by General Jones.

April 27. Morgantown, Monongalia County, was surrendered to General Jones by the citizens. Three citizens were shot near town by the Rebels.

April 28. The suspension bridge across the Monongahela river at Morgantown was set on fire by the Confederates, but they permitted the citizens to extinguish the fire before much damage was done.

April 29. The Confederates under Imboden advanced to and occupied Buckhannon, in Upshur County.

April 29. General Jones attacked and captured Fairmont, Marion County, after a sharp skirmish. He captured 260 prisoners.

April 29. The large iron railroad bridge across the Monongahela above Fairmont, which cost over $400,000, was blown down with powder. The first blast of three kegs of powder placed under a pier, failed to move it, and the Confederates proceeded to burn the wood-work, considering it impossible to destroy the iron superstructure. But after several hours of undermining, a charge of powder threw the bridge into the river.

April 29. Governor Pierpont's library at his home in Fairmont was burned by the Rebels.

April 29. Colonel Mulligan, who had been in Barbour County fighting Imboden, came up and attacked the Confederates under Jones, while they were destroying the bridge above Fairmont, and sharp fight ensued. Mulligan saw that he could not save the bridge, and fell back to Grafton.

April 30. Imboden lost 200 soldiers at Buckhannon by desertion, because he would not permit them to steal horses for their private benefit.

April 30. Skirmish at Bridgeport, Harrison County. General Jones captured 47 prisoners, burned a bridge and trestle, and run a freight train into the creek.

May 2. General Jones occupied Philippi, and from there sent across the Alleghanies, by way of Beverly, several thousand cattle and horses taken from the people. On the same day he formed a junction with Imboden's troops.

May 2. Lieutenant G. M. Edgar, with a detachment of Confederates, was attacked by Federals at Lewisburg, Greenbrier County. He defeated them.

May 4. General Jones invested Clarksburg, where several thousand Union troops had collected from the counties south of that place, but he did not make an attack.

May 5. Imboden skirmished with a small Union force at Janelew, Lewis County.

May 6. Imboden moved from Weston toward the southwest, Jones having moved west from Clarksburg toward Parkersburg. Up to that time Imboden had collected 3,100 cattle from the country through which he had raided.

May 6. Jones moved against West Union, in Doddridge county, but upon approaching the town he saw that the Union troops collected there were prepared to make a stand and fight, and he declined battle and moved on west.

May 7. Jones captured Cairo, Ritchie County, and the small garrison at that place.

May 8. Colonel James A. Galliher was fired upon by bushwhackers at Capon Bridge, Hampshire County.

May 9. Jones burned 100,000 barrels of oil at the oil wells in Wirt County. The tanks broke and the crude petroleum flowed into the Little Kanawha River, took fire and the spectacle of a river in flames for miles was never before seen. The destruction of everything combustible along the river was complete. The Confederates advanced no nearer the Ohio. Both Imboden and Jones turned southward and eastward and recrossed the Alleghanies late in May. Instead of procuring "several thousand" recruits, as Imboden had expected, more soldiers were lost by desertion than were gained by recruits. General Lee expressed disappointment with the result, and Imboden excused the failure to increase his army by saying that the inhabitants of West Virginia were a "conquered people," in fear of Northern bayonets, and not daring to espouse the Confederate cause.

May 12. Imboden defeated a small Union force near Summerville.

May 19. Fayetteville, in Fayette County, was attacked by General McCausland, but after bombarding two days the Federals forced him to retreat.

May 23. General B. S. Roberts was superseded by General William W. Averell in command of the Federal forces in the northern part of West Virginia. General Roberts was relieved because he offered so little opposition to the advance of Jones and Imboden. When Imboden crossed the mountains and took Beverly, the war department at Washington urged General Roberts to collect his forces and fight. To this General Roberts replied that the roads were so bad he could not move his troops. The answer from Washington was sarcastic, asking why the roads were too bad for him and yet good enough to enable the Rebels to move with considerable rapidity. From all accounts, the roads were worse than ever before or since. Imboden left Weston with twelve horses dragging each cannon, and then found it necessary to throw away ammunition and the extra wheels for the guns, in order to get along at all, and then sometimes being able to make no more than five miles a day. When General Averell took command he changed

3000 infantry to cavalry, and trained it to the highest proficiency, and with it did some of the finest fighting of the war. The Confederates feared him and moved in his vicinity with the greatest caution. His headquarters at first were at Weston.

June 7. General Lee ordered Imboden into Hampshire County to destroy railroad bridges, preliminary to the Gettysburg campaign.

June 10. General Averell urged that the mass of mountains forming the great rampart overlooking the Valley of Virginia should be fortified and held. He referred to the Alleghany, Cheat Mountain, Rich Mountain and others about the sources of the Greenbrier, Cheat, Tygart and Elk Rivers. In his letter to General Schenck he said: "It has always appeared to me that the importance of holding this mass of mountains, so full of fastnesses, and making a vast re-entrant angle in front of the enemy, has never been appreciated."

June 14. A portion of General Milroy's forces were captured by Confederates at Bunker Hill, near Martinsburg.

June 14. Martinsburg was captured by Confederates under General A. G. Jenkins. General Daniel Tyler, who had occupied the town, retreated.

June 16. Romney was captured by Imboden.

June 17. South Branch Bridge, at the mouth of South Branch, was burned by Imboden, who advanced through Hampshire County, forming the extreme left of General Lee's army in the Gettysburg campaign.

June 24. A Union scouting party from Grafton to St. George had a skirmish with guerrillas, killing five and capturing several horses.

June 26. Skirmish at Long Creek, in the Kanawha Valley. Captain C. E. Hambleton, with 75 men, was attacked and defeated by Confederates under Major R. A. Bailey, with a loss of 29 prisoners and 45 horses.

June 29. General William L. Jackson, with 1,200 Confederates, moved against Beverly to attack the forces under Averell.

July 2. The Confederates under Jackson attacked the troops at Beverly and were repulsed.

July 4. The Confederates under W. L. Jackson, who had fallen back from Beverly, were attacked and routed at Huttonsville by General Averell.

July 13. An expedition set out from Fayetteville, crossed into Virginia and cut the railroad at Wythville, being absent twelve days, skirmishing with small parties of Confederates.

July 14. Skirmish on the road between Harper's Ferry and Charlestown, resulting in the defeat of the Confederates.

July 14. Confederates defeated in a skirmish at Falling Waters.

July 15. Colonel C. H. Smith defeated Confederates near Charlestown.

July 17. Skirmish at North Mountain, Berkeley County. The Rebels were defeated, with 17 captured.

July 19. Fight near Martinsburg, in which General Bradley T. Johnson was defeated by General Averell, who had just arrived from Beverly and was opposing the western wing of General Lee's army retreating from Gettysburg. Johnson was destroying the railroad when Averell drove him away, capturing 20 prisoners.

August 5. General Averell moved from Winchester through Hardy County on his expedition to Greenbrier County.

August 5. Skirmish at Cold Spring Gap, in Hardy County, by a portion of Averell's force under Captain Von Koenig, and a detachment of Imboden's command. The Confederates lost 11 men captured.

August 6. Averell sent a squad of cavalry to Harper's Mill, from Lost River, Hardy County. Several prisoners were taken, but the Federals subsequently fell into an ambuscade and lost the prisoners and had 13 men captured and 4 wounded. The Confederates had 3 killed and 5 wounded.

August 19. The Federals destroyed the saltpeter works near Franklin.

August 21. Wilkinson's Brigade skirmished with Confederate guerrillas near Glenville, killing 4.

August 22. Confederates were defeated by Averell near Huntersville.

August 25 Averell crossed from Huntersville to Jackson River and destroyed saltpeter works.

August 26. Battle of Rocky Gap, in Greenbrier County. Averell with 1300 men fought General Sam Jones with over 2000. The battle continued two days, when Averell's ammunition ran short and he retreated to Beverly. His loss in the battle was 218, the Confederate loss 162. This was one of the most hotly contested battles in West Virginia. Captain Von Koenig was killed. It has been said it was done by one of his men whom he had struck while on the march. It is also said that this soldier did not know Averell by sight, and supposed it was Averell who had struck him, and when he shot Von Koenig, supposed he was shooting Averell.

August 26. Lieutenant Dils with 40 Federals killed 3 bushwhackers ten miles from Sutton, Braxton County.

August 26. Union troops were fired upon by bushwackers on Elk River, five miles below Sutton.

August 27. Forty guerrillas under Cunningham attacked a Federal detachment under Captain C. J. Harrison, on Elk River, near Sutton. The guerrillas were defeated.

August 27. In a skirmish with Confederate guerrillas on Cedar Creek, fifteen miles from Glenville, Gilmer County, Captain Simpson defeated them, killing 4.

September 4. Skirmish at Petersburg Gap, in Grant County. A Union detachment marching from Petersburg to Moorefield was defeated.

September 11. Confederates under McNeill made a daybreak attack upon Major W. E. Stephens near Moorefield and defeated him, killing or wounding 30 men and taking 138 prisoners. The Federals were endeavoring to surprise McNeill, but were surprised by him. The Rebels had 3 wounded.

September 15. One hundred Federals under Captain Jones attacked 70 Confederates at Smithfield, capturing 11. Captain Jones was wounded.

September 20. A Federal picket on the Senaca Road, where it crosses Shaver Mountain, was attacked and defeated by the Confederates who lost 4.

September 24. A scouting party of 70 sent from Beverly by Averell lost 2 men in a skirmish at Greenbrier Bridge.

September 25. Sixty Confederates under Major D. B. Lang of Imboden's command, surprised and captured 30 of Averell's men at the crossing of Cheat River by the Senaca trail.

October 2. A petition was signed and forwarded to the Confederate Government, asking for the removal of General Sam Jones from the command in Western Virginia, and the assignment of some other General in his place. Among the signers were members of the Virginia Legislature from

CHRONOLOGY OF THE WAR. 161

the West Virginia counties of Mercer, Roane, Putnam, Logan, Boone and Wyoming. There were many other signatures. Those counties were represented in the Virginia and the West Virginia Legislature at the same time. The petition charged incompetency against General Jones. He was soon after relieved of command in West Virginia.

October 7. Confederates under Harry Gilmor defeated Captain G. D. Summers and 40 men at Summit Point, Jefferson County. Captain Summers was killed.

October 13. Fight at Bulltown, Braxton County. Confederates under W. L. Jackson were defeated with a loss in killed and wounded of 50 by Captain W. H. Mattingly, who was severely wounded in the action.

October 14. When Jackson retreated from Bulltown he was pursued by Averell's troops, who came up with him and defeated him at Salt Lick Bridge.

October 15. Twenty-seven of Harry Gilmor's men who had been sent to burn the Back Creek Bridge, were captured in a skirmish near Hedgeville by Federals under Colonel Pierce.

October 18. Attack on Charlestown by 1200 men under Imboden. The Confederates captured 434 of Colonel Simpson's command and then retreated, hotly pursued. Some of Imboden's infantry marched 48 miles on the day of the fight, thus beating the record made by Napoleon's soldiers, who marched 36 miles and fought a battle in one day.

November 1. General Averell moved from Beverly into Pocahontas County with about 2,500 men, and General Duffie moved from Charleston to co-operate with him. They expected to form a junction in Greenbrier County.

November 3. Skirmish at Cackleytown, Pocahontas County. Confederates were defeated by Averell.

November 5. Confederates were defeated by Averell at Hillsboro, Pocahontas County, and at Mill Point.

November 6. Battle of Droop Mountain, Pocahontas County. Averell attacked General Echols, who had 1700 men strongly posted on the summit of a mountain. It was a stubborn contest and the Federals gained the day by a flank movement, Echols retreating with a loss of 275 men and three cannon. Averell's loss was 119. The Confederates made their escape through Lewisburg a few hours before General Duffie's army arrived at that place to cut them off, while Averell was pursuing. By blockading the road, Echols secured his retreat into Monroe County. Averell attempted pursuit, but received no support from Duffie's troops, who were worn out, and the pursuit was abandoned.

November 6. Confederates at Little Sewell Mountain were defeated by General Duffie.

November 7. Lewisburg was occupied by General Duffie.

November 7. In a night skirmish at Muddy Creek the Confederates were defeated by General Duffie's troops.

November 8. A squad of Confederates driving cattle was attacked on Second Creek, on the road to Union, in Monroe County, and lost 110 cattle.

November 12. The Saltpeter Works in Pendleton County, used by the Confederates in making gunpowder, were destroyed by Averell's troops.

November 15. General Imboden sent Captain Hill into Barbour County to waylay wagon trains on the road from Philippi to Beverly.

November 16. At Burlington, in Mineral County, 100 Confederates under McNeill captured a train of 80 wagons and 200 horses, killing two men, wounding 10 and taking 20 prisoners. The wagon train was under an escort of 90 men, commanded by Captain Jeffers.

December 8. Averell moved from Keyser with Federal troops upon his great Salem raid, which he concluded on Christmas Day. He had 2500 cavalry, and artillery. It was a momentous issue. General Burnsides was besieged at Knoxville, Tennessee, by General Longstreet, and it was feared that no re-inforcements could reach Burnsides in time to save him. The only hope lay in cutting Longstreet's line of supplies and compelling him to raise the siege. This was the railroad from Richmond to Knoxville, passing through Salem, sixty miles west Lynchburg. Averell was ordered to cut this road at Salem, no matter what the result to his army. He must do it, even if he lost every man he had in the execution of his work. An army of 2500 could be sacrificed to save Burnsides' larger army. With his veteran cavalry, mostly West Virginians, and equal to the best the world ever saw, Averell left Keyser December 8, 1863, and moved through Petersburg, Monterey, Back Creek, Gatewood's, Callighan's, Sweet Sulphur Springs Valley, Newcastle to Salem, almost as straight as an arrow, for much of the way following a route nearly parallel with the summit of the Alleghanies. Four Confederate armies, any of them larger than his, lay between him and Salem, and to the number of 12,000 they marched, counter-marched. and maneuvered to effect his capture. Still, eight days he rode toward Salem in terrible storms, fording and swimming overflowing mountain streams, crossing mountains and pursuing ravines by night and by day, and on December 16 he struck Salem, and the blow was felt throughout the Southern Confederacy. The last halt on the downward march was made at Sweet Sulphur Valley. The horses were fed and the soldiers made coffee and rested two hours. Then at 1 o'clock on the afternoon of December 15, they mounted for the dash into Salem.

From the top of Sweet Springs Mountain a splendid view was opened before them. Averell, in his official report, speaks of it thus: "Seventy miles to the eastward the Peaks of Otter reared their summits above the Blue Ridge, and all the space between was filled with a billowing ocean of hills and mountains, while behind us the great Alleghanies, coming from north with the grandeur of innumerable tints, swept past and faded in the southern horizon." Newcastle was passed during the night. Averell's advance guard were mounted on fleet horses and carried repeating rifles. They allowed no one to go ahead of them. They captured a squad of Confederates now and then, and learned from these that Averell's advance was as yet unsuspected in that quarter. It was, however, known at that time at Lynchburg and Richmond, but it was not known at what point he was striking. Valuable military stores were at Salem, and at that very time a train-load of soldiers was hurrying up from Lynchburg to guard the place. When within four miles of Salem a troop of Confederates were captured. They had come out to see if they could learn anything of Averell, and from them it was ascertained that the soldiers from Lynchburg were hourly expected at Salem. This was 9 o'clock on the morning of December 16. Averell's men had ridden twenty hours without rest. Averell saw that no time was to be lost. From this point it became a race between Averell's cavalry and the Lynchburg train loaded with Confederates, each trying to reach Salem first. The whistling of the engine in the distance was heard, and Averell saw that he would be too late if he advanced with his whole force.

So he set forward with three hundred and fifty horsemen and two rifled cannon, and went into Salem on a dead run, people on the road and streets parting right and left to let the squadron pass. The train loaded with Confederates was approaching the depot. Averell wheeled a cannon into position and fired three times in rapid succession, the first ball missing, but the next passing through the train almost from end to end, and the third following close after. The locomotive was uninjured, and it reversed and backed up the road in a hurry, disappearing in the direction whence it had come. Averell cut the telegraph wires. The work of destroying the railroad was begun. When the remainder of the force came up, detachments were sent four miles east and twelve miles west to destroy the railroad and bridges. The destruction was complete. They burned 100,000 bushels of shelled corn; 10,000 bushels of wheat; 2,000 barrels of flour; 50,000 bushels of oats; 1,000 sacks of salt; 100 wagons; large quantities of clothing, leather, cotton, harness, shoes; and the bridges, bridge-timber, trestles, ties, and everything that would burn, even twisting the rails, up and down the railroad sixteen miles.

At 4 p. m., December 16, Averell set out upon his return. Confederate troops were hurrying from all sides to cut him off. Generals Fitzhugh Lee, Jubal A. Early, John McCausland, John Echols and W. H. Jackson each had an army, and they occupied every road, as they supposed, by which Averell could escape. Rain fell in torrents. Streams overflowed their banks and deluged the country. The cavalry swam, and the cannon and caissons were hauled across by ropes where horses could not ford. The Federals fought their way to James River, crossed it on bridges which they burned in the face of the Confederates, and crossed the Alleghanies into Pocahontas County by a road almost unknown. More than 100 men were lost by capture and drowning at James River. The rains had changed to snow, and the cold was so intense that cattle froze to death in the fields. Such a storm had seldom or never been seen in the Alleghanies. The soldiers' feet froze till they could not wear boots. They wrapped their feet in sacks, Averell among the rest. For sixty miles they followed a road which was one unbroken sheet of ice. Horses fell and crippled themselves or broke the riders' legs. The artillery horses could not pull the cannon, and the soldiers did that work, 100 men dragging each gun up the mountains. Going down the mountains a tree was dragged behind each cannon to hold it in the road. The Confederates were hard in pursuit, and there was fighting nearly all the way through Pocahontas County, and at Edray a severe skirmish was fought. Beverly was reached December 24, and thence the army marched to Webster, in Taylor County, and was carried by train to Martinsburg. Averell lost 119 men on the expedition, one ambulance and a few wagons, but no artillery.

December 11. Confederates under Captain William Thurmond attacked General Scammon at Big Sewell and were repulsed. General Scammon was marching to attract the attention of the Confederate General Echols, and thereby assist Averell on his Salem raid.

December 11. Confederates under General W. L. Jackson were defeated at Marlin Bottom, Pocahontas County, by Colonel Augustus Moor, who marched into that country to assist Averell, by attracting the attention of the Rebels.

December 12. Lewisburg was taken by General Scammon, General Echols retreating.

December 12. Troops sent by General Scammon drove Confederates across the Greenbrier River.

December 13. Skirmish at Hurricane Bridge. Confederates attacked a small force of Federals under Captain Young. Both sides retreated.

December 14. Skirmish on the Blue Sulphur Road, near Meadow Bluff. Lieutenant H. G. Otis, with 29 men was attacked by Rebel guerrillas under William Thurmond. The guerrillas fled, having killed 2 and wounded 4 Union soldiers, while their own loss was 2.

1864.

January 2. Confederates under General Fitzhugh Lee invaded the South Branch Valley. This raid, following so soon after Averell's Salem raid, was meant as a retaliation for the destruction at Salem. The weather was so cold and the Shenandoah Mountains so icy that Lee could not cross with artillery, and he abandoned his guns and moved forward with his troops.

January 3. Petersburg, Grant County, besieged by Fitzhugh Lee.

January 3. An empty train of 40 wagons, returning from Petersburg to Keyser, was captured by Confederates.

January 6. Romney was occupied by Fitzhugh Lee.

January 6. Springfield, in Hampshire County, was captured by Confederates under McNeill and Gilmor.

January 30. General Rosser, with a strong Confederate force, captured a train of 93 wagons, 300 mules and 20 prisoners, at Medley, Mineral County. Among the prisoners taken was Judge Nathan Goff, of West Virginia, whose horse fell on him and held him. He was then twenty years old. The wagon train was in charge of Colonel Joseph Snyder.

January 31. Petersburg, Grant County, was evacuated by Federals under Colonel Thoburn upon the advance of an army under General Early. Colonel Thoburn retreated to Keyser by way of Greenland Gap.

February 1. General Early advanced and attacked the fort near Petersburg, not knowing that Colonel Thoburn had retreated and that the fort was empty.

February 2. General Rosser destroyed the railroad bridges across the North Branch and Patterson Creek, in Mineral county.

February 3. Forty Rebels under Major J. H. Nounnan attacked and captured the steamer Levi on the Kanawha, at Red House. General Scammon was on board and was taken prisoner.

February 11. Confederates under Gilmor threw a Baltimore and Ohio passenger train from the track near Kearneysville, and robbed the passengers.

February 20. Twenty Federals under Lieutenant Henry A. Wolf were attacked near Hurricane Bridge. Lieutenant Wolf was killed.

February 25. General John C. Breckenridge was assigned to the command of the Confederate forces in West Virginia, relieving General Sam Jones. General Breckenridge assumed command March 5.

March 3. Colonel A. I. Root marched from Petersburg and destroyed the Saltpeter Works operated by Confederates in Pendleton County.

March 3. Skirmish in Grant County. Lieutenant Denney with 27 Federals was attacked and defeated near Petersburg with a loss of 7 men and 13 horses.

CHRONOLOGY OF THE WAR. 165

March 10. Major Sullivan was killed by Mosby's guerrillas in a skirmish at Kabletown.

March 19. Eight men, of Imboden's command, who had been in Barbour County attempting to waylay a wagon train, crossed into Tucker County and robbed David Wheeler's Store, three miles from St. George.

March 20. Skirmish at the Sinks of Gandy in Randolph County. The Rebels who had robbed Wheeler's store were pursued by Lieutenant Valentine J. Gallion and Captain Nathaniel J. Lambert and defeated, with 3 killed, 2 captured, and the stolen property was recovered.

April 19. Confederates were attacked and defeated at Marlin Bottom, Pocahontas County.

May 2. An expedition moved from the Kanawha Valley under Generals Crook and Averell against the Virginia and Tennessee Railroad. This is known as the Dublin Raid, so called from the village of that name in Pulaski County. The cavalry was under the command of General Averell, while General George Crook was in command of all the forces. On May 9 occurred a desperate battle on Cloyd Mountain, near the boundary between Giles and Pulaski Counties, Virginia. General Crook commanded the Union forces, and the Confederates were under General Albert G. Jenkins. For a long time the issue of the battle was doubtful; but at length General Jenkins fell, and his army gave way. He was mortally wounded, and died soon after. His arm had been amputated at the shoulder by a Federal surgeon. In the meantime General Averell, with a force of cavalry, 2000 strong, advanced by wretched roads and miserable paths through Wyoming County, West Virginia, into Virginia, hoping to strike at Saltville or Wytheville before the Confederates could concentrate for defense. When the troops entered Tazewell County they had numerous skirmishes with small parties of Confederates. When Tazewell Court House was reached it was learned that between 4000 and 5000 Confederates, commanded by Generals W. E. Jones and John H. Morgan, had concentrated at Saltville, having learned of Averell's advance. The defences north of that town were so strongly fortified that the Union troops could not attack with hope of success. Averell turned, and made a rapid march toward Wytheville, to prevent the Confederates from marching to attack General Crook. Arriving near Wytheville on May 10, he met Jones and Morgan, with 5000 men, marching to attack General Crook. Averell made an attack on them, or they on him, as both sides appeared to begin the battle about the same time. Although out-numbered and out-flanked, the Union forces held their ground four hours, at which time the vigor of the Confederate fighting began to slack. After dark the Confederates withdrew. The Union loss was 114 in killed and wounded. Averell made a dash for Dublin, and the Confederates followed as fast as possible. The bridge across New River, and other bridges, were destroyed, and the railroad was torn up. Soon after crossing New River on the morning of May 12, the Confederates arrived on the opposite bank, but they could not cross the stream. They had been unable to prevent the destruction of the railroad property, although their forces out-numbered Averell's. The Union cavalry rejoined General Crook, and the army returned to the Kanawha Valley by way of Monroe County.

May 3. Bulltown, Braxton County, was captured and the barracks burned by Confederates under Captains Spriggs and Chewings.

May 4. Captain McNeill with 61 Confederate cavalry captured Piedmont, in Mineral County, and burned two trains, machine shops, and captured 104 prisoners.

May 6. Lieutenant Blazer's scouts attacked and defeated a troop of Confederates near Princeton, Mercer County.

May 8. Fifty Confederates attacked a Federal post at Halltown, Jefferson County, and were defeated.

May 9. Skirmish on the summit of Cheat Mountain between a scouting party from Beverly and 100 Rebels.

May 10. The Ringgold Cavalry was attacked and defeated at Lost River Gap, Hardy County, by Imboden. The Federals were hunting for McNeill's men, and Imboden had hurriedly crossed from the Valley of Virginia to assist McNeill to escape.

May 11. Romney was occupied by General Imboden.

May 15. A scouting party moved from Beverly under Colonel Harris against Confederate guerrillas in Pocahontas, Webster and Braxton Counties, capturing 36 prisoners, 85 horses, 40 cattle, and returning to Beverly May 30.

May 19. General David Hunter was appointed to the command of Federal forces in West Virginia. He assumed command May 21.

May 24. In a skirmish near Charlestown the Confederates under Mosby were defeated.

June 6. Skirmish at Panther Gap. Rebels were defeated by Colonel D. Frost.

June 6. Fight near Moorefield. Eighty Federals under Captain Hart were attacked and lost four killed and six wounded, but defeated the Confederates.

June 10. Colonel Thompson was defeated near Kabletown by Major Gilmor.

June 19. Captain Boggs, with 30 West Virginia State troops from Pendleton County, known as Swamp Dragons, was attacked near Petersburg by Lieutenant Dolen, with a portion of McNeill's company. The Confederates were at first successful, but finally were defeated, and Lieutenant Dolen was killed.

June 26. Captain McNeill, with 60 Confederates, attacked Captain Law and 100 men at Springfield, Hampshire County. The Federals were defeated, losing 60 prisoners and 100 horses.

June 28. A detachment of Federals was defeated at Sweet Sulphur Springs by Thurmond's guerrillas.

July 3. Skirmish at Leetown. Confederates under General Ransom attacked and defeated Colonel Mulligan after a severe fight. A large Confederate army under General Early was invading West Virginia and Maryland, penetrating as far as Chambersburg, Pennsylvania.

July 3. Confederates under Gilmor attacked Union troops at Darkesville, Berkeley County, and were defeated.

July 3. General Early captured Martinsburg.

July 3. Skirmish at North River Mills, Hampshire County.

July 4. General Imboden attacked an armored car and a blockhouse at the South Branch Bridge, in Hampshire County. He blew the car up with a shell, and attempted to destroy the bridge, but the blockhouse could not be taken, and he retreated.

July 4 Rebels under Captain McNeill burned the railroad bridge across Patterson Creek, Mineral County.

CHRONOLOGY OF THE WAR. 167

July 4. An attack on the North Branch Bridge, in Mineral County, was repulsed by the Federals.

July 4. Harper's Ferry was invested by Confederates. They besiged the place four days, but the heavy guns on the heights drove them back and shelled them to the distance of four miles. General Franz Sigel was in command at Harper's Ferry.

July 6. General Imboden attacked Sir John's Run, Morgan County, and burned the railroad station-house, but was driven off by iron-clad cars.

July 6. Big Capon Bridge, Morgan County, was attacked by Imboden. He was driven off by iron-clad cars.

July 14. Romney was occupied by McNeill.

July 23. Romney was taken by McNeill and Captain Harness.

July 25. Federals under General George Crook were defeated at Bunker Hill, Berkeley County.

July 25. Fight at Martinsburg. The Confederates in strong force fought General Duffie all day.

July 30. Confederates under General W. L. Jackson were defeated near Shepherdstown.

August 2. The Confederates under General Bradley T. Johnson captured Green Spring, Hampshire County, Colonel Stough being in command of the Federals. The Rebels had advanced toward Cumberland, and made an attack on the Federal defenders, but did not push the attack. These Confederates were returning from their plundering raid in Pennsylvania.

August 2. Confederates under McNeill destroyed three railroad culverts between Keyser and Cumberland.

August 2. The suspension bridge across the South Branch of the Potomac near Springfield was cut down by order of General Early.

August 4. Confederates under Generals Bradley T. Johnson and John McCausland attacked Keyser and were repulsed.

August 7. General Averell overtook and routed the forces of McCausland and Johnson, near Moorefield. These Confederates had burned Chambersburg, Pennsylvania, because the people would not pay $400,000 ransom. Averell entered Chambersburg within two hours after the Confederates left, and he pursued them through Maryland into West Virginia, and came upon them at daybreak near Moorefield and surprised them, captured all their artillery, 420 prisoners, 400 horses, retook the plunder carried from Pennsylvania, and drove the disorganized forces ten miles into the mountains. The Rebels believed that no quarters would be given them because they had burned Chambersburg.

August 21. Skirmish at Summit Point between a detachment of Confederates and the New York Dragoons.

August 21. General Sheridan was defeated at Welch's Spring with a loss of 275.

August 22. Confederates at Charlestown were defeated by Colonel Charles R. Lowell.

August 22. General Sheridan's troops defeated the Confederates at Halltown.

August 29. The Confederates were defeated four miles from Charlestown. This fighting, and that which followed and preceded it in the same vicinity, was between the armies of General Sheridan and General Early.

September 1. Martinsburg was captured by General Early's troops. Averell retreating.

September 2. Confederate cavalry under Vaughn was defeated by Averell at Bunker Hill.

September 3. Federals under General Crook defeated General Kershaw near Berryville, killing and wounding 200.

September 3. Averell defeated McCausland at Bunker Hill.

September 4. Cavalry fight near Berryville between Mosby's and Blazer's men, in which Mosby lost 19 men, killed and captured.

September 14. Skirmish near Centerville, Upshur County, between Federals under Captain H. H. Hagans and 30 horse thieves.

September 17. Confederates under Colonel V. A. Witcher, to the number of 523, among them Captain Philip J. and Captain William D. Thurmond's guerrillas, moved from Tazewell County, Virginia, upon a raid into West Virginia, returning September 28 with 400 horses, 200 cattle, and having lost only one man.

September 18. General Early's troops recaptured Martinsburg.

September 23. Confederates under Major James H. Nounnan moved from Tazewell County upon a raid into the Kanawha Valley. They returned to Tazewell October 1.

September 26. Colonel Witcher captured Weston and robbed the Exchange Bank of $5,287.85; also captured a number of Home Guards.

September 26. Captain William H. Payne, of Witcher's command, occupied Janelew, Lewis County.

September 27. Witcher defeated Federal cavalry at Buckhannon and captured the town.

September 28. The Rebels having moved up the river from Buckhannon, and Federals, under Major T. F. Lang, having occupied the town, Colonel Witcher made a dash and recaptured the place and took Major Lang and 100 men prisoner, and destroyed a large quantity of military stores.

September 30. Skirmish at the mouth of Coal River. Rebels under Major Nounnan were defeated.

October 11. Skirmish two miles south of Petersburg between 198 Home Guards under Captain Boggs and Rebels under Harness.

October 26. Colonel Witcher attacked the town of Winfield and was defeated. Captain P. J. Thurmond was mortally wounded, taken prisoner, and soon after died.

October 29. Major Hall, with 350 Rebels, attacked Beverly and was repulsed with a loss of 140, Hall being mortally wounded and taken prisoner. The Federals, 200 in number, were in command of Colonel Youart. He lost 46. The Confederate attacking force was made up of men from 21 regiments.

November 1. Green Spring, Hampshire County, was captured by Confederates under Captain McNeill; about 30 Federals were taken prisoner.

November 5. Colonel V. A. Witcher captured and burned the steamers Barnum and Fawn at Buffalo Shoals, Big Sandy River.

November 7. Colonel George R. Latham, with 225 Federals, defeated McNeill at Moorefield, taking 8 prisoners.

November 27. Colonel R. E. Fleming with a small force attacked 2,000 Confederates under Rosser at Moorefield, and was defeated, with a loss of 20 men and one cannon.

November 28. Major Potts, with 155 men, was defeated by Confederates of Rosser's command at Moorefield.

November 28. General Rosser surprised Keyser, capturing or dispers-

CHRONOLOGY OF THE WAR. 169

ing the Federal garrison of 800, and taking several cannon, burning government and railroad property, and carrying away hundreds of horses.

November 28. Confederates under Major McDonald were defeated at Piedmont by 27 men under Captain Fisher.

1865.

January 11. General Rosser captured Beverly. The Federals were in command of Colonel R. Youart. They lost 6 killed, 23 wounded and 580 prisoners.

January 11. A Federal scouting party, under Major E. S. Troxel, moved from Keyser, passing through Pendleton County.

January 15. Skirmish at Petersburg. Major Troxel defeated McNeill.

January 19. Rebel guerrillas wrecked a train on the Baltimore and Ohio Railroad near Duffield.

February 4. Train thrown from track and robbed by Confederates near Harper's Ferry.

February 5. Major H. W. Gilmor was captured by Federals under Colonel Young, near Moorefield.

February 21. Generals Crook and Kelley were captured at Cumberland by 61 Confederates under Lieutenant Jesse McNeill, son of Captain J. H. McNeill. There were 3500 Union troops in Cumberland at the time.

February 26. General Winfield S. Hancock was assigned to the command of the Federal forces in West Virginia.

March 15. Rebel guerrilas were defeated on the South Fork, above Moorefield, by Captain McNulty.

March 22. Lieutenant Martin defeated Confederates of McNeill's command on Patterson Creek, in Mineral County, killing 2, wounding 3.

March 30. A railroad train was derailed and robbed near Patterson Creek Bridge, in Mineral County, by McNeill's command.

April 2. General W. H. Emory was assigned to the command of Union forces in West Virginia.

April 6. Confederates under Mosby captured Loudoun County Rangers near Charlestown.

April 10. General Emory proposed to Governor Boreman that the West Virginia civil authorities resume their functions, re-open the courts and dispense justice, inasmuch as "no large bodies of armed Rebels are in the State."

April 12. Lieutenant S. H. Draper raided a Rebel rendezvous on Timber Ridge, Hampshire County.

April 15. Captain Joseph Badger moved from Philippi with a scouting party, passing through Randolph and Pocahontas Counties, returning to Philippi April 23.

May 8. McNeill's company surrendered at Romney.

June 1. Colonel Wesley Owens left Clarksburg with 400 men and made a twelve days expedition through Pocahontas and Pendleton Counties, hunting for Governor William Smith, of Virginia, who had not surrendered. He was also collecting Government property, mostly horses, scattered through those counties. No trace was found of the fugitive governor. The country was exhausted and desolated. Only two families were found in Huntersville, Pocahontas County. The paroled Confederate soldiers were coming home and were trying to plant corn with but little to work with. By the terms of surrender granted Lee by Grant, the Confederate soldiers who had horses or mules were permitted to keep them. Old cavalry horses and artillery mules were harnessed to plows, and peace again reigned in the mountains of West Virginia.

West Virginia furnished 36,530 soldiers for the Union, and about 7000 for the Confederate armies. In addition to these there were 32 companies of troops in the state service, some counties having one company, some two. Their duty was to scout, and to protect the people against guerrillas. The majority of them were organized in 1863 and 1864. These companies with their captains were as follows:

Captain	M. T. Haller	Barbour County.
"	A. Alltop	Marion County.
"	H. S. Sayre	Doddridge County.
"	J. C. Wilkinson	Lewis County.
"	George C. Kennedy	Jackson County.
"	John Johnson	" "
"	William Logsdon	Wood County.
"	William Ellison	Calhoun County.
"	Alexander Donaldson	Roane County.
"	Hiram Chapman	" "
"	H. S. Burns	Wirt County.
"	John Boggs	Pendleton County.
"	M. Mallow	" "
"	John Ball	Putnam County.
"	J. L. Kesling	Upshur County.
"	William R. Spaulding	Wayne County.
"	M. M. Pierce	Preston County.
"	William Gandee	Roane County.
"	Nathaniel J. Lambert	Tucker County.
"	James A. Ramsey	Nicholas County.
"	John S. Bond	Hardy County.
"	William Bartrum	Wayne County.
"	Ira G. Copeley	" "
"	William Turner	Raleigh County.
"	Sanders Mullins	Wyoming County.
"	Robert Brooks	Kanawha County.
"	B. L. Stephenson	Clay County.
"	G. F. Taylor	Braxton County.
"	W. T. Wiant	Gilmer County.
"	Isaac Brown	Nicholas County.
"	Benjamin R. Haley	Wayne County.
"	Sampson, Snyder	Randolph County.

PART SECOND.
County History.

MAP OF AUGUSTA COUNTY.

RESIDENCE OF MELVILLE PECK.

CHAPTER XVIII.

―:o:―

SETTLEMENTS AND INDIAN TROUBLES.

The territory embraced in what is now Barbour County did not become the home of white men until settlements had been planted in all the bordering territory. The present counties of Randolph, Upshur, Lewis, Harrison, Taylor, Preston and Tucker were colonized before Barbour. It is, therefore, proper to speak briefly of the advent of the pioneers into the surrounding country before the earliest history of this county is taken up; otherwise the settlement of Barbour could not be presented as it should. Randolph was the scene of the earliest colonization. The first white men's homes on the waters of the Monogahela were in Tygart's Valley in 1753, and they built their cabins, one on the site of Beverly and the other two miles above, the latter named David Tygart from whom the river was named, and the former, Robert Files (or Foyle) from whom Files Creek received its name. Nearly thirty years elapsed after settlements were planted on the upper waters of

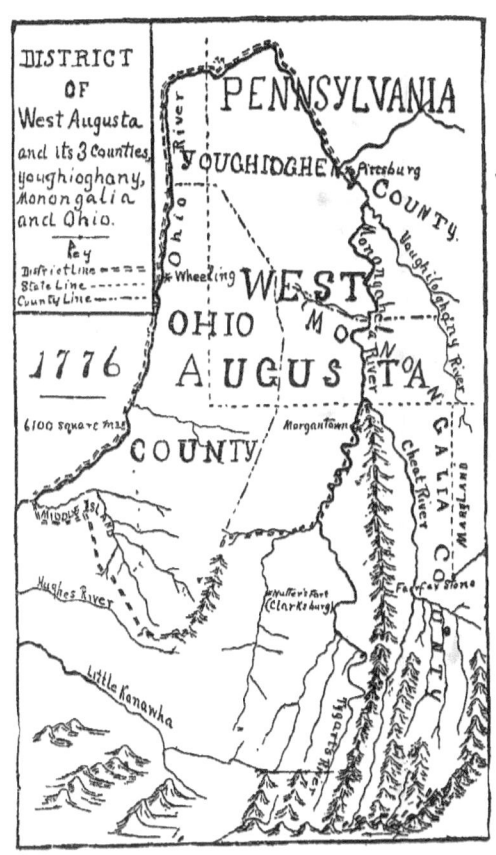

DISTRICT OF WEST AGUSTA 1776.

the Potomac before the tide of emigration crossed the Alleghanies and took possession of the valleys of the West. That range of mountains was for a third of a century a barrier which the white man did not cross. The country beyond the mountains, was called "the waters of the Mississippi," because the streams having their sources on the western slope flowed into the Mississippi, while those rising eastward of the summit found their way into the Atlantic Ocean. It was usual from about 1760 to 1780 for the Virginia records to distinguish between the eastern and the western country by designating the former "Hampshire County," and the latter "the waters of the Mississippi," because Hampshire included the most important settlements between the Valley of Virginia and the summit of the Alleghanies, and did not include any territory on the western side except about eighty square miles in the present county of Tucker. The country beyond the mountains gradually became known from reports of hunters and others who crossed from very early times. It is proper that mention should be made of the routes and trails by which the explorers and settlers found their way over the Alleghanies into the valleys of the Monongahela and its tributaries. The subject has been much neglected by writers who have pretended to cover the field, they having given their attention to the great highway west from Cumberland to Pittsburg, losing sight of other paths of great importance. Before proceeding to a consideration of some of them, a due regard for the cause of history requires that a brief account of the highway west from Cumberland be given, by which settlers to the lower Monongahela found their way.

About 1750, the Ohio Company, a wealthy corporation engaged in trading with Indians and dealing in western land, employed Colonel Thomas Cresap, who lived fifteen miles east of Cumberland, to survey a path by which traders could carry their merchandise to the Ohio River. Cumberland was then called Will's Creek, and the company had a store and fort there. Colonel Cresap offered a prize to the Indian who would mark out the best route from Cumberland to the site of Pittsburg. An Indian named Nemacolin received the prize. Part of the way the path followed a buffalo trail by which those animals had crossed the mountains for ages. Traders with pack horses traveled that path from that time, by the hundreds, although they had a path to the Ohio before that. Two years before (in 1748) three hundred traders reached the Ohio, some by way of the Kanawha, some by Cumberland and some by other routes. In 1754 George Washington widened the Nemacolin trail and took wagons over it as far as the Youghiogheny. This was the first wagon road over the Alleghanies into the Mississippi basin. The next year, 1755, Braddock with his army widened the path and moved wagons and artillery over it to within nine miles of Pittsburg. He was defeated and the road remained unfinished. The National Road west from Cumberland now follows nearly the route of the old Nemacolin trail. After Braddock was defeated, his road remained a quarter of a century without a wagon, loaded with merchandise, passing

SETTLEMENTS AND INDIAN TROUBLES.

over it. Goods were still packed on horses. The first wagon load of merchandise reached the Monongahela in 1789.

Prior to that time a project had been set on foot for opening a canal from tidewater, along the bank of the Potomac, and up the North Branch of that stream to the base of the Alleghanies. The terminus of the canal was located in the present county of Grant, where the Northwestern Pike now crosses the North Branch. From there a road thirty miles long was to lead across the mountains to the waters of the Monongahela. The exact point of intersection was not definitely determined, but the most practicable route led down Horse Shoe Run to Cheat River at the Horse Shoe, in the present county of Tucker. From the point determined upon, a canal down the river was designed to be continued till the stream became navigable. The prime mover in this scheme was George Washington, who in 1775 was about to organize a company to build the canal, but the Revolutionary War came, and nothing more was done till the war closed. Then he again took up the scheme. He believed that easy and adequate communication should be opened between the Atlantic coast and the great valleys west of the Alleghanies; because, as he argued, if those valleys should remain cut off from the East by the mountain barrier, the settlers who were flocking there by thousands, would set up an independent government and seek an outlet down the Ohio and Mississippi, and their commercial interests would lead to political ties which would bind them to the Spanish Colonies then in the Mississippi Valley. He, therefore, urged that two canals be built, one by way of the Potomac and the Monongahela; the other by the way of the James and the Kanawha. In 1784, the year after peace was declared with England, he crossed the Alleghanies and visited the Monongahela on a tour of observation, as well as to look after large tracts of land which he owned in the West. He visited Morgantown and ascended Cheat River and crossed the Alleghanies to Staunton. The wisdom of America's greatest man is shown no more in his success in war and in his foresight in politics, than in his wonderful grasp and understanding of the laws governing trade, and the effect of geography on the history of a country. And with equal foresight he mapped the most practicable routes for highways. The survey made forty years after, for a canal from Alexandria to the Monongahela, followed almost the identical line marked by Washington, including the roads across the mountains. The canal was never built further than Cumberland because the invention of railroads checked canal building. Washington was opposed by the Maryland Assembly in his canal schemes, but when, in 1784, he

WASHINGTON'S MAP.

again took up the work, Maryland joined Virginia, and in December of that year both made appropriations for opening a road "from the highest practicable navigation of the Potomac to that of the Cheat River or the Monongahela."

Having thus spoken of the highways and the proposed highways between the Potomac and the Upper Valley of the Ohio, it remains to be shown that those were not the only paths across the mountains. The paths yet to be mentioned were more local, but, within a narrower sphere, were of no less importance. So far as Randolph, Tucker, Barbour and Upshur Counties were concerned, the paths amounted to more than the great highways through Pennsylvania, for the early settlers came over the trails of which there were three important ones and a fourth (McCullough's) of lesser importance. The McCullough trail passed from Moorefield to Patterson Creek, up that stream to Greenland Gap in Grant County; crossed a spur of the Alleghanies to the North Branch, following the general course of the Northwestern Pike to the head of the Little Youghiogheny, in Garrett County, Maryland; thence to the Youghiogheny, west of Oakland, and on to Cheat River, near the Pennsylvania line. But a branch of it led down Horse Shoe Run to the mouth of Lead Mine Run, where it intersected another path to be spoken of later. Another trail led up the North Branch of the Potomac striking the face of Backbone Mountain near where Bayard now stands; thence reaching the summit near Fairfax Stone. Passing to the western slope, it descended to the mouth of Lead Mine, ten miles east of St. George. It reached Cheat River at the mouth of Horse Shoe Run, three miles above St. George. Thence one branch led down Cheat, across Laurel Hill to the Valley River below Philippi, and thence westward to the Ohio. The other branch followed up Cheat, reaching the head of Leading Creek, in Randolph County, and after joining the Seneca Trail, near the present village of Elkins, passed up the river to its source, where dividing, one part led down Elk River, one down the Little Kanawha and a third crossed to the Greenbrier. The majority of the settlers on Cheat, above and below St. George, came to the country over the North Branch Trail, as did many of those on Leading Creek, and the early settlers on the Buckhannon. There is no record of the marking of the trail near Fairfax Stone. It was there at the earliest visit of white men, and was no doubt an Indian trail antedating history. The first white man to follow the trail was probably William Mayo in 1736. He ascended the North Branch that year and discovered the tributaries of Cheat. History does not say how far westward and northward he followed the stream; probably not far. In 1745 other explorers, following the same route, reached the present territory of Tucker County, and a map made of the region soon after is fairly accurate.

Twenty miles south of Fairfax Stone, another path crossed the Alleghanies, the most important in West Virginia north of Greenbrier. It was

SETTLEMENTS AND INDIAN TROUBLES. 179

called the Seneca Trail, or the Shawnee Trail. The latter name was given it because it was traveled by Shawnee Indians, notably by Killbuck's bands in raiding the South Branch Settlements. It was called the Seneca Trail, because, after crossing the Alleghany Mountains at the head of Horse Camp Creek, it passed down Seneca Creek, in Pendleton County, to the North Fork. The Shawnee Trail, or a continuation of it, was an old Indian war path, perhaps used centuries ago. It came from Pennsylvania, passed through Maryland, crossed the Potomac at the mouth of the South Branch, ascended that stream to Moorefield where the McCullough Trail struck off; thence it ascended the river to the mouth of the North Fork; up that stream

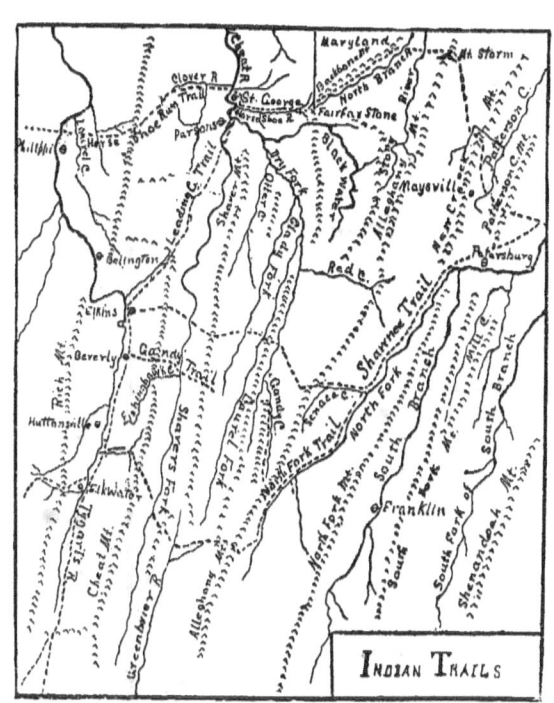

EARLY TRAILS CROSSING THE ALLEGHANIES.

to the mouth of Seneca; thence across the mountains and the tributaries of Cheat to Tygart's Valley at Elkins. From there it became one with the trail, coming by way of Fairfax Stone. The Shawnee Trail was the chief highway between Tygart's Valley and South Branch for a century. In the early times, hundreds of pack horses, loaded with salt, iron and merchandise, passed over it every year, and many a drove of cattle went by that route to the eastern markets. During the Civil War it was frequently used by soldiers. Many of the horses and cattle captured by the Confederate Generals, Jones and Imboden, were sent across the mountains by that trail. General Averell who had command of the Federal forces in this part of West Virginia, found it necessary to post strong pickets on the path. A wagon road has since been made following the same general course, and the old trail is no longer used, but sections of it remain, deeply worn through the wilderness of pine and laurel. A century will not suffice to destroy the old highway over which Indians passed before a white man had seen the valleys of the West. Killbuck's Indians retreated by that trail after the Fort Seybert massacre in 1758.

Thirty miles south of the Shawnee Trail was another path leading from the South Branch of the Potomac into Pocahontas County, and thence into Tygart's Valley. It was a branch of the Shawnee Trail, and instead of crossing the mountains at Seneca, it continued up the North Fork to Dry Run in Pendleton County; passed up Laurel Creek into Highland County, Virginia, and crossed the mountain on the general route of the Staunton and Parkersburg Pike, coming into Tygart's Valley probably at the mouth of Riffle's Run or Becca's Creek, where it joined the trail up the valley already described. Many of the settlers in the upper end of Randolph came over this trail. Thus the routes by which immigration entered the upper valleys of the Monongahela were three: that down Horse Shoe Run, in Tucker County; that by way of Seneca Creek, and that through northern Pocahontas County. The majority of the settlers on Cheat, Tygarts', Buckhannon and the upper West Fork, traveled these trails. A few worked their way up the river from the vicinity of Brownsville, Pennsylvania.

A study of the physical features of the country lying between Cheat River and the Potomac, stretching fifty miles along the Alleghanies, will show why so few paths crossed from the valleys on the east to those on the west. The tract, embracing more than 1000 square miles, was and is one of exceeding difficulty to the traveler. Between Fairfax Stone and the head of the South Branch, the Alleghany Mountains and the parallel and crumpled ridges lying on both sides, are pushed together in rugged and stupendous masses; broken and cleft; steep and bleak; cut by ravines; battlemented by crags and pinnacles; and had all the thickets been removed, the region would still have presented serious obstacles to the passage of the emigrant and explorer. But, added to the rocks and cliffs, the whole country along the upper tributaries of Cheat and over to the Greenbrier, was one unbroken wilderness of pines and tangled laurel. Nearly a century passed after the settlement of the country on both sides before roads were constructed through this wilderness, even in the most favored places; and to this day there are scores of square miles with scarcely a cabin. The dense beds of laurel even yet appall the hunter.

Settlements in Randolph.

Having seen some of the difficulties in the way of the early settlers in reaching central West Virginia, it is proper to speak of the settlements made immediately around the borders of the territory now in Barbour; and first, mention should be made of Randolph County, on the south, for there was the first settlement on the waters of the Monongahela in West Virginia, and there occurred the first massacre by Indians in West Virginia. Robert Files and David Tygart, located with their families at and imme-

SETTLEMENTS AND INDIAN TROUBLES. 181

diately above Beverly in 1753. Files had six children, and Tygart several. There was no war with Indians at that time, and the pioneers apprehended no danger, even in that remote place. But exposed frontiersmen and their families were never entirely free from danger in those days. During the summer of 1753 they had not raised bread enough for their use and were preparing to return to the South Branch to spend the winter, when a party of Indians, who had been on a thieving expedition in the vicinity of Moorefield, came over the Shawnee Trail (as is supposed) and discovered Files' cabin. They murdered seven members of the family, but one son, who was absent when the attack was made, fled to Tygart's and alarmed that family in time for all to escape. No other settlement was made in Randolph for eighteen years, 1772. It is believed that David Tygart was among those who settled the valley a second time, but of this the evidence is not conclusive. Among the settlers, whose names became identified with the history of Tygart's Valley were Benjamin Hornbeck, Darby Connolly, John Stewart, John Crouch, Jacob Riffle, Matthew Whitman, John, David and William Haddan, Jacob Stalnaker, John White, Jacob and James Westfall, William Currence, Jonathan Smith, Samuel Wamsley, Colonel Benjamin Wilson, John McLain, John Nelson, James Ralston, James Crouch, Jonathan Buffington, and Jonas Friend. Nearly all the land in Tygart's Valley was located in 1772, or earlier, but few patents were obtained for it till ten or fifteen years later.

SITE OF FILES' CABIN.

RANDOLPH COUNTY COURT HOUSE 1789.

In 1774 the Dunmore War came, and two forts were built in Randolph, Westfall's at Beverly, and the Currence fort near Huttonsville, ten miles above. The settlers escaped without being visited by Indians till 1777. By that time three other forts had been built in Tygart's Valley. Friend's fort at the mouth of Leading Creek; Wilson's fort, at the mouth of Wilson's Creek, four miles below Beverly, and Haddan's fort, at the mouth of Elkwater, twenty miles above Beverly. Late in the fall of 1777 Indians murdered the family of Darby Connolly, about three miles above Haddan's fort. Their common grave is to be seen in a field to this day. The savages also murdered John Stewart, his wife and child, and carried away as a prisoner a girl named Hamilton. Colonel

GRAVE OF THE CONNOLLYS

Wilson with thirty men pursued the Indians five days in rain and snow, but could not overtake them.* The next year the Indians came again and murdered Lieutenant John White. Again Colonel Wilson pursued them into Gilmer County, but failed to inflict any punishment. In 1780 savages came again and raided Tygart's Valley, above the mouth of Elkwater, where they set an ambuscade and attacked a party of men on their way to Greenbrier County. The fight occurred about a mile above Haddan's fort. John McLain, John Nelson and James Ralston were killed, and James Crouch was wounded. Soon after this Mrs. John Gibson was murdered and her children carried into captivity, probably by these same Indians who escaped without punishment. The next year, 1781, a large body of Indians, after passing through the present county of Barbour where John Minear, Daniel Cameron and Jacob Cooper were murdered, fell upon the settlement on Leading Creek in Randolph, and a general massacre was the result. Half a dozen grown persons were killed, and between twenty and thirty children, besides several persons taken prisoners. Among the the killed were Mrs. Jonathan Buffington, Mrs. Benjamin Hornbeck, Mrs. Daniel Dougherty and all their children, Alexander Roney, and others. Laden with prisoners and plunder, the savages set out for the Ohio, but they were not to escape unpunished. A man whom they had shot at in Barbour, but had missed, fled to Clarksburg, and gave the alarm. In the meantime Colonel Wilson of Randolph, with as many men as he could raise on short notice, went in pursuit. There was some doubt whether all the Indians had retreated, and Colonel Wilson's men became uneasy for their own families, and refused to proceed until the safety of their own wives and children was assured. Only four men were willing to go forward. They were Colonel Wilson, Richard Kittle, Alexander West and Joseph Friend. It was useless to follow the Indians with so small a number, and Colonel Wilson returned home. Meanwhile the scouts sent out from Clarksburg discovered the trail of the Indians on Isaac's Creek, in Harrison County, and Colonel William Lowther, of Hacker's Creek, Lewis County, raised a company and fell upon the savages on a branch of Hughes River in Ritchie County, and defeated them with slaughter, capturing everything they had except one gun, and liberating the prisoners, except one who had been accidentally killed by the fire of Colonel Lowther's men.

In 1782 between twenty and thirty Indians under the leadership of Timothy Dorman, a renegade Englishman, penetrated Randolph County, after having burnt the fort at Buckhannon, and shot Jacob Stalnaker. They then proceeded to the present county of Pendleton where they murdered Miss Gregg.

---

*While Colonel Wilson was pursuing the Indians, his own family nearly fell victims to another party of savages, who had entered the lower part of Tygart's Valley. Mrs. Wilson escaped on a wild horse across the river to Wilson's fort, with two small children in a sack slung across the horse, and a third in her arms.

Town of Philippi.

SETTLEMENTS AND INDIAN TROUBLES.

Tygart's Valley was not again invaded for nine years, and then only once. On May 11, 1791 they murdered Joseph Kinnan near Elkwater, and carried his wife into captivity.

Settlements in Upshur.

The first settlement in what is now Upshur County has special interest for Barbour, not only because of its proximity, but because the first white men ever to set foot on Barbour County's soil, so far as known, took up their abode in Upshur, and became that county's first settlers. Through them we obtain our first glimpse of Barbour at a time when no human being claimed it as his home.

In the interval between the close of the French and Indian War and the beginning of Pontiac's War, the large garrison kept at Fort Pitt (Pittsburg) had little to do, and four soldiers, perhaps becoming weary of doing nothing, deserted and set off into the wilderness. This was in 1761, and they were not heard of for a year. But it was subsequently learned that they had been roaming about the mountains of Pennsylvania, and had finally taken up their abode in the Glades in Western Maryland. Their names were John and Samuel Pringle, William Childers and Joseph Lindsay. In 1762 they strolled into the settlement of Lunice Creek, Grant County, where they were recognized as deserters, and Lindsay and Childers were arrested, but the two Pringles escaped to their camp in Maryland where they fell in with John Simpson, a trapper and trader, who employed them to attend his traps. They remained there two years, and until hunters from the South Branch began to frequent that wilderness. Fearing discovery and arrest, they decided to move further west, and Simpson went with them. They passed down Horse Shoe Run, no doubt following the old Indian trail, and crossed Cheat River at the Horse Shoe. Here a quarrel arose between Simpson and one of the Pringles, and they divided the packs, and parted company. The route of Simpson to the Valley River is not definitely known, except that he arrived at the mouth of Pleasant Creek, the present boundary between Barbour and Taylor Counties. The geography of the county renders it probable that he descended Cheat River seven miles to the mouth of Bull Run, ascending that stream to the top of Laurel Hill, and descended Sandy Creek to the Valley River. He traveled to the head of Simpson Creek (which he named) and thence made his way to Elk, and descended it to the site of Clarksburg where he made a camp. He remained there a year without seeing a human being, and then returned to the South Branch and sold his furs. He again took up his abode at Clarksburg and remained till the country about him began to be settled, which was about 1772, with settlements in neighboring sections somewhat earlier.

The Pringles, after they separated from Simpson, continued their journey to the Valley River, reaching it below the mouth of the Buckhannon.

Continuing up the river till they reached the mouth of the Buckhannon, they ascended it to the mouth of Turkey Run, a short distance below Buckhannon, and there took up their abode in a hollow sycamore, on a farm afterward belonging to Webster Dix. They remained there three years and until their ammunition was exhausted. John Pringle returned, with furs, to the South Branch, leaving Samuel at the forest camp with only two loads of powder.

One of these he wasted in an effort to kill a deer, but was so fortunate as to kill a buffalo with the other. When John returned he reported that there was peace, and they went back to the South Branch. The next year Samuel Pringle and several prospective settlers visited the Buckhannon Valley and in 1769 a number of families settled there. Among them was John Jackson with his two sons, George and Edward.* They settled at the mouth of Turkey Run.

Other settlers were, John Hacker, who located where Bush's fort was afterwards built; Alexander and Thomas Sleeth near the mouth of Turkey Run; William Hacker, Thomas and Jesse Hughes, John and William Radcliff, John Brown, John and Benjamin Cutright and Benjamin Rule. That fall, 1769, after their corn was raised they returned to the South Branch for their families. When they came back they found that buffaloes had devoured their corn. They worked hard and prospered, but in 1773 the colony nearly starved because of the scarcity of corn. Settlements followed in all the country surrounding Barbour. In 1770 Booth's Creek was colonized by Captain James Booth and John Thomas; Simpson's Creek was settled in 1772 by William Lowther and others. He had married a sister of Thomas, Jesse, Job and Elias Hughes.

Indian warfare was very severe in the years following 1777 in the region about Buckhannon, and in 1782 the settlement there was broken up, and Timothy Dorman and his Indians burned the deserted fort.

The Settlements of Tucker County.

Emigrants traveling from the South Branch in search of new homes in the West, would naturally reach Cheat River before arriving in Barbour,

---

*John Jackson was the great grandfather and Edward Jackson the grandfather of the Confederate General, Thomas J. Jackson. (Stonewall.) He was an Englishman by nationality, but was born in Ireland, 1719. While yet a boy he moved to London with his father and two uncles. In 1748 he settled in Cecil County, Maryland, and seven years later married Miss Elizabeth Cummins, an Englishwoman, and when they settled in Upshur County, Mrs. Jackson, with money she had inherited, bought part of the land on which the town of Buckhannon was built. She died in 1825 at Clarksburg, aged 101 years. John Jackson had died in 1804, aged 85 years. Both John Jackson and his son, Edward, were soldiers in the Revolutionary War. At George Jackson's house the first court in Harrison County was held, July 20, 1784. At that court Col. Benjamin Wilson was elected Clerk, Colonel William Lowther was recommended as Sheriff, Henry Haymond as County Surveyor, Col. Benj. Wilson, Colonel of the militia, Henry Delay, Lieutenant Colonel, Wm. Robinson, Major, John P. Duval, County Lieutenant. After one day the court adjourned to the house of Hezekiah Davisson, Clarksburg.

provided they pursued the Horse Shoe Run trail. Consequently, the region about St. George was settled several years before the first colony was planted in what is now Barbour. So far as now known, all of the early colonists in Tucker entered the country over the Horse Shoe Run trail. This locality receives its name from a bend in Cheat River, and the Horse Shoe contains some of the finest lands along that stream. Eight or nine years elapsed after the Pringles passed that way in 1764 before another white man came.* The next man who came was Thomas Howell whose home was on the South Branch. He had been taken prisoner by Indians during the French and Indian War, and had been carried beyond the Ohio. After several years he determined to make his escape and rejoin his friends on the South Branch. From his description of the route he traveled, in connection with the known location of Indian trails at that time, his journey can now be traced with tolerable certainty. It seems that he followed the Indian trail up the Little Kanawha and crossed to the head of Tygart's Valley River (probably at the mouth of Elkwater, twenty miles above Beverly). He supposed that he was then on the headwaters of the South Branch, and with this belief he followed the stream downward two days, when it turned abruptly to the west and broke through a range of mountains. This was evidently in the vicinity of the site of Elkins.† Being now satisfied that the stream was not the South Branch, he turned eastward and came to Cheat River, probably near the mouth of Shaver's Fork, where the town of Parsons now stands. Concluding that this was surely the South Branch he descended the stream. The bottoms were covered with forests of oaks, walnut, sugartrees and sycamore, some of the later of enormous size.‡ He was doomed to disappointment again; for, when he passed the Horse Shoe, he observed that the river bore off to the northwest, breaking through mountains after mountains, and in the distance skirting the eastern base of Laurel Hill and disappearing from view. The direction was wrong and it could not be the South Branch. He crossed to the mouth of a large creek coming in from the east, and ascended that. It was Horse Shoe Run. He followed an Indian trail and it lead him to the South Branch, where, as tradition states, he died in a few days from overfeeding after a month of almost unbroken famine. But before he died he

---

*This may not be strictly correct, for it is probable that both the Pringles and John Simpson subsequently visited the Horse Shoe in passing to and from the South Branch; and that the Buckhannon colonists also traveled that trail as early as 1767 and 1768.

†The fact that Howell followed the river from near its source to that point without finding inhabitants is proof that it was before 1772, or early in that year, as the country about Beverly was settled in 1772.

‡A sycamore opposite the mouth of Horse Shoe Run, still standing within the memory of persons now living, had a hollow more than eleven feet in diameter.

told of the fine valley which he had discovered, and the route by which it might be reached.*

Among those who listened to Howell's narrative was Captain James Parsons, a prominent citizen who lived near Moorefield.† He noted carefully the route, and soon set out to see the country. He was pleased with it and afterwards located claims covering nearly all of the Horse Shoe and the adjacent lands as far as Holly Meadows, and settled his three sons on the lands, but he never became a resident of that part of the country himself. The first settlement was made in the Horse Shoe in the spring of 1774. In April of that year the land, as far as Holly Meadows, was surveyed by Joseph Cresap, who lived near the mouth of the South Branch.††

The Parsons family did not occupy the country alone. About the time of their coming, another land hunter entered the country. This was John Minear, a hardy German, born in 1730, and emigrating to America in 1767

---

*On the muster roll of Captain John Ashby's company, dated October 21, 1757, the name of Thomas Howell is found. (See *Virginia Historical Magazine* for 1895.) It is not improbable that he was the man who made the journey detailed above. Captain Ashby's company served in the South Branch Valley, and on Patterson Creek, in the present County of Mineral, in the French and Indian War. Soldiers were frequently killed or captured during that period by Indians, and it is not improbable that Howell was captured in that vicinity while serving as a soldier.

†James Parsons was an officer in the Hampshire militia. He is first mentioned in history in connection with an occurrence in 1756. Indians broke into the settlement on Lunice Creek, near Fort George (now Petersburg, Grant County) and killed Jonathan Welton and wounded and captured others. They retreated across the Alleghanies to Cheat River, at Dunkard's Bottom, near the Pennsylvania line. Captain Parsons, with a squad of men, overtook them in the night. He crawled up to reconnoitre, and seated himself upon a pole just outside the light of the fire. Presently an Indian began rebuilding the fire, which was burning low, and needing more fuel, he walked a short distance away and took hold of the pole on which Captain Parsons was sitting. The Captain quietly raised himself and permitted the Indian to pull the pole from under him, which the savage did without discovering that anyone was near. The white men were, all this time, lying nearby with guns cocked ready to fire. Captain Parsons gave the signal, and a deadly volley was poured into the camp, killing several Indians, and also, by accident, a white prisoner. It was on that occasion that Samuel Bingamon, a powerful man and a noted Indian fighter, pursued an Indian, caught him and beat him to death. In 1774 a company of soldiers from the South Branch took part in the Dunmore War. Captain Parsons was of the number, but whether he was at Point Pleasant or marched by way of Wheeling with Lord Dunmore is unknown. He was present at Camp Charlotte when the treaty was made, as was his neighbor, Captain Michael Cresap, who lived near the mouth of the South Branch.

††A considerable number of surveyors and settlers were in the party, and while at work in the Holly Meadows, some hunters from Tygart's Valley discovered them and mistook them for Indians. They hurried home, collected a company of men and returned to the Holly Meadows to attack the party, but fortunately discovered them to be white men. This was in a time of peace. The settlements on Cheat River, at and near the Horse Shoe, may be considered to date from April, 1774.

SETTLEMENTS AND INDIAN TROUBLES. 189

with his wife and children, the eldest of whom was David, twelve years old. He was a man of good education, of great energy, of sound judgment, and he has left his imprint upon the history of West Virginia, being the leader and mainstay of the Cheat River colony in its early years, and being the first white man to lose his life within the present borders of Barbour County. A detailed account of his death will be found in the following pages. He was a landowner on the South Branch, in the present County of Hardy, before he visited Cheat River. Having examined the new country, he organized a company of colonists and led them across the Alleghanies. Among those who came with him were, Daniel Cameron, Philip Washburn, (John Minear's son-in-law), Andrew Miller, Jacob (?) Cooper, Salathiel Goff, Robert Cunningham, Henry Fink, Stephen Radcliff, and others whose names are no longer remembered.

John Minear planted his colony in the Horse Shoe. He claimed the land, but subsequently he disposed of his claim to James Parsons, who also laid claim to it, and Minear's colony moved down the river two miles, and located near and below where St. George now stands. But that was two years later, in 1776, and intervening events of great importance must be mentioned. The settlement in the Horse Shoe was made in the spring of 1774. That summer the Dunmore War came, and John Minear built a fort in the Horse Shoe, on land now included it the Tucker County Poor Farm. It was a stockade enclosing an acre or more, with a log house near a spring. There is no record that anyone was killed in the colony by the Indians that year, but the savages prowled about the settlement, and on different occasions persons venturing out were pursued and narrowly escaped. Becoming weary of constant watching and anxiety, the colony abandoned the

THE HORSE SHOE FORT BUILT IN 1774.

Horse Shoe in the fall of 1774, and returned to the South Branch. From that time until the spring of 1776 there was not a white man within the limits of what is now Tucker County, so far as known.

There was no Indian war in 1776, and John Minear conducted his colony back to Cheat River, and made the site of St. George the center of the settlement. His land covered the site of St. George and extended a mile down the river. On the opposite side was the land of his son Jonathan Minear, two miles below. Jacob Cooper settled four miles below St. George at the base of Miller's Hill. Daniel Cameron located on the east side of the Cheat, opposite Miller's Hill. Salathiel Goff's claim was just east of John

Minear's. Stephen Radcliff built his cabin on Horse Shoe Run, six miles above St. George. The location of other settlers is not now known. In 1777 the Indian war began again, and a fort was built at St. George, on the site of the present court house. This fort was on the same plan as that built in the Horse Shoe, but the palisaded space was smaller, enclosing not more than a quarter of an acre. A mill was built about the same time to grind grain, and soon a saw mill was added. This is believed to have been the first grist mill and saw mill built in West Virginia, between Laurel Hill and the Alleghany Mountains.

MINEAR'S FORT AT ST. GEORGE 1777.

The site of Minear's mill at St. George was long forgotten, but in 1875 a flood cleared out the accumulation of gravel from the channel of Mill Run where it flows through the town, and on the bedrock the old logs of the mill dam were brought to view.*

In 1781 Virginia had begun issuing patents for land west of the Alleghanies. Before that date the settlers had no legal titles to it, except so much title as a "tomahawk right," or "corn right" might give them.† In April of that year John Minear, Andrew Miller, Salathel Goff, Daniel Cameron and Jacob Cooper went to Clarksburg to meet the land commissioners and obtain patents. While returning and just before crossing the Valley River below Philippi, and half a mile above the mouth of Hacker Creek, they were fired upon by Indians in ambush near the trail. The savages had hung a leather gun-case over the path to attract attention, and it had the desired effect. The men halted and Minear, suspecting the truth, exclaimed, "Indians!" and wheeled his horse in the narrow path. At that moment the Indians fired, and he fell. Cameron and Cooper were also killed. Salathiel Goff and Andrew Miller sprang from their horses and fled, both hotly pursued. Miller ran up the hill, and Goff toward the river. The former was so closely pressed that he despaired of getting away, but he gained the top of the ridge, ran through a thicket of brush where the Indians lost sight of him, and made his escape back to Clarksburg. Meanwhile other Indians were pursuing Goff whose course of flight took him toward the river. Arriving on the bank, and his pursuers that moment

---

*In 1884 the writer examined the old dam, and found the logs to be in a sound condition, more than a century after they had been placed there. The ax marks on them were plainly seen. The dam had been buried beneath gravel so long that the oldest inhabitant could not remember when it occurred. An old cant-hook used on the saw mill is still in existence and is still doing service on a country mill in that vicinity, a venerable relic of a former century.

† See page 23 of this book.

being out of sight, he threw off his coat to facilitate his swimming. But as he leaped down the bank, a cracking of brush near by announced that the savages were at hand. On the impulse of the moment he threw his coat into the river, and crawled under a hollow bank for concealment. The Indians were by that time on the bank above him. He heard their voices, and once caught a glimpse of a reflection in the water, made by the gleam of the sun on a gun or tomahawk. Then he saw their images mirrored distinctly in the water beneath him, and he gave up hope. But an unexpected circumstance saved him. His coat was floating off down the river and it caught the eyes of the Indians, and they began moving off along the bank, following the garment. Whether they succeeded in recovering it, will never be known. Goff did not wait to see, but at the first opportunity he crawled from his place of concealment and made his escape, leaving the savages a hundred yards below.

SCENE OF THE MURDER OF MINEAR, COOPER AND CAMERON 1781.

The accompanying sketch shows the site of the murder as it is to-day. The narrow space between the hill and river was an admirable place for an ambuscade, and it is to be wondered that any of the men escaped, for the Indians numbered between twenty and thirty. The hill up which Miller made his escape is very steep. An examination of the river bank at the present day discovers no underground hiding place for a man; but there is record evidence that the bank has fallen into the river since then. Trees which formerly stood there, and particularly a corner tree to a tract of land, have been undermined and have fallen into the river. It is, therefore, reasonably certain that the bank was undermined and hollow at the time of the ambuscade and that Goff found a hiding place under the overhanging roots of a tree.* The men were shot about where the small cabin (belonging to Hugh Culverson) now stands. There is a tradition that some of the Indians lay concealed in a hole made by a tree falling by the roots, between where an old oak stump now stands and the foot of the hill. It is probable that another party of the Indians were in the rear of the men at the time of the attack; otherwise Goff and Miller would have fled back on the trail instead of taking what to them seemed the only avenues of escape, the one up the hill, the other toward the river.

When news of the tragedy reached St. George, David Minear with a dozen men proceeded to the place and buried the dead. Many years afterward some men who were digging in that vicinity exhumed the bones of the three men. A very old man was present who had been acquainted with Minear and Cameron, and he identified the skeletons by the teeth. Minear had two front teeth missing. So had one of the skulls. Cameron chewed tobacco, and his teeth were worn short. So were they in one of the skulls. The bones were reinterred in a grave between a white-oak tree and the foot of the hill, and was marked by plain stones. The stump of this tree is yet to be seen. The oak was spared many years after the land about it was cleared, because it marked the graves, and also the spot where the Indians lay in the root-hole when they fired.

Lewis Wilson, who is still living in his eighty-second year, remembers distinctly when the grave-stones were there and when the oak had old blaze marks on it, pointing to the graves. The grave-stones were subsequently pulled up and used in the foundation of a cabin built near the spot by Richard Male.†

The Indians continued their journey toward St. George after they had scalped the dead, but meeting James Brown and Stephen Radcliff, and being unable to kill or capture them, the savages concluded that it would be useless to proceed in the hope of surprising the settlement on Cheat, and they turned south and massacred the settlers on Leading Creek an account of which has already been given.

Sometime after the killing of Minear, Indians paid a visit to Cheat River and murdered Bernard Sims, son of John Sims, who lived on the land

---

*Salathel Goff was afterwards President of the first County Court of Randolph County.

†Richard Male gave this land to his two sons, Wilmer and Hezekiah. They died soon after, leaving each a widow. Their father-in-law, wishing to secure them a home, built them a cabin exactly on the line dividing their two tracts of land, giving as his reason for it, that by so doing, one daughter-in-law could not drive the other out; but if they could not live in common and at peace, each could retire to her own side of the house and the same roof would cover both. This cabin long ago disappeared, but the rocks used in its foundation are visible. The land now belongs to Alexander Norris, except a lot of one acre belonging to Hugh Culverson.

RESIDENCE OF ALSTON GORDON DAYTON.

SETTLEMENTS AND INDIAN TROUBLES. 195

of James Parsons, four miles below the present town of Parsons. He had smallpox, and when the Indians discovered that he was afflicted with a disease greatly feared by them, they fled without scalping him, yelling as they ran: "Smallpox! Smallpox!"*

The troubled times on the borders, and the many murders by the Indians, induced the Governor of Virginia in 1782 to send troops. The number sent to Monongalia County was only seventy, and they were militia from Hampshire County. At that time Monongalia embraced the present counties of Tucker, Randolph, Harrison, Barbour, and northward to Pennsylvania, and westward to the Ohio. Seventy soldiers were too few. These seventy were divided into squads, and before June 30, 1782, had been stationed in Tygart's Valley near Beverly, on the West Fork, near Clarksburg, and on Cheat River near St. George.† It is stated in General Irvine's report that in Monongalia County he only had 300 effective men.‡

There were several visits by the Indians to the Cheat River settlement, the dates of which cannot now be fixed. Without giving the date, it can be stated that on one occasion an alarm of Indians was sounded and the settlers fled to the fort. A family living at the mouth of Clover Run, half mile from the fort and on the opposite side of the river, were working in a cornfield, and in the haste of the older members of the family to reach the fort, they forgot a boy, eight years old, in the field. When he called he was answered, as he supposed by his parents, and was thus decoyed into the woods, out of sight of the fort, where the Indians took him prisoner and carried him to the Ohio. He never got back.§

The night following the capture of the boy, Indians appeared four miles below the fort at the house of Mrs. Cameron, widow of Daniel Cameron who had been killed with John Minear and Jacob Cooper. The savages approached the cabin in the night. The widow with two small children was alone. Looking through a crack in the wall, she discovered in the vague shadows, an Indian's head and shoulders above the garden fence, as he stood motionless, apparently listening to detect the whereabouts and meaning of some uncertain sound. She quietly lifted her sleeping babies from their cradle, and carrying them in her apron, ran into the woods and

---

*The date of the killing of Sims is uncertain. While Withers gives no date, he leaves it to be inferred that it occurred about 1779. This was probably just ten years too early, as there is a well founded tradition in Tucker County that he was killed the day before Jonathan Minear met his death, 1789.

†In Colonel John Evans' official report to General Irvine at Pittsburg, June 30, 1782, he says the troops were sent to "the Horse Shoe;" but that was then and for many years afterward, the common name for all the settlements on Cheat River for miles above and below. The fort was at St. George and no doubt the troops were stationed there.

‡Two years before that, in 1780, the militia enrollment in what is West Virginia, was given in *Jefferson's Notes on Virginia* as follows: Monongalia 1000, Greenbrier 502, Hampshire 930, Berkeley 1100; total 3532.

§A pet crow which was with him in the field, followed him as far as the Ohio River where the Indians, actuated by superstitious fear, shot it.

reached the fort in safety. The Indians burned the house that night.*

In 1787 Indians came into the settlement and stole five horses from Henry Fink. The settlers barricaded themselves in the fort for several days. Believing that the savages contemplated an attack on the fort, which then contained only six men, the others having gone to Winchester for salt, great pains were taken to impress upon the enemy the belief that the place was well defended. The men would change their clothes frequently, and walk out where the Indians, who were concealed on a bluff across the river, could see them. The trick had the desired effect, and the Indians made no attack.

In 1789† Indians again invaded the Cheat River settlements, and in March drove the settlers into the fort. After some days the enemy were supposed to have departed, and the people returned to their farms. Among them were Jonathan Minear, son of John, and Philip Washburn, brother-in-law of Jonathan. Their land was two miles below the fort, on the opposite side of the river, at the mouth of a creek known to this day as Jonathan's Run. Indians waylaid them and killed Minear and took Washburn prisoner as he was carrying a load of fodder to feed the cattle. The savages had siezed him before he suspected their presence. At the same instant they fired upon Minear and broke his leg. He tried to reach the river, but was overtaken on the bank, and while running around a beech tree, propping himself with one hand against the tree, he was tomahawked.‡ The firing was heard by a settler on the opposite side of the river, and men from the fort went in pursuit of the Indians, under the leadership of David Minear, brother of Jonathan. The savages retreated up a steep ridge below Jonathan's Run, and the ridge is still known as Indian Point. They hurried to the Valley River in what is now Barbour, and there the trail was lost. The white men hunted for the trail all next day, and late in the evening found it, and after following it a mile or two, discovered the camp of the enemy. It was subsequently ascertained that the Indians, who seemed to think that pursuit from St. George was not to be feared, had spent the day hunting for the cabins of settlers in the vicinity of the Valley

---

*At the October term of the County Court in Randolph in 1801 a note occurs which probably gives the ages of the Cameron children at the time their mother carried them to the fort. It is stated that when Daniel Cameron was killed he left a widow and one daughter, Catherne, a year old, and that five months after his death, a second daughter, Elizabeth, was born. If Mrs. Cameron's flight from Indians was in 1783, the children were about three and two years old, respectively. Both daughters grew to womanhood, but no record of their marriage is found in Randolph County. After the death of Daniel Cameron, his widow married Thomas Cade. No record of this marriage occurs in Randolph; so if it took place in Randolph territory, it must have been before the county was formed.

†The date of this occurence was long disputed, and is not yet settled with absolute certainty; but a minute entered on the court records of Randolph County in April, 1789, renders it highly probable that the occurrence was in March of that year.

‡While striking at Minear, the Indian's tomahawk frequently struck the tree, and the cuts in the bark left scars which could be seen for a hundred years. While thus striking they cut off the fingers of Minear's hand. They scalped him, broke his skull into fragments and drove the pieces into a stump. His dog guarded the body till men came from the fort.

SETTLEMENTS AND INDIAN TROUBLES. 197

River, but had found none that were occupied. They were thus off their guard when Minear's party attacked them. Two or three were too severely wounded at the first fire to escape and were overtaken and killéd. The remainder of the Indians fled, some taking their guns, others running off without them and eluding further pursuit. Their only prisoner, Philip Washburn, was rescued, and on April 29, 1789, the county court of Randolph appointed him administrator of the estate of Jonathan Minear.*

The Minears, and their descendants, became related with many of the people, not only of Tucker County, but of Barbour also. Of John Minear's children, Mary Ann married John Saylor in 1795. He is supposed to have perished in the woods while hunting. A small stream near St. George, where he was last seen alive, is still known as Saylor's Run. Sarah, another daughter of John Minear, married Benjamin Marsh in 1799, and their descendants are still living. John Minear's sons who survived him were, Philip, David and John; the Minears now living in Tucker County being descendants of David, through his son, Enoch; while Adam, another son of John Minear, settled in Barbour, near the Taylor line, on the river. He had marrid Miss Cobb, a native of Pennsylvania, and their daughter, Nancy Minear, who was born in 1801, was the wife of John Howe Woodford, of Barbour County, and thus became related with a large family of that name.

The first settlers within what is now Barbour County, so far as can now be ascertained, were Richard, Cotteral and Charity Talbott, and their mother. Richard was sixteen years old, Cotteral about eighteen and Charity twenty. They came in 1780 and settled two miles northwest of Philippi, and by intermarriages afterwards became related with the Woodford and Reger families. The account of this settlement will be found in the biographical part of this book, under the name of Richard Talbott. In another chapter which treats particularly of the settlement and development of Barbour, the colonization of the various localities will be considered in detail, together with early developments and improvements in each.

---

*At the fire of the whitemen, the savages fled in panic while the victors rushed into the camp. A few moments later an Indian came bounding back into the midst of the white men, caught up something from the ground, looking like a small pouch, and escaped with it so suddenly that no one had time to shoot him. The old settlers often discussed the question whether it was a bag of money or a pouch of medicine which the savage valued so highly that he risked his life for it. It was probably neither money nor medicine, but the scalp of Jonathan Minear.

CHAPTER XIX.

Notes From the Records.

The County of Barbour was named from Philip Pendleton Barbour, who was a son of Thomas Barbour, was born in Orange County, Virginia, May 25, 1783, died February 24, 1841. He studied law while young, and when only seventeen years of age went to Kentucky to look after some business for his father. He was unsuccessful in managing the business, and his father was so much displeased that he disowned him. He attempted to teach, but could procure no school. He took up the study of law again, and when nineteen years old returned to Virginia, and borrowing money, entered the college of William and Mary as a law student. Subsequently he returned to Orange County and soon became a successful lawyer. In 1812 he was elected to the Virginia Legislature, and was earnest in his support of the administration in its war with England. Two years later he was elected to Congress and was afterwards chosen speaker. When the University of Virginia went into operation, about 1825, he was offered the professorship of law in that institution, and although pressed by Mr. Jefferson to accept it, he declined, and was soon after appointed judge of the general court of Virginia. In 1827 he resigned the judgeship and was elected to Congress. He was president of the Virginia Constitutional Convention of 1829. On account of weak lungs, which prevented him from speaking in public, he accepted a judgeship in the circuit court of the United States for the Eastern District of Virginia. In 1836 he became judge of the United States Supreme Court, which post he held till his death.

Boundaries of Barbour.

The act of the Virginia Legislature passed March 3, 1843, establishing Barbour County, fixed its boundaries as follows:

"Beginning opposite the mouth of Sandy Creek, on the east side of the Valley River, in the now county of Randolph; thence down the said Valley River, with the several meanders thereof, to Daniels' Ferry; thence a straight line to the dividing ridge on the waters of Simpson's Creek and Bartlett's Run, (so as to include Ruben Davisson's farm in the new county); thence a straight line to the old farm now occupied by Samuel Bartlett; thence to the head of Goodwin's Run; thence a straight line to William Bean's on Gnatty Creek; thence a straight line to the head of Peck's Run; thence with the dividing ridge between the head of Peck's Run and Hacker's Creek to the gap of said ridge where

NOTES FROM THE RECORDS. 199

the road crosses leading down Hacker's Creek; thence a straight line to Samuel Black's residence (including the farm of the said Black in the new county) on Buckhannon Run; thence a straight line to the mouth of Sarvis' Run, on the Middle Fork of the Valley River; thence a straight line to the gap of Laurel Hill Mountain where the Widow Corley's corner tree stands; thence with the top of the said mountain until it comes to the Preston County line; thence with the Preston and Randolph County line to the beginning, the whole to form one distinct and new county, and to be called and known by the name of Barbour County, in honor to and in memory of Philip P. Barbour of Virginia."

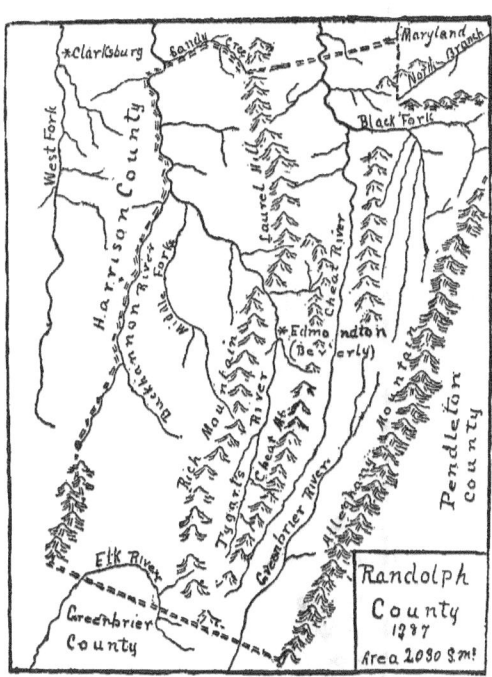

MAP OF RANDOLPH COUNTY FROM WHICH BARBOUR WAS TAKEN.

From a minute entered in the proceedings of the county court it is inferred that the actual line was surveyed entirely around Barbour County in 1843, as in July of that year the sum of eighty-six dollars was set aside to pay the surveyors, including guides, but no record of such a survey is found on the books of the County Surveyor. It became a matter of importance to have part of the lines accurately surveyed, and in 1894 the sum of $944.50 was paid for that purpose. The commissioners who made the survey between Barbour and Taylor were C. M. Cornwell, J. E. Hall and M. F. Hall on behalf of Barbour, and J. F. Ross, M. W. Kinkaid and Upton Foreman on behalf of Taylor, with J. Nelson Baker as umpire. The calls of that survey were:

"Beginning at a stone pile on the corner of Harrison, Barbour and Taylor, west of Simpson's Creek, thence north 86 degrees 53 min., east 2422 feet, passing 83 feet south of the residence of John Lough, to a stone on the ridge on the John H. Woodford farm; thence south 89 degrees, 30 min., east 10942 feet to the Pleasant Creek Ford; thence north 68 degrees, 53 min., east 19086 feet to the mouth of Pleasant Creek, at L. Keller's residence on the line, and so crossing the river as to have 1772 feet of railroad in Pleasant District; thence up Sandy to the mouth of Little Sandy, which is the corner of Preston, Barbour and Taylor."

The commissioners who surveyed the lines between parts of Barbour and Randolph were, Milton Hart and H. C. Rosenberger on behalf of Barbour; A. C. Findley, C. M. Mosteller and Jefferson Scott on behalf of Randolph, and David Poe, umpire. The line is as follows:

"Beginning (line south 82 degrees, 45 min. west) at a hickory on top of Laurel Hill;

900 feet to a cliff; 2,800 feet to a small stream; 4,550 feet to a small stream; 5,100 feet to P. Stipe's land. 8,400 feet to Tom Corley's land; 11,030 feet to Nixon Shomo's land; 12,300 feet to Visquesney's line; 13,400 feet to George Hayes' land; 17,176 feet to Beaver Creek; 20,495 feet to Valley River: 24,660 feet to the north bank of the river, after crossing the second time, nearly opposite the mouth of Zebb's Creek; 26,486 feet to the river again; 27,500 feet to H. G. Davis' land; 30,012 feet to Patrick Judge's land, 31,175 feet to T. Kavanaugh's land; 33,300 feet to Patrick Glannon's land; 34,281 feet to Taylor's graveyard; 53,447 feet to the mouth of Sarvis Run on the west bank of Middle Fork."

The First Court.

The minute book of Barbour County's first county court begins with an entry made April 3, 1843, and it is therein stated that the court was held at the house of William F. Wilson, and all the acting Justices of the Peace of the county were present. They were: David Holder, Jacob Keller, William Shaw, Jacob Bennett, Joseph Teter, Henry Sturm, William F. Wilson, William W. R. Callihan, Samuel Elliott, Elam D. Talbott, Isaac Booth, John H. Woodford, Joseph McCoy, William McCoy, Noah E. Corley, John Reger, Samuel Stalnaker, John Kelley, Michael H. Nevil, George Nestor and William Johnson. At that time, under the Virginia constitution of 1830, the county court was composed of the Justices of the Peace, and the Justices were appointed by the Governor. The Sheriff was nominated by the Justices and appointed by the Governor. He was usually the oldest Justice, that is, the one who had been longest in office. The Justices also elected the County Clerk. All of the Justices of the Peace who lived in the territory taken from Randolph (east of the Valley River and Buckhannon River) had been Justices in Randolph County; and it is said that all the others had been Justices in Lewis or Harrison Counties.

The first duty to which the new court gave its attention was the election of a Clerk for the term of seven years. Three candidates presented their names to be voted upon viva voce, Lair D. Morrall, Michael H. Nevil and Thomas Hall. The result was, Morrall received 11 votes, Nevil 5 and Hall 3; Morrall being elected. He at once entered upon his duties but first gave bond in the sum of $3,000, his sureties being Samuel Stalnaker, William F. Wilson, E. D. Talbott, Henry Sturm and George Harris all but the last being members of the court.

SIGNATURES OF EARLY JUSTICES IN RANDOLPH CO.

The court was now organized and ready for work. Six lawyers came forward and asked to be admitted to practice, all of them being attorneys well-known in the county at that time. They were, John S. Carlile, John S. Duncan, Edgar M. Davisson, U. M. Turner, Bernard L. Brown and David Goff. They took the required oath and were admitted to practice before the county court. At that time there was much more business in the county court for lawyers than there is under the present constitution, by which much of the business formerly done in that court is now transferred to the circuit court.

At that time, as now, the office of Sheriff was one of the most important in the county; but it was not, as it now is, open to any voter of the county who might choose to try for it, but no one except a Justice of the Peace was eligible, only in rare cases of vacancy when a temporary appointment of "cryer" (a substitute for Sheriff) might be made. The court might nominate whom it pleased, among its own members; but it was customary (a custom perhaps never varied from) for the oldest Justice to be nominated. All the Justices in Barbour had held office in the county the same length of time, and there was no "oldest." But the court recognized the Justices who had longest served elsewhere and Isaac Booth and Joseph McCoy were the candidates. Booth had been Sheriff of Randolph as long ago as 1813 and a Justice there as early as 1801. It cannot be ascertained what length of time McCoy had been in office. The voting gave Booth 2, and McCoy 16. The latter was, therefore, recommended to the Governor for appointment as Sheriff: It was customary to make a second and third choice for appointment, to be considered in case a reason should arise for not giving the appointment to the man first chosen. As second choice, John H. Woodford was named; and William Shaw was third choice.

SIGNATURES OF EARLY RANDOLPH COUNTY SHERIFFS.

Next came the naming of a candidate for Coroner, to be appointed by the Governor. The first vote stood: John Sargent 3, Peter Zinn 10, Samuel Keller 7. No choice. On the second ballot Zinn stood 12, and Keller 6. Keller was then named as second choice.

Following this came the election of a Prosecuting Attorney. The court had the election of this officer without presenting the name to the Governor for approval. There were three candidates, John S. Carlile, John S. Duncan and Mortimer M. Johnson. On the first vote Duncan received 9, Carlile 5 and Johnson 3; no choice. On the second vote Duncan was chosen.

The important question of selecting a site for a court house was then taken up. A committee was appointed to make the selection, and chose the ground on which the present court house stands. The minutes of the court do not state what offers, if any, were made by different parts of the county. The committee appointed to select the ground was composed as follows: W. W. R. Callihan, Jacob Bennett, John Kelley, Michael H. Nevil and William F. Wilson. No formal report of this committee is on file; but there is reason to believe that a report was made the next day, and the site selected which has since been the place of the court.

Provision was made for an election in the county. Only three voting places were named. That would seem to be inadequate, but it was much better than in Randolph when the first election was held there. That were county was six times as large as Barbour, yet only three voting places provided there. In Barbour the voting places were, first, the house of Jesse Phillips at Sandy Creek Cross Roads, with George Nestor, Joseph Teter and John Holsberry as commissioners to superintend it; second, the house of Isaiah Welch, on Elk Creek, with James Dilworth, John C. Holden and Thomas Hall as election commissioners; and third, at the court house, with William Shaw, William F. Wilson and Peter Zinn as commissioners. This completed the business of the first day of court.

The next day, April 4, court met, and the first preacher in the county to be licensed to solemnize the rites of marriage, received that license. He was a Methodist minister named George L. Warner, and his bond was fixed at $1500. He gave as bondsmen, Edgar M. Davisson, Noah B. Wamsley and Samuel Stalnaker. On the same day a license of the same kind with equal bond was granted Joel Pitman, a Methodist preacher. With that, the court adjourned to William F. Wilson's mill, and there resumed busines.

No sheriff had yet been appointed, and to provide an officer the court elected a "cryer." The bond was fixed at $10,000. Five candidates entered the list, and the first vote was as follows: Noah E. Corley 4, Elias Alexander 2, James Benson 2, Samuel Keller 1, Flavius J. Holden 1. There was no choice, and not until four votes had been taken was an election made, it being required that the successful candidate receive a majority of the votes cast. Elias Alexander was chosen.

The county was then divided into two constable districts, the first including all of Barbour that was taken from Harrison and Lewis; and the second, all that was taken from Randolph. The constables for the first district, were John Weaver, Isaac Johnson, George W. Gall, James Welch, James Benson, Noah B. Wamsley and Alpheus Teter; in the second district Absalom Hardin, Elias Alexander, Martin D. Kittle, Samuel Keller, Isaac

PHILIPPI BRIDGE,
Built 1852. The First Bridge Captured in the Civil War.

BARBOUR COUNTY COURT HOUSE.
From its Dome Floated the First Confederate Flag in West Virginia.

Coffman, William Simpson, Francis O. Shurtliff and Flavius J. Holden. In the first district the bond of each constable was $3000, and in the second district $2000.

The county was divided into two districts to be in charge of the Overseers of the Poor. The first coincided with the first constable district, and the second with the second constable district. In the first James Teter, Soloman Jarvis and Robert Talbott, were overseers; and in the second, John Holsberry, William Simpson and Absalom Phillips were overseers; and John S. Carlile was appointed agent for the Overseers of the Poor. Just what the duties of that officer were is not plain, but he was paid a tolerably liberal salary, in comparison with salaries of other officers.

In two days the court had been held in two places, and on the second day the question came up again. Two places were considered, and when the vote was taken, "the new meeting house" on the land of Peter Zinn, had three votes, and the residence of John R. Williamson, near Hite's Ferry, received seven votes, and was selected as the place of holding court.

On April 5, a committee, consisting of John S. Carlile, John Holsberry, James D. Hall, Elam D. Talbott, and Jacob Talbott, was appointed to draft plans for public buildings. The committee reported on the first day of next court, May 1.

Alpheus Wilson was appointed deputy county clerk. On April 5, the first mention in the records is found of the town of Philippi. The exact language is this: "Ordered, that the county seat of this county be known and called Phillippa." Not until the May term, 1844, is the name Philippi, as now spelled, found on the records.

On May 1, 1843, the first road overseers were appointed. They were, Johnson Ward, James D. Hall, John Radcliff, Alpheus Zinn, Albert E. Corder, Jacob Talbott, Henry Robinson, Elisha Talbott, John Reed, Henry Wilson, Daniel Post, Eli Hudkins, Absalom Roberts and John Martin. On the same day the first tavern in Barbour County was granted a license. John R. Williamson was the proprietor, and it stood in "Phillippa." It was, presumably, the same building then being used as a court house. That closed the term of court for April. Court was held every month.

Barbour's Court House.

As stated already, the first court of Barbour was held in the residence of William F. Wilson, the next in his mill, and then it was moved to the residence of John R. Williamson. A brief history of the building of the first public court house (the present one) will now be given. The committee appointed to draft plans made its report at the May term, 1843, submitting two plans for the court house, and two for the jail. Plan No. 1, in each case was called the "Hampshire Plan," because modeled after the public building of Hampshire County. No. 2 was called the "Barbour Plan," and was original. The court adopted the Hampshire plan for the court house and the Barbour plan for the jail. The Hampshire jail had a small yard, with brick walls twenty feet high, enclosing a space where prisoners for debt were permitted to walk about and see the sky. The Barbour court, when the plan was explained, decided to try something else, and then adopted the model on which the present jail was built. Barbour's court house and Hampshire's are practically of the same size and style.

Having adopted plans, the court appointed a committee to see to the building. This committee consisted of Elam D. Talbott, Henry Sturm, John S. Carlile, William W. R. Callihan, and Michael H. Nevil. Its duties were to advertise for bids, to enter into contracts, and, last but not least, to borrow money with which to put up the buildings. It was stipulated that, in case the committee should be unable to borrow sufficient money to pay for the work, it should have no power to enter into contracts. The court instructed the committee to advertise for bids in the "*Scion*" *of Democracy* published at Clarksburg, and to let the contract on June 1, 1843.

On June 29 the court met again, and the building committee came forward with a report that it had contracted with Felix Davis, of Hampshire County, to build the court house and jail for $8000, to be paid in five annual installments of $1600. The court refused to ratify the contract, and the committee resigned. A second committee, consisting of Thomas M. Hite, William Carroll, William F. Wilson and G. D. Camden was at once appointed to report a plan for a jail. The next day the court entered into a contract with William Carroll and John S. Murdock to build the court house and jail for $5300, to be completed in two years, and to be paid for in five annual installments.

Four days later Joseph McCoy, Sheriff of Barbour, came into court and lodged a formal protest against being held responsible for the escape of any prisoner, because there was no jail. This method of procedure was quite common in early times, not only in Barbour but in other counties. The Sheriff from time to time would protest against being held responsible for the escape of prisoners.

At the September court, 1843, the court house plan was modified, although it is not stated in what particular. A new committee had been appointed, consisting of William F. Wilson, Martin Sinsel, Edwin D. Wilson. It reported a modified plan for the court house which the court approved; and the contractors agreed to complete the building for $3820. This evidently did not include the price of the jail. A new committee, consisting of Lair D. Morrall, Edwin D. Wilson, John H. Woodford, David Holder and Isaac H. Strickler, was appointed to superintend the building; and the contractors were ordered paid $1090 for work done on the jail. Three months later William Carroll assigned his contract to Amos Carroll. On May 15, 1844, the jail was so far completed that court was held in it, and in the following September it was completed and accepted from the contractors; but in the January following the Sheriff again protested that the jail was insufficient. John H. Woodford was then Sheriff.

In April, 1845, the contractors were formally notified that the foundations, so far as done, were not according to contract, and would not be accepted, and in May following, the court decided that the contract was "illegal, null and void." The minutes of the session do not state what the trouble was, nor is it rendered clear in what way the matter was smoothed over; but when it was proposed to enter into a new contract with the builders the motion was defeated by a vote of 11 to 8; thereby, as it appears, authorizing the contractors to proceed under their old contract. Then came the qustion of raising money to complete the building, and the proposition of levying a tax was supported by a vote of 13 to 5. David Holder, the presiding justice, was opposed to the course taken, claiming that it was illegal, and he refused to sign the minutes of the day, "because the contractor had been paid $1273.33⅓ on his job." Thereupon the minutes were signed by William Shaw.

In May, 1845, the court met in the court house, although the building was not completed, and at that session ordered that William K. Hall be paid $1180 "for extras on the court house." In July an order was made that in the future the court would meet in the court house. In October, 1846, the building was pronounced done "with a few slight exceptions." One of the last changes was to order the cupola made "eight square instead of round."

Early Court Proceedings.

The first special term of court was held May 29, 1843, for the purpose of trying the suit of Jacob Watson against Eugenus Coburn. The complaint alleged that Watson had been forcibly driven off his land (29 acres), by Coburn, and the court was asked to restore him to his possessions. The jury empaneled to try the case was the first summoned by the county court and consisted of the following: William Elliott, John Phillips, Felix Ryan, Henry Shaffer, Peter Zinn, Jacob Bolyard, William Moore, Richard Phillips, Amos Poling, Michael Boyles, Roger Poling and Ely Phillips. The case was decided in favor of Watson.

On June 29, 1843, the first grand jury called by the county court, was empaneled, consisting of John Robinson, Isaac B. Marsh, Abraham Phillips, Thomas Bartlett, Philip Haddix, Joshua Glascock, William Robinson, William Vanscoy, Jacob Woodford, Elias Robinson, Henry Knapp, William Bolton, Gideon Ellison, Henry Shaffer, David Thompson, Thomas Thompson and Abel Morrall.

William F. Wilson was recommended to the Governor for the first County Surveyor, and subsequently was appointed. County surveyors, under the laws of that time, were required to pass an examination before a board composed of professors of William and Mary College.

Joseph McCoy, who had been appointed first Sheriff of Barbour, appointed as deputies Isaac Reger, Benjamin McCoy and John McCoy. It was permissable at that time, (and it was frequently done) for the Sheriff to sell the emoluments of his office to some one or more of his deputies. In other words, he would accept so much, and turn over all the work and all the receipts to another. There is nothing in the records to show that this was ever done in Barbour, but it was a not unknown procedure in Randolph before Barbour was formed.

On July 3, 1843, the court ordered the overseers of the poor to bind John Greathouse to Thomas Thompson till 21 years of age. This is mentioned not because of its historical importance, but because it is the first order of its kind found on the court records of Barbour, and it shows what the method was at that time of disposing of the paupers. It was customary to bind them to responsible citizens, if they were under twenty-one years old, and require their masters to pay them a small sum, usually from $20 to $70 each, when they were of age. If the pauper was old, or unable to work, the county hired some one to provide a home, clothing and food for him. In June, 1851, an election was held to decide whether the county should buy grounds and build a poor house. The result was a defeat for the proposition. Forty years elapsed before a poor house was built.

At this term, July, 1843, the estimate was made for the county expenses of the year, and $558.79½ was ordered paid, the principal items being:

John S. Duncan, services as Prosecuting Attorney. $100
Lair D. Morrall, services as County Clerk... 100
Blank Books for the use of the County...... .... 108 47¼
Expenses of surveying the County line................. 86

The court fixed bounties on old wolf scalps of $10 each; young wolves half price; old red foxes 75 cents; young foxes half price. No record has been found showing the number of wolves killed in the county, but the number was probably not large as those animals were nearly extinct in Barbour at the time the county was formed; but in Randolph, on the south, and in Tucker, on the east, wolves were sometimes killed for many years, the last killed in Tucker County being in 1894, and the last in Randolph in 1897.

In September, 1843, the County Surveyor appointed as his deputies Isaiah Wilson, Benjamin Heatherly, David Goff and Josiah W. Goff.

The first official recognition of public education in Barbour is found on the County Court's minute book for the October term, 1843, when twelve commissioners were appointed. It is probable that the county had been at that time divided into twelve school districts, but the earliest record of such division is not found till October, 1846, three years later. It was the beginning of public schools, but the beginning was small. The twelve commissioners appointed by the court were, John H. Woodford, Abraham Reger, Joseph Rightmire, James Dilworth, Thomas Proudfoot, Samuel Cleavenger, Lair D. Morrall, Abel Morrall, William Johnson, Daniel Nestor,

NOTES FROM THE RECORDS.

Felix Ryan, Noah E. Corley. These commissioners elected one of their number County Superintendent. It is said that Lair D. Morrall was chosen at that time, but the record is silent on the subject until 1847 when the name of Morrall occurs as County Superintendent, and he held the office seventeen years after that time.

In November, 1843, the court fixed the charges for taverns, and every subsequent year, up nearly to the war, they did the same. The rates fixed n the year named were as follows:

Meals, each,............16⅔ cents	Horse to hay 24 hours....12¼ cents
Lodging, per night ..... 6¼ cents	Apple brandy, per ½ pint. 6¼ cents
Oats or corn, per gallon.. 8 cents	Whiskey, per ½ pint ...... 6¼ cents
French brandy, per ½ pint 12½ cents	Peach brandy per ½ pint.. 6¼ cents

The court also fixed a scale of prices, seemingly very low, for keeping property while under execution and in the hands of an officer. The prices were:

For keeping a slave 24 hours............................	25 cents
For keeping a horse or mule 24 hours	4 cents
For keeping horned cattle 24 hours, each.	2 cents
For keeping a sheep or goat 24 hours...................	½ cent
For keeping a hog or shoat 24 hours....................	½ cent

The first citizen of Barbour licensed to practice law, who had not practiced before the county was formed, was Albert G. Reger. The preliminary step to his obtaining the license was taken January 1, 1844, when the county court certified that he merited a license. It was customary at that time for a young lawyer who desired a license, to obtain a recommendation from the county court, and he would present this recommendation to the circuit court by which he would be licensed, if he could pass the required examination.

At that time, and for several years later, the Sheriff's bond was $30,000.

On June 22, 1844, Solomon Yock was indicted for "giving a challenge to fight a duel." So far as found by an examination of the records this was the first and only indictment for that offence in Barbour. One year later he was tried and acquitted.

In 1844 William F. Wilson was appointed by the court to "lay off the prison bounds." That was required by a law unknown under the constitution of West Virginia. It was lawful, and by no means uncommon, to imprison a man for debt; but he was usually granted privileges not accorded other prisoners. A certain space around the jail building, sometimes including two or three acres, was laid off as the prison bounds, and the prisoner for debt was granted liberty to walk about these bounds, but, on his honor, he promised not to cross them. At night he must return to prison to sleep. The bounds were usually coincident with certain streets and squares. The record does not show what bounds were set in Philippi. No prisoner for debt could be kept in jail at public expense. The creditor who secured his imprisonment was compelled to feed and clothe him, and this expense usually made the creditor weary of the business and the prisoner would be turned out. There was also a provison in law by which a prisoner for debt could obtain his freedom by surrendering his property and declaring himself to be a bankrupt. The minntes of the county court do not show that there ever was a man imprisoned for debt in Barbour; but it is probable that if all the justice dockets were examined, cases would be found.

In June, 1847, the court ordered all county roads cleared of brush eighteen feet wide, and graded twelve feet wide. In December of that year the coroner held an inquest on the body of John O'Neal, finding that he had been killed by a blow dealt by Benjamin Heatherly, and that Heatherly had fled. The coroner discovered that property worth $275 belonging to Heatherly could be seized, and it was taken, as the law directed at that time.*

In 1850 the court elected another Clerk. The candidates and the votes which each received were as follows: Lair D. Morrall 21, Thomas Hall 8, Henson L. Hoff 1, Isaac Booth 1. At the same court Thomas Proudfoot was chosen to assess the lands of Barbour.†

In July, 1852, Justices of the Peace were elected by the vote of the people for the first time. Prior to that they were appointed by the Governor. Their term was for four years. At the same time the first Prosecuting Attorney was elected, Charles S. Hall.

In January, 1853, there was a smallpox scare. The court entered of record that Oliver Cromwell had died of that disease and that his family were afflicted with it, and they were ordered to be quarantined. In February the court ordered the vaccination of all persons within one and a half miles of the residence of William Castello, deceased.

In 1856 Lair D. Morrall was commissioned a notary public, the first on record in the county.

From May 8, 1861, to October 7, 1861, there is no record of a county court. That was the opening of the war, and many of the public men who had been prominent in the county's affairs up to that time, went into one or the other army, some never to return. New names are found in many places when the minutes of the court are examined after the re-establishment of the Federal authority in Barbour.

On September 27, 1861, the record states, Lewis Wilson was elected County Clerk "to fill a vacancy." This election was held under the reorganized government of Virginia. At the same election James Trahern was chosen Sheriff, also "to fill a vacancy;" while another vacancy was declared in the office of Prosecuting Attorney, and Nathan H. Taft was

*This was in accordance with a law passed in 1792. See page 87 of this book.
†In accordance with the act of March 20, 1850.

elected to fill it. The office of assessor was likewise vacant and was filled by the election of Josiah L. Hawkins and Samuel S. Lackney. The constables elected at that time filled vacancies. Thus there was a change in most of the offices of the county.

In February, 1862, the jail of Taylor County was adopted as the Barbour Jail. No reason for it is given.

The last county court held under Virginia's authority convened June 1, 1863. West Virginia became a State twenty days later.

On February 9, 1895, the county court record contains the following entry:

"Be it remembered that, commencing on the 26th day of December, 1894, there fell a snow something like 22 inches deep in this part of the county; and from that time up to and including this date, we have had, according to the remembrance of the oldest inhabitants, the coldest and most severe winter since the year 1856.*

In 1896 there was a hydrophobia scare. The county court ordered all dogs in the county killed, and also all animals that had been bitten by dogs. But the owners of dogs might muzzle and confine them, instead of killing them.

Notes from the Circuit Court Records.

The first circuit court in Barbour was held Wednesday, May 10, 1843, at the residence of John R. Williamson. Edwin S. Duncan was Judge. Edwin D. Wilson was appointed Clerk by the court, and his bond was fixed at $10,000 and his bondsmen were, Gideon D. Camden, George Hay Lee, William Calder Haymond, John S. Duncan and George Lee. The court appointed Geoge Hay Lee Prosecuting Attorney and allowed him $50 for his service.

The first grand jury impaneled by the circuit court (and the first in the county) consisted of the following named men: Henry Sturm, foreman, James Teter, Abraham Reger, John Black, Robert Talbott, Michael Boyles, John Hoff, John Gall, Bryan Sturm, Daniel Howdershelt, Jacob Smith, Abner Schoonover, Martin D Poling, John Trimble, Hezekiah Mitchell, and Martin B. Poling.

The first foreigner naturalized in Barbour was Charles Alfred Viquesney, October, 1847. The second man was John Miles, a native of England, naturalized in the county court, March 21, 1851.

In 1853 occurred the first murder trial in the county. Thomas Board waylaid and shot his nephew, Strickler I. H. Chrislip, a small child, and was indicted for the offence in April, was tried in July and hanged in October.

There is no record of any circuit court in Barbour from May, 1861, to November, 1866. There was court during every year between these dates as is shown by papers filed in the Circuit Clerk's office, but no minute book

*For mention of the winter of 1856, and other hard winters, see page 79 of this book.

is known to be in existence, and no one knows what became of it. That was during the war, and eighteen months after its close.

Last Wills and Testaments.

In the first twenty years of Barbour's existence there were placed on record in the county 102 wills. Below will be found a list of the testators and the dates when the documents were placed on record. The date does not necessarily imply that the person who made the will died at or near that time; but such was usually the case, and unless there is reason for believing to the contrary, it is reasonably safe to conclude that the will was recorded shortly after the death of the testator. Following is the list:

1843.
Lawrence Mitchell
Sarah Thompson
Isaac Phillps

1844.
Rebecca Hudkins
Edward Reed
Edward Stewart
Robert Foster
William Hartman

1845.
Christopher Nutter
Richard Male
Job Kesling

1846.
Simeon Curkendall
Jacob Nestor
Garrett Johnson
Jacob Lesher

1847.
William Chrislip
William Cole
Jonas Vanscoy
Solomon Jarvis

1848.
Hezekiah Thompson
Tevalt Moats
William Male
Adrain Heatherly
John Carlin

1849.
John Parrill
William Sargent
Edmond Cleavenger
Samuel Black
John Premble
Eppa Bartlett
Francis Thompson

1850.
Alexander McCoy
Dorcas A. McCoy
Isaac L. McCoy
Robert Carter
Amos Hilliard
John Simpson
John Foy
John P. Moore
Jacob Teter
John Johnson
Mesheck Hyatt

1851.
Benjamin Simon
William Poling
Jesse B. Wells
William Ryan
Levi Coberly
Jacob Carpenter
James Heatherly
John Walter

1852.
Asa Skidmore
Joel O'Neal
Joseph Paugh
Oliver Shurtliff
John Thompson
William Chambers
Edwin D. Wilson
Oliver Shutliff
Frederick Hills
Abraham House
John H. Sample
Joseph Corder

1853.
Jacob Simon
Asa Bennett
Joseph Phillips

1854
William Pickens
George Nutter
James Campbell
John McGee
John Mitchell
James Ramsay
Samuel Poling
John Dorton
Joshua W. Cole
John Rider

1855
Levi Johnson
James McGlamary
James Poling
Jacob House

1856
George Maple
Solomon Mitchell
William Benson
Thomas Bartlett
Henry Pride

1857
William F. Wilson
Charles S. Hall
Samuel George
George Chrislip
George Rodabaugh
Christian Markley

1858
William McLean
Isaac Booth
Matthias Hilliard

1859
Enoch Hall
Martin D. Poling
Christian Carr
Isaac Norris
Christopher Costeloe

Residence of Samuel Vanhorn Woods.

NOTES FROM THE RECORDS. 215

1860	James W. Haines	Robert Morrison
Samuel Cleavinger	William Murphy	John Holsberry
Charles W. Parrott	Malinda Bartlett	Banister P. Stephens.
Benjamin Winans	1863.	
1862.	Thomas J. Sharp	
John I. Poling	Samuel Cooper	

The First Deed Book.

When the county was organized, one of the first duties of the court was to provide a book in which to record the deeds. There was a discussion of considerable length whether it would be better to buy one large book or two small ones, and finally it was decided that one large one was preferable, so that all the deeds could be recorded in one volume. It was agreed among the members of the court that one book (if large) would contain all the deeds that would ever be filed for record in Barbour County. Accordingly, the large book was bought. It was filled in eight years. Since then 39 other books have been filled with recorded deeds, and a new one is required each year.

Early Marriage Licenses.

Following is a list of the marriages solemnized in Barbour in the first five years of the county's existence:

1843.

MAN'S NAME	WOMAN'S NAME	BY WHOM MARRIED.
Baylus England	Rebecca Wright	Joel Pitman
Isaac Kelley	Lucinda Rohrbaugh	"
John R. Thompson	Mary Day	"
Nicholas Poling	Rachel Robinson	G. S. Warner
Nicholas Gainer	Phoebe Poling	"
Adam Coontz	Sarah Stalnaker	"
William Chrislip	Nancy Ward	Francis H. Reed
John Jenkins	Sarah Cleavinger	Edmund Dennison
John M. Corley	Ann Maria Wilson	Joseph Wrightman
William Leonard	Prudina Bennett	"
Hamilton G. Bartlett	Catherine McKinney	"
Jesse Reed	Rebecca Cole	"
Jacob Proudfoot	Cyrena Vanscoy	B. F. Sedgwick
William McClaskey	Catherine Proudfoot	"
Nathan Reed	Malinda Vanscoy	"
Francis Hathaway	Leanna Proudfoot	"
Jesse Mitchell	Eliza Walker	Henry G. Bonnett

MAN'S NAME	WOMAN'S NAME	BY WHOM MARRIED
Simon Phillips	Susanna Fitzwater	Simeon Harris
John B. Poling	Martha Jane Phillips	"
Jesse Fitzwater	Sarah Harris	Simeon Harris
Levi Moore	Barbara Harris	"
William S. Harris	Agnes Phillips	"
Noah B. Wamsley	Elizabeth House	Moses Tichnell
Absalom Strader	Catherine Ward	"
Jacob W. Reger	Anne Nealy	"
Absalom Roberts	Rebecca O'Neal	"
Joel Bonnett	Barbara Hoover	Rezin White
Joseph Decker	Elizabeth Cummins	"
Stephen Debar	Catherine Rohrbaugh	"
Samuel H. Purkey	Phoebe Phillips	Oliver Shurtliff
Lathrop P. Rude	Ruth Phillips	"
Christian Smith	Elizabeth Welch	P. W. Holder
James Romine	Mary Hudkins	John Dennison
David Cole	Lucinda Thompson	"
Jonathan Hornbeck	Jane Lipscomb	G. Martin

1844

MAN'S NAME	WOMAN'S NAME	BY WHOM MARRIED
Elias England	Rosa Yock	Joel Pitman
James W. McGuffin	Ann Rebecca Carter	"
E. Yoke	Margaret Goldsberry	"
Joshua Newman	Rachel Newman	"
John Day	Elizabeth Thompson	"
Abner Turner	Rebecca Thompson	"
Anthony S Rohrbaugh	Clarissa Morrison	"
David B. Riser	Elizabeth Nealy	Francis H. Reed
Marshall Dean	Louisa Kesling	"
James T. Hartman	Mary Burner	"
Adam Wamsley	Rachel Pifer	"
Jacob H. Wolf	Lucy Ann Carr	"
Lair Dean	Sarah Lanham	"
Wellington Hickman	Eleanor Reed	John Dennison
Eppa Hathaway	Mary Robinson	B. F. Sedgwick
Robert R. Talbott	Jane Virginia Stickle	Joseph Wrightman
James Thompson	Elizabeth Virginia Stickle	"
Thomas Corder	Elizabeth Zinn	"
Anthony Simon	Minerva Corder	"

NOTES FROM THE RECORDS.

MAN'S NAME	WOMAN'S NAME	BY WHOM MARRIED
John Reed	Margaret McCalley	Joseph Wrightman
Lewis Wilson	Ann Keys	"
Simon M. Switzer	Lucy Ann Proudfoot	"
Simon Swick	Surrilda Weaver	"
Elam B. Bosworth	Evaline Switzer	Joseph Wrightman
John O. Smith	Dian Phillips	Simeon Harris
Samuel O'Neal	Mary Crites	Alexander Morrison
William C. Jenkins	Mary White	"
John Daniels	Elizabeth Hawkins	J. S. Patterson
Daniel O'Neal	Mary Reed	"
James Chriss	Eliza Chrislip	"
James Morrison	Mahala Crites	Rezin White
Jeremiah Lanham	Elizabeth Crites	"
William Brown	Emily Wright	Oliver Shurtliff
James P. Yokum	Hulda Kuykendall	"
Esau Bennett	Rachel Hudkins	"
Francis O. Shurtliff	Eliza Booth	"
Jacob Hudkins	Rachel W. Holder	Peter W. Holder
Abraham K. Holder	Emily Hudkins	"
James W. Ryan	Deborah Moore	Jacob Keller
Philip F. Poe	Lydia Martin	"
Daniel Howdershelt	Mary Walter	"
George Binegar	Elizabeth Constable	John Davidson
James W. White	Catherine Reed	James Little
Henry Gall	Eunice Marteney	G. S. Warner

1845.

Michael Simon	Catherine George	Joseph Wrightman
Ephraim Welch	Mary Daniels	"
Clarles B. Cleavenger	Mary Welch	"
Aaron McDaniel	Statira Glascock	"
Alexander Zinn	Mary Ann Reed	"
David Hall	Matilda Dickenson	'
Joseph Marteney	Margaret Finley	"
Andrew Miller	Rebecca Nutter	"
Alpheus Zinn	Mary Woodford	"
John Proudfoot	Rebecca McVicker	"
George Weaver	Guilda Duckworth	"
Edwin L. Rude	Mary Poling	Oliver Shurtliff
Jacob Abel	Malinda England	"
George W. Brake	Abigail Workman	Alexander Morrison

MAN'S NAME.	WOMAN'S NAME.	BY WHOM MARRIED.
Daniel Wilson	Naomi Reger	John W. Alvis
Ormsley B. Lowden	Amelia White	J. S. Patterson
Abraham R. Chrislip	Sarah H. Kirby	"
William Price	Bethany Payne	A. J. Warren
Thomas Bartlett	Martha Swick	Job Wolverton
Henson Stout	Mary Jane Swearingen	Joel Pitman
George Smith	Jane Hoff	"
Fielder W. Swearingen	Mary Ann B. Stout	"
David Wilson	Jane Amanda Carter	"
Absalom Digman	Susanna England	"
John W. Kittle	Eliza Skidmore	"
Perry Green H. Hudkins	Mary Castello	R. W. Holder
William Nestor	Elizabeth Harsh	G. Nestor
Frederick Booth	Emily Stalnaker	Jacob Keller
Collins Skidmore	Sarah Gainer	"
David M. Auvil	Eliza Keyser	"
John Auvil	Catherine Cox	"
Martin G. Poling	Hulda Limber	"
John D. Black	Cyrena Walter	"
George W. Howdershelt	Mary Stalnaker	"
Samuel W. Nestor	Elizabeth Smith	"
James Edwards	Emily England	"
Thompson M. Norman	Elizabeth Boyce	"

1846

Elias Coffman	Ellen Corley	Jacob Keller
Levi Kuykendall	Sarah Ann Cokenour	"
Adam G. Mustoe	Nancy Wilson	"
Peter Shafer	Amelia Nestor	"
William Engle	Tabitha Chriss	J. S. Patterson
Loman Reed	Elsie E. Engle	"
Lemuel Chrislip	Salnia Peck	"
Valentine Hinkle	Matenda Lewis	"
Saul Simon	Nancy Black	"
John Swick	Rachel Black	"
Alva Teter	Mary A. Hartman	"
Francis Marion Will	Eleanor Zirkle	Joel Pitman
Samuel C. Jackson	Mary Ann Harris	"
Bazael J. Mills	Elizabeth Skidmore	"
Joseph Sargent	Lucinda Lanham	"

NOTES FROM THE RECORDS. 219

MAN'S NAME.	WOMAN'S NAME.	BY WHOM MARRIED.
Isaac Price	Mary Elizabeth Stonestreet	Joel Pitman
Jesse Rightman	Mary Ann E. Stemple	A. J. Warren
George Gainer	Maria Poling	"
Asa Phillips	Mary Phillips	"
Ambrose Himes	Zephery Phillips	Simeon Harris
Simeon Harris	Sarah Phillips	"
Jacob Shaver	Judy Fitzwater	"
Joseph P. Cross	Emily Phillips	"
Martin Poling	Sarah Wells	"
Isaac I. Post	Mary Brake	Alexander T. Morrison
D. Yates	Mary C. Sinsel	John Davidson
James E. Carver	Minerva Lanham	James Little
Matthias Ross	Nancy Douglass	"
John G. White	Martha Jane Boatwright	"
William Reed	Sarah Robinson	A. A. Reger
John W. Chrislip	Belinda George	Gideon Martin
Morgan H. Burner	Sarah Ann Baker	"
Joshua Wood	Elizabeth Martin	"
Noah Lantz	Catherine Teets	"
Edward F. Grant	Ann Eglantine Jarvis	John W. Alvis
Emanuel Cool	Nancy Ann Reed	Gideon Martin
Washington Martin	Matilda Cool	James F. Burris
Martin Chrislip	Sarah Ann Chrislip	"
Michael Shaw	Emeline McVicker	David P. Murphy
Elmore McCollough	Susan Trimble	Adam C. Rider
Isaac Trimble	Belinda Jane Neal	"
Elisha Skidmore	Harriet Wright	Benjamin Bailey
James Smith	Hanna Cottrill	Benjamin Stickley

1847

Ellerton Phillips	Hannah Ball	Jacob Keller
Levi W. Richman	Anna Nestor	"
John W. Marsh	Eva Gainer	"
Alexander K. Wilson	Miranda Fravel	"
William Auvil	Nancy Valentine	"
John Sturm	Minerva Ann Curry	"
David P. Murphy	Francis Murphy	"
Levi Barb	Appaline V. Fravel	"
Peter Shafer	Amelia Nestor	"
Robert Phillips	Nancy Valentine	"

MAN'S NAME.	WOMAN'S NAME.	BY WHOM MARRIED.
Thomas H. Isner	Caroline Furguson	Jacob Keller
Arnold Poling	Lydia Hudkins	"
Andrew Sturm	Margaret Harris	"
Nestor Hardin	Margaret Stalnaker	"
Edward Hill	Catherine Digman	"
Nathan Rogers	Susan Amanda Jamison	James Little
Levi I. Queen	Nancy Ritchie	"
Adam White	Rachel Talbott	H. Reger
Daniel W. Shurtliff	Jane Holder	Oliver Shurtliff
George H. Phillips	Martha Hillyard	"
Perry Hillyard	Sallie Phillips	"
Alpheus Murphy	Mary McVicker	David J. Murphy
Isaac Haddix	Malinda Weaver	"
Israel Poling	Rachel Limbers	Henry Clay Dean
Michael Poling	Sarah Sturm	"
Thomas F. Bartlett	Nancy Pepper	Benjamin Bailey
Marshall Pepper	Mary E. Bartlett	"
Stewart Chapman	Mary Jane Paugh	James Wrightman
Samuel Heatherly	Helen A. Corder	"
Isaiah Michael	Darinda Duckworth	Benjamin Stickley
Asa Crites	Nancy Boatwright	"
William Frymire	Elizabeth Crites	"
Fountani Moody	Eleanor Frymire	"
William Adams	Delila Lipscomb	Joab Wolverton
James Zinn	Catherine Criss	Gideon Martin
James Dean	Eliza Black	"
James L. Hickman	Susanna Benson	Hanson Reger
Hiram Cotrill	Lucy Ann Peck	"
Daniel Wilson	Naomi Reger	John W. Alvis
Page D. Carter	Mary Ann Perry	"
Henry H. Boatwright	Rhoda Hudkins	"
John Bolton	Nancy Jones	Joel Pitman
Jacob Shockey	Nancy Wilmoth	"
James Heatherly	Mary Ann Engle	"
Edgar Poling	Mary Weaver	"
John W. Kittle	Sarah Yeager	"
Harvey Poling	Mary Markley	"
Eli J. Swearinger	Anna Poling	"
Abraham Wells	Mary O'Neal	"
Samuel Knapp	Catherine Delawder	"

MAN'S NAME	WOMAN'S NAME	BY WHOM MARRIED
Samuel S. Shockey	Lucinda Payne	Joel Pitman
William L. Parks	Margaret Smith	"
Stewart Chapman	Mary Jane Paugh	Joseph Rightmire
Samuel Heatherly	Helen A. Corder	"
Eppa H. Carter	Austin Fravel	Robert Carter
Isaac Coontz	Mary Price	"
Austin Reader	Maria Wright	John Davisson
Ephraim McCalley	Rebecca Robinson	Joshua S. Corder
William W. Wood	Lucinda Heatherly	"
John Pickens	Hannah Corder	"
John H. Proudfoot	Sarah Ann Modesitt	"
Benjamin Reger	Prudence Talbott	"

Election Returns.

During the fifty-six years of Barbour's existence, elections have been held at least once a year, but the poll-books are not to be found for the elections prior to 1874, nor are they complete for all elections since that time. For the early years of the county the only source of information concerning the election of officers is contained in the proceedings of the courts, and this information is meager. Following will be found a summary of the results of general elections since 1873.

Election October 13, 1874.

Candidates. *Votes.* *Majority.*

CONGRESS.

Charles J. Faulkner, Democrat...................... 804   339
A. R. Boteler, Republican............................. 465

Election October 10, 1876.

GOVERNOR.

Henry M. Mathews, Democrat...................... 1187   295
Nathan Goff, Republican.............................. 892

Election November 7, 1876.

PRESIDENTIAL ELECTORS.

Democratic... 1117   252
Republican.. 865

Election October 8, 1878.

Candidates.	Votes.	Majorities.
CONGRESS.		
B. F. Martin, Democrat	1202	803*
Frank Burr, Republican	399	
John A. Thompson	357	

Election October 12, 1880.
GOVERNOR.

Jacob B. Jackson, Democrat	1240	384*
George C. Sturgiss, Republican	856	
N. B. French	221	

Election November 2, 1880.
PRESIDENTIAL ELECTORS.

Democratic	1017	175
Republican	842	

Election October 10, 1882.
CONGRESS.

William L. Wilson, Democrat	691	
John W. Mason, Republican	769	78*
B. M. Kitchen	111	

Election October 14, 1884.
GOVERNOR.

E. W. Wilson, Democrat	1359	75
Edwin Maxwell, Republican	1284	

Election November 4, 1884.
PRESIDENTIAL ELECTORS.

Democratic	1263	22
Republican	1241	

Election November 2, 1886.
CONGRESS.

William L. Wilson, Democrat	1256	
W. H. H. Flick, Republican	1257	1

Election November 6, 1888.
PRESIDENTIAL ELECTORS.

Democratic	1508	35
Republican	1473	

*Plurality.

SAMUEL VANHORN WOODS.

NOTES FROM THE RECORDS. 225

Election November 4, 1890.
CONGRESS.
William L. Wilson, Democrat...................... 1477   112
George Harman, Republican...................... 1365

Election November 8, 1892.
PRESIDENTIAL ELECTORS.
Democratic.. 1462   59
Republican.. 1403

Election November, 1894.
CONGRESS.
William L. Wilson, Democrat...................... 1456
Alston G. Dayton, Republican.................... 1605   149

Election November 4, 1896.
PRESIDENTIAL ELECTORS.
Democratic.. 1645   72
Republican.. 1573

Election November 8, 1898.
CONGRESS.
John T. McGraw, Democrat...................... 1503
Alston G. Dayton, Republican.................... 1557   54

Lawyers Who Have Practiced in Barbour.

William E. Arnold............1847
Daniel M. Auvil...............1853
Henry D. Auvil...............1860
Stark W. Arnold..............1878
Thomas J. Arnold............1874
John W. Arbuckle............1898

Bernard L. Brown............1843
Jonathan M. Bennett.........1843
Benjamin Bassel, Jr..........1843
William G. Brown............1845
George W. Berlin.............1846
Caleb Boggess................1847
James M. Bennett............1850
A. C. Bowman................1877
Thomas A. Bradford.........1857
Thomas Brown...............1847
Frederick Berlin..............1848
Richard A. Brown............1849
Edward C. Bunker...........1854
John J. Brown 1859
J. Alexander Brown..........1860

Simon Buckingham..........1865
Thomas P. R. Brown.........1869
John Bassel...................1873
A. C. Baker...................1873
James A. Bent................1889
W. E. Baker...................1897

John S. Carlile 1843
G. D. Camden................1843
Jesse C. Canfield.............1892
Gustavus Cresap............1845
Samuel Crane................1849
William C. Carper............1854
C. J. P. Cresap................1860
W. D. Carlile..................1874
J. Philip Clifford..............1889
A. W. Corley..................1892
W. G. Conley.................1894
John F..Corder...............1898

John S. Duncan..............1843
Edgar M. Davisson..........1843

Burton Despard..............1843
Spencer Dayton..............1847
Edwin S. Duncan.............1849
Alston G. Dayton............1878
James B. Dorman.............1847
John A. Dille...............1849
E. S. Daniels...............1883
C. P. Dorr..................1884
M. K. Duty..................1892
C. W. Daily.................1892

Mathew Edmiston.............1843

John S. Fisher..............1855

David Goff..................1843
Claude Goff.................1856
William A. Gibson...........1860
David W. Gall...............1881
William T. George...........1897

William Calder Haymond......1843
Charles A. Harper...........1843
Charles S. Hall.............1843
Edwin S. Hewitt.............1843
John S. Hoffman.............1844
William A. Harrison.........1844
John N. Hughes..............1854
J. S. Hall..................1881
Alpheus T. Haymond..........1843
Joseph Hart.................1843
Marcellus B. Hagans.........1849
Ephraim B. Hall.............1852
Felix H. Hughes.............1859
Willoughby Harrison.........1874
John H. Holt................1883
T. W. Harrison..............1886
Lloyd Hansford..............1887
Charles G. Harrison.........1888
J. F. Harding...............1888
C. C. Higginbotham..........1889
Jasper L. Hall..............1870

William T. Ice..............1866

Robert Johnson..............1843
Waldo P. Johnson............1843
James M. Jackson............1843
Leonidas S. Johnson.........1846
Robert Johnston.............1843

W. B. Kittle................1894
Leland Kittle...............1882

Charles Lewis...............1843
George R. Latham............1859
David H. Lilley.............1863
George H. Lee...............1843
Robert Lynn.................1845
George W. Lurty.............1853
Philetus Lipscomb...........1886
L. M. LaFollette............1889
Lewis C. Lawson.............1889

Addison McLaughlin..........1843
David J. Morgan.............1845
Benjamin F. Myers...........1845
Charles M. Murphy...........1892
John McWhorter..............1851
Henry O. Middleton..........1859
John B. Mason...............1868
John N. Martin..............1869
Benjamin F. Martin..........1873
John W. Mason...............1874
James Morrow................1888
Edwin Maxwell...............1888
E. T. Moreland..............1894
W. B. Maxwell...............1886
C. D. Merrick...............1889

James Neeson................1844

Hezekiah G. Pinnell.........1843
Melville Peck...............1881
A. M. Poundstone............1867
Aldine S. Poling............1892

Albert G. Reger.............1844
S. L. Reger.................1881
Ira E. Robinson.............1891

Augustine J. Smith..........1843
James K. Smith..............1844
J. H. Stewart...............1877
J. G. St. Clair.............1887
Chapman J. Stewart..........1844
S. M. Sommers...............1857
Eugene T. Sommerville.......1879
Robert M. Strickler.........1878
Eugene Sommerville..........1887
W. Scott....................1889
James T. Scott..............1892
George B. Scott.............1897
Fontain Smith...............1866
C. W. Smith.................1873

Uriel M. Turner...............1843	Samuel Woods...............1848
Cabell Tavener...............1843	Benjamin Wilson 1849
Nathan H. Taft...............1846	Enoch T. Withers............1843
Joseph A. Thompson..........1859	Frank Woods................1877
H. G. Thurman...............1883	J. Hop. Woods..............1878
E. D. Talbott................1883	J. B. Ware..................1898
W. G. L. Totten..............1886	Samuel V. Woods............1881
R. E. Talbott................1893	
Alonzo L. Taylor.............1886	U. G. Young................1889
A. J. Valentine..............1886	John Zinn..................1858
	Henry A. G. Ziegler........1869
W. D. Williams...............1846	

Constables.

1843. John Weaver, Isaac Johnson, G. W. Gall, James Wilch, James Benson, Noah B. Wamsley, Alpheus Teter, Absalom Hardin, Elias Alexander, Martin D. Kittle, Samuel Keller, Israel Coffman, William Simpson, Francis O. Shurtliff, F. J. Holder, Asa W. Talbott, John Martin, Joseph Corder, Samuel Holsberry, Garrett Johnson, William W. Jones, Samuel Haddix, Jackson Cash, John Kelly, George Harris, Nestor H. Kittle, Michael Boyles, George K. Digman, Absalom Roberts, Elmore Harrow, Mason Overfield, Jonathan Yager.

1844. John Douglas, Westfield Overfield, James Kesling.

1845. Abraham R. Chrislip, George Simon, Joshua Glascock, Jesse Teter, Samuel Cleavinger.

1849. John Dilworth, James W. McGuffin, Israel Poling, David Wilson, Stephen J. Thompson, Daniel Yager.

1851. James H. Prim, Joshua Wood, Jr., Absalom Wilmoth, Thomas D. Boyles, Gilbert Boyles.

1852. Absalom Digman, William Corder, Jacob Sturm.

1855. Adam Kerr, Asberry Rogers, Philip Digman.

1858. Spencer Glascock, Anthony B. Vannoy, Peter Johnson, Francis Snodgrass, Charles A. Holt, James F. Harvey, Anthony Rohrbaugh.

1859. Levi Bennett, Hansford Glascock.

1861. Minor S. Reynolds, John H. Wilson, Charles M. Groves, Milton C. Atherton, Henson L. Stout.

1862. Abraham R. Ward, N. E. Warder, Benson Simon, Isaac Price.

1863. David Foy, Jacob Waugh, Benjamin Simon, Solomon Coffman.

1864. Stephen Bolton, John Reeves, Isaac F. Hays, Simon Philips, Bartholomew Rosenberger, Salom Smith, Simpson Phillips.

1865. Robinson Woodford, Lewis Zirkle, Philip Rusmisel, John W. Cox, William P. Wilson, Richard Crutchard, Leper Rogers, Michael Simon, Thomas Williams.

1867. Henry A. Markley, William G. Martin, William Cunningham,

Thomas K. Ford, John Stalnaker, Isaiah Poling, John Beaver, Robert G. Thorn, Reuben E. Walden.

1868. Stingley Shaffer, Matthew Edmunds, Daniel M. Williams, William Cade, William W. Johnson, William P. McCoy.

1870. Jacob B. Shroyer, W. G. Martin, Perry F. Poling, William M. George, John R. Shafer, A. C. Leyman, William Simon, John B. Stout, H. J. Thompson, H. Combs.

1872. Nelson Peck, Elmore B. Philips, George W. Fry, Levi H. Campbell, Jesse B. Poling, Robert B. Bartlett, William W. Hudkins, John E. Hulderman, Henry Hovatter, Washington Phillips, J. W. Greathouse.

1874. David S. Talbott.

1876. William Phillips, G. D. Harris, Jethro Bennett, William Price, Sanford Coffman, Terah Osborn, Benjamin K. Knight, William Murphy, Christian Post, I. R. Murphy.

1880. Cornelius Corley, George A. Lough, Francis L. Swick.

1882. William W. Jones, Joseph B. A. Simon, George L. Corder, William S. Scott, Charles W. Haller, Jethro Moore, G. G. McVicker, James Nutter.

1884. G. M. Hovatter, B. W. Gainer, Wesley Bean, William S. Cutright, Matthew R. McVicker, William P. Townsend, Franklin P. Knight, Joseph P. Yager, Simpson Cross.

1888. James D. Thacker, F. A. Simpson, Isaac A. Baughman, Johnson Phillips, Solomon E. Yoke, James H. Bean, Daniel H. Myers, Henry C. Myers, John B. Knapp.

1890. William A. Mason, Charles Cross, F. L. Dennison, Abraham Ware.

1893. E. V. Golden, W. G. Golden, A. J. Cline, Loyal Marsh, Isaac W. Stemple, Monroe Phillips, Enoch Moore, John M. Good, R. A. Chapman, I. H. Miller, Edward England, John Good, L. J. R. Sandridge, J. D. Wentz, Silas Douglass, W. S. Haddix, S. M. Moore.

1894. Haymond Cade, William England, Lee M. Moore, A. J. Golden, A. E. Alexander.

1896. Monroe Shomo, Z. I. Kines, John Harris, Porter Sipe, David Nutter, R. E. Jones, George Price, M. P. Rinehart, Johnson Phillips, George W. McDaniel, Henry O'Neal, Peter T. Reed, John Purkey, H. C. Upton, Ira Harris.

1898. W. J. Lutz, Floyd Ward, Scott H. Shaw.

Justices of the Peace.

1843. David Holder, Jacob Keller, Jacob Bennett, Joseph Teter, Henry Sturm, William F. Wilson, William W. R. Callihan, Samuel Elliott, Elam D. Talbott, Isaac Booth, James T. Hartman, Abraham T. Reger, Jr.,

Jacob H. Burner, Jacob Simon, Jonathan Coburn, Absalom Knotts, Jacob Woodford, Charles Zinn, John H. Woodford, Joseph McCoy, William Shaw, Noah E. Corley, John Reger, Samuel Stalnaker, John Kelley, Michael H. Neville, George Nestor, William Johnson, Thomas Hall, Robert B. Stewart, Abraham Hudkins, Thomas Proudfoot, Robert Talbott, John Hoff, Samuel Cleavenger, Daniel Howdershelt, Absalom Hardin, David Thompson William W. Foster.

1852. Anthony H. Wells, William K. Hall, David Zinn, George W. Bedford, Henry D. Martin, William Biggs, Daniel Yeager, George W. Gall, John N. Hall, Enoch Hall, Solomon S. Leonard, Jesse Teter, Isaac W. Carper, Samuel Haddix.

1856. Joshua Glascock, Sanford Mason, Samuel Holsberry, F. J. Yowell, William W. Jones, Richard Phillips, John P. Thompson, Henry Hovatter, Henry A. Barron, Noah B. Wamsley.

1860. Edward F. Grant, David R. Poling, John Shoeyer, George K. Digman, Hiram Smith, James Proudfoot, Richard T. Talbott, Washington Martin, Joshua Wood, Matthias Benson, Joseph N. B. Crim.

1861. Anthony Rohrbaugh, Martin Myers, Samuel Kelley, Johnson Ward, Arnold Rogers, George M. Yager, Daniel Boyles, Enoch Sayers, Arnold Right.

1862. J. F. Harvey, Leonard Stout.

1863. A. P. Wilson, Aguilla J. Ward, Silas Bennett, James P. Robinson, James Nestor, Allen V. Wilmoth, Daniel Felton.

1865. Henson L. Hoff, William Price, John Douglas, Holsberry Stalnaker, James W. George.

1867. Charles M. Groves, Michael Simon, John B. Ryan, John W. Cox, Abraham Hudkins.

1869. Samuel A. Shanabarger.

1872. Benjamin R. Greathouse, Christopher C. Hovatter, J. D. Martin, Henry Deahl, Franklin E. Payne, J. W. Gawthrop, Lair D. Morrall, John Beaver.

1876. Job H. Glascock, S. M. Cornwell, E. M. Keyser, John E. Clem, A. B. Vannoy, John W. Corder.

1880. David A. Fridley, William J. Bartlett, James D. Corder, Isaac R. Murphy, Washington Phillips.

1882. F. B. Durrett, Simon Swick.

1884. M. Gainer, Phillip Ramsay, John E. McVicker, Joseph H. Lutz.

1888. George M. Kittle, E. A. Waugh, Washington Phillips, Garrison J. Stalnaker, J. W. Wheeler, William H. Swiger, John W. Greathouse, Marion Gainer, Solomon W. Harris.

1890. Ai Cleavenger, Thomas J. Patterson, Sylvanus H. Talbott.

1893. A. W Jones, Lafayette Corrick, A. D. Zirkle, D. B. Ward, E. B. Hudkins, J. C. Felton, John W. White, Jethro Bennett.

NOTES FROM THE RECORDS.

1894. James Coffman, James O'Neal, W. I. Wood, Elsworth McVicker, Franklin Phillips.

1896. W. A. Mason, Nelson H. Harris, A. Rohrbaugh, James H. Nestor, L. N. B. Paugh, William G. Keys, Alonzo G. Bartlett, Isaac I. Murphy, John W. White, D. B. Harsh, David Nutter.

1898. R. M. Nestor, T. A. Law.

County Clerks.

Lair D. Morrall 1843
James T. Hartman 1858
Lewis Wilson 1861
Luther C. Elliott 1879
Granville E. Taft 1891

Circuit Clerks.

E. D. Wilson 1843
L. D. Morrall 1852
David M. Myers 1863
Lewis Wilson 1866
Job H. Glascock 1867
Isaac V. Johnson 1873
James H. Felton 1891
R. E. Talbott 1897

SIGNATURES OF BARBOUR COUNTY CLERKS.

Judges.

Edwin S. Duncan 1843
David McComas 1847a
Joseph L. Fry 1848
George H. Lee 1850
G. D. Camden 1852
George W. Thompson 1853b
Edward P. Pitts 1860b
W. A. Harrison 1862
T. W. Harrison 1863
John Brannon 1873
William T. Ice 1881
A. B. Fleming 1882c
A. B. Parsons 1885c
John Bassel 1886c
Joseph T. Hoke 1889
J. H. Holt 1897
J. Hop Woods 1899f

SIGNATURES OF BARBOUR'S CIRCUIT CLERKS.

SIGNATURES RANDOLPHS CIRCUIT CLERKS.

a—special for Duncan; b—special for Camden; c—special for Ice; f—special for Judge Holt.

NOTES FROM THE RECORDS. 231

Prosecuting Attorneys.

John S. Duncan	1843	William T. Ice	1866
George Hay Lee	1843	H. A. G. Zeigler	1868
Charles S. Hall	1845	Thomas P. R. Brown	1873
G. D. Camden	1846	A. G. Dayton	1885
Daniel M. Auvil	1860	C. F. Teter	1889
Nathan H. Taft	1861	Melville Peck	1893
Spencer Dayton	1863	Charles M. Murphy	1897
Charles S. Lewis	1866		

SIGNATURES OF CIRCUIT JUDGES.

Sheriffs.

Joseph McCoy	1843	James Knotts	1870
John H. Woodford	1845	James W. Talbott	1872
William Shaw	1847	Jacob Hudkins	1873
George Nestor	1849	James E. Heatherly	1881
Henry Sturm	1851	Jacob W. Robinson	1885
John R. Williamson	1852	James A. Williamson	1887
William McClaskey	1854	John W. Shank	1889
William W. Daniels	1860	Truman T. Elliott	1893
James Trahern	1861	John Howell	1895
Spencer Glascock	1863	B. B. Rohrbaugh	1889
Augustus A. Modisett	1866		

County Surveyors.

William F. Wilson	1843	Thomas Wilson	1872
Lewis Wilson	1850	Daniel J. Taft	1885
Joseph Howes	1860	C. Cornwell	1889
Peter Johnson	1867	Alva Wolverton	1893
Orlando P. Hoff	1870	S. L. O'Nael	1897

NOTES FROM THE RECORDS.

Assessor

Jacob Keller	1843
John Callihan	1844
Joseph Teter	1845
Flavius J. Holden	1846
Samuel Elliott	1847
Phineas Phillips	1848
David Holder	1849
Noah B. Wamsley	1850
William M. Simpson	1852
Robert Talbott	1852
Philip Digman	1858
Joseph Marteney	1858
Josiah L. Hawkins	1861
Samuel S. Lackney	1861
G. A. Compton	1862
Daniel Boyles	1864
William P. Keys	1867
Samuel Haddix	1867
William M. Hays	1868
Joseph Marteney	1870
H. H. Stalnaker	1877
Gilbert H. Himes	1885
J. W. Gawthrop	1885
George W. Heltzell	1889
William B. Corder	1889
Isaac M. Poling	1893
John K. Murphy	1893
E. H. Compton	1897
Isaac C. Woodford	1897

School Commissoners Before the War.

Abraham Reger	1843
Joseph Rightsman	1843
James Dilworth	1843
Thos. Proudfoot	1843
Samuel Cleavinger	1843
Lair D. Morrall	1843
Abel Morrall	1843
William Johnson	1843
Daniel Nestor	1843
Felix Ryan	1843
Noah E. Corley	1843
Thomas Hall	1844
John H. Woodford	1844
M. J. Martin	1844
Joseph Teter	1844
Abraham Hudkins	1845
James T. Hartman	1846
Samuel Stalnaker	1846
Elias Alexander	1846
James D. Hall	1846
John R. Williamson	1847
Noah B. Wamsley	1850
Joshua W. Reeves	1850
Daniel Yager	1850
Henson L. Hoff	1852
Henry D. Martin	1852
Isaiah Wilson	1852
Daniel M. Auvil	1853
James O. Carter	1853
George W. Gall	1854
Isaac Johnson	1854
James B. McLean	8516

SIGNATURES OF BARBOUR'S SHERIFFS.

RESIDENCE OF JOHN HOPKINS WOODS.

NOTES FROM THE RECORDS. 235

Robert B. Stewart............1860
Abraham R. Talbott..........1860
Sandford Mason..............1860
Charles Mustoe..............1860

County Commissioners.

Benjamin H. Woodford.......1882
James A. Williamson........1882
William P. Keys............1882
B. B. Durrett..............1882
A. J. Hartman..............1882
Hartzel E. Hoff............1883
Isaac Martin...............1883
F. J. Yowell...............1885
H. H. Stalnaker............1887
M. D. Riley................1891
Thomas B. Mason............1893
Willis Lantz...............1897
J. Ed. Stewart.............1899

Supervisors.

George W. Gall.............1863
G. A. Compton..............1863
Jonas Cooper...............1863
Samuel Knapp...............1863
William C. Trimble.........1863
Jacob Hudkins..............1863
Joseph Teter...............1864
David Zinn.................1864
James Boyles...............1864
Hansford Glascock..........1865
William U. Showalter.......1865
George T. Pickens..........1865
Adam M. Woodford...........1866
James Nutter...............1866
Samuel Holsberry...........1866
N. B. White................1866
Aquilla J. Ward............1866
Samuel Knapp...............1867
A. M. Talbott..............1867
John N. Hall...............1867
Joseph K. Baker............1867
Jesse Fitzwater............1867
Simon Buckingham...........1868
Levi H. Cross..............1868
William J. Bartlett........1868
F. G. W. Ford..............1869
David H. Townsend..........1869
Andrew J. Wilmoth..........1870
Isaac Hovatter.............1870
Jacob Bennett..............1870
John W. Corder.............1871
A. B. Vannoy...............1872
E. T. Brandon..............1872

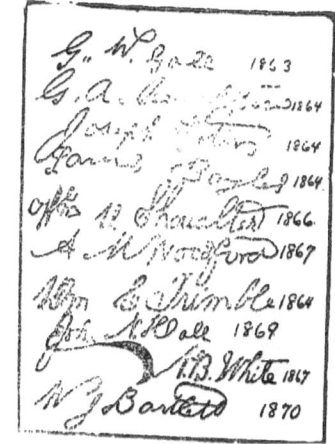

SIGNATURES OF THE PRESIDENTS
OF THE BOARD OF
SUPERVISORS.

School Superintendents.

Lair D. Morrall............1847
Peter Zinn.................1864
Levi Johnson...............1864
Robert A. McClutcheon......1869
Simon Buckingham...........1872
Perry Marteney.............1875
W. D. Zinn.................1885
John L. Malcom.............1887
Simon S. Talbott...........1889
M. C. Lough................1891
George C. Poling...........1893
Charles I. Zirkle..........1895
Le Roy V. Holsberry........1899

Early Prices of Farm Stock.

Prices of some kinds of farm stock have changed since the early days of Barbour County, as will be shown by the following extracts from the records. In June, 1844, at a sale of the property of William Proudfoot, who had recently died, the sums realized seem small in comparison with present values:

2 steers	$13.00	9 hogs	$ 7.50
3 yearlings and 1 calf	10.50	20 geese	2.00
3 cows	25.50	30 bushels of corn	11.25
3 horses and 1 colt	66.12	2 loom	2.00
31 head of sheep	14.98		

The estate of Martin Life, who had also recently died, was settled by appraising and selling his personal property. The sale took place February 22, 1845, and the following list will show the value placed by the appraisers and the amount realized at the sale:

NAME OF ARTICLE.	APPRAISED AT.	SOLD FOR.
1 wagon	$15.00	$10.00
11 head of sheep	9.00	9.16
1 sorrel mare	20.00	9.10
1 grey mare	20.00	5.51
1 grey mare	18.00	3.01
1 cow	8.00	6.00
4 sows and pigs	8.00	5.00
1 wooden clock	8.00	3.50

In 1847 the property of William Chrislip, deceased, was appraised by order of Court, and the following items are selected, with the values given them:

8 head 2-year-old cattle	$56.00	1 yoke of 4-year-old oxen	$30.00
6 yearling cattle	24.00	1 " " 3 " "	30.00
1 sorrel mare, blind of one eye	25.00	14 head of sheep	14.00
1 red cow with white face	12.00	9 head of lambs	4.50
1 red-sided, white-backed cow	10.00	1 old saddle	1.50

CHAPTER XX.

THE CIVIL WAR IN BARBOUR.

The amount of fighting in Barbour County during the Civil War was not large in comparison with southern and eastern counties; yet Barbour occupies a place in history different from others because here was fought the first important engagement. It was not the first fighting, for prior to that time there had been encounters at Gloucester Point, Baltimore, and Sewell's Point, but the action of Philippi June 3, 1861, is regarded as the opening fight of the war.

Causes and events leading up to this great struggle are outlined in former chapters of this book, as far as West Virginia was immediately concerned; and in this chapter affairs of Barbour County will be specially considered. An effort has been made to collect and set down a plain statement of facts concerning the movement within Barbour County immediately preceding and during the Civil War. When Virginia seceded from the Union, the people of Barbour divided into hostile camps. In fact they had divided into parties before that time, one loyal to the Union, the other loyal to Virginia whether in the Union or out. The vote on the Ordinance of Secession showed that a majority were secessionists, but the majority was not large. No record of the vote is found in Barbour. Before that election there were nearly one thousand Confederate troops in Barbour, under Colonel Porterfield, and their presence had an influence in augmenting the vote of the secessionists. Prior to that time several meetings had been held in the county by those in sympathy with secession, and only one meeting had been held by Union men. As early as January 25, 1861, Thomas A. Bradford and Samuel Woods announced themselves candidates for election as delegates to the Richmond Convention, which subsequently passed the Ordinance of Secession; but to be a candidate, at that time, did not imply that they favored secession. Therefore each candidate issued a circular informing the people how he stood on the vital issues. The following is an extract from the circular by Mr. Woods:

"The Union of the United States is a Union of independent sovereignties, except so far as they have surrendered portions of their sovereignty to the Confederacy of the United States for the purposes specified in the Constitution of the United States. Every State adopted the Constitution of the United States as part and parcel of the State constitution. It may of right assume all its rights and sovereignty for such causes as it may deem sufficient for itself without giving just cause of offense to any other State that may decline to do so. The allegiance which the citizens of each State owe to the Federal Government of the United States is subordinate to that due to each State, and may be lawfully withdrawn by each State whenever it may deem it to its interest to do so. When any State exercises these rights by seceding from the present Union of the United States, every citizen of such State is bound to render obedience and allegiance to it alone. There exists no lawful authority in any government, State or Federal, to coerce any State to return to the Union that may have in its sovereign capacity seceded from it, and any attempt to do so is an invasion of the sovereignty of such State, and is equivalent to a declaration of war against it and ought to be resisted at every hazard and to the last extremity. The Constitution of the United States, while its provisions have been observed, has given to the people peace and security at home and power and influence abroad; and if preserved will give the same to our posterity. Every effort and sacrifice, not inconsistent with the sovereign rights and honor of Virginia, should be made to preserve the same from destruction."

Mr. Bradford was considered the secession candidate while Mr. Woods was looked upon as more favorable to the preservation of the Union. Mr. Bradford announced his platform January 21, 1861, in a circular from which the following is an extract:

"I hold that, although the Federal Constitution created a government, yet that government and that constitution were as much dependent upon the will of the people of the several States for its creation and perpetuation as any other constitution in the country. The constitution was ratified by the individual States, each acting for itself as an independent sovereignty, and when the powers delegated by that constitution are perverted to the injury and oppression of any or either of the States, they have the indisputable right to resume them. This right to resume the power delegated to the Federal government was expressly reserved in the ordinance of the Virginia convention which ratified the constitution. This is a right which has always been held sacred by the people of Virginia because it furnished them with a remedy against unbridled majorities. If it be not so, and if the separate States do not enjoy this right, then the idea of State rights and State sovereignty, which has always been the Polar Star of Virginia politics, is a delusive dream, and this a great, consolidated government. But, if a State does secede, has the Federal Government the constitutional right or power to coerce her into submission? I think not. Coercion is war, and the President has not the power to make war upon any country, much less one of the original parties to the Federal compact. Coercion is disunion, certain, inevitable and irreversible; and this state of things I maintain no President, under the flimsy pretext of enforcing the laws, has a right to precipitate upon the country. I believe it is the duty of Virginia to present an unbroken front to her enemies and demand with stern determination all the rights which belong to her and her southern sisters. These rights should be guaranteed upon a basis so firm and stable that the recurrence of our present troubles would be placed beyond the reach of Northern aggression. If we fail in this, I am for Virginia's resuming the powers she delegated to the General Government, and forming such other government as may best secure the liberty, safety and happiness of her people.

"All the evils which now threaten the very existence of our Government have been produced by the lawless and unconstitutional aggressions of the non-slaveholding States. For the last thirty or forty years they have persistently engaged in every species of injustice and insult toward us. They have traduced and slandered us before the nations of the earth. They have denied us equal participation in the common territories of the United States. They have sent their hired mercenaries among us for the express purpose of inciting our slaves to insurrection, and alienating the affections of our people from each other. They have sent their bands of Myrmidons among us to murder our people and steal and destroy our property, and when these infamous malefactors escape into those State they are protected by their executives from the just penalties which our laws denounce against them. In thirteen of the free States they have passed their so-called personal liberty bills by which a felon's punishment is meted out to our citizens if they should go in pursuit of their property which may have escaped or been stolen from them. And finally, they have, by an exclusively sectional vote, repudiating the idea of nationality, elected Abraham Lincoln who is openly pledged to the miserable dogma that the negro is the equal of the white man. I shall favor submitting the action of the convention to the people for ratification or rejection."

Before the close of January a mass meeting was held on Hacker's Creek, with Jacob Woodford as president and Robert Talbott as vice-president. This was designated a "State's Rights" meeting, and after endorsing the candidacy of Mr. Bradford, it passed resolutions favoring the secession of Virginia, declaring:

"The cause of South Carolina is our cause, and we will see her righted to the bitter end, and when she falls, Virginia must fall with her."

Early in February, 1861, a similar meeting was held on Stewart's Run, of which Abraham Simon was president and Anthony Reger vice-president. Milton D. Reed was secretary. There were several speeches made, all favoring Virginia's secession, or, as the minutes of the meeting show, "all taking strong grounds in favor of defending the rights, the independence and the honor of the South at every hazard and to the last extremity." Speeches were made by James D. Hall, R. D. Talbott, L. E. Gall, Granville Carlin, W. W. Carlin and Gideon Reger. In the election which followed, Samuel Woods was chosen from Barbour County. On February 21 he offered the following series of resolutions before the Richmond convention:

"Resolved, that the allegiance which the citizens of Virginia owe to the Federal Government of the United States of America is subordinate to that due to the State of Virginia, and may, therefore, lawfully be withdrawn by her whenever she deems it her duty to do so.

"That in case the State of Virginia should exercise this authority, her citizens would be in duty bound to render allegiance and obedience to her alone.

"That the State of Virginia recognizes no authority in any government, State or Federal, to coerce her or any of her citizens, to render allegiance to the United States, after she may, in her sovereign authority, have withdrawn from it; and that she will regard any attempt at coercion as equivalent to a declaration of war against her, to be resisted at every hazard and to the last extremity.

"That the States of South Carolina, Georgia, Florida, Alabama, Mississippi, Louisiana and Texas, having severally and formally withdrawn the allegiance of their respective people from the United States of America, a faithful, earnest desire to avert civil war, and the sound, conservative sentiment of the country, alike, indicate to the government of the United States the necessity and policy of recognizing their independence."

These resolutions were received in Philippi in the latter part of February, and on March 7 a mass meeting was held at the court house, at which Mr. Woods' resolutions were read and approved. That meeting went as far in its endorsement of secession as any meeting held in the South. John H. Woodford was chairman, Colonel Henry Sturm was secretary, and D. M. Auvil made the opening address. Upon motion of Lair D. Morrall a committee of five was appointed to draft resolutions, and the following persons were appointed on the committee: Lair D. Morrall, D. M. Auvil, J. R. Williamson, R. T. Talbott, and Nathan H. Taft. The committee reported as follows:

"Resoved, that this meeting approve the resolution offered by Samuel Woods, Esq., at the Richmond convention, and that we clearly and distinctly announce and proclaim the doctrine of State's Rights, State sovereignty, and our unalterable opposition to the doctrine of Federal consolidation.

"That we repudiate and denounce the doctrine of Federal coercion, as a principle fatal and destructive to the doctrine of State sovereignty, and which, if attempted to be carried out in any form, will inevitably lead to bloodshed and, in the end, to an exterminating war of section against section.

"That in the opinion of this meeting it is the duty of the Federal Government to immediately acknowledge the independence of the seceded States.

"That in the opinion of this meeting it is the duty of the State of Virginia to immediately withdraw the allegiance of the citizens of this State from the Federal Government."

The records of the meeting do not show that there was a voice raised against the resolutions. Speeches in support of them were made by A. G. Reger, T. A. Bradford, N. H. Taft and D. M. Auvil. In the meanwhile supplementary resolutions were written by Mr. Reger and were adopted as follows:

"Whereas, we, a portion of the people of the county of Barbour, believe that all honorable means have failed on the part of Virginia to reconcile the differences between the North and the South, and that the interest of Virginia is inseparably connected with that of the South, and that the time has come when Virginia should espouse the common cause of the slaveholding states,

"Resolved, therefore, that the State of Virginia should lose no time in making common cause with her sister States of the South, who for years have borne so patiently the encroachment of Northern fanaticism.

"That any attempt on the part of the Federal Government to coerce the States which have seceded, will be regarded by us as a declaration of war upon the whole South."

One man only, a native of New England, but a citizen of Barbour, attempted to speak for the Union, but was driven out while a gun was leveled at his breast.* The requirements of history do not impose upon the historian the duty, at this late day, of recording all the personal dangers and persecutions endured in those troubled times by men on account of their opinions. The statement, however, can be truthfully made that the charge of

---

*This man was Spencer Dayton, father of Congressman A. G. Dayton. He escaped by jumping through a window of the court house.

tyranny, so far as Barbour County is concerned, can not be laid upon those who favored secession, without, at the same time, laying it with equal force upon those who upheld the Union. While Confederate troops were in power here, the Union citizens had a hard lot. When the Federals came into power, the sympathizer with the South often preferred self-exile to the wrongs which he must endure if he remained at home. So, upon this phase of the county's history the curtain will not be raised.

One of the most potent factors in stirring up the people of Barbour against the Government was a newspaper published at Philippi by Thompson Surghnor, the *Jeffersonian*. No paper in Richmond surpassed it in violence of utterances. The editor, however, had the courage of his convictions, and fought and died in the war. His name will be found on other pages of this book. No better idea of the state of feeling in Barbour County, from the secession standpoint, can be given than that set forth by editorials in the *Jeffersonian* at the time. That which was published immediately after the meeting in the court house, March 7, 1861, is selected because it is valuable as an historical document.

"We have no faith in the convention.* The good men of that body are powerless, and their hands are tied by a majority of demagogues whose little, narrow souls cannot rise above party considerations. The Union shriekers hold in check the patriots who would strike for the honor and safety of Virginia. These Union-shrieking knaves and traitors care nothing about the rights and honor of the State. They are preparing for a spring campaign, and their animosity against the Democracy of Virginia is ten fold more intense than their hatred of Abolitionism. These Union-shrieking tories are divided into classes—demagogues and fools. Such men as Willey, Carlile,† and a few others, can lead their small fry into any traitorous design which their sordid natures and their hatred of Democratic principles may contemplate. How the noble spirits of Wise, Montague and Tyler and other patriots must chafe at the disgusting spectacle! It is a wonder they do not retire and leave these base Submissionists full scope to hatch ruinous plots against the State and prepare for a spring campaign when Knownothingism will be fought over again under the Abolition colors of Abe Lincoln.‡

"It never was the intention of a majority of that convention to do anything else but further their designs against the Democratic party of Virginia.§

The leaders are old politicians which the crisis has galvanized into life, and the black bile which has been secreted by years of disappointment will soon be poured fourth upon our people. But if the people will elect such men to office, they must abide the consequences—only it is hard that the true and the good must suffer. The crisis has swept over the country with startling effect and made two nations where only one pre-existed. The return of the Southern Confederacy is now beyond the range of any reas-

---

*The secession convention then in session at Richmond.
†Waitman T. Willey and John S. Carlile.
‡President Lincoln was inaugurated eleven days before this was published.
§At that time the convention at Richmond had not passed the Ordinance of Secession, and there was a general belief that it would not do so. On March 9, (six days before this editorial was published) a test vote had been taken at which secession was defeated by a vote of 89 to 46.

onable expectation. They are free—free from a subtle, designing foe, and by the help of God, and their own self-reliance, they intend to remain free.

This is the plain statement and it is high time that it should be distinctly understood. Men who continue to talk of the Union and saving the Union, are either knaves or fools. The question now is, where shall Virginia go? Shall she go to the North and be ruled by the pharisaical folly that has perverted one of the best systems of government, or shall she go with the South as their co-equal, and where she will be honored and loved? The good men of the State have urged this matter upon their consideration; but thus far the Union-shriekers have turned a deaf ear to their entreaties; nor do we believe that any inducements will cause them to forego this purpose of Abolitionizing Virginia.

"Virginia is now contemned by the North on account of her foolish peace propositions. The mighty Commonwealth which in time past was so noble and so bold, the foremost in fight and the first in council and in field, now stands trembling before Abolition dictation, and vainly begs after compromises from her most deadly foes. Her threats about coercion did not deter Lincoln in his inaugural from taking an opposite position. But let the true patriots in Virginia be not discouraged. Do not leave her now, naked to her enemies. The Satanic ingenuity of those cold-blooded politicians who struggle for the ascendancy of the hour will be instrumental in opening the eyes of the people to their degradation and shame."

Early in 1861, when Virginia politicians had fully made up their minds that Virginia should secede, a close censorship of the United States mails was ordered, and papers and documents, supposed to be hostile to the cause of secession were taken from the mails and destroyed. In Philippi a bonfire was made in the streets of papers sent to subscribers in that vicinity. The post master refused to deliver these papers to the persons to whom they were addressed, but turned them over to secessionists who publicly burned them. A similar course was pursued in other towns of West Virginia.

The inaugural address of President Lincoln was published in the *Jeffersonian*, and an editorial commented upon it, giving the editor's opinion that the President (whom he called "old Abe"), intended to use force against the South. "Too much time," says the editorial, "has already been lost in tomfoolery after visionary compromises. There can be no compromise where fanaticism is arrayed against honor and justice. Lincoln repudiates all compromise and intends to coerce." The article proceeds as follows:

"Business called us to Washington at the time of the inauguration, and we witnessed the ceremony. Would that the entire population of the State could have seen it! If there is one spark of patriotism in the bosoms of those base Submissionists, who have caused so much trouble and delay, the sight would have fanned it into flame. The military display made by old Scott was greater than when we marched into the City of Mexico, and the precautions taken to preserve the life of old Abe were more studied than any Scott had ever used to guard the lives of his soldiers in an enemy's country. Lincoln, weak, foolish and cowardly, was surrounded by cavalry four deep. Is such a creature fit to be the Chief Magistrate of a great nation? Yet this guilty, cowardly, traitorous miscreant is worshipped by the Union shriekers who are endeavoring to Abolitionize Virginia. Mr. Lincoln designs to use the power of the Government to hold, occupy and possess the property and places belonging to the Government, and to collect the duties

JUDGE SAMUEL WOODS.

and imposts. This language applies directly and unmistakably to the seceded States. and enunciates war with the Confederate States of America as plainly as language can do it."

When the Richmond Convention passed the Ordinance of Secession, the movement began in western Virginia for the reorganization of the State Government, or the formation of a new State, or both. Meetings were held in half the counties now forming West Virginia, and delegates were appointed to a convention to meet at Wheeling May 13, 1861. Circumstances were such in Barbour at that time that a meeting of Union men could not be held openly without risk of interruption. There was no lack of Union men, but they were not organized, and in the face of the armed and unarmed secessionists in the county, they could not organize. But when the Confederate forces retired, and the Federals came in, the Union men were found to be numerous. In January 1861, the Palmetto or Confederate flag was raised over the court house in Philippi, and remained there until hauled down by Union troops under Colonel Kelley on June 3, 1861.

Finding that no public meeting to uphold the Union cause could be held in Philippi, a small number of citizens met secretly for the purpose of appointing delegates to the Wheeling Convention. This meeting was afterwards styled, the "Shoeshop Convention," because it met secretly and at night in a shoeshop belonging to Martin Myers. The windows were darkened and the door locked, and only sufficient candle light was used to enable the clerk to do what writing was necessary. Not one word of the proceedings of the meeting have been preserved in writing. The minutes and resolutions were taken to Wheeling and were lost. Not many persons were there. The list, so far as it can be now ascertained, consisted of the names of Martin Myers, Hanson L. Hoff, William K. Hall, Edwin Tutt and Spencer Dayton. Mr. Hoff was chairman and the resolutions were written by Mr. Dayton. Delegates to the Wheeling convention were appointed, namely, H. L. Hoff, Joseph Teter, Sr., Rev. Alpheus Zinn and Spencer Dayton. From some cause the resolutions were not signed that night, and the next day Mr. Dayton carried them to Mr. Hoff, the chairman, for his signature. The chairman took the pen to sign the paper, but hesitated, and laid down the pen, saying:

"I have been thinking about this since last night. I am an old man, and all I have in the world will be taken from me and I will be driven from home if I sign this. The secessionists will not let me stay here if I sign these resolutions. Whether the good these resolutions will do will justify this sacrifice on my part, I don't know."

After a discussion between Mr. Hoff and Mr. Dayton, certain parts of the resolutions, which the secessionists might deem particularly hostile to their designs, were stricken out, and the paper was then signed. The delegates to Wheeling met in Philippi to make ready for the journey. As yet it had not become public that a Union meeting had been held, but it was suspected that Barbour would likely be represented at Wheeling, and the closest watch was kept to thwart any attempt in that direction. Guards were posted at the bridge and no one, suspected of being a Union man, was permitted to cross unchallenged.* When the delegates-elect had reached Philippi and held an informal conference on a street corner, and when the difficulties and dangers in the way of going to Wheeling were understood, all the delegates, except Mr. Dayton, excused themselves from going. Mr. Dayton said he would go if it cost him his life The other delegates returned to their homes, and that night Mr. Dayton prepared to leave Philippi. He saddled his horse and waited till long after midnight when the streets were quiet, and he supposed the guards at the bridge would be asleep. It was his intention to dash past the picket, if challenged. When he reached the vicinity of the bridge, he laid whip to his horse and went through at a dead run, and out upon the pike to Webster. He saw no picket and never learned whether a picket was on duty at that time. At the Wheeling convention Barbour was accredited with three members, Spencer Dayton, E. H. Manifee and J. H. Shuttleworth. Mr. Manifee lived in the Coves, and Mr. Shuttleworth had a farm on Gnatty Creek near the line. Neither of them had been appointed by the meeting of Union men at Philippi. When Mr. Dayton returned from the convention, he reached home late at night, and hoped to enter his house undiscovered; but in this he was not successful. The next day the soldiers went to his house to arrest him, but he was in hiding up stairs and they did not find him. That evening, at dusk, he escaped to the hill back of his house, and succeeded in making his way to Grafton which had been occupied at that time by the advance guard of McClellan's army.

Confederates Occupy Philippi.

Governor Letcher issued a call May 1, 1861, for the militia to take up arms. Four days later Colonel George A. Porterfield was appointed to the command of the troops in Northwestern Virginia, and about the middle of May he reached Philippi and began to organize his troops.† Companies of militia were already there, or joined him within a few days. After his retreat he wrote a letter (June 6) to General Garnett in which he spoke in

---

*The guard was stationed at a small store at the east end of the bridge, kept by Charles W. Russell, a native of Winchester. He also kept the toll-gate at the east end of the bridge.

†On May 14, Colonel Porterfield reached Grafton on his way to Philippi, and the same day wrote to General Lee that volunteers and officers whom he expected to find there had not put in an appearance. He was on the point of setting out for Philippi, and said, "There is great dissatisfaction in this and adjoining counties, and opposition to the lawful action of the State is certainly contemplated. Please direct my letters to Fetterman, one mile west of Grafton, and the only post office in the county to which letters can be sent with safety." It was the intention of the Confederate authorities to have Colonel Porterfield's force in Grafton in time to influence the vote for Secession, on May 24. (See Records of the Rebellion, vol. 2, page 848.)

THE CIVIL WAR IN BARBOUR. 247

disparaging terms of the character of the troops which had joined him, saying:

"This force is not only deficient in drill, but ignorant, both officers and men, of the most ordinary duties of the soldier. With efficient drill officers they might be made effective, but I have to complain that the field officers sent to command these men are of no assistance to me, and are, for the most part, as ignorant of their duties as the company officers, and they as ignorant as the men."

A company of militia, called "the Barbour Greys," afterwards mustered into the Confederate service, was early in the field. Captain A. G. Reger was in command, but later Captain Thomas A. Bradford took charge. The troops were quartered in the court house before Colonel Porterfield came. On May 14, 1861 this company's roll was as follows: Thomas A. Bradford, Captain; George P. Thompson, First Lieutenant; James C. Cline, Second Lieutenant; Micheal M. Rider, First Sergeant; Hiram Smith, Second Sergeant; Hanibal Hill, Third Sergeant; Obediah Phillips, Fourth Sergeant; William D. F. Jarvis, Fifth Sergeant; Edwin D. Williamson, First Corporal; William J. Bonner, Second Corporal; Lemuel Poling, Third Corporal; James E. Hall, Fourth Corporal; George Armstrong, William Barrett, John H. Campbell, James H. Campbell, John J. Golden, James M. Golden, George W. Henderson, David W. Harris, James P. Heckman, William M. Humphreys, Lorenzo D. Humphreys, William Isner, William F. Holt, Mortimer C. Johnson, James E. Lynch, Hickman Minear, William Mustoe, Franklin A. Poling, Allison D. Robinson, Patrick Riley, Fredrick Sandridge, Emanuel Stone, Andrew J. Thompson, Josiah Thompson George W. Thompson Perry M. Talbott, Alexander Whiteley, John C. Wallace, Anthony H. Wells, David Wagoner, John Woodford, David Wilson, Henry H. Barron, John Berry, Charles B. Carter, Eldridge Golden, Thomas B. Johnson, John T. Kent, John M. Sturm and Albert C. Wilson.*

The oldest commissioned Captain of cavalry militia in Virginia at the commencement of the war was Captain W. K. Jenkins, of Barbour County. His troop of cavalry was organized September, 1858, and he was commissioned Captain October 12, 1858. This cavalry was called out by Governor Letcher, and was mustered into service at Philippi, under Colonel Porterfield, May 22, 1861. The roll of the company was as follows:

W. K. Jenkins, Captain; Hanson L. Cross, First Lieutenant; Cregan

---

*This list is taken from the original muster roll of the company dated April 30, 1862. Some of the orignal members of the company may have been killed or may have left the company before this roll was taken. Those who joined the company between May 14, 1861 and April 30, 1862, were as follows: W. H. Benson, W. E. Campbell. James P. Callihan, Elam T. Corder, Francis M. Cunningham, David Dilworth, Granville Evick, Elliott Jones, Isaac Jones, John W. Jones, Joseph M. Jones, William D. Kelley, Joshua Lunsford, John A. Marshall, Franklin Marshall, Oliver Mulleunix, William B. Poling, Harrison Paugh, William Sibert, Charles C. Slenart, Mathias Turner, Sinclair Turner, George W. Trimble, F. M. Trimble, Benjamin Varner, John F. Varner, Hezekiah Bowers, John Beveridge, Cornelius Colan, Daniel Colan, Joseph Church, Solomon Flesher, George Hanger, Abraham Life, Champ Thornhill, Jacob Peck, John W. Lemmons, W. F. Varner, Solomon White, Peter White and George Wymer.

Burner, Second Lieutenant; William Hall, Third Lieutenant; Thompson Surghnor, Fourth Lieutenant; Edward Corder, First Sargeant; Wesley Dilworth, Second Sargeant; Philip A. Reed, Third Sargeant; Samuel Marteney, Fourth Sargeant; James Smith, First Corporal; Jeremiah Harvey, Second Corporal; John M. Radcliff, Third Corporal; Wilson Paugh, Fourth Corporal; S. M. Callihan, First Bugler; Wesley W. Hudkins, Second Bugler; Samuel Cleavenger, Saddler; Adam O. Starker, Farrier; John H. Hite, James P. Callihan, Benjamin J. Cleavenger, William Bartlett, John Cooper, Squire Crouso, Isaac Jones, Elliott Jones, William Reed, Benjamin J. Knight, P. G. Chislip, John Cleavenger, Robert J. Humphreys, Ruben Waldron, Wesley Waldron, George M. Yeager, Van Buren Ward, Champ Thornhill, Worthington Teter, Martin Reger, M. D. Reed, Felix Stewart, Alpheus Corder, Nathan Reed, E. G. Chrislip, Noah Welch, Hezekiah Sargeant, John Welch, Charles Callihan, William Lemmon, Lewis Hickman, Wellington Hickman, Jacob Thrasher, Enoch Talbott, Middleton Jenkins, Dod Long, Gideon Reger, Demetrius Dickenson, Allen Simon, Lemuel O. Marks, John N. Heatherly Elijah Cotteral, E. B. Ward, W. W. Daniels, Richard Hudkins, William H. Dougherty, Daniel Reed, John Pickens, Benjamin J. Rohrbaugh, Alexander Wiley, John Powers, James Teter, George W. Kerr, George Burner, Joel Reger, William Mouser, John Wells, Sansom Zinn, Anthony Zinn, H. L. Shaw and Hanson Mowry.

Captain Hill's Company.

The roll of company E, 62d Virginia Regiment Volunteer Infantry was as follows: Hannibal Hill, Captain; H. H. Stalnaker, 1st Lieutenant; Andrew Valentine, 2nd Lieutenant; Elliott Stalnaker, 3rd Lieutenant; G. S. Hymes, 1st Sargeant; B. H. Woodford, 2nd Sargeant; Jasper Huffman, 3rd Sargeant; J. E. Moore, 4th Sargeant; I. B Talbott, 5th Sargeant: Charles Callihan, Corporal; Valentine B. Poling, Corporal; Metress Dickenson, Corporal; Marion Gainer, Corporal. Privates, Allen Boner, ——— Bolton, James Coontz, Robert Corder, Thomas Carrico, Simpson Cross, Charles Cross, Elam Cross, John Carter, Ahab Canfield, Frank Dadisman, J. N. Dadisman, William Dadisman, Samuel Dickenson, G. W. Dickenson, Silas Dawson, Albert England, Hamilton Fink, Jacob Fink, Frank Finley, Joseph Fitzwater, John Grinnon, Ed. Hall, N. Hall, Nicholas Holsberry, Jacob T Huffman, Jasper Harris, Silas Harris, Isaac Hendrick, Thomas Isner, Henry Isner, William Johnson, Joseph Johnson, Abraham Johnson, Coleman Jones, Cephas Jones, Baxter Kalor, George Kalor, John T. Kent, Melville Lang, Adam Moore, Granville Moore, Edward Mason, George Morris W. H. Murphy, Robert Moran, Joseph Moran, Solomon Myers, Michael Myers, Burrell Nutter, Theodore Nutter, Jesse Poling, Isaac Poling, Uram Poling, Alexander Poling, Hamilton Poling, Israel Poling, Edward Poe.

THE CIVIL WAR IN BARBOUR. 249

George Pitzer, Gideon Reeder, Isaac Rease, Gipson Rease, Martin Sherman, Alexander Sayers, Israel Smith, Harrison Sherman, Ferguson Sherman, Salathiel Talbott, F. M. Talbott, William Wilson, Monroe Wells.

Colonel Porterfield had fourteen companies at Philippi, five of cavalry and nine of infantry. The cavalry companies were commanded by Captains W. K. Jenkins, McNutter(from Rockbridge), Robert McChesney (from Rockbridge), F. F. Sterrett (from Augusta) and McNeill (from Pocahontas); and the infantry companies were commanded by Captains Stoner (from Pocahontas) Anderson and Moorman (from Pendleton) A. G. Reger and Sturm (Barbour), C. C. Higginbotham (Upshur), Felix H. Hull (Highland), Thompson (Marion) and Robinson (Taylor.) This force was about one thousand men.* They were poorly armed and in no condition for fighting There were only one thousand cartridges for muskets, and some of the muskets were flint locks, and some of the men had no guns at all. Captain Jenkins' company had forty sabers, one pistol and one knife. Four hundred rifles were stored in the jail and not an ounce of ammunition for them. The guncaps sent for the muskets were found too small. The company from Upshur was unarmed, and Colonel Porterfield was compelled to send to their homes for want of arms a cavalry company from Pocahontas County and an infantry company from Barbour.

It was not the purpose of Colonel Porterfield to make Philippi his headquarters. He halted there to organize his forces for a movement upon Grafton. It was the avowed purpose of the Confederates not to permit the Federal authorities to use the railroad. The Confederates hoped to hold the whole country to the Ohio, but the immediate object when Colonel Porterfield advanced beyond Philippi was to sieze and hold Grafton and thus control the railroad. He knew he had not men or arms enough to do it, if he should meet much opposition; but he hoped to augment his force of men and arms before he should be attacked. He intended to march to Grafton, telegraph to Harper's Ferry for arms, and have them sent to Grafton by rail. Government forces held the railroad at Cumberland as it turned out and no arms could pass that point. Colonel Porterfield took possession of Fetterman May 24 and of Grafton May 26. A few Union troops were at Grafton, but fell back as the Confederates advanced. It is not the purpose

---

*The evidence given at the court of inquiry, called at Beverly, June 20, 1861, to try Colonel Porterfield, states that his force at Philippi June 3 was 600 infantry and 175 cavalry, total 775.

†See pages 130, 131 and 132 of this book.

‡In order to delay the advancing Federals and gain time to retreat (by way of Fetterman) Colonel Porterfield sent Colonel Willey accompanied by Thompson Surghnor and two others on an outgoing train toward Wheeling late in the evening. Thirty-six miles from Grafton they jumped off the train, burned two small bridges and walked back to Grafton that night. Other parties were arrested and punished for burning the bridges who had nothing to do with it.

of this chapter to review the events in the vicinity of Grafton as the Federals advanced and the Confederates fell back; that has been done elsewhere. Colonel Porterfield saw the necessity of a retreat and he retreated while he could.

On the evening before the retreat from Grafton, Governor Letcher sent a telegraphic order to Colonel Porterfield to seize a train of cars and make a rush on Wheeling and capture the arms which the Federal authorities had sent there. Colonel Porterfield saw the impossibility of executing such an order, and he quietly disobeyed it, never explaining to Governor Letcher why he had not gone to Wheeling. Had he started upon that mission, there is little probability that the train would have reached Wheeling; and had he reached Wheeling, certain capture or destruction would have awaited his command.

The Fight at Philippi.

On June 3, 1861, came the affair at Philippi. Colonel Porterfield, whose forces found it necessary to retreat, was an officer in the Mexican War, and was at or near Buena Vista during most of that time. He graduated from the Virginia Military Institute in 1844 and two years later assisted in raising the first company which Virginia sent to that war. When the Civil War began he was living on his farm in Jefferson County, and offering his services to the Confederate cause, he was sent to this part of the State, as already narrated. He served till 1862, then retired from the army and resumed civil life at his old home. In 1871 he became a banker at Charlestown, West Virginia, where he still resides. Below will be found an account of the fight at Philippi from his own pen, written for this History of Barbour County:

Charlestown, W. Va., Aug. 12, 1899.

Hu Maxwell, Esq., Dear Sir:—Having been requested, by Mr. J. Hop Woods, to send you an account of the surprise of my command at Philippi on the morning of the 3d of June, 1861, I respectfully submit the following report:

I received information on the 2d of June that a strong United States force had reached Grafton, and that my position would probably soon be attacked. The roads leading towards Grafton had been scouted during the day and no enemy seen. After a council held in the evening there was a general understanding that we would retreat, but no time was fixed at which it should begin. Infantry pickets were posted as usual on the roads leading towards Grafton, and the cavalry officers were ordered to scout the same throughout the night. A drenching rain began near midnight and continued for several hours. The guards being without cartridge boxes, and carrying their ammunition in their pockets, which, by exposure to the rain, would become wet and unserviceable, left their posts and came in without being relieved. No report was made to me during the night. The roads being thus left unguarded, the approach of the enemy was not made known. One force, composed of more than two infantry regiments and two pieces of artillery, advanced by the road entering the town from the northwest,

THE CIVIL WAR IN BARBOUR. 251

Another of about the same number came by the road from the northeast. Both reached the north side of the town about the same time, near 4 o'clock, A. M. Their artillery was put in position on a hill to the northwest of the town, and began the fire upon our cavalry camp in the valley below, just north of the town. This fire gave the alarm and caused the cavalry to stampede through the town. The infantry retreated in better order. There was no pursuit.

Whilst on the main street I observed a company in blue uniform—a Union company—standing in line at the north end of the street, which I mistook for one of my own companies, having a similar uniform, and I rode down sufficiently near it to discover my mistake, when I turned and rode slowly away to avoid being recognized. Upon my return I was joined by Robert Johnston, Esq., of Clarksburg, Acting Adjutant, formerly Auditor of Virginia; and we were not discovered and fired upon until near the southern end of the street. We were the last of the command to leave the town.

Colonel Kelley, of the Union side, was wounded as he was about to enter the town. Two or three of our cavalrymen were severely wounded by the artillery fire.

We lost our baggage, a few boxes of old rusty flint-lock rifles and muskets, two kegs of powder and some lead—all the ordnance stores we had. We had neither medical, commissary's nor quartermaster's stores, except the tents of one cavalry company, the only company with the command which had tents. Our subsistence was procured from the surrounding country as needed, and our transportation was by hired or impressed teams.   Yours respectfully,

GEORGE A. PORTERFIELD.

After retreating into Randolph County, and after having for some time endured censure, which all people now admit was undeserved, Colonel Porterfield demanded a court of inquiry which met at Beverly, June 20. If the authorities at Richmond did not openly find fault with him, they remained silent while others found fault; while the truth of history shows that he was not to blame. The fault was with those who sent him to the front, and utterly failed to support him, expecting him, with raw, unarmed troops, in a hostile country, to withstand an attack from troops which could be thrown against him to a number ten or twenty times his strength. On this subject General G. A. Carman, an officer in the Union Army and author of the book *"The West Virginia Campaign in 1861,"* says in one of his letters written to Colonel Porterfield, in 1881: "Your conduct of affairs in West Virginia was a failure only in this, that you had no tools to work with. You advised the authorities and did everything that a soldier loyal to his cause could do, and the result was logically due to the fact that you were not properly supported and your views properly appreciated. You were simply overwhelmed, and no amount of skill or strategy could have saved you."

The court of inquiry at Beverly, June 20, found that he had acted with coolness on the occasion of the surprise; that he had taken precautions against surprise; that he erred in not taking extraordinary precautions in face of the threatened attack, and that the retreat was conducted in good order and that the lesson ought to have good effects throughout the war.

After his retreat from Grafton, on May 29, Colonel Porterfield received

252   THE CIVIL WAR IN BARBOUR.

information which left little doubt in his mind that he would be attacked. About three thousand Federal troops had reached Grafton by the evening of June 1, under command of General Thomas A. Morris. Colonel Benjamin F. Kelley planned the attack for the morning of June 2; but on the evening of June 1, General Morris reached Grafton from Indiana, and countermanded the orders for an attack that night; but he arranged for it the next night following. It was the plan not to drive the Confederates out of Philippi, but to capture them, and to that end, the attacking force advanced in two columns, one east of the river under Colonel Kelley, consisting of 1600 men, and the other west of the river, under Colonel Ebenezer Dumont, with 1450 men, and two brass six-pounders. Colonel Kelley's troops left Grafton on the morning of June 2, on the cars going toward the east. It was announced that they were bound for Harper's Ferry. This was to deceive any spies who might be waiting to communicate with Confederates at Philippi. The soldiers left the cars at Thornton, about six miles east of Grafton, and under the guidance of Jacob Baker, a citizen of Cove District, Barbour County, set out upon the march for Philippi under orders to camp in the afternoon where the men could rest and eat, and resume the march in time to reach Philippi at exactly four o'clock the next morning. This column was to approach on the road leading by the cemetery, but before reaching that point it was the plan to cross the hill and come into the eastern and southern end of town and cut off retreat on the Beverly road. The column under Colonel Dumont left Grafton on the cars on the evening of June 2, and moved to Webster, five miles west, and there left the cars, under orders to march upon Philippi so as to arrive before the town at precisely four o'clock, and to divert the attention of the Confederates until the real attack should be made by Colonel Kelley.

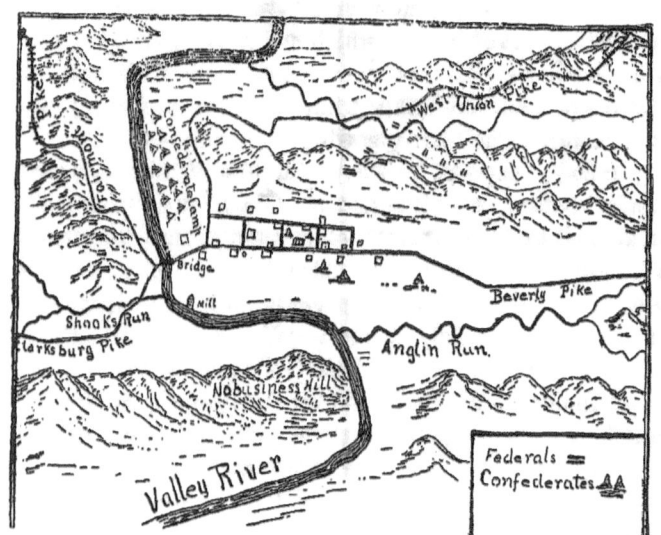

MAP SHOWING THE POSITION OF TROOPS AT THE ATTACK ON PHILIPPI.

The night of June 2, was dark, and soon after night-fall rain set in and

Col. George A. Porterfield.

continued all night. Colonel Kelley had the longer march, and the rougher road, but he had more time and proceeded without incident, but arrived at Philippi about fifteen minutes past four, and a little too late to cut off the retreat. Colonel Dumont's column moved from Webster some hours after dark. Colonel F. W. Lander led the advance and had immediate charge of the cannon. He was not an officer in the army at that time, only a volunteer. The rain impeded their progress, and at a quarter till three o'clock they were five miles from Philippi. From that point they marched on the double quick and at four o'clock had reached their destination. Having thus followed the movements of the attacking forces from Grafton to Philippi, it is proper to speak of the Confederates during that night in and about Philippi.

On the night of June 2, Captain James Dilworth, who had been a militia officer, collected about fifty men at a point seven miles west of Philippi, on the Clarksburg pike, and prepared to dispute the passage of General McClellan's army, which was then supposed to be marching toward that neighborhood. The men were not militia, but the citizens who were armed with corn-cutters, scythes, pitchforks and a few old flintlocks. Captain Dilworth had a sword. The women and children of the neighborhood had been sent to a place of safety. The men marched to a cross-roads, set an ambuscade in a thicket, and waited for the enemy. About midnight the rain set in, and becoming discouraged, the men held a council of war which decided to go home; thus once again verifying the old adage that a council of war never fights. However, the Federal army which attacked Philippi the next morning advanced by another road, and it was no doubt very fortunate that it was so.

Colonel Porterfield on that night had sent a picket down the road toward Webster, and had sent Captain Jenkins with a strong cavalry picket out the Clarksburg road and toward Elk City. The road by which the enemy would be likely to advance being thus picketed, Colonel Porterfield lay down to sleep in fancied security, believing that ample notice of any danger would be given. Captain Jenkins remained on duty all night at Elk City. But the picket on the Webster road came in after midnight. The rain was pouring down, and the pickets concluded that "no Yankees will venture out tonight, by jeeminy," and returned to Philippi. Thus the road was open, and as the Federals advanced they did not encounter a single picket. Colonel Dumont's force reached the top of the hill overlooking the town and on the opposite side of the river, undiscovered, and placed the two cannon in readiness for the fight as soon as Colonel Kelley's force should be in position. But the attack was made a few minutes sooner than was intended.* The Confederates did not make a stand. The cavalry was

---

* It is stated on authority which seems to be unquestionable, that the attack was commenced because of a mistaken signal, a pistol shot fired by a woman, Mrs. Thomas

camped in the lower end of the town, near where the freight depot now is. Of the infantry, some was in the court house and other was quartered in other buildings. The affair on that morning was styled "The Philippi Races." There was little fighting. About half a dozen rounds were fired from the cannon, solid shot being used. One of these balls took off the leg of a cavalryman named Hanger, who had run to the stable for his horse. The stable occupied the present site of C. I. Zirkle's house. The wounded man lay in the stable loft till his leg was amputated by a Federal surgeon. He was cared for by friends in the vicinity of Philippi, and after the war he went to Washington and engaged in the business of manufacturing artificial limbs. A cadet from Lexington, Virginia, named Dangerfield, who had come to Philippi to drill the troops, was wounded nearly in front of the court-house. At that instant a Confederate cavalryman galloped by and lifted the wounded man on the horse behind him and carried him to Beverly, where his leg was amputated. The Federals captured his trunk, and from the similarity of the names they supposed it belonged to Colonel Porterfield and sent it to Huttonsville. They also sent Colonel Porterfield's to him.

The Confederates began their retreat upon the first fire. After the retreat from Grafton to Philippi the strictest orders had been given to waste no powder, and when the time came for the fight, the small supply on hand was mostly abandoned.* The cavalry in the lower end of town went out rapidly, and the infantry followed in considerable confusion. Colonel Porterfield gave no order for retreat. While the Confederate forces were decamping before the fire from the hill beyond the river, Colonel Kelley's troops began to arrive. One body came over the hill back of the

---

Humphreys, and to this circumstance is due the escape of the Confederates, who thus had time to retreat before cut off by Colonel Kelley. Mrs. Humphreys lived on the hill at the old Talbott place, near the road along which the Federals were marching. She was awakened by the passing of the army, the cannon in advance; and being anxious to warn the Confederates of their danger, she waked her son, put him on a horse and started him toward Philippi. He was within full view of the Federals and they arrested him at once. Seeing her son pulled from the horse, Mrs. Humphreys sallied forth to give battle, and she dealt many a blow with sticks, and rocks, and fists, and finally rescued her son. Had she retired to her house at that stage she would probably have been permitted to do so; but no sooner was her son free from the clutches of his captors than she put him on the horse again and attempted to send him to Philippi. He was again pulled from the horse and Mrs. Humphreys renewed her attack upon the Federal army; but she was no longer content to fight with rocks: but pulling a pistol from her bosom she fired it point-blank at the soldiers' faces. Fortunately the bullet missed. The soldiers raised their guns to fire, but an officer forbade it, and in the confusion of the moment she hustled her boy into the house and shut the door. But the pistol shot had had its effect. The cannon had already been planted on the hill and overlooking Philippi; and the order was not to fire unless a signal by a pistol shot should be heard. Mrs. Humphreys' pistol was heard, and the Federals supposing that it was the expected signal, the artillery opened upon the Confederate camp.

*It is related that Captain Higginbotham or Upshur was at the river washing that morning when the artillery opened on the hill. At the second shot he exclaimed, "There's a man who's not afraid to burn powder," and immediately hit the road for Beverly.

THE CIVIL WAR IN BARBOUR. 257

court house, and another body passed through the gap further south, and opened fire. But they were too late to cut off the retreat, but were in ample time to accelerate it.* A detachment sent further south to come into the pike a mile above the town was too late. Colonel Kelley was at the head of his troops, and he reached the main street before the Confederates were out, and while pressing the pursuit and when near the site of the present school house he was shot through the breast by a man who was making his escape from an orchard in the rear of the school house. The officer was carried into Jacob Ashenfetter's house.† A Federal soldier, Alfred Work, was wounded near the eastern edge of Philippi by Confederates in the woods who were making an effort to cover the retreat. He was carried to the house of William K. Hall where his wound was dressed. Colonel Kelley recovered and fought till the close of the war.‡ The retreating Confederates were not pursued far, and they continued their retreat to Beverly.§ Above Belington they met re-enforcements hurrying towards Philippi to render assistance. The cannon had been heard at Beverly,

---

*The excitement among citizens in town was intense. People fled in all directions. One woman forgot her baby in the cradle. Another, Mrs. Mary Rogers, daughter of Captain James Dillworth, fled up the hill back of the residence of Judge Woods. Meeting the advancing Federals in that quarter she raised a white garment on a pole in token of surrender. An officer assured her that she would be protected. She afterwards married Jacob Strader and died at Carthage, Illinois.

†There is much disagreement among the people of Philippi as to the exact point where Colonel Kelley was wounded, and also as to the circumstances under which he received the shot. The official report of General Morris, written June 7, at Grafton, says: "After the bridge was taken, Colonel Lander pressed forward and joined Colonel Kelley, rode into the enemy's ranks, and captured the prisoner reported to have shot Colonel Kelley. He had great difficulty in restraining the Virginia Volunteers from summarily dispatching the man, who is a noted secessionist and a quarter-master of the rebel forces." * * * Colonel Kelley, whilst leading the attack of his column, fell severely wounded by a pistol shot in his left breast." In a report dated Cincinnati, June 3, General McClellan says: "Colonel Lander captured the officer who shot Colonel Kelley."

‡The West Virginia soldiers made Colonel Kelley a present of a splendid horse which he named Philippi in commemoration of his victory. He rode this horse till the night of February 20, 1865, when it was taken at Cumberland, Maryland, by sixty-one Confederates under Lieutenant Jesse McNeill, who also on that occasion carried away from the city General Kelley and General Crook, who were kidnapped in the midst of an army of 4,000 men, and carried to Staunton.

§A mile or two out from Philippi, Major A. G. Reger rode up to Captain Bradford and said: "Captain, wouldn't we better halt the Barbour Greys and give them a round anyhow?" The Barbour Greys were Major Reger's old company, and were armed with shotguns. Captain Bradford, in very emphatic language, and without slacking his pace, answered that

and the militia there moved toward Philippi. But, when the true situation was learned, the re-enforcements fell in line and marched back to Beverly, and after a short halt, proceeded to Huttonsville, eleven miles further south.*

There was one company of cavalry, under Captain Jenkins, which was cut off from the main body when the Confederates retreated. As already stated, Captain Jenkins had been sent out on the Clarksburg road the evening before the fight. His orders were to remain out all night and the next morning report at Philippi. In obedience to these orders he proceeded to Elk City, and after sending out scouts and posting pickets, went into camp. On that night the first man wounded in Barbour County during the war was shot in front of Captain Jenkin's headquarters. The man was Washington Dickenson, not a soldier, but he was for that night, standing picket in place of his brother who had been detailed for that duty. During the night a Federal scout, named Clark, came up the Clarksburg road and fired at Dickenson and wounded him in the hand.† The next morning about nine Captain Jenkins moved toward Philippi, and was almost in the edge of the town when the citizens informed him that the Confederates were gone and the town full of Federals. With that he took to county roads and made his way into Randolph and joined Colonel Porterfield at Huttonsville. About a dozen of Captain Jenkin's men being Union in sentiment and unwilling to fight for the Confederacy, had deserted before reaching Huttonsville. When this was reported to Colonel Porterfield he sent for Captain Jenkins and upbraided him for having a company of Abolitionists. A quarrel ensued between the Colonel and the Captain, and asking for Captain Jenkin's commission, Colonel Porterfield wrote his discharge across the face of it, and handed it back to him, and discharged the whole company. Some of the men returned home and some went into other companies.

Captain Jenkins sold his horse and returned to Philippi where he was arrested by the Federals as a spy, but after a trial he was set at liberty, took the oath not to take up arms against the United States, and during

---

he didn't think it prudent for shotguns, and not a cartridge for them, to oppose long-range artillery. That was the only proposition to stop and fight that was made during the retreat.

*It is peculiar that the sound of the cannon was heard at Beverly, 24 miles in an air line, with a mountain between, while not a sound was heard at Elk City, less than four miles in an air line, over an open country.

†This man Clark subsequently went to Randolph County in August, 1861, as a spy to discover the plans of General Lee who was threatening Elkwater and Cheat Mountain. He was captured and spent eighteen months in Castle Thunder, at Richmond. He was exchanged, was made a lieutentant of cavalry, and was killed at Winchester. His body was aken to Bridgeport, in Harrison County, and was there buried.

the remainder of the war he remained at his home at Elk City. He served fifteen days in the Confederate army.

The hill from which the Federals fired their first cannon was then in woods. It is now cleared of timber and in pasture. The spot has an historical importance as it marks the place where the rising powers of the North struck the first blow against the arms of the South. From the firing of that cannon, the roar of artillery seldom ceased, until the Southern Confederacy was a thing of the past and the chains had been struck from millions of slaves. A monument should be erected to mark the historic spot, and the American flags hould float perpetually over it.

HILL FROM WHICH THE FIRST CANNON WAS FIRED.

General Garnett in Barbour.

When Colonel Porterfield retreated over Laurel Hill, there remained no armed Confederates in Barbour County. Men returned to their homes in the county who had found it necessary to leave because of their Union sentiments. On the other hand, many men whose sympathies were with the South, went away with the retreating Confederates. The Federal troops who occupied Philippi on the morning of June 3, did not fall back to Grafton, but remained as a garrison;* and within a short time others arrived, and before the end of the month of June General Morris had about 4000 troops at Philippi, and there were four times that many at Grafton, Rowlesburg, Clarksburg and elsewhere in the vicinity. General McClellan had crossed the Ohio in person (June 19) and had taken command of this army of 20,000 with which he expected to clear all the northern part of West Virginia of Confederates. He was never ordered into West Virginia, by the War Department at Washington. He came without orders. Soon after the fight at Philippi there were numerous applications from West Virginia to be mustered into the Union service, and on June 6, Winfield S. Scott, then Lieutenant General of the United States Army, ordered General McClelland to muster them in. On June 10, the Secretary of War countermanded this

---

*The Federal soldiers raided the office of the *Jeffersonian*, broke up the press and threw the type in a well. The editor, Thompson Surghnor, retreated with the Confederates. The Federals also raided the Bank of Philippi, and not finding any money in sight, they blew open the safe. But it was empty also. All the funds of the bank, and other things of value, had been removed to Beverly the day before.

order. Within the four days, between Scott's order and the countermand, nearly enough had applied at Grafton to make a regiment. The two conflicting orders created confusion, and on June 11 General Morris, at Grafton, telegraped to General McClellan at Cincinnati, as follows:

"If we don't muster Virginians into the service according to proclamation and arm them, we must quit the territory or prepare to hold it with Federal troops. The strong motive of the move here is gone unless their volunteers are received. Such as volunteer for the service will not enter unconditionally, having not State aid. Small force of rebels can control numbers. Have already mustered some informally. When a regiment is ready it will not do to disband. The effect would be disastrous. It is the cheapest way to defend Western Virginia. It is the only way to unite her citizens. Other methods will fail."

McClellan urged the enlisting of West Virginians, and it was done, subsequently, to the number of over 36,000.*

The Federals showing no inclination to fall back from Philippi, the Confederates pushed reinforcements over the mountains from Staunton into Randolph; first, for the purpose of preventing the further advance of the Union forces, and, second, for the purpose of pushing northward and re-capturing the railroad. General Garnett superseded Colonel Porterfield in command. He had no doubt of his ability to prevent the Union forces from advancing, after he had fortified Laurel Hill and Rich Mountain; but he did not think he would be strong enough to make an advance. He had about six thousand troops, of which 4000 were at Laurel Hill in Barbour, 1300 at Rich Mountain in Randolph, and about 700 at other points. General Garnett had reached Huttonsville June 14; on the 15th with 2000 troops he left Huttonsville, and on the 16th occupied Rich Mountain and Laurel Hill. On June 25 he wrote to Richmond saying that he had blockaded all the roads crossing Laurel Hill between Cheat Mountain and St. George, by cutting trees across them, to prevent the Federals from getting in his rear. He sent out heavy escorts towards Philippi and Buckhannon to collect grain and cattle, and spoke of widening the road from St. George to Rowlesburg

---

*At the time the Federal army moved into West Virginia, a foolish and unnecessary fear seized the people that a terrible example was to be made of them. Reports flew thick and fast. One was that sixty thousand Union troops had been scattered along the Baltimore and Ohio Railroad with orders to sweep southward and destroy all property of Southern sympathizers, and drive the people from their homes. Of course, everybody should have known better. In Barbour County there are instances of families congregating at one place, in expectation meeting death from the advancing Federals, while the men, with what guns they had, stood ready to fight for their families till death. The scene appears ridiculous now, but it was terribly serious at the time. General McClellan's proclamation, promising protection and safety, evidently had not yet circulated through the interior of the State. See page 132 of this book.

and by that route reach the railroad; but he added that with his present force he feared the railroad was beyond his reach.

"My best chance of getting at the railroad at present seems to be by the Morgantown road running from Yeager's to Evansville. When once to Evansville, I should threaten equally Grafton and Cheat Bridge, at both of which points they now have a force which they would be compelled to keep in this position, and thus enable me to get at the road at Independence, destroy it there, and then fall upon the force at Cheat Bridge, before it could be reinforced from Grafton. The objection to this operation is that it enables the enemy at Philippi to throw himself upon my rear. My moving force, however, of 3000, will not be sufficient, I fear, for the operation."

At that time there were 20,000 men opposed to Garnett; and he estimated them at 17,000; yet, he seriously considered attacking the railroad with 3000 troops. Speaking further in his letter to Deas on June 25, he says:

"At Philippi the enemy occupy the heights beyond the town' in the direction of Grafton. They have mined the bridge and thrown abatis in the ford. It is further said that they have blocked up the road on this side of Philippi."

On July 1 General Lee wrote to Garnett and urged him to strike the railroad if possible, saying: "The rupture of the railroad at Cheat River would be worth to us an army." On July 6 General Garnett wrote from Laurel Hill: "I don't think it probable that the enemy, notwithstanding his superiority of numbers, will attempt to attack my position unless the necessity of his force elsewhere becomes very imperative, for the simple reason that he has as much of Northwestern country as he probably wants." To this General Lee replied on July 11 saying that he did not believe the Federals would remain at Philippi and the other points which they then held, but would endeavor to push over the mountain to Staunton.*

Such were the Confederate plans, fears and hopes. The Federals who opposed them also had fears and hopes. General McClellan, late in June, began to concentrate troops for attacking the Confederates at Rich Mountain and Laurel Hill. The chief point of attack was Rich Mountain. Believing that he could capture that point, McClellan expected to cross to Beverly and compel Garnett to retreat from Laurel Hill. The attacking column moved from Clarksburg and other points to Buckhannon, ready to advance up the Beverley Pike.

General Morris, with 4000 soldiers, was at Philippi, and the task assigned him was to advance to Belington and threaten Garnett at Laurel Hill and hold him there while McClellan executed the contemplated move-

---

*Colonel Porterfield had been ordered to destroy the Baltimore and Ohio Railroad, and particularly the bridge across Cheat River at Rowlesburg, but was provided with no tools for doing it. He attempted to destroy Cheat Bridge after his retreat to Philippi, and sent Lieutenant Lemuel Chenoworth to Rowlesburg for that purpose; but the attempt was a failure.

ment by way of Buckhannon to Beverly. About July 2, General Morris became excited over a rumor that the Confederates intended to attack his force at Philippi. He urged McClellan to send reinforcements. To this McClellan at Buckhannon, replied, saying: "I am not a little surprised that you feel the defense of Philippi so hazardous and dangerous an operation. If 4000 of our men, in a position selected and fortified, are not enough to hold the place against any force these people can bring against it, I think we had better all go home. You have only to defend a strong position, or at most, to follow a retreating enemy. I propose taking the really difficult and dangerous part of the work on my own hands. I will not ask you to do anything that I would not be willing to do myself. But let us understand each other. I can give you no more reinforcements. I cannot consent to weaken any further the really active and important column which is to decide the fate of the campaign. If you cannot undertake the defense of Philippi with the force now under your control, I must find someone who will. Do not ask for further reinforcements. If you do, I shall take it as a request to be relieved from your command and to return to Indiana. I have spoken plainly. I speak officially. The crisis is a grave one, and I must have generals under me who are willing to risk as much as I am. Let this be the last of it. I wish action now and determination."*

Three days later General Morris was ordered to advance to Belington. On July 6, General McClellan, still at Buckhannon, sent him an order, of which the following is an extract:

"Advance from your present position tomorrow morning and take up a position within two miles of the enemy, near Elllott's farm, in preference on the south side of Barker's Mill Run, on the heights in the rear of William Yeager's house. It is preferable to avoid the defile north of the Elliott house by crossing the river somewhere near the nineteen mile post from Beverly, and recrossing at the ford where the Middle Fork road crosses. At all hazard accomplish the object proposed. Occupy Belington by a strong advance guard, and place a strong detachment to cover the paths leading from the Rebel camp to the left flank of your position. Watch closely day and night. Have everything ready to pursue them should they retreat. Arrange your hour of starting from Philippi so that you will reach the Elliott farm within an hour or two after sunrise. Induce them to believe that you will make the main attack; the object being to cut them off at Beverly."

No sooner had General Morris reached Belington than the Confederates opened fire on him, and there was constant skirmishing, but not much

---

*It is the opinion of some military men that General Morris was the wiser of the two on that occasion. General J. D. Cox, writing years afterwards, in "The Battles and Leaders of the Civil War," said that if Garnett had been as strong as McClellan supposed him to be, there was nothing to prevent him from overpowing Morris at Philippi, and when this was done, the road to Clarksburg would be open and there would have been a race between him and McClellan which could get there first.

FLOURING MILL AT MANSFIELD.

DYER & SWITZER'S STORE AT MANSFIELD.

THE CIVIL WAR IN BARBOUR.

damage was done.* On July 9, General Morris wrote from Belington, saying: "Our advance position is behind Belington some 200 yards. The cleared grounds extend some 200 yards beyond Belington. A heavy body of timber then commences, which is now occupied by the enemy in large force. Skirmishing has been going on since the occupation of our position. Yesterday they appeared in such force that we threw severel shells into the woods and attempted to occupy it with our pickets; but we were driven in with a loss of two killed and three wounded. Our total loss up to this time, in killed, is 4, wounded 6, missing 1. * * * * The enemy were in motion several times yesterday and their columns were seen marching in our direction. We are sure they were last night in rear of a round hill in front of Belington, and within three-fourths of a mile, and in numbers at least two or three thousand."

The events which followed took place outside of Barbour County and will be briefly mentioned. On July 11 McClellan attacked and defeated the Confederates at Rich Mountain, and thus opened the way to Beverly, where he would be able to cut off the retreat of General Garnett in the direction of Staunton. The fight at Rich Mountain was really made by 300 Confederates on the summit of the mountain at Hart's house, who were attacked by 1900 Federals who had marched ten miles through the woods and thus flanked the Confederate post. The main body of the Confederates at that time was at the western base of Rich Mountain, nearly two miles from the battle ground. The Federals defeated the Confederates on the mountain, gained the Beverly pike and cut off the main body of Confederates, 600 of whom surrendered two days later, after

BATTLEFIELD OF RICH MOUNTAIN.

---

* General Garnett was afraid that his rear would be attacked by troops who would go up the Cheat River road, cross by way of Pheasant Run to Leading Creek and come in south of his position. The Federals could have flanked him without so much trouble. Their infantry could have crossed Laurel Hill anywhere, and no doubt would have done so had it been necessary; but the flank movement at Rich Mountain decided the day, and there was no necessity of attacking Laurel Hill. Military men have expressed surprise that General Garnett supposed his position strong enough to hold. Had he fallen back to Cheat Pass, above Huttonsville, he probably could have held his ground a considerable time.

vainly trying to escape through the mountains. At one o'clock on July 12 McClellan reached Beverly, and thus cut off Garnett's retreat over Cheat Mountain, just what he had set out to do. But Garnett was no longer at Laurel Hill. He learned of the defeat of his force at Rich Mountain, and he hurriedly decamped in hope of getting through Beverly before too late. He could have done so, but for mistaken information. His scouts saw soldiers in Beverly on the morning of July 12, and supposed them to be Federals; but they were really Confederates, a squad of fifty or more under Captain Nat. Tyler, who had escaped from Rich Mountain, and after wandering all night in the woods, had reached Beverly, from which point they retreated south.

When General Garnett, on his retreat from Laurel Hill, reached Leedsville, where the town of Elkins now stands, he turned up Leading Creek and crossing into Tucker County, tried to escape in that direction. General Morris was in pursuit from Belington. On the morning of July 13, at one o,clock, he reached Leadsville, and halted two hours for rest. He had only four wagons of bread and pork to feed an army of 3000, having left Belington in such a hurry that he could not wait for more supplies. At 4 a. m. he continued the pursuit, the Confederates at that time being from six to ten miles ahead of him, and cutting trees across the road at every opportunity. About 8 a. m. the advance guard fired upon the Confederates on Pheasant Run, and about noon at Kalor's Ford another skirmish took place. At 2 p. m. the Confederates halted at Corrick's Ford, a mile above the present town of Parsons, on Shaver's Fork, and the Battle of Corrick's Ford was fought there. It was not a severe fight, but each side suffered a small loss, the Confederates losing the most. They continued the retreat nearly a mile further to another ford where General Garnett with a small squad made another stand, and he was killed. His army continued the retreat, throwing away ammunition, guns and supplies, and after narrowly escaping capture at Red House, 24 miles beyond Corrick's Ford, by an army under General Hill, the remnant of the Confederate force reached Petersburg, Grant County, and after a rest of a couple of days, proceeded to Highland County. The Federals under Morris were not in condition to continue the pursuit beyond Corrick's Ford. They were starving, and returned to Belington by way of St. George and Clover Run.

Internal Affairs During the War.

Nearly all the county and district officers of Barbour County, at the outbreak of the Civil War, were sympathizers with the South. Those who did not go away with Colonel Porterfield, or soon after, did not choose to carry on the country's business, and there was a period of several months during which there was no execution of law, except such as the Federal officers took a hand in. On May 8, 1861 the county court adjourned and there is no record of any other court till October 7, of that year. On September 27 there was an election held "to fill vacancies". Lewis Wilson was elected County Clerk, James Trahern Sheriff,* Nathan H. Taft Prosecuting Attorney, Josiah L. Hawkins and Samuel S. Lackney Assessors. Constables were elected. This was the first election under the Re-organized Government of Virginia. Philippi was almost deserted. Lawyers who had joined the Confederates left their offices and books, and these were looked after by nobody. Many books, as well as much household goods, were carried away by thieves. Valuable portions of some libraries were preserved by Spencer Dayton who, when the war was over, restored them to their owners. This was particularly the case with Thomas A. Bradford's books. Although he was an active Secessisnist, and Mr. Dayton a strong Union man, yet they had been before, and ever after were warm friends, and Mr. Dayton cared for his library and restored it to him, notwithstanding an effort was made at one time by a Federal officer to confiscate the books (no doubt for his own benefit). When Union soldiers were not occupying the town, often not a human being was to be seen on the streets. The country people preferred to stay at home, and few citizens of the town occupied their houses. Occasionally detachments of Union troops passed through the town; and at intervals long trains of wagons, hauling supplies to Beverly or other points, would break the monotony of the scene.

On page 86 Minute book No. 8, of the county court of Barbour, under date of June 2, 1862, the following resolution, offered by Spencer Dayton, is recorded:

"Whereas, on this date one year ago our court-house and county were in possession and under the domination of organized bands of rebels who, by force of arms, deprived our citizens of their peaceful rights of resort to courts of justice, and in effect declared war against existing laws and authority, and against citizens who recognized or appealed to such laws; and in place of the Federal banner, they unfurled from the roof of this house a miserable badge of disloyalty and treason. But, on the following

---

*In the winter of 1862-3 Sheriff Trahern was taken from his home by a detail of seven Confederates who had been sent for that purpose by General Imboden who was in winter camp in Augusta County. The Sheriff was taken to Richmond and was held sometime, when he returned home. Five of his captors were Barbour County men, and after his return he informed on four of them, and they were compelled to leave Barbour. The fifth man befriended Mr. Trahern, and gave him money to mitigate his suffering while a prisoner, and when the others were informed against at the close of the war, this man's name was not mentioned, and he remained in Barbour, and is today one of the prominent business men of the county. The kidnapping of the Sheriff had deplorable results. The next night two prominent citizens of Barbour, Henry Bowman and Henry Wilson, who were Southern in their sympathies, were assassinated under the mistaken belief that they had been implicated in the kidnapping of Sheriff Trahern.

day, June 3, 1861, the traitors were routed and driven from our midst in base and cowardly confusion by volunteer soldiery of the United States, through whose timely aid our citizens were relieved from an abhorred despotism and have since enjoyed protection and the rights and blessings of civil liberty under the government to which they were reared.

"Now, therefore, we the body of Justices for the County of Barbour, State of Virginia, as a court, this day assembled at Philippi, do for ourselves, and on behalf of the people, enter in our record our sincere thanks to the Federal soldiers engaged in the battle of Philippi, and to their national-head and commander-in-chief, Abraham Lincoln, President of the United States. We especially congratulate him upon the firm, energetic and just manner in which the present war has been conducted on the part of the United States since the first blow was struck here one year ago. We tender him our sympathy and support in his responsible labors, commending to him, under the constitution, a merciful regard for the rights of the several States and the citizens thereof held by the confederated enemy, rigidly enforcing only during the war the laws of the forfeiture of property in slaves just so far as may become a military necessity for the suppression of the rebellion or the submission or extermination of those actively engaged in it. A copy of this entry is directed to be forwarded to the President of the United States and furnished to the press at large for publication."

On October 6, 1862, the county court levied a poll tax of forty cents and a property tax equivalent to 32 per cent of all taxes imposed, and thus raised money to pay a bounty of fifteen dollars each to citizens of Barbour who would volunteer in the Union army.

The Imboden Raid.

In the spring of 1863 occurred the memorable raids under General John D. Imboden and General William E. Jones, when 5,000 Confederates swept across West Virginia. Barbour County was not much concerned in the raid, in comparison with other counties of the State, as only a few bands of Confederates penetrated to Philippi. Late in April Imboden, with 3,700 troops, crossed the Alleghanies into Randolph, and at the same time a column of 1,300, under Jones, crossed the Alleghanies from Grant County, through Maryland, into Preston County. It was the intention to unite the two columns about Clarksburg. Jones met a set-back at Greenland Gap, which delayed him eight hours. Captain Wallace with eighty men fortified a church in the pass and held it until the building was set on fire. After capturing the pass, Jones pushed on, struck the railroad at Oakland, again at Terra Alta, cut down the suspension bridge across Cheat River at Albrightsville, three miles from Kingwood, captured Kingwood; attacked Rowlesburg, but failed to take it; broke the railroad at Independence; captured Morgantown; set on fire the bridge there, but permitted the flames to be extinguished; and marched to Fairmont and commenced undermining the bridge there to blow it up. Leaving Jones there for the present, it is necessary to follow Imboden's column as it advanced through Randolph. He moved against Beverly which had a Federal garrison of 878 men under Colonel George R. Latham, who held his ground some hours, but finding that he was being surrounded, he retreated toward Philippi at 5 p. m. The roads were so muddy that horses struggled along half buried in mire and water. The Confederates pursued to the base of Laurel Hill, and a small detachment under Major D. B. Lang, was sent toward the railroad to gain intelligence of the whereabouts of General Jones. The main body under Imboden moved out on the Buckhannon road. It is now necessary to leave Imboden for the present, west of Beverly, and speak of another factor which influenced the results. The Federal troops in this part of the State had fallen back to Clarksburg at Imboden's approach. General Mulligan with about 800 Federals had crossed from Keyser, and was near Grafton when he heard of Imboden's advance toward Barbour. Thus on April 26 the affairs stood—Jones with Confederates near Morgantown, Mulligan with Federals near Grafton and Imboden with Confederates west of Beverly. Taking up the account here, Imboden in his official report says:

"On the evening of the 26th I crossed Middle Fork and encamped about midway between Philippi and Buckhannon, some twelve miles from each, sending all my cavalry forward to sieze and hold the bridge across the Buckhannon River near its mouth. Considerable cannonading was heard at this time in the direction of Philippi, which I supposed to proceed from the enemy we had driven from Beverly, in an endeavor to prevent Major Lang from going toward the railroad where I had expected him to find General Jones. But at 11 o'clock Colonel Imboden informed me that the Beverly force had passed up toward Buckhannon at sunrise that morning, and that there was a fresh brigade at Philippi, reported by the citizens to have arrived the night before from New Creek, under command of General Mulligan, and that the cars had been running all the night previous and that other troops were in the vicinity. He requested me to send two regiments of infantry and a section of artillery to the bridge that night, as he was apprehensive of attack. He also informed me that he had captured a courier from Buckhannon and that two others had escaped and gone back to that place. * * * Knowing that General Mulligan was east of the Alleghanies when our expedition set out, and not hearing from General Jones, it was the opinion of all present that he had failed to reach or interrupt communication on the Baltimore and Ohio Railroad, and that our position was exceedingly critical * * * and if we were beaten, the enemy could cut off our retreat at Laurel Hill and at Buckhannon or Weston. I concurred in the opinion of my colonel that in the face of this new information it woule be extremely imprudent to advance farther or remain where we were, with the danger of being overwhelmed and cut off in a few hours, and that the safety of the command required that we should fall back to a position where escape would be possible if we were overpowered. Accordingly, we marched back to Roaring Creek on the 27th. The road was so bad that it took nine hours to accomplish two miles."

General Mulligan, after penetrating into Barbour,* learned that Gen-

---
*On this campaign General Mulligan wore green clothes. He was an Irishman, and his whole brigade was Irish, and had a reputation as fighters. Mrs. Mulligan accompanied her husband on this expedition, as was her custom. She shared with him the

eral Jones was threatening Fairmont, and he hastened to fight him, but arrived too late to prevent the destruction of the bridge at that place. Mulligan then fell back to Grafton, and Jones proceeded to Philippi, and passed on to Buckhannon, and to Weston, joining General Imboden. Jones intended to destroy the bridge at Philippi, and his soldiers had straw piled on it ready for firing; but upon the urgent request of Southern citizens, chief of whom was Elder Joshua S. Corder, the bridge was spared. No doubt the Confederates were influenced in this by the argument that they might need the bridge themselves before many days while on a retreat. On May 2, General Jones, at Philippi, collected all the cattle and horses taken in Monongalia, Preston, Marion, Barbour and Tucker Counties, thousands in number, and sent them south by way of Beverly. General Jones paid for some of these in Confederate money, and some were stolen from the people. At Morgantown his men with swords galloped along the streets, cutting the halter-straps of horses found hitched, while other men corralled the animals and drove them off, offering to pay for nothing. Nearly the same course was pursued at Kingwood and Fairmont.*

The "cannonading heard in the direction of Philippi," spoken of by General Imboden, was done by General Mulligan during an encounter with Major Lang's detachment of Confederates. The men under Lang advanced down the pike to the large rock about a mile south of town, where they met some of Mulligan's men. The Federals fell back, and the Confederates did likewise.

In 1863 another levy was made in Barbour County to pay a bounty of fifteen dollars to all Federal soldiers who had enlisted before that date. The rate was twenty cents poll and sixteen per cent of the full rate of property.

Federal Soldiers from Barbour.

No list has ever been compiled of the Union soldiers who went to the war from Barbour County. Many went to other counties, and some to

---

hardships of camp life. He was killed in the vicinity of Martinsburg near the close of the war. A fortification built by him on the hill overlooking Petersburg, in Grant County, is still called Fort Mulligan.

*When it was learned that Confederates were approaching Philippi, Spencer Dayton hurriedly secured the most valuable of the county records, filled a coffee sack with them and carried them to Joshua Glascock's house, in Pleasant District, where Mr. Glascock assisted in concealing them. West Virginia at that time was just succeeding in achieving its Statehood, having separated from Virginia; and the Confederates were particularly anxious to destroy records and worry officers of the Re-organized Government. Before Imboden set out upon this raid, as early as January 20, 1863, General Lee wrote to him as to his conduct in West Virginia, instructing him to "render the position of Sheriff as dangerous as possible." The Confederates, when raiding in this State, never lost an opportunity to carry away the records and worry the officers of this State. The Sheriff in Randolph, J. F. Phares, was shot, and in Barbour the Sheriff, James Trahern, was carried as a prisoner to Richmond.

THE CIVIL WAR IN BARBOUR. 271

other states, and enlisted. In March, 1864, the county court voted a bounty of $200 for each volunteer credited to Barbour, and negotiations were entered into by the Board of Supervisors to borrow money from the Bank of Clarksburg to pay the bounty. In case the money could not be obtained at Clarksburg, the agent appointed for the purpose was authorized to go to Wheeling for it. No record is found in the court house here by which it is shown whether any money was obtained; but probably none was procured at that time, for on May 31, 1864, the court ordered that two notes, of $100 each, payable in nine and twenty-one months, with interest, be given to soldiers as their bounty. Following is a list of the soldiers entitled to the notes.

John Chips
Bernard W. Fisher
Lloyd Wright
Noah J. Sipe
Joseph H. Satterfield
A. F. Wilson
John Crits
Philip Coonts
George H. Richardson
John R. George
Adam Minear
James F. Harvey
Henry Fortney

Calvin Courtney
Samuel Randall
John Yates
John Anderson
Henry H. Guseman
Otha Moore
William M. Duffield
Rolley Wright
John Millan
Joseph E. Hill
David H. Cox
David D. Riley
James W. McAtee

John D. Reese
Preston Campbell
Francis Loman
Henry H. Clutter
Thomas F. Wilson
Samuel W. Boyles
Allen C. Marsh
Andrew J. Wilmoth
Joseph H. Clayton
Wesley Bolton
Francis B. McDermott
J. M. C. Harris
William E. Walker

In June, 1864, an additional list of soldiers is found who were ordered to be paid the bounty. The names are given below:

William W. Cain
Remembrance L. Ferguson
John Hoge
Joseph B. Johnson
William B. Martin
Vernon M. Clary
Thomas J. Ashley
George H. Bistell
Silas Cornwell
Samuel Riggs
Euric Strasnider
Armor Strasnider
William Van Horn
Lewis B. Workman

J. F. Cumberledge
Braly Gump
Robinson Hostuttle
Noah J. Meriner
Daniel White
Henry S. White
George W. Ashley
Emory B. Clary
Sabeus Main
Rezin W. Reger
Stephen Shrisler
Francis M. Stansberry
William T. White
David W. Heatherly
William Howell

Joseph S. Durrah
Hiram Gump
Abraham Hostuttle
Alfred McMaster
William O. Hennen
Stephen Stiles
John Boller
Elias N. Cornwell
Thomas H. Neal
Ozias T. Richardson
John L. Scritchfield
Henry Taylor
Hamilton Wise
Abraham Jobuson

272   THE CIVIL WAR IN BARBOUR.

The Union soldiers from Barbour were exempt from poll tax. In September, 1864, the bounty was raised to $300, payable in three installments in four, eight and twelve months. At the same time a bounty was provided of $10, to go to the recruiting officer for each volunteer whom he might induce to enlist. The volunteer was required to be a citizen of Barbour. This measure was deemed necessary to prevent volunteers from other counties coming to Barbour to get the bounty. All counties did not offer the same bounty, and men who contemplated volunteering would go to the county which paid the highest bounty. Preston County, which was very liberal with bounties, paid them to many a volunteer from other counties. Additional soldiers from Barbour who were paid bounties, were Samuel Shanabarger, L. A. Egan, John Minear, Nehemiah Howell, C. G. Walsh, J. F. Wilson, A. Harris and Isaac Husk.

In November, 1864, the supervisors ordered the sheriff to nail up all the doors and windows of the court house, except the front door, which was to be kept locked. Soldiers and the public generally had disfigured and defaced the building, and it was the purpose to keep trespassers out. After the war closed the supervisors employed Edwin Frey and W. G. L. Totten, of Buckhannon, as the attorneys of Barbour County in its claim against the Government for damage done the court house and jail by United States troops. Their fee was to be fifteen per cent of all they could collect off the Government. There is no record that any money was ever collected.

Captain Haller's Home Guards.

After the formation of West Virginia, and toward the close of the Civil War, thirty two companies called Home Guards were equipped in this State under as many captains. Their duty was to protect their counties from Confederate raids and from the depredation of thieves and mauraders. The company intended for the defense of Barbour was at first cavalry, with George Yeager as Captain; but for economic reasons the company was dismounted and became infantry, and Michael T. Haller was elected Captain, and he remained in command until he was killed in an ambush set by a Confederate scouting party led by a man named Moore. Captain Haller and two of his men, William Martin and Andrew Nestor, were taken prisoners, and being sentenced to die, they were granted the privilege of praying. While kneeling, they were shot. Captain McNeill then took charge of the Home Guards. The roll of the company, as made out by those still living was as follows:

Michael T. Haller, captain; Andrew Nestor, orderly; William Wagner, 2d sargeant; William H. Weaver, 3d sargeant; William G. Nestor, 4th sargeant; George H. Nestor, Coleman Boyles, Melker Boyles, William Martin, Stingley Hoffman, Jonas Nestor, James L. B. Kelley, John England,

Residence of Granville E. Taft.

Elias Haller, James Kirby, David Vance, Abraham House, Philip Coontz, Isaac Smith, James Harris, William Cox, James Fry, Henry Myers, Stogdon Compton, Marshall Boyles, George Johnson, Abraham Nestor, Cornelius Bowman, William Jaynes, Sanford H. Nestor, James Osburn, Sanford H. Moats, Marion Nestor, Samuel Harsh, Hezekiah Mitchell, John Coontz, John England, sr., Augustus J. Cline, John Vance, Henry Vance, John Knavenshoe, Andrew Martin, Marion Weaver, George Lohr, Dr. William Coffman, Robert Coffman, Jesse Ritsman, William Jenkins, Matthew Edmonds.

CHAPTER XXI.

MISCELLANIES.

Booth's Ferry (now Philippi) was an important place nearly half a century before the formation of Barbour County. It was named from Daniel Booth, who owned it about the year 1800. Prior to that time the locality was called Anglin's Ford. Daniel Booth lived there or in that vicinity as early 1787, as is learned from the records in Randolph County, where it is ordered that a road be surveyed from Beverly to Sandy Creek, passing by Daniel Booth's. Two years later, 1789, a road was ordered surveyed from Jonas Friend's, the present town of Elkins, to Anglin's Ford over the Valley River. It would appear from this that there was a ford at Philippi as early as 1789; and it was probably named from William Anglin, who settled there at a very early day and who was the original owner of the land on which Philippi stands. No record has been found of William Anglin earlier than 1789, but it is by no means improbable that he lived where Philippi now stands as early as 1783 or 1784, but not as early as 1780, as some have claimed. Although the river was fordable at ordinary stages at Philippi, yet the old ford was two miles below. That old ford and the trails which led to it are spoken of elsewhere in this book. When the river was unfordable, travelers from the east, or visa versa, would patronize the ferry, and proceed over the trail to Clarksburg or elsewhere. About the time the ferry was established, that is, about 1800, the road from Clarksburg to the Valley River was widened for wagons, and the work of opening the road toward Beverly by way of Sugar Creek was pushed. After that road was opened, the old ford two miles below Philippi was not much used, and Booth's Ferry became the most important crossing between Beverly and the Monongalia line.

The old ferry was situated at the bend of the river, at the mouth o Anglin Run, and the western landing was at the foot of the sharp ridge which breaks abruptly down to the river at that point, and is called "Nobusiness Hill." Traces of the old road leading upward and around its side can yet be seen. At that time the western bank of the river was in Harrison County and the eastern bank in Randolph. In 1825, at Booth's Ferry, a murder was committed which made a profound impression in the community. Samuel Anglin

NOBUSINESS HILL.

shot and killed Jonas Grimes who was crossing the river in a canoe. There had been trouble between them. Grimes had married Alsay Wilson, sister of William F. Wilson, and at his death left two small children, Wilson and Harvey. After the murder, Anglin ran into the woods, hid his gun a short distance from the scene of the tragedy and disappeared so completely that no trace of him could be found for years. It was reported and currently believed that he had joined the Indians among the Rocky Mountains. After a few years his family left the country and no one knew their destination. It is now known that Anglin did not join the Indians, and that he came back some years after in disguise and removed his family to the vicinity of Cahokia, Illinois, opposite St. Louis, where he died some time in the forties. Lewis Wilson, who was traveling through that country in 1839, discovered him on the bank of the Mississippi and talked with him.

Ferries across the river were established from time to time at different places; but the most important below Philippi was the McDaniel Ferry, near the present station of Cecil. The Booth Ferry changed hands and was sometimes called the Hite Ferry. At the time Barbour County was formed it belonged to William F. Wilson and William Shaw. They entered into an agreement with the county court to ferry all citizens of Barbour County, during court days, across free of charge, but the county agreed to pay them two dollars a day for the service. The building of the bridge, which was completed in 1852, was the end of the old ferry.

The Philippi Bridge.

The Valley River at Philippi is crossed by a double bridge, of two spans, each span supported by four wooden arches, rising from either bank and resting on a span in the middle of the river. The structure is 312 feet long, and is of wood throughout. It is a fine specimen of architecture of a peculiar order and of an old fashion. Bridges of that kind are no longer common in West Virginia. Iron or steel is now almost exclusively used in

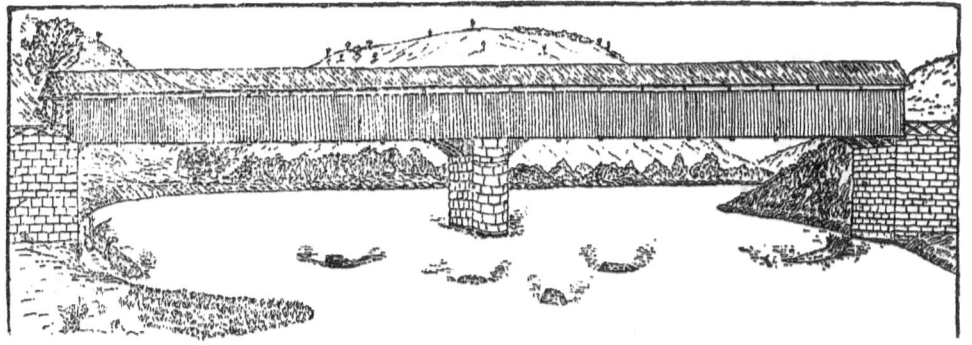

THE PHILIPPI BRIDGE

thier construction. The few that remain in this part of West Virginia are venerable curiosities, for the most part dating back before the Civil War when the building of pikes was more common than now. Among the old patterns that remain may be named; that across Cheat River five miles above Rowlesburg; that across Shaver's Fork in Randolph County; at Beverly in Randolph; across the Greenbrier River, seven miles from Huntersville; and at Philippi. A number of these old wooden structures were detroyed during the Civil War; and the two longest yet remaining, that above Rowlesburg and that at Philippi, narrowly escaped burning at the time of the Jones raid in 1863. Orders were issued for burning both of them by General Jones, but he retreated from the Cheat Bridge in such a hurry that he could not set it on fire; and the Philippi bridge was spared through the intercession of citizens with Southern sympathies, chief among whom was Elder Joshua S. Corder.

The Philippi bridge was built in 1852, the stone work by Emmett J. O'Brien, and the wood work by Lemuel Chenoweth of Beverly. Mr. O'Brien was then a citizen of Barbour, but afterwards of Lewis County. Mr. Chenoweth was a bridge architect by profession, and his designs were original with him, and every principle was worked out with mathematical accuracy. He knew beforehand the shape and size of every piece of timber used in the frame work of his bridges. Nearly half a century has shown that his work was of a superior order. He was born in 1811, son of John I. and Mary (Skidmore) Chenoweth, of Beverly. He took an active part in politics, and was a man in many ways superior to ordinary men, both in education and natural endowments.

The contract were let at Richmond for the bridges which Virginia was then building in the western part of the State, and had been extensively advertised. Bidders were present in large numbers from the East and the North, with all sorts of models and plans, including iron structures, wire cables, cantilevers, stone arches, and wooden bridges of many kinds. Mr. Chenoweth was there with his model made of hickory wood, as strong as it could possibly be made, not to exceed the required size. So far as appearances went, some of the New England Yankees had models of perfect form and beauty, painted and enameled in the highest art. On the appointed day the bidders all assembled before the Board of Public Works, and each showed his model, and set forth his claims of what weight his bridge would sustain. Mr. Chenoweth was one of the last called forward to show what he had. His plain wooden model did not attract much attention; but he created consternation among the other bidders when he placed his model on two chairs, one end resting on each, and then stood on his little bridge, and called on the other architects to put theirs to the test by doing the same. Not one would do it, for they knew their models would be crushed. If the Philippi bridge were as strong in proportion to its size as Mr. Chenoweth's model, it would sustain the weight of a man six hundred feet high. The test decided the contest, and Mr. Chenoweth was given the contract for the bridges. He built one at Beverly, at Middle Fork, at Buckhannon, at Weston, at Philippi; and many smaller ones. The one at Philippi, and a small one across Stone Coal Creek near Weston are believed to be the only ones built by him before the war that are still standing.

The county seat of Barbour was located at the place where Philippi now stands before there was a town and before the place was named. It was then a farm belonging to William F. Wilson, and the locality had long been known as Booth's Ferry. The land was first the property of William Anglin, and in succession was owned by John Wilson, Daniel Booth, Ely Butcher, Elmore Hart, Thomas H. Hite and William F. Wilson, who divided it into lots and disposed of the most of it within a few years after the establishing of the county seat. The county was named after Philip Pendleton Barbour, and it was the intention of the county court when it selected a name for the town to honor the given name of Mr. Barbour; giving it the feminine form, however, in conformity with the Latin language. The feminine of Philip is Philippa, and it was meant that such should be the name of the town. But because of misspellings and a misunderstanding of the origin of the name (confounding it with Philippi, an ancient city) the name finally took the form which it now has. On April 5, 1843, the third day of the first county court, it is "ordered that the county seat of this county be known and called PHILLIPPA." Except that the name had too many "l's" the form was proper, according to what was originally intended. Later the name became Philippi, but even then it was oftener misspelled than spelled correctly.

Before the town was given legal existence by act of the legislature it was laid out in lots of one-fourth acre each, and a number of them had been sold. The following list comprises all, or nearly all, of the lots sold before the town had been created by act of the legislature. All of them were sold by William F. Wilson.

Purchaser.	No. of Lot.	Price	Purchaser.	No. of Lot	Price
The County (a gift)	1¼ acres, 16 poles	——	John Overfield et al.	39	$ 23
Thomas M. Hite	56 and 57	$210	Thomas A. Hoffman	26	20 50
John Bennett	36	40	Martin B. Sinsel	Part of 6 & 7	100
Edwin D. Wilson	54 and 55	165	William Pickens	4	90
Solomon Jarvis	52	116	J. R. Williamson	Part of 6 & 7	100
Isaiah W. Reeves	26	22	John Curry	21	50
Anthony Wells	——	25	Elam D. Talbott	Part of 50	100
John S. Carlile	51	1	Thomas B. Curtis	Part of 50	1
Elisha Finley	85	40	William Woodford	17	40
Samuel S. Montgomery	29	20	Eli Hudkins	19	33
Randolph Chenoweth	53	71	Miner Cleavenger	33	50
William Shaw	58 and 59	87	Thomas Thompson	27 and 29	45
Ludwick Day	71	25	Lewis Wilson	¼ mill and lot	1
Harrison Hagans, et al.	12 and 13	242	Hugh Collett	70	30

On February 14, 1844, the Virginia Legislature passed the act forming Philippi, and named the first trustees as follows: Lair D. Morrall, James L. Bunbridge, William Shaw, John R. Williamson and William F. Wilson.

The law fixing the county seat stipulated that if the grounds for the court house should be acquired by gift, the quantity should not exceed two acres. Accordingly, when William F. Wilson gave the land the square contained one acre and ninety-six poles. After the establishing of the county seat, the first house built in Philippi stood where the passenger depot is now located and was built by William F. Wilson. The next, located nearly on the ground now occupied by the Commercial hotel, was built by Lair D. Morrall. John S. Carlile built the next, and Edwin D. Wilson the next. None of these is now standing. There were farm houses on the site of Philippi long before there was a town. William Anglin probably built the first house on the site of Philippi, and Moses Kinkaid the next, although this matter is not of record, depending only on traditions handed down. The families residing in Philippi in 1850 were those of:

Lair D. Morrall	Robert Tutt	Noah Corley
Lewis Wilson	Henry Barron	James Prim
William F. Wilson	Daniel Capito	Rev. Josiah Reeves
Spencer Dayton	Mrs. Elizabeth Jarvis	William Shaw
John P. Thompson	Isaac H. Strickler	A. G. Reger
Samuel Woods	William Simpson	John S. Carlile
Edwin Tutt	Dr. Haymond	Stephen B. Holt
Martin Myers	Charles S. Hall	D. M. Myers
Daniel M. Auvil	Henry Thompson	A. P. Wilson

The town of Philippi was incorporated by act of the Legislature February 1, 1871. After the town government was organized, the first ordinance passed ordered that all hogs and horses running at large should be "arrested." Four years later a similar ordinance was passed concerning geese. Following are lists of the town officers, no mention being made of the second or succeeding term of the same man, the first only being given.

Mayors.

C. P. Thompson............1871	W. Chenoweth............1885
John P. Thompson...........1873	Samuel V. Woods............1886
Albert G. Wilson............1874	D. W. Gall 1889
Andrew Simon..............1875	Granville Peck............1891
A. P. Wilson 1876	Charles F. Teter............1893
J. P. Newlon...............1877	L. D. Robinson............1896
Harrison Mason 1879	J. N. B. Crim 1897
C. C. Hovatter..............1881	William A. Mason...........1898
Granville F. Grant...........1882	Fred O. Blue 1899

Treasurers.

Isaac H. Strickler 1871	W. Chenoweth 1891
L. D. Morrall...............1873	G. E. Grant................1893
Melville Peck...............1885	

MISCELLANIES. 281

Recorders.

Lewis Wilson 1871	John W. Poling 1890
Luther C. Elliott.............1877	Charles L. Steel............1892
J. S. Cornwell...............1881	J. H. Knapp................1893
L. D. Morrall 1883	N. I. Hall..................1896
D. W. Gall..................1885	A. D. W. Strickler..........1899
Lloyd D. Robinson 1888	

Assessors.

William P. Keyes.............1871	Melville Peck...............1889
W. D. F. Jarvis 1876	J. H. Daniels...............1892
C. C. Hovatter...............1877	A. S. Poling................1893
L. D. Morrall................1883	L. D. Robinson..............1897
A. D. W. Strickler...........1887	

Sergeants.

Stingley Shaffer.............1871	William A. Mason............1884
C. C. Hovatter...............1874	John T. Kent................1885
Solomon R. Jarvis............1875	William T. Hulderman........1887
J. N. Gans 1875	A. L. Taylor................1887
W. D. F. Jarvis 1876	G. C. Bennett...............1889
William Price................1877	A. Holden...................1891
Andrew Simon 1880	W. L. Chrislip..............1892
George C. Corder.............1881	John H. Daniels.............1892
John B. Knapp...............1882	E. Holsberry................1894
John T. Prim.................1882	James P. Robinson...........1896

Councilmen.

Job H. Glascock..............1871	Jehu M. Talbott..............1883
James A. Grant 1871	A. G. Dayton................1883
Simon Buckingham............1871	S. T. H. Holt................1884
T. P. R. Brown...............1871	Lewis Wilson................1884
John P. Thompson............1872	J. Hop Woods................1885
William T. Ice...............1873	G. W. Diddle 1888
A. G. Reger..................1873	A. D. W. Strickler...........1888
D. F. Byrer..................1873	W..Chenoweth................1888
D. W. Gall...................1874	C. F. Teter..................1889
L. D. Morrall................1874	D. J. Taft...................1891
I. H. Strickler...............1875	J. W. Conner................1891
I. V. Johnson................1875	G. W. Gall...................1891
T. A. Bradford...............1876	R. F. Rightmire.............1892
J. J. Newlon.................1876	J. H. Felton.................1892
John W. Bosworth............1876	G. E. Taft 1893
George P. Sargent 1878	J. M. Proudfoot..............1894
J. N. Hathaway..............1878	Melville Peck 1896
William F. Byrer.............1879	W. S. Wilson.................1896
Isaiah Wilson 1879	Fred O. Blue 1897
James E. Hall................1881	George L. Woodford 1899
Jacob W. Robinson...........1881	

Banks in Barbour.

There have been three banks in Barbour County. The first was established about 1855, known as the Bank of Philippi. Lair D. Morrall was president, and Charles W. Parratt, cashier. Upon the latter's death, John W. Payne became cashier, and continued in that position till the bank came to a sudden end. When Colonel Porterfield retreated from Grafton to Philippi in 1861, Mr. Payne saw the handwriting on the wall, and packed up the money, effects and movable property of the bank ready for flight. He was a Secessionists, and did not relish the chance of falling into Union hands. Early Sunday morning, June 2, he started—just twenty-four hours in advance of the Federal troops. It is not known just how much money he took with him; but probably not much, for as he was leaving Philippi he borrowed sixty dollars of J. N. B. Crim, and departed with the bank forever. An effort was made to re-open it at Wytheville, but not much business was done. It may be stated in passing that Mr. Payne, after the war, repaid the sixty dollars. When the Union troops captured Philippi, they raided the bank building, blew open the safe, but found no money. The old safe, with its broken door, still lies in a vacant lot. Notes of the old bank were subjects of speculation years after the war. J. N. B. Crim bought thousand of dollars of them in Baltimore; and sold $10,000, face value, of them to one man, Benjamin McCoy, Sheriff of Barbour.

In 1875 the Farmers' Bank was established in Philippi. A. B. Modissett was president and J. W. Talbott, cashier; but later J. E. Heatherly became president and G. W. Gall, jr., became cashier. On April 1, 1886, the building and fixtures were sold to the Tygart's Valley Bank, and the Farmers' Bank ceased to exist. Its affairs went into the hands of a receiver, and the courts were called upon to settle its business.

The next day, April 2, 1886, the Tygart's Valley Bank opened its doors for business. J. N. B. Crim was president and G. W. Gall, jr., was cashier. On March 15, 1893, J. F. Manown became cashier. The bank attained and held a leading and influential position in the financial and business affairs of the county. The Board of Directors, in 1899, was as follows: J. N. B. Crim, Charles M. Bishop, A. G. Dayton, James E. Hall, Lewis Wilson, L. C. Elliott and D. J. Gibson.

Trails and Roads.

The beginning of roads in Barbour County differed little from their beginning in the other counties of the State. The first were trails leading in a few directions and followed at uncertain intervals by the settlers on business and pleasure, and by emigrants on their way to new fields. About one hundred years have elapsed since the first wagon road was built in what is Barbour. Before that time a path which could be followed by

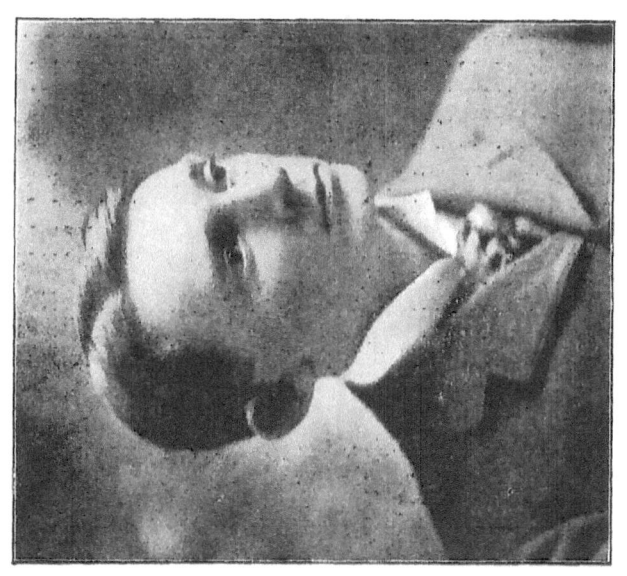

STUART H. BOWMAN.

LUTHER HAYMOND,
The engineer who located the Beverly and Fairmont Pike,

pack-horses without scraping the packs off against trees, was considered a great convenience, if not a luxury. The first step toward transforming a trail into a road was to "bush it out," and make it "passable for pack-horses and men on horse-back," as the old records express it. As early as 1788 the trail leading from Clarksburg to Winchester, passing through Barbour, crossing into Tucker at the head of Clover Run and crossing Cheat River at St. George, was spoken of in the records as the "State Road." If one mile of it at that time had ever known a wheel, certainly it was not in Barbour or Tucker, and probably not in Harrison. Still it was called a road, and was sometimes distinguished as the "Pringle Packroad," because it was probably marked out (or, at least, followed, for it was an old Indian trail) by the Pringles and other early settlers on the Buckhannon River. It crossed the Valley River a mile below Philippi, passed up Ford Run on the east side and Hacker on the west side of the river. It was the highway from the east to the west, through Barbour and Tucker. Very little of it ever became a wagon road.

Lest there be a misunderstanding, it is proper to state that it was not an impossibility to take a wagon long distances through the woods without a road. It was occasionally done by the pioneers. About 1783 (the exact date is not certain) a wagon was taken from Hampshire County to the Horse Shoe, in Tucker County, by Thomas Parsons, when there was no pretense of a wagon road for the fifty miles crossing the Alleghanies. The wagon was empty and drawn by four horses. A number of slaves accompanied it, and when the hills were so steep, the rocks so abundant or the trees so thick that the wagon could not pass, it was taken to pieces and carried by the negroes over the difficult places, when it was again set up and was drawn by horses. By cutting out a sapling or a log occasionally, the wagon could be taken, at times, several miles without unhitching the horses; and the progress was more rapid than might be supposed. It passed up the North Branch of the Potomac, crossed the Alleghany near Fairfax Stone, descended Lead Mine Run and Horse Shoe Run to Cheat River. So far as any known facts warrant the assertion, that was the first wagon to cross the Alleghanies in West Virginia, north of Greenbrier County, and if the date, 1783, is correct, it was absolutely the first wagon crosssing the Alleghanies within the limits of West Virginia. Jacob Warwick took a wagon to Pocahontas County very soon after 1783. There were plenty of good wagons in Hampshire County twenty years before that time; and it is probable that home-made wagons were in use in Randolph County and in Monongalia County as early as 1788, but none had yet been seen at Clarksburg. Even in the older and more prosperous settlements on the Monongahela in Pennsylvania, the statement has been made, and has long gone uncontradicted, that a wagon, loaded with merchandise, did not reach the Monongahela till 1789.* Those old wagons were different in one important particular from modern wagons. The tire was made in four sections, each one a quarter-circle, and these sections were fastened on the felloes by bolts, with large heads, which were so numerous that they gave the wheel the appearance of a cogwheel. Now the tire supports the felloes, then the felloes supported the tire.

Returning to a consideration of the old trails of Barbour County, it may be stated that, as settlements became scattered here and there, they were connected by trails marked by blazing the trees. These were called "blazes." An old order in Randolph County calls for "a road along Currence's blazes square across the valley." It was customary, but not the universal custom, to blaze only one kind of a tree on a certain trail. For example, one path would follow blazes on chestnut trees; on another path, oaks would be blazed; on another, beech; and so forth. Thus the beech blazes would lead to the mill; the oak blazes to the deer lick; the chestnut blazes to a certain house or settlement. A stranger inquiring his way to the mill would be told to follow the beech blazes, and if he found himself on a path differently marked, or if the path forked and he would turn into the trail where the oaks were blazed, he would know that he was wrong.

As early as 1787 the trail from Clarksburg to Beverly passed through what is now Barbour County. It was the old State Road from Clarksburg to the point where it crossed the river a mile above the mouth of Hacker Creek. There the Beverly road branched off, crossed the hill to Anglin Run about half a mile above Philippi, passed to the head of that run, over to Sugar Creek and up that stream and over the hill to where Belington now is, and thence over Laurel Hill into Tygart's Valley. The fact that this trail was used as early as 1787 in traveling between Clarksburg and Tygart's Valley is fixed by a noted wedding which occurred that year, the wedding party traveling over that trail. Colonel John Haymond, of Clarksburg, was married, four miles below Beverly, to Mary, eldest daughter of Colonel Benjamin Wilson. Colonel Haymond was accompanied from Clarksburg by a large company of young people of both sexes; and the first night, on their way to Beverly, they camped at the large rock a mile above the site of Philippi. The rock was formerly a well-known land mark; but it has been nearly destroyed by blasting for macadam.

The first wagon road on the east side of the river, in Barbour County, was made by William F. Wilson in 1800. It was seven miles long and led from the site of Philippi to Bill's Creek, where Mr. Wilson then lived. He built it for seventy-five cents a rod, and it went up the points of hills and followed the tops of ridges, over the tops of knobs, rather than to grade round them, to save digging. This road was subsequently extended to

---

See Veach's "Monongahela of Old."

Beverly. It had before that time been constructed on the west side of the river, then Harrison County, from Philippi to Clarksburg. At any rate, as early as 1803 wagons could pass from Philippi to Clarksburg.

In 1801 an order was passed for a road, a part of which was probably within the present limits of Barbour. The order was to "view a way for a road from John Jackson's Mill to the top of the mountain at the head of the creek above John Bozar's [Bozarth?] on the old road that goes to Hecker's [Hacker's?] Creek, so as not to go through improvements, or alter the road that is laid off through William Vandevender's and Widow Reger's lands." That order betrays the secret of many a steep, crooked or swampy road in West Virginia, where it might have been comparatively straight, level and dry. The roads passed round fields, even if to do so they must climb hills or cross swamps. Travelers through West Virginia for a hundred years have been climbing hills because the short-sighted pioneer made the original path that way to get round his neighbor's corn patch. Five dollars in damages were probably saved in the start, but five hundred dollars have been wasted in keeping the bad road in repair and traveling it. When a road is first surveyed it should be put in the proper place, no matter whose cornpatch it cuts in two. Then all subsequent improvements upon it will be permanent. How often can the trace of a very old road be seen standing on its end against the side of the mountain, and near it the abandoned bed of a later road, not quite so steep, and perhaps a third road, also abandoned, while the modern highway winds gracefully round the base of the hill, the discovery having been made after a hundred years that it was not necessary for the road to go over the hill at all. Early road makers did not know that a pot bail is as long standing as lying, or that a road round a hill was often no longer than a road over it.

The pike building in Bourbour began about 1848, and the principal highways of that class within the county now are the Beverly and Fairmont, the Beverly and Morgantown, the Gnatty Creek and West Union, the Philippi and Clarksburg, the Philippi and Buckhannon, and the Middle Fork Pike. About 1850 the survey for the Beverly and Fairmont Pike was completed. It was made by Luther Haymond, of Clarksburg. In crossing Laurel Hill, above Belington, he did not follow the route of the old road, but left it to the north. The route on the eastern side of Laurel Hill was the occasion of a bitter controversy by persons who wanted the road located for their special benefit. In entering the town of Philippi there was another controversy. The route as surveyed passed through David Byrer's tannery, and Mr. Byrer, being much opposed to it, proposed to the engineer, Mr. Haymond, that they should settle the matter by shooting at a target with rifles. In the contest Mr. Haymond won, but did not insist on the terms, and located the road below the tannery. The piers of the Philippi bridge were commenced in 1851.

Newspaper History in Barbour.

Journalism in Barbour County dates from August, 1857, at which time *The Barbour Jeffersonian* was founded by Thompson Surghnor, a soldier who had served in the Mexican War. It was a weekly, the subscription price being $1.50 per annum, "if paid in advance; otherwise $2.00." Advertising rates, except for long contracts, averaged two and a half cents a line, each insertion. The paper was all printed in Philippi, there being no "patent side." The motto at the head of the paper was: "The Union—according to the Constitution," indicating plainly where the paper would be found on the questions which were the vital issues leading up to the Civil War, and which were settled for all time by that war. The paper was published nearly four years, and until about June 1861. It was a Secession organ, strong in its support of Virginia's opposition and hostility to the United States. When the Federal troops, June 3, 1861, drove the Confederates out of Philippi, the editor went with them, joined the army and was subsequently killed at Beverly. His body was brought to Philippi by Christopher C. Hovatter, where it was buried. The Federal soldiers wrecked the newspaper office and threw the type into a well.

Few copies of the old *Jeffersonian* are now in existence, but such as are found are full of local history. A copy of October 16, 1857, now owned by D. W. Gall, of Washington, D. C., is the earliest to be had. From it the following items of local interest are taken. Lawyers, whose cards are found in it, were:

Samuel Woods, Philippi	John Brannon, Weston
D. M. Auvil, Philippi	Norval Lewis, Clarksburg
Spencer Dayton, Philippi	Burton Despard, Clarksburg
Thomas A. Bradford, Philippi	Edwin Maxwell, Clarksburg
A. G. Reger, Philippi	Charles S. Duncan, Clarksburg
Claudius Goff, Beverly	Charles Lewis, Clarksburg
Samuel Crane, Beverly	Wilson Sommers, Clarksburg
G. W. Berlin, Buckhannon	John S. Carlile, Clarksburg
John S. Fisher, Buckhannon	Johnson D. Hansbrough, Pruntytown
J. M. Bennett, Weston	

The doctors mentioned in the paper were, E. D. Talbott, James B. Reeves, Philippi; and Dr. Harter of Webster, W. Va.

In the advertising columns are found business announcements as follows:

A new marble yard in Philippi which is to be "permanent," by J. H. Viquesney.

A land agency at Beverly, operated by John N. Hughes and James H. Logan.

A saddle and harness manufactory at Philippi, by John C. Byrer.

Tin and sheet iron ware, and Arthur's self-sealing fruit cans, opposite the bank, by S. M. Holt.

Daniel Capito announces that "the Barbour House" is open to the accommodation of the public, and he solicits a continuation of past patronage.

The announcement of Thomas A. Hoffman that he has fitted up "the Red House," at Simpson, formerly Claysville, as a tavern.

J. T. Simms advertised a marble yard at Webster.

The Philippi School, opened for a five months term; tuition for reading, writing and elementary arithmetic, five dollars for the term; for arithmetic, English grammer, history and natural philosophy, six dollars; for contingent expenses, fifty cents per scholar; no deduction for loss of time. The teacher was Jacob Z. Chadwick.

Leather for sale and hides wanted; "no new book accounts opened; no credit asked," by David F. Byrer.

Brady, Haines & Grace announced that theirs was the cheapest line of goods ever opened in the county, adding: "Persons accustomed to going to the Rail Road to trade will find it to their advantage to give us a call, as we will sell as low and give as much for Trade as can be had at the Rail Road."

"The Farmer's Exchange," a store owned by McClaskey & Crim, advertised goods at low prices, including ready made clothing.

One marriage notice is found in the paper, David Kittle, of Philippi, to Melinda Bartlett; Rev. James Gawthrop, officiating.

From market quotations, the price of commodities in Philippi at that time are learned, as follows:

Butter	$ .12½	Flax Seed	$1.00	Oats	$ .25
Bacon	.11	Flour, per bbl	5.00	Potatoes	no sale
Hams	.12½	Ginseng	.30	Wheat	.80
Corn	.50	Honey	.12½	Snakeroot	.30
Cheese	.10	Jeans, (country made)	.75	Timothy seed	2.75
Dried Apples	.75	Linen, " "	.25	Tallow	.12½
Feathers	1.00	Lard	.10	Rye	.45

Dr. Elam D. Talbott is announced as a candidate for the Legislatue.

As for news, the *Jeffersonian*, to judge from the issue of October 16, 1857, was very poor. That issue contained only one item which could properly be classed as local news, and that was:

"The Circuit Court is now in session, Judge Camden presiding—the proceedings will be given next week."

There is one other paragraph which in some measure savors of local news. It is as follows:

"We do most humbly beg of our worthy mail contractor the kind favor to have mail brought more regularly from Webster. This is the second or third time that he has left the mail at that place. His neglect gives us a great deal of annoyance and trouble, as when the mail fails, we have to select our matter from Jayne's almanac and a cook book."

It probably did not occur to the editor that if he would publish a little more home news, and "select" less matter his paper would have been more valuable, if not to his subscribers, at least to the future historian in search of information regarding Barbour County. Mr. Surghnor's paper, of the date mentioned, contained thirteen and one half columns of reading, with only one and one-half inches of local news. Some of the leading articles were as follows: "Bank Convention" in Charlottsville, Virginia, one column and a half; "The Canal Across the Isthmus of Darien," one column; "Senator Hunter and the Enquirer," half column; "Baltimore as It Is," half column; "The Old Banks against Independent Banks," half column; "Slavery in Oregon," "Fight with a Bear," and "Tomb of Napoleon," one column; "Notes of the Independent Banks," one-third column; "Man Overboard," three columns; "The Quaker's Corncrib," nearly a column.

A short time after the *Jeffersonian* suspended publication, another paper, *The Old Flag*, was started and was continued for sometime. But no copy of it can be found, nor are many facts concerning it be ascertained. It did not last long, and was probably published by Federal soldiers; or at least, it was published under their auspices and protection.

On November 29, 1873, the *Plaindealer* came into existence, edited by David W. Gall who retained connection with it twenty-five years. It had the field to itself for some years, and was a good newspaper. There were differences in politics in Barbour at that time, even within the ranks of the same party, and some persons believing that certain measures should be represented in a different manner, were instrumental in launching another paper, the *Jeffersonian*, which was started by George P. Sargeant in 1876, and in 1883 it was bought by J. Hop Woods and D. W. Shaw. After a time it was merged with the other paper, and the name became the *Jeffersonian-Plaindealer*, and was so continued till 1898 when Mr. Gall sold his paper to John T. Reger who dropped the first name, and soon changed it from a weekly to a twice-a-week paper.

The first issue of the *Philippi Republican* was dated October 9, 1880, and H. C. Shearer was editor and proprietor. The paper's politics was indicated by its name. On November 24, 1881 Marion F. Hall became the proprietor and editor of the paper and retained his connection with it till September 10, 1896, when he sold it to Myron C. Lough and Charles I. Zirkle. On September 2, 1897, Mr. Lough sold his interest in the paper to John H. Zirkle, and the brothers still publish it.

On May 9, 1889, Melville Peck and J. H. Knapp published the first number of *The Tygart's Valley Star*, at Philippi. In a short time Mr. Knapp retired from the business and his place was taken by Mrs. Peck who superintended the office and much of the writing until the paper was sold in 1891.

On July 6, 1893, the *Barbour Democrat* was founded by Aldine S. Poling who still owns the paper and has constantly been its editor. In politics it supports the party whose name it bears.

In 1897 *The Belington Independent* was founded at Belington by H. K. McCutcheon, and in 1899 I. D. Martin became associated with him in the publication.

The Geology of Barbour County.

Barbour County is less rugged than the counties south and east of it. The mountains are not so high, nor the valleys so deep as those of Tucker and Randolph. While there are cliffs of some boldness along the water courses, there are few of the pinnacles and peaks so common east of Laurel Hill and along the spurs of the Alleghanies. The mountains of the region further east sink into hills with rounded tops in Barbour. Still, Barbour has no wide valley, like the magnificent one lying in Randolph between Rich Mountain and Cheat Mountain; nor has it a valley to compare with some of the bottom lands along Cheat River in Tucker; but in Barbour the level or nearly level lands lie, for the most part, on the ridges and uplands. Taken all in all, the geography differs widely from that of the region between Laurel Hill and the Alleghanies, and this difference is due to certain facts in geology which it is necessary to understand in order to make plain the reason why Barbour's mountains are not high nor its valleys deep and wide.*

The period of disturbance succeeding the Carboniferous epoch, which compressed the rock formations of the Alleghany region into vast folds, expended its strength in uplifting the rocks which have since been excavated into mountains, range beyond range, in parallel ridges, beginning with the Shenandoah Mountain, North Fork Mountain, Alleghany Mountain, Backbone Mountain, Cheat and Rich Mountains. In looking at a map it will be seen that the last large mountain of the Alleghany system on the west is Rich Mountain in Randolph, and its continuation through Barbour and Tucker, known as Laurel Hill. East of that ridge the mountains roll, fold beyond fold, until they reach the Valley of Virginia. But west of Laurel Hill and Rich Mountain the rocks are not much folded, and no high mountains are found. East of Laurel Hill the strata are crumpled, broken, set on edge, turned this way and that at all angles; but west of the great ridge the rocks lie more nearly horizontal, layer upon layer, extending toward the Ohio River, in almost unbroken regularity. To this fact is due Barbour County's lack of deep valleys and high and rugged hills. No vast rocks have been tilted on edge to form pinnacles. No steep inclines have assisted erosion to cut deep valleys.

---

*The chapter beginning on page 71 of this book should be read as an introduction to the present chapter; for the facts stated there will not be repeated here.

A few words concerning Laurel Hill and the geological lesson it teaches are in order. That ridge forms the boundary between Barbour and Tucker, and between Barbour and part of Randolph. Geographically it is a well-defined mountain, shedding the rainfall down the southeastern slope into Cheat River and Leading Creek, and down its northwestern slope into Valley River. Between Belington and Elkins the Valley River cuts through this ridge, and from there to its source, flows on the eastern side. South of the gap cut by the river the ridge is called Rich Mountain, but it is a continuation of Laurel Hill, both in a geographical and geological sense, and it is proper to consider both as one and the same mountain. Laurel Hill is peculiar in its formation. It is only the stump of a mountain, in comparison with what formerly was there. What remains is only the western edge of a vast ridge, now worn away, for the most part. If it could be fully restored there would be a range overtopping the Alleghanies. Its eastern base would run nearly north and south through Tucker County, near St. George, and its summit (a broad, stupendous arch) would lie some four or five miles east of the present top of Laurel Hill, and perhaps three thousand feet higher. All the central part, and nearly all the eastern escarpment of that ancient mountain are now worn away; but the western base, fragmentary as it is, remains—Laurel Hill.

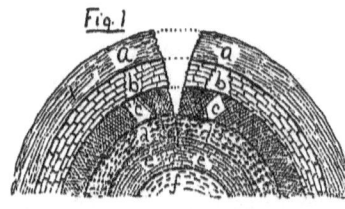

LAUREL HILL—First Stage in Life-History

LAUREL HILL—2nd Stage

LAUREL HILL—PRESENT STAGE.

The structure of this mountain can be studied to much better advantage in Randolph County than in Barbour and Tucker, because in Randolph both the eastern and western flanks remain, while the middle part is scooped out and now forms Tygart's Valley. The western flank is now Rich Mountain; the eastern is Cheat Mountain. The accompanying cut will show the relation which these two mountains bore to the greater mountain which once rested between and above them. Cheat Mountain, the eastern base of the old mountain, shows the fragments of the old arch very nicely; but that ridge disappears, in its northern course, about the Tucker County line, and from that point through to Maryland (parallel with Laurel Hill)

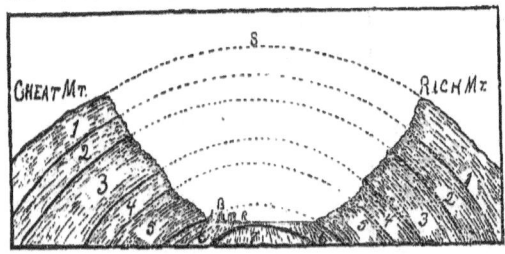

SCULPTURE OF TYGART'S VALLEY.

SALATHIEL L. O'NEAL.

RESIDENCE OF JAMES E. HALL.

only fragments of the old mountain can be recognized. But the western base can be traced one hundred miles, in Randolph as Rich Mountain; in Barbour and Tucker as Laurel Hill, and in Preston as Briery Mountain. Below Rowlesburg Cheat River, which south of there flows on the east side, breaks through and emerges on the west side. Were the ancient mountain restored, its summit would lie directly over Beverly, over the valley of Leading Creek, nearly over Limestone Mountain in Tucker, and over Terra Alta in Preston. Were the mountain thus restored, a person in ascending it from the west side would not be half way to the top when he had reached the present summit of Laurel Hill. It would, perhaps, be superfluous to state that the old mountain has been worn away by the action of water, mostly by tributaries of Cheat River, in Tucker and Preston, and by Tygart's Valley River in Randolph. The waters flowing from Laurel Hill westward have made comparatively small impression on that ridge, with its capping of hard Pottsville conglomerate rock, which acts as a roof to protect the softer rocks below. It is supposed by some persons, and is not improbable, that when the great arch forming the old mountain was forced up, the strain ruptured the strata along the top, forming a chasm longitudinally with the summit, and that water taking advantage of this channel speedily widened and deepened it, and undermined both sides until in some places the eastern side has well nigh disappeared, while enough of the western side remains to form a respectable mountain (Laurel Hill) and is the dividing ridge between the waters of Cheat and those of the Valley River.

Rocks Nearly Horizontal.

Westward from Laurel Hill, as already stated, the layers of rocks are not much tilted or folded, but lie nearly horizontal. There are some wide, low arches, which have considerable magnitude when taken as a whole, but they are so regular that they do not disturb the general contour of the country. The lowest rock showing on the surface within the county's borders is the Pocono sandstone near the head of Teter's Creek. This rock lies 1022 feet under Philippi, as shown by the log of the oil well near the town. It is known in the Manington oil field as the "Big Injun sand," and some of the best wells in the State are in it. The fact that the Pocono sandstone is on the surface in the southern part of the county, and at Philippi is 1022 feet below the surface, shows that it dips toward the north and west.

Lying just above the Pocono sandstone is the Greenbrier limestone. It

296 MISCELLANIES.

takes its name from Greenbrier County, where it reaches its fullest development, attaining a thickness of 1400 feet. In Barbour it is not more than 150 feet thick. It is sometimes called "Mountain" limestone. It is found on high mountains (and sometimes in the valleys) over much of Pocahontas County; it forms the Mingo Flats in Randolph and sweeps in a thick belt from one end of Randolph to the other, along the faces of Cheat and Rich Mountains; in Tucker it covers nearly the whole extent of Dry Fork, and following the face of Backbone Mountain, extends to Maryland; it forms a band entirely around Limestone Mountain, and is a famous rock. Barbour has but a small area of it.

Formation	Thickness feet
UPSHUR Sandstone	350
PUGH	300
Great Conglomerate	400
CANAAN	1200
Greenbrier Limestone	400
POCONO	100
HAMP-SHIRE	1000
Jennings	700

ROCK-COLUMN IN RANDOLPH COUNTY.

NAME OF FORMATION	Thick
Monongahela Series	100
Redstone Coal	
Pittsburg coal	
Conemaugh Series	500
Mahontown Coal	
Upper Freeport Coal	340
Lower Freeport Coal	
Alleghany Series	
Davis Coal	
Clarion Coal	
Pottsville Series	300
Hart coal	
Mauch Chunk Red Shale	250
Greenbrier Limestone	150
Pocono Sandstone	100

ROCK-COLUMN IN BARBOUR COUNTY.

Next above the limestone is the Canaan formation, 250 feet thick. In Pennsylvania it is called the Mauch Chunk Shale. It takes the West Virginia name from Canaan in Tucker County, where it is 750 feet thick.

Next above the Canaan formation is the Pottsville Conglomerate, sometimes called the Blackwater formation because of its great development on Black Fork of Cheat, in Tucker County, where it is 645 feet thick. In Upshur County it is known as the Pickens Sandstone, from its development near Pickens where it is 500 feet thick. In the old geological survey of Virginia, sixty-five years ago, it was called "No. 12." In Barbour it is not more than 300 feet thick, but it has played an important part in the county's geography. It forms the crest of Laurel Hill, and being very hard, it has acted as a roof, protecting the softer formations below from erosion. It has been largely instrumental in preserving the mountain from being cut to pieces by the action of the elements. The rock is made up largely of white, water-worn pebbles, which, ages ago, were washed and fretted on a seabeach before being formed into rock.*

Overlying the Pottsville Conglomerate is found the Alleghany series. It is equivalent to the Savage and Bayard formations, the former named

---

*See page 75 for further mention of this remarkable rock, the most remarkable from the history of ancient lands which it suggests, of all the rocks of West Virginia.

from the Savage River in Maryland, and the latter from the station of Bayard on the West Virginia Central Railroad. In Upshur County the two are known as the Pugh formation. This rock makes cliffs along the Valley River below Belington, and on Roaring Creek.

Overlying the Alleghany series of rocks is the Conemaugh series, which crops out at Philippi, and makes cliffs in that vicinity. The lower portion of it, 150 feet thick, is called the Mahoning sandstone in Pennsylvania. In Tucker County it is known as the Fairfax formation, so named from the Fairfax Stone, the corner of Maryland. In Upshur County it is called the Upshur sandstone. The whole Alleghany series in Barbour is about 500 feet thick. The upper half is called the Elk Garden formation in Mineral County, and the Braxton formation in Upshur and Braxton Counties. The same rock, extending over a wide area, has different names in different localities.

The topmost layer of rock in Barbour County is only about 100 feet thick, and belongs to the Monongahela series. It caps the hills northeast of Belington, and in the western part of the county. It lies above the Pittsburg coal.

It will thus be seen that the total thickness of rock exposed in Barbour County is about 1740 feet. That is, if all the layers which the streams have cut through, were piled one upon another, they would from a cliff that high. This is a small showing in comparison with some other counties of the State. For example, in Tucker County, just east, the streams have cut through strata whose aggregate thickness is more than 4000 feet; and in Grant County, just east of Tucker, the depth which erosion has reached is more than 13,000 feet. Nor is that the deepest cut into the earth's crust to be found

DIAGRAM SHOWING DEPTHS OF EROSION IN BARBOUR TUCKER AND GRANT COUNTIES.

within West Virginia. In Pendleton County nearly 16,000 feet of rock have been cut through, and in Mercer County the depth reached is over 17,000 feet—ten times that of Barbour.

Veins of Coal.

There are nine veins of coal in Barbour County, but they are not all of commercial value. There may be other veins of small size. The Pittsburg coal, eight feet thick, is found on the tops of knobs northeast from Belington, and near the top of some of the hills in the western part of the county. Above this, and within one hundred feet of it, is the Redstone coal, three or four feet thick. About 350 feet below the Pittsburg coal, is the Masontown vien, from three to five feet thick, mined at Belington. Below this, 150 feet, is the Upper Freeport coal, mined at Philippi, Junior and Roaring Creek. It is from four to eight feet thick. The vein is worked at Thomas, in Tucker County. Forty or fifty feet below this is the Lower Freeport coal, found in the bank of the river just below Philippi. The slate and coal together are ten feet thick. About 200 and 300 feet lower are two veins not much developed in Barbour. They are the Davis and Clarion veins.

In the Pottsville Conglomerate is a vien of coal which in some places is worth mining and in others is not. The Hart Mine on the Buckhannon pike, five miles west of Beverly, is in this vein; and it is mined on Backbone Mountain in Tucker County, but little attention has been given to it in Barbour. There is a vein of cannel coal on Beaver Creek, not developed.

"Captive Watercourses."

In the process of chiseling out the valleys and mountains, whereby the whole appearance of a landscape may be changed in the course of long ages, it sometimes happens that streams are turned aside from their original channels, and the water is carried off in an opposite direction. An example of this is found in Barbour County. Indian Fork of Elk, and all the tributaries of Elk above the mouth of Indian Fork formerly emptied into the Valley River a short distance above Philippi. They now reach the West Fork at Clarksburg. By consulting a map it will be seen that Indian Fork and the main stream of the Elk have their sources five or six miles west of the Valley River, and that they flow eastwardly, directly toward the river until they approach within a short distance of it, and then, as In-

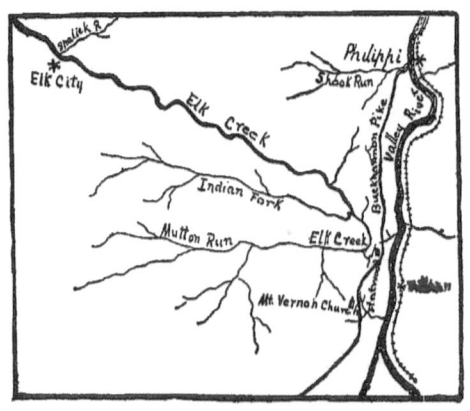

MAP OF FLATWOOD AND VICINITY.

dian Fork and Elk unite, they turn back toward the west-northwest, and flow in a direction almost opposite to the former course and reach the West Fork at Clarksburg. Thus, the streams which once were tributaries of the Valley River are now tributaries of Elk. They are what geologists call "captive watercourses." The process by which Elk was able to cut them off and divert them from their former channels is easily understood when a few facts concerning the geological history of the region between Philippi and Clarksburg are taken into consideration. The inquiry takes us back many thousand years and deals only with well-established geological truths written in the countour and sculpture of the region as it now exists.

During one of the later periods of geology, long after the close of the Carboniferous age, the country between Philippi and Clarksburg, as well as on all sides round, was more nearly level than now. Then the bed of the river at Philippi and the bed of the West Fork at Clarksburg were practically at the same altitude above the sea, and were both probably lower than they are now. Today the river at Philippi is nearly 400 feet higher than the West Fork at Clarksburg. At the time under discussion the divide between the waters of the West Fork and those of the Valley River was as far west as Elk City, or probably further west. A change took place, however, which has pushed the divide eastward until now it is in several places within a mile of the bed of the Valley River, and in some places not half a mile distant.

This change is a result of a tilting of the region. An uplift raised the country along the Valley River several hundred feet and tilted it toward the northwest. Thus, the streams tributary to the West Fork were made to flow down a steeper incline. They began to cut deeper channels because of the increased power given by their steeper gradients. As they deepened their gorges they wore the divide back toward the east, encroaching rapidly upon the headwaters of the streams emptying into the Valley River. At that time Elk was a shorter stream than now. Its source was at the divide near Elk City. But it deepened its channel and lengthened its course by cutting through the old divide and pushing the new watershed further and further east until today it has approached in places within less than a mile of Valley River.

With what has been said it is easily understood by what process it intercepted creeks flowing east. Its deeper gorge cut across their courses and diverted their water toward the west. Indian Fork was first cut off, and then Mutton Run, or as it is called in its lower course, Elk. All the headwaters of Elk Creek formerly flowed into the Valley River.

Those who look for the old channel by which those creeks reached the river must bear in mind that an immense period of time must be taken into account. What was then the surface of the country has been worn entirely away, and in places cut to great depths. The channel of the river has probably been lowered as much as 300 feet since then. In this cutting and chiseling of the surface of the landscape, it would be little less than miraculous if any part of the old channel should remain. However, there is strong evidence and much probability for locating it through the wide gap in the divide on the farm of of Jacob Shank, about three miles southwest of Philippi, in that region called "Flatwood." The flatness of the region is due to the fact that it occupies the old valley through which Indian Fork and the upper tributaries of Elk once flowed on their way to the Valley River. This old valley (now on top of a mountain) has been much cut and disfigured by gullies, ravines and brooks which have destroyed what was once a level valley floor; but even yet the general level appeals at once to the eye when seen from such distance that the local irregularities are obscured.

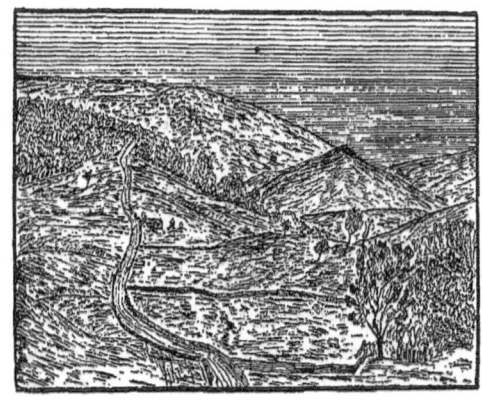

SECTION OF PRE-HISTORIC VALLEY OF ELK AT FLATWOOD.

Instances of the capture of portions of the drainage of one river basin by streams of another are met with in other parts of West Virginia. Glady Fork and Spruce Fork, in Upshur County, formerly emptied into the Buckhannon River, but they have been cut off and diverted by the encroaching channel of Stone Coal Creek, and now follow that stream to the West Fork at Weston. Another instance is found further south, where Laurel Creek, Cow Run and Get Out Run, formerly tributaries of French Creek, emptying into the Buckhannon, have been intercepted by streams emptying into the Little Kanawha. The same tilting of the region toward the northwest which caused Elk Creek to cut back nearly to the Valley River, was also responsible for the encroaching of Stone Coal Creek and the sources of the Little Kanawha upon the waters of the Buckhannon.

The same conditions still exist and the same agencies are still active; and so sure as the conditions continue, that sure will Elk Creek cut back the divide toward the channel of Valley River. Already it has cut the divide away and pushed it eastward fully five miles. The question may well be asked, what will happen if the watershed is pushed back a little further? One more mile toward the east will cut off the Valley River, and divert its waters, by way of Elk Creek, to the West Fork at Clarksburg. And that will happen as surely as effect follows cause. But no one now living need feel alarm. The present owners of the fine farms along the valley of Elk Creek that are destined to be torn out and carried down the West Fork, have no occasion for anxiety. A thousand centuries will pass before the floods of the Valley River will leave their ancient channel and pursue their new course down the valley of Elk Creek.

Masonic Lodges in Barbour.

There have been two Masonic lodges in Barbour County, the first, Bigelow Lodge, No. 28, organized November 19, 1849, and ceasing to exist at the breaking out of the Civil War; and Bigelow Lodge No. 52, organized April 16, 1870. A portion of the minutes of the meeting held November 19, 1849, is in the following words:

Whereas, a dispensation was received from the Most Worshipful James Points, Grand Master of the Grand Lodge of Ancient, Free and Accepted Masons of the State of Virginia, appointing John S. Carlile Worshipful Master, Thomas B. Curtis Senior Warden, and Benjamin F. Lewis Junior Warden, authorizing the said brethren to open and hold a lodge at Philippi, Virginia, by virtue of which dispensation they held their first communication on November 19 A. D. 1849, A. L. 5849. Present, John S. Carlile, W. M., Thomas B. Curtis, S. W., Benjamin F. Lewis, J. W., Stephen M. Holt, S. D., John Clark, J. D., Moses Shehan, Tiler.

The first members initiated were William E. Herndon and Nathan H. Taft. The next day another meeting was held at which Granville E. Jarvis was initiated and Mr. Herndon and Mr. Taft were passed to the degree of Fellow Craft. The first meeting under the charter was held April 10, 1850. There were a number of visitors present from Morgantown, Clarksburg and elsewhere. At that meeting Edwin D. Wilson and Elam D. Talbott were initiated. At the meeting held June 15, 1850, Michael Crim was admitted as a member, and the following officers were elected: John S. Carlile, W. M; Stephen M. Holt, S. W., William E. Herndon, J. W.; Elam D. Talbott, Treasurer; Edwin D. Wilson, Secretary; Nathan H. Taft, S. D.; Granville E. Jarvis, J. D., Michael Crim, Tiler. There are no minutes of the lodge meeting from October 15, 1850, to July 20, 1852. At that date the officers were, Elam D. Talbott, W. M.; Michael Crim, S. W.; William Johnson, J. W.; Stephen M. Holt, Treasurer; Nathan H. Taft, Secretary; Granville E. Jarvis, S. D.; Rezin B. Wilson, J. D.; Thomas B. Curtis, Tiler. From this date until the record closes the officers were as follows:

1853.

Michael Crim, W. M.
William Johnson, S. W.
Granville E. Jarvis, J. W.
Stephen M. Holt, Treas.

Nathan H. Taft, Sec.
Rezin B. Wilson, S. D.
Thomas B. Curtis, J. D.
Elam D. Talbott, Tiler.

1854.

William Johnson, W. M.
Nathan H. Taft, S. W.
Rezin B. Wilson, J. W.
Stephen M. Holt, Treas.

Samuel Woods, Sec.
William McClaskey, S. D.
Elam D. Talbott, J. D.
Michael Crim, Tiler.

MISCELLANIES.

1855.

Nathan H. Taft, W. M.	John P. Thompson, Sec.
Samuel Woods, J. W.	Charles B. Hall, J. D.
Henry D. Auvil, S. D.	William Johnson, Tiler.
Stephen M. Holt, Treas.	

1856.

Samuel Woods, W. M.	John C. Byrer, Sec.
Charles B. Hall, S. W.	J. P. Thompson, S. D.
Stephen M. Holt, J. W.	Henry D. Auvil, J. D.
Elam D. Talbott, Treas.	Nathan H. Taft, Tiler.

1857.

Nathan H. Taft, W. M.	John C. Byrer, Sec.
J. P. Thompson, S. W.	Elam D. Talbott, S. D.
William McClaskey, J. W.	William Johnson, J. D.
Stephen M. Holt, Treas.	Samuel Woods, Tiler.

When the Federal soldiers entered Philippi in June, 1861, there was much confusion. Some of the citizens who hurriedly departed for the South carried with them what they considered most valuable. In that confusion some of the records of the Masonic Lodge were lost never to be recovered. The die of the seal of the lodge was not heard of for twenty-five years when it was found in the road near Graysville, Ohio, and the person who found it had sold it to I. A. Wilcox of that place, and it finally was returned to its lawful owners. One book containing the minutes of the lodge from 1858 till the war, has never been found. The earlier book, however, was recovered, with the following note written in it.

June 26, 1861. This book was taken from some rubbish and preserved for its proper owner. Therefore, in the absence of the proper person to receive it, I pass it for safe keeping to Squire Grant and I feel fully convinced that he will place it in the hands of its proper guardians.
          JAMES H. M. JENKINS,
              Assistant Provost Marshal.

Before the book reached the hands of its proper owners, it appears to have been used as a record book in the military camp at Philippi, as the following entries indicate.

Edward F. Grant enters a complaint against Colonel McCook's 9th Ohio Regiment for breaking into the houses and gardens of Haynes and Hovatter, June 25, 1 p. m.

June 25. Two privates in the guard house for crossing dam without a pass.

Two o'clock. Two privates in the guard house for stealing glassware and vegetables.

Three o'clock. Four men in the guard house for theft. Discharged.

Ninety-six men in guard house for breaking into dwellings and houses.

The following list of members took the three degrees in the Bigelow Lodge No. 28, between the organization of the lodge till sometime in the year 1858. No later record of that lodge exists, and there were other members who joined later, but whose names cannot now be obtained.

William E. Henderson	Nathan H. Taft	Granville E. Jarvis
Elam D. Talbott	Edwin D. Wilson	Isaac H. Thompson

Sincerely yours,
Will H. Wentz

William Johnson	Benjamin W. Kirk	Charles B. Hall
John W. Reger	William McClaskey	Samuel Woods
John P. Thompson	Benjamin McCoy	John Stalnaker
Alfred Lester	William P. Woodruff	Henry D. Auvil
Samuel Jones	Rezin B. Wilson	John C. Byrer
E. C. Marple	William Biggs	Wilson Swindler
Joseph N. B. Crim	Charles W. Parrott	James W. Haines
James A. Grace	Daniel M. Auvil	Alexander Johnson
F. H. J. King	Lamar M. Hoff	Charles B. Willis
Fenelon Howes	James Teter	Philip Digman
John R. Williamson	Joseph Teter, Jr.	Zebedee Warner

The present lodge was established April 16, 1870. Those present were William Johnson, W. M., John P. Thompson, S. W., Elam D. Talbott, J. W., and John R. Williamson, Granville E. Jarvis, William McClaskey, Philip Digman, James A. Grant, C. F. Hanshaw, James E. Jett and Samuel Wood. The visitors were John J. Davis, John Bassell and Benjamin F. Martin. The officers elected were William McClaskey, treasurer, Samuel Woods, secretary, C. F. Hanshaw, junior deacon and J. E. Jett, tiler.

Samuel Woods was appointed to constitute the lodge under the charter granted in 1872, and on February 3, 1873, assisted by W. H. Purkey and Marion F. Hall, this was done, and William Johnson was installed W. M.; John P. Thompson, S. W., and E. D. Talbott J. W. The list of officers was completed by electing William McClaskey, treasurer; Samuel Woods, secretry; Marion F. Hall, S. D.; Granville A. Grant, J. D., and Ballard Shaffer, tiler. Following is the list of officers of the lodge:

Officers of Bigelow Lodge.

Worshipful Master—1872 William Johnson, 1873 Samuel Woods, 1874 Job H. Glasscock, 1875 T. A. Bradford, 1876-7 L. C. Elliott, 1878 M. F. Hall, 1879 T. P. R. Brown, 1880-81 James M. Woodford, 1882 to '84 and '91-2 A. D. W. Strickler, 1885 J. E. Hall, 1886 Robert M. Strickler, 1887 C. F. Teter, 1888 John M. Simpson, 1889 M. F. Hall, 1890 Jacob M. Proudfoot, 1893 N. I. Hall, 1894 G. A. Byrer, 1895 B. H. Woodford, 1896 A. S. Bradford, 1897 J. W. Talbott, 1898 C. B. Williams, 1899 L. D. Robinson.

Senior Warden—1872 John P. Thompson, 1873 Job H. Glasscock, 1874 T. A. Bradford, 1875 L. C. Elliott, 1876-7 T. P. R. Brown, 1878 R. M. Strickler, 1879 and 1883 J. M. Woodford, 1880 G. A. Grant, 1881 A. D. W. Strickler, 1882 and '84 J. E. Hall, 1885 G. A. Byrer, 1886 C. F. Teter, 1887 and 1894 B. H. Woodford, 1888 M. F. Hall, 1889 J. M. Proudfoot, 1890 W. A. Williamson, 1891 and '93 John T. Reger, 1892 Monzell M. Hoff, 1895 A. S. Bradford, 1896 J. W. Talbott, 1897 N. I. Hall, 1898 L. D. Robinson, 1899 R. H. Woodford.

Junior Warden—1872 E. D. Talbott, 1873 M. F. Hall, 1874, 1883 and 1886 L. C. Elliott, 1875 T. P. R. Brown, 1876-'77 I. V. Johnson, 1878 Perry Marteney, 1879 G. A. Grant, 1880 C. W. Proudfoot, 1881 J. E. Hall, 1882 J. D. Corder, 1884 and '94 A. S. Bradford, 1885 C. F. Toter, 1887 John W. Simpson, 1888 J. M. Proudfoot, 1889 W. A. Williamson, 1890 John T. Reger, 1891-2 N. I. Hall, 1893 C. C. Douglas, 1895 Guy C. Elliott, 1896 L. D. Robinson, 1898 R. H. Woodford, 1899 Richard E. Talbott.

Treasurer—1872 William McClaskey, 1873 to 1876 J. W. Talbott, 1877 to 1886 A. M. Woodford, 1887 to 1892 I. V. Johnson, 1893 to 1899 M. F. Hall.

Secretary—1872 Samuel Woods, 1873-4 I. V. Johnson, 1875 George E. Grant, 1876 and 1879 S. H. Morrall, 1877 M. F. Hall, 1878 W. F. Byrer, 1880 and 1885 to 1890 A. D. W. Strickler, 1881-2 L. C. Elliott, 1883 and 1890-5 and 1895 to 1899 George A. Byrer, 1884 Monzell M. Hoff, 1885 to 1890 A. D. W. Strickler, 1894 N. I. Hall.

Senior Deacon—1873 Granville A. Grant, 1874 George E. Grant, 1875 and 1880 S. H. Morrall, 1876, 1882 and 1885 B. H. Woodford, 1876 Chester W. Proudfoot, 1877 J. M. Woodford, 1879 L. C. Elliott, 1880 J. E. Hall, 1881,'84, '88 G. A. Byrer, 1883 W. F. Byrer, 1886 S. H. Johnson, 1887 and 1897 J. M. Proudfoot, 1889 M. M. Hoff, 1890 C. C. Douglas, 1891 D. W. Gall, 1892-3 B. H. Paugh, 1894 T. T. Elliott, 1895 S. A. Moore, 1896 R. H. Woodford, 1898 R. E. Talbott, 1899 Floyd T. Holden.

Tiler—1872-3 and 1878 to 1890 and 1895 to 1899 Ballard Shaffer, 1874-5 Philip Digman, 1876 H. L. Stout, 1877 G. A. Grant, 1892 to 1896 J. M. Proudfoot.

Following will be found a list of members who have died and have been buried with masonic honors since the organization of the lodge in 1870: Alexander H. Elliott, killed in a railroad wreck July 27, 1873, buried at the Elliott Graveyard at Meadowville. John M. Jenkins, drowned in Gnatty Creek July 30, 1875, buried at the Hall Graveyard. John R. Williamson, died January 31, 1876, buried at Silent Grove. Eugene T. Brandon, died November 25, 1876, buried at the Philippi Graveyard. Perry Marteney, died December 11, 1880, buried at Mount Vernon Graveyard. Augustus B. Modisett, killed by the falling of a lumber pile February 26, 1881, buried at Modisett Graveyard, afterwards removed to Mary's Chapel Cemetery. Dr. Elam D. Talbott, died June 23, 1881, buried at Philippi Graveyard. Waitman M. Corder, died suddenly at Martinsburg, West Virginia, September 24, 1882, buried at Mary's Chapel Cemetery. William F. Byrer, died July 27, 1884, buried at Philippi Graveyard; was afterwards reinterred in Fraternity Cemetery, Philippi. Rev. Cyrus Kittle, died April 26, 1885, buried at Philippi Graveyard. William McClaskey, died July 1, 1886, buried at Philippi Graveyard. Captain Thomas A. Bradford, died March 30, 1888, buried at Philippi Graveyard. Samuel H. Morrall, killed by lightning on the hill east of Philippi June 7, 1892, buried at Philippi

Graveyard. Colonel William Johnson, died February 2, 1893, buried at Little Bethel Graveyard, near Meadowville. Major Albert G. Reger, died November 20, 1893, buried at Fraternity Cemetery, Philippi. Colonel John Harvey Woodford, died at Weston, West Virginia, March 1, 1894, buried at Mary's Chapel Cemetery. James Knotts, died October 26, 1895, buried at the Elliott Graveyard, Belington, West Virginia. Judge Samuel Woods, died February 17, 1897, buried at Fraternity Cemetery, Philippi. William S. Elliott, died September 18, 1897, buried at the Elliott Graveyard at Meadowville.

The following have been admitted as members of the lodge:

Isaac V. Johnson	Charles J. P. Cresap	James W. Talbott
Joseph Teter	Cyrus Kittle	Artemus McCoy
Joseph E. Wasson	Christopher B. Graham	S. Harvey Johnson
Mansfield McWhorter	James W. Windom	David B. Douglas

The following were members of Bigelow Lodge No. 28, and became charter members Lodge 52 when it was organized, or were afterwards admitted as members:

Granville E. Jarvis	Elam D. Talbott	William Johnson
William McClaskey	Samuel Woods	John P. Thompson
Benjamin McCoy	Joseph N. B. Crim	Philip Digman
John R. Williamson	Joseph Teter	

The following are now members of Bigelow Lodge, No. 52:

George W. Baughman, Fred O. Blue, Alexander S. Bradford, George A. Byrer, Edward H. Compton, Joseph N. B. Crim, J. Minter Dennisson, David Dilworth, C. Columbus Douglas, David B. Douglas, Truman T. Elliott, Luther C. Elliott, David W. Gall, Granville A. Grant, George E. Grant, Marion F. Hall, James Ed. Hall, Nathan Isaac Hall, Monzell M. Hoff, Floyd T. Holden, Arthur G. Hooper, Peyton B. Lake, Lloyd B. Lovett, Porter L. Lovett, J. Frank Manown, Isaac D. Martin, Samuel A. Moore, Artenius McCoy, B. Escridge McCoy, Theophilus McCoy, Mansfield McWhorter, Morgan Parsons, Arthur Parsons, Aldine S. Poling, Jacob M. Proudfoot, John Thomas Reger, Warren W. Right, Lloyd D. Robinson, Amos F. Rohrbough, Charles S. M. See, Lewis S. Semmelman, Ballard Shaffer, George C. Stone, Robert M. Strickler, Arthur D. W. Strickler, Granville E. Taft, James W. Talbott, Dowden C. Talbott, Richard E. Talbott, Marone C. Talbott, William Worth Teter, Charles F. Teter, E. Clark Trimble, Charles B. Williams, William A. Williamson, James W. Windon, James M. Woodford, Benjamin H. Woodford, Robinson H. Woodford, B. Holly S. Woodford, J. Hop. Woods.

Philippi Lodge No. 59, I. O. O. F.

The Independent Order of Odd Fellows' Lodge and named "Philippi

Lodge No. 59," was instituted Dec. 16th, 1871, and was organized by Grand Secretary Thomas G. Steele, of the Grand Lodge of W. Va.; a charter having been granted on the 4th day of November, 1871, by the Grand Lodge I. O. O. F.

Since its organization two hundred and fifty four members have been received either by initiation or by card.

This lodge has erected a large and commodious brick building with an iron front; the ground floor fitted for store room, the largest and most commodious in the town, with a spacious hall above, where the lodge holds its stated weekly meetings (on Saturday evening.)

In addition to this, the lodge owns one half of Fraternity Cemetery in conjunction with the Masonic Order—in all about seven acres for burial purposes, and conveniently located, near a half mile below the town of Philippi on the east side of Tygart's Valley River. The valuation of the property, real and otherwise, is estimated at from six to seven thousand dollars, belonging to the lodge. Since the organization hundreds of dollars have been paid out of its treasury for the relief of sick brothers, burial of the dead and to many of its members in distress.

The present membership of Philippi Lodge, No. 59, I. O. O. F. is as follows:

Officers elected July 1st, 1899.

W. T. George, N. G.　　　　　　　　Geo. L. Woodford, V. G.
J. W. Bosworth, R. Sec'y.　　　　　　W. Chenoweth, P. Sec'y.
W. S. Wilson, Treas.

PAST GRANDS.

*Bosworth, Jno. W.	Hovatter, C. C.	Kent, John T.	Reger, S. L.
Barnes, Geo. W.	Holsberry, E.	Knapp, John B.	Switzer, John B.
Chenoweth, W.	Holt, S. T. H.	Lough, Geo. A.	Talbott, S. S.
Curry, D. J.	Hulderman, W. T.	Murphy, C. M.	Taft, Gran. E.
Dayton, A. G.	Ice, Wm. T.	Talbott, R. Ed.	Walter, Lewis
Call, D. W.	Johnson, I. V.	Switzer, P. A.	

THIRD DEGREE MEMBERS.

Andrick, Geo W.	Davis, W. O.	Nutter, A. J.	Talbott, Jehu M.
Brandon, C. W.	Griffith, J. W.	Murphy F. B.	Talbott, R. Ed.
Byrer, C. M.	Hoff, M. M.	Payne, C. A.	Talbott, C. C.
Burgess, Rev. J. M.	Holsberry, M.	Poling, Jno. W.	Talbott, W.T. W.
Bartlett, A. G.	Harvey, G. B.	Proudfoot, J. M.	Thompson, E. B.
Burner, R. B.	Hall, M. F.	Parks, Noah S.	Wilson, A. G.
Brooks, S. Lee	Jones, A. W.	Phillips, Jas. M.	Woodford, Jno. F.
Callihan, Nathan	Knapp, J. Letcher	Robinson, Ellis B.	Wilson, W. S.
Chrislip, A. G.	Kelley, Noah	Reed, Rob't T.	Wilson, E. C.
Cutright, W. S.	Keller, Layfayette	Reed, Geo. W.	Ward, C. C.
Corder, W. E.	Lough, Geo. A.	Rice, Andrew J.	Watring, F. M.
Douglass, Irvin	Magee, Wm. F.	Smith, Dr. Isaac	Walter, J. Woodbridge
Dennisson, J. M.	McDaniel, Abram	Shaw, David W.	Woodford, Jos. M.
Fry, J. W.	Mann, Jno. C.	Showalter, W. U.	Williamson, J. O.
Greynolds, Geo. E.	Murphy, C. M.	Stalnaker, White.	Yokum, A. S.
Gall, G. W., Jr.	Moore, Sam A.	Simpson, F. M.	Yokum L. G.
Cox, W. A.	Moore, W. C.	Switzer, C. L.	Zinn, John A.
	Nutter, A. G.	Hawkins, A. F.	

*J. W. Bosworth, G. Rep. to Sov. Grand Lodge for 4 years.
†A. G. Dayton, Grand Master of the State Grand Lodge.

The encampment branch of the order, called "Tygart's Valley Encampment, No. 28 I. O. O. F.," meets in this hall semi-monthly. It was instituted in 1877, on 21st day of April by Gr. Rep. Thomas S. Spates, acting as Grand Patriarch, and has a good membership.

Settlements and Development.

Ebenezer Kelley in 1795 settled near Meadowville and his children were Mary, Eunice, Isaac, Rebecca, Osa, Hannah, Samuel, Jane, Johnson. Two years later John Hoffman, a German, settled near Kelley; and the father of Andrew Stalnaker was a near neighbor. James Poling was living in that vicinity five years earlier. In 1788 Robert Johnson made his home east of Meadowville on a stream which bears his name, and ten brothers and sisters came with him. He had been a Revolutionary soldier. Some members of the family give the name as Levi, but the record of the marriage of his daughter Rachel with Ebenezer Kelley shows that the name was Robert. He had eleven children, ten of them remembered by name. One daughter married George Gainer, and her name is not remembered. The other children were, Garrett, who, in 1797, married Mary, daughter of James England; Isaac, who married Hannah Poling; Francis, who married Elizabeth England; Benjamin, John G., who in 1806 married Elizabeth Poling; William, who married Catherine Hovatter; Levi, who married Rebecca Cross; Robert, who married Elizabeth Hoffman; Rachel, who married Ebenezer Kelley; and Rebecca, who in 1806 married William Hoff. Henry Phillips, a Welchman born January 7, 1766, settled at Meadowville and built a fort there in 1784. He married a sister of Simeon Harris, the Baptist preacher; and he had seven brothers and one sister, as follows: Isaac Phillips, born January 19, 1769, married Elizabeth daughter of Jacob Kittle, in 1793; Joseph, born December 26, 1769, married Margaret, daughter of Jacob Kittle, 1816; John I., born June 12, 1772, married Bertha, daughter of Phineas Wells, 1793; Thomas, born January 25, 1775; William, born December 20, 1776; Susanna, born December 8, 1779; Thomas, born July 23, 1783, married Peggy, daughter of Jacob Westfall, 1815; Moses, born December 7, 1785. Evidence that the brother and sister of Henry Philips, whose marriages are not given above, lived in Barbour, has not been found. There was a Thomas Phillips, not mentioned above, who lived somewhere in the south-eastern part of Barbour as early as 1787; for in that year he was appointed Overseer of the Poor, together with Aaron Richardson and William Wilson, who lived near him. Thomas Phillips, William Wilson and Simeon Harris were on the first grand jury in Randolph County, 1787. In 1803 the election was held at the house of Henry Phillips. There were then only three voting places in Randolph County, one at Henry Philips', one at David Minear's (St. George) and one near Beverly. The will of Thomas Phillips was recorded in 1806 and that of John Phillips in 1815.

MISCELLANIES.

In 1783 a man named Smith settled on Sugar Creek. There is disagreement as to his given name, Joseph or William. The evidence is not conclusive, but there is strong reason for believing that he was William Smith, son of Jonathan Smith, one of the first settlers in Randolph. Some of the stones under his cabin now lie in the yard of William H. Smith.

Simeon Harris, one of the most noted preachers in this part of the State, lived near Meadowville in 1786. The chimney of his cabin is yet pointed out. It was large enough to receive a back log ten feet long.

OLD CHIMNEY OF SIMEON HARRIS.

Joseph Pitman, an Englishman who married Nancy Edwards, settled on Bill's Creek in 1803, with his son Joel, who subsequently became a noted Methodist preacher. In 1812, Joseph Pitman's daughter Elizabeth married Samuel Skidmore; in 1813 his daughter Esther married William Smith; in 1816 his daughter Judah married John Skidmore. His son Joel married Sarah, daughter of Samuel and Elizabeth Currence. Mrs. Currence was a daughter Cornelius Bogard. Samuel Currence died in the war of 1812 and was given a military burial. Joseph Pitman was a soldier in the Revolutionary War, and his son Joab died while a soldier in 1812. George Pitman, son of Joel, married a daughter of Leonard and Rachel Stout, Mrs. Stout being a niece of Henson L. Hoff.

John Yock came from Germany and was one of the first settlers near Belington. His children were John, Elias, Solomon, Jerry, Debby, Mary, Lucinda, and two other daughters.

Soon after the close of the Revolution, Benjamin Vannoy, who had been a solder in that war, took up his home near Meadowville. John Holsberry, in 1800, came from Pennsylvania by way of Ohio, and made his home on Teter's Creek, near Kalamazoo. He was a soldier in the War of 1812, and his children were Samuel, William, Nicholas, Martin, Rachel, Elizabeth Catherine and Nancy. Other early settlers on Teter's Creek were Nicholas Sturm, who married Annie McClaskey, and George Gainer, whose daughter Mary married Francis Vansy [Vanscoy?] in 1814. William Woods, grandfather of Willis Lantz, was an early settler near Calhoun. John England and his son John had their home near Belington at an early date. In 1797 Mary, his daughter, married Garrett Johnson, and Robert Maxwell performed the marriage ceremony.

There is a clan of partly-colored people in Barbour County often called "Guineas," under the erroneous presumption that they are Guinea negroes. They vary in color from white to black, often have blue eyes and straight hair, and they are generally industrious. Their number in Barbour is estimated at one thousand. They have been a puzzle to the investigator; for their origin was not generally known. They were among the earliest settlers of Barbour. Prof. W. W. Male of Grafton, West Virginia, belongs to this clan, and after a thorough investigation, says: "They originated from an Englishman named Male who came to America at the outbreak of the Revolution. From that one man have sprung about 700 of the same name, not to speak of the half-breeds." Thus it would seem that the family was only half-black at the beginning, and by the inter-mixtures since, many are now almost white. George Male settled near the mouth of Hacker. and on the opposite side of the river lived Richard Male. Reese Male, son of George, was born in 1815. Soon after 1790 Samuel Morris lived on the hill just below the Kelley Mine.

James Booth lived at the Felton place, five miles below Philippi; and William Booth settled on the head of Ford Run.

Christopher Nutter settled about 1784 where James Nutter now lives in Union District.

Christopher Hovatter of Maryland, ancestor of all the name in Barbour and Tucker Counties, settled in Cove District about 1790. The family of Hardins, said to have come from Kentucky, settled also in Cove about the same time.

The village of Elk City was surveyed and named by Isaiah Wilson in 1869. The first lot was bought by W. K. Jenkins and he built the first house. The creek was named Elk because in early times those animals frequented a lick now on the property of Henry Holsberry, near Elk City.

The village of Hall, on the Buckhannon River, contained 75 people in 1899 John Harrow, 1839, was the first settler on the site of the place.

After half a century of experiments in keeping the poor, Barbour County purchased 175 acres on Taylor's Drain for a poor farm, and placed it in charge of Jasper Wince who speedily made the enterprise self-sustaining.

About 1835 Silas Talbott bored a salt well on Sugar Creek near Vannoy's Mill, to a depth of 700 feet. There was plenty of salt, but it was damaged by petroleum which accumulated in the well. The drill became fast in the hole and the work was abandoned.

Edmund R. Dyer was the first to bring to Barbour a wheat drill, a hay tedder and a manure spreader. He was the first to operate farm machinery by a gasoline engine.

The first corn drill and the first ball-bearing mowing machine in the county were brought by Albert G. Chrislip.

Sylvanus W. Zinn produced a new variety of wheat, "Zinn's Golden," by crossing the Fulse and the Golden Strains. He also crossed and introduced a new variety of corn, and his other inventions or introductions were, spike-toothed lever harrow, a land roller and a wire-fence weaving machine.

The Early Harvest potato was introduced by James M. Phillips.

MISCELLANIES.

Isaac Sturm is authority for the statement that the first thrashing machine chaff piler was brought to Barbour in 1837 by a man named Ranshaw, who five years later brought a horsepower separater.

Augustus J. Zinn claims that the first wheat reaped by machinery in Barbour County was on his farm on Shook's Run.

Bronze turkeys and Light Brahma chickens were introduced into this county by Noah S. Parks; and he likewise brought from Kentucky the first Reuben Turner Horses seen in Barbour; and brought the first traction engine for thrashing machines.

The first wagon factory in Barbour was operated at Hopewell by David P. and J. Newton Hamrick in 1868.

In 1881 Hiram Male was the possessor of a ewe eighteen years old which had raised thirty lambs, which had been sold for thirty dollars.

The largest clearing in one year was by John Harvey Woodford, forty acres. In the fall of 1883 the land was woods. The next spring it was planted in corn.

A lemon tree was planted in 1875 by Mrs. James E. Hall, and was sheltered from the cold. It began to bear when four years old, and during the first five years produced two hundred pounds of lemons.

Rev. John M. Mason claims that he was the first person in Barbour County to engage extensively in the sheep business (about 1877).

On the old Talbott homestead, on Baker's Run, is a coal bank which has been operated fifty years.

Ginseng was exported from Barbour County as early as 1786.

On the river bottom, opposite the mouth of Ford Run, is said to have been the starting place for "cheat"—a worthless growth resembling rye—in Barbour. That was a camping place for travelers and emigrants over the Pringle Trail, and the seeds of "cheat" were carried by the horses from the Alleghany Mountains.

David Riley Woodford introduced the first full-blooded Hereford cattle into Barbour County, and John F. Woodford the first Polled Angus cattle, and the first Clydesdale horses. The first Durham cattle were brought to Stewart's Run by John G. Carlin.

The first steam grist mill on the east side of the river was set up in 1867 by C. J. Fisher, near Fisher's store. Near the same place, many years earlier, Jacob Sargeant built a small water mill.

The sheltering of hay and stock on an extensive scale was first practiced in Barbour County by J. E. Heatherly.

It is said that the first horse-power thrasher and separator came to Barbour in 1852.

The first steam flouring mill at Philippi was built in 1882 by J. W. Talbott and others.

LEWIS WILSON.

Isaac McDaniel claims to have brought to Barbour the first horsepower thrasing machine, in 1846.

About 1800 George Hayes operated a tanyard above Philippi, and about the same year a man named Elkhart built a mill on Sugar Creek, one mile south of Vannoy's Mills, and about the same time John Bozarth built a mill on Buckhannon River, near Teter's Mill. He built a sawmill also. In 1825 Cornelius Hoff built a grist mill above Elk City.

Near Meadowville is a willowtree sixteen feet in circumference, in the yard of F. C. Phillips. About 1795 this tree was a riding switch and at the end of a long day's journey the rider stuck it in the grond where it grew.

The village of Burnersville was built on land belonging to Isaac Reger and the first cabin near the town was built by Jacob Reger. The first store belonged to Solomon Dinkle. The name is from Jacob Burner who settled there in 182. He was the first postmaster there.

On July 21, 1896, at Belington the river rose eight feet in one hour, and sixteen feet in three hours. All of the creeks in Barbour were very high. On August 3, 1898, a severe thunder storm, accompanied by two and a half inches of rain, passed over Philippi, and lightning struck several times in or near the town. On February 10, 1899, the thermometer was 28 degrees below zero in Barbour. The "year without summer" was 1816. The greatest drought known in this region was in 1755. In 1784 there was a summer frost which killed trees. In 1846 there was a flood which stood nineteen inches deep at the crossing of the street in front of the court house. The flood of 1888 lacked a foot of that mark.

The first mill at Philippi was built by William F. Wilson in 1818. It was burned. In 1830 Solomon Wyatt built where Lewis Wilson's mill now stands. That also was burned. The mill which now occupies the site was built in 1857 by Lewis Wilson.

Bill's Creek was named from William Barker an early settler.

The Belington bridge was built in 1886.

In 1882 Barbour County subscribed for 500 shares ($100 each) of the Grafton and Greenbrier Railroad.

An examination of the wills recorded during the first fifteen years of Barbour's existence shows that only one library was mentioned and listed. It was that of Edwin D. Wilson, of seventy-six volumes.

From June 11 to June 23, 1881, six persons died in Barbour whose aggregate age was 476 years. Their names and ages were, Reuben Board 83, Edward F. Grant 68, John Harris 93, Martin Waters 81, Dr. E. D. Talbott 71, William Price 80.

In 1881 and 1882 an organization known as the Red Men existed in Barbour County. Their avowed purpose was to improve society by punishing those whom the law failed to reach. A number of well-meaning citizens belonged to the secret organization at first, but within two years the body degenerated into an association of vicious persons whose principal objects were revenge or plunder. Persons were taken from their homes at night and unmercifully flogged. On the night of November 2, 1881, they compelled the jailor at Philippi to open the door and release two of their number. On August 12, 1882, a mail carrier near Belington was robbed by them; and they plotted to assassinate Judge Samuel Woods, Prosecuting Attorney Thomas P. R. Brown and Deputy U. S. Marshal W. W. Teter because these gentlemen had done their duty in upholding law and order. Finally the organization was broken up, after the conviction and punishment of several of the members.

Shook's Run received its name from Monus Shook. In early days Isaac Minear built a mill on that stream, half mile from its mouth.

In 1863 the Legislature passed the law for the division of counties into districts. The commissioners to make the division in Barbour were, David Zinn, Henry Martin, Johnson Ward, Jesse Teter and Enoch Sears. Seven magisterial districts were made at that time, Cove, Pleasant, Elk, Philippi, Union, Glade and Barker. Valley District was added later by division of Barker.

In 1850 Barbour had 222 free negroes and 113 slaves. In that year its real estate was valued at $1,193,712.

On August 12, 1894, the body of F. M. Russell was found in the road by Howard Radcliff between Brushy Fork and Overfield. Three bullet holes were in his body. Russell had recently been tried on the charge of murdering Mrs. Amanda Welch, and acquitted. It was never ascertained who shot him.

The first mill on Taylor's Drain was near its mouth. It would run by water or horsepower. The stones are there yet, and part of the dam. Just above the mill site was the first blacksmith shop in that section, and beside the shop was the second Methodists church built west of the river in the county.

In 1850 David Byrer bought property in Philippi of James A. Burbridge and entered the tanning business, selling leather at home and abroad. He hauled hides from Uniontown, Cumberland and Parkersburg. Mr. Byrer brought the first steam engine to Philippi and used it in his tannery. He bought it in the oilfields near Brownsville, Pennsylvania. It is still in fair condition; and likewise is the carpetsack in which Mr. Byrer carried his earthly posessions when he came the first time to Philippi.

In 1851 the first church in Philippi was built, the M. E.

Gideon Martin, a pioneer M. E. preacher in Barbour, about 1835, had a yearly salary of sixty dollars, and a monthly circuit of three hundred miles, including appointments at Beverly, Belington, Jerusalem, (not in Judea) White Oak, St. George, Terra Alta, Oakland and others.

In 1870 a small corner of Barbour County, near the summit of Laurel

MISCELLANIES. 317

Hill, was added to Tucker. It was done on petition of Elijah Phillips and fourteen other citizens of Barbour, and the petition was presented in the senate January 27, 1870, by Spencer Dayton.

In June, 1853, a memorable hail visited Philippi, the stones being as large as hen eggs. Many fruit trees were killed, and scarcely a pane of glass was left in windows facing the west. There was only one box of 8x10 glass in town. Judge Samuel Woods bought that, and other people stopped windows with old clothes until glass could be procured from a distance.

The land where the town of Peel Tree stands was cleared by William Reed.

Cornelius Queen built a mill on Elk Creek about 1800.

Squire Crouso claims to have brought the first combined reaper and binder to Peel Tree.

About 1865 Bartholomew Severe, who lived near the old iron furnace on Brushy Fork, in Cove District, while leveling a mound in his garden dug out a large heap of Indian bones. No one who is now living counted the skulls; but Captain A. C. Bowman, who saw them "heaped in a pile like pumpkins," estimated the number at one hundred. So indignant were the neighbors because Mr. Severe had disturbed the resting place of the dead that they threatened him with arrest; but he justified his act by saying: "They are nothing but Injuns," and the skulls were left scattered about the premises until they finally disappeared.

In 1848 a commendable effort was made to develop the iron resources in Cove District. Iron ore is there found over an area of 10,000 acres,  chiefly on Brushy Fork. Some of it is in veins and ledges from one foot to fourteen feet thick. Other lies on and just beneath the surface, forming a very coarse and rocky soil. But the ore which lies near the surface is probably the remains of old ledges which have been partly worn away and lie scattered on the surface. Without entering into a discussion of the deposits of iron, from the geological standpoint, it may be stated that iron ore, such as is found on Brushy Fork, is a water deposit, of the same age as the rocks with which it is associated. The rocks in that locality were formed about the beginning of the Carboniferous age,* and while the sands or shells of which they were made, were being deposited in the bottom of the water, the material forming the iron ore was also collecting. Iron is abundant in all parts of the earth's crust with which man is acquainted. Few rocks can be found, and few soils which do not contain more or less iron. It is iron which gives rocks and soils their red color. The grains of sand which, in

---

* For an account of rock formations see Chapter VIII, beginning page 71 of this book.

the aggregate, form thick beds of solid rock, are often bound together by a cement or matrix of iron. Remove the iron and the rock would fall to sand. Water trickling over rocks, and percolating through soils, takes up more or less of the iron with which it comes in contact and carries it away. If this water flows into a lake, or a swamp, it will evaporate and leave behind it the iron and other solids which it held in solution. This gradual accumulation will finally form thick beds of iron ore. If there is decaying vegetation in and about such lake or swamp it will hasten the deposit of iron, because of a chemical combination. This is what occurred in ages long past in the Brushy Fork region. That the district was at times swampy is proved by the coal seams in the vicinity of the iron ore, for coal is formed (of wood) in swamps and shallow water. Springs and brooks flowing from the higher grounds into the marshy tracts came laden with iron held in solution, and this iron was deposited and was afterwards mixed and covered with sand and other impurities, and the whole mass hardened and became ledges of rock, were elevated by foldings of the strata, and were worn and cut into hills and valleys until today we find iron, coal, limestone, sandstone, and mixtures of all. Iron ore is sometimes found in nodules of concentric layers, like the layers of an onion. The belief, not uncommon, that this form is due to the supposed fact that the molten ore was thrown from a volcano and assumed a spherical shape while cooling high in the air, is without foundation. There were no volcanoes in this part of West Virginia; and if molten iron should be thrown high in the air, the resulting body would be quite different in appearance from the iron globules found in Barbour County. Molten matter thrown high from a crater returns to earth as dust or shreds. The iron nodules were more likely formed in swamps, with vegetable substance and mud as a center, about which the subsequent layers formed. They are sometimes hollow, or partly hollow, and the central mass is usually a little richer in iron than the concentric layers. In the Brushy Fork region the central part is half pure iron, the outside about forty-seven per cent pure.

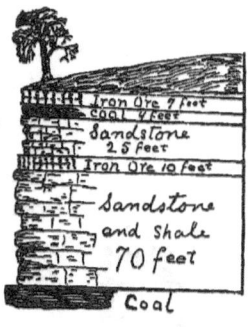

ROCK FORMATION, BRUSHY FORK

The furnace on Brushy Fork was built in 1848 and was used six years. The blast was operated first by water power and afterwards by an engine (believed to have been the first in Barbour County, about 1850). It was thirty-nine feet high when built, but is little more than half of that now, much of the stone of which it was built having been removed for various purposes. The fuel was charcoal, and about 9000 pounds of iron were produced a day. This was hauled by mule teams to Fairmont, where it was loaded on steamers. The furnace stands on a seam of coal, which was not used for fuel. The old stack is now overgrown with weeds and brush. In 1890 a well was bored to a depth of 2100 feet on the opposite side of the river from Philippi. Traces of oil were found, but a strong flow of artesian water interfered with the development of the oil prospects. At a depth of 1022 feet the Pocomo sandstone was reached. This rock rises to the surface near the head of Teter's Creek, showing a dip of more than a thousand feet between that point and Philippi.

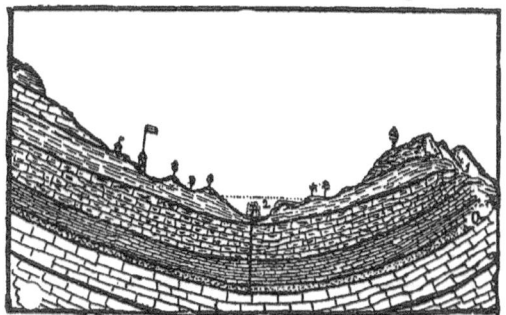

AN ARTISIAN WELL FORMATION.

The Pocono sandstone is a great oil producer further north, where it is known as "Big Injun." The Philippi well flows water the year round, and it does not freeze near the mouth of the well, even in the coldest weather.

The bridge at Moatsville, a two-span arched structure, was built by J. B. Nicola in 1890,

ARTESIAN WELL AT PHILIPPI.

Twelve miles below Philippi, in the river, are the Wells Falls, so named because of holes, like wells, in the rock forming the bed of the river at that place. There are more than thirty of these holes, ranging in size from a few inches deep and as many in diameter, to ten or fifteen feet in diameter. The tradition of the country is that some of them defy all attempts at sounding, and that no bottom has been reached. This is not well founded, and the error of the tradition can be demonstrated by anyone at no great trouble. More notions that are false are held regarding caves and other dark caverns than in any other department of human experience or speculation. Caves classed as "miles in extent," are seldom many rods; and cliffs "hundreds of feet up," or holes "thousands of feet down," nearly always disappoint the expectations of the man who measures them. It is so much more convenient to stretch the imagination than to stretch a line, that most persons employ the former system of mensuration. The writer of this visited the Wells Falls on August 30, 1899, when the river was very low, and within two hours and at not much trouble or danger, the bottom of every well was found and the depths measured. The deepest is twenty-four feet. This one is in a rock above low water mark, and the only appliance needed to measure it is a long fish-pole. The next deepest is twenty-one feet. The measuring of it is more difficult, because it is in the bottom of the river, immediately under the falls, and some caution is necessary to reach a shelving rock from which to let down the sounding pole. The other large wells are ten or fifteen feet deep. They are all due to the same agency; rocks whirled round by the currents, cutting downward like drills. The theory that the wells are of human make deserves no consideration. The falls there, including the rapids above, have a height of some twenty-four feet, and are capable of developing, for three-fourths of the year, perhaps, four hundred horse power, enough to drive the machinery for a considerable town. It could be carried by electricity thirty or forty miles without much loss.

The first carriage brought to Barbour belonged to Uriah Modisett.

The original forest on Teal Run contained walnut trees six feet in diameter, the stumps of which yet remain.

The attempts to find oil in Barbour have thus far not been crowned with success, although efforts have been made and some encouragement met with. Geologists have so far mastered the knowledge of oil-bearing rocks that they have largely reduced to a science what was formerly pure chance. They cannot tell to a certainty where oil is, but can often point out with accuracy where it is not. Experience has shown that oil is seldom found except near the tops of anticlines; that is, in the large folds of rocks, bending like arches. Dr. I. C. White, of West Virginia, first pointed out the fact. Water, oil and gas accumulating under a fold of strata, arrange themselves according to their several specific gravities. The water is heaviest and sinks deepest; oil lies on top of the water, and gas being still lighter, rises to the top of the arch and is there held. The boring which penetrates the rock is liable to encounter the three in succession. In a country where the rocks are worn by streams, and the anticlines are cut deeply, oil need not be expected, because if there ever was any, it long ago ran out and escaped. The accompanying cut shows an ideal section of an anticline, the gas in the highest part of the rock-arch, the oil just below, and water still lower. The most experienced geologists cannot always determine, from the surface of a region, whether or where an anticline exists beneath, but their judgment is always of value. It may be remarked that such anticlines are often large, ten, twenty or more miles across, and very much longer.

AN OIL-BEARING ANTICLINE.

About 1824 a gum made of a hollow log was set in a sulphur spring on the farm of George Phillips near Belington. Seventy-five years later the gum was taken up, and was found not only sound, but the wood was green.

In 1876 a cottonwood switch was brough from Ohio to Philippi, and Lewis Wilson planted it in front of his mill—the only cottonwood in the county. Afterwards the railroad was built and dirt was piled eight feet deep round the sappling. Instead of dying, the tree put out new roots near the surface of the ground, flourished, and is now eighteen inches in diameter.

The Mount Olive Primitive Baptist Church was constituted at the Rice house, two miles west of Philippi, June 21, 1817, by Phineas Wells and Simeon Harris with about ten members. Elder Wells continued as the minister until too old for active service, and was succeeded by Simeon Harris, Hamilton Goss, John Curry, Cornelius Hoff, Benjamin Holden and James Tisdale, and the church increased to seventy members. The first association was held there in 1823. The separation or division of the church on point of doctrine, occurred in 1839, and the pastor after the division was Elder Thomas Collett; the second Elder John Dennison; the third Elder John Thompson; the fourth Elder Joshua S. Corder, who is the present pastor. Elder J. N. Bartlett is a member of this church. The membership is forty-five. During the war the edifice was burned by Union soldiers, and no payment for it was ever made. A new church was built.

Zebe's Creek was named from Zebe Cotterall who was an early bear hunter in that region.

The early name of the region about Belington was Barker Settlement, and that was the name of the first post office there.

Robert F. Dunham, living near Belington, was born in Taylor County in 1815, has been a member of the Baptist Church 64 years and a minister 40 years.

In Union District, on the land of Daniel O'Brien, is a deposit of alum and copperas, formed by water trickling from ledges of rock. It is often called green vitriol. Copperas contains no copper, but is a combination of water, sulphuric acid and iron; and where copperas abounds, alum is almost sure to be present also, as both minerals are composed largely of water and sulphuric acid.

Near Elk City is a gas well which at certain periods, after a few days of quiet, jets forth, to the height of sixty feet, water and spray, after the manner of a geyser, except that in a geyser the expelling force is steam and in the gas well it seems to be gas which accumulates until it acquires sufficient force to lift the column of water, whereupon, it blows the water out.

John Gibson with his wife and several children was among the first, if not the very first, to settle on Sugar Creek. The first mention of them there is the record of their murder by Indians, believed to have been about 1782, although it may have been at the time of the Leading Creek massacre in April, 1781. They were at their sugar camp when Indians surprised them and took them prisoners, and before proceeding far, they murdered Mrs. Gibson in the presence of her children. One son afterwards came back. Nothing is known of the fate of the other members of the family.

Mrs. Gibson was the first citizen of what is now Barbour County to be killed by Indians. It was then part of Monongalia County.

Only twice in the history of Barbour County did Indians murder its citizens. The first was the Gibson family, mentioned above. The last was the Bozarth family living on the Buckhannon River near where Teter's mill is now located. This event is remarkable also from the fact that it was the last murder committed by Indians east of the Ohio River. It is strange that at that time, when settlements had been made to the banks of the Ohio, Indians should penetrate as far as Barbour County before finding an opportunity to commit murder. This band of Indians was discovered while passing through Gilmer County, and the settlers on the Buckhannon as well as on the Valley River were warned, but they refused to heed the warning, as no Indians had visited those settlements for thirteen years. Withers has left an account of this murder in the *Border Warfare*, from which the following extract is taken.

Pursuing their usual avocations in despite of the warning which had been given them, on the day after an express had sounded an alarm among them, as John Bozarth, sr., and his sons John and George were busied drawing grain from the field to the barn, the agonizing shrieks of those at the house rent the air around them, and they hastened to assertain, and if possible avert the cause. The elasticity of youth enabled George to approach the house some few paces in advance of his father; but the practiced eye of the old gentleman first discovered an Indian only a small distance from his son, and with his gun raised to fire upon him. With parental solicitude he exclaimed: "See, George, an Indian is going to shoot you!" George was then too near the savage to think of escaping by flight. He looked at him steadily, and when he supposed the fatal aim was taken, and the finger just pressing on the trigger, he fell and the ball whistled by him. Not doubting that the youth had fallen in death, the savage passed by him and pressed in pursuit of the father. Mr. Bozarth was enabled to keep ahead of his pursuer. Despairing of overtaking him, by reason of his great speed, the savage hurled a tomahawk at his head. It passed harmlessly by, and the old gentleman got safely off. When George Bozarth fell as the Indian fired, he lay still as if dead, and supposing the scalping knife would be next applied to his head, determined on seizing the savage by the legs as he stooped over him, and endeavor to bring him to the ground, when he hoped to be able to gain the mastery over him. Seeing him pass on in pursuit of his father, he arose and took to flight also. On his way he overtook a younger brother who had become alarmed and was hobbing away on a sore foot. George gave him every aid in his power to facilitate his flight until he discovered that another of the savages was pressing close upon them. Knowing that if he remained with his brother, both must inevitably perish, he was reluctantly forced to leave him to his fate. Proceeding on, he came up with his father, who not doubting but he was killed when the savage fired at him, broke forth with the exclamation, "Why, George, I thought you were dead," and manifested, even in that sorrowful moment, a joyful feeling at his mistake. The Indians who were at the house wrought their work of blood upon such as would have been impediments to their retreat; and killing two or three smaller children, took Mrs. Bozarth and two boys prisoners. With these they made their way to their towns and arrived in time to surrender their captives to General Wayne.

The graves of the two (not three) murdered children are still to be seen on a hill near where the house stood. The place is a short distance east of Burnersville.

Asa Wesley Woodford.

Farm of Asa Wesley Woodford.

MISCELLANIES.

No person in Barbour County has been found who can tell when or why Teter's Creek was named. No member of the Teter family can give information. The first Teter to come to Barbour, according to the genealogy of the present members of the family, was Jacob, who moved from Pendleton County to the vicinity of Belington about the year 1800. Yet the land books at Richmond show that Teter's Creek was named at least seventeen years before that time and within three years after the first cabin was built in what is now Barbour County. The land books state that John Hardin, jr., located 1000 acres of land on Teter's Creek in 1783. It was then in Monongalia County. The same land books at Richmond record another item which does not prove, but may suggest, whence the creek obtained its name. An entry shows that in 1786 George Teter located 224 acres of land on Tygart's Valley River, in what was then Harrison County. The present territory of Barbour was all included in Harrison at that time. It has not been learned who this George Teter was, nor whether he was related to Jacob Teter. He located the land fourteen years before Jacab came here. It is not improbable that the creek was named from him.

In 1787 Samuel Talbott located 545 acres on Tygart's Valley River. It cannot be learned to what branch of the Talbott family he belonged, as the records of the family in this county contain no mention of him. He was here within seven years after the first settlement in the county.

Morrall Schoonover of Glade District produced a new variety of wheat in 1898 by crossing fulse and longberry.

On the farm of E. B. Bennett on Stemple Run, a branch of Laurel Creek, is a ledge of purple-blue flint one and a half inches thick. Indian arrow points made of that flint are found in the vicinity. Within a few feet of the flint is a black substance, in a vein six inches thick, resembling asphaltum. It is said that a metal can be obtained from it by smelting.

Jonathan Adams, a Revolutionary soldier from New Jersey, is accredited with building the first brick house in Barbour County. It was in Elk District.

The first man buried in the Chrislip graveyard, west of Philippi, was an unknown stranger. Sawed lumber for his coffin could not be obtained; and a large poplar tree was cut, and a coffin was hewn from its trunk.

The first mill at Hall was built by David Hall who was born in Pendleton County in 1812, and was a son of David and Elizabeth (Skidmore) Hall. In 1836 he married Nancy, daughter of Abraham Reger.

Abraham Reger and John Harrow, while hunting near Middle Fork Bridge, killed a bear with their knives, while it was in the act of killing their dogs. The last bear in Union District was killed by Abraham Reger about fifty years ago, on the farm now owned by Charles F. Shirk, one mile from Hall.

The town of Belington was named from John Bealin, who moved from

Philippi to that place and built a store before the war. Bealin subsequently moved to Kansas, and his building was burned during the war. The only house in the original town which is now standing is the "Aunt Polly Lemon House." The town now has 700 people, three churches, three hotels, fourteen business houses, and is the terminus of the B. & O., the W. Va. Central, and the Roaring Creek Railroads.

Sugar Creek was named from the sugar trees along its course.

Wolf Run was so named because a wounded wolf, pursued by Philip Coontz, died in the creek.

Hunter's Fork was so named because of the choice hunting grounds in that vicinity.

John Hill, a Revolutionary soldier, who went to the army as a substitute for his brother, was an early settler on Sugar Creek, but the Gibson family and the Hunter family were there before him, and the ruins of their cabins are still pointed out. Mr. Hill built a stone house with two stories and a basement, the corners of split stone and the walls of cobbles, largely taken from Indian graves nearby, in which large bones were found. This house was occupied by Garrett Cade as late as 1863, and parts of it stood ten years longer. John Hill ultimately became blind from injury to his eyes while building this house. At the time of his death he was over eighty years old and owned 400 acres on the waters of Sugar Creek. All the Hills in that part of the county are his decendants. The stone house was long a favorite stopping place for travelers.

Webster Hillyard who lives on General Garnett's camp ground at Laurel Hill, has in his possession two bombshells (one still loaded) picked up by him in the vicinity. He also has a Confederate officer's table, made of cherry, which was left when the Confederates retreated.

Miss Martha Mustoe, who lives in Barker District, possesses a curious quilt, supposed to have been brought from Virginia in 1863 by one of Averill's soldiers returning from the Salem Raid. Miss Mustoe's mother bought it from the soldier for four dollars. It is an autograph quilt, with a name in each of the thirty-six squares written with indelible ink. The dedication states that it was presented to Mrs. C. Skeen by a friend whose name is illegible. The quilt was muddy when bought by Mrs. Mustoe. Some of the names and mottoes written on it are as follows:

> May all the names inscribed here in the Lamb's Book of Life appear.
> E. T. Gilbert, Greenbrier City, Va.

"Be perfect, be of good comfort, be of one mind, live in peace, and the God of love and peace be with you."

Mary Skeen, Covington, Va., F. L. Hunter, Greenbrier Bridge, R. A. Dickson, Locust Hill, Martha Hamilton, Creenbrier City, Elizabeth Peery, Jeffersonville, Martha Fudge, Covington, 1851. To Kate Skeen, from her mother, 1853.

In 1877 G. S. Hymes, Elmore B. Phillips and W. S. Lang, excavated for coal on a high knob on the farm of Mr. Pillips. The coal proved too thin to pay for mining. The slate thrown out dissolved by the weather and left sea shells of several species in perfect form. They belong to the upper series of the Carboniferous age,

In 1894 while sawmill men were digging a well on the farm of Charles R. Stipes, on Beaver Creek, they discovered a nineteen inch vein of cannel coal, overlaid and underlaid with bituminous coal and slate. No effort has been made to develop the coal. It gives a brilliant light when burning. While digging a well at his house, seventeen feet below the surface, Mr. Stipes found perfect specimens of fossil ferns embedded in the rock. They were of the Carboniferous age.

The largest sandstone cave in Barbour County is on a spur of Laurel Hill, on land belonging to Charles Stipes, 3 miles southeast of Belington. It is 155 feet long, 44 feet wide at the mouth, 30 at the extreme end, and 15 feet high; the floor is level fifty feet back, then covered with bowlders. A crevice from the top lets in rainwater, which in winter freezes, forming ice in all fantastic shapes which sometimes nearly blocks up the cavern. In former times when deer were plentiful they frequented the cave in hot weather to escape the flies, and were frequently killed there by hunters who shot them as they came out. Sheep now lie in the cave in hot weather.

The remains of General Garnett's camp, near Belington are yet visible on the lands of Columbus and James Mustoe at the foot of Laurel Hill, at the bend in the pike. The sugartree under which the general had his headquarters still stands; there remains also a clump of apple trees under which the confederates buried their dead; and in the bottom is a well still used that was dug by the Confederates. The positions of their batteries which commanded the roads and the country towards Belington are still marked, one near the graves of James Mustoe and wife; southwest of this on top of the hill a few hundred yards distant was another battery. A line of entrenchments runs diagonally up the hill from the   ground southwest of James Mustoe's house, to a large sugartree on top of the first hill. North of the pike stood another battery, and a line of entrenchments ran from the foot of Laural Hill above the turn in the pike.

The Mt. Morris M. E. Church was built in 1839, at a cost of $200 and the trustees were William Walter, Levi Miller, George Walter, John Holbert.

Melker Baker built one of the first mills, if not the first, in Cove District It was near Rockford.

Before the building of the Northwestern pike (1835-1849) merchandise for Barbour County was hauled from Baltimore in wagons. The road passed through Hampshire County to Piedmont, thence near Oakland to Aurora in Preston County, down Mill Run to St. George, thence up Clover and over Laurel Hill to Meadowville. The last Barbour County man who wagoned from Baltimore was John Elliott.

An eccentric pedagogue who taught school in Barbour about 1830–1860 was William Ferguson. He was noted for the severity of his punishment when pupils failed to get their lessons, He pulled their hair and cracked their heads together, exclaiming as he bumped them: "Abomination on your abominable heads! Can't I learn you nothin'!" He always carried his pockets full of pills, saltpetre, sulphur, ipecacuanha, mandrake and other nostrums, and if a child in school complained of being sick he proceeded to dope it with all the ingredients of his heterogeneous pharmacopoeia until the remedy became worse than the disease. However, some of his pupils remember him with great veneration. He lived in the Coves and died in the county,

The Kelley Mine, a mile below Philippi, was incorporated in 1896. The president was James E. Hall; secretary and treasurer, C. F. Teter. The company owns 8000 acres of coal land and has machinery which cost over ten thousand dollars. The boilers have 300 horse-power capacity. The mine was developed largely through the energies of Columbus Kelley.

On the farm of J. D. Holsberry, in Glade District, stand the walls of a Methodist Episcopal church which was built sixty-five years ago by John Holsberry and his neighbors. It was of logs, eleven rounds high, and 26 by 30 feet, with a gallery. The roof has long since fallen in, but the old pulpit remains among poison vines which have grown to the top of the walls. Within the walls of that old edifice the Scriptures have been expounded by some of the most noted preachers of the land. Among them was Samuel J. Clawson with his eccentricities. Hon. Henry Clay Dean, before he left the ministry for politics, preached many a time there. Once while preaching in this church a member of the congregation was making a disturbance, when Dean took a chestnut from his pocket and struck the unruly member in the forehead to remind him of his conduct. This church was used until the close of the war, when most of its members united with the M. E. Church, South, and the old house of worship went to ruin.

The origin of surnames is often discussed, and much has been written on the subject. It is well authenticated that at least one surname originated in Barbour in 1792; but the name belonging to a woman, it was lost when she married, One Monday morning, in 1792, an infant was found on the doorstep of Solomon Yock, of Barker District. The identity of her parents was never discovered; and from the fact that it was Monday when she was found, they named her Elizabeth Monday, shortening her name to Betsy Monday. In 1816 she was married to James Skidmore (by John Rowan of Beverly) and the license gives her name Elizabeth Monday. She lived to the age of ninety-nine years, and had eleven children, four of whom are still living, Collins, Solomon S., Martha, Christina and Felix. She lived with the last-named son, and died in 1891. She was always called Betsy Monday. It may not be amiss to mention that a surname is known to have originated in Preston County nearly in the same way. Soon after the building of the Baltimore and Ohio railroad a crew of repair hands found an abandoned child, and named him "Repair." He retained the name as long as he lived, served by that name in the Union army, drew a pension by that name, and now his children are perpetuating the name. It is probable that nearly all surnames originate in some small incident or occurrence.

Little Bethel Church, of the Primitive Baptist denomination, stands near Meadowville, occupying one acre, deeded in 1836 by Eli and Isaac Phillips to John Harris and William Price as trustees. The first organization of the church was in 1795, probably the year following the arrival of Elder Simeon Harris at Glady Creek from Hardy County. The old church book is lost, and the present book gives only the date of organization and not the names of the members. This church appears to have been the first in Barbour's territory. In 1836 a second house was built on the site, and in 1876 the present one. The minutes of 1835 say that William Price was moderator and John Harris clerk. The next year Simeon Harris was moderator; and at present Elder Jacob B. Cross is moderator, and E. B. Phillip clerk.

There are several sinkholes in the limestone belt along Laurel Hill. One called Simbad's Cave, long suspected, but never explored till October 20, 1899, is on the head of Johnson's Mill Run. On that date it was entered by Guy C. Elliott, Dr. W. A. Campbell, Warren W. and J. Mike Johnson, W. S. and Boyd O. Lang. The entrance is through a funnel-shaped depression, 35 feet across and about ten feet deep. An old opening has become filled with logs and earth within the memory of the citizens; but a new one declining at an angle of thirty-five degrees for as many feet, admits one with difficulty to a more level floor. Some distance further a small brook is reached, which presently disappears. The cave, in places very narrow, can be followed 160 feet further, where an offset four or five feet down is met. Beyond this the opening is larger a few yards, and then to the end is so low that it can be entered only by crawling. The opening, apparently, has been closed by mud and gravel carried in by water. There are well-formed stalactites, due to dripping lime-water, and in places the walls are white with deposits resembling porcelain. It is supposed that this cave is connected with the limestone spring on Y. B. Elliott's land.

PART THIRD.

Family History.

CHAPTER XXII.

―――:o:―――

FAMILY HISTORY.

A

WILLIAM EDGAR ARNETT, born in Monongalia County, 1845, son of Solomon and Mary Arnett, was married in Mason County, June 27, 1876, to Caroline, daughter of Davis and Milla (Dawson) Pritchard. Children, Della May, Hugh Glenn, Bessie Day, Minnie Milla, Frank Elsworth. He is a member of the M. E. Church, a Republican, a farmer and stock-dealer, living two and a half miles west of Philippi where he owns 160 acres of the old Adam Woodford farm, nearly all improved. He was educated in the public schools of Monongalia County, and takes an active interest in educational matters. The ancestry is German and Dutch, his grandfather having come to West Virginia from Delaware. The Pritchards are also of Dutch origin, William Pritchard, Mrs. Arnett's grandfather, having come to West Virginia from Maryland, about 1818.

B

CAPTAIN ADAM COLEMAN BOWMAN (autobiography.) My life is uneventful and unimportant, and I am disinclined to write one word concerning myself, yet I have been so importuned by my children, and the publisher of this work, that I forego my own feelings and give a sketch for the gratification of others. I was born May 1, 1839, on Cheat River, near Licking Creek, in the present County of Tucker; was married May 24, 1874, to Tacy Jane Wilmoth; our children are three, Stuart Hampton, Thomas Armstead Bradford and Tacy Maud. To their mother is due their health, good looks and moral and intellectual training. I was born at a time when there were no educational opportunities, to speak of, and my parents being poor, I by dint of perseverance and the help of an old college professor, Wm. Ferguson, was enabled to obtain a smattering education far in advance of most people of my day. I obtained from Professor Ferguson, not a classical education, but knowledge of English, some Latin and a good idea of mathematics and surveying. I was also good in history. When about 19 years of age I conceived the idea of being a lawyer; but

---

*Mrs. Bowman is a daughter of Isaac W. Wilmoth, formerly a representative man of Barbour, but now dead. He was a son of John Wilmoth, and John was a son of Thomas who was one of five Wilmoth brothers who settled on Shaver's Fork of Cheat River, east of the present town of Elkins, when that region was Monongalia County, now Randolph. The brothers were Jonathan, Nicholas, Thomas, John and James. The last named was killed by Indians.

had not a book or a dollar to buy one. I went to members of the profession and got the loan of books, and advice as to the course of study. After two years' studying and teaching school at intervals, I presented myself for examination before Judges Gideon D. Camden, George W. Thompson and William Jackson, who signed my license and congratulated me upon passing a very satisfactory examination.

Just as I had entered upon the practice of law, the Civil War was upon us. I, with a number of others, regarded the cause of the South just; and in the spring of 1861, was arguing for the South and encouraging the enlistment of volunteers for the war. We held meetings at old Valley Furnace, and so high was our blood and effective our arguments, that we soon enlisted a number of young men, who were organized into a company and mustered into the service of the Confederate States. Our first rendezvous was Grafton which we occupied with great satisfaction to ourselves, deluded with the idea that to meet the enemy was to vanquish him at sight, having become impressed with the idea that a Southern dog was better than a Northern lion. Our commander Colonel Porterfield had a much better conception of the fighting qualities than his soldiers. Hearing that the enemy was approaching he wisely retreated. Our retreat to Philippi was accomplished in good order and without incident except a false alarm that the Yankees were upon us and an order to flank and take the woods, which order was executed with alacrity by all except our company, the "Mountain Guards," and which order, for lack of knowledge and because of an utter misconception of the enemy, I foolishly countermanded, and formed our company into line of battle, firmly believing Yankees were cowards. Our company got then and there great credit for daring and bravery, all on account of an order without authority. The next incident was our flight from Philippi. To call it a fight is a misnomer. Here the Mountain Guards again showed a lack of appreciation of the situation, refused to run, formed in line and marched out in good order, and only retreated a short distance until they concluded the Yankees didn't amount to much, and hearing the report of cannon, decided to go back and capture the cannon. They actually marched back a considerable distance and only were prevented from the undertaking by citizens and cooler heads who realized the folly of the undertaking. I have always regretted that we did not go on for there never was more blundering or greater lack of generalship than the taking of Philippi, and I firmly believe, with the light now before me, that 100 disciplined, well equipped men could have routed the army of General Kelley.

The next army incident was at Laurel Hill. There, came the first revelation to me of war in earnest. A new and graver conception was forced upon my mind. I found that the Yankees could shoot and fight. We engaged them on the skirmish line without faltering, and I began to realize that the idea of a southern dog whipping a northern lion existed only in imagination. General Garnett would have defeated the enemy but for the capture of Rich Mountain. When that occurred retreat was the only hope. It was accomplished without confusion or hurry, until we were overtaken by a straggling few at Corrick's Ford where a few shots were fired and General Garnett killed. Then what had been orderly retreat became a rout. The army ran wild; officers had no control; the swiftest were able to get ahead, soldiers fell out of the ranks; took to the woods and fields; and in their frenzy, it was every man for himself. I not being accustomed to marching and unable to endure fatigue, was soon in the rear. A circumstance occurred here that made a deep impression on my mind. A comrade, John R. Phillips, and myself, friends from boyhood, both belonging to the same company, had fallen exhausted and unable to go farther, when a wagon came along, and Henry Sturm, our captain, who was riding a horse, saw us lying by the road. He called to the wagon and got Phillips on, saying that he was a lieutenant. I tried to get on the wagon and was pushed off, while Phillips went on. I followed on until I, with other straggling soldiers, got near a point called the Red House, and found the enemy there ahead of us. There we took to a swamp so thickly grown with brush, that it was almost impenetrable. Here we lay concealed three days and nights without blankets or rations. I was huddled with three Confederate officers who on the third day decided to surrender. They left me in the swamp with a solemn promise not to betray me. Hunger and thirst were so great I finally succumbed and crawled out, and got to an old Dutchman's by the name of Enos Sell. Fever set in, they nursed me three weeks, when I rode home horseback. In a few days I was captured, and was held prisoner until exchanged, then returned to the South and resumed hostilities. I recruited a company, joined the command of Wm. L. Jackson, and followed the fortunes of the Confederacy until the close of the war; participating in the battles of the Wilderness, Antietam, Petersburg, and the campaign of Early in the Valley of Virginia; was Captain of Company K, 19th W. Va. Vols.; was wounded twice, and surrendered with General Lee at Appomattox.

During the time I was in the army I had many sanguinary conflicts, many hair breadth escapes and many blood curdling experiences, but nothing so chilled my blood, and was so ground into my nature as the killing of my father, Henry V. Bowman. From that time my nature changed and revenge took the place of the common, ordinary soldier; and nothing was too daring for me to undertake that was within the bounds of legitimate warfare. I was to the front in every engagement and led my company with a fierceness that surprises me at this time. The instigators of the fiendish and hellish act were known to me soon after my return home. They are all dead now and gone to their reward. While the fire of the furies burned in my nature, and does now, while I write this, yet I never took the slightest revenge upon prisoners though numbers fell into my hands, or punished innocence for a crime dark as hell.

Since the war I have been engaged in peaceful avocations, merchandising and practicing law. The law was really my forte and I now exceedingly regret that I did not give it my entire attention. To me it was enjoyment and a financial success.

The Bowman genealogy to me is limited. They are German, or rather Dutch. The only one we can date from is George Bowman, who came from the state of New York with the Van Meters, and settled on the South Branch of the Potomac, in what is now Hardy and Hampshire Counties. George Bowman's son Adam married Rachel Van Meter, daughter of Abram Van Meter, and at an early day migrated with James Parsons to Cheat River, in what is now Tucker County. Adam Bowman had a numerous family, my father Henry Van Meter Bowman being his second son and child. There is nothing peculiar or striking about the Bowmans, so far as I know, except an utter disregard of ornamentation and especially jewelry. Not one was ever known to wear a finger ring, shirt stud, breast pin or diamond. While too poor to indulge in these luxuries, that is not the only reason. The fact is they abhor these; and never was a Bowman known who could dance or touch a musical instrument. Instrumental music to them is a dead language. Among the Bowmans are lawyers, doctors and one preacher, Bishop Bowman, of the M. E. church, who is a lineal descendant of George Bowman. None have won particular distinction or great wealth, but are all respectable, none ever guilty or accused of a crime.

I give this sketch, with this admonition especially to my children: There are greater things than money and some things for which money is no equivalent. Your honor, honesty and integrity are above price. Let money be no temptation to barter with these. Live honestly, justly and uprightly, and you will always have the confidence and esteem of the good, and will quit this life happily.

STUART H. BOWMAN, son of Captain A. C. Bowman, was born at Valley Furnace, Barbour County, June 28, 1875, and attended the county schools until fifteen years of age, when he obtained a certificate in Tucker County and taught the Location school, five miles east of St. George. He subsequently taught ungraded schools and summer normals in Barbour County while working his way through college. In 1893 he graduated from the Fairmont Normal School, the highest in a class of twenty-one, and valedictorian of his class. The next year he entered the Peabody Normal College at Nashville, Tennessee, and graduated in 1895 with the degree of L. I. (Licentiate of Instruction). He won the gold medal in the inter-society debate between the Erosophian and Adelphi Literary Societies of the University of Nashville the same year; and in 1896 graduated from that University with the degree of A. B., being class representative. For two years while in the University of Nashville he was connected with the editorship of the *Peabody Record*, the official organ of the University, the second year being editor-in-chief. In 1896-'7 he was third assistant in the Fairmont Normal School, and edited that school's journal which was established that year. He delivered the address before the Alumni at the commencement in June, 1897. He was for two years a member of the Barbour County Board of Examiners, during which time a vigorous and successful effort was made by the board to prevent dishonest practices among applicants. In 1897 he entered the West Virginia University and graduated with the degree of A. B. in 1898. His studies at the University were chiefly along the lines of political science and political economy.

In 1898 he was nominated by the Democratic party of Barbour County for the House of Delegates, and elected by a majority of about sixty, having run more than one hundred votes ahead of his ticket. He at once took a prominent place in the House, was chairman of the Committee on Education and member of the Committee on Taxation and Finance, and of other committees. He introduced and pushed through the House the bill for increasing the tax on telegraph companies, which the Senate failed to pass; and also the "Bowman Express Bill," for increasing the tax on express companies, which passed both houses but was vetoed by the Governor. He advocated the idea in the Legislature that the first and most important duty of that body is to reduce the burden of taxes and to provide for a better equalization of taxes by reducing the State levy and by bringing under tribute the various forms of invisible wealth, and the property and public franchises held by corporations. To that end he introduced a set of resolutions directing the Committee on Taxation and Finance to take under consideration the advisability of enacting a State Income Law, a movement which was heartily approved by leading newspapers of the State. Mr. Bowman was also identified with other measures of an educational and literary character. He is a member of the Board of Directors of the Acme Publishing Company, a large printing and binding plant at Morgantown, and is financially interested in other business enterprises. He has taken up the study of law and expects to make that his profession.

LEONARD CLARK BOWMAN, born in Tucker County 1845, son of Henry Van Meter and Margaret (Wilmoth) Bowman, was married near Corrick's Ford, Tucker County, April 28, 1874, to Margaret Catherine, daughter of Jacob and Sarah Ryan (Long) Kalor. Mr. Bowman is a Democrat and a farmer, residing on Glady Creek, where he owns 200 acres of land, principally cleared, and underlaid with coal. He cleared nearly 100 acres of the farm himself after his return, about 1881, from Kansas, where he had resided five years and pre-empted 160 acres of land, which he sold. His farm is in good condition, with good residence and other buildings, and will graze twenty head of cattle, fifty sheep, besides stock to run the farm, and meadow to cut twenty-five or thirty haystacks yearly. He was educated in the public schools, and held the office of Justice of the Peace. He is a leader in educational matters, and while in Kansas was a school officer and assisted in organizing a free school system in his part of the country. Mrs. Bowman was living at the mouth of Pheasant Run, in Tucker County, in 1861, and the skirmish at Kalor's Ford, two hours before the battle at Corrick's Ford, was fought round the house where she lived, and many bullets struck the house.

ELDER JOHN N. BARTLETT, born 1850 on Simpson's Creek, son of William P. and Edith (Bailey) Bartlett, was married February 24, 1870 to Ann Belle, daughter of Elder Joshua S. and Virginia A. (Grant) Corder. Children, Edward Marshall, William P., Joshua Corder, Virginia Belle, Farris E. The subject of this sketch is a minister of the Primitive Baptist Church; in politics a Democrat, and resides on the headwaters of Simpson's Creek where he owns a fine farm of 190 acres, underlaid with coal. In 1862 he joined the Missionary Baptist Church at Mt. Vernon. In 1879 at Mt. Olive Church, he joined the Primitive Baptist Church, and in 1884 was licensed to preach. Two years later he was ordained a minister, and since then has been regularly visiting Primitive Baptist Churchs in Tygart's Valley River Association and also in the Redstone Association in Pennsylvania, and has done it without charge, engaging all the while in extensive farming operations. He has baptzied and received into the church of his faith a large number of persons. Edward Marshall Bartlett, his oldest son, was born January 25, 1871; and after completing the public schools of the county, he attended the Fairmont Normal, Salem College, (Salem, W. Va.) Pen Art Hall, Delaware, Ohio, and in 1894 graduated therein the commercial course; and then he attended the University at Logansport, Indiana. After leaving school he traveled in twenty-three Western and Southern States, and at present has taught nine years in the public schools of Barbour. As a penman he ranks among the very best in the State. William P., Elder Bartlett's second son, was born June 28, 1873; and is a skilled mechanic and undertaker, in business at Flatwoods, Braxton County.

The genealogy of the Bartlett family of Barbour and adjoining counties is more accurately preserved than is the record of most families as old as that. There is some obscurity concerning the earliest in American, but after that the record is not much broken. Four Bartlett brothers came from England to America about 1700. One settled in Virginia, one in New Hampshire, and the descendants of the other two have not been located. The Virginian is the ancestor of the Bartletts of this part of West Virginia.*

---

*There is a tradition that the Bartletts are of Turkish origin, but investigation shows that the tradition is not well founded. Early in the history of New York a Turkish boy came to that city, apparently friendless, and was cared for at the house of a man

FAMILY HISTORY.

William Bartlett, the earliest of the name born in America, so far as known, was born in Virginia in 1720. Subsequently he made his home in Loudoun County, where he raised a family of seven boys, (no daughter, so far as known). The sons came into Western Virginia soon after the close of the Revolutionary war, and were among the pioneers west of the Alleghanies. Their names and places of settlement were as follows: William settled near Simpson in the present County of Taylor; Thomas settled in the Glades of Preston County; Benjamin settled near Bridgeport, Harrison County; Robert and John settled on the West Fork a few miles below Clarksburg; James settled at Clarksburg, and Sanford lived at the same place, but was never married. He was a recruiting officer for the United States army in the War of 1812.

William Bartlett, the eldest of the seven brothers, was born about 1755 in Loudoun County, and in 1777 married Elizabeth Hathaway who was born and raised near Alexandria. They had eleven children, seven boys and four girls and their names and marriages are as follows: Thomas married Malinda, daughter of Robert Bartlett; Eppa married Rebeca Barron of Fairfax County, Virginia; It is not known whom William married; James married Catherine Strother; Robert married Lydia Wells, of Randolph County; Josiah married Abigail Goff of Clarksburg, aunt of Judge Nathan Goff of that city; Benjamin married Mary Goff, sister of Abigail Goff; Cynthia died young. At the time of her death she was engaged to Samuel Selvy. Sarah married Mr. Lister; Dolly married Samuel Selvy, to whom Cynthia had been engaged at the time of her death; Hulda married Samuel Powell.

Each of the above marriages resulted in a numerous progeny. Thomas, Eppa and James enlisted for the War of 1812, but peace was declared before they reached the front. Ten children were born to Eppa and Rebecca Bartlett. Their names and marriages are as follows: Daniel married Sarah Cole; William P. married Edith Bailey; John G. married Nancy Goodwin; Thomas T. married Jemima Bartlett; James married Hannah Cole; Eppa died at the age of fourteen; Hamilton Goss married Catherine McKinney; Sarah married John Goodwin; Mary married William A. Cole; Nancy married John McDonald, and is the only survivor of the family. (1899).

Thirteen children were born to William P. and Edith (Bailey) Bartlett. Seven died early in life; three are still living, Thornbury B., John N. and Lydia. The names and marriages of the six who reared faimilies are as follows: Thornbury B. married Rhoda Ann Hudkins; Gideon Martin married Rebecca Marple; John N. married Ann Belle Corder; Rebecca married John Flint; Mary E. married Marshall Pepper; Lydia married William Judson Bartlett.

Thomas Bartlett, grandson of William Bartlett, the first, and son of

---

named Bartlett where he lived some years, and finally adopted the name of his benefactor. The tradition probably originated in that incident.

FAMILY HISTORY.

William the second, married Malinda Bartlett, and became the father of six boys and three girls, and following are their names and marriages: Samuel married Mary Fleming; William married Miss Hustead; John married Sarah Fleming; Thomas married Viar Bartlett; James married Sarah Bartlett; Elijah married Rebecca Bartlett, Susan married Thomas St. Clair; Emily married Rev. Richard Marshall; Sarah married Mr. Meeks. Six children were born to John and Sarah (Fleming) Bartlett, and their names and marriages are as follows: Thomas married Nancy Pepper; Lorenzo died young; James V. married Elizabeth Newlon; William Judson married Lydia Bartlett; Jemima married Calvin Tyson; Emily Ann married Meredith Powell.

GIDEON MARTIN BARTLETT, born in Taylor County in 1843, died May 10, 1899, son of William P. and Edith (Bailey) Bartlett, was married in Harrison County, May 21, 1876, to Rebecca, daughter of Amos G. and Siba (Chrislip) Marple. Their son's name is Morton B. Mr. Bartlett was a Baptist, a Democrat, a farmer and stockdealer, living on the waters of Simpson Creek where he owned 240 acres, nearly all improved. His grandfather was Eppa Bartlett.

WILLIAM JUDSON BARTLETT, born in Taylor County 1838, son of John and Sarah (Fleming) Bartlett, was married September 27, 1860, to Lydia, daughter of William P. and Edith (Bailey) Bartlett. Children, Cora, Edith, Lora A., Ervin Lee and Bertha. He was a member of the Missionary Baptist Church, a Democrat, and a farmer living on Laurel Creek. For four years he held the office of Justice of the Peace; for six years member of the Board of Education, and two terms was a member of the Board of Supervisors, and was defeated by only three votes as Democratic candidate for County Commissioner. He was a charter member of the Silent Grove Missionary Baptist Church, and was its clerk from its organization in 1875 until his death, 1899. He owned 305 in Philippi District, and a house and lot in Parsons, West Virginia.

BENJAMIN B. BARTLETT, born in Taylor County, in 1847, son of Thomas F. and Jemima Bartlett, was married near Pleasant Creek, in 1868, to Rebecca Jane, daughter of William and Mary Cole. Children, Mary Alsona, Lora May, William Thomas, Otis, Ina May, Jemima Pearl. Mr. Bartlett is a Missionary Baptist, a farmer and stockdealer residing on Pleasant Creek where he owns 280 acres of highly improved land, underlaid with coal. On the paternal side his grandfather was Eppa Bartlett and on his mother's side Benjamin Bartlett. William A. Cole, Mrs. Bartlett's father, was born in 1812.

HAMILTON CREED BARTLETT, born on Pleasant Creek in 1866, son of Hamilton G. and Catherine (McKinney) Bartlett, was married January 16, 1890, on Baker's Run, to Victoria, daughter of Franklin J. and Zepporah Yowell. Children, Ercel C., Aubrey Randall, Gladys and Otis. Mr.

FAMILY HISTORY. 345

Bartlett is a Democrat and an Odd Fellow; and his farm of 61 acres on Pleasant Creek is underlaid with coal.

GEORGE WESLEY BARNES, born at Cumberland, Maryland, November 3, 1853, son of George W. and Mary Constantine (Lentz) Barnes, was married at Clarksburg, September 16 1880, to Ida A., daughter of Corbin B. and Nancy (Woodford) Bradford. Children, Taisa E., George C., William C., Annie E., Pearl E. and Nettie May. He is a member of the M. E. Church, an Odd Fellow, K. of P. and K. of M. He is a Republican, and a farrier and smith, living in Philippi. He was educated in Barton and Cresaptown, Maryland. His paternal great, great grandfather came from England, and settled in Pennsylvania; and his great grandfather and grandfather (Abraham Barnes) were soldiers in the Revolution, fought through the war, and the latter was wounded in the neck and knee and drew a pension. He had three houses, on the same site, burned by Indians, and had three children killed by them, on Sideling Hill Creek, Pennsylvania. Mrs. Barnes' father fought in the Mexican War. The grandfather Lentz came from Baden Baden, Germany, 1828. He settled in Maryland. The mother of the subject of this sketch was then eight months old. Mr. Barnes came to Barbour in 1881. He has patented a brake-lever known by his name, and has other patents pending.

DANIEL BOLYARD, born in Barbour in 1826, son of Jacob and Sarah (Poling) Bolyard, was married in 1849 to Sarah, daughter of Gilbert and Nellie (Goff) Boyles. Children, Ann Eliza, John Wesley and James. He is a Democrat, living on Sugar Creek, where he owns 76 acres, nearly all improved. When sixteen years of age he injured his right leg by jumping off a fence, and it became necessary to amputate it five years later, and he learned the shoemaker trade. He worked in Philippi eighteen months and received as pay a set of shoemaker's tools, consisting of one hammer and a pair of pincers. He then worked a few months near Rowlesburg, and then went to Fellowsville. He afterwards married and settled at Gourdtown, now Kalamazoo, where he worked till the close of the war and then moved to where he now lives, and has been working ever since. "Uncle Dan Bolyard's" shoes and boots are very much in demand. His daughter, Ann Eliza, married Bedford Bryan; John W. married Genettie Sturm, and moved to Tucker County in 1893, and three years later was elected Justice of the Peace on the Democratic ticket; James married Elizabeth Hersh, and spent four years in the West before marrying, and after his return engaged in threshing, having bought the first new steam thresher east of the Valley River, in the county. His children are Gilbert, Maude, Claude, Cayton, Elcey and Walter. He owns 58 acres, all cleared.

DANIEL BOOTH was one of Barbour County's earliest settlers, and he lived near Belington. Few facts concerning him are now known. He was lieutenant of militia in 1787, and he and his wife were buried at Belington.

He had six children, Isaac, James, William, John, Stephen and Jane. All of the sons were soldiers in the War of 1812, and John and Stephen died while in the army at Norfolk in 1814. Jane Booth married William F. Wilson; William Booth married Deborah, daughter of Edward Hart, in 1803; in 1804 he was Constable in Randolph, and he subsequently moved to Illinois. James Booth married Phœbe, daughter of Terah Osburn, in 1797, and died on the Felton place below Philippi. He was an ensign of militia in 1798. Isaac Booth was the most prominent of the family. He was born January 1, 1796. He lived on the farm now owned by Rev. Robert Dunham, near Belington, and died March 14, 1858, and at his death owned 1700 acres, and had formerly owned twice that much. He had two children, Peyton C. and Eliza, who married Oliver Shurtliff. He was buried in a field a quarter of a mile northwest of Belington, and his grave is now unknown. In 1801 he was a Justice of the Peace in Randolph, in 1805 a major of militia, in 1813 Sheriff. He always took a prominent part in military affairs, and for years attended every muster, riding a large gray house. He served twenty-one years in the Virginia Legislature. He was a colonel in the War of 1812, and after the close of the war was appointed brigadier general. Peyton Booth, son of Isaac, married Harriet Phillips. Their son John married Rachel R., daughter of Peter and Elizabeth (Deems) Coyle, and their children were Isabel, Emma, Cicero, Washington I., Frederick, Ella M. and Mattie.

ROBERT M. BIBEY, born 1877, son of William M. and Mary Elizabeth (Cade) Bibey, is a member of the U. B. Church, of the Junior O. U. A. M., and in politics he is a Democrat and by occupation a clerk at Junior, and was educated in the common schools. In 1899 he was chosen to represent his lodge in the State meeting at Morgantown.

JOSEPH PERRY BROCK, born 1850 in Pennsylvania, son of John A. and Jane (Kiger) Brock, was married September 1, 1872, to Mary, daughter of Seth and Drusilla (Swisher) Harris. Children, Florence, Frank, Birdie, Nellie and Nita. He is a member of the M. E. Church, South, an Odd Fellow, member of the Knights of Pythias, a Democrat, and a merchant residing at Philippi. He attended school at Waynesburg, Pennsylvania, and began teaching school when sixteen years of age and taught six years in Marion and Monongalia Counties. He came to Barbour County in 1896 and became the owner, in succession, of a drug store in Philippi, one in Belington, and a general store in Philippi. He owns 114 acres of land in Green County, Pennsylvania, underlaid with coal and oil. He also owns oil interests in West Virginia. His father, John A. Brock, was born in Pennsylvania in 1807; his grandfather, Joseph Brock, was born in Ohio; and his great-grandfather, William Brock, was of German extraction, but was born in England, and emigrating to America, settled on the Muskingum River, in Ohio, being one of the pioneers. The wife of the subject of this sketch was born in Marion County, and belongs to the family of Swishers who were early settlers about Spring Hill, then Augusta County, Virginia.

FREDERICK O. BLUE, born 1872 at Grafton, son of George F. and Mary Martha (See) Blue. On November 26, 1895, at Philippi, he was married to Maggie J., daughter of Judge William T. and Columbia A. (Jarvis) Ice. Their son Frederick William was born June 29, 1897. Mr. Blue is a Baptist, in politics is a republican, belongs to the Masonic order, and by profession a lawyer, residing at Philippi. He was educated in the Grafton schools.

THOMAS ARMSTEAD BRADFORD, born August 30, 1825, in Orange County, Virginia, son of Alexander and Hannah (Burton) Bradford, was married in Randolph County, August 4, 1859, to Lucie M., daughter of Dr. Squire and Hannah (Buckey) Bosworth. Their children were two, Stella V. and Alexander S. Mr. Bradford was one of the California pioneers in the days of the gold excitement, but subsequently returned to his native State, studied law and located in Pocahontas County, where he was elected prosecuting attorney. In 1856 he removed to Barbour and ever after made it his home, dying of paralysis in 1888. He was one of the foremost of the many able men of Barbour County. In the Civil War he advocated the cause of the South, assisted in organizing the Virginia forces in this part of the State, and was present in Philippi and acting captain of a company under Colonel Porterfield at the time of the Philippi fight, June 3, 1861. He went south with the retreating Confederates and did not return till the close of the war. He then came home to find his law practice ruined, his library scattered, his property of little value, and himself debarred from many of the former rights of citizens, because of his participation in the rebellion. A portion of his library had been saved by Spencer Dayton, and after the war it was restored to him. He and Mr. Dayton, although as opposite in politics as it was possible for men to be, were always warm personal friends. Mr. Bradford speedily regained his lost practice, and to the end of his life he was regarded as among the ablest and most conscientious lawyers of the State. In 1872 and 1879 he was elected to the West Virginia Legislature, and was at different times prominently considered as a candidate for congress; but the selection of that candidate is often determined more by geographical lines than by the fitness of the men, and Mr. Bradford's time never came.

ALEXANDER STUART BRADFORD, born 1861, at Tinkling Spring, Augusta County, son of Thomas A. and Lucy Marie (Bosworth) Bradford, was married December 8, 1898, at Belington, to Emma, daughter of Truman T. and Lummie (Lynch) Elliott. Mr. Bradford is a Presbyterian, belongs to the Masonic Order and to the Independent Order of Red Men. In politics he is a Democrat, and resides at Philippi. In 1891, in connection with

Edward S. Taft, he founded the first daily paper at Newport News, Virginia. He sold his interest three years later.

REV. STANBERRY BARB, born near Morgantown in 1845, son of Peter and Sarah (Lynch) Barb, was married November 17, 1864, to Mary A., daughter of Robert B. and Nancy (Hamilton) Tallman. Children, Silas Columbus, Philip G., William H., Robert P., George Clarence, Elza Lee, Flora B., Rosa M. and Roscoe. He is a Baptist minister and a Democrat, residing at Hall. His education was obtained in the country schools, and he has held the office of member of the Board of Education. The grandfather, William Barb, was a Virginian, but emigrated at an early date to West Virginia. His ancestors were German and Irish. Rev. Barb has organized more churches of his denomination than any other preacher in Barbour County, having been in the active service twenty-five years, and now has charge of five congregations.

NAPOLEON BONAPARTE BOLTON, born near Philippi in 1850, son of William and Clarinda (Jones) Bolton, was married March 31, 1870, to Louisa, daughter of Garrett, and Elizabeth (Thompson) Johnson. Children, John O., Ella B., Edna, Myrtle and Lula May. He is a member of the M. E. Church, and is a Republican and farmer, living on the waters of Bill's Creek. His grandfather and father were natives of New York, and came to West Virginia at an early date. Mr. Bolton traveled a year in the West making his headquarters in Nebraska; but he returned to West Virginia to make his home. He moved to Monongalia County in 1893, but the next spring returned to Barbour.

WILLIAM T. BOLTON, born 1856, son of James A. and Druzilla (England) Bolton, was married January 1, 1878, to Christina, daughter of John and Mary (Spearga) Wagner. Children, Morris, Delbert, Atlee Burpee, Lillie, Winnie (namesake of the "daughter of the Confederacy"—Winnie Davis) and Dessa Helma. He is a Baptist, a Democrat and a farmer, living on a spurr of Laurel Hill where he owns 344 acres, one-third improved, a portion of the Payton C. Booth farm. Since the building of the town of Elkins, eight years ago, he has sold large quantities of fruit in that market. In 1894 his second son, Delbert, aged 14, was killed by a falling tree while fighting a forest fire on Laurel Hill. The boy had been a member of the Baptist Church eighteen months and was deeply religious. Mr. Bolton raises English Berkshire hogs, one of which in 1898, when 31 months old, weighed 810 pounds, which was probably the largest hog ever in Barbour County.

CHARLES S. BENNETT, born near Burnersville, 1870, son of Levi and Malinda (Campbell) Bennett, was married December 28, 1892, near Moundsville, to Clara, daughter of William and Nancy (McCombs) Finsley. Children, Walter and Nora Blanche. Mr. Bennett is a member of the Christian Church, and is a farmer and stonemason, living near Mt. Zion. His great grandfather Bennett came from Ireland, while on his mother's side his ancestry was English.

SYLVESTER L. BROOKS, born 1857 near Clarksburg, son of F. M. and Martha (Whiting) Brooks, was married in September, 1883, at Clarksburg, to Nannie T., daughter of Samuel and Mary (Randolph) Thompson. Children, Howard T. and Samuel B. Mr. Brooks is an Odd Fellow, Knight of Pythias and Modern Woodman of America; a Democrat, a merchant, a member of the firm of Brooks & Jackson, at Belington, in Barbour County. He was educated in the common schools and in the West Virginia College at Flemington.

ENOCH W. BÆHM, born 1868, son of Henry H. and Sarah (Minear) Bæhm, is a member of the M. E. Church, and a teamster residing on Ford Run. His ancestors were German, his grandfather, Jacob Bæhm, coming to West Virginia from Virginia in early times, first settling in Pendleton County. Jacob Bæhm s wife's names was Margaret Mouser. The subject of this sketch owns, in partnership with his mother, 27 acres of coal land.

JOHN T. BROCK, born 1850 in Pocahontas County, son of Andrew and Nancy (Smith) Brock, was married in Braxton County, July 26, 1871, to M. E. Dillon, (born in Rockbridge County, February 24, 1851,) daughter of Joseph Dillon whose wife's maiden name was Moss. Mr. Brock is a member of the M. E. Church, South, is a Democrat, and a jeweler, residing in Philippi.

JAMES M. BURGESS, born 1847, at Haymarket, Prince William County, Virginia, son of Addison and Mary A. (Utterback) Burgess, was married September 17, 1868, at Richmond, Virginia, to Mary S., daughter of William B. and Jane (Lee) Lewis. His second marriage was to Maude M., daughter of George and Florence (Fleming) Utterback. Children, Ora L., William A., James Edwin, Charles L and Nela, the last named by his second marriage. He is a minister in the Baptist Church, and an Odd Fellow, and resides in West Philippi. He was educated at Bethel Academy, Virginia, and at New Baltimore, same State, and spent three years in the Confederate army, belonging to the artillery branch of the service, and took part in the battles at Fredricksburg, Chancellorsville, Gettysburg, Brisbane Station, the Wilderness, Spotsylvania Court-house, Hanover Court-house, Cold Harbor, Siege of Petersburg, New Market Heights, Dutch Gap and many skirmishes. Although he had many narrow escapes, and was in the hardest fighting of the war, he escaped without a wound. Near the last days, he was taken prisoner. His great, great grandfather Burgess was a Scotchman who settled in Virginia, and on the other side, his grandfather, Stephen Tompkins, was an Englishman and also settled in Virginia. Mr. Burgess taught school fifteen terms, seven of them as principal of the Flemington school, and has been in the Baptist ministry seventeen years. In 1874 he came to West Virginia, and spent twelve years at Flemington where he had charge of four churches, and eight years at Philippi, where he had charge of six churches. He is an earnest advocate of education.

R. B. BURNER, born 1853 near Greenbank, Pocahontas County, son of Henry and Sarah (Kerr) Burner, was married at Vannoy's Mill, December 28, 1873, to Sarah Margaret, daughter of William H. and Ann (Pfau) Dougherty. Children H. Burt, Lloyd, Gennettie Belle, Robert Brady, Clarence Truman, Dora May, Iva Grace, Silva Gertrude. He is a member of the Christian Church, is an Odd Fellow, a Democrat and a farmer, living near Jerusalem where he owns 140 acres, mostly improved. He was educated in the public schools. Willis Burner, his great grandfather, came from Ireland and settled in Pocahontas County and was drowned in Greenbrier River. Joshua Kerr was grandfather of the subject of this sketch. Lieutenant R. D. Kerr, who served in the Spanish-American War, graduated at West Point, and is a cousin of R. B. Burner. William H. Dougherty, Mrs. Burner's father, served in the Confederate army, and was eighteen months a prisoner at Camp Chase. His father, Joshua Dougherty, came from Ireland and settled in Rockingham County. The sons, Burt and Lloyd Burner, are teachers.

DAVID F. BYRER, born 1826, son of Frederick and Susanah (Cobaugh) Byrer, was married in 1850 to Mary E., daughter of Samuel and Ruth (Criswell) Lewis. He was a tanner in Philippi, and further mention of him will be found in this book.

DANIEL BOYLE, born on Teter's Creek, 1829, son of James and Catherine (Watring) Boyle, was married in 1851 to Joanna, daughter of William and Martha Smith, and after her death he married Harriet, daughter of Elisha and Lucinda (Waldo) Kittle. Children, James D., Louisa, Evaline, Dama, Randolph and Truman. Mr. Boyle is a member of the M. E. Church of the Grand Army of the Republic, is a farmer near Calhoun where he owns 140 acres, underlaid with coal and mostly improved. Mr. Boyle attended subscription schools. Gilbert Boyle was his grandfather, and was a soldier in the War of 1812, dying 1835. He was one of the early settlers in Cove District. John Watring, Mr. Boyle's grandfather on his mother's side, came from Germany and settled in Preston County. Mr. Boyle was a Union soldier, and had six brothers in the Union army, a record seldom equalled. He was lieutenant in Company F., 15th W. Va. Infantry, and saw much hard service. His wife's grandfather was Dr. Waldo.

BARNET BOYLE, born near Vannoy's Mill, 1831, son of James and Catherine (Watring) Boyle, was married in 1857 to Sally Ann, daughter of John and Mary (Yock) Kelley. For a second wife he married Sarah Amanda, daughter of Andrew and Barbara (Marple) Trimble. Mrs. Boyle died in 1892. The children by his first marriage were, Mary Catherine, William Posten, John Wesley, Amanda Alice, James Oscar; by the second marriage, Truman, Loretta, Dowden, Armora, Belle, Charles, Armintie,

Joel Lyman. Mr. Boyle is a Republican and a farmer, living two miles northeast of Philippi. He attended public schools, was in the Federal army, and saw much service as a scout. His great grandfather came from Ireland and settled on Teter's Creek. He owns 44 acres, mostly improved, in the Kelley Coal Field.

JOHN IRWIN BOYLE, born 1860, son of Samuel and Delilah Ann (Upton) Boyle, was married October 16, 1879, to Cordelia Jane, daughter of Stephen and Elizabeth (Delawder) Strawderman. Children, Jerome Calvin, Lily Dana, Bertie Ann, Bessie L. He is a member of the M. E. Church, a Republican and a farmer, living on the head of Bear Run where he owns 20 acres, underlaid with coal. His great-grandfather came from Germany, and his father was a Union soldier.

CHARLES WILLIAM BOYLE, born May 9, 1863, near Tacy, son of Marshall and Mary A. (Hushman) Boyle, was married December 31, 1883, to Almira Belle, daughter of Peter G. and Mary C. (McGuffin) Poling. Children, James Delbert, Melvin P., Lily Atlantic, Zora Lee, Zella May, Minnie Gay and Herbert M. Mr. Boyle is a Republican, a farmer and a carpenter, residing near Laurel Creek Bridge at Dantown, where he owns 90 acres, mostly improved and underlaid with coal. He was educated in public schools. His father was a member of Haller's Home Guards; and his grandfather on his mother's side was Dr. Abraham Hushman, a noted physician of Virginia who came to West Virginia half a century ago.

C

ELDER JOSHUA SIMMONS CORDER is of English and Irish descent. His grandfather, Joseph Corder, came from England and settled in Virginia about the close of the Revolution. He had four sons and four daughters. The sons were James, Joseph, William and John. James moved to Ohio and settled near Circleville; John located near Logansport, Indiana; Joseph crossed the Blue Ridge in 1838 into western Virginia; and William, the father of the subject of this sketch, was born March 29, 1785, in Frederick County, now Fauquier, Virginia, and on September 14, 1811, was married to Sarah Cole, of Loudoun County. She was of German descent. Three years after their marriage they set out for West Virginia They crossed the Alleghanies and penetrated the wilderness beyond. Mr. Corder was a man of energy, industry and honor; but he came with few of this world's goods. The habits of thrift, which he possessed, he transmitted to his descendants. In December, 1814, he arrived in what was then Harrison, now Barbour, with his wife and two small children, and bought fifty acres of land, for $450, of Peter Robinson, on Hacker's Creek. He built a small cabin of unhewn logs, and took up his abode within its walls, surrounded by forests.

Mr. Corder had a good dog, but no horse or cow. Occasionally the howl of the wolves was heard. The low lands were usually swampy and somewhat unhealthful, and few persons settled in them. Mast was generally plentiful, and swine raising was profitable to the extent that the family's supply of meat from that source seldom failed. Grain was raised in small patches and was ground on hand-mills before better were to be had. Shoes for children in the summer time were not thought of, and often the winter was well on the way before the feet of the young members of the household were clad. William Corder and his wife worked up from that humble beginning until they owned 1200 acres of farming land on Hacker's Creek, and a farm or two besides. They had eleven children, Joseph, William, Joshua, James, John, Edward, Elizabeth, Martha Ann, Mary, Ingaby and Hannah. One thing here should be said: when he owned only fifty acres of land, the Mount Olive Primitive Baptist Church was constituted at the Rice House, on the Philippi and Clarksburg pike, now owned by D. M. Proudfoot. This was on June 21. 1817. and by Phineas Wells, and perhaps Simeon Harris, with about ten members. They could not purchase a lot to suit them on which to build a church house, and Mr. Corder said to them: "I am not a member of your body, but the Lord has given me what little I have, and I will give you a lot on the corner of my little tract." The church accepted his offer and built on the lot a hewed log house, twenty-four by thirty feet, with a gallery and a pulpit after the English style. It was not long until Mr. Corder and his wife were baptized into the fellowship of the church. The subject of this sketch was their third son, and was born February 15, 1820, and was so sickly that there was little hope of his living. But his health and strength improved, and he was baptized into the fellowship of the Primitive Baptist Church when he was but fifteen years old. He composed a song commemorating his experience, from which the following verses are taken:

>Come saints of God and hear me tell
>>What dreadful thoughts I had of hell.
>
>I felt myself so far from God
>>The earth did tremble where I trod.

>Though I was young, quite in my youth,
>>I longed to hear and know the truth;
>
>And often went in secret prayer
>>To find my God in mercy there.

>I often wept myself to sleep
>>And prayed the Lord my soul to keep,
>
>Lest I should drop into the lake
>>And never, never more to wake.

>The year of eighteen thirty-three,
>>It pleased the Lord to set me free;
>
>My age was only twelve and one
>>When Peace and Joy came through His Son.

ELDER JOSHUA SIMMONS CORDER.

FAMILY HISTORY.   355

The division of the Baptists took place in this country in 1839, and Elder Corder was numbered with the Oldside, as they were called in that day; and the next year he was licensed by the church to preach. He was then but twenty years old and was limited in education. He attended the Clarksburg Academy and Rector College at Pruntytown, and afterwards took a tour to the West, preaching among the churches of Ohio and Indiana. He taught in Indiana eight terms of school, and in the meantime preached to a number of churches. In September, 1843, having returned to West Virginia, he was ordained by his home church. Then he returned to the West, as he supposed to make his home; but in his traveling and preaching he came home to see his parents, and went to visit the Virginia churches, and near Front Royal he became acquainted with a young lady, Virginia Ann Grant, to whom he became engaged.

On June 18, following, that is 1850, Elder Corder and Miss Grant were married and built a nice dwelling. Then came the War of 1861, just as they were becoming well situated. Nearly everything they had was distroyed by Federal troops. Wagon loads of household goods, books and furniture were hauled off, and bacon and grain were taken without payment. The family were driven from the house, a guard was put round it and the family were not permitted to return. After the soldiers had used the house nearly four years they burned it, together with nearly two miles of fence. This was done by the Federal soldiers because Elder Corder owned a few slaves)which came into his possession through heirship) and was true to his own State. He never attempted to injure any person, being a minister of the Gospel. He had appealed to the Federal authorities for protection. His loss was not less than $8000. He saved the Philippi bridge from being burned at the time of the Imboden raid, 1863. He successfully appealed to the soldiers to spare it after they had piled straw on it to burn it. When the Mount Olive Primitive Baptist Church was rebuilt (after the Union soldiers destroyed it) he gave $250 toward the work, and borrowed at ten per cent interest the money. He is now about eighty years old and has been a preacher fifty-nine years, and never asked for a dollar in his life for preaching. He thinks that the Gospel should be preached without charge. He is now the pastor of Mount Olive Primitive Baptist Church on Hacker's Creek, has baptized over forty members into the fellowship of the home church, and more than a hundred into other churches of the same faith and order; has been the Moderator of the Tygart's Valley River Association of Baptists nearly thirty years; and has united in marriage over three hundred couple. He has been offered several political offices in Barbour County, but he always declined, saying that preachers had no business with political offices.

Elder Corder has three children, Ann Belle, who married Elder J. N. Bartlett; Blue Dell, who married J. E. Cole; and Semma Ell, who is single.

He has written verses and hymns all his life. Some of his songs are popular in church service. The following hymn was written when he was seventy-five years old:

> Without thy strength, O God, I'm weak,
> Without thy grace I'm poor;
> Oh, bring me to thy feet to seek
> Thy name for evermore.
>
> Show me the riches of thy grace,
> My God, my God, my all,
> That I may see thy lovely face,
> Then I shall never fall.
>
> O, let me taste those heavenly joys,
> Which I have felt before,
> Then I will part from all my toys,
> And learn to seek thee more.
>
> So many things step in my way
> To keep me back from truth
> That I am often made to say
> And cry, like ancient Ruth:
>
> "O, keep me, gracious God of love,
> To fix my thoughts on thee
> And then my mind will soar above
> And better things will see."
>
> Lift up my head, my hands, my feet;
> Show me the path of life,
> That I may walk the golden street
> Beyond the reach of strife.

WILLIAM B. CORDER, born 1858, son of William and Trena (Devers) Corder; was married December 25, 1877 to Bertha J., daughter of James K. and Sally Bartlett. Children, Guy Emmett, Iva, Ila, Sadie, L. R., Waitman D., William Everett, H. Wade, L. B., Rossie A., Roxie B. and Sally F. He is a Baptist, a Republican and a farmer, living on Simpson's Creek, where he owns 304 acres underlaid with coal. He was educated at the West Virginia College at Flemington. He has held offices as follows: Member of the Legislature, Assessor, Member of the Board of Education, Postmaster at Simpson, railroad agent at the same place. The ancestry of the Corders is given in the sketch of of Joshua S. Corder. The Devers were French, and Mrs. Corder's grandfather, James Devers, served seven years in Washington's army in the Revolution. He married Anna Barker.

WILLIAM ALONZO CORDER, born 1862, on Hacker's Creek, son of James W. and Mary C. (Bond) Corder, was married June 19, 1884, to Nannie R., daughter of Benjamin S. and Lucy (Pell) Reynolds. Their child's name is James Stanley, born October 11, 1887. Mr. Corder's mother was born in Harrison County, daughter of Reuben Bond. Mr. Corder is a Primitive

FAMILY HISTORY.   357

Baptist; is a farmer and stockdealer, living three miles north of Philippi on the Beverly and Fairmont Pike, where he owns 350 acres of improved land underlaid with coal, and devoted largely to cattle grazing and grain. The farm is one of the finest in Barbour County. In early life he was in the mercantile business, and was post master at Switzer's. Mrs. Corder, born October 20, 1863, graduated from the Fairmont Normal School in 1881.

Benjamin S. Reynolds, the father-in-law of the subject of this sketch, was born in Harrison County, August 21, 1821. He accumulated a fortune from a beginning of 200 acres given him by his father, Thomas P. Reynold's also a native Harrison County, where he was born April 11, 1798, and where he was married to Miss Margaret Thompson, (born in Harrison). After their marriage the young couple settled on Limestone Creek where they purchased a large farm and reared their children, Benjamin S. and Mary J. On this farm Mr. and Mrs. Reynolds died, the former in 1854 and the latter in 1881. The grandfather of B. S. Reynolds was John Reynolds. He was born in Culpeper County, Virginia, where he resided till 1785 when, with his family, he removed to Harrison, hauling his household goods in a covered wagon, said to be the first to reach that county. Mr. Reynolds located on West Fork, five miles above Clarksburg, and was one of the pioneers in that vicinity. He made yearly trips to Winchester for salt and other supplies, paying with ginseng and deer skins. On those occasions he used an enormous bull as a pack animal, carrying on him a load of 500 pounds from Winchester to Clarksburg. John Reynolds' father was Cornelius Reynolds, probably a native of Ireland, but an early settler in Culpeper County where he died. The maternal grandparents of Thomas P. Reynolds were Thomas Phillips and his wife Mary, who were natives of Wales, who emigrated to America in 1770 and five years later to West Virginia. They had two children, both daughters. One married John Reynolds, the other Robert Bartlett. The father gave each daughter 400 acres of land, and retained 200 acres for himself, which he afterwards gave to his name-sake, Thomas P. Reynolds. Mr. Phillips was a remarkable man, in one respect at least; he was never known to be angry. The maternal grandparents of B. S. Reynolds were James and Jane (McCaully) Thompson, natives of County Down, Ireland, where they were married. They landed at Baltimore after a stormy voyage of fifteen weeks. On September 5, 1849, Benjamin S. Reynolds was married to Lucy Ann, daughter or Hezekiah Pell, of Preston County. His father was a New Yorker who came to Preston at an early day.

WILSON P. CORDER, born 1845 at the old Corder homestead on the head of Hacker Creek, son of Joseph and Catherine (Patton) Corder, was married June 2, 1870, to Marietta, daughter of Bennett I. and Nancy Hudkins. Children, Cony E., John F., Richard D., Ettie and Nettie (twins), J. Wayne, Mettie, Grover and Flora May. He is a Democrat, farmer and stockraiser, residing on Brushy Fork of Elk, where he owns 220 acres of fine land, underlaid with coal. He was educated at the Pruntytown Academy. Cony E. Corder, his son, is one of Barbour's progressive teachers, and was educated in the public schools, at the Buckhannon Seminary, and at the Fairmont Normal School. John F., his second son, taught four terms of school, attended the Fairmont Normal School, and in 1898 graduated in law at the West Virginia University, and located in Grafton for the practice of his profession. Richard D., another son, is a teacher and a student at the Fairmont Normal School.

JOHN MARSHALL CARDER, born in Philippi 1851, son of Noah and Tabitha (Bennett) Carder, was married June 1, 1882, in Greenbrier County, to Mary E., daughter of John and Elizabeth Rinker. Children, Florida and Lena May. Mr. Carder is a Democrat, a farmer and a stockraiser, owning 190 acres on the Fairmont and Beverly Pike. He raised 350 bushels of oats and 320 of wheat in one year; he also introuduced a new variety of wheat into the county; he spent a short time in Illinois, as a carpenter. A very fine sugar grove is among his possessions. His father, Noah Carder, was nine years a blacksmith in Philippi, and was married twice, his second wife being Sarah A., daughter of Barnett and Jennie (Sturm) Poling. Three children were born to each marriage.

REUBEN B. CARDER, born 1854 at Philippi, son of Noah and Tabitha (Bennett) Carder, was married September 28, 1885, at Philippi, to Mary A., daughter of Daniel and Rachel (May) Fridley. Children, Albert M. and Danah. He is a Democrat, a farmer and a stockraiser, living four miles south of Philippi on the Fairmont and Beverly Pike, where he owns 450 acres, mostly improved, and all underlaid with coal. In 1898 he handled 800 sheep in addition to his agricultural business. Mrs. Carder is the possessor of an elegant set of glass dishes brought from Ireland by her great-great-grandfather, whose name was Nicely. Noah Carder, father of the subject of this sketch, introduced the first mowing machine into Barbour County. He was one of the most progressive farmers of his time. The family is of German origin, coming to Virginia in 1740, and his immediate ancestors settling near Philippi early in the present century.

JOHN G. CARLIN, born on Stewart's Run in 1846, son of John and Sarah (Gall) Carlin, was married December 12, 1866, to Hester, daughter of Lemuel and Jemima (Chrislip) O'Neale. Children, Rosetta and Laura B. He is a Democrat, a farmer and stockman living on Stewart's Run, where he owns 129 acres, all improved and underlaid with coal. The first Durham cattle on Stewart's Run were brought by him. The record of the Carlin family dates back to 1740, at which time John Carlin was born in Ireland. In 1772 he was married, and he raised a family of three children, viz: John, born 1773; Margaret, born 1775; Edward, born 1777. The family came from Ireland to Wheeling about 1774, and the history of the son John only

FAMILY HISTORY.   359

is known. He grew to manhood at Wheeling, and in 1798 married Catherine, daughter of William and Abigail Reed. They had twelve children, viz: Robert, born 1800; William, 1802; John, 1804; Edward, 1806; Abigail, 1808; Margaret, 1810; Elizabeth, 1812; Thomas, 1814; Amos, 1816; Katie, 1818; Asa, 1820; Mary, 1823. Of these children, John, in 1835, married Sarah Gall, and their children were, Granville, Luther, Melvin, John G. (subject of this sketch), Miranda, Margaret and Matticia.

JOHN R. COLE, born on Pleasant Creek in 1856, son of Jesse and Elizabeth (Knotts) Cole, was married March 9, 1882, near Grafton, to Laura E., daughter of Lewis and Harriet (Wilson) Lewellyn. Their child's name is Everet E. Mr. Cole is a member of the M. E. Church, a merchant and farmer, residing on Pleasant Creek; he was educated in the public schools of Barbour. The sword carried by his father through the Civil War now belongs to Mr. Cole, who values it highly. His farm contains 205 acres of highly improved land, principally devoted to grazing cattle.

ALBERT G. CHRISLIP, born near Elk City, 1859, son of Irvin G. and Mary (Daniels) Chrislip, was married near Boothsville, October 27, 1898, to Ella, daughter of Allen Nuzum. Mr. Chrislip is a member of the M. E. Church and his wife is a Baptist. He is an Odd Fellow, and a wholesale and retail merchant in Philippi. The Chrislips came from Germany and the Daniels from Holland. He began life on the farm; tried the West three years; taught two years in the Philippi schools, introducing the word method; clerked in the store of Job Glascock, and then wrote in the County Clerk's Office under Luther C. Elliott, and finally went into the mercantile business in connection with his brother, William L. Chrislip, dealing in farm implements, and fertilizers. They introduced the first corn drill and the first ball-bearing mowing machine into Barbour County. They handle 50,000 pounds of wool a year, and their sales of merchandise aggregate $40,000 annually. This business has been built up in nine years.

The Chrislip family has been in Barbour 107 years the first comer, Jacob, settled six miles west of Philippi in 1792. The name comes from Germany where it is written Christleib, and in Pennsylvania and the West it is still often spelt that way. The family is traced back through Germany to a Turk who, when a child, at the storming of Belgrade, on the Danube, by Prince Eugene in 1688, fell into the hands of the Germans. The Turks had been defeated, and some mother, unable to save her child, hid him in an oven where he was found and saved. He was taken to Germany, educated there, and became a decorator of the Royal Court. The translation of the name Christlieb is "Christ-love." The first to come to America was Frederick Charles, who had married Anna Catherine Buck, a widow, and their two sons were Frederick Charles and Jacob, the latter born 1747. They landed at Baltimore 1765, and settled in Pennsylvania, where Jacob, in 1779, married Nancy Singer, who was born in 1755. In 1792 they made their way into what is now Barbour and purchased land six miles west of Philippi. Following are the names of their children and dates of birth: George, 1782; Jacob, 1787; John, 1789; William, 1794; Abram, 1795; Isaac, 1797; Samuel, 1800; Mary, 1780; Elizabeth, 1781; Christina, 1785; Catherine, 1786; Nancy, 1790; Margaret, 1797, and Sarah, 1802. The father, Jacob, died 1822 and his wife 1824.

Of the children, George married Mary Rice, and died 1857. Their children were Thomas B. and Jacob. Jacob married Elizabeth Reger, and died 1868. Their children were, Lemuel, Abram and Jacob A. John married Margaret Harvey, and their children were, Nathan, William, Martin, Malinda, Elizabeth, Jemima and Matilda. William married Hannah Ward, and died 1847. Children, Peregrine G., William Turner, Johnson B., Sebia, Drusilla, Hannah, Rachel, Minerva, Susan and Sarah Ann. Abram married Amanda Britton, and died 1887. Children, Ervin G., Julia, Eliza, Elizabeth J., Elmer Lee. Isaac was unmarried; died 1881. Samuel married Eleanor J. Board, and died 1889. Children, Melissa, Virginia, Deniza, Lee, Harriet, Gibson and Marcellus R. Mary married David Willett; Elizabeth married Nicholas Crouse; Christina married James A. Connor, and died 1818. Nancy married Jacob Owens, and Margaret married David Jenkins. Sarah married Solomon Chrislip and died 1885.

JAMES K. CLEAVENGER, born on Simpson's Creek, 1846, son of Samuel and Kizziah (Cole) Cleavenger, was married November 24, 1870, in Harri- County to Elizabeth A., daughter of John W. and Rebecca Flint. Children, Cora May, Ira, Ara, Eva, Stella. He is a member of the Missionary Baptist Church, is a Democrat and a farmer, living on Simpson's Creek, where he owns 208 acres, mostly improved. His education was obtained at the Corder school house. His ancestry was English, and his father, still in good health, is 89 years old, and never took more than two doses of medicine in his life.

CHARLES W. CLEAVENGER, born on Foxgrape Creek, 1856, son of Minor M. and Mary (Knotts) Cleavenger, was married November 9, 1884, in Taylor County, to Minerva, daughter of Patrick F. and Mary (Hustead) Fleming. Children, Cecil Wayne, Buford and Mary. He is a Republican, a farmer and stockdealer, residing on Simpson's Creek, where he owns 225 acres, and on Foxgrape Creek he owns 100 acres. He follows grazing mostly, and pastures seventy-seven cattle and twenty sheep at present. His father's brothers were, Frank, Charles, Samuel, John and Garrison. Their sister, Salley, married Cyrus Bartlett. Mrs. Cleavenger's grandfather, Samuel Bartlett, was the father of twenty-one children. She was descended from James Fleming, and as he has many descendants in this and neighboring counties, it is proper to give a sketch from his family record. James Fleming was born March 21, 1775, and on March 16, 1797, he married Elizabeth Welch, who was born November 29, 1777. He died

October 11, 1846; she died March 15, 1847. Their children were, Lawrence Fleming, born July 26, 1798, married Miss Lake. Patrick Fleming, born April 15, 1800, married Margaret McDonald. Ann Fleming, born March 25, 1802. Jemima Fleming, born April 7, 1804; married William Reynolds, and died November 13, 1785. Mary Fleming, born June 10, 1806; married Samuel Bartlett. Sarah Fleming, born March 17, 1809; married John Bartlett. Emily Fleming, born September 14, 1811. M. Sylvester Fleming, born November 30, 1812; married Matilda Bartlett. Johnson Cassel Fleming, born October 13, 1815; married May Bartlett, October 13, 1843. James and Elizabeth Fleming, born June 14, 1819; Elizabeth married John G. Cleavenger, and died July 3, 1884. Benjamin James Fleming, born June 2, 1822.

AI CLEAVENGER, born on Simpson's Creek, in 1860, son of John G. and Elizabeth C. (Fleming) Cleavenger, was married September 24, 1784, to Cora B., daughter of C. E. and Elizabeth J. (Lake) Batson. Their daughter's name is Sadie May. Mr. Cleavenger is a Missionary Baptist, a farmer and stockdealer, living on Simpson's Creek, where he owns a valuable farm of 340 acres of highly improved land, underlaid with 20 feet of coal in two veins. He owns the property known as "the J. D. Corder farm." He deals extensively in cattle and sheep. He has filled the offices of President of the Board of Education and Justice of the Peace. He was educated at the West Virginia College at Flemington; and in politics he takes much interest in the cause of the Republican party.

JAMES W. CLEAVENGER, born 1853, son of Minor M. and Mary (Knotts) Cleavenger, was married July 11, 1876, to Melissa Ann, daughter of Richard S. and Margaret (Weaver) Talbott. Children, Anna and Ada. He is a member of the U. B. Church, a Republican and farmer, residing on Indian Fork, where he owns 137 acres, well improved. He was educated in the common schools and in the West Virginia College at Flemington.

JOSEPH N. B. CRIM, son of Michael and Catherine (Strickler) Crim, was born in 1835, in Rockingham County, Virginia, and when twelve years old removed with his parents to Barbour County and settled on a farm six miles from Philippi; but soon afterwards moved to Philippi and made his home with an uncle who was engaged in merchandising. He at once entered the store, attending schools when he could, and thus learned by practice the principles of business and acquired the habits of industry which ever afterwards characterized him and placed him the foremost of the business men of the county. About the time of his majority he went into business for himself, and soon became the leading merchant of the county, which position he held for years, in the meantime buying extensive real estate interests. William McClaskey, afterwards Sheriff of Barbour, was his first partner in the merchantile business. Mr. Crim owned a store at Elk City from November, 1861, till March 4, 1894. In 1878 he became a partner with L. D, Morrall in Philippi, and at the end of three years sold his interest to his partner. From 1867 till 1872 he was in partnership with W. W. Daniels in a store at Peel Tree; and had a store also at Overfield, with T. B. Douglas as a partner; and also a store at Belington; and later he was a member of the firm E. H. Crim & Company, at Philippi. He became largely identified with the banking business, and at present is the president of the Tygart's Valley Bank, one of the solid institutions of Barbour County. He might have turned his attention to politics, and, so far as one can judge, the way was open for his advancement to high places; but he did not choose to do so, except that, 1866, he was a candidate for Sheriff, and in 1872 a candidate for the Constitutional Convention of the State. In the former instance, at the primary election, he carried the county by 460 majority, but did not go on the ticket at the general election. In 1872 he was elected to the Constitutional Convention by 350 majority. Mr. Crim married Almyra J., daughter of John N. and Harriet (Rightmire) Hall, and they have two children, E. H., who is a merchant of Philippi, and Cora May, who is the wife of Melville Peck, Esq. Mr. Crim's grandparents were Peter and Elizabeth (Shaffer) Crim, of Rockingham County, Virginia, where he owned a mill. He was a native of Pennsylvania. Mr. Crim's grandfather, on his mother's side, was Joseph Strickler, a farmer of Page County, Virginia.

GEORGE CAMPBELL, M. D., born 1855 in Barbour, son of George G. and Elizabeth A. (Bryan) Campbell, was married July 26, 1882, to Burnettie daughter of James and Hannah (Skidmore) Nestor. Children, George Howard and Delores Elizabeth. In politics he is a Democrat; by profession a physician and farmer, living at Danville, where he owns 125 acres, principally cleared. He devotes much of his attention to stock-raising. He was educated at the University of Maryland, and takes a deep interest in schools. His father, George G. Campbell, was born in 1824 in Baltimore, and was a son of George Campbell, of whom Judge Samuel Woods said: "He was the most remarkable man I ever knew." Geo. G. Campbell in 1845 came to the farm on which he now lives, and engaged in the mercantile business with his half brother, George W. Bedford, until the beginning of the war. He married Elizabeth A., daughter of William and Barbara (Swisher) Bryan, February 8, 1854. Children, George, Bedford, Mary William, Albert, Florence B., Leander, Littlewood and Rosa Alice. He owns 700 acres. Among his possessions is a writing desk which his father carried across the Atlantic Ocean nineteen times, and the papers left in it at his father's death 1866, are still in it.

GEORGE CAMPBELL, father of the above named, was an Englishman. In 1893 Judge Samuel Woods was a witness in a suit in court connected with the Campbell estate, and his deposition now on file in the Supreme Court, Judge Woods thus speaks of George Campbell:

Isaac V. Johnson.

FAMILY HISTORY 365

"He informed me frequently that he removed from England and settled in Boston, Mass., in the year 1797; that he was 22 years of age at the time he settled in Boston; that he continued to reside in Boston till the spring of 1804, when he removed to Baltimore, where he continued to reside from that time for 50 years, when he came to Barbour County in 1854, and that he died in Barbour County in the winter or early spring of 1866, when he must have been between 90 and 91 years old. From 1854, after he removed to Barbour County, and up to the time of his death, I was intimately acquainted with him and saw and conversed with him frequently, except the four years during the Civil War. I saw him but once or twice after the war, a short time before his death. He was the most remarkable man I ever met. He was a thoroughly well informed man. He was the only living man I ever met that was the connecting link between the Elder Robert Peel, Prime Minister to England, and Sir William Pitt and other modern English statesmen who had passed away fifty years ago. He was the only man I ever saw who could say to me that he had seen and had conversed with the celebrated John Wesley and Bishop Coke, the first Bishop of the Methodist Church. He told me that he was present at the first general conference of the Methodist Church in Baltimore. He told me that he had been engaged as a shipowner, engaged in importing goods and passengers from England and Ireland to the United States, during a period of thirteen years, and that he had crossed the Atlantic Ocean nineteen times, and that he was wrecked twice. To sit and talk with him was like reading the history of modern times. His life had been contemporary with all the great men of the United States, and in England, for more than fifty years, and his extensive commercial transactions had brought him in personal contact with nearly all the distinguished men of the United States during that period. In 1814 he was one of the patriotic soldiers that defended the city of Baltimore from the British forces in its attack upon that city."

George Campbell, born in 1777, married Mrs. Julia Bedford, and had two children, Littlewood, who died in Carroll County, Maryland in 1840, aged 18, and George C., now of Barbour County.

WILLIAM COLE, an early settler in this part of the State, whose wife was Elizabeth, had children as follows: Joshua, born July 1, 1770; Mary, born 1772; William, 1774; Hezekiah, 1776; Elizabeth, 1781; Nancy, 1784; Joanna, 1886, and Sarah, 1789.

JAMES COFFMAN, born 1858, son of James H. and Elizabeth (England) Coffman, was married first, December 8, 1881, to Nancy Ramsay, and second, April 26, 1890, to Martha Channell. Children, Almonta Grace, Eliza beth B., Nancy C., Alston G. D., James G., Arnett, Avis, and one which died unnamed. He is a member of the United Brethren Church, is a Republican, and in business is a butcher; was formerly a carpenter and blacksmith. He attended public schools and now lives at Belington where he fills the office of Justice of the Peace, and has never had but one judgment reversed in the six years he has held office. His people came from Germany, where the name is spelled Kaufman. He taught school ten years. In 1880 he began with only fifty dollars and nine years later he had property worth $7000. He took a prominent part in having the town of Belington divided.

WILLIAM A. COX, born in Monongalia County, 1859, son of William P. Cox, married first, 1881, to Ada Fimple; second, 1894, to Lily Shomo; third,

1898, to Celia Brady. Children, Mary J., Fred, Grace, Howard, Myrtle, Charles. He belongs to the orders K. of P. and I. O. O. F., and is foreman of mines at Junior. He was educated in the common schools, and is of English and German ancestry.

E. H. COMPTON, was elected Assessor for Barbour County. He is a Republican and a merchant, residing at Moatsville. He was educated in the public schools and at a private school at White Oak.

PHILIP COONTZ, a German, born in New Jersey, 1762, for awhile a citizen of Pennsylvania, was an early settter where Huffman postoffice now stands. He was a large man, high tempered, but was a good citizen. His hunting shirt reached his heels, and he was a veritable Nimrod. After leaving Pennsylvania he lived awhile with a sister near Hagerstown, Maryland; then located at Cumberland, and finally took up his abode in Cheat Valley, where the magnificent hunting charmed him. While there his first wife died. He then pushed into Barbour and took up his abode near Huffman. In that vicinity lived John Barnhouse, whose daughter Barbara became the second wife of Mr. Coontz. They were married in 1795, by Robert Maxwell, a Justice of the Peace on Leading Creek. On the marriage license the name is spelled "Kunce." The date of his coming to Barbour is in doubt. It is related that he was following a wounded wolf when news reached him of the murder of Adam Stalnaker, who was killed near Beverly in the summer of 1782 by Timothy Dorman and his band of Indians. This would place him among the earliest settlers of Barbour. While living at Huffman several of his children were born (he had seventeen). He was a mill-builder, and wherever he went he could be tracked by his mills. He had a mill and a distillery near Huffman and his place was famous among travelers. He built his second mill at the mouth of Hunter's Fork. This mill was burned by a forest fire. He built his next at the mouth of Mud Gut, and here he erected a three-story house and spent the remainder of his days, dying in 1856, aged 94 years. The ruins of his house and mill are still seen. He could remember the Revolution, and his brother volunteered for service. His sister died in 1852, aged 104 years.

The descendants of Philip Coontz are scattered far and wide. Thirteen of his children grew up to be men and women. One of his daughters married and went to Texas; another daughter and a son, Lawrence, went west and were never heard of. Henry and Philip went to Ohio (Marietta) in 1841. John was the oldest son, and was born in 1800, settled on Sugar Creek and raised nine children, all of whom remained in Barbour County. John Coontz was noted for the fine horses which he kept. Adam settled at Little Laurel, on the Valley River. Frederick was a great hunter and a noted traveler. He claimed that he built the first cabin on the site of Chicago. He lived awhile with the Indians, and finally returned to his old home and died on Sugar Creek, leaving a snug fortune to his five children. He

FAMILY HISTORY.

died at the age of 84 years. During the Civil War members of the family fought in both armies.

SAMUEL M. D. COONTS, born 1844, son of Adam and Sarah (Stalnaker) Coonts, was married in Taylor County, 1871, to Isabel F., daughter of William B. and Mary (Davis) Poe. Children, Zura M., Amanda M, William J., Adam T. and Grover C. He belongs to the M. E. Church, South, is a Democrat, a farmer and a mechanic, living on the west fork of Sugar Creek. His farm, of 135 acres, is nearly all improved. A log house on this land has a strange history. The four men who carried up the corners were all subsequently killed. They were Jacob Schoonover, Jacob Hill, William Coontz and Jonathan England. Schoonover was killed in Missouri by Quantrell's Guerrillas; Hill was killed by Federal soldiers, supposed to be Captain Howe's company, in 1864, near the head of Teter's Creek on a farm belonging to Jasper Harris; Coontz was killed on the west fork of Sugar Creek in 1863, by Hudson Ramsey; England was killed in 1870, near the head of Bill's Creek by a log rolling over him.

ISAAC J. COONTS, born 1851, son of Adam and Sarah (Stalnaker) Coonts, was married April 17, 1878, near Meadowville, to Mary E., daughter of Captain M. T. and Sarah (Nestor) Haller. Children, Irvin D., William H., Adam J., Merrill, Floyd F., George L., Orem S. and Isaac J. He is a member of the M. E. Church, a Democrat and a farmer and mechanic, living on the west fork of Sugar Creek, where he owns 265 acres, 200 improved. The land on which the unfortunate Gibson family was murdered by Indians belongs to him; also the old "Hunter Field," and the old stone house, the ruins of which are still visible. A portion of his land is underlaid with a twelve-foot vein of coal.

FREDERICK MONROE COONTS, born 1860, son of Jesse and Lydia Coonts, was married November 10, 1880, to Amanda, daughter of Frederick and Emily (Stalnaker) Booth. Their child, Effie, born May 22, 1881, died in infancy. Mr. Coonts is a member of the M. E. Church, South, a Democrat and farmer, residing on Mud Creek, where he owns 41 acres of improved land. He was educated in the common schools. Frederick K. Booth, father of Mrs. Coontz, was born August 13, 1822, and was raised by his uncle, Frederick Hill, and lived for years in the "Old Stone House." He married Emily, daughter of Andrew Stalnaker. Their children's names were, Stephen, John, Andrew, William, Burnett, Jeremiah, Catherine, Amanda and Lee Ida. He was an industrous farmer and accumulated over 550 acres of land, and after giving liberally to his children, he had 200 acres left. He built a saw-mill and a grist-mill on Hunter's Fork of Sugar Creek.

D

SPENCER DAYTON, born in Litchfield County, Connecticut, January 22, 1820, is a son of Henry and Lavina (Culver) Dayton. His father was a tanner and shoemaker. When about twelve years old Spencer Dayton left home in order to live with a relative where school facilities were better. He was at home occasionally afterward; but while yet young he became an apprentice to learn the mill wright trade, and succeeded so well that he was able, in a few years, to command the highest wages, ($300 a year.) While learning his trade he was a constant reader, at all leisure hours; and the habits then formed have remained with him through life. Believing that he could do better for himself than to remain a mill wright, he began the study of law, and in 1846 successfully passed the examination required by the laws of Connecticut, and was admitted to practice. The family to which he belongs is one of the oldest in New England. The earliest members of the Dayton family came to America before 1640, and Samuel Dayton, the great, great, great grandfather of the subject of this sketch, was one of the founders of Setauket, Long Island. His descendants established themselves in Connecticut, where the Honorable Isaac Dayton, of New Haven, son of Samuel, was married December 29, 1708, to Elizabeth, daughter of Michael Tod,* of New Haven, and had twelve children, as follows:

Rebecca married Ebenezer Gilbert; Hannah married Stephen Jacobs; Elizabeth married Daniel Doolittle; Charity married Jehiel Tuttle; Sarah married Benjamin English, of New Haven, who gave his life in defense of his native city when attacked by the British, July 5, 1779;† Deborah married Nathan Mansfield, from whom was descended Rear Admiral Hull Foote, of the U. S. Navy, whose "Unconditional Surrender" message at Fort Henry was duplicated a few hours later by General Grant to Fort Donaldson. The sons of Isaac Dayton were, Giles, who served in the Revolution and settled at Blandford, Massachusetts; Jonathan, who married Mary Yale,‡ and was captain in the Revolution, commanding the New Haven troops when the city was attacked by the British. Isaac, another son, lived at Newport and fought in the Revolution, and was several months a prisoner of war; Israel married Widow Dinah Clark, and his son, Israel, was a Revolutionary soldier, and the ancestry of Hon. H. B. Warner, of Washington, D. C., and Michael, youngest son of Hon. Isaac Dayton, married Mehitable Doolittle, settled at Watertown, Connecticut, and had thirteen children, viz: Charles, David, Miriam, Michael, Justus, Mehitable, Polly, Elizabeth, Isaac, Samuel, Lyman, Abel and Olive. The father was

---

*Elizabeth Tod was born in 1690. Her father was born in 1653, son of Christopher Tod, who was born in Ireland. Governor Tod, of Ohio, is a descendant of Christopher. When Governor Tod was asked why he did not spell his name with two d's, he replied. "The Author of all never spelled his name with two d's, and I don't propose to put on more style than God Almighty."

†One of their grandsons, Hon. James E. English, was twice Governor of Connecticut and in 1875 was elected United States Senator. Another grandson was Hon. E. D. Mansfield of Cincinnati, a noted author, and a son of Jared Mansfield, Surveyor General of the Northwest under President Jefferson, and long a professor at West Point.

‡A near relative of Elihu Yale, the founder of Yale University.

FAMILY HISTORY.

a Revolutionary soldier and officer, and died in the service. He was born June 4, 1722, married, January 29, 1749. His son, Justus, (sometimes spelled Justice) was the grandfather of Spencer Dayton, and was born June 30, 1754, was married June 10, 1777, to Hannah Titas, and had eleven children, viz: Spencer, Russell, Rhoda, Jonah,* Mehitable, Beulah, Henry, Justus, Chester, Archibald, Elizabeth. Of the above named children, Michael and Justus served in the Revolutionary War; the former in the ill-fated expedition against Quebec in the winter 1775-6, but survived for other fields; the latter as captain in the Twenty-sixth Connecticut Regiment. In 1777 he was one of 300 volunteer who marched from Connecticut under General Oliver Walcott and took part in the capture of General Burgoyne's army. He was wounded, but recovered, and died in 1825.†

Thus the ancestors of Spencer Dayton are traced: Spencer the son of Henry; Henry the son of Justus; Justus the son of Michael; Michael the son of Isaac; Isaac the son of Samuel, the first in America.

Spencer Dayton was married in Upshur County, November 12, 1849, to Mrs. Sarah Barrett, widow of Samuel Barrett. Children, Eldon Lee, born March 31, 1851; Imogene L., born December 2, 1853; Ida V., born October 19, 1855, and Alston Gordon, born October 18, 1857. Mrs. Dayton's maiden name was Bush, she being a daughter of Zadock and Abigail (Dewey) Bush, and was born October 3, 1819. She belongs to the same family as Admiral George Dewey, who, on May 1, 1898, in a two hours engagement, destroyed the Spanish fleet in the harbor of Manila. The ancestry of Mrs. Dayton is traced as follows: She is a daughter of Abigail Dewey (Bush), who was born October 3, 1777, at Westfield, Massachusetts; Abigail was a daughter of Timothy Dewey, born January 24, 1755, at Westfield, Massachsetts; Timothy was a son of David Dewey, born July 20, 1725, at Westfield, Massachusetts; David was a son of David Dewey, born January 28, 1700, at Westfield, Massachusetts; David was a son of David Dewey, born January 11, 1676, at Windsor, Connecticut; David was a son of Israel Dewey, born September 25, 1645, at Windsor, Connecticut; Israel was a son of Thomas Dewey, born in Sandwich, England, and came to Dorchester, Massachusetts, about 1630. All the Deweys in America, now numbering

---

*Jonah Dayton was a noted inventor, particularly of musical instruments. At Daytonville, Connecticut, (named in his honor) thousands of organs have been built at his factories, and many of the ablest workmen employed in the largest factories in the United States learned their trade under him.

†The Samuel Dayton, named as the oldest known ancestor, had a brother from whom are descended other Daytons of prominence, including General Elias Dayton of the Revolutionary army. His son, Jonathan, was a member of the convention which framed the Constitution of the United States, and his name ("Jona. Dayton") is signed to it. He was subsequently Speaker of the House of Representatives and U. S. Senate. The city of Dayton, Ohio, was named in his honor. His son, William L. Dayton, was one of the founders of the Republican party, and in 1856 was a candidate for vice-president on the ticket with John Fremont, and was a candidate for President in 1860 and received a respectable vote againt Lincoln and who subsequently made him Minister to France. He died in 1864.

about 15,000, are descendants from Thomas Dewey. The admiral is descended from Josiah Dewey, who married Hepzibah Lyman, and who was a son of Thomas Dewey. The Lyman family is traced, without a break, from Hepzibah back thirty-two generations to Charlemagne, emperor of France, in the year 742.

Having thus briefly traced the ancestry of Spencer Dayton, and also of his wife, a brief account of his life, after he became a man, will now be given.

Having completed his law studies in Connecticut and having decided that the South offered a field for those practicing the legal profession, Mr. Dayton set out for Virginia in 1847, carrying in his pocket a few hundred dollars, the sum of his savings, and in a valise an extra suit of clothes. At Winchester he was admitted to practice in the court of Frederick County; but not wishing to locate there, he crossed into Greenbrier, traveling part of the distance by stage, and part leisurely on foot. He had not decided where he would locate, but hearing that court would soon be in session in Nicholas County he proceeded from Lewisburg to that county. There he met for the first time Edwin S. Duncan, judge of the court; and the acquaintance there commenced grew into a friendship which was never interrupted. However, it is proper to relate that the first few meetings were not calculated to promote strong feelings of mutual attachment; but each learned to respect the other. The court of Nicholas County was held at Summersville, and Mr. Dayton applied for license to practice law, and Judge Duncan ordered the license issued. The next court of the circuit was at Sutton in Braxton County, and Mr. Dayton proceeded to that point and applied for license to practice in that county, and the license was ordered. But a few minutes later Judge Duncan recalled the applicant and informed him that the laws of Virginia required one year's residence in the State before license to practice law be issued, and therefore, if he wanted to practice in Virginia he must first reside here a year. Johnson N. Camden was clerk at Sutton at that time.

Finding that the judge would not admit him to practice, and believing that it was in a measure due to prejudice against him because he was from the North, he turned about and retraced his steps to Summersville. Some of the residents and visitors at Sutton did not conceal their pleasure at what they supposed was the discomfiture of the young Yankee. But he kept his counsel and bided his time. At Summersville he procured from the clerk, John Hamilton, a certified copy of the order of Judge Duncan admitting him to practice, and with this document in his pocket he set out for Weston, passed through Clarksburg and Fairmont, on foot, and crossed into Pennsylvania. There was at that time an understanding (which amounted to a law) between Virginia and Pennsylvania that each would admit to its courts lawyers from the other State. Knowing this, Mr. Dayton proceeded

FAMILY HISTORY. 371

to Somerset County, where Judge Jere S. Black was on the bench, and presented the certificate that he had been admitted to practice in Nicholas County, Virginia. Thereupon he was admitted to practice in Pennsylvania. The Pennsylvania license, in its turn, and under the rules of reciprocity, would give him the right to demand license in Virginia, and no judge would feel at liberty to refuse the demand. Thus he set out for Virginia to hunt Judge Duncan. By that time the Randolph Court was in session and Mr. Dayton went thither, and through Colonel David Goff presented his papers and asked to be admitted to practice. Judge Duncan examined the papers, in evident impatience and ill-humor, but seeing that he had been trapped, he ordered the clerk to make the entry admitting Mr. Dayton to practice; and then addressing the members of the bar and the people in the courthouse, he said: "If any of you have any dealings with this young Yankee, I would advise you to lookout for yourselves. He played a genuine Yankee trick on me, and I cannot help myself." Mr. Dayton, from that incident, became known in the vicinity as "the young Yankee who outwitted Judge Duncan."

Not having yet decided on a place to locate, but being favorably impressed with Clarksburg, Mr. Dayton returned from Beverly to Philippi and there met John S. Carlile who then resided in Philippi and who persuaded Mr. Dayton to become his law partner. This business arrangement caused Mr. Dayton to locate in Philippi where he made his permanent home and extended his practice to Randolph, Upshur, Lewis, Tucker, Taylor, Grant, and to other counties, as well as to the higher courts. His care in the preparation of cases, and the information at his disposal, soon gave him a high rank among lawyers. On one occasion in Tucker County, some attorney objected to a paper in the suit, claiming that it was improperly drawn. Judge Samuel Woods (who was not interested in the suit) glanced at the writing and exclaimed: "Why, that cannot be so! Spencer Dayton wrote this paper, and in matters of law and forms he is as infallible as the Apostle Paul."

As the trouble leading up to the Civil War thickened, Mr. Dayton became the champion of the Union cause in Barbour, and he upheld that cause at the risk of his life. His acquaintance with the people of the North and South convinced him that, in the war, the South must ultimately be crushed beneath the weight of the moral and physical courage, the wealth and the perseverance of the North. He knew that the North would be slow to begin, but would never turn back nor hesitate when once in the field. The chapter in this book, concerning the war in Barbour County, details the part taken by Mr. Dayton, and it need not be repeated here. It should be stated, however, for the truth of history, that he did all he could to alleviate the hardships of the war while it was in progress, and when it was ended, he was among the first to say, let us have peace. He was many times in a position to do acts of kindness to his political enemies during the war and immediately after its close; and he never let such an opportunity pass. More than one proscribed man, in danger of his life or liberty because of his actions or opinions, was helped by Mr. Dayton without ever knowing the source from which the help came.

He assisted in the Wheeling Convention in 1861 in reorganizing the State of Virginia, which reorganization ultimately led to the formation of West Virginia. That convention and the part which he took in it is spoken of elsewhere in this book. In 1869 he was elected to the State Senate and took a formost place in the movement at that time looking to the re-enfranchisement of those who had lost their civil rights because of taking part against the government in the war. The leaders who acted with him were W. H. H. Flick and William M. Welch. They were called "Let-up Republicans" to distinguish them from the radical and extreme Republicans who still insisted upon keeping the heel upon the necks of those who had assisted the South in the rebellion five years before. In that contest in the Legislature upon the question of removing the restrictions which then existed against Southern men, Mr. Dayton was the pivotal member, and his vote and influence turned the scale and led to the repeal of the restrictive measures. The Flick Amendment was opposed in the Legislature by the extreme Republicans and the extreme Democrats, and its passage and the good results from it were due to the moderate members who championed the cause of political toleration.

Mr. Dayton was always a careful and extensive reader, and by that means acquainted himself with the leading authors of the English language. He also, as a recreation, learned French and Greek, and has read the entire Bible in those languages, as well as in English. He has held the office of Prosecuting Attorney in more counties, perhaps, than any other man in the State, having been elected to that position in Barbour, Randolph, Pocahontas and Tucker, and in all he was elected on the same day.

ALSTON GORDON DAYTON, son of Spencer Dayton, was born in Philippi, October 18, 1857, and on November 26, 1884, was married to Miss Lummie; daughter of Arthur Sinsel of Grafton. Their son's name is Arthur Spencer. After attending the public schools, Mr. Dayton entered the West Virginia University and graduated with the degree of A. B. in 1878; and on October 18, of the same year, it being his twenty-first birthday, he was licensed to practice law and entered into a partnership with his father. Two years later he was appointed Prosecuting Attorney of Upshur County; and immediately thereafter he received the nomination on the Republican ticket for that office in his native county. He was defeated by a small majority, but ran ahead of his ticket, and in 1884 his party again nominated him for the place, and he was elected, being the first Republican to fill the office after the war. In 1888 he was a candidate for judge of the circuit

ALSTON GORDON DAYTON.

court and failed by only two votes of receiving the nomination. Two years later his friends presented his name before the Republican Convention at Piedmont as a candidate for congress in the Second West Virginia District, which position was then held by Hon. William L. Wilson, author of the Wilson Tariff Bill. Mr. Wilson was a formidable antagonist, and the belief was general that only a man from east of the Alleghanies could defeat him; and in the convention the choice fell on Hon. George Harman, a wealthy farmer of Grant County, while Mr. Dayton received a strong support from counties west of the mountains. In 1894 he was nominated for congress in the convention at Elkins; and Mr. Wilson, who was still in congress, was again in the field, the champion of a party confident of victory. The campaign was a memorable one, and was fought from start to finish with a bitterness seldom equalled in politics. Mr. Dayton, figuratively speaking, asked no quarter and gave none in the discussion of the political questions brought into the campaign. The result was an overwhelming victory for Mr. Dayton, whose majority was over two thousand. In 1896 he was again elected, and again in 1898, and his present term will expire in 1901.

Mr. Dayton's career in congress has been one of steady increase of influence. Soon after he entered that body he was appointed on the Naval Committee, and he at once became a working member, and later a leader in the important measures originating in or formulated by that committee. When he entered congress we had three battleships in commission and three in course of construction. He was a believer in a strong navy, and on every occasion he advocated the construction of war ships of the most powerful class, instead of small vessels that could be built cheaply. He wanted something that could pound and withstand pounding. The result is—and it is due in no small measure to his efforts—we now have complete and in course of construction nineteen battleships. The naming of the powerful armored cruiser "West Virginia" was largely as a compliment to him. This vessel is designed with a displacement of 12,000 tons, and 23,000 horse-power, and it will belong to a class of the most formidable fighting machines in the world. It will have the speed of the cruiser and the fighting ability of a battleship. When Mr. Dayton first took his stand in favor of battleships, as against torpedo boats and other small craft, there never had been a battleship in action. That class of vessels was an experiment. But with the battle of Santiago, July 3, 1898, it was demonstrated that the solid work is done by the big ship. Mr. Dayton took a foremost place in the controversy in congress, concerning the construction of dry docks. Before the Fifty-Fifth Congress the ruling had been that appropriations could not be made for dry docks unless a bill had been passed, establishing dry docks; but Mr. Dayton was instrumental in having that ruling reversed, and dry docks were classed with the naval establishment; and the result was that four such docks were provided for, at Portsmouth, New Hampshire; Boston, League Island, Pennsylvania; and Algiers, Louisiana.

Mr. Dayton introduced a bill which passed the senate, providing for promotion upon the retired list of Lieutenant R. M. G. Brown, of the navy, in recognition of his services in saving lives and property during the great storm at the Simoan Islands. Lieutenant Brown is a native of Preston County. Mr. Dayton was largely instrumental in securing the appropriation of over $5,000,000 to open up the Monongahela to free navigation and to build locks and dams between Morgantown and Fairmont. He also was prominent in an important feature of the United States Geological Survey. Although the work of surveying had been in progress over fifteen years, by a strange oversight no provision had ever been made for setting up monuments to mark permanently the work, so that additional investigation or survey might be taken up anywhere with exact data at hand from which to begin measurements. Mr. Dayton called the attention of congress to this defect, and provision was made for setting up a stone in every county seat in the United States, on which the true north and south line of the place is marked.

The territory of Alaska was purchased from Russia in 1866, and provision was made that the laws of Oregon should be in force in Alaska, and thus the matter stood until 1898, although in many particulars the Oregon laws did not suit the different conditions in the far north. A congressional committee was appointed in 1898 to provide a code of criminal law for Alaska, and Mr. Dayton was a member of the committee, and did a large share of the work of framing and writing the laws. A committee consisting of the whole House debated the bill, containing the code, ten days, and Mr. Dayton championed the measures and debated them successfully with the best lawyers in congress, and the bill passed.

Perhaps the most noted and lasting work done by Mr. Dayton was in connection with the Navy Personnel Bill. The object of this bill was to regulate the line of promotion in the navy; to give all an equal chance; to equalize the pay received by naval and army officers, and to change the course of study in the Naval Academy at Annapolis. It should be explained that graduates from the Naval Academy were arbitrarily divided into two classes; the one became engineers and machinists; the other became officers who might rise to the highest grade. The new law places all on an equal footing as to promotion. Under the old law it was nearly impossible for an officer to rise above a lieutenant until he was over fifty years of age, because promotion was more on account of age than of service; and the Civil War had left so many officers that they became lieutenants, and seldom could get beyond it. The new law removed this disability and provided avenues for promotion without much increasing the expense of service. The pay of the officers of the navy was made equal with that of the officers of corresponding rank in the army. Provision was made for the enlistment of competent machinists who had never attended the Naval Academy; and other important provisions were made which practically changed the whole service of the navy. It brought about a reform of the most sweeping kind. There had been about fifty ranks in the navy. This clumsiness was abolished. Mr. Dayton was recognized as the champion of the bill when it came before the House in 1899. It was of the greatest importance to naval men, and they watched its progress with anxiety. Mr. Dayton made a number of speeches on the bill, showing that he had thoroughly mastered the subject, and had become an authority on naval affairs. The bill successfully passed and became a law. The naval officers at Washington gave a banquet to the congressmen who had championed the cause which at last had brought relief to the navy. It was a work whose good results will be seen in future years.

Rear Admiral W. T. Sampson, the hero of Santiago, who took a deep interest in this measure, stated publicly that Mr. Dayton's speeches on this bill disclosed the most accurate knowledge of the difficult and obscure mechanical and other details of naval affairs and personnel, and the clearest insight into them, ever displayed in debate in congress, and that the naval corps generally conceded this. The extent of this commendation can only be appreciated by those who know how little the Admiral is given to passing compliments.

After the blowing up of the Maine in Havana Harbor there was a time of waiting. Congress had appropriated money to be spent in preparations for war, but the first speech in the House of Representatives, plainly intimating that Spain must be pushed from Cuba, was made by Mr. Dayton. His concluding remarks on that occasion were:

> Two hundred and sixty-six brave men are dead today as a result of the *Maine* tragedy. Over 200,000 are dead in Cuba and 250,000 more, largely helpless women and children, are being held in imprisonment and starved to death there today. We do not know as yet that the Spanish authorities blew up the *Maine* and destroyed the lives of our seamen, but we do know that Spanish authority is responsible for this wholesale deadly murder in the first degree going on within a hundred miles of our shores. With food and raiment in one hand and with its strong power backed by the righteous will of 70,000,000 of freemen, this Administration must intervene, stop this horror, and give Cuba her freedom. This intervention may be done, I hope, peacefully. If so, God be praised; but if not, and it can only be done by war, let it come. Humanity, mercy, charity, and all the attributes of God himself will be with us, and Cuba will be free.

During his terms in congress Mr. Dayton has kept up his law practice and has engaged extensively in outside business, operating in coal lands and in other properties. He is now a director of the Tygart's Valley Bank at Philippi. He is a member of the Presbyterian Church, is an Odd Fellow and a Knight of Pythias.

JAMES MINTER DENNISSON, born at Weston, Lewis County, December

7, 1863, son of Calvin C. and Margaret E. (Morrison) Dennisson, was married July 27, 1898, at Weston, to Lucy L., daughter of Samuel and Elizabeth P. (Speirs) Lockhart. He is a Presbyterian, a Mason and a Democrat, and is railroad agent and Telegraph operator at Philippi. He was educated at Oberlin, Ohio.

FRANCIS BRAXTON DURRETT, born 1849, son of Braxton Byrd and Ann Elizabeth (Williams) Durrett, was married October 18, 1877, to Martha, daughter of Anthony and Clarissa (Johnson) Rohrbaugh. Children, Zora Mildred, Ada May, Jessie Avah, Bessie and Flossie. He was a member of the Missionary Baptist Church, a Democrat and a farmer; was educated in the public schools and served twelve years as Justice of the Peace. Mr. and Mrs. Durrett owned 185 acres with 125 cleared. He taught school seven terms. His father was born in Spotsylvania County, and died 1895 in Valley District, Barbour County. In 1880 he was elected County Commissioner, but on account of failing health, he resigned before the end of his term. He was a prosperous farmer and owned one of the largest apple orchards in Barbour County. His grandparents were natives of France.

JOHN A. DAVIS, born in Augusta County, Virginia, 1846, son of William W. and Saphrona Davis, was married in 1863 at Beverly, to Elizabeth daughter of John and Elizabeth (Fleming) Selby. The daughter, Lucy E., married J. E. Sprigg. Mr. Davis is a Methodist, a Democrat and a blacksmith at Junior. He was educated in the public schools, and served in the Confederate army, taking part in many battles.

EDMUND R. DYER, born in Pendleton County, 1851, son of Allen and Martha (Miller) Dyer, was married at Jane Lew, Lewis County, June 22, 1882, to Phileua, daughter of Mansfield McWhorter. Children, Otto M., Allen, Audrey, Roscoe F., Ruth, Paul, Anna, Harry, Cecil, and one that died unnamed. He is a member of the M. E. Church, and is a Republican, engaged in farming and stock raising, besides owning and operating a saw mill and flour mill at Mansfield. The town, Mansfield, is named from Mrs. Dyer's father, Mansfield McWhorter. Mr. Dyer is a member of the mercantile firm of Dyer & Switzer. His farm near Mansfield contains 450 acres nearly all improved. He introduced the first wheat drill into Barbour, and stretched the first telephone wire of the Philippi Extension Telephone Company, of which he was a member. This was the beginning of the Woodford system. The capacity of his flour mill is forty barrels a day. In addition to his extensive property in Barbour County, he owns a half interest in 1600 acres in Randolph County, on Shaver Mountain and Laurel Fork, about 300 acres of which is in grass and grazes 100 head of cattle, and 130 sheep. The balance is heavily timbered; and he owns 130 acres in Preston County, partly improved.

JEFFERSON DAVIS DIGMAN, born 1861 at the old Digman homestead on Laurel Creek, son of Samuel and Sarah (Sturm) Digman, was married October 18, 1883, to Laura Virginia, daughter of Francis C. and Elizabeth C. (Mouser) Snodgrass. Children, Zella Bryan, Granville Floyd and Baby. He is a member of the Methodist Protestant Church, a Democrat, and a farmer residing on Laurel Creek, where he owns 150 acres, mostly improved and underlaid with coal. His grandfather's name was Charles Digman. The mother of the subject of this sketch was born 1819, and is a daughter of Colonel Henry and Elizabeth (Stalnaker) Sturm, and was married on Sugar Creek, 1838. Her mother's maiden name was Elizabeth Gainer. Their children were Thomas Benton, Martha J., Susan, Elizabeth, Clarinda, John, Nancy Catherine, Charles Henry and Jefferson Davis. She has belonged to the Methodist Protestant Church 57 years.

IRA LEE DADISMAN, born 1873 in Taylor County, son of William and Sarah M. (Gawthrop) Dadisman, is a member of the Baptist Church, in politics is a Democrat, and by occupation a teacher, residing near Hall. He was educated at the Mountain Business College, and at the Fairmont Normal School. His ancestors came from England to Maryland and settled on Lord Baltimore's possessions. The grandfather, George Dadisman, was born in Paige County, Virginia, in 1815, near the Luray Cave, where his son William was born. In 1857 he came to Taylor County and lived near Grafton till his death. William Dadisman came to Barbour in 1873 and located on a farm on the Buckhannon River. I. L. Dadisman began teachin 1892. He assisted in compiling this History of Barbour County.

CHARLES G. DADISMAN, born near Cecil, Taylor County, July 19, 1873 is a son of Joseph and Margaret (Halterman) Dadisman. He is a member of the Order of Red Men, and of the Junior Order Improved. In politics he is a Democrat, and by occupation a teacher and farmer. He was educated in the public schools of Barbour, and now lives on Big Laurel Creek, where he owns real estate. He is a progressive and successful teacher and has been engaged six years in the work.

GEORGE WASHINGTON DICKENSON, born 1834, son of Robert and Elizabeth (Swadley) Dickenson, was married April 12, 1865, to Deniza J., daughter of Albert E. and Margaret (Talbott) Corder. Children, Charles Burdell and William Ashford. He is a member of the M. E. Church, South, a farmer and stock raiser residing near Elk City. He served three years in the Confederate army, and had two brothers in the service, Demetrius, who died at Richmond, and Samuel, who was honorably discharged. He owns 262 acres of improved land, and a fine residence. His sons died of diphtheria within a week of each other. The finest monument in the State marks their grave. The monument weighs 40,000 pounds and cost $3450. The Dickenson ancestry is Dutch. The great grandfather of the subject of this sketch came from Holland and settled in Virginia, and his son, Samuel Dickenson, was born and died in Pendleton County. Samuel's son Robert removed to what is now Barbour shortly after marriage, and his children were, Jacob, Matilda, Samuel, George W., Rachel, Demetrius and Harriet.

HENRY C. DAUGHERTY, born 1857, son of Jacob and Jane (Pitman) Daugherty, was married March 12, 1880, to Mary, daughter of Henry and Jane (Kerr) Burner. Children, Ida Belle, Dora J., Gordon Thomas, David Loring, Corbett Vane, Madge Irvin. Mr. Daugherty is a member of the Christian Church, and is a carpenter and contractor residing near Mt. Zion Church. His ancestry was Scotch and Irish; his grandfather served in the Mexican War, his father in the Union Army in the Civil War. His daughter Ida is a school teacher

E

COLONEL WILLIAM ELLIOTT, son of David Elliott, was born in Loudoun County in 1802. His grandfather was born in Scotland, and his father settled near Webster, Taylor County, in 1814, and died there at the age of eighty. About 1827 William Elliott, accompanied by his brother, Samuel, settled at Meadowville and engaged in the mercantile business, hauling their goods by wagons from Baltimore. Their business prospered and they bought land and became stockdealers. About 1837 William Elliott married Rebecca, aged sixteen, daughter of Dr. Solomon Parsons, who lived near St. George. Their children were as follows: Melvina (Knotts), E. C., Solomon P., Jane (Poling), Truman T. and Henrietta (Rosenberger). About 1852 the Elliott brothers dissolved partnership, and four years later the subject of this sketch bought out Solomon Yeager at Belington, and moved his family to that place where he lived until his death, which occurred June 3, 1883, and he was buried in a vault at Belington. He had been a member of the Missionary Baptist Church. Up to the war he was a Whig. He then became a Democrat and remained so until the end of his life. He never would accept an office other than military, and was Captain, Major and Colonel in the Virginia militia. His son, Truman, has his sword which he keeps, together with one which he himself captured in battle.

REV. JAMES BAXTER ELLIOTT, born at Meadowville, August 25, 1837, son of Samuel and Elizabeth (Scranage) Elliott, was married October 30, 1871, to Anna Rebecca, third daughter of John C. and Catherine (Parsons) Johnson. Mrs. Johnson was a daughter of Captain Job Parsons of Tucker County. In 1882 Mrs. Elliott died, and six years later Mr. Elliott married Mrs. Myra Wilson, who was a daughter of Joseph Reed, of Marion County. Mr. Elliott's children were, Frank Marion, (deceased), Ottice, Charles Murrill, Marcine Johnson, John Samuel, Ann Rebecca, (deceased) Lena, Rayburn, Ethel and Reed. He is a member of the M. E. Church, South, a Democrat and a farmer, merchant and stockdealer, residing at Meadowville. He was educated at Alleghany College, Meadsville, Pennsylvania.

He owns 450 acres in Glade District, 350 improved; 1300 in Tucker County, 300 improved; 115 in Randolph, 50 improved. He owns a valuable ledge of limestone on Laurel Hill, and extensive deposits of iron ore. The celebrated "cold spring" on the head of Johnson's Mill Run, belongs to him. He is an active member of his church and contributes to its support and has been a local preacher for several years. Since the dissolution of the firm of D. T. Elliott & Brothers, he has had control of the general mercantile business at Meadowville, known by the name of J. B. Elliott. The Elliotts were early settlers in Barbour County, and have always been men of character, enterprise and ability.

LUTHER CREED ELLIOTT, born 1844, son of Samuel and Elizabeth Elliott, was married May 14, 1887, to Julia A., daughter of John and Josina (Coplin) Elliott. He is a member of the M. E. Church, South, in politics is a Democrat, belongs to the A. F. & A. M., is a farmer residing at Meadowville, and was educated at Alleghany College, Meadsville, Pennsylvania. He has been captain of militia; in 1873 he was appointed deputy sheriff under J. W. Talbott; in 1878 he was elected County Clerk, and was re-elected in 1884. When his term was out he moved to the old homestead at Meadowville and has since engaged in general farming and stockdealing. He owns 900 acres in Barbour, mostly improved; 2700 in Tucker County and 700 in Randolph. The land on which the old Henry Phillips fort stood belongs to him, and he also owns the Keller Hill. He is a very active member of his church, and is seldom absent from services.

TRUMAN THEODORE ELLIOTT, son of William and Rebecca (Parsons) Elliott, born 1844. His children were, Alice, Guy C., Emma, Minnie, Nettie, Carl, Stella, William, Mary P. and two who died in infancy. He is a member of the Missionary Baptist Church, a Mason, a Democrat and a farmer, living at Belington, which town was laid out on his farm in 1886. In 1892 he was elected Sheriff. He was a cavalryman in the Confederate army.

GUY CLAYBORNE ELLIOTT, born 1870, son of Truman T. and Mary Columbia (Lynch) Elliott. He is a member of the Missionary Baptist Church and a Democrat. He was educated in the Belington public schools, Fairmont Normal School and Sadler, Bryant and Stratton's Business College, Baltimore. He was a deputy sheriff of Barbour under his father. He is a partner in the mercantile business at Meadowville, in the firm of Parsons & Elliott, Arthur Parsons being his partner. Mr. Elliott is general manager and has full charge, Mr. Parsons being on the road for Ruhl, Koblegard & Co., Clarksburg, West Virginia. Mr. Elliott is a member of the following secret orders: Bigelow Lodge, No. 52; A. F. and A. M., Philippi; Copestone Chapter, No. 12, and De Molay Commandry, No. 11, Grafton; Osiris Temple, A. A. O. N. M. S., Wheeling, and of Belington Lodge, No. 104. K. of P. He is of Scotch and Irish descent.

FAMILY HISTORY.

JOSIAH HENRY EKIS, born 1845, son of Benjamin and Mary Ann (Hardin) Ekis, was married November 7, 1872. to Sarah Miller. Children, Rosa, born 1873; Hester Ann, 1875; Andrew B., 1878; Mary, 1880; Hattie, 1883. Mr. Ekis is a Republican and a farmer, living on Cove Run. He was a member of Haller's company of Home Guards (Federal) during the Civil War.

WILLIAM A. ELBON, born in Green County, Virginia, 1837, son of Harold P. Elbon, was married in 1857 to Mary Dolly, and in 1873 to Mrs. Eliza J. Auvil. Children, John H., Mary Ellen, French S., Lucy K., Laura Belle, and others that died in infancy. Mr. Elbon is a carpenter and millwright at Junior, is a Democrat and has held the positions of post master, and Mayor of Junior. He was in the Confederate service, worked in the Richmond arsenal and was superintendent of lead mines in Tennessee. Afterwards he saw active service in the field and as ranger among the mountains.

F

SAMUEL D. FELTON, born March 26, 1862, at the old Felton homestead, son of Daniel and Lucinda (England) Felton, was married October 10, 1894, at Belington, to Emma Florence, daughter of Alpheus and Lucinda (Yock) Moore. Children, James Frederick and baby. He is an Odd Fellow and a Republican. Mrs. Felton is a member of the Missionary Baptist Church. He is a farmer and lumber dealer and lives near Alden. He was educated in the public schools of Barbour. His ancestors came from England. The grandfather lived in Maryland and died in Preston County near Kingwood. Daniel Felton lived on the home place about fifty years. On the mother's side the ancestry was Irish. James England, the great-grandfather, and John England, the grandfather, lived near Belington.

CAPTAIN JOHN C. FELTON, born in Preston County, September 5, 1842, son of Henry and Catherine Felton, was married in Barbour County, July 1, 1869, to Susanna M., daughter of H. D. and Maggie Martin. Children, Henry W., born July 13, 1870, died April 14, 1891; George C., born 1882; Jacob F., born 1873; Maggie C., 1875; Edgar C., 1878; Harlin A., 1880; Elizabeth E., 1883; William U., 1888. Captain Felton is a member of the M. E. Church, of the G. A. R., is a Republican and a farmer, residing in Philippi District. He was raised near Rowlesburg and saw the first locomotive cross Cheat River at that place. When the Civil War came on he joined the Union army and fought till the close of hostilities. He enlisted at Albrightsville, Preston County, July 4, 1861, to serve three years. On April 12, 1863, he was commissioned sergeant. When his three years were up he enlisted for three years more. In 1864, while fighting in front of Petersburg, he was promoted. Subsequently he became First Lieutenant of the 7th West Virginia Infantry, and within a few days was again pro-

The Dickenson Monument.

moted to be Captain in the 7th West Virginia Veterans, and held the place till discharged July 1, 1865. He took part in several of the hardest battles of the war, including Gettysburg. He was with Grant's army in the advance against Richmond and in the siege of Petersburg. On one occasion he was under fire for thirty days and nights.

NAYLOR FOREMAN, born 1835 in Preston County, son of Alexander and Jemima (Graham) Foreman, was married to Elizabeth, daughter of Jacob and Sarah (Miller) Shroyer. Children, Jacob B., Clara Jane, John Alexander, Isaac Miller, Joseph N., George R. He is a member of the M. E. Church, is a Republican and a farmer of Cove District. He has held the offices of township treasurer, member of the board of education, and others. Mr. Foreman is a leader in farm and stock improvements in his neighborhood. In 1870 he introduced the Southdown sheep; and at the same time he introduced the Chester hogs; in 1890 the Shropshire sheep; in 1880 the Marino sheep; and he has also introduced new varieties of wheat and corn. His wife died in 1868, and in 1869 he was married to Appalonia Miller. His great-grandfather, Robert Forman, was born in England July 17, 1754, and Mary Naylor, his wife, July 20, 1745. Joseph Foreman, son of Robert, and grandfather of the subject of this sketch, was born in Pennsylvania, March 24, 1771, and married Miss Conner. Alexander Foreman, son of Joseph, was born April 9, 1802, and married Jemima Graham, March 26, 1828.

ISAAC FRIDLEY, born in Harrisonburg, Virginia, 1818, son of Isaac and Elizabeth (Sellers) Fridley, was married 1852 to Sophia, daughter of Philip Miller. Children, Mary Jane, Mary E., Josephine E., Francis M., Oliver P., Joseph T., John E., Lewis R. He lives on Shook's Run.

G

HON. DAVID W. GALL, born in Barbour County July 25, 1851, son of John J. and Rebecca (Sayre) Gall, is of French, German and English descent. His early life was spent on a farm. His early education was neglected, except instruction given by his mother and sister. When he entered the public schools his progress was rapid, and he soon was a teacher. He entered the West Virginia College at Flemington where he completed his education, but before leaving college he entered the field of journalism by establishing the *Plaindealer* at Philippi, November 29, 1873. While performing the duties as an editor he was preparing himself for the practice of law, and in 1881 passed an examination before Judges John Brannon and A. B. Fleming, of the Circuit Court and Judge Okey Johnson of the Supreme Court. Mr. Gall has always been public-spirited, and has taken an interest in the affairs of his native town, having been three times elected member of the Town Council and twice Mayor. He has also been active in church work, and in 1890 was elected lay member of the general conference of the M. E. Church, South, at St. Louis. Thirteen consecutive years he served as superintendent of the Sunday School at Philippi, and was once elected president of the Barbour County Sunday School Convention. In 1890 he was nominated by the Democrats in the 10th District for State Senator. At the previous election the district had given Hon. Thomas E. Davis, Republican, 825 majority; but Mr. Gall went in to win, and transformed the 825 Republican majority into 36 Democratic majority. He carried Barbour by 83 majority, while the congressional candidate, Hon. W. L. Wilson, received only 35 majority. In the Cleveland campaign of 1892, he was chosen chairman of the Democratic County Executive Committee, and with his associates on the committee, so successfully managed the campaign that the entire Democratic ticket was elected, a thing which had not before occurred in years. Mr. Gall, in 1891, delivered a memorial address at the decoration of graves of Odd Fellows at the Bluemont Cemetery at Grafton.

The people of Barbour are indebted to him for much that was accomplished (and much that was prevented) at the sessions of the Legislature of 1891-3. The independent school district at Belington, and also that at Elkins, were largely due to his efforts. There was a determined fight made against independent school districts. He succeeded in breaking that opposition. A peculiar combination was made against his bill, and an effort was made to compel him to support measures distasteful to him. At that time an effort was made to raise the school tax five per cent. and he was opposed to it. When his bill for the independent school district had passed the Senate, it was laid on the table in the Lower House. This was done with the hope of forcing him to support the measure for increasing the taxes in return for assistance in passing his own bill. But he refused to do it, and in a commendable fight won a clear victory.

In the senatorial contest of 1893, he was for Senator Faulkner, believing by that choice that he was reflecting the sentiments of his constituents more nearly than he would do by voting for Hon. J. N. Camden. He was a strong candidate for President of the Senate in 1893, and he would have been elected had he permitted his friends to support him for the place. In the same year he was a prominent candidate for the Collector of Internal Revenue for West Virginia, but failed in the appointment. However, he was appointed the head of a division in the Treasury Department at Washington until October 5, 1897, when he was reduced to a clerkship, class 3, because a Republican was preferred as Chief of Division. In November, 1898, he was removed from the service. When he retired from the office, sixty of his clerks signed the following testimonial and presented it to him:

"We, the clerks in the office of the Auditor for the Post Office Department, who have been on the work of the Inspecting Division, from July 1, 1893, to October 5, 1897, or any part of the time, bear testimony to the honorable and impartial manner in which D. W. Gall, the then Chief of the Division, conducted the business. During that entire period, or the time that we were in this Division during Mr. Gall's official life there, we cannot recall a single dishonorable act done by him, either officially or personally. He advanced the work of the Division, elevated the standard and conducted the affairs of the office so as to make things harmonious and pleasant. He showed a high degree of efficiency and retired from his official position with the esteem of all."

Mr. Gall was one of the delegates appointed by Governor Atkinson to the Pure Food Congress at Washington in 1898. Although not in the service of the Government he still resides in Washington, but claims Philippi as his home.

He was married in June, 1876, to a daughter of Mr. and Mrs. A. G. Reger, and to them were born a daughter and two sons: Minnie R., J. Camden and Albert D. His newspaper life of twenty-five years, was a trying one. When he began the publication of the *Plaindealer* there was no other paper in the county, and the people were unaccustomed to a local paper, and did not appreciate its value. But Mr. Gall had the pleasure of seeing his town and county develop. Soon after he started his paper, a very strong and persistent rival came into the field in the *Jeffersonian*, but competition only stimulated Mr. Gall to greater exertion, and, after ten years of struggle, he became the owner of both papers, merged them into one, the *Jeffersonian-Plaindealer*, which name it retained until the first part was dropped by its present owner. From the establishment of the paper, 1873, until he sold it, 1898, he was actively connected with its publication, except while a civil service employee, holding the Philippi post office, during Cleveland's first term, being the first Democratic post master there since 1861. He is an Odd Fellow and a Mason (thirty-second degree) and is president of the board of trustees of Fraternity Cemetry at Philippi.

ANDREW J. GALL, born 1829 in Pendleton County, son of John and Margaret (Arbogast) Gall, was married April 11, 1867, in Barbour, to Mary F., daughter of A. E. and Margaret (Talbott) Corder. Children, Robert B., Emma E., Ella A. and Rissa. He is a member of the M. E. Church, South, a Democrat and a farmer, residing on the waters of Stewart's Run, where he owns 408 acres. He served in the Confederate army form 1862 till 1865 under Jackson and Early. His grandfather served under Washington in the Revolution, and his great grandfather, Gall, came from Germany, and settled in Rockbridge, and his great grandfather, Arbogast, came from Holland and settled in Pendleton County.

JAMES WILLIAM GAWTHROP, born 1844 at Pruntytown, son of Enos D. and Ruth (Wiseman) Gawthrop, was married in 1871 to Mary, daughter of Jacob and Nancy (Martin) Reger. They have no living children. He is a member of the Baptist Church, is a Democrat and a farmer, living near Burnersville. The ancestors of Mr. Gawthrop were English and Irish; his father being born and raised at the Gawthrop homestead near Pruntytown. Mr. Gawthrop followed teaching several years; was three times elected Justice of the Peace; once County Assessor; once a member of the Legislature, and in 1899 was appointed Assessor for the western district of

Barbour. For fourteen years he has been superintendent of the Bethany Baptist Sunday School. In 1861, when seventeen years of age, he enlisted in the Confederate army, and was in the fight at Philippi in June of that year, remaining in the army till the close of the war; was captured and taken to Point Lookout, and later to Elmira, N. Y., where he was held a prisoner nine months. He came into West Virginia on the Imboden raid in 1863, and was in the fighting about Richmond before Lee's surrender. He came to Barbour County in 1868.

GRANT GRAHAM, born 1867 at Kingwood, West Virginia, son of James and Nancy (Field) Graham, was married June 28, 1899, at Buckhannon, to Etta, daughter of Archibald Hinkle. He is an Odd Fellow, a Modern Woodman, in politics a Republican, by occupation a druggist at Belington, where he located in 1899. He was educated in the public schools. His father was a Union soldier.

WILLIAM TAYLOR GEORGE was born, October 3, 1869, near Talbott's store, in Valley District, son of John R. and Gaytura (Taylor) George. On December 11, 1892, at Marietta, Ohio, he was married to Dora May, daughter of John and Mary (Brown) Howell. Children, Buena May, born near Stockton, California, September 28, 1893, Ada L., born at Visalia, California, February 17, 1896. He is a member of the M. E. Church, is an Odd Fellow, in politics is a Democrat, and by profession is a lawyer, residing at Philippi. He attended the United Brethren Academy at Buckhannon, and graduated at the Stockton Normal School, California. In 1891 he was a member of the Barbour County board for the examination of teachers. He taught four years in West Virginia and three in California, in which State he holds a State diploma. In 1895, upon examination before the Supreme Court at San Francisco, he was admitted to practice law, and the next year, having returned to West Virginia, he was licensed to practice in Barbour, and subsequently in Tucker, Taylor, Randolph, Upshur, Harrison, and in the U. S. District and Circuit Courts, and the Supreme Court of West Virginia. The grandfather of the subject of this sketch was Samuel George. He came from eastern Virginia and settled in the upper end of Barbour, and was one of the earliest settlers there. His father was John R. George, of Virginia. The father of the subject of this sketch served in the Union army from 1861 to 1865 and took part in many battles. He spent three years in a Confederate prison, having been captured near Richmond.

JOHN MOSHIME, GOODE, born in Shenandoah County in 1839, son of George and Rebecca (Schmucker) Goode, was married May 7, 1861, in Pendleton County, to Susan, daughter of Abraham Simmons. Children, Sarah Alice, Louisa Elmeda, Alba Ellsworth, George Cornelius, Albert Page, William Johnson, Ida May, Frances Virginia, James Garfield, Annie Jane, Howard Guy. Mr. Goode is a member of the U. B. Church, is a

Republican and a carpenter, living in Valley District. He was educated in the public schools and has filled the office of Constable.

ROBERT S. GODWIN, born 1841, son of Isaac and Mary (Coffman) Godwin, was married April 15, 1866, to Sarah Ann Phillips. Children, James R., Charles E. and Clemantine. He lived with his father thirteen years in Tucker County, then returned to Barbour. He was in the Confederate army under Captain John Riley Phillips, was wounded in the head at Camp Alleghany, in the hip at Port Republic, and in 1864 was captured at Spotsylvania Court House, and imprisoned at Point Lookout and at Elmira, New York, until the war closed. When he reached home he weighed ninety pounds, having lost one hundred pounds during captivity. He is now a prosperous farmer near Valley Furnace.

MRS. SALLY GAINER. This venerable lady, the widow of Bryan R. Gainer, is in her eighty-fourth year, and although totally blind can spin her "dozen cuts" a day. She became blind in 1884, was blind thirteen years, then recovered her sight one year, and once more became blind. She relates an incident of pioneer life, originating a local proverb known as "David's Dumplings." In early times the settlers banded together to do their farm work, as defense against Indians, thus going from farm to farm. One of them, David Williams, was so long from home that a dish of dumplings, which he had left on his table, was covered with mold upon his return. Peeping into the house to see that the coast was clear, he caught sight of the dumplings, and mistaking them, woolly as they were, for an opossum which had taken possession of his table, he fired at the object, broke the plate and scattered the dumplings. After that, anything very old and stale was "David's Dumplings."

JOHN W. GAINER, born 1863, son of Isaac and Margaret (Semple) Gainer, was married November 17, 1891, near Meadowville, to Suffrona J., daughter of Elmore B. and Juliann (Wilmoth) Gainer. Their child's name is Sylva Autumn. Mr. Gainer is a Democrat and a farmer, living on Sugar Creek, where he owns 39 acres, nearly all under cultivation. His grandfather, John Gainer, served in the War of 1812.

H

GRAHAM H. HAMRICK was born September 18, 1821, in Rappahannock County, Virginia, a son of Peter Hamrick. He moved with his father to Rockingham County, and on April 16, 1844, was married to Margaret, daughter of David Whitmer, and lived thirteen years in that county. In 1857 he moved to the John N. Hall farm on Elk and remained there ten years, and then moved to the farm of Joshua S. Corder on Hacker's Creek, and three years later bought the small farm on the same creek where he spent the remainder of his life, and died February 11, 1899. He was a member of the Primitive Baptist Church. His wife died July 20, 1882. Their family consisted of eight children, David P., the wagon maker, and J. Newton, the merchant of Hopewell; Dorcas, wife of James Cleavenger, a merchant; R. W., a silversmith of Spencer, West Virginia; Mollie, wife of George Cunningham, a teacher of Randolph County; Margaret, wife of Perry Phares, a machinist of Cumberland, Maryland; Augusta (now dead), wife of J. M. Talbott, Justice of the Peace at Parsons, West Virginia, and Eliza (now dead), wife of Samuel Felton, a gunsmith. On September 24, 1885, he married Mary C. Compton, of Clarksburg.

RESIDENCE OF G. H. HAMRICK.

Mr. Hamrick's fame rests on a discovery made by him of an embalming process by which vegetables, meats, and even human bodies may be preserved for a time, the length of which is not yet known. Two human bodies embalmed by him in February, 1888, were in a perfect state of preservation after the lapse of eleven years. Time only will tell how much longer they will be preserved. Mr. Hamrick was not an educated man. About the only book he studied was the Bible, and in it he claimed to have discovered his embalming process. Years before he announced his discovery, he occasionally would seek information from his friends on his favorite theme by asking them if they knew of any book which would give an account of ancient embalming, and whether there was any historical mention of embalming antedating the death of Jacob, as told in the 50th chapter of Genesis. He was unacquainted with ancient history, and was not aware that Egyptian mummies, older than Jacob, are now in existence in the museums. The cost of a first-class embalming in Egypt was about $3600; while by Mr. Hamrick's method the cost would probably not much exceed the one hundredth part of that.

Mr. Hamrick began his experiments about twenty-years ago by immersing green ears of corn, tomatoes and other perishable vegetables in a fluid which he made. This fluid, when pure, was as clear as water. He kept his secret and experimented for years. Finally he began to preserve small animals and pieces of meat, and so successful was he that he became very anxious to try his method on a human body. Through the assistance of Judge Samuel Woods he obtained two bodies at the Weston Insane Asylum, and was permitted to experiment on them in a room for forty days, with no one else present. After forty days the officers and doctors of the asylum were admitted to the room, and found the two bodies perfectly preserved, without a sign of decomposition. From that day Mr. Hamrick's fame began to go forth.

Mr. Hamrick had not obtained a patent. He applied for one, and his application was rejected, on the grounds that the fluid described in his formula, would not produce the result claimed for it. The only answer he could make to this was to offer to give a practical demonstration of it in Washington under conditions named by the commissioner of patents. This offer was accepted, and he took the two mummies from Weston to Washington, with a certificate from the asylum officers setting forth when the bodies had been embalmed, nearly two years before. In addition to this, a subject was procured, and in the presence of several officials, including a representative of the Smithsonian Institute, Mr. Hamrick embalmed the body. A patent was given him without further question. Within a few hours Mr. Hamrick received an offer of $10,000 for the right to use the process in Pennsylvania. Instead of accepting or declining the offer, he left Washington, and went home. He never made much money out of his discovery. He was an old man, and lacked ability, in a business way, to turn his patent into cash. He sold shoprights in many parts of the United States, and his income could easily have been made large, but his health failed, and on February 11, 1899, he died of consumption. On December 24, 1891, he was elected an honorary member of the Paris Inventors' Academy, of France, and was subsequently granted a bronze medal, and still later a gold medal, all without expense to him. When he drew near the end of his life, he prepared embalming fluid for his own body, and instructed his friends how to use it. He died at a time when the weather was intensely cold, the thermometer having been below zero for four days, and part of the time as much as 22 degrees below. All of this time the fluid which he had provided for himself was remote from the fire, in a glass jar, as much exposed as if out of doors, and it was not frozen. He was buried at Mary's Chapel Cemetery, five miles north of Philippi.

DAVID PEYTON HAMRICK, son of Graham H., and Margaret (Whitmer) Hamrick, was born in Rockingham County, Virginia, 1845; and on March 11, 1875, on the Valley River, below Philippi, he was married to Isora, daughter of Isaac and Jane (Hoffman) Woodford. Their son's name is Troy. Mr. Hamrick resides at Hopewell, and is a blacksmith and wagonmaker, having followed the business thirty years. He was in the mercantile business seven years; and is the owner of 30 acres of highly improved land.

JOSEPH NEWTON HAMRICK, son of Graham H. Hamrick, was born in Rockingham County, Virginia, in 1851, and on May 17, 1887, at Philippi, he was married to Barbara E., daughter of Benjamin and Susan (Mank) Smith. Children, Hallie F., and Rossie and Roxie (twins). He is a merchant, residing at Hopewell, four miles north of Philippi, and he owns a half interest in 50 acres of improved land. For twenty-five years, in partnership with his brother, he was in the wagon-manufacturing business, the first in Barbour, and the wagons were noted far and near on account of their substantial character.

HANSON LEWIS HOFF, a native of Loudoun County, Virginia, and son of Anthony Hoff, was born May 15, 1805, and died October 4, 1890. He was married three times, first to Anna Rightmire, second to Sarah Rightmire, and third, to Mrs. Emily Coplin, in 1858. His first wife was a daughter of John and Anna (Ashby) Rightmire. His children by his first marriage were Granville, Sophia J., Lamar, William D.; by his second marriage, Hartzel Eldridge, and Orlando Purcell. His second wife was born in 1817 and died in 1855. His third wife survived him. Mr. Hoff came to Barbour County when young, and lived at Cherry Hill, where John F. Woodford now lives. He was a Baptist and a farmer, was educated in the country schools, and in politics was a Republican. He was chairman of the meeting held in Philippi which sent Spencer Dayton as a delegate to the first Wheeling Convention in 1861, by which the first steps were taken to re-organize the Government of Virginia and to create the new State of West Virginia.

HARTZEL ELDRIDGE HOFF, son of Henson L. Hoff, was born in Barbour County in 1843, and died 1895. He married Anna E. Coplin, and they had one daughter, Sallie G., born 1881, and in 1899 was married to O. W. Hall of Barbour County. Mr. Hoff was collector of internal revenue from 1863 to 1873, and for several years was a member of the Barbour County Court. In 1891 he was ordained a minister of the Baptist Church, and preached until his death, dying regretted by all who knew him.

MANZELL M. HOFF, M. D., born August 20, 1859, son of Lamar M. and Malissa E. (Chrislip) Hoff, who were married in 1857. The subject of this sketch was married September 4, 1890 to Ida M., daughter of Jesse and Elizabeth Teter of Belington. Mrs. Hoff's grandfather was Jacob Teter, and his father was also Jacob (the first of the name to settle in Barbour) and Jacob's father's name was Philip Teter, a Pennsylvanian. The Teters came from Germany. Dr. Hoff is a grandson of Hanson L. Hoff, and a great grandson of Anthony Hoff, and a great, great grandson of John Hoff, of Trenton, N. J. The Hoff family came from Germany in 1750 and settled in New Jersey, and later some of the family moved to Virginia, and some to Ohio. Three brothers came from Germany, one spelling his name Hoff, another Huff and the third, Hough. All of these spellings are now in use. Mrs. Hoff's ancestors, on her mother's side, came from Virginia, her grand parents being Thomas and Sarah (Lemmons) Phillips. The subject of this sketch is a member of the M. E. Church; in politics is a Republican, and belongs to the following lodges and secret societies: Bigelow Lodge No. 52, A. F. and A. M. of Philippi; Copestone Chapter No. 12, R. A. M., and DeMolay Commandry No. 11, Knights Templar, Grafton; I. O. O. F. Lodge

First Court House in Harrison County, 1787.
Drawn by Bruce Haymond from the original specifications on file at Clarksburg.

Second Court House in Randolph Co. Built 1808.

WESTFALLS'S FORT AT BEVERLY.

This building was erected in 1774 as a defense against Indians, and is the oldest house in West Virginia west of the Alleghanies. From a photograph taken in 1899. The windows were cut in it after the Indian Wars.

No. 59; Tygart's Valley Encampment No. 28, I. O. O. F., Ivan Lodge No. 61, K. of P. Dr. Hoff was educated in the high schools and summer normals, and commenced the study of medicine in 1885, attended the Maryland University School of Medicine, Baltimore, and graduated in April, 1889. He is a member of the Barbour County Medical Society, West Virginia Medical Society, has been a member of the Barbour County Board of Health, and is now president of pension examining surgeons, at Philippi. He was also member and secretary of the board during President Harrison's administration. He performed military service while a member of the Illinois State Volunteers.

ORLANDO PURSELL HOFF, born 1847, son of Hanson L. and Sally (Rightmire) Hoff, was married October 11, 1874, to Martha E., daughter of David and Nancy (Reger) Hall. Children, Gertrude, Mary Leona and Florence Lois. He is a Republican and a farmer, living near Hall. He served one year as County Surveyor, and since then has occasionally engaged in surveying. His farm is a valuable one, well stocked with cattle.

JOHN HOWELL, born 1843, at the old Howell homestead, son of Nehemiah and Rebecca (Limbers) Howell, was married first to Mary E. Ringer, of Fayette County, Pennsylvania, January 11, 1866; second, to Mary E., daughter of Robert and Emaline Brown. Children, Columbia E., Annie M., Dora May, R. B. Hayes, and an infant unnamed born in 1873. He is a Republican, a farmer and stock dealer, owning about 1800 acres, of which 450 acres are under cultivation; and he plows 150 acres annually, planting 40 in corn, 75 in wheat, and the balance in oats, buckwheat and potatoes. In one year he raised 1000 bushels of potatoes, 1050 of wheat, and 2000 of shelled corn. The stock he handles is of the improved varieties, usually 300 cattle yearly. When he was in the lumber business from 1873 to 1895, he owned two saw mills and was an exporter of lumber. His dealings in fertilizers are extensive, amounting to 300 tons a year. He lives on a part of the old home farm. He served about one year in the Union army. He has always taken an interest in the success of his political party, and has been three times nominated for office. In 1888 he was defeated by a few votes for Sheriff; in 1892 was elected, on the face of the returns, to the legislature, but was counted out on technicalities. In 1894 he was elected Sheriff of Barbour by a large majority. All of his land is underlaid with coal, there being four veins, including the Roaring Creek vein 12 feet thick. Mr. Howell was seven years post master at Calhoun, during his mercantile career. He was one of the stockholders in the narrow-guage railroad, the first in the county. Mrs. Howell was born 1847, and her ancestors were English, her great grandfather having come from that county and settled in Pennsylvania.

GRANT TRUMAN HOWELL, born 1861, son of Nehemiah and Rebecca (Limbers) Howell, was married October 18, 1893, to Anna Belle, daughter of Eldridge and Darothy (Bartlett) Golden. Children, Eva Maude, Harold George and Jessie. He is a member of the M. E. Church; of the A. O. F. A., is a farmer and lumber dealer, owning 164 acres near the old homestead mostly improved. He was educated in the public schools of Barbour. The great grandfather came from Scotland and settled near Philadelphia, and Nehemiah Howell was born in Preston County 1815, and died 1885. Nehemiah's father's name was John, and he was born in 1792. The grandfather, John Limbers, was born in France, and with his parents settled in Green County, Pennsylvania, about 1835. Rebecca Howell was born 1823. William Howell, brother of Nehemiah, was in the Union army under Averell, and was in the battle of Droop Mountain and at other places, dying of a wound received at Cedar Creek in 1864. The children of Nehemiah and Rebecca Howell, were as follows, with the dates of their births: Sarah, 1841; John, 1843; William, 1845; David, 1847; Lewis, 1848; Rachel, 1850; Martin, 1852; James, 1854; George, 1856; Samuel, 1858; Grant, 1861; Mattie E., 1865.

R. B. HAYES HOWELL, born 1877 in Barbour County, son of John and Mary (Brown) Howell, was married October 9, 1898, at Philippi, to Lummie, daughter of Mr. and Mrs. Lewis Jones. He is a member of the Missionary Baptist Church, and is a farmer and stock raiser, living near Clements. He is in partnership with his father in the fertilizer and machine business. When he was only fifteen years of age he began transacting business, and soon developed a judgment and knowledge which enabled him to compete successfully with men who had the experience of years. The most of the stock handled by him is of improved varieties.

THE HOLSBERRY FAMILY. The great-grandfather of John D. Holsberry came to Pennsylvania from Germany when sixteen years of age. All the people in this county of that name are descended from him. He had three sons, Samuel, Conrad and John. Samuel married in Pennsylvania but died without children; Conrad and John went to Ohio and bought land near Zanesville. Other settlers, from New Jersey, located there about the same time. The locality proved unhealthful, and after much sickness the colonists arranged to return to the East. They arrived in Barbour and settled among the foothills of Laurel Hill in Glade District. Among the families so settling was one named Poling, and Margaret Poling belonged to the family. Before she left Ohio John Holsberry became acquainted with her, and desirous of possessing so estimable a young lady for a wife, he sold his land for almost nothing (it afterwards became very valuable) and followed the Poling family to Barbour, where he was soon successful in winning the hand of the charming girl. They built their house where Kalamazoo now stands. When the War of 1812 began, John Holsberry volunteered, and became a commissioned officer and went to Norfolk; but on account of sickness in his family he resigned before the close of the war. His family consisted of six children, all of whom married and now have descendants living in Barbour County. The children were Rachel, who married Andrew Stalnaker; Nancy, who married John Regan; Samuel, William, Catherine and Martha, who is now the only one living. John Holsberry died in 1862 at the age of eighty-two, and was laid to rest in the M. P. White Oak Cemetery by the side of his companion who had gone on before. The descendants of Conrad Holsberry drifted from Ohio down the Mississippi and are now in Texas.

JOHN D. HOLSBERRY, born 1848, son of Samuel and Magdalena (Digman) Holsberry, was married in Randolph County in 1870 to Marietta, daughter of Thomas and Basbaba (Nutter) Schoonover. Children, French S., Leroy Virgil, Della, Granville Cicero, Hattie and Chloe Rue. He is a member of the M. E. Church South, a Democrat and a farmer, owning 215 acres in Barbour County, principally cleared, and a half interest in 1050 acres of woodland in Tucker County. He lives at Kalamazoo. His father was born in 1810 and died 1878; and his mother was a daughter of Charles Digman, who was drowned on Hunter's Fork of Teter Creek. Their children who are living are, Nicholas, Nancy, who married Wilson Stalnaker; Malissa, wife of J. E. Moore; Amanda, wife of Lemuel Nestor; the subject of this sketch; and Johnson, who died in youth.

LEROY VIRGIL HOLSBERRY, born in Glade in 1873, son of John D. Holsberry. He is a member of the M. E. Church, South, in politics is a Democrat, and by profession an educator. In 1896 he graduated from the State Normal School at Fairmont, and soon afterwards was elected Superintendent of the schools of Barbour County. Such time as he can now spare from the duties of his office he spends in the West Virginia University as a student.

JAMES K. HOLSBERRY, born 1849 on Teter's Creek, son of William and Rebecca (Vannoy) Holsberry, was married in 1868 on Teter's Creek to Elizabeth C., daughter of George and Mary (Stalnaker) Howdershelt. Children, Liona, Devilla F., William W., Effie M., Sophronia F., Nora V., Howard F., E G. and Tracy H. He is a member of the German Baptist Church, a Democrat, a farmer and a stockman, residing on Teter's Creek, where he owns 750 acres. William Holsberry was born at Kalamazoo in 1819, and was a farmer and miller, owning the Holsberry Mills on Teter's Creek. His father was John Holsberry, born near Pittsburg in 1780, and came to Barbour about 1800 and

LEROY VIRGIL HOLSBERRY.

settled near Kalamazoo. On the farm of James K. Holsberry, on April 24, 1865,, Captain M. F. Haller, Lieutenant Nestor and William Martin, Home Guards, were killed by Confederates.

THOMAS HAWKINS, born 1851, son of John and Mary Hawkins, married Elizabeth, daughter of Silas and Sarah (McKinney) Talbott. Children, Arta Frank and Astley Silas. He is a Missionary Baptist, a Republican, a farmer and miller, living three miles east of Philippi. He has been a member of the board of education. The Hawkins family came from Virginia to West Virginia in early times. They are descended from Lord John Hawkins of England. The subject of this sketch was left an orphan early in life and made his own way. He is a progressive farmer and an influential man in the community.

A. F. HAWKINS, born July 6, 1876, near Philippi, son of Thomas E. and Elizabeth (Talbott) Hawkins. He is a member of the Baptist Church, is an Odd Fellow, in politics is a Democrat, and by occupation a teacher. He attended the public schools; entered, in 1893, the West Virginia Cenference Seminary at Buckhannon, and graduated in 1897. He had begun teaching when sixteen years of age. The year after his graduation he was elected principal of the Beverly school, in Randolph County and the summer following he taught a private Normal school at that place. He was then appointed principal of the Public School at Parsons, in Tucker County; and in 1899 he was chosen as principal of the public schools at Philippi, thus each year gaining promotion in grade and salary. In the spring and summer of 1899 he assisted in collecting material for this history of Barbour County, his work being done chiefly in Philippi, Elk and Pleasant Districts. His people, on one side, are related to the Talbotts the first settlers of the county, and on the other side, the Hawkins family originated in England where the name is frequently met in the history of that country.

MARION FRANCIS HALL, born in 1844, in Preston County, son of William K. and Elizabeth (Simpson) Hall, was married in 1893, to Mary Martha, daughter of Milton Hart. Mr. Hall is a member of the M. E. Church, a Mason and an Odd Fellow, and is a merchant at Philippi. Further mention of him will be found in this book.

JAMES E. HALL, son of John N. and Harriet (Rightmire) Hall, was born on Elk Creek, November 27, 1841, and on August 19, 1869, at Philippi, he was married to Elizabeth, daughter of Lewis and Annie (Keyes) Wilson. Their only child, Lillian, was born October 6, 1870, and is the wife of Charles F. Teter, of Barbour County. Mr. Hall is a member of the M. E. Church, South, a Democrat, a member of the Masonic Order, and by business is a coal operator, residing at Philippi. The first members of this family came from England about 1745, and Samuel Hall was one of the first settlers in Barbour, and his son, John N. Hall, was born here and was identified with public affairs. Both he and his wife were born in 1815, and she was a daughter of John Rightmire, a merchant. Their children were, Julia, Allie J., wife of Joseph N. B. Crim; Emma I., wife of Colonel N. J. Coplin, Clarksburg; James E. and Jasper L., who died in New Mexico. The subject of this sketch was educated in the Ohio University. He entered the Confederate army, became adjutant of his regiment and was in much of the fighting up to Gettysburg, where he was wounded and taken prisoner, and was confined at Fort McHenry, Fort Delaware and Point Lookout, and near the close of the war he was exchanged, and reached the Confederate lines in time to be included in Lee's surrender. After the war he returned to Barbour and engaged in farming and other business. In 1878 he moved to Philippi. For five years he was manager of the Grafton and Greenbrier railroad, and was, and still is, interested in enterprises looking to the development of the county's resources.

JAMES E. HEATHERLY, born near Mt. Olive Church 1853, died 1897, son of Samuel J. and Helen A. (Corder) Heatherly, was married at Philippi, February 8, 1877, to Laura E., daughter of John R. and Susan (Sinsel) Williamson, children, Rissa Dale, Grace Lucile, Wayne Williamson. His wife is a member of the Baptist Church. He was a Democrat, a farmer and stock dealer living three miles east of Philippi. He was educated at the West Virginia College at Flemington. In 1880, at the age of twenty-seven, he was elected Sheriff of Barbour County, being the youngest Sheriff in the State. In 1888 he was again elected, but on account of failing health he was unable to fulfill the duties of his office, and the County Court appointed a successor. Before his election to the office of Sheriff he had been largely engaged in farming and stockdealing, and during his term of office he was extensively identified with the mercantile business at Philippi. A considerable block of stock of the Grafton and Greenbrier railroad was owned by him. During the latter years of his life he devoted his energies solely to farming and stock dealing, handling annually as many as 10000 sheep and 2000 cattle, and raising thousands of bushels of grain, on his highly improved farm of 1000 acres. It is all underlaid with coal. The first telephone in Barbour County is said to have been introduced by him. Mr. Heatherly was killed by lightning July 18, 1897 while taking shelter in a barn during a rainstorm. Commodore Strawderman was killed at the same time, and the barn was set on fire. There bodies were carried from the barn by James Phillips before the building was consumed. Since Mr. Heatherly's death, his wife has successfully managed the large property, making it highly remunerative. His daughter Rissa Dale graduated with high honors from Broaddus College and is now a teacher in that institution.

JAMES M. R. HOVEY, born 1825 in Lawrence County, Ohio; son of James and Maticta Hovey, was married in 1842 in Meiggs County, Ohio, to

Lucy Brown, daughter of William and Cynthia Stevens. Children, Margurita, Ida, Francilla, William, Franklin and Edmond. He is a member of the Baptist Church, of the G. A. R., and a carpenter, living at Hall. He was educated at Rutland, Ohio, and served three years in the Federal army, holding the office of corporal. In 1870 he made his home in Barbour County. At his second marriage he married Sarah E. Kinney, and their children are, Harvey I., Cassie, Dora, Henry, James, Elijah, Manser and Maggie.

JOHN P. HATHAWAY, son of Eppa and Hannah (Woodford) Hathaway, was born near Pleasant Creek in 1853. On September 2, 1875, he married, near his present home, Rachel E., daughter of David R. and Eunice (Kelley) Poling. Children, Homer G. and Birdie E. He was educated in the public schools of the county, is a member of the M. E. Church, is a farmer and a carpenter, at the latter trade having worked twenty-five years, frequently superintending extensive work. He owns 37 acres of land, underlaid with coal and largely improved, three miles east of Philippi.

JOHN I. HOFFMAN was born near the mouth of Laurel Creek in 1841, son of Israel Putnam and Anna (Black) Hoffman. On September 30, 1869, he was married to Elizabeth A., daughter of Andrew and Barbara (Marple) Trimble. Children, Lunetta, Barbara, Arthur D., Almeda Belle, Ida M., Delbert M., Okey, Irskene and Bliss. Mr. Hoffman is a member of the G. A. R., is a farmer and lives near Arden, which town he named. He spent seven years in the mercantile business, and six years of the time was postmaster. John Hoffman, his grandfather, was a German and came from Loudoun County, Virginia, and settled near Meadowville in 1797, when the father of the subject of this sketch was six or seven years old. Daniel Hoffmnn, brother of Israel, was in the War of 1812. John Black, the grandfather of the subject of this sketch, on his mother's side, came from what is now Garrett County, Maryland, and settled near Meadowville. John Hoffman joined the Union army and fought with Averell in all his campaigns. At the battle of Rocky Gap, when the rebel bullets came like hail, Mr. Hoffman took shelter behind a stump, but immediately discovered that he was in a yellow jacket nest. The Confederates made the attack hot in front and the yellow jackets made a bayonet charge in the flanks. Mr. Hoffman had his choice: stay where he was and stand the yellow jackets, or get out and face the bullets. He was not long in deciding that he preferred bullets in front to yellow jackets in the rear, and out from behind the stump he came.

GEORGE A. HARRIS, born 1872, son of Gideon Draper Camden and Rachel (Hosseflute) Harris, is a Democrat in politics, by occupation a farmer and teacher residing on Sugar Creek, where he owns 131 acres, nearly all improved. He has taught six terms in Barbour County. Rev. Simeon Harris, the well-known preacher, was his great grandfather.

WILLIAM TANDY HULDERMAN, born 1845, in Pleasants County, West

FAMILY HISTORY. 401

Virginia, son of Amasa and Mary E. (Jones) Hulderman, was married October 12, 1878, in Barbour County, to Laura E., daughter of William and Matilda (Bailey) Sharps. Mrs. Hulderman is a member of the M. E. Church, South, and the subject of this sketch is an Odd Fellow, a Democrat and a hotel keeper in Philippi, proprietor of the Valley House. He attended the public schools. His father's children were, John E., Martha A., James E., Amariah H., Salathiel T., Charles A., Nathan S., William T. and Coleman L. The grandfather of the subject of this sketch was John Hulderman, born about 1770, in Germany, settled at Shinnston, in Harrison County, and died at the age of ninety-nine years. His children were, Henry, Amariah F, Absalom, William and Jane.

GILBERT SIMEON HYMES, born 1842, in Barbour County, son of John and Malinda (Phillips) Hymes, was married January 4, 1866, to Susan Malinda, daughter of Jesse and Sarah (Harris) Fitzwater. Children, Thomas Jackson, (died 1886) Laura and Sallie Matilda. He is a Democrat and a farmer, owning 146 acres in Barbour and 97 in Randolph, of which 170 are improved. He is also engaged in stock raising. He was educated in the public schools. In 1884 he was elected Assessor in the eastern part of Barbour for four years. He was in the Confederate service under General Imboden from 1862 till the close of the war, and was wounded in the left leg at the battle of New Market, and was slightly wounded at Williamsport. He was orderly sergeant in Captain Hannibal Hill's Company, 62d Virginia.

FLOYD TRIPLETT HOLDEN, born 1869, on Beech Lick of Elk Creek, son of John Benton and Columbus (Chenoweth) Holden, was married June 17, 1897, at Philippi, to Harriet Columbia, daughter of Nathan Harmon and Mary Ellen (Jarvis) Taft. He is a member of the Baptist Church, is a Mason, Knight of Pythias and a Democrat. He is a teacher, residing at Philippi, and was educated at the Fairmont Normal School and at the Conference Seminary at Buckhannon. The name in the Norse language was Olden, and the family came from Normandy to England about the time of William the Conqueror (1066.) They were possessed of property, and well to do for six hundred years, when they met financial reverses and came to America, where Benjamin settled in New Jersey and became the ancestor of the Holdens in West Virginia, and probably of those in the West also. He had three sons, Alexander, Benjamin and one whose name is lost. The two sons were American soldiers in the Revolutionary War, and subsequently moved to Ohio, where Alexander served in the legislature and in other offices. Later the brothers returned to West Virginia and bought and inherited land in Harrison and Barbour Counties. Benjamin's descendants live in Harrison County. Alexander had three sons and one daughter. The eldest was John Chamberlain Holden, born 1791, and a soldier under General Harrison in the War of 1812. In 1813 he married, and in 1815, settled on a farm of 730 acres on Beech Lick, Isaac's Run and Elk. He had two children by his first wife who died soon after, and in 1819 he married Prudence Kittle, of Randolph County, and to them were born fifteen children, one of whom was John Benton, born in 1841, who was in the Confederate army. On February 3, 1869, he married Columbia Chenoweth and they had three sons, the youngest dying in childhood. The second son, William L., born 1873, married Ella Findley, October 21, 1894, and two children were born to them, Otto F. and Stella E. The mother of these children died 1898. William L. afterwards married Ethel Schurman. The wife of John B. Holden was a daughter of Newton Chenoweth, and granddaughter of John Chenoweth, of Hampshire County, and a Revolutionary soldier. The Chenoweths are of a very ancient family of Welsh origin. The name was originally Trevelisich; but one of them having built Chenouth Castle, the family took the name of the castle. The family settled in Maryland very early, and one branch intermarried with the family of Lord Baltimore, and another with the Cromwells, thereby becoming related with the great Oliver. The Holdens, now wide-spread, have always been men of prominence and culture, filling chairs in educational institutions, seats in the legislative bodies, and pulpits in churches. They have usually been Baptists, and seven of Benjamin Holden's descendants have been preachers of that denomination, among them being Rev. L. W. Holden, Rev. Alexander Holden and Rev. Charles Horace Holden still living.

ADOLPHUS HAMILTON, born in Monongalia County, on Decker's Creek, 1839, son of John J. and Matilda (Castola) Hamilton, was married January 3, 1867, in Barbour County, to Elizabeth S., daughter of Jeremiah and Nancy (Irons) Harvey. Children, Wade Hampton, Okey Johnson, Maude, George, Agustus F. He is a member of the United Brethern Church, a Democrat and a farmer, residing on Sandy Creek. He attended school at Evansville, Preston County. His wife died in 1892. He served in the Union army as a wagoner, from 1861 to 1864, when he was taken prisoner by Mosby's men and was incarcerated in several southern prisons, including Andersonville. In the latter part of the year he was exchanged and came home in broken health. He worked on the railroad for one year and then began farming.

JOHN FRANKLIN HEWITT, born 1872, son of Joel and Hulda (Hayes) Hewitt, was married March 20, 1898, to Margaret, daughter of Andrew and Emily (Wiseman) Monehan. Their child's name is Lily. Mr. Hewitt is a Republican, and a teacher and artist, living on the waters of Hanging Rock Run. He was educated in the public schools.

RYLAND G. HASKINS, born 1860, son of G. W. Haskins, was married August 30, 1883, in Mineral County, to Josephine, daughter of Joseph Pennington. Children, Earl, Effie, Fairfax and Letta. He is a Knight of Pyth-

ias and a Mason; in politics a Republican, and by occupation a superintendent of mines and a merchant at Junior. He formerly lived at Davis, in Tucker County. He has held the position of post master, and was educated in the public schools.

GEORGE ELAM HALLER, born 1859, son of Eli Francis Morrison and Catherine (Nestor) Haller, was married April 8, 1883, near Nestorville, to Generva Palestine, daughter of Henry and Hannah (Vannoy) Stalnaker. Children, Gay and Ottis Roy. Mrs. Haller died in 1896, and two years later he married Mrs. Bludel Stemple, daughter of Anthony and Sally (Stalnaker) Poling. His child by the second marriage is Genevi Pearl. Mr. Haller is in business with Wesley Bennett and Lee Poling at Nestorville, where they have a roller process flouring mill and a planer. He owns 75 acres of land, all cleared, and two houses and lots in Nestorville, and is also engaged in general farming and stock raising, and takes a special interest in sheep and hogs. His uncle Captain Michael Haller, was killed near Holsberry's Mill near the close of the war.

I

JUDGE WILLIAM T. ICE, born March 9, 1840, in Marion County, son of Andrew and Elizabeth (Alexander) Ice; was married in 1866, to Columbia, daughter of Rev. Solomon Jarvis. Children, Lizzie B., Robert B., Maggie J., William T. jr., Nellie M., Grace and Columbia V. Of these, Robert died in 1880; Maggie J. was married to Fred O. Blue, a lawyer of Philippi, in 1895; and William T. jr., is now partner of his father in the practice of law, at Philippi, having graduated from the West Virginia University in 1897, and the next year was graduated from the law department of the same institution. The Ice family is English, and the great, great grandfather of Judge Ice was one of the pioneers in West Virginia, the locality now Marion County, and he assisted in defending the early settlements against the Indians. He was a farmer. The Alexanders were Scotch and settled in Culpeper County, Virginia, where they were merchants and farmers. Judge Ice's mother died in 1848 and his father in 1885, a member of the Christian Church. In early life the subject of this sketch worked on his home farm and obtained such an education as was within his reach. When twenty years of age he began reading law with Fenton Smith and remained in Mr. Smith's office four years, when he was admitted to practice, and soon afterwards located in Philippi which has been his home ever since, and where he has always enjoyed a large and lucrative practice. Soon after locating in Barbour he was elected Prosecuting Attorney; in 1875 he was elected to the legislature and served two terms. In 1880 he was elected Judge of the Third Judicial Circuit, composed of the counties of Taylor, Tucker, Barbour, Preston and Randolph, and served eight years. He has always been a Democrat, and has exercised an influence with his party. He owns a handsome residence in Philippi, several town lots, an improved farm, and in Randolph County he owns valuable timber lands. He is a member of the Missionary Baptist Church.

MARTIN ICE, born 1862, son of Daniel and Emily (Poling) Ice, was married November 6, 1887, to Mary Belle, daughter of Henry and Eliza Ridgeway. Children, Minnie Olive, Everett Earl, Alley Dale, Okey J. He is a member of the State Grange, a Democrat and a farmer, and was educated in the public schools.

JAMES B. ISNER, born near Meadowville, 1858, son of Henry and Julia Ann (Sherman) Isner, was married September 29, 1881, at Hezekiah Poling's on Bear's Run, to Sarah Virginia, daughter of Hezekiah and Elizabeth Poling. Zora Emma, their child, was born May 31, 1886. He is a member of the M. E. Church; a Republican and a farmer, living on the head of Sand Run, where he owns 85 acres of finely improved land. He was educated in the public schools of the county. His father was captured by Federal soldiers and sent to prison at Camp Chase, where he died.

J

HON. I. V. JOHNSON. The following biography of Mr. Johnson was published in the *Charleston Mail*, while he was Auditor of the State:

"Isaac Vandeventer Johnson, Auditor of West Virginia, was born in Randolph, now Barbour, November 15, 1837. His father, Col. William Johnson, was a farmer and tanner and was a prominent and influential citizen, representing Barbour County in the Virginia House of Delegates from 1859 to 1865. The subject of this sketch received a limited education in the public schools of that day which was supplemented by a year and a half at Emory and Henry College. He entered the Circuit Clerk's office of Barbour County at the age of sixteen as deputy clerk, and continued in that position until the breaking out of the war, with an intermission of the years 1857 and 1858, which years he spent in Illinois. Espousing the cause of the South, he assisted in organizing early in April, 1861, the "Barbour Grays," of which he was elected Second Lieutenant (the late lamented Thomas A. Bradford being the Captain.) He was badly wounded in the knee at the battle of Allegheny Mountain on the 13th day of December, 1861. At the reorganization of the army in 1862, he was elected First Lieutenant of his company, the 31st having become a part of "Stonewall" Jackson's command. Finding toward the close of that campaign that he could not, on account of his wound, stand the infantry service, he resigned his commission and attached himself to the Brigade of General Imboden, where he was assigned to duty by the Secretary of War in the Quartermaster's department, where he continued until the close of the war, when he returned to his home in Barbour County. In 1866 he entered the service of the Baltimore & Ohio Railroad Company, where he was employed as brakeman, baggage-master and clerk in the Parkersburg railroad office until 1870. In the latter year he returned to Barbour County and engaged in farming and

FAMILY HISTORY. 407

teaching until 1872, when he became a canditate for and was elected clerk of the circuit court of that county under the new constitution, going into office on the 1st of January, 1873. He was twice re-elected to the same office, retiring on the 31st of December, 1890, after a continuous service of eighteen years. He became a candidate for the Democratic nomination for State Auditor, and was nominated and elected to that office in 1892 for the term of four years.

"Auditor Johnson has been twice married, his first wife being Miss Fannie Link, of Bridgewater, Virginia, to whom he was married on the 24th of December, 1874, who died August 25th, 1891, and by whom he had three children. His second wife was Miss Fannie Kemper, of Shendun, Virginia, to whom he was married on the 20th of September, 1893. He is a Master Mason, a member of Bigelow Lodge, No. 52, Philippi, Barbour County, W. Va., and an Odd Fellow, a member of Philippi Lodge, No. 59, and is a member of the M. E. Church, South."

At the close of Mr. Johnson's four years' term of service as Auditor, not being a candidate for re-nomination or re-election, he turned his office over to his Republican successor, Mr. L. M. La Follette, and moved to Roanoke, Virginia, where he now resides, being engaged principally in farming pursuits. During Mr. Johnson's term of service as auditor, his office was kept in the perfect order and system characteristic of his nature and disposition. He made many valuable and original recommendations to the Legislature concerning the improvement of the service and change in the administration of the office. No defaults in the collection of the revenue occurred during his term, and defaults in previous terms were prosecuted. It is but justice to say that West Virginia never had a better Anditor, or more deserving and popular official. The loss which West Virginia sustained by his removal was a positive gain to the "Old Commonwealth," for whom Mr. Johnson, by reason of his birth, education, association and service there during the Civil War, retained an affectionate remembrance.

Mr. Johnson's children are Miss Ivy, the eldest, named in imitation of of the initials of her father's Christian name, and who is now the wife of Mr. Mark Cordier Price, of Roanoke; and Frank and Virginia, all of whom, with Mrs. Johnson and himself, during his term at Charleston, participated in and formed part of the social functions of the administration at the Capital.

JOSEPH LINDEN JOHNSON, born 1846 at Meadowville, son of Hon. William and Lydia Ann (Wells) Johnson, was married January 12, 1869 to Ella Rebecca, daughter of Michael and Catherine (Strickler) Crim. Children, Lillian Amanda, Lennie Crim, Clifford C., Warren Wellington, William Michael and Emma Virginia. He is a member of the M. E. Church, South, a Democrat, and a farmer and merchant residing at Meadowville. He was in the Confederate service, on General Imboden's staff. Mr. Johnson owns

86 acres, all improved. Part of the Keller Hill is on his lands. Indian graves and flint arrow-heads in that vicinity render it probable that aborigines lived there in considerable numbers.

LEVI JOHNSON, born 1849 on Teter's Creek, son of John G., and Catherine (Parsons) Johnson, was married in 1873 on Teter's Creek, to Helen A., daughter of Emory and Catherine (Gainer) Poling. Children, Bernice C., Herman G., Otie E., Johnnie, Emory, Lloyd S., Stewart L., Helen A. In politics he is a Democrat, and is a member of the M. E. Church, South. He resides on Teter's Creek where he owns 238 acres, largely improved and he is a very successful farmer.

RICHARD M. JOHNSON, born 1841 on Mill Run, son of John G. and Catherine (Parsons) Johnson; was married in 1859, on Teter's Creek, to Nancy, daughter of Samuel M. and Elizabeth (Carpenter) Gainer. Children, Orvilla D., Orlando, James, W. W., Troy, John G., Raymond. Mr Johnson is a member of the M. E. Church, South, a Democrat, and a farmer owning 126 acres, 90 improved, on Teter's Creek. He has always lived in Barbour, except nine months spent in Texas in 1879, and has dealt in horses which he takes to Virginia and North Carolina where he trades them for cattle.

CAPTAIN MORTIMER C. JOHNSON, born 1836, son of William Johnson of Meadowville, was married to a daughter of James Poling, and had two daughters. At the commencement of the Civil War, he entered the Confederate service, in the Barbour Greys. In 1862 he was discharged because of deafness, and came home and raised a company of his own, known as Company H., 62 Regiment, Virginia Infantry, Imboden's Brigade. Just before his death he had come home on a furlough, and was killed while returning to the South. The names of those with him were, H. L. Yock, Samuel Cleavenger, David Cleavenger, Ezra Reger, Harrison Coberly, Peter Reed, and Lorenzo Adams. They passed through Tucker County, and were pursued by Captain Nathaniel J. Lambert, of the Home Guards, and were fired upon at the Sinks of Gandy in Randolph County, and Captain Johnson and one other Confederate were killed, and Lorenzo Adams was wounded in eighteen places, but subsequently recovered.

CAPTAIN WILLIAM KESTER JENKINS, born 1824, near Franklin, Pendleton County, son of William and Jane (Kester) Jenkins, was married January 11, 1848, at Elk City, to Roda, daughter of John and Nancy (Brown) Daniels. Children, John Morgan, born 1849; Margaret Jane, 1851, married Adam Corrick, of Santa Rosa, Cal.; Mary E., 1853; Lydia J., 1855; Henry A. Wise, 1856, married Mary J. McKenzie, of Louisa, Ky.; James Hall, 1858, married Anna Weeks, of Cal.; Albert, 1860, married Kate B. Weeks, of Logansport, Ind.; William K., 1863, married Mary McCracken; Roda Belle, 1866; Joseph Lee, 1867, married Zella M. Moore, of Cal.; Burton Claude, 1870. Captain Jenkins married the second time, June 18, 1872, to

Mrs. Mary Jane Reed, widow of William N. Reed. Her maiden name was Callihan, born 1835, daughter of John and Malinda Callihan. Her first marriage occurred in 1851, and her children were, Caroline, Charles C., who married Fannie Dillon, of Cal.; James D. H., married Hattie S. Woodford, daughter of Adam Woodford; Emma, Etta. Captain Jenkins is a member of the M. E. Church, South, is a Democrat, and has been a Notary Public fifteen years at Elk City. His ancestors, on his father's side, were English, his father coming from England and settling in Rockingham County, Virginia, where the parents of the subject of this sketch died when he was five years old and he was taken to raise by his aunt, Mary (Kester) Findley. The Kesters were a noted family in border history. They came from England, although the name would suggest a German origin. They were among the earliest settlers in Pendleton County, and lived in the southern part of that county during the French and Indian war. James Kester, (son of the first Kester who came to America) had two brothers and an only sister in 1758, when Killbuck, the Shawnee Indian, invaded Pendleton County at the head of fifty or sixty savages. The settlers fled to Fort Seybert, which surrendered without fighting, although it could have probably held out against the Indians. James Kester saw his only sister tomahawked by the Indians, and he, and presumably his two brothers, were carried into captivity, together with James Dyer, the ancestor of E. R. Dyer, now of Barbour County. James Kester returned from captivity and subsequently served seven years in the American army during the Revolution. Fred Kester, an uncle of Captain Jenkins, served in the War 1812. Captain Jenkins bought the first lot in Elk City.

HENRY MIDDLETON JENKINS, born 1836, on Stewart's Run, son of Jonathan and Amanda (McKensie) Jenkins, was married November 6, 1863, near Flemington, Taylor County, to Mary Ann, daughter of Lewis and Cynthia (Bailey) Fleming. Children, Ella C., Hattie, Amanda V., Martha P., Albert G., Patrick H., Jonathan Lewis, Chester M. and Corder J. He is a member of the Missionary Baptist Church, a Democrat and a farmer, living on Hacker's Creek, where he owns 128 acres, largely improved. He has been a member of the Board of Education, and was eight years Overseer of the Poor. His daughter, Ella, married John C. Moats and lives five miles east of Philippi; Hattie married Robert E. S. Holden and lives in Philippi; Amanda married Mr. Rowe and lives in Taylor County; Martha married Boyd W. Doak and lives in Pennsylvania. His great grandfather came from Ireland and settled on Goose Creek, Loudoun County, Virginia; and his grandfather, Jesse Jenkins, served in the War of 1812, as well as his uncle, William McKinney, who, with his brother, Thomas, (grandfather of the subject of this sketch) were early settlers in Barbour, locating on Stewart's Run. His great grandmother, Jenkins, came from Wales. The

Baileys and Flemings were Irish, the McKinneys Scotch. Edward Fleming, great grandfather of Mrs. Jenkins, served in the Revolutionary War. Mrs. Jenkins' brothers, John and Lewis, served in the Union army, and Patrick in the Confederate army.

REV. JOHN L. B. JONES, PH. B., was born in 1865, at Calhoun, Barbour County, son of Solomon S. Jones, a family originally from Virginia. He attended public schools of the county, the West Virginia College, Flemington, the Conference Seminary, at Buckhannon, Butler, Missouri, the Music School, at Pittsburg, the Dubuque Vocal Institution, Iowa. In addition to these schools, he attended instruction under several private teachers, last of whom was Portius, and the Mountain Lake Park Chautauqua. Early in 1899 the Taylor University, of Upland, Indiana, conferred upon him the degree of Bachelor of Philosophy for special work done. He married Adaline, daughter of John T. Moss, of Barbour. They have six daughters, Winnie, Alice, Grace, May, Agnes, Ruth. In 1891 he entered the ministry, and has had charge of Ireland, Flatwoods and Aurora circuits. He is a hard student, an excellent scholar and an able preacher. He has given much attention to music, and is a successful composer of Church and Sunday School music; nor does he confine himself to sacred music, but composes both songs and music, patriotic and sentimental. He has set to music many of the songs written by Miss Ida L. Reed, Barbour County's talented hymn writer. He supplies Christmas and Easter music for churches in New York, Boston, Philadelphia, Baltimore, Pittsburg, Cincinnati, St. Louis and elsewhere. Among his best known music are, "America is Good Enough for me," "The Parting Hour," "Only a Song and a Memory," etc.

ALBERT W. JONES, born near Calhoun in 1853, son of Ephraim and Malinda (Yoke) Jones; was married April 22, 1880, in Barbour, to Ida, daughter of Benjamin and Jemima (Morgan) Shafer. Children, Effie Dove, Frona May, Benjamin Franklin, Dora Beulah, Charles Manzell, Frederick E. and Emma Gay. He is a member of the M. E. Church, an Odd Fellow, a Democrat, farmer and carpenter, and lives near Calhoun, where he owns 100 acres, mostly improved, and bearing choice fruit. He attended the county schools, and was four years a Justice of the Peace. His wife is a decendant of Morgan, the Indian fighter. His uncle, William Jones, died in the Federal army, after three years of service.

MATHIAS JENNINGS, born 1849, in Washington County, Pennsylvania, was married at Kingwood, West Virginia, to Miss Conley, daughter of Elias Conley. Their child's name is Marietta. He is a member of the M. E. Church, is an I. O. O. F. and Junior O. U. A. M. He is a Republican, and since 1894 has been proprietor of the Valley House at Belington. He attended the common schools, and is of English and Irish decent, and his wife in descent is German, Irish and Welsh.

ROBERT EDWARD JACKSON, born 1863 at Jane Lew, Lewis County, son of James W. Jackson, was married at Lightburn, Lewis County, in 1891 to Mollie R., daughter of J. J. Lightburn. Children, Joseph Goodloe and Edith Lyle. Mr. Jackson is a member of the Baptist Church, and belongs to the orders I. O. O. F., K. of P. and M. W. of A.; in politics is a Democrat, and by occupation a merchant, of the firm of Brooks & Jackson, at Belington. He was educated at the West Virginia University, and at Eastman Business College, Poughkeepsie, New York. He was Mayor of Belington in 1898. He is a relative of General Stonewall Jackson.

K

JAMES LEWIS BURBRIDGE KELLEY, born near Philippi in 1847, son of John and Mary (Yoke) Kelley; was married in Barbour, May 11, 1874, to Annie M., daughter of Jacob and Margaret (Arndarf) Boehm. Children, Corbin L., Alpheus B., Augusta, Jacob Woodbridge, Carrie O., Rachel L., Margaret M., Henry M. Mr. Kelley is a Republican, and a farmer on Ford's Run, owning 51 acres underlaid with coal. His grandfather, Ebenezer T. Kelley, came from New Jersey and settled near Meadowville about 1795, and his father, John Kelley, was a Justice of the Peace in Randolph County before Barbour was formed. He joined Captain Haller's company of Home Guards in 1864 and served till May 30, 1865. His father was in the War of 1812, and helped defeat the British army which attempted to capture Baltimore.

The Kelley family has kept a record more fully than most families, and it is possible to give the family history more fully. Samuel Kelley, the great grandfather of the subject of this sketch, lived in Somerset County, New Jersey, as early as 1763, and his wife's name was Eunice. On October 2, 1763, their son, Ebenezer T. Kelley, was born. When he was 27 years old, in Alleghany County, Maryland, (Dec. 2, 1790), he married Rachel, daughter of Robert and Mary Johnson. Rachel Johnson, was born October 22, 1769, in New Jersey. They lived in Maryland two years, then moved to Hampshire County, Virginia, where they remained three or four years and then crossed the Alleghanies into Randolph (now Barbour) and settled near Meadowville in 1795 or early the next spring. Following is a list of children, with births and deaths: Mary, born in Alleghany County, Maryland, January 15, 1792; Eunice, born in Hampshire County, Virginia, September 27, 1793, married a man named Cade, and died in Monroe County, Ohio, 1835. In the old family record is written this verse:

> Eunice Kelley is my name and virtuous is my life,
> And happy is the man who gets me for a wife.

Isaac and John L. Kelley who seem to have been twins, were born February 20, 1796, in Randolph County. Isaac died in Monroe County, Ohio, 1845, and John L. in Barbour in 1866; Rebecca was born June 8, 1798, in Randolph, married a man named Carpenter, and died 1860 in Iowa; Osa was born March 25, 1800 in Randolph, died in Barbour in 1875; Hannah, born in Randolph, June 8, 1802, married a man named Yoke, and died 1843 in Barbour; Samuel was born September 9, 1804 in Randolph, died 1863 in Barbour; Jane was born August 5, 1807, in Randolph; Johnson was born July 25, 1810 in Randolph. The children of John L. Kelley were: Isaac, born August 9, 1823; Rebecca, born November 29, 1824; one died young; Solomon, born November 14, 1827; Stingley, born November 30, 1830; Elias, born January 8, 1833; Oscar, born January 13, 1835; Sarah Ann, born November 11, 1837; Cymon and Garrett, born April 18, 1840; Elam, born February 25, 1842; James Lewis Burbridge, born May, 4, 1847.

COLUMBUS KELLEY, born 1854 near his present home, is a son of Elias and Catherine (McGee) Kelley, was married May 6, 1884, near Arden, to Jemima, daughter of James and Julia (Hoffman) Fry. Children, Edwin L., Lenora M. and Eva. He is a member of the M. E. Church and an Odd Fellow, and he owns part of the Kelley land, and his farm of 125 acres around the mine is improved. The mine was largely developed through his industry and perseverance, and is named from him. A history of the mine will be found elsewhere in this book, and need not be repeated here.

WARREN BRANCE KITTLE, born 1872 at Belington, son of George M. and Charity Ellen (Poling) Kittle, was married June 30, 1897, at Philippi, to Zonie, daughter of W. S. and Virginia (Baker) Wilson. Their child's name is Virginia. He is a member of the M. E. Church, is a Republican and a lawyer, residing at Philippi. He took the degree of L.L. B. in the West Virginia University in 1894. His father is a son of Cyrus and Tirza (Stalnaker) Kittle, and was born in Randolph in 1847, and in 1871 he married Charity Ellen, daughter of Martin G. and Hulda (Limbers) Poling. Their children were Warren B., George Bruce, Rutherford M., Lucy Rebecca, Anna Mary and Francis Gordon. Cyrus Kittle was born in 1819 and died 1885. He was a politician of considerable importance, and held fourteen offices in Randolph County. He was a Union man during the Civil War and was concerned with military affairs and had several narrow escapes. In 1862 he was in St. George at the time of the Imboden raid and escaped by burying himself in the hay in Adam Tait's barn, although the soldiers unwittingly prodded him with pitchforks while throwing out hay for their horses. Again, the next spring he was in Beverly when Imboden attacked that place, and he had barely time to hit the road for Philippi before the Confederates cut off retreat. He narrowly escaped Confederates in Barbour, and hurried into Taylor and took the road for Fairmont just in time to run into another Confederate army above Fairmont, under Jones. Taking to the open country he fled into Pennsylvania and reached Pittsburg penniless. He worked in the iron mills and earned money enough to take him home. He was at that time Colonel of the West Virginia Militia. He was a member of the first West Virginia Legislature, and was on the

LIEUT.-COL. DAVID BERKLEY LANG.

Shortly before Lieut.-Col. Lang was killed, a comrade painted his portrait on a pine board, and from that portrait the above engraving was made.

FAMILY HISTORY. 415

committee which designed and adopted the State Seal and Coat of Arms. He found the design on a tombstone in a Wheeling cemetery and had it copied. He was ten years a minister in the M. E. Church. The children of Cyrus Kittle were, Levi, George M., Creed, Amassa, Mary L., Emmett, Ulman Wirt, Eliza L., Cenna, Grant and Ellen (twins), Waitman T. Willey. The father of Cyrus Kittle was Elijah, born 1798, who married Lucinda, daughter of John Waldo. Their children were, Cyrus, John Waldo, Amassa, David A., Alva, Hulda, Prudence, Pauline, Emmeline, Harriett, Sally and Louisa. The grandfather of Cyrus Kittle, John Waldo, lived on Booth's Creek, now Marion County. He spent many years a prisoner with the Indians. The father of Elijah Kittle was Abraham, who married a daughter of John Chenoweth, who was an American soldier in the Revolution. This Abraham was a son of Abraham Kittle, the first of the name in West Virginia. He was born in New Jersey in 1735 and died in 1816. His grave is yet to be seen in the old Collett graveyard four miles below Beverly. His children were, Richard, Jacob, Abraham, George, John and one daughter.

JACOB HENRY KNAPP, born in Barbour County January 8, 1868, son of John B. and Sallie Ann (Smith) Knapp, was married near Elk City, Sept. 7, 1893, to Florence Emma, daughter of Mordecai D. and Armettie (Hudkins) Riley. Children, Jacob H, Jr., born Aug 4, 1894, and Florence Marjoram, born March 22, 1899. Mr Knapp is a Baptist, a Knight of Pythias, a Democrat and a merchant residing at Philippi. He was educated in the free schools of Barbour. From July 1, 1893, to December 1, 1898, he was U. S. Deputy Collector of Internal Revenue. His grandfather, Henry Knapp, came from the State of New York and was a Barbour County pioneer, working for years at the trade of chair maker. His grandmother Smith was a pioneer settler on Sugar Creek, near Meadowville, and was a woman of remarkable intellect and business management. The subject of this sketch began working from home at the age of thirteen, and kept it up for about seventeen years, following many lines of work. He applied the principle that persistent labor will bring results and he thinks that want and poverty would be materially lessened if all boys and young men would try the same principle.

ADAM KERR, born 1820 in Pocahontas County, son of Robert and Susan (Arbogast) Kerr, was married in 1845 to Hannah, daughter of Moses and Mary (Waybright) Arbogast; in 1856 to Rosanna Rogers; in 1869 to Rebecca Thompson; in 1875 to Martha Gordon; in 1888 to Virginia Pugh. Children, Ezra, William Bailey, Enoch and Margaret Jane. He resides on the Buckhannon River.

JAMES KNOTTS, who was Sheriff of Barbour in 1871, was born at Knottsville, Taylor County, son of James and Susanna (Miller) Knotts. On October 29, 1857, at Belington, he was married and lived one year at Knottsville, then moved to Barbour, where he followed farming and merchandizing. He resigned the office of Sheriff after one year, because of poor health. He was a member of the M. E. Church, South. He died October 26, 1895, and was buried at Belington.

BENJAMIN J. KNIGHT was born in Taylor County, son of Thomas and Catharine (Rosier) Knight.

LIEUTENANT COLONEL DAVID BERKLEY LANG* was born January 31, 1831, near Bridgeport, Harrison County, West Virginia. His father, Lemuel Lang, married the daughter of Thomas Berkley, who laid warrant on the land that the town of Astor, Taylor County, is built upon.

A few months after David's birth the two families moved to Missouri, and while on the way David's mother died with cholera, and his father, leaving the child with its grandparents, returned to his former home, and in about three years married Miss Surrepta Bartlett, and went back to Missouri and brought David home, who was three years old, but remembered how his Grandmother Berkley lamented when they parted.

His youth was spent upon the farm in summer, and he attended country schools in winter, and obtained a good English education.

He was married August 24, 1851, to Elizabeth Powell, daughter of Burr and Elender Powell, of Taylor County, and settled at Fairview, Taylor County, (now Astor) where he engaged in the mercantile business, a few years. After disposing of his store, he built a steam flouring mill on Simpson's Creek, near Flemington, but the business did not prove a financial success. He lost over $500 in one year by investing in wheat when it was high. In the spring of 1859 he moved to a place three miles south east of Belington, having exchanged the mill with Mr. Shepler for a farm, (now owned by Charles Stipes) where he farmed and practiced medicine in that part of Barbour and the north western part of Randolph until the Civil War. He had studied medicine before he was married and while he was running his store. In 1861 he was having a very successful and lucrative practice. In boyhood days he had somnambulistic habits. His father often found him on the rungs of the ladder that led to his bed room, sound asleep with his book in his hand. At one time he awakened and found the covers off of his bed. Not being able to find them in the room he lit a candle and while hunting for them he discovered them wound around the outside post of an unfinished portico frame. He had walked out of the door of the upper room, on the joist, while asleep, and he would not walk out to take them down when he found them, but procured a pole and unwound them with it. There had been no recurrence of this strange habit from his boyhood days until the fall of 1860. In that year his wife awakened one night and saw him by the light of the moon sitting by his stand writing. When he came to bed she awoke him, and asked him what he had been writing.

---

*This sketch was written by an intimate friend of Major Lang for the History of Barbour.

He said, "nothing." But when he procured a light he found a letter on the stand written to Lemuel E. Davidson, of Flemington, Taylor County, in which he spoke of a war between the States, and said that he had taken side with the South, and his friend that of the North, which proved to be the fact in the years that followed. Mr. Davidson, however, did not take part in the conflict, but was a Union man, and a member of the first legislature of West Virginia and a member of the committee that designed the Coat of Arms of the State. The letter was very well written, with the exception of a few places, where the ink on his pen had become exhausted before refilling. He often showed this letter to his friends as a curiosity, and the strange part of it was, that at the time it was written he was very much opposed to Virginia's seceding from the Union, and made several speeches against the Ordinance of Secession, but when a majority of her citizens said, "she must secede," he, like R. E. Lee and T. J. Jackson, being strongly in favor of State's Rights and believing that his allegiance to his native State was greater than to the General Government, cast his fortunes with the South, and yet he was always opposed to slavery.

On the Sunday morning that General McClellan's forces made an attack on General Garnett at Laurel Hill, he, in company with Colonel William Johnson, of Meadowville and some other citizens, who had spent the night at his home, went to the Confederate camp two miles away, not knowing that there was any possibility of an attack, and expecting to return home in the evening, but the pickets were put on duty, and no one was allowed to pass the lines, and it being a part of his nature not to be inactive, he procured a gun and went into the skirmish, and took a very active part until Garnett's forces left Laurel Hill. He returned home, and after staying a few hours mounted his horse, and with his double barreled shot gun followed the retreating Confederate forces. He overtook them in the vicinity of Corrick's Ford and participated in that battle.

There stood a sugar tree on the farm of Peyton C. Booth, near the Confederate camp at Laurel Hill, which he stood behind and exchanged several shots with the enemy; and for years could be seen the marks of the balls that struck the tree. The few days that passed during the Laurel Hill skirmish were the most trying to his wife and children of all they had ever endured. They had looked for him home on Sunday evening, and when he did not return his wife went to the Confederate lines daily to hear from him, but the pickets did not know him, nor would they let her pass, and the frequent volleys of musketry and artillery not far away increased the anxiety for her husband and made her heart almost break with grief.

After going to the South he was employed by General William L. Jackson as a scout, and was in many close places with the enemy. He came through the mountains home in the latter part of November, 1861, and spent a few days with his family, leaving his horse with a friend on

Cheat Mountain. On making his return he become lost in the dense hemlock and laurel thickets between the forks of the Greenbrier River. He first left his saddle so he could get through the brush better, and after cutting his way through the laurel with a heavy knife he had to abandon his horse and would have perished in the snow had not some Confederate scouts found him, supposing they had caught a Yankee spy. They conveyed him to Camp Alleghany, on top of the mountain, and after they had warmed, they permitted him to go through their winter quarters to find some one to identify him. Meeting A. G. Reger, of Philippi, he was released. Jacob Burner, of Pocahontas County, found the saddle three years after the war, hanging where he had left it.

In writing to his wife and children, December 4, 1862, from Camp Washington, Augusta County, he said: "We are with J. D. Imboden, and on the 9th of last month captured a company at St. George, Tucker County, with all their stores." This letter was written with a pen made of elder. He also speaks in this letter of the hardships that he had endured in the past eighteen months as a scout, and that he was "urged by his friends to accept a more honorable position in a regiment." He received the appointment from the War Department shortly after as Major of the 62d Virginia Regiment. He had served as Major of the Militia while he lived in Taylor County, and was very well versed in military tactics. He was with Imboden when he made the attack on Beverly, April 24, 1863, and on the 25th, with part of Captain Taylor's company and some others, he came down to General Garrett's old camp at the foot of Lauruel Hill in pursuit of Colonel Latham's command, which had retreated from Beverly. His men camped for the night, and he came home, it being the last night he ever spent with his family. The next morning he left home and the writer went with him to where the house of John Pharis now stands—one mile above Belington—and leaving him, he said, "Be good to your mother." He and his men hurried toward Philippi, and in his diary he says that he and fourteen others made a dash on Philippi, causing the enemy considerable fright. Colonel Mulligan and some of his officers were near Big Rock, which has since been partly taken away to macadamize the main street of the town, and it is said that they came on them so suddenly that the Colonel lost his hat, and as he went galloping into camp he hallooed: "Fire that cannon," while he was still between the Rebels and the guns. The Rebels fell back and camped on the bank of the river near Washington Jones' and the next night camped at the the Hillery Place, near where the town of Mabie now is in Randolph County, and the next day fell in with Imboden near Buckhannon.*

On the night of of September 25, 1863, he, with a large troop of men,

---

*For further mention of Major Lang's expedition into Barbour, see the History of Randolph page 260.

captured thirty of General Averell's men at the Burned House, at the crossing of Cheat River, on the Seneca Trail.* He went into their camp under disguise, after they had lain down, and, ascertained their number and position, and returned to his men on the mountain, and captured the company, all but one man who made his escape. His intention had been to surprise a company stationed at Belington; but finding this company at the river, he took it and returned South. In a letter written to his wife July 13, 1864, from Blair's House near Washington, he said, he had been under fire every day since May 7, and had marched over 600 miles, and had escaped with nothing more than a few holes through his clothing, until the day before. He had been given the post of honor, and was put in front, and drove the enemy five miles to the fort. In the fight his spur was struck by a ball which slightly disabled him. The spur saved his foot from amputation. On September 5, 1864, while commanding the skirmish line at Bunker Hill, eight miles below Winchester, he fell mortally wounded, and died the next day at Winchester, having been carried off the field by his comrades. He said that "If he could see his wife and little children he could die happy," and that he "asked no greater compensation from the Confederate government for his services than the education of his children." As you enter the Stonewall Cemetery, at Winchester, from the south gate his grave is the second on the right of the sleeping Virginians, marked by a plain marble slab, (the same as all the Virginians) "Lieut. Col. David B. Lang, 62d Va. Reg., Died Sept. 6, 1864." He believed in the virtue and triumph of the cause he had espoused, and said in one of his letters to his wife that, " If this unholy war should last until my youngest son is eighteen years old, you would inspire such patriotism in each of them that they would shoulder their muskets in defense of their country." In another he said, "I shall see Virginia free or be buried beneath her sod." He was a cool and brave officer, respected and beloved by his men. He was always delighted to be in command of the skirmish line, and was cheerful and hopeful in all vicissitudes of life.

Colonel Lang was sued on a security debt a year or so before the war, and, having some creditors of his own who desired to be secured, he gave a deed of trust on his property, and his wife signed her interest in it. It was not sold until after the close of the war, when it took everything to pay off his debts, and left his wife and children without anything, but courage; yet there was never a murmur or regret that she had signed her interest to secure his creditors. Their children were, Winfield S., who married Catherine Fitzwater; Margaret E., who married Marshall Scott; Martha P. married Jesse Phillips and died 1888; Payton P. married Alice Gainer and died 1895; David B. married Grace V. Vanscoy; George W.

---

*See page 263 of the Randolph History.

married Ella Wilmoth. The last three lived in Randolph County Mrs. Lang died November 19, 1898, at the home of her son, David, near Kierans, Randolph County, at the age of 70 years.

WINFIELD SCOTT LANG, born 1852 in Taylor County, son of Colonel David B. and Elizabeth (Powell) Lang, was married near Meadowville in 1872 to Catherine, daughter of Jesse and Sarah (Harris) Fitzwater. Children, Emma Olive, Thurman, John Lemuel, Minnie A., Jesse David, Boyd Otto, Martha Susan. He belongs to the M. E. Church, South; is a Democrat and a farmer, residing on Glady Creek. The office of Assessor for the eastern district was held by him in 1882, and for several terms he was Justice of the Peace. He assisted in collecting data for this History of Barbour County, his work lying chiefly in Barker, Glade and Cove Districts.

MYRON CARLETON LOUGH was born four miles south of Philippi, June 25, 1870, and is a member of the Baptist Church and of the Junior O. U. A. M. He was reared on a farm. Until sixteen years of age his winters were spent in the country schools and his summers on his grandfather's farm. He began teaching in his seventeenth year. When he was eighteen he led the county in the teachers' examination, giving him a standing in the teachers' ranks. He attended the summer normal school taught by Prof. J. F. Ogden, at Philippi, W. Va., for three years, and received much inspiration from that noble man. At the age of twenty he entered the Business College run in connection with the West Virginia Normal and Classical Academy at Buckhannon. He paid his tuition there by teaching in the school. In the spring of 1891, one month before he was twenty-one years of age, he was elected County Superintendent of Free Schools of Barbour County, on the Republican ticket. In the fall of the same year he entered the M. E. Conference Seminary at Buckhannon, from which institution he graduated in 1894, having completed both the scientific and normal courses, with the degree of Bachelor of Pedagogy. The next year was spent at the same institution, and he was graduated from the classical department. While at the Seminary he was on three annual contest debates, winning two and losing one. He has the record of being on for more public performances than any person who has ever graduated at the Seminary. He was the orator of the class of 1894.

In 1895 he received a scholarship at Denison University, Granville, Ohio. He attended that institution one year. His reputation as an orator and debater followed him there. He was chosen to represent the the leading society of the University and won a cash prize of $40—no small honor for a West Virginia boy. In the summers of '95 and '96 he and Mr. C. I. Zirkle taught very successful summer schools at Belington, Barbour County. At the close of their last normal there, Messrs. Lough & Zirkle purchased the Philippi Republican, Mr. Lough being elected principal of the Graded Schools at Belington at the same time. In 1897 he was elected to his present position, that of teacher in the Fairmont State Normal School. While teaching at Fairmont he has been pursuing work leading to the Bachelor of Arts degree, at the West Virginia University. He is now a Senior at that institution. He will take the degree the present year, as he has been granted a leave of absence from the Normal School until the spring term of 1900. Take it all in all, Mr. Lough's life has been a very busy one, as will be noticed from the great number of things he has accomplished while securing his education. He has earned every dollar of money spent on his education and is now entirely out of debt. He claims December 25, 1898, as the happiest day of his life, for it was upon that day that the sweetheart of his youth, Miss Emma Parks, also of Barbour County, became his wife. They seem to have many years of usefulness before them.

Mr. Lough is a graceful and forceful writer, both in prose and verse. The following is from his pen:

THEY'RE SMARTER'N US.

I've read the papers a good deal of late
Of boys with nothing who've made themselves great.
It makes me so blamed discouraged sometimes,
Out here on the farm of brambles an' vines.
That I almost wish I'd never been born.
All day a-plowin' an' hoein' the corn
Ain't very much fun to a feller like me,
Who'd like to be something, but knows he can't be.
I tell you what, Jim, I'm down in the mouth,
When I read of the boys in the North an' the South
Who've ris from the lowest an' porest of homes,
While I'm left a-diggin' in these ol' stones.
An' Jim, my ol' boy, you're right here with me,
There's a reason fer 't all, as plain as can be;
We'd as well give in, an' without any fuss,
  They're smarter'n us, Jim,
  They're smarter'n us.

I read t'other day that our own congressman
Was once a young lad all yellow an' tan
With the rays of the sun; that he worked all the day
From morning till night; never had time to play:
But now jes look at him and see what he's done.
Can't explain it, you say? 't's as easy as fun.
I've thought it all out an' see it, you mus'.
  He's smarter'n us, Jim,
  He's smarter'n us.

An' our President, Jim, was once a pore lad,
Worked hard ever' day in good weather and bad;
How he ris is a wonder in some people's mind,
'N' how he managed through all a plain way to find

To come to the front. But, Jim, I know,
An' if you think a minute, you'll see it's so,
That no matter'n what else he put his trus'
    He's *smarter'n* us, Jim,
    He's *smarter'n* us.

There is many another as I've hearn tell
With odds against 'em who've come out well;
But we're too old, Jim, an' its now too late
Fer us to be tryin' to change our fate.
All we can do, then, at this late day
Is to comfort ourselves as ever we say,
"We know it's not fair an' we think its not jus'."
    But they're smarter'n us, Jim,
    They smarter'n us.

Some people may say that's a pore excuse;
But I've seen it tried, and what's the use
Of a feller who's built for the farm and the plow
To make a to-do an' a great pow-wow
An' try to be somethin'. Jim, do as you please,
I'll not try to catch 'em, but live at my ease,
An' run my ol' plow, just to keep off the rus'.
    For they're smarter'n us, Jim,
    They're smarter'n us.

Great people are not always happy, I'm told,
But ever are greedy and graspin' fer gold;
An' seekin' fer honors still higher than they
Have ever seen a comin' their way.
Forever impatient an' lookin' ahead,
They'll never be satisfied till they are dead,
An' all of their bones hev returned to the dus',
    But they're smarter'n *us*, Jim,
    They're smarter'n *us*.

An' will they be satisfied when they are dead?
Will each have a golden crown then on his head?
'F it's true what I've heard 'bout a few of them, Jim,
'T strikes me their chances 'll be pretty slim.
But they ought to be satisfied, don't you think so?
For all through this wilderness down here below,
Whether counted as wrong, er reckoned as jus',
    They've been smarter'n us, Jim,
    Been smarter'n us.

WILLIS LANTZ, born 1853, near his present home, son of William and Martha (Woods) Lantz, was married at the old Sturm homestead, February 13, 1876, to Arminda, daughter of Jesse and Delita Ann Sturm. Children, Pheny, David, Thomas, Estella, Martha Ann, Athie Minerva, Willis, Ertle. He is a Missionary Baptist, an Odd Fellow, a Democrat, a farmer and blacksmith, and lives near Calhoun where he owns 320 acres, mostly improved.

Myron Carleton Lough.

William Judson Bartlett.   Columbus Kelley.

FAMILY HISTORY. 425

His great grandfather came from Germany and settled on Peck's Run. Mrs. Lantz's grandfather was Colonel Henry Sturm; and her grandfather, Thomas Wood, came from New York to West Virginia. The father of Mr. Lantz served in the Confederate army, and his uncle, Henry Lantz, was killed at the battle of Gettysburg. He was elected president of the county court in 1896.

WILLIAM HENRY LANTZ, born 1862 near Buckhannon, son of William and Martha (Woods) Lantz. On January 11, 1885, in Barbour, he was married to Marietta Sturm. Children, Ida Belle, Idella, Florida May, Willie A., Lovy Grace and Baby. He is a member of the M. E. Church, South, and a hard-working, progressive farmer near Calhoun where he owns 120 acres, mostly cultivated or in grass. The fruit on his place is of excellent grade. A new variety of bearded wheat was introduced by him into Barbour. His ancestors were German.

THOMAS ALONZO LAW, born on Hacker's Creek, Lewis County, in 1858, son of Oscar and Barbara (Post) Law, was married November 4, 1880, in Taylor County, to Rozaltha, daughter of John and Elizabeth (McDonald) Cleavenger. Children, John, Arnett, Edison Oscar, George and Ethel. He is a member of the M. P. Church, and belongs to the order of I. O. O. F. and K. of P. He is a Republican and a farmer, residing on Simpson's Creek. His great grandfather Law was a native of Ireland, and his great grandfather Post was from New Jersey. Mr. Law owns 81 acres of highly improved land on Hacker's Creek, in Lewis County. He imported the first Aberdeen-Angus cattle into the northern part of Barbour County, where he moved in 1893.

M

THOMAS JACKSON MURPHY, born 1866, on Haddix Creek, in Tucker County, son of Herbert and Jane Amanda (Price) Murphy; and was married in 1887 on Sugar Creek to Doretta, daughter of Nathan and Lydia C. (Shoemaker) Bennett. Children, Naomi, Ira Hamon, Essie C., Oda May, Charles Gordon, and Wilma Belle. He is a Democrat and farmer, residing on the head of Sugar Creek, where he owns 46 acres, three miles from Meadowville. His father lives in Randolph, near Montrose, and his grandfather, Elder David P. Murphy, was a noted minister of the Primitive Baptist Church.

BENJAMIN FRANKLIN MURPHY, M. D., born 1868 near Burnersville, son of Isaac R. and Nancy (VanGilder) Murphy, was married at the residence of Albert G. Wilson, Philippi, August 3, 1898, to Alice C., daughter of Albert and Jennie (Jones) Wilson. He is a member of the Missionary Baptist Church, an Odd Fellow, in politics a Democrat, and by profession a physician. Dr. Murphy attended school at the West Virginia Conference Seminary at Buckhannon; and then took up the study of medicine in the

Medical College of Virginia, at Richmond, remaining two years and graduating in April, 1895. He located in Philippi, where he built up an extensive and lucrative practice, being frequently called into other counties. Drs. Murphy and Williams performed the first operation in Barbour County for the restoration of double hairlip, being so successful as to greatly relieve the deformity and to establish speech. Dr. Murphy has been especially successful in his treatment of fever, having lost but one case during his practice. On his father's side his ancestors were Irish, and on his mother's side German. His grandfather, Marshall Murphy, came from Virginia.

ANDREW MILLER. This man was one of the pioneers of Barbour and settled in the Coves when that was in Monongalia County, but the exact date of his settlement there has not been ascertained. It was, however, subsequent to April, 1781, for he was at that time living on Cheat River, four miles below St. George, and a ridge named from him is called Miller Hill to this day. He came from the South Branch of Potomac to St. George when sixteen years of age, a member of the colony which John Minear planted on Cheat River in 1776. It is not certain whether Miller was a member of the Horse Shoe Colony, planted by Minear in 1774, and broken up by Indians the same year; but he was certainly a member of the second colony in 1776. He was born February 25, 1760. He remained on Cheat River several years, and in the spring of 1781 accompanied John Minear an others to Clarksburg to meet the land commissioners and obtain certificates on which to base claims for land patents. The disaster which befell them while returning, in which Minear and two others were killed by Indians below Philippi, is fully detailed elsewhere in this book. On that occasion Miller's horse was killed. Sarah, the wife of Andrew Miller, was born January 11, 1756. The names of their children and the dates of birth of each are as follows: John, September 25, 1786; Mary, March 5, 1789; Elizabeth, August 17, 1792; Andrew, August 15, 1794; Susanna, September 5, 1797, Sarah, January 9, 1800. Andrew Miller died on New Year's day, 1834, in his seventy-fourth year. His wife died March 4, 1840, aged eighty-four.

JOHN MILLER, son of Andrew and Sarah Miller, born 1786, was married to Abalonia Baker who was born February 20, 1788, and the names of their children and the dates of their births were as follows: Sarah, born December 26, 1809; Melker, February 20, 1812; Andrew, January 20, 1814; John, April 29, 1816; George, October 25, 1818; Elizabeth, March 16, 1821; Jacob, August 9, 1823; Martin, November 9, 1825; Henry, August 1, 1828. John Miller died May, 12, 1868, and his wife died November 16, 1875.

JACOB MILLER, son of John and Abalonia (Baker) Miller, born 1823, was married November 3, 1848 to a daughter of Nathan and Mary Hall.*

---

*Nathan Hall, born 1799, was married to Mary, daughter of Isaac Means in 1820. He was nearly all his life a Justice of the Peace or a member of the Legislature, and at

FAMILY HISTORY.

The names of their children and the dates of their births are as follows: Mary A., born April 5, 1850; Isaac H., November 2, 1851; Sarah E., December 10, 1853; Nathan W., October 5, 1855; Syrena C., August 13, 1857; Sophrona J., July 2, 1859; John H., January 28, 1863; George W. B., July 22, 1865. Mr. Miller is a member of the M. E. Church, a Republican and a farmer, living on Gap Run, where he owns 250 acres, well stocked. He and his wife have celebrated their golden wedding. On his mother's side, his grandfather, Melker Baker had a gun factory in Pennsylvania. He was several years a captive with the Indians, and made himself useful by repairing their guns.

ANDREW MILLER, son of Andrew and Sarah, born 1794, married Hester Ann Poling, and their children are as follows: John Z., born July 17, 1842; Sarah, March 25 1844; Susanna, July 27, 1846; Lucinda, January 29, 1849; Lucinda, April 18, 1851; Mary, September 17, 1853; Andrew K., September 17, 1855.

ANDREW K. MILLER, married Sophia Shanabarger, and their children were, Theodore, born October 29, 1881; Mattie, March 29; 1883; Addie Grace, 1885; Andrew Boyd, April 1886; George L., January 15, 1888; Floyd, March 23, 1890; Bradford, March 15, 1892; Goldie, January 22, 1894; Benjamin D., November 19, 1895; Brisco, September 25, 1897.

JACOB MCLEAN, born in Randolph County 1838, son of William and Hannah (Wees) McLean, was married March 13, 1862. Children, James William, Samuel Henry, Malissa, Hannan F., Arthur, Charles L., Fleming, Edwin Parsons. He is a member of the M. E. Church, South, a Democrat, and a farmer, living on the Valley River, where he owns 200 acres, with 115 under improvement. His son Samuel is a graduate of the Fairmont Normal School, and studied law in the West Virginia University. He is now principal of the Beverly school, and is an able and progressive educator. Another son, Arthur, is a minister in the M. E. Church, South, and is now preaching on the Cedar Grove Circuit, Kanawha County. Mr. McLean is post master at Orpha, Barbour County.

ISAAC D. MARTIN, born in Cove District, 1878, son of Isaac and Susanna (Knotts) Martin. He is a member of the M. E. Church, belongs to the society of Modern Woodmen, of the Masons, of the Junior O. U. A. M., and in politics is a Republican, and in business is a clothing merchant at Belington, and is joint editor of the Belington *Independent*, and an enterprising business man. He was educated in the public schools.

ROBERT ANDREW MCCUTCHEON, born 1833, son of James and Ellen (Benson) McCutcheon, was married at Beverly in 1861, to Margaret, daughter of George and Elizabeth (Hart) Buckey. Children, Almonta Benson, George P., Golden Frank, Howard Kerr, and Robert E. He is a Meth-

one time he owned part of the land on which Grafton now stands. He died in 1846, and his wife in 1863. They had eleven children.

odist, an Odd Fellow and a Republican. He is post master at Belington, and proprietor of Mountain View Hotel, and was educated in the schools of Staunton and Washington College and Massay Creek Academy. From 1868 to 1872 he was Superintendent of the schools of Barbour. His paternal ancestors were Scotch Irish; and his brother, J. S. K. McCutcheon, was a Colonel in the Confederate army, and now lives at Exeter, California.

GEORGE MCKINNEY, first of the name in Barbour, came from Ireland to Virginia, and later to Overfield in what is now Barbour. He had married Mary James, a Welsh woman, and their children were, Nancy, who married Jacob Talbott; Sally, who married Samuel Talbott; Margaret who married a Mr. Dennison; Polly, a school teacher; Joseph William, who married Mary Reed; George who married Margaret, daughter of Simeon Harris. George had a family of the following names: Mary, who was married to Levi Phillips; Hannah, who was married to Daniel Poling; Sarah who married Silas Talbott; Nancy, who married George Phillips; Elizabeth, Pheobe, who married Joseph Poling; Catherine, who married Hamilton G. Bartlett; David James, who married Sarah St. Clair; Rachel, Bessheba, who married Thomas Pepper. The children of James McKinney were, Melissa Victoria, Thaddeus G., Berthena, Clinton T., Cleophus J., Lair D., Florence and William Delbert. The last named was born in 1868, and on August 2, 1897, married Stella McDonald. They have one child, Nellie.

CLINTON T. MCKINNEY, born 1856, son of David J. and Sarah (St. Clair) McKinney, was married October 20, 1887, to Lucinda A., daughter of David and Susan Virginia (Williamson) Sturm. Children, Guy Everett, Way David James, Frederick Glenn. He is a Missionary Baptist, a Democrat, and a farmer, living on Sand Run, where he owns 110 acres. He was educated at the West Virginia College at Flemington.

JONATHAN EMORY MEANS, born 1854 in Marion County, son of James C. and Mary (Case) Means, was married September 20, 1877, at Palatine, West Virginia, to Olive, daughter of Eugenus E. and Drusilla (Burner) Lyman. Children, Edna, Maggie, George Howard, Lelia, Bertha May and Sally. He is a member of the M. E. Church, an Odd Fellow, a Republican and a carpenter, residing at Philippi. He served three years in the Federal army, and his father was a volunteer for the Mexican War, but was never called into service. His grandfather Means, was a native of Pennsylvanian, born in 1800 and died in 1895; his father was born 1826, and his mother in 1830, and died 1889.

LAIR DAVIS MORRALL, born October 12, 1814, son of Samuel M. and Elizabeth (Davis) Morrall, was married 1843 to Elizabeth, daughter of Henry Harper. Children, Elizabeth Virginia, Albina Louisa, Samuel Henry, Lucy Amanda. Mrs. Morrall was born in 1818, at the Burnt Bridge, above Beverly. Soon after their marriage they moved to the newly formed county of Barbour, and from that time until his death, Mr. Morrall was constantly identified with the county's interests, for the most of the time being an officer. A detailed account of his services in that capacity will be found elsewhere in this book. Mrs. Morrall, who died in 1893, was for ten years the only Presbyterian in Philippi; and she assisted in building the first church of that denomination in the county, which was erected at Belington under the immediate patronage of Mrs. Jacob See. The ancestors of Mr. Morrall were early settlers in Virginia; his grandfather, Samuel, marrying in 1757, and having a family as follows: Elizabeth, Jane, John, Rachel, Samuel, Mary, Sarah, William D., James, Jessie, Esther. Of these, Samuel was the father of Lair D. Morrall, and was born in 1767.

JOHN C. MANN, born 1836 in Rockingham County, Virginia, son of Oliver and Harriett (Cathrea) Mann, was married May 2, 1867, at Meadowville, to Sally, daughter of William and Lydia (Wells) Johnson. Children, William M., Okey J., Anna A., Daisy E., J. Rush, Oliver, John Bassell. He is a member of the Baptist Church, of the Odd Fellows, a farmer and plasterer, and lives on the Beverly and Fairmont pike, one mile west of Philippi. He served four years in the Confederate army, seeing his first service at Philippi, June 3, 1861. At Rich Mountain he saw his next service, and from there fell back with the Confederates to the Alleghanies, and later fought Hunter at Lynchburg and was in active duty, surrendering at the close of the war at Harrisonburg. He was taken prisoner at Cold Knobb, Greenbrier County, in December, 1862, and was sent to Camp Chase. His son Rush, enlisted in the army in 1898 for the war against Spain. Mr. Mann's ancestors were English and Irish. Henry Mann, one of his ancestors, more than a century ago was apprenticed as a turner in London, and the article of indenture is still preserved by the family. On his mother's side, his grandmother, Sophia Lewis, daughter of Thomas Lewis, was a niece of Colonel Charles Lewis, who was killed at the battle of Point Pleasant in 1774.

SUSAN MONTGOMERY, born in Cove District, 1847, daughter of Samuel and Sarah (Sturm) Digman, was married December 20, 1863, to Adam, son of Samuel and Nancy (Edwards) Montgomery. Children, John, Sarah E., Clorinda C., Nancy J., Mary A., Samuel B., Bertie C. and William S. Mr. Montgomery was a member of the M. P. Church, and in politics was a Democrat, residing at Tunnelton, Preston County.

SABEUS MAIN, born in Green County, Pennsylvania, 1832, son of Joseph and Lydia (Mariner) Main, was married March 12, 1894, at Philippi, to Sarah Jane, daughter of William F. and Jane (Booth) Wilson. He is a member of the Missionary Baptist Church and belongs to the G. A. R. He is a farmer, residing two miles south of Philippi. He was in the Union army three years. Mrs. Main's first husband was William M. Simpson, and they were married in 1847; her second husband was Henson L. Yoke, married in 1870. Mr. Main is her third husband.

JETHRO MOORE, born 1857, son of William and Sally (Bennett) Moore, was married in 1878 to Ellen, daughter of H. and Sarah (Ramsey) Coonts. Children, Cora, Ernest, Lizzie, Walter, Frank, Charles, William, Mattie, Albina, Ada Dale. He is a member of the U. B. Church, of the Junior O. U. A. M., and in politics is a Democrat, and by occupation a miner at Junior. He was educated in the public schools, and in 1893 was constable.

SAMUEL ALBA MOORE, born 1870 near Meadowville, son of Jasper and Melissa (Holsberry) Moore, was married at Philippi, March 3, 1895, to Estrella, daughter of Mrs. Laura A. Peck. Their daughter is named Mildred Margerie. He is a member of the M. E. Church, South, is an Odd Fellow and a Mason, and by occupation a merchant at Philippi. Mr. Moore was raised on a farm, began teaching when fifteen years old, and taught three years in this county. Then he was traveling salesman in this State for three years, at the expiration of that time going to New York as general agent for the Brown Manufacturing Company. In 1893 he returned to Philippi and took charge of the affairs of Moore & Holsberry, two years later succeeding to the business, and has continued in that capacity ever since, meeting with great success in his undertakings.

SANFORD MASON, born in 1822 in what is now Taylor County, son of Thomas N. and Lydia (Goodwin) Mason, was married December 5, 1839, near Pruntytown, to Rosanna, daughter of Edward and Nancy (Prunty) Fleming. Children, Emily, Edward J., Elmore, Perry P., Mary Etta, John F., Lydia Jane and Thomas N. He is a member of the Missionary Baptist Church, a Republican, a farmer living on the waters of Pleasant Creek. Mr. Mason was one of the first superintendents of the Fairmont and Beverly pike, was three times elected Justice of the Peace. The grandfather, Thomas T. Mason, came from New Hampshire and settled in Harrison County, and the grandfather on his mother's side, Franklin Goodwin, came from England, and according to a custom of the time, was sold into servitude for a stated time to pay for his passage across the sea, and he afterwards settled in Harrison County, now Taylor. Thomas T. Mason was born in Taylor County in 1794, and his wife two years later. He fought in the War 1812. The subject of this sketch came to Barbour in 1847 and settled on the river where he lived till 1865. His Grandfather Mason's children were Nancy, Martha and Benjamin, and his father's were Sarah, Mary, Nancy, Sanford, Henson, Harrison and Thomas N. Pruntytown was named from the father of Nancy Prunty.

THOMAS BYRNE MASON, born 1833 in Maryland, son of William F. and Jane Mason, was married September 23, 1869, to Catherine, daughter of Nestor and Margaret (Stalnaker) Hardin. Children, William Nestor, Margaret Jane and Estella Blanche. He belongs to the M. E. Church, is a Mason, a Democrat and a farmer, living on Sandy Creek, where he owns 364 acres of improved land. He attended school at Garner Valley, and was a teamster in the Civil War, and for six years was a member of the county court. His father died 1878, and was a native of Preston County; his mother died 1872. They had five daughters and two sons.

REV. JOHN F. MASON, born 1850 near Philippi, son of Sanford and Rosanna (Fleming) Mason, was married December 28, 1876, at Pleasant Creek, to Margaret Martha, daughter of John and Mary (Zirkle) Lough. Children, Ida V., Leslie A., and Alley and Calley (twins). He is a minister in the Missionary Baptist Church, a farmer and stockraiser. He owns 233 acres of improved land, and was the first man in Barbour to engage extensively in the sheep business. For twenty-five years he has been in the ministry, laboring in Taylor, Harrison, Marion, Lewis, Tucker, Preston and Doddridge, having had charge of thirteen churches in all; marrying forty couple, adding 250 members to the church, and preaching 800 sermons.

ORESTES T. MARKS, born 1873 on Camp Run, son of Lemuel and Indiana (Talbott) Marks, was married on Pleasant Creek, August 18, 1895, to Adah, daughter of Lewis and Terrena (Woodford) Lough. Children, Lotus, Arnett D., Olen E. He is a Baptist and a farmer, living on Flag Run, Taylor County. He was educated at the West Virginia College, Flemington.

He was two years a member of the board of examiners for teachers. He taught six years in Barbour. On his father's side his grandfather was Benjamin Marks, and on his mother's side, Jesse Jenkins, a Revolutionary soldier.

O

SALATHIEL LANE O'NEAL, elected in 1896 to the position of County Surveyor, was educated at Hillsdale, Michigan. In politics he is a Democrat; he is an Odd Fellow and belongs to no church, although a believer in religion. He is noted for his inventive ability, and is the inventor of a platting, drafting and self-computing machine; a transit compass, and a telemeter for computing distances between distant objects, such as ships at sea or from one mountain to another. His district map of Barbour County was constantly consulted as the highest authority in compiling this history of Barbour. The map is on a scale of 200 poles to the mile, the largest yet made of the county.

P

MELVILLE PECK (autobiography). The first sentence in David Copperfield is, "I am born." This was my introduction into the world, as I am informed, on January 3, 1855, in that beautiful and fertile portion of Barbour County, Virginia, (now West Virginia), known as Elk district, on Isaac's Run, one-half mile west of the Ebenezer Church. A small mansion house still marks the place. I received a limited education in the free schools, and the West Virginia College, began teaching at the age of eighteen, taught eight schools, entered the mercantile business as a clerk in February 1877, became the acting member of the firm of Crim and Peck in 1879, sold out the business in 1880, was admitted to the bar in December 1881, located at Clarksburg, entered the law department of the West Virginia University, September 1882, received the degree of LL. B., June 1883, located in Philippi, July 4, 1883, where I still live and practice my profession. With J. H. Knapp, Esq., as a partner, on May 9, 1889, we issued the first number of *The Tygart's Valley Star*, a weekly newspaper, at Philippi. After a time Mr. Knapp retired from the firm, and his place was taken by my wife who superintended the office, and did much of the writing, till the plant was sold in 1891. This paper was aimed to be a leader, not a follower, of public sentiment. In 1892, I was elected Prosecuting Attorney of this county, and held the office four years. During this term the two famous murder trials of Russell and Chambers were had in our circuit court, resulting in the acquittal of the former and the conviction of the latter. Twice it has been my lot to be Mayor of Philippi, and during my first term I was arrested by a constable, the only time in my life, for moving a saw-mill off the street. My course was fully vindicated by the courts from the two justices who tried me to the Supreme Court of Appeals. The second term was resigned because a majority of the councilmen held different views from me on the liquor question in the town. In the beginning of my law practice, I recorded deeds at twenty-five cents each, by the kindness of L. C. Elliott, Esq., Clerk of the county court, held the office of commissioner of accounts, and later commissioner in chancery, all of which were in due time given up for an increasing law practice.

My grand father, on the paternal side, Josiah Peck, was born in Virginia, January 31, 1778, was married to Sarah Smith, a Virginia lady, January 24, 1808, served as a captain in the War of 1812, died in Roane County, West Virginia, about the year 1874. Of this union five daughters and two sons were born. Nelson Peck, the elder son, married Hannah Means, of Logan County, Ohio; lived and prospered there to a ripe old age and died without children. Josiah Peck, Jr., was born in Augusta County, Virginia, June 13, 1819, was married to Laura A. Matheney, daughter of William and Jane (Grim) Matheney, and grand daughter of John and Elizabeth Grim, October 12, 1846, and to them were born nine children in the following order: Nelson, Henderson, George Washington, Melville, Columbus, Marcellus Ethelbert, Chesley R., Ira Aldus, and Estella Maud, wife of Samuel A. Moore. Two of the sons, Columbus and Ira A., are dead, two are ministers of the Gospel, two are physicians, and two are lawyers. Our mother was born January 24, 1829, and is still living. Father died April 13, 1880.

On August 4, 1876, I was united in marriage with Cora May Crim, only daughter of Hon. J. N. B. Crim and Almira J. (Hall) Crim, of Elk City, this County. On the paternal side my wife is the granddaughter of Michael Crim and Catharine (Strickler) Crim, and the great granddaughter of Peter

CHARLES W. SHOMO. JAMES K. WARE.

Crim and Elizabeth (Shaffer) Crim, of Rockingham County, Virginia. On the maternal side, she is the granddaughter of Hon. John N. Hall and Harriett (Rightmire) Hall, and the great granddaughter of Samuel Hall and Elizabeth (Owens) Hall, and was born in Philippi, October 31, 1859. We have two sons and one daughter: MWood Crim, Herbert Cromwell, and Edna Gay, all of whom have completed their second year in college, this June '99, the sons at the West Virginia University and daughter, at R. M. W. C., Lynchburg, Va. We are members of the M. E. Church, South, at Dogget Chapel, Philippi.

CAPTAIN JOHN RILEY PHILLIPS, born August 24, 1839, near Meadowville, son of James and Osa (Johnson) Phillips, grandson of Jacob Phillips, great grandson of Isaac, and great-great-grandson of Moses Phillips, an Englishman who settled on the South Branch, and subsequently in Randolph County. Isaac Phillips married Miss Kittle, of Randolph, and Jacob married Sarah Bennett. Osa Johnson was a daughter of John Johnson and granddaughter of Robert Johnson, a Scotchman. The subject of this sketch had one sister, Sarah Ann, and no brother. His parents were very poor, possessed but little education, married young and settled first in the eastern part of Barbour, then a wild region. Subsequently they moved to Clover Creek, which was still wilder, and again they moved, this time to Brushy Fork in Barbour, where they made a permanent home. John Riley Phillips was a man of unusually brilliant mind. Had he been educated he would probably have gained a national reputation as a thinker and lecturer. He was an orator of unusual ability, and a careful reader of such books as came within his reach. His education was limited to the schools of the neighborhood. Among his teachers was William Furguson who made a deep impression upon the young man's mind. A literary society in that neighborhood, attended by Captain Phillips, Captain A. C. Bowman and others, was an association for good, and in point of intellectual strength its equal could be found in few rural districts anywhere.

Captain Phillips and Captain Bowman studied law at home, intending to go to Texas to enter professional life; but their plans never matured. The Civil War came on, and they espoused the cause of the South, were the very first in the field, marched to Grafton, retreated to Philippi, fled to Beverly, joined Garnett's army; were in that general's retreat from Laurel Hill, and were separated in the route. Phillips fought through the entire war, in some of the hardest battles, in victory and defeat. He received wounds from which he never recovered, although he lived till October 24, 1894. On March 7, 1867, he was married to Elizabeth E. Parks, and had one child, May. The lines of Gray can be applied with truth to Captain Phillips:

> Full many a gem of purest rays serene
> The dark, unfathomed caves of ocean bear;
> Full many a flower is born to blush unseen
> And waste its sweetness on the desert air.

SAMUEL ELLIOTT PHILLIPS, born in Randolph County, 1832, son of Eli and Mary (Kittle) Phillips, was married November 9, 1854, near Meadowville, to Sarah, daughter of James L. and Prudence (Phillips) Yeager. Children, Prudence, Elam H., Cordelia, Naomi, Louisa A., Irvin, Rebecca, Octava, Virginia J. and Joshua Corder, who was born December 15, 1875 and died April 20, 1899. He is a Democrat and a farmer, living on Glady Creek, where he owns 96 acres, nearly all improved, and partly underlaid with a three-foot vein of coal. There is an excavation and a ruin on his land which have been supposed to be traces of a furnace. It has been attributed to Indians. It should be borne in mind, however, that Indians were unacquainted with the process of smelting ores, and mined nothing except native copper, which they could hammer into shape. Therefore, if the ruin really was a furnace, it was probably made by the first white settlers, and the circumstances of its building have been forgotten.

WASHINGTON PHILLIPS, born 1846 on Glady Creek, son of William and Delila (Coonts) Phillips, was married on Gladys Creek in 1868, to Eliza, daughter of Samuel and Jemmia (Taylor) Wilmoth. Children, Charles L. and Ida May. He is a member of the German Baptist Church, in politics is a Democrat, and by occupation a farmer on Glady Creek, where he owns 160 acres, half improved. He has held the office of Constable eight years and Justice four years in Glade District, and has lived in Barbour all his life.

GRANVILLE PHILLIPS, born 1843, near Meadowville, son of George and Nancy (McKinney) Phillips, and he was married December 17, 1865, to Julia Ann, daughter of John and Sarah (Hines) Sherman. Children, Rachel, Elizabeth, Ruhama, Catherine, George Monroe. He is a Baptist; in politics a Republican, and is a member of the G. A. R., and by occupation is a farmer, living one mile below Philippi. He served eleven months in the Confederate army, then joined the Union army, and served till the end of the war, experiencing many hardships, both on the march and in the field. His great grandfather, Isaac Phillips, came from England and settled near Meadowville, and his grandfather, Noah Phillips, lived near the same place. On his mother's side, his grandmother was Peggy McKinley, of Irish ancestry. Mrs. Phillips' first husband was Henry Isner, and they had two children, James B. and Sarah Rosanna. The former married Virginia Poling. Rachel E. married Isaac Lantz, and Monroe married Mary Snyder. The Shermans were Germans and came to West Virginia from Virginia.

JAMES MARION PHILLIPS, born 1852, near Meadowville, son of Simeon and Susanna (Fitzwater) Phillips, was married March 14, 1876, to Masalona, daughter of Isaac and Mary Coonts, and was married a second time, November 1, 1890, at Philippi, to Evaline, daughter of Daniel and Harriet (Kittle) Boyles. Children, Gilbert H., Dota Susanna, Lummie Ruth, Burnett D.,

Erca May. He is a member of the M. E. Church, South, is an Odd Fellow, a Democrat and a farmer, living near Calhoun, where his farm of 120 acres is nearly all improved. He introduced the variety of potatoes known as the Early Harvest into Barbour. He was educated in the public schools. On his father's side, his people were English and German; on his mother's side his grandfather, John Fitzwater, was a native of Hardy County, and came to Barbour at an early day.

THE POLING FAMILY. These people were very early settlers in Barbour, but all efforts to trace them to a common ancestor have been fruitless. They are connected with a family of the same name in Hampshire County, and it is said that they originally came from New Jersey and that the name was Poland, so called from the country from which they came to America. But this cannot be stated with certainty, for the evidence is not conclusive. In the early records of Randolph County the name was always spelled Poland. In 1806, Elizabeth, daughter of Peter Poland, was married to John Johnson, by Robert Maxwell, a Justice of the Peace. In 1809, George Nestor was married to Millie, daughter of Martin Poland, by Simeon Harris. In 1810, Martin Poland was married to Mary, daughter of William Wilson, grandfather of Lewis Wilson. In 1815 the name is spelled Poling for the first time. In that year Jonas Poling was married to Phoebe, daughter of Cary Headley. Simeon Harris solemnized the ceremony. In 1816 Samuel Poling was married to Elizabeth Marks, and in the same year Andrew Foreman married Rachel Poland, and Martin Poling married Annie, daughter of William Right.

ISAAC S. POLING, born 1832, died 1897, was a son of Barnett and Jennie (Sturm) Poling, and was married July 27, 1867, at Churchville, Virginia, to Louisa May, daughter of William and Mary Ann (Keshner) Rogers. Children, William B., Mary Jane, George Franklin, Lloyd, Lucinda, Luther, Minnie L., Susan Virginia and Appie. He was a member of the M. E. Church, was a Democrat, and a farmer living on Whitman Run, where he owned 126 acres, nearly all improved; and still in possession of his widow. He served three years in the Confederate army under Imboden, and took part in many battles. He was a prisoner of war six months. His grandfather came from Maryland. Mrs. Poling's people came from Holland and were early settlers in the Valley of Virginia.

REV. CYRUS POLING, born on the old Poling homestead, July 28, 1850, son of George and Rachel (Kelley) Poling, was married April 8, 1873, near Meadowville, to Loretta, daughter of Jacob and Catherine (Stalnaker) Hudkins. Children, May, born February 11, 1874; George Jacob Webster, born December 3, 1877; Lulu Braxie, born April 19, 1880; Odie Belle, born December 11, 1883; Minnie Blanche, born April 23, 1888; Nora Beverly, born September 15, 1890. The subject of this sketch taught school thirteen years in Barbour County. He entered the ministey of the M. E. Church in

1877, and since that time he has officiated in 113 marriages, and has received 3000 into the church. He has aided in the building of twenty-three houses of worship. Among the places of his labor are Webster, Sutton, Fremansburg, Belington, Troy, Beverly, Elkins, Tunnelton, Pruntytown, Bridgeport, Farmington. He now resides at the latter place. He was educated at the West Virginia College at Flemington. He owns 165 acres, mostly improved and underlaid with coal. His son Webster owns 115 acres, devoted to graizing and fruit. His daughter May, married Dr. R. M. McMillan, of Wheeling. Rev. Poling's mother is a daughter of Samuel and Delila (Rolands) Kelley. She was married October 14, 1849. Rev. Poling's father was a son of Amos and Sarah Poling, born 1822, died 1895.

ALDINE S. POLING, thirty-two years old, son of Isaac and Elfenzine (Corder) Poling, was married at Philippi, to Lizzie W., daughter of Major Edward F. Grant. They have two children. Mr. Poling graduated at the West Virginia University, and soon afterwards began the publication of the *Barbour Democrat*, to which he has since given his attention.

WADE POLING, born 1869, son of Isaac and Jane E. (Elliott) Poling, was married October 9, 1895, to Rosa V., daughter of Josiah H. and Sarah (Miller) Ekis. Children, Dellet T. and Cecil R. He is a member of the M. E. Church, South, is a Democrat and a farmer, residing on Glady Creek, where he owns 303 acres, of which 285 acres are cleared. He cuts 35 stacks of hay, raises from 100 to 200 bushels of wheat, and from 500 1000 bushels of corn annually, which he feeds to his stock. He can graze thirty head of three-year-olds, and takes special interest in growing cattle and sheep. His farm is all underlaid with coal, and has a good ledge of limestone on the "Streets Farm," which adjoins his other lands. His father was born in 1836, son of James and Elizabeth (Vannoy) Poling, and was married (1865) to Elfenzie S. Corder, who died in 1867, leaving one child, Aldine S. Poling, editor of the *Barbour Democrat*. In 1868 he married Jane E. Elliott, daughter of Colonel William Elliott, of Belington, from which union six children were born, viz.: Wade, Etta, Solomon, (deceased), Frona, Bertie, and Rebecca Elizabeth, who died in 1891.

ISAAC M. POLING, born 1833, near Valley Furnace, son of Jacob and Louisa Poling, was married near Calhoun, May 3, 1888, to Mary A., daughter of Marshall and Sarah J. (Galliher) Phillips. Children, Minnie Belle, Orange Glenn and Lulu Blanche. He is a member of the Christian Church, in politics is a Democrat, and by occupation a farmer and teacher, residing near Calhoun. He was educated in normal schools of Barbour County. In 1892 he was elected Assessor of Barbour County, (east side), and served four years. He taught twelve years in the public schools of Barbour; now owns 66 acres of highly improved land, and is one of the leading men of his part of the county, being an able advocate of enlightened methods of farming, and an influential member of the Democratic party.

FAMILY HISTORY.

IRA C. POLING, son of Martin G. and Rebecca (Stemple) Poling, was born near the George Poling farm, June 15, 1867, and on September 11, 1888, at Nestorville, he was married to Rosa Belle, daughter of Jesse and Mary (Sturm) Stalnaker. Children, Raymond, born September, 3, 1890; Jessie M., September 4, 1893; Nora B., October 19, 1895, and Virgia M., July 2, 1898. Mrs. Poling was born October, 25, 1869. Mr. Poling is a member of the M. E. Church, and is a farmer, living two miles east of Philippi, where he owns 115 acres of improved lands, underlaid with coal. He was educated in the public schools of Barbour. Mrs. Poling's grandfather was Henry Stalnaker.

MRS. RACHEL H. POLING, born at the old Howell homestead, 1850, daughter of Nehemiah and Rebecca (Limbers) Howell, was married December 9, 1869, to James W., son of Martin and Sarah (Wells) Poling. Children, Sylvester, Alice M., Rosa Belle, Sarah R., George H. She is a member of the Missionary Baptist Church, and was educated in the public schools. She is proprietor of the Pennsylvania Hotel at Davis, Tucker County, West Virginia. Her son Sylvester, married Appie V. Parks; her daughter Rosa, married Nelson T. Bowman, and Sarah married James T. Darkey of Old Town, Maryland.

LOMAN SALATHIEL POLING, born on Teter's Creek in 1859, son of Emory and Catherine (Gainer) Poling, was married in Randolph County in 1880 to Genetta Estelline, daughter of Solomon and Mary Jane (Triplett) Ferguson. Children, Maudie A., Mattie E., Emory L., Solomon F., J. S., Hattie P. and Lulu G. Mr. Poling is a Democrat, and a farmer with good buildings, residing on Teter's Creek, where he owns a farm; also a mountian farm in Tucker County. He has taught nineteen terms of school in Randolph, Tucker and Barbour Counties. Mrs. Poling, a granddaughter of Robert Ferguson of Randolph County. Emory Poling, his father, was born at Meadowville in 1836, son of James and Elizabeth (Vannoy) Poling. He married a daughter of Samuel M. Gainer, and their children were Helen Angeline, James S., Loman S., Anzina Elizabeth, Josephine Augusta and Solomon S. James Poling and James' father were both born near Meadowville, the latter being one of the earliest inhabitants.

JAMES SAMUEL POLING, born 1856 on Teter's Creek, son of Emory and Catherine (Gainer) Poling, was married at Vannoy's Mills, 1875, to Louisa, daughter of William and Lucinda (Vanscoy) Workman. Their daughter's name is Florna. He is a member of the M. E. Church, South; is a Democrat, and a farmer and stockraiser, living on Teter's Creek; and he owns 300 acres, half improved, of which 88 acres are in Barbour and the remainder in Tucker County. He was educated in the public schools of the county, and began life as a teacher in Randolph County where he taught two terms; then two in Tucker, and nineteen in Barbour, in all of which he was successful.

RILEY D. POLING, born on Bear Run, 1873, son of Hezekiah and Elizabeth (Woodford) Poling, was married four miles south of Philippi, August 22, 1895, to Cora Virginia, daughter of Spotswood and Isabella (Reed) Thacker. Their child's name is Dowden E. He is a member of the M. E. Church, and by occupation a farmer, residing on the waters of Sugar Creek, where he owns 130 acres of land, partly improved and all underlaid with coal. He was educated in the public schools of Barbour. His mother was born one mile west of Philippi in 1836, daughter of William and Sarah (Jackson) Woodford. She was married in 1860 to Hezekiah, son of William and Elizabeth (Payne) Poling. Their children were Maria, Sarah Virginia, Ulyses S., John Wesley, Columbia Ann and Riley D. Her grandfather, William Jackson, was born in Ohio.

COLUMBUS H. POLING, born near Philippi in 1876, son of Albert W. and Catherine (Moore) Poling. In politics he is a Republican, and by profession a teacher, living at Philippi. He was educated in the public and private schools, and began teaching at the age of seventeen, and by his habits of industry and economy he has acquired some valuable real estate near Philippi.

WILLIAM ARTHUR PITTS, born 1853 at Scottsville, Virginia, son of Charles and Cassandra (Thurman) Pitts, was married at Philippi, 1883, to Alberta, daughter of A. G. and Mary R. (Seay) Reger. Children, Alma Virginia, Mamie Reta and Thurman Reger. Mr. Pitt is a grandson of Elisha G. Thurman of Virginia, who was a brother of Hon. Allen G. Thurman of Ohio. He is a member of the M. E. Church, South, and in politics a Democrat. By occupation he is a real estate broker, residing at Kerens, Randolph County, and was educated at Stony Point College. Charles Pitts was born at Glasgow, Scotland, and came to America while young. In the Civil War he fought on the Confederate side under Fitzhugh Lee. Previous to the war he was a merchant, and since the war has been a farmer and stockraiser. W. A. Pitts was for a number of years a railroad contractor, first in Virginia and after 1881 in West Virginia, in the Kanawha Valley; then, in 1882, on the Weston & Buckhannon Railroad; in 1883 on the Grafton & Greenbrier; in 1887 was a contractor on the West Virginia Central, and the next year located at Kerens, where he has since remained in the employ of that company.

NOAH STOUT PARKS, born 1863 near Romine's Mill, son of Granville and Susan (Hardman) Parks, was married January 20, 1887, on Elk Creek, to Mary Etta, daughter of John Riley and Amanda (Simon) Zinn. Children, Lula Anna May, Rosa Bara Jane, Opal Jennie Belle, Sarah Van Leer. He is a member of the United Brethren Church, and of the orders I. O. O. F. and T. K. O. M. In politics he is a Democrat and in business a traveling salesman for the McCormick Machine Company, and lives at Mansfield. Noah Parks, his great grandfather, was an Englishman and was an early

FAMILY HISTORY. 441

settler on Brushy Fork. Mr. Parks introduced the bronze turkeys and Light Brama chickens into Barbour; also introduced the Reuben Turner stock of horses from Kentucky into Barbour; also introduced the first traction engine for threshing machine purposes, in 1893. He owns a half interest in a patent car coupler and is a stockholder in an oil well at the Kelley mines. Mr. Parks' father was a prisoner at Camp Chase in the Civil War.

SAMUEL D. PEPPER, born 1848 on Bartlett's Run, son of Johnson and Roanna (Bailey) Pepper, was married in Doddridge County, December 8, 1876, to Naomi, daughter of Ralph M. and Roxalina (Williams) O'Neill. Children, Earl, Inez, Raymond L. and Roxalina. Mr. Pepper is a member of the Missionary Baptist Church, in politics is Republican, and by occupation is a farmer and stockdealer, residing on Bartlett's Run, where he owns 256 acres, underlaid with coal. The family is English. William Pepper, the great grandfather of the subject of this sketch, came from England and settled in Delaware, and after his marriage removed to Virginia, before the Revolutionary War. His son, William Pepper, was born in Virginia and married Nancy Johnson. Their children were, William, Scarber, Parker, Vina, Anna, and Johnson, the last being father of the subject of this sketch. These children came to West Virginia in 1808 and settled near King's Knobb, on the Brushy Fork of Elk. Johnson Pepper was born July 8, 1801, and his wife 1810, and is still living (1899). Johnson Pepper's children were as follows: Marshall, Nancy, Mary, Thomas, Edith, Thornbury, Benjamin, Eleanor, James B., Samuel D., Roanna. The Baileys are English, and the great grandfather of the subject of this sketch married Hannah Thornbury, of Scotch-Irish extraction, and he lived in Virginia, reaching the advanced age of 103 years. His son, Thornbury Bailey, was born in Virginia, and at an early date came to West Virginia, where he married Mary, daughter of Thomas Bartlett. The history of the Bartletts is given elsewhere in this book.

WILLIAM G. W. PRICE, born 1828 near Belington, son of William Price, was married in 1848 to Elizabeth England. Children, Israel, James M., Cordelia, Eliza Jane, Francis M., Charlotte, Henry H., Lucretia. He is a member of the M. E. Church, in politics a Republican, by occupation a shoemaker and resides above Belington; was educated in the common schools, and was a soldier and officer in the Civil War, beginning as a private and rising to lieutenant. He belonged to Company F, Fifteenth W. Va. Infantry, and served under Crook and Sheridan, in the Shenandoah Valley, in Kentucky and Tennessee, taking part in sixteen engagements. His son, Henry H., was born in 1868, married in 1895 at Belington to Laura, daughter of John England. Their child's name is Rhea Bernice. He is a Methodist, a Junior O. U. A. M., and a Republican and by occupation is a shoemaker and confectioner. He was educated in the public schools. Among the battles in which Lieutenant Price took part were the following:

Cloyd Mountain, New River Bridge, Middle Brook, Lynchburg, Snicker's Ferry, Winchester, Fisher's Hill, Cedar Creek, and many others. He was under Generals Crook, Hunter and Sheridan, and in 1864 his regiment lost 285 men. His brother, Isaac, was in the same regiment, and lost both his arms, and one and a half pounds of flesh shot from his thigh by the explosion of a shell at Cedar Creek.

CHARLES E. PAYNE, born on Stewart's Run 1871, son of Francis E. Payne, was married June 11, 1898, at Clarksburg, to Effie, daughter of John G. and Julia (Lafollette) Fleming. In politics he is Democratic, belongs to the I. O. O. F., and is a farmer residing on Stewart's Run where he owns 170 acres, well improved. His father was born in Loudoun County, Virginia, in 1832, son of Travis and Mary (Wise) Payne; and was married December 11, 1855, in Barbour, to Virginia, daughter of Abram and Mary (Yeager) Simon. Children, Mary Florence, Lewis A., W. Benjamin, Richard F., Andrew J., Emma I., John B., Claude C. He is a member of the M. E. Church, South; in politics is Democratic, and by occupation a farmer on Stewart's Run. He was County Assessor of lands, was nine years a Justice and one term County Commissioner. His grandfather came from England and settled in Fairfax County, Virginia; his father moved from Fairfax to Loudoun County; and the subject of this sketch moved from Loudoun to Frederick, from Frederick to Taylor (1852), and five years later came to Barbour, where he now lives with his daughter, Mrs. Emma Woodford, who owns 150 acres on Stewart's Run. His father was a soldier in the War of 1812.

JAMES R. PROUDFOOT, born on Taylor's Drain, 1828, son of William and Margaret (Mouser) Proudfoot, was married in 1854 to Ann M. Mouser. Children, Jacob, Francis H., Sylvester, and one unnamed. He is a member of the M. E. Church, a Republican and a farmer, living on Taylor's Drain, where he owns fine property. He attended school in the vicinity, and in 1860 was a Justice of the Peace. He is one of the substantial men of Barbour County.

JOHN PROUDFOOT was born in Scotland and emigrated to Virginia, married Leanor Hitt, who was of German descent and a native of Virginia, and they had born to them in Fauquier County, Virginia, seven children. Mrs. Proudfoot's uncles, John and Peter Hitt, were American soldiers in the Revolution. She was a professed Christian but never a church member. She died in 1829 and was buried at Mary's Chapel on Taylor's Drain. John Proudfoot died 1823 and was buried at Mary's Chapel. He was a Presbyterian and was highly educated. Their children were Mary, John, Elias, Alexander, William, James and Thomas. Sketches of their lives follow.

MARY PROUDFOOT, daughter of John and Leanor, was born in Virginia June 12, 1787, died on Taylor's Drain. She married John Robinson

JOSEPH TETER.

FAMILY HISTORY. 445

(For names of children see sketch of John Robinson.)

JOHN PROUDFOOT, son of John and Leanor, was born in Virginia, died on Taylor's Drain, married first Agnes Glasscock, and second Rebecca Thompson. Children, William, Alexander, Sarah Ann, Lucy, Polly, Nancy, Mahala, Henry and Susan.

ELIAS PROUDFOOT, son of John and Leanor, was born in Virginia and died in Missouri. He married Edith Read.

ALEXANDER PROUDFOOT, son of John and Leanor, was born in Virginia and died on Middle Fork, Barbour County. He married Elizabeth Cole, and their children were John, William, Joshua, Leanor and Nancy.

WILLIAM PROUDFOOT, son of John and Leanor, born in Virginia, died 1843 on Taylor's Drain, married Jane Robinson. (For names of children see sketch of Jane Robinson.)

JAMES PROUDFOOT, son of John and Leanor, born in Virginia, died 1855 on waters of Hacker's Creek in Barbour, buried on Taylor's Drain. He married Elizabeth Reed, who died in 1865 and was buried on Taylor's Drain. Their children were McGowen, Arah Jane, Francis, James William, Edith and Matilda Ann.

THOMAS PROUDFOOT, born in Virginia, died 1890 at Des Moines, Iowa; married Elizabeth Robinson. (For the names of his children see sketch of Elizabeth Robinson.)

JOHN H. PROUDFOOT, born on Pleasant Creek, 1822, son of Alexander and Elizabeth (Cole) Proudfoot, was married in 1846 to Sarah A., daughter of Uriah and Joanna (Cole) Modisett. Children, Anna E., Chester W., Joanna Martha, Delbert M., Ira B. and Isa M. He is a member of the Primitive Baptist Church, and is a farmer on the waters of Hacker's Creek. When public schools were introduced the school houses were located in Pleasant District by a committee composed of Mr. Proudfoot, John Harvey Woodford and Richard Crutcher. The grandfather of the subject of this sketch, John Proudfoot, came from Scotland and settled on Taylor's Drain.

DELBERT MARSHALL PROUDFOOT, born in Barbour, 1857, son of John H. and Sarah A. (Modisett) Proudfoot, was married in Pleasant District, May 28, 1882, to Nancy J., daughter of Isaac and Jane (Hoffman) Woodford. Children, Grace and John H. Mr. Proudfoot is a member of the Primitive Baptist Church, a Democrat, a farmer and dairyman, living on the Clarksburg pike, west of Philippi. He attended the West Virginia College at Flemington. His great grandfather was a native of Scotland and was educated for the church. Mrs. Proudfoot's grandfather was John H. Woodford, one of the leading men of the county. Mr. Proudfoot's grandfather, Uriah Modisett, was a man of large influence in Barbour County, and his uncle, Augustus Modisett, was Sheriff of Barbour in 1866, and was a member of the West Virginia Legislature. Later he removed to Indiana. Mr. Proudfoot owns 80 acres, highly improved, and a fine dairy of improved stock. It was the first dairy in Barbour County. Mrs. Proudfoot was born August 17, 1857, and is a member of the M. E. Church.

R

ROBINSON AND PROUDFOOT FAMILIES. Among the first settlers of what is now Barbour County were the Robinson and Proudfoot families. More than a century ago these families came from the East and settled on Taylor's Drain. That beautiful valley with its rich state of cultivation, as it is today, was made so by the energy and industry of the two families named, together with the Woodford family, which married into the Robinson family. The hum of the bee and the song of the bird have taken the place of the howl of the wolf. Just across the Delaware in New Jersey lived James Robinson and Elizabeth Davis (who became his wife) when the old Liberty Bell proclaimed that Independence had been declared. No doubt they joined with the populace in that greatest of all American celebrations, July 4, 1776. Some twenty years later, James Robinson and his family, consisting of his wife and two sons, Job and John, came to what was then Harrison County, stopping a short time in Fayette County, Pennsylvania, where their daughter Elizabeth was born. The four other children, William, Jane, Mary and James, were born in their new home on the headwaters of Taylor's Drain. James Robinson and his wife were of English descent, and she was a Quaker, possessed of the estimable qualities of that religious sect. He died in 1835 and his wife in 1840. They were buried in the beautiful cemetery of Mary's Chapel, which is near the site of their old homestead. The history of their children is as follows:

JOB ROBINSON; son of James and Elizabeth, was born in New Jersey, died in Barbour County and was buried at Mary's Chapel. He married Nancy Thompson, and their children were John S., Henry, Elizabeth, Job, Rebecca and Nancy.

JOHN ROBINSON, born March 28, 1793, son of James and Elizabeth, was born in New Jersey, died in Barbour, was buried at Taylor's Drain. He married Mary Proudfoot, born June 12, 1787, and their children were James, Elias, Leanor, John, Elizabeth, Mary, Agnes, William and Jacob. Of these, Jacob, the youngest, is the sole survivor. This family and part of Job Robinson's family are the only ones of the numerous descendants of James Robinson that remained in Barbour County. All the others migrated to the West. John Robinson was an American soldier in the War of 1812.

ELIZABETH ROBINSON, daughter of James and Elizabeth, was born in Pennsylvania and died in Iowa. She married Thomas Proudfoot, and their children were Jacob, Catherine, Jane, James, Harriet, Elias, Emily, Caroline, Charles and Martha Ann.

WILLIAM ROBINSON, son of James and Elizabeth, born in Barbour died in Calhoun County, married Katherine Weaver. Their children were,

FAMILY HISTORY.   447

Frank, Job, Harvey, Abbey, Rachel, Louisa, James, Loucetta and Elizabeth.

JANE ROBINSON, daughter of James and Elizabeth, was born in Barbour, died in 1858, was buried at Taylor's Drain. She married William Proudfoot. Their children were, Edith, Leanor, Elizabeth, John, James R., Julia Ann, Edward and Sally.

MARY ROBINSON, daughter of James and Elizabeth, was born and died in Barbour, and was buried at Mary's Chapel, which was named for her. She married Jacob Woodford, and their children were, William, Robert, James, Benjamin, John and Hannah.

JAMES ROBINSON, son of James and Elizabeth, was born in Barbour and died at or near Gallena, Illinois.

WILLIAM ROBINSON, son of John and Mary (Proudfoot) Robinson, was born in what is now Barbour, then Harrison County, September 20, 1827, and spent the greater portion of his life on Taylor's Drain, in Pleasant District. In 1850, when he was twenty-three years of age, he was married to Mary Sayre, and they made their home near the place of his birth. He owned a large farm which engaged his attention, although he worked nearly all his life at his trade, shoemaking. Ten children were born to them of whom nine attained the ages of maturity, one dying in 1863, at the age of eighteen months. Those living, named in the order of their ages, beginning with the eldest, are, Mrs. Isaac Means, residing at Evansville, Preston County; Frank P., near Grafton, Taylor County; Louisa V., who married Lon Wilson, of Barbour County; Sarah A., who married Thomas J. Allen, of East Peru, Iowa; Mary M., Rev. John S. Robinson, now of Weston, West Virginia, of the M. E. Conference; David W. and Charles W., (twins) the latter is cashier of the Bank of Mannington, at Mannington, Marion County; Rose, who married Scott H. White, of West Superior, Wisconsin; and Ira E., of Grafton, Prosecuting Attorney of Taylor County.

The Robinsons were southern Democrats, but they remained loyal to the Union and to the Stars and Stripes during the Civil War. William Robinson left his home on Taylor's Drain early in the war, and moved to near Knottsville, in Taylor County, where he would be less exposed to annoyances from Confederates and their sympathizers. Having previously purchased a farm and tannery there, he took up the pursuits of peace in his new home, and industriously followed his calling. He operated the tannery at Knottsville during the war and after its close. He resided at Knottsville fourteen years, a model citizen, a man without enemies, whose character was a guide to the young. He was a member of the M. E. Church, and held an official position in it nearly all his life. After his residence in Taylor he returned to his former home in Barbour and made it his place of residence till the end of his life. His death, due to paralysis, came suddenly November 23, 1896, and he was buried at Taylor's Drain. He was never an office seeker. In 1890 he was nominated on the Republican ticket in Barbour for the legislature, without his consent and without his knowledge; and although Barbour was then strongly Democratic, he lacked only sixty-eight votes of being elected.

JACOB W. ROBINSON, son of John and Mary (Proudfoot) Robinson, was born on Taylor's Drain, Barbour County, February 20, 1829. He was twice married, first on November 20, 1855, to Elizabeth Ann daughter of Albert and Mary (Thompson) Carter, and four sons were born to them, William Fletcher, James P., Lloyd D. and John A. He was married the second time on July 1, 1869, to Belinda, daughter of Philip and Christina (Miller) Wolf, and they have two sons, Ellis B. and Clarence Elliott. Nearly the whole of the first fifty years of his life was spent on Taylor's Drain; and in 1877 he moved to Philippi to make it his home and to perform the duties of deputy sheriff and jailer, to which position he had been chosen. Prior to that time he had, for four years, from 1866 to 1870, filled the office of District Treasurer for Pleasant District, and as such he collected disbursed and accounted for the taxes of that district. During that time the majority of the school houses in that district were built and he paid for them with the public money. When he moved to Philippi it was to act as deputy for J. W. Talbott, who was then Sheriff. When Jacob Hudkins was elected Sheriff in 1876, Mr. Robinson was appointed his deputy for the west side of the county and collected the taxes there. He served in that capacity until 1880, and then became proprietor of the Robinson House, now the Valley House, in Philippi; and in 1883 built an addition to it. In 1885 he was elected Sheriff and filled the office four years. Afterwards, when a vacancy occurred in the office, he was appointed to fill it; and when B. B. Rohrbaugh was elected Sheriff in 1896, Mr. Robinson was again chosen as deputy and jailer. He is a member of the M. E. Church, South, and a Democrat.

LLOYD D. ROBINSON, born on Taylor's Drain, December 22, 1861, son of Jacob W. Robinson, was married October 19, 1887, at Philippi, to Prudie S., daughter of Edward F. and Lydia A. Grant. Children, Opal, born December 29, 1890; Neil, born April 27, 1893, died June 29, 1894; Harry Grayden, born May 26, 1896. Mr. Robinson is a member of the M. E. Church, of Bigelow Lodge No. 52, A. F. and A. M.; in politics is a Democrat; lives at Philippi, and has held the following offices: Deputy Sheriff three years; Recorder of Philippi several years; Mayor of Philippi 1896; was the first postmaster in the State appointed under Grover Cleveland, and held the position four years and twenty-seven days. In 1896 he was chairman of the Democratic Executive Committee, and is now a member of the Congressional Executive Committee for Barbour County.

MAJOR MILTON D. REED, born 1836, near Philippi, son of Peter and

Ruth (Lewellyn) Reed, was married May 30, 1861, to Margaret J., daughter of John and Elsie Stuart. Children, Stuart F., Ocea Lewellyn, Rosa Belle. He is a member of the Missionary Baptist Church, a Republican, and a farmer and stockraiser, living on Elk Creek. Mr. Reed was a major in the Virginia militia, and for twenty years was secretary of the Board of Education. His farm of 245 acres is in a fine state of improvement, and is underlaid with coal. His daughter Ocea, in 1895, was married to Edward Minter Jackson, of Buckhannon, a well known farmer and stockman of Upshur County; and his daughter Belle, in 1898, married Charles C. Wentz, of Parkersburg.

STUART F. REED, son of Milton D. Reed, was born in Elk District, January 8, 1866. At the age of sixteen he began teaching, and in 1884 entered the Fairmont Normal School, graduating in ten months. He then entered the West Virginia University as a cadet, taking the classical and law course. In 1889 he graduated with the degree of L.L. B., and has been admitted to the bar in the State and the United States Courts. During his student days he was selected orator on several public occasions, to represent the Parthenon society. He was one of the founders of the *Athenaeum*, the magazine of the University. In 1891 he bacame managing editor of the Clarksburg *Telegram*, one of the leading Republican papers of the State. He took an active part in politics and literary work, and was elected three consecutive times President of the West Virginia Editorial Association, and declined a fourth election. As a compliment to the ability with which he had filled the position, the editors of the State presented him with a solid gold watch, chain and diamond-set charm. Mr. Reed personally conducted the memorable excursion of West Virginia editors to the Atlanta Exposition. In 1894 Mr. Reed was nominated without opposition for the State Senate, and was elected by a large majority; and on his twenty-ninth birthday, in the Senate Chamber of West Virginia, he selected his desk and chair as the youngest member of that body. His first speech was that placing Hon. Stephen B. Elkins in nomination for the U. S. Senate. The speech on that occasion was highly complimented by the press and by public men. Another notable speech made by him, and one of great influence on the history of the State, was that protesting against the appropriation of State funds for private and sectarian schools. Mr. Reed has held other positions of trust, but they have been more honorary than lucrative. He is a trustee of Broaddus Classical and Scientific Institute at Clarksburg, and for three years was a Regent of the State University. In 1892 he was an alternate delegate to the National Republican Convention at Minneapolis. He has served as member of the Republican State Committee, and as president of the National Republican League. He was a member of the World's Literary Congress at Chicago in 1893, and was publicly complimented by the president for the part taken in a debate. He is a Royal Arch Mason and a Knight Templar.

In 1897 Mr. Reed tendered Governor Atkinson his resignation as State Senator and Regent of the University and accepted a commission from the President as Post-master at Clarksburg. In 1898 he was married to Miss Bonnie Smith, of Clarksburg, who is a graduate of Broaddus College, and who had taken a special course in art and literature at Lebanon, Ohio. Mr. Reed has built a residence at Clarksburg. His example can be cited for the guidance of young men in the struggle of life. Every step in his course has been the result of hard work, patient perseverance, confidence in self, and a clear appreciation of the duties of citizenship; not over zealous in his own advancement, yet ready to accept the honors as well as the responsibilities which might fall to his lot. In achieving honors for himself he has also brought honor to his native county.

IDA L. REED, daughter of James and Nancy J. (Lelliardt) Reed, was born 1865 on Rock Camp Run, Barbour County. Her ancestors were Scotch, English and German, but were early settlers in Virginia and were soldiers in the Rovolutionary War. Her brothers and sisters were Lucy B., Hampton H., John R., Eugene F., James L., Ira Milton and Isadora. She is a member of the M. E. Church, and resides on a farm near Arden, her father having died in 1892. Her facilities for obtaining an education were limited; but she taught five years in the public schools. She early began a literary life and has contributed largely to the religious literature of her time, chiefly hymns, cantatas and special exercises for Christmas, Easter, Harvest Home and Sunday School exercises for children. More than five hundred of her hymns and thirty cantatas have been published and widley circulated by printing houses in New York, Chicago, Cincinnati, St. Louis and elsewhere. In addition to these, she has written many poems, which have been published in the newspapers. Extensive quotations from her hymns cannot be given. The following will suffice:

CHRISTMAS BELLS.

Hark, the music soft and low,
  Merry, merry, Christmas bells,
Ringing out across the snow,
  Merry, merry Christmas bells.
Tell the story o'er again,
  Ring the happy, happy strain,
Peace on earth, good will to men,
  Merry, merry Christmas bells.

CHORUS

Ring, ring, O hear them chime;
Ring, ring, 'tis Christmas time!
Peace on earth, the chorus swells,
From the merry Christmas bells.

> At the sound the pulses thrill,
>   Merry, merry Christmas bells,
> Peace and joy each heart doth fill,
>   Merry, merry, Christmas bells.
> Now the tidings glad proclaim
>   Tell abroad the Savior's fame,
> Chime ye praises to his name,
>   Merry, merry, Christmas bells.
>
> Now let strife and warrings cease,
>   Merry, merry Christmas bells;
> Ring in joy, good will and peace,
>   Merry, merry Christmas bells.
> Over every hill and plain
>   Ring the glad triumphant strain,
> King of kings our Lord doth reign,
>   Merry, merry Christmas bells.

REV. IRA MILTON REED, Ph. D., brother of Miss Ida L. Reed, whose sketch is given above, is a writer of ability who has published treatises on scientific and theological subjects, and has written with force on other themes. Although his chief work has not been in the field of poetry, the following two verses show that he possesses ability in that line:

WHO IS THE CHRIST?

> A Christ is the glory of one great mind,
>   And the God of that mind expressed
> Through the love and goodness of all mankind
>   In robes of humanity dressed.
>
> A picture he is that all should paint
>   On the canvass of their life,
> Through the lights and shadows of sinner and saint
>   But blending in oneness from strife.

In 1895, in Baltimore he published a book, "*Earth-Life and the Borderland,*" which aimed to give a new direction to religious inquiry, by taking a middle ground between materialists and spiritualists, or rather by adopting portions of the doctrines of both and attempting to found a religion upon them. The doctrines set forth in the book would scracely be accepted by the orthodox churches. On the one hand it suggests what Drummond expounded in his "*Natural Law in the Spirit World;*" and on the other hand it comes very nearly the position of the Persian, Omar Khayyam, who exclaimed:

> I sent my Soul through the Invisible,
>   Some letter of that After-life to spell;
> And by and by my Soul returned to me
>   And answered: "I Myself am Heaven and Hell."

Mr. Reed, perhaps, lays himself liable to the criticism that he fails to draw the distinction between what really exists and what, to a person under the spell of a hypnotist, seems to exist, as when he says of the Hindoo fakirs:

They are able to communicate mentally with a brother master in a distant city, reverse the power of attraction, cause music to be heard in the air without an instrument, with one finger suddenly cause a weight of several tons to be lifted and remain suspended in the air. They change your whole order of vision and send you away to some strange and beautiful land unlike anything the natural mind can conceive of.

Below will be found a few quotations from Rev. Reed's book, disconnected and selected at random, but showing the tenor of his discourse and the direction of his teaching.

The universe evolves Gods, Christs, Shakespeares and spiders all at the same time. It is all simply according to the degree of fineness and quality of which the thing is composed.

There is more pharisaism, bigotry, and rivalry now in our religious society than there was then (in the time of Christ), all because we have too many salvation bosses and peddlers of denomination stationed wherever they can drive the biggest sale or get the biggest salary.

For aught I know, in the far future of eternity somewhere I will become a god of some country or planet or sphere.

Heaven is not a place to pick stringed instruments and blow horns all the time, and say amen and hallelujah and glory.

I used to warn sinners to flee the wrath to come, and tell them of an awful doom gaping before them, when, ten chances to one, they were better than I.

It is the duty of the minister of God to show men their good qualities and not their imperfections—to be the deliverer, not the executioner.

Humanity is getting tired of wrathful gods, devils and hells.

Oh, unprofitable Pharisees of the nineteenth century! Ye love to be called Rev. and Dr. of Divinity, and hold the upper seat in the synagogue, and recite tales of ribs and burning bushes and big fish, while millions of men are thirsting for a knowledge of their own souls.

Life is what we make it. Devils in hell or a God on some distant star have nothing to do with it. If I were such a God for one day I would stop the mouth of every man who prays for deliverance from a sin-cursed earth, the vale of tears, as he calls it.

Men make their own hells and heavens, likewise their devils and gods.

JOHN RYAN, who settled on a branch of Teter's Creek, was one of the earliest settlers. His father was an Irishman of whom but little is known. There is account of three of his children, John, James and William. The first two went to Ohio. William married Rebecca Bennett, June 27, 1816, and settled where his son, John Ryan, now resides. They had six children who lived to maturity; of these, Mary married Squire Richard Phillips; Jacob went to Iowa while a young man and married Caroline Lewis; James married Deborah Moore and still lives in Cove District; Daniel married Emily Coffman, moved to Iowa, then back to Ritchie County, West Virginia; Michael D. married Mahala Poling, and Jane married Henry Sturm, and they both live on Laurel Creek.

HENRY H. RYAN, born 1857, son of Michael and Mahala (Poling) Ryan, was married March 25, 1879, to Mary C., daughter of Henson H. and

Mr. and Mrs. Lair Davis Morrall.

Nancy E. (Boyles) Poling. He is a member of the M. P. Church, of the Junior O. U. A. M., is a Democrat, and is employed on public works. He lives at Tacy, at which place he attended school. He is of Irish and German ancestry. On his mother's side his grandparents were Roger (born 1798, died 1878) and Mary Poling (born 1800, died 1888), who lived near Meadowville. William and Rebecca Ryan were his paternal ancestors, living on Teter's Creek, the former dying in 1851, the latter in 1858.

GEORGE MCCLELLAN RIGHT, born 1862, son of Arnold and Elizabeth (Hayes) Right, was married November 1, 1885, to Laura Amanda, daughter of Dr. Charles and Jane A. (Capito) Willis. Children, Grace M. and Lena. He is a member of the M. E. Church, an Odd Fellow, Knight of Pythias, a Republican and a merchant, at Belington. He was educated in the public and private schools, and was deputy sheriff under J. W. Robinson.

M. D. RACER, born 1829 in Rappahannock County, Virginia, son of John and Martha (Simons) Racer, was married October 3, 1896, at Philippi, to Albina L., daughter of Lair D. and Elizabeth (Harper) Morrall. He is a member of the Presbyterian Church and resides one mile east of Philippi, where he is engaged in farming. He served four years in the Confederate army, and his father was a soldier in the war of 1812.

MORDECAI DUNHAM RILEY, born in Harrison County in 1842, son of William H. H. and Margaret (Dunham) Riley; was marriel November 14, 1867, in Barbour County, to Annetta, daughter of Abraham and Maria (Morgan) Hudkins. Children, Walter G., Florence, Edna D. and Roscoe H. His daughter Florence, married Jacob Knapp of Philippi, and Edna married Herman Tyson. Mr. Riley is a member of the Missionary Baptist Church, a farmer and stockraiser living on the waters of Elk Creek where he owns 325 acres, half of it underlaid with coal, and all in fine state of cultivation. He moved to Barbour thirty years ago, lived first on Simpson's Creek, and then moved to his present farm. Ten years he served on the Board of Education of Elk District, and four years he was a member of the county court, one year as its president. While a member of the court he introduced machines for working the roads. Mr Riley's great-great-grandfather came from England to America before the Revolution and was a soldier in that war. Three brothers came with him to America. One located in Fauquier County, Virginia, and two in Maryland. About 1810 the grandfather of the subject of this sketch, with a large family, moved to Harrison County, and took part in the War of 1812, marching to Norfolk, under Colonel Joseph E. Johnson, who was afterwards Governor of Virginia. He took part in the fighting about Washington and Baltimore in 1814 which culminated in the defeat of the British at North Point. William H. H. Riley, father of the subject of this sketch, was born 1813, and his children were, Julia Ann, John W., Jonathan G., M. D., Mary, James K. P. Leonard, Elizabeth, and Amanda.

FAMILY HISTORY.

HENRY CLAY ROSENBERGER, born 1843 in Jefferson County, son of David Rosenberger, was married September 15, 1874, to Henrietta, daughter of William Elliott. Children, William David and Elizabeth (Mrs. Right). Mr. Rosenberger is a Baptist and I. O. O. F., a Democrat and a farmer living at Belington. He lived from 1875 to 1884 in Tucker County. In early life he was a miller. His education was obtained in public and private schools. He has a clock that has been running more than a century, and still keeps good time. It belonged to his grandfather.

BURTON BIGGS ROHRBAUGH, born November 22, 1863, in Barbour, son of Anthony and Clarissa (Johnson) Rohrbaugh, was married, first, in 1882, to Adaline E., daughter of Arnold and Elizabeth (Hayes) Right; the second time September 19, 1899, to Emma E., daughter of Andrew J. Gall. Children, Effie Estella, Nora May, Windell Wilson. Mr. Rohrbaugh is a member of the M. E. Church, South; of the Odd Fellows, Masons and Knights of Pythias, is a Democrat, and now Sheriff of Barbour County. He was educated in the public schools and in a private school at Meadowville. He was formerly postmaster at Belington; was a farmer till twenty-five years old; then a merchant at Belington, near which place he owns 139 acres of improved land. His grandfather was John Rohrbaugh.

CLARK LEE ROHRBAUGH, M. D., was born 1856 in Upshur County, son of John and Martha (Butt) Rohrbaugh, and was married January 27, 1885, to Hulda May, daughter of Creed Carpenter. Children, Jessie Pearl, Otis Clark, Flossie, Hazel. Dr. Rohrbaugh is a member of the M. P. Church, is a K. of P. and I. O. O. F.; is a Republican, and a physician and surgeon, at Belington where he has practiced nine years, having practiced at Talbott's before that time. He began his education in the public schools, and in 1893 graduated from the Medical College of Ohio.

AMOS F. ROHRBAUGH, born 1871, son of Albert and Mary O. (Thornhill) Rohrbaugh, was married October 18, 1893, in Taylor County, to Emma G., daughter of Mr. and Mrs. Reuben Hall. Their child's name is Leona. Mr. Rohrbaugh is a member of the M. E. Church, South; is a Democrat, belongs to the order A. F. and A. M., and K. of P., and by occupation is a merchant at Belington, where he was postmaster from 1895 to 1897, and is now deputy sheriff. His education was obtained in the public schools, and he spent his early life on a farm. Then he took up the lumber business with Curtin and Pardee Lumber Company, and later entered the mercantile business. His wife died April 30, 1899.

S

DAVID WILLIAM SHAW, son of William and Edith (O'Neal) Shaw, was born May 18, 1852, at Philippi, and on March 12, 1879, was married to Barbara Ellen, daughter of William W. and Jane (Thompson) Woodford. Children, David Blain and William Ralston. The family is Scotch, and

William Shaw, grandfather of the subject of this sketch, emigrated to America and settled in Preston County, then Monongalia, in the latter part of the eighteenth century, and on June 13, 1795 his son, William, father of the subject of this sketch, was born. In early life he came to what is now Barbour County, and made his home where Philippi now stands. As early as 1830, he was a Justice of the Peace in Randolph, and upon the creation of the new county he was one of the Justices who organized Barbour. He was the third Sheriff. In private life he was a miller, a stone mason, a farmer, and for some time was one of the owners of the ferry at Philippi. He was a county officer for twenty-five years, was one of the original trustees of Philippi, and was always a Democrat. He was a soldier in the War of 1812 and was stationed at Norfolk. The last years of his life were spent on his farm one and a half miles west of Philippi, where he died June 19, 1876. The farm now belongs to his son, the subject of this sketch. David W. Shaw was educated in the common schools of Philippi and the West Virginia College, at Flemington, Taylor County, from which he graduated in the class of 1876. He then entered the profession of teaching, devoting his winter months to teaching, and farming during the summer. This arrangement continued until 1885, when he relinquished teaching and devoted himself exclusively to agriculture, until June, 1894, when he was elected to the position of Superintendent of the West Virginia Reform School at Pruntytown. In the autumn of 1886 he was elected n member of the State Legislature, and was re-elected to the four successive terms. The session of 1893 he served in the important capacity of speaker of the house. He was chairman of the committee on education during the first three sessions. He introduced the bill providing for the abolishing of the special school elections. He was also instrumental in framing and securing the passage of a bill providing for the broadening of the common school curriculum, so as to provide for the teaching of civil government, book-keeping, and physiology. He is a member of Philippi Lodge, No. 59, I. O. O. F., and of the Methodist Episcopal Church, South.

JOHN COMBS SHAW was born near Kasson, Barbour County, is a son of Samuel and Elizabeth (Shroyer) Shaw. He is a member of the M. E. Church, of the Knights of Pythias, in politics Republican, and by occupation a teacher, employed in the State Normal School at West Liberty, West Virginia, but his home is in Barbour. He graduated in 1889 from the Fairmont Normal School; in 1891 from the Peabody Normal, Nashville, Tennessee; in 1892 from the University of Nashville with the degree of B. S., and in 1894 with the degree of M. S. In 1895-6 he was Scholar in Pedagogy at Clark University, Worchester, Massachusetts, and the next year in the same institution he was Fellow in Psychology. The great grandfather of Mr. Shaw came from England and settled at Barton, Maryland. He raised five sons, the youngest of whom was Joseph, who married Florence Smar and raised three sons and three daughters. After two of the children were married, the family moved to Cove District, Barbour County. Samuel, the second child, is the father of the subject of this sketch. His children are Julia, John Combs, Joseph Columbus, Francis Elizabeth and Maggie Belle.

COLONEL HENRY STURM, was born in Cove District about 1794. He was the son of Nicholas Sturm, an Englishman, and one of the earliest settlers in Barbour, coming here from Virginia. Henry Sturm represented Randolph County in the Legislature; and in the War of 1812, he joined our army at Norfolk. In the Civil War, though old, he again entered the army. Nicholas Sturm, (sometimes written Storm), was a Justice of the Peace in Randolph County in 1811, and Henry, his son, was Constable in 1821, Justice 1831, and Ensign of Militia the same year. He was twice married, first to Susan Alexander, a widow, and a daughter of Frank and Elizabeth (England) Johnson. The children of Colonel Sturm were, William, Jackson, John, James, Lair, Thomas, Samuel, Rachel, Elizabeth and Sally. Samuel, son of Colonel Henry, furnished the timbers for the Philippi bridge. His children were, Jesse, David, Elizabeth, Harvey, Henry, Amanda, Eldridge, Phoebe Ann, Charles, Deniza Ann, Catherine.

ISAAC STURM, born near Meadowville, 1821, son of Nicholas and Anna (McClaskey) Sturm, was married 1841 to Isabel, daughter of Jonathan and Sarah (Poling) McKinney. Children, Melissa Ellen, Hulda J., Nicholas J., Sarah A., Mary C., Harriet and Wade H. He is a member of M. E. Church and a farmer and lives near Olive Hill School House.

DAVID STURM, born 1841, son of Samuel and Matilda (Vannoy) Sturm, was married October 11, 1864, at the old Williamson homestead, to Susan Virginia, daughter of John R. and Lucinda (Sinsel) Wiliamson. Children, Lucinda A., Charles Bruce, George Frederick. He is a member of the Missionary Baptist Church; a Democrat, a farmer and a carpenter, residing on the waters of Sand Run. He has held the office of member of the Board of Education. Facts concerning the ancestry of Mr. Sturm are given in the biography of Colonel Henry Sturm.

JACOB W. STURM, born in Barbour in 1852, son of Melker J. and Mary (Bolyard) Sturm. On July 18, 1877, on Ford Run, he married Lucy, daughter of John E. and Elizabeth (Knapp) Bennett. Children, Hatzel, Charles, Harman and Vidie. He is a member of the M. E. Church, and is a farmer, residing near Olive Hill. His education was obtained in the public schools of Barbour; owns 55 acres underlaid with coal, and chiefly devoted to grazing purposes.

WILLIAM WALLIS STALNAKER, born in what is now Barbour, 1827, son of Samuel and Isabel (Ryan) Stalnaker, was married in Taylor County, April 29, 1852, to Elizabeth, daughter of John and Sarah (Haymond) Lewellen. Children, Adolphus Waitman, Sarah Olive and William Henry. He is a Methodist, a Republican and a farmer, living on Teter's Creek, where

ASTLEY SILAS HAWKINS.　　　　　　　ARTA FRANK HAWKINS.

he owns 263 acres, nearly all cleared; and in partnership with his son, William H., he owns 650 acres, including land on which his grandfather, William Stalnaker, settled when he moved from Beverly to this vicinity. They are engaged in general farming and stockraising, cutting fifty stacks of hay, handling over 100 cattle and from fifty to seventy-five sheep a year. The land is underlaid with coal and also contains a deposit of potter's clay, which was worked for some years by Burley & Bennett on Teter's Creek. His son Adolphus moved to Texas in 1877 and married, December 6, 1882, Sarah C. Marsh, of Texas, and has been successfully engaged in stockraising and owns 1160 acres, under wire fence. He and his brother, William H., and their sister, Mrs. Sarah Cole, own 640 acres on Red River, a gift from their father. His daughter, Sarah C., married Andrew Cole, a successful farmer of Pleasant Creek, Barbour County; and William H. married Alice, daughter of Colonel Truman T. Elliott of Belington. She died July 5, 1897, leaving two children, Lena Gladys and Hugh Elliott.

HARRISON HAGANS STALNAKER, born 1827, son of James and Elizabeth (Neptune) Stalnaker, was married 1850 in Tucker County to Catherine, daughter of William R. and Catherine J. (Ward) Parsons. Children, James, William (deceased), George Washington, Imboden and David Floyd. The subject of this sketch belongs to the M. E. Church, South, is a Democrat and a farmer, living on Mill Run of Teter's Creek, where he owns 440 acres, 250 cleared. In 1862 he enlisted in the Confederate service and served till the close of the war, under General Imboden, and laid down the last Confederate flag at Buchanan, Botetourt County, Virginia. At Port Republic he received a wound in the head, rendering him unconscious. He took part in all the battles with Imboden. While on a visit home in 1864 he narrowly escaped capture by Home Guards under Captain Haller. Just after dinner they came upon him so suddenly he did not have time to get away, and his wife concealed him behind a three-cornered cupboard, and was quietly washing the dishes when the Guards entered. They searched the house, but failed to find him. He was twice elected Assessor of the Eastern District, and served six years as County Commissioner.

WILLIAM STALNAKER, brother of Adam Stalnaker, who was killed by Indians near Beverly in 1782, was one of the early settlers on Teter's Creek, living where W. W. Stalnaker now resides. The exact date of his location there is not known. He married Margaret McHenry, near Beverly. His children were, Elizabeth, who married Colonel Henry Sturm in 1815 (the ceremony being performed by Simeon Harris); Samuel, who married Elizabeth Ryan; Mahala, who married William Marteney; Andrew, who married Rachel Holsberry; James, who married Elizabeth Neptune; Willis, who married Nancy, daughter of Charles Digman, who was drowned on Hunter's Fork of Sugar Creek; Isabel, who married Alexander Shaw; John, who married Margaret Black, and Dorcas, who married Daniel Marteney, brother of William Marteney. Mr. Stalnaker's only neighbor was John Ryan, Sr. They put bells on their horses and cattle and turned them out to range in Nelson's Low Gap, of Laurel Hill, in the spring, leaving them there till fall, or till needed. A combat between a bear and a panther, in their native wilderness, is not oftened witnessed; but Mr. Ryan once saw such an encounter, which he described as follows:

> A tree had fallen across a ravine and the bear started to cross the log, and at the same time the panther started to cross from the opposite end, and they met near the middle. Neither would give way to the other, and the bear dealt the panther a blow with his paw and knocked him off into the ravine. The panther deliberately walked back to the same end of the log and met the bear again, for the bear instead of proceeding across while the way was clear, had sat down on the log to wait. As the panther came up the bear again struck him a blow and the second time knocked him off. Once more the panther returned to the same end of the log and for the third time faced the bear. But this time the panther was more cautious, and instead of walking up within range of the powerful paw, he crouched a few feet away, and sprang on the bear and fastened his claws in the animal's head. Both tumbled off the log together, and the battle in the ravine was fast and furious. But the bear was too strong for his antagonist, and bore him down, and seizing him by the throat and clutching him in his arms, held him in a death grip and soon killed him. But it was a dearly-bought victory; for the panther had so lacerated the bear with his claws that he almost disemboweled him. The bear walked a few paces, lay down and died.

GARRETSON J. STALNAKER, born in Randolph County, 1858, son of Granville and Jane (Hilkey) Stalnaker, was married May 25, 1879, to Mary M., daughter of Burr P. and Sally A. (Lake) Newlon. Children, Alman J., Lenora, Baxter B., Oral and Mary F. He is a member of the M. E. Church, a Republican, and a manufacturer of lumber at Belington. He has filled the position of Justice of the Peace. He owns 50 acres near Belington and 45 acres in Randolph County. He has a bayonet plowed up in Belington in 1897. It had probably lain buried since 1861.

WARD P. STALNAKER, born near Meadowville in 1857, son of Holsberry and Caroline (Parsons) Stalnaker, was married February 19, 1880, near Philippi, to Carrie M., daughter of William J. and Lydia Bartlett. Children, Judson Clay, Dale Holsberry, Osban, Gideon Guy and Lydia Beatrice. Mr. Stalnaker is a member of the M. E. Church, South, and his wife is a Baptist. He is a farmer on Laurel Creek, near Fisher's Store, where he owns 150 acres, and he was educated in the public schools. The great grandfather of the subject of this sketch came from England and settled near Meadowville. Two brothers crossed the ocean with him. One settled in Randolph and one in Gilmer County. Andrew, father of Holsberry Stalnaker, married Rachel Holsberry, and accumulated property valued at $15,000 at the time of his death. He dealt largely in horses.

CHARLES K. SWITZER, born near Petersburg, Grant County, 1853, son of David N. and Francis A. (Wilson) Switzer, was married May 29, 1879, of Fort Syebert, Pendleton County, to Minnie M., daughter of Allen and

Martha (Miller) Dyer. Children, Ola G., Fannie D., Neva V. He is a member of the M. E. Church, a Democrat, and a merchant at Mansfield, of the firm of Dyer & Switzer. He owns 26 acres of improved land near Mansfield, and a nice residence. Mrs. Switzer is a sister of E. R. Dyer, of Mansfield. The Switzer family is of German and Swiss origin and was founded in America by three brothers, John, Valentine and Nicholas, sons of John Switzer who never came to America. About 1770 the three brothers settled in Hardy, then Hampshire County. John Switzer's sons were Michael, John, Isaac and Phillip, and his daughters, Margaret, (who married Paul McKeever), Elizabeth, Sarah, Nellie and Catherine. The children of John, the son of John, were Catherine, Madeline, Rebecca, Maria, Elizabeth, Christina, Isaac, Adam, Michael, Stephen, John, Henry, Anthony, David, William, Kile and Jacob. The children of Nicholas, the son of John, were Daniel, Valentine, Simon, Phoebe, Magdalen, (who married Jacob Oldacre). Of these, Daniel married Mary Ogden, and their children were Jessie, Abram, David N., Simon, Eveline, Perry, Valentine and Isaiah. Of these, Simon married Harriet Rogers, and their children were Minerva and William.

PHILIP ANDERSON SWITZER, born at Upper Tract, Pendleton County, 1857, son of David M. and Frances A. (Wilson) Switzer, was married July 1, 1887, in Baltimore to Rachel Virginia, daughter of Silas B. and M. J. (Lemon) McClung. Children, Lena Virginia, Charles McClung and Ethel Clarence. He is a member of the M. E. Church, a Democrat and a member of I. O. O. F. and of K. O. T. M. His education was acquired in the public schools of Pendleton County, and he is by occupation a miller, being a stockholder in the E. R. Dyer & Company flour mill at Mansfield, Barbour County, and he also owns a comfortable home at the same place.

CHARLES K. SWITZER, born 1853 in Hardy, now Grant County, is a son of David N. and Francis A. (Wilson) Switzer. He was married in Pendleton County, May 29, 1879, to Minnie M., daughter of Albert and Martha (Miller) Dyer. Children, Ola G., Fannie D., Neva. He is a member of the M. E. Church, is a Democrat, and resides at Mansfield where he is in the mercantile business. He was educated in the public schools of Pendleton County, and is of Scotch-Irish and German ancestry. Mrs. Switzer is a sister of E. R. Dyer, member of the firm of Dyer & Switzer. He owns 26 acres near Mansfield, and a fine home in the town.

J. ED. STEWART, born 1850 on Elk Creek, son of John and Elsie Stewart, was married October 8, 1875 to Emily J., daughter of Abram and Maria (Morgan) Hudkins. Children, Hope, Dorothy, Stanley, Mathew, Mercea, Nellie, Victor. He is a member of the Missionary Baptist Church, a Republican, a farmer and stockdealer residing two miles below Elk City. He attended the West Virginia College at Flemington. In 1898 he was elected Commissioner of the county court. His great-grandfather, William Stewart, came from Ireland, married Miss Upshur, a Scotch lady, and settled in Highland County, Virginia. Edward Stewart was his grandfather, who married Margaret Callihan, and about 1837 they settled in what is now Barbour County. Their children were, Edward, William, Robert, Adam, John, Charles, Anna, Peggy, Polly and Jennie. Mr. Stewart's father was married in Highland County in 1834, and his children were: Felix, Hugh, Margaret, and J. Ed. Of these, Felix married Ingoby Nutter, Hugh married Catherine Fisher, Margaret married M. D. Reed, who is the father of Stewart F. Reed, of Clarksburg. The grandfather, Edward Stewart, was a Revolutionary soldier. Mr. Stewart owns 200 acres of valuable land. He was a teacher in his early life. His daughters, Hope and Dorothy, graduated at the Buckhannon Seminary.

ALEXANDER STEWART, born 1853, son of Silas and Zeporah Stewart, was married at Grafton, 1881 to Ida M., daughter of George and Julia Dilworth. The Stewarts came from Ireland to Virginia, and from Bath and Highland Counties, John, Robert, Edward, William and Silas Stewart came to Barbour and Harrison Counties.

ARTHUR W. STRAWDERMAN, born on the waters of Sugar Creek, 1865, son of Stephen and Elizabeth (Delawder) Strawderman, was married October 17, 1886, at the residence of Isaac Talbott, on Hacker's Creek, to Angelina, daughter of Isaac and Martha (Mitchell) Talbott. The subject of this sketch is a member of the Missionary Baptist Church, a Democrat and a farmer, carpenter and stonemason, residing three miles from Philippi, on Hacker's Creek, where he owns 28 acres, underlaid with coal and mostly improved, with a young orchard.

SAMUEL G. STRAWDERMAN, born 1852, son of Stephen and Elizabeth (Delawder) Strawderman, was married April 6, 1872, to Mary M., daughter of Vincent and Charlotte (Jordan) Gribble. Children, James Commodore, Francis Edward, Delbert Otto, Asta Esker, Ida Dell. He is a Missionary Baptist, a Democrat, a farmer and blacksmith, living east of Philippi, where he has plied his trade for seventeen years. He was educated in the public schools of the county.

ELIZABETH STRAWDERMAN, born 1832 in Hardy County, daughter of Jacob and Barbara Delawder, was married June 4, 1854, to Stephen, son of Sarah Strawderman. Children, Elam T., Malinda, Samuel G., Cordelia J., George, Albana, Jefferson D., Olive E., Arthur W., Savanna, Marcellus B. and John R.

CHARLES R. STIPE, born in Frederick County, Maryland, May 17, 1850, son of George E. and Mary M. (Rector) Stipe, married Jane, daughter of John and Mary (Yeager) Hillyard, March 17, 1875. She died the next year, and he married Catherine, daughter of Martin and Mary (Mustoe) Hillyard (cousin of his first wife), November 16, 1879. She died June 9, 1880. On October 2, 1884, he married Fannie C., daughter of Simeon S. and Louisa

RICHARD E. TALBOTT.

WARREN BRANCE KITTLE.

DAVID W. GALL.

ALBERT G. CHRISLIP.

M. (Bartlett) Lake, of Taylor County. Children, Cordelia, George, Edward, Thurman, Clay, Minnie, Pearl. He owns 323 acres, one-third cleared and well improved. The land contains two veins of bituminous and one of cannel coal.

ISAAC HARRISON STRICKLER, born July 27, 1816, in Page County, Virginia, son of Joseph and Mary (Miley) Strickler, was married at Philippi September 30, 1850, to Margaret J., daughter of Rev. Solomon and Elizabeth (Rightmire) Jarvis. Children, Robert Mann, Joseph Thomas (died young), Arthur DeWitt, Mary Alice, Sarah Belle (died young), Anna Elizabeth, Catherine Crim, Etta Jane, Clora Antonia. He was a Baptist, Odd Fellow, Good Templar, Democrat and a merchant. His was the first store in Philippi, and it stood in the rear of the present school building, near the old ferry. It was the firm of Almon & Strickler for a year. The store was opened (1843) in a stable. Three years later he built a brick store. He was the first postmaster in Philippi and held the office seventeen years. He went to the South during the war, served as a soldier, an officer, and later as a contractor. He also kept store for a time at Buckingham Court House with L. D. Morrall. In 1866 he opened a store in Philippi with Granville E. Jarvis, whom he subsequently bought out, and continued the business till his death in 1885. His son, Rev. Robert Mann Strickler, married Laura R., daughter of Colonel Mann Spitler, of Luray, Virginia. The Stricklers came from a German canton in Switzerland to Pennsylvania soon after the settlement of Philadelphia. Of the four brothers, one located in Philadelphia, one in Lancaster, one in York, and the fourth, Abraham, in Chester; and in 1728 settled on the Susquehanna River. Jacob, son of Abraham, went to the Valley of Virginia about 1731 and bought 1000 acres of Jacob Stover on the Massanutton, and 640 acres on South River. He was a Menonite preacher. Later (about 1750) another Strickler, of the same family, settled in what is now Page County, Virginia, and he had a son Joseph, who was president of the Page County Court, Assessor and Clerk, and died in 1856. This man was the father of Isaac H. Strickler. There is in the family a Bible printed at Zurich, Switzerland, in 1536.

ARTHUR DEWITT STRICKLER, son of Isaac H. and Margaret J. Strickler, born December 26, 1855, was married February 20, 1884, at Philippi, to Kate Rosalie, daughter of William and Catherine (Proudfoot) McClaskey. Their child, Robert Parvin, was born April 11, 1885. The subject of this sketch is a Baptist, a Democrat, and at present holds a position in the National Bank of Elkins, West Virginia. He has held the position of deputy in the Circuit and County Clerks' office of Barbour. He spent four years as clerk in the State Auditor's office, in Charleston, under Auditor I. V. Johnson, and remained seven months after the expiration of Mr. Johnson's term. Other positions held by him have been commissioner in chancery, notary public, town councilman and recorder of Philippi. The positions he has held in secret societies are as follows: He was a member of the Good Templars, Philippi Lodge No. 20, a number of terms W. C. T. The lodge ceased to exist in 1892. On October 15, 1877, he was initiated in Bigelow Lodge No. 52, A. F. and A. M.; passed November 19 and raised December 3, same year; appointed Senior Deacon in June, 1878; elected Secretary in 1880; Senior Warden in 1881; was Worshipful Master 1882, and served three years; re-elected Secretary in 1885, and served six years; was re-elected Worshipful Master in 1891 and 1892; in 1880 was appointed Deputy Grand Lecturer by Charles H. Collier, Grand Lecturer for the Sixth Masonic District, and served as such till 1886; served as Deputy Grand Lecturer of the Seventh District in 1895; in 1896 was reappointed for the Sixth District and is filling that position at present.

In 1887 he was appointed District Deputy Grand Master of the Sixth Masonic District, by Charles H. Collier, G. M., and served one year.

In 1884 he was appointed Grand Marshal of the Grand Lodge of West Virginia, of A. F. and A. M., by George E. Thornbury, Grand Marshal; was again appointed Grand Marshal by John M. Collins, G. M., in 1895; appointed Senior Grand Deacon in November, 1896, by Braxton D. Gibson, G. M.; elected Junior Grand Warden in 1897, and Senior Grand Warden in 1898.

On March 17, 1887, he was appointed Representative of the Grand Lodge of Ohio, near the Grand Lodge of West Virginia, by S. Stacker Williams, Grand Master of Ohio, and he still fills the position.

In 1880 and 1881 he received the several degrees in and became a member of Copestone Chapter No. 12, Royal Arch Masons, Grafton, West Virginia, remained a member till 1894, when he was dimitted to join Tyrean Royal Arch Chapter No. 13, Charleston, West Virginia, and in it served as Grand Master of Second Veil; Principal Sojourner; Captain of the Host, and Scribe. In 1887 he was appointed Grand Marshal of Grand Royal Arch Chapter of West Virginia. On Decemqer 5, 1891, he was appointed Representative of the Most Excellent Royal Arch Chapter of Kansas, near the Grand Chapter of West Virginia.

On November 9, 1882, he received the several degrees in and became a member of Crusade Commandry No. 6, Knight Templar, Fairmont, West Virginia, and remained a member till 1894, then was dimitted and joined Kanawha Commandry No. 4; in 1895 was elected Junior Warden, in 1896 Senior Warden, in 1897 Captain General, in 1898 Generalissimo. He is a member and Past Chancellor of Ivan Lodge, No. 61, K. of P., of Philippi.

CHARLES W. SNODGRASS, born 1868 on a tributary of Laurel Creek, is a son of Francis C. and Elizabeth (Mouser) Snodgrass, and married March 20, 1895, to Florence, daughter of George W. and Sarah (Stalnaker) Stemple. Their child's name is Gusta. He owns 85 acres, nearly all

FAMILY HISTORY. 469

cleared and largely used for grazing. It is on the waters of Laurel Creek. His grandfather, Francis Snodgrass, was an Englishman.

JACOB SHANK was born May 15, 1815, near Martinsburg, Berkeley County, son of John and Elizabeth (Johnson) Shank, and grandson of Christian Shank, who came from Germany when fourteen years old, his father and mother dying on the sea during the voyage over. On November 15, 1849, the subject of this sketch was married to Susanna, daughter of John and Margaret (Arbogast) Gall. Children, John W., Margaret Jane, Sarah E., Virginia E. and Rosa L. He is a member of the M. E. Church, South, and resides three miles west of Philippi. He is the only survivor of the Mexican War now residing in Barbour County. Christian Shank, his grandfather, was a Revolutionary soldier, and drew a pension many years. The subject of this sketch was three years a merchant, and eighteen years a tanner in Philippi. When the Federal army under McClellan reached Philippi, the soldiers destroyed $1000 worth of Mr. Shank's property, burning his tanbark and carrying his leather away.

JOHN W. SHANK, born west of Philippi, 1851, son of Jacob and Susanna (Gall) Shank, was married in Elk District, Barbour County, December 22, 1888, to Lee Ann, daughter of Samuel and Mary [Emmitt] Dickinson. He is a member of the M. E. Church, South, and by occupation a farmer, living three miles west of Philippi, where he has 170 acres, one-half improved. He attended the West Virginia College at Flemington and taught school in Barbour twelve years with unusual success. In 1880 he was elected Assessor for the west side of the river and served four years; and in 1889 he was appointed Sheriff by the county court and served two years.

ANDREW SIMON, born September 7, 1844, on Stewart's Run, Barbour County, son of Abram and Mary [Yeager] Simon, was married January 17, 1871, to Ella Syrena, daughter of William and Catherine [Proudfoot] McClaskey. Children, Paul Modisett, born January 25, 1872; Willie McClaskey, November 16, 1873, died August 8, 1874; Charles Hanshaw, May 17, 1876 [now in the U. S. Navy, stationed in the Philippine Islands]; Carlton Andrew, September 21, 1878; Cathleen Willis. September 14, 1880; Carrie Cowan, September 9, 1882; Tony Abram, August 2, 1884; Mona Bradford, December 10, 1886; Thompson Jackson, March 4, 1887; Virginia Payne, June 1, 1894. The subject of this sketch spent eighteen years as a commercial traveler, for the most part in West Virginia. He assisted in collecting material for the History of Barbour County. The Simon family came to Barbour from Hampshire County, where Benjamin Simon, grandfather of the subject of this sketch, was born August 9, 1781. He married Elizabeth Stump, who was born in the same county August 18, 1786. Their children were as follows, with dates of birth: Catherine, born February 11, 1806; John, October 2, 1807; Margaret, January 7, 1809; Polly, August

7, 1810; Abram, April 20, 1812; George, July 12, 1815; Christian, February 15, 1817; Sarah, May 24, 1819; Anthony, November 25, 1821. Of the above children, Abram was married December 22, 1833, to Mary Yeager. He died December 1, 1865. Their children were, Sarah [now Mrs. William Talbott], born November 9, 1834; Virginia [now Mrs. F. E. Payne], July 23, 1837; Benjamin A., May 20, 1841; Andrew, September 7, 1844; James K., January 19, 1849; Lewis H., March 3, 1855.

SAMUEL LEWIS SEMMELMAN, born 1845 in Baltimore, Maryland, son of Albright and Mary Ann (Neeb) Semmelman, was married March 4, 1877, at Newburg, Preston County, West Virginia, to Mrs. Mary M. Hubbard, daughter of William and Nellie (Harden) Dehaven. Children, Alice M., Jessie L., Charles A., Lula Gay, John Henry, Bobbie, (deceased) and Carrie May. He is a member of the following secret orders: A. F. and A. M. Lodge No. 52, Philippi; Copestone Chapter No. 12, A. F. and A. M., and DeMolay Commandry No. 11, Knights Templar, Grafton, West Virginia. In politics he is a Republican, and lives on Teter's Creek, where he owns 160 acres, 130 cleared. It is the farm on which lived John Ryan, one of the earliest settlers. He also owns two houses and eight acres of land in Old Moatsville. He is engaged in general farming, stockraising and merchandizing. He came to Barbour in 1879 from Thornton, Taylor County, where he had been operating a store for N. Rogers. He was engaged in the mercantile business at Nestorville till 1884, when he sold out to C. W. Haller and moved to the farm he now owns. In 1890 he moved to Scottsdale, Pennsylvania; then moved to Moatsville, where he had a store five years, and then sold the stock to J. M. Compton, and moved back to the farm where he has cleared thirty acres in the last two years. He was educated in the public schools of Baltimore.

JOHN WILSON SHROYER, born 1856, son of John and Elizabeth (Gawthrop) Shroyer, was married July 12, 1888, in Taylor County, to Rebecca, daughter of William and Hester (Osborn) Means. Children, Ethel, Mabel Edna, Lulu Hazel, Nilia Grace. Mr. Shroyer is a Republican and a farmer living in Cove District, where he owns 173 acres. He was educated in the public schools, and has held the office of school trustee. On January 17, 1865, Mr. Shroyer's father was shot and killed at Gregg's by a gang of horsethieves who attempted to break into his stable. He drove them away and while pursuing them he was shot. A bullet passed through the clothes of his son, the subject of this sketch. The thieves them returned, broke into the stable and took the horses.

AARON STRADER, born 1838 in Upshur County, son of Michael and Eva (Radabaugh) Strader, was married in 1859 to Priscilla, daughter of William and Mahala (Simon) Ward. Children, Ruhanna E., Ulysses Grant, William Michael, Dorcas E., Wellington L., Granville Lee, Jemima Catherine, Burton M., Asa, Asha, Mary Jane and Martha Ann. He is a member

A. F. ROHRBOUGH.

JOHN H. ZIRKLE.

JOHN T. REGER.

B. B. ROHRBOUGH.

FAMILY HISTORY. 473

of the M. E. Church, of the G. A. R., a Republican and a farmer on Peck's Run. In 1862 he enlisted in the Union army at Buckhannon. Soon afterwards his leg was broken by the kick of a horse, and after recovery he was placed on guard duty where he served till the close of the war. The Straders came from Holland and settled in New Jersey, half a century before the Revolutionary War. About 1740 some of them settled on the South Branch in the present County of Hardy.

CHARLES W. SHOMO, born 1873, son of George N. and Virginia (Visqusney) Shomo, was married May 31, 1896, at Junior, to Maude M., daughter of S. R. and Mary C. (Williams) Elbon. Their child is Hazel B. He is a member of the M. E. Church, of the K. of P., and in politics is a Republican, and by profession a teacher, having been educated in the common schools. He has a library of 400 volumes, and is a careful reader. His grandfather was D. J. Shomo.

BESSHEBA M. SMITH, born 1847, on Hacker's Creek, daughter of Silas and Sarah (McKinney) Talbott, was married August 27, 1872, to Levi J. B. Smith, son of John and Mary (Swisher) Smith. Their son, Esker T., was born August 9, 1873. Eighteen months later her husband died, and she moved with her son to Barbour County, and now resides on Baker's Run. She has been a member of the Baptist Church since 1863. Levi Smith served six months in the Union army, being discharged at Wheeling in 1864. His father was John Smith who was born in 1796; his grandfather was also John Smith, and was of Irish parentage. Mrs. Smith has been an invalid since 1888. She owns 45 acres of highly improved land underlaid with coal. David Smith was born October 29, 1773, died November 7, 1864, was of English decent, born in New Jersey. He was Justice of the Peace, captain of Malitia and Sheriff of Lewis County. He married Sarah Hacker who was born June 24, 1775, and died 1855. She was of Irish descent. Their son, John Smith, was born October 24, 1796 and died October 12, 1880. He was a local preacher over fifty years. On January 28, 1819, he married Mary Swisher, who was born November 4, 1801, and died May 29, 1878. Her father was Peter Swisher, native of Maryland, born March 11, 1777, died September 27, 1830, (killed by falling tree). On January 27, 1801, he married Susanna Rinehart, who was a native of Maryland, was born December 1, 1779, and died at the age of seventy-five.

RICHARD TALBOTT, probably the first white man to make his permanent home in Barbour County—together with his brother, Cotteral, and sister, Charity,—was born in Fairfax County, Virginia, November 16, 1764. He was a son of William Talbott, a native of England, who came to Virginia long before the Revolution. The Talbott family is one of the oldest in England, where it is usually spelled Talbot. In this country the spelling is sometimes Tolbert, which conforms fairly well with the common pronunciation of the name. The ancestors of the family crossed from Normandy

(France) to England with William the Conqueror in the year 1066, and from time to time members of the family rose to great prominence in England. Upon the death of his father Richard Talbott was bound out. Whether the two older children were also bound out cannot now be ascertained, but they were probably old enough to take care of themselves. The man to whom Richard was apprenticed was not good to him, and he decided to run off. Having communicated his purpose to his sister, Charity, she laid plans to assist him, and the scheme was a bold one. Knowing that it would be useless for her brother to escape from his master if he remained in the country, for he would be taken back and, perhaps, subjected to worse treatment, she determined to get all things ready, and the three children, she being the eldest, accompanied by their mother, would cross the mountains and seek a new home in the wilderness of the west.

The preparations for flight were made so secretly that they were unsuspected, and when all things were ready, Charity assisted Richard to escape from his master, and they departed secretly for the new land beyond the Alleghanies. They completed their long journey through the wilderness, crossed only by trails, and, in 1780, arrived in Barbour, then Monongalia County, and selected a site for their home. It must be confessed that no small degree of courage and self-confidence were exhibited by these people who thus braved the dangers of the frontiers at a time when the Indian war was raging in all its fury. They selected land on the waters of Hacker's Creek, and made that their home. Their nearest neighbors on the south were about Beverly and Leading Creek; on the east at St. George; on the north, about Simpson, and on the west and southwest near Buckhannon and Clarksburg. It is recorded that they were several times obliged to leave their homes on account of the hostility of the Indians, and twice fled east of the Alleghanies. None of the family fell victims to the savages. Eight years after they came to Barbour, Richard Talbott married Margaret Dowden, whose parents were about to move away with her. She was born December 25, 1776, lacked three days of being twelve years old. To them were born thirteen children. Their names and the dates of their births are as follows: Samuel 1790, Mary Ann 1792, Jacob 1794, Abraham 1796, Isaac 1798, Robert 1801, Elisha 1804, Silas 1806, Absalom 1807, Elam 1810, Zachariah 1513, Margaret 1815, Elizabeth 1819. Nearly all the Talbotts of Barbour County are descendants of the above named children.

In 1788 Cotteral Talbott married Elizabeth, daughter of Jacob Reger. The marriage ceremony was performed by Isaac Edwards, a noted preacher of that early time, who traveled through Randolph and adjoining counties and concerning whose birth and death nothing seems to be known.

Robert Talbott, son of Richard, married Mary Woodford, daughter of William and sister of John Howe Woodford. (See sketch of the Wood-

FAMILY HISTORY. 475

fords.) Their children were, John, Richard T., David, William Woodford Salathiel, Marion, Robert M., Perry, Margaret, Hannah, Josina and Mary.

ISAAC D. TALBOTT, born 1823, on Hacker's Creek, son of Elisha and Millie (Stephens) Talbott, was married October 21, 1841, to Martha, daughter of Robert and Sallie (Keller) Mitchell. Children, Anna Amelia, Augusta, William Riley, Sallie, Simon Switzer, Mary M., Angeline and Theodosia. He is a Baptist and in politics a Democrat, and by occupation a farmer on Hacker's Creek. Mrs. Talbott is of Irish descent. The Mitchells were early settlers in Barbour.

SIMON SWITZER TALBOTT, born 1852, son of Isaac D. and Martha (Mitchell) Talbott, was married in Preston County, West Virginia to Mary Elizabeth, daughter of James and Amanda (Blackwood) Snyder. He is an Odd Fellow, a Democrat, and a farmer and stockdealer, residing on Hacker's Creek, where he owns 200 acres of well improved land. He attended the West Virginia College, at Flemington, and has held the office of County Superintendent. Mrs. Talbott's grandfather, Henry Snyder, came from Germany to Virginia, and in 1827, near Newburg, Preston County, his son, James, Mrs. Talbott's father, was born. Mrs. Talbott was educated at the Fairmont Normal School and taught three years; Mr. Talbott taught twenty-three schools.

ROBERT M. TALBOTT, born 1840, son of Robert and Mary (Woodford) Talbott, was married December 29, 1869, to Mary Florence, daughter of John R. and Lucinda (Sinsel) Williamson. Children, Anna Laura, Susan A., Maggie, James Guy, Alba Ray, Lucinda, Patrick G. and Emma. Mr. Talbott is a Missionary Baptist, and is a farmer, living near Arden. He was educated at the Morgantown Academy, and at a Commercial College in Philadelphia, and has taught twenty-four schools, and spent seven years as a merchant at Vannoy's Mill and at Flora, on Sugar Creek. He owns 120 acres in Barbour and owns a half interest in 900 acres in Randolph. Alba Ray, his son, was a soldier in the Spanish War of 1898.

WILLIAM WOODFORD TALBOTT, born 1825, son of Robert and Mary (Woodford) Talbott, was married June 12, 1853, to Sarah, daughter of Abram and Mary (Yeager) Simon. Children, Salathiel M., Melvin, Lewis Wilson, Elam Dowden, Abram Ira, Fitzhugh Lee, William Floyd, Waitman T., Robert Dellett, Mary Florence, Virginia B., Rosa May. He is a member of the Missionary Baptist Church, a Democrat, and a farmer, residing on Stewart's Run, where he owns 340 acres of land.

ELAM DOWDEN TALBOTT, son of William Woodford Talbott, was born 1857, and was married June 15, 1886, to Lutie Lee, daughter of Squire Newton and Florence A. (Brown) Bosworth, of Beverly. Children, Eva Bosworth, Marguerite, Eugenia, Winifred and William Donald. Mr. Talbott graduated at the West Virginia University, and entered upon the practice of law, locating at Beverly, Randolph County, and has become one of the foremost members of his profession in that part of the State. His brother, Dr. Lewis W. Talbott, located in Randolph County also, and is a leading physician at Elkins.

JAMES WESLEY TALBOTT, born 1839, son of Zachariah and Mary (Ellison) Talbott, was married November 21, 1861, to Almira, daughter of Henry A. and Eunice (Marteney) Gall. Children, Emma Rosetta, Estella Lee, Minnie May and Adela. In 1895 his daughter Minnie was married to Charles Bruce Sturm, of Philippi. Mr. Talbott is a Missionary Baptist, a Mason, and in politics a Democrat. He is proprietor of the Commercial Hotel in Philippi, and is a traveling salesman for a Philadelphia firm. For six years he was Sheriff of Barbour County, two years by appointment and four by election. Immediately after his marriage he entered the mercantile business at Mansfield, and later at Overfield. In 1865 he went into the saw-mill business and followed it five years, until he became Sheriff. Five years later he became cashier of the Farmers' Bank of Philippi, and held the position nine years, in the meantime engaging extensively in other business, and was promoter of the first steam flour mill in Barbour County, built at Philippi, in 1882; and was prominently identified with the building of the Grafton and Greenbrier railroad. The father of Mrs. Talbott's mother, Gideon Ellison, came to Barbour from Eastern Virginia and married Elizabeth Stephens, sister of Elisha Talbott's first wife. His children were, Zachariah, John, Isaac H., Samuel W., Robert F., Edward G., Mary, Julia, Louisa, Emaline, Kaziah. The children of Zachariah Talbott, by his first wife, were, James Wesley, Almira, Ervin A., Asa Burton, Robert Clinton; by his second wife, who was Kaziah Ellison, sister of his first wife, the children were, Gideon P. and Baby; by his third wife, who was Margaret J. Zinn, one child, Madera Elizabeth Belle. Mr. Talbott has a copper tea kettle which was brought to Barbour by his grandfather, Richard Talbott, in 1780.

SYLVANUS H. TALBOTT born 1854, son of Silas and Sarah (McKinney) Talbott, was married November 30, 1884, to Edith, daughter of William and Lydia Bartlett. Children, Iva, William Bruce, Hazel, Ruby, Esker Wayne. He is a member of the Baptist Church, a Democrat, a farmer and stockdealer, living on Baker's Run, where he owns 105 acres of improved land, underlaid with coal. Mr. Talbott was five years a Justice of the Peace. The ancestors of Mr. Talbott have been given. Silas Talbott was born 1806, and his wife 1811; he died 1877 and she in 1899. Their children were, Margaret, Abraham, Daniel P. Jane M., Joseph P., Indiana, Sarah A., Elizabeth E., Besshēba M., John M., Wicena, Sylvanus H.

RICHARD EDWARD TALBOTT, born February 21, 1867, son of Richard T. and Margaret (Weber) Talbott, was married June 5, 1895, at Philippi, to Etta, daughter of Isaac H. and Margaret (Jarvis) Strickler. Their child's name is Margaret. Mr. Talbott is a member of the Baptist Church, is a

WILLIAM WOODFORD TALBOTT AND FAMILY.

Lewis Wilson　　Abraham Ira　　Salathiel M.　　Floyd　　Elam Dowden　　Waitman T.
　　　Mary Florence　　Mr. Talbot　　Mrs. Talbott　　Fitzhugh Lee
　　　　　Virginia B.　　Robert Dellett　　Rosa May

FAMILY HISTORY.

Democrat, an Odd Fellow, a Mason and a lawyer. He formerly held the office of Recorder of Philippi, and is the present Circuit Clerk. He was educated in the public schools, in private schools and in the West Virginia University, graduating from that institution in the law department in 1893. His father, in early life, spent several years in Illinois and other western States, chiefly in the lead mines. While there, April, 8, 1849, he was married by a Catholic priest to Miss Weber. Immediately after that event he and his wife returned to Barbour County, passing down the Mississippi to the mouth of the Ohio, up that stream to Parkersburg, thence overland by stage to Barbour. He purchased a farm of George Woodford, and settled on the head of Simpson's Creek, where the new town of Heatherly is now building. There he became a prosperous farmer, and his children were as follows. Mary Elizabeth, Virginia, Melissa Ann, Josina (died February 28, 1897, at Pratt, Kansas), Robert Dowden (died young), John Lawrence, Lora Linden, David Albert, Richard Edward, Margaret Alice (died May 22, 1893, near Oklahoma City, Oklahoma;) William Howe, Alonzo (died young), Arthur Lee, Kyle Weber. The Weber family are German, and Lawrence Weber, grandfather of the subject of this sketch, was born in Merlenbach, Germany, and in 1819 was married to Elizabeth, daughter of John Keil, of Kraumbach. On June 8, 1830, they left for America, and arrived in Baltimore September 20, with four children, namely: John, born December 10, 1819; Katharine, born January 8, 1822; Eva, born August 16, 1825; Elizabeth, born November 23, 1828. The other children were born in America, namely, Margaret, born in Pennsylvania, February 21, 1833; Mary Ann, born March 31, 1836; Sarah, born March 5, 1841; Louisa, born September 25, 1844. The family removed to Illinois. Richard T. Talbott, born April 17, 1821, is a son of Robert, and Robert was a son of Richard and Mary (Dowden) Talbott, the first settlers in Barbour.

COLUMBUS TALBOTT, born 1864, son of Abram R. and Irena Talbott, was married November 15, 1893, to Mattie, daughter of Captain William C. and Rebecca (Conway) Parker. He is a member of the M. E. Church, South, an Odd Fellow, a Democrat and a farmer, living near Burnersville. He was educated at the Fairmont Normal School. His father, who was a son of David and a grandson of Cotteral Talbott, was born in 1827. His mother's maiden name was Ruth Wamsley. Abram Talbott married (1849) Irena, daughter of Stephen and Catherine (Reger) Martin. Their children were, Elizabeth, Leroy H. and Columbus. He is a member of the M. E. Church, South, is a Democrat and a farmer, living near Burnersville.

JACOB TETER. According to the traditions of the family, Jacob Teter was the first of the name to make his home in what is now Barbour County, coming from Pendleton and settling near Belington about the year 1800. However, it is shown by the Virginia land books that George Teter owned land here as early as 1787; and the same books show that Teter's Creek was named as early as 1788. It is probable, therefore, that there were two families of Teters who figured in the early history of what is now Barbour. Jacob Teter was married before he came to Barbour, and his son Joseph was born in Pendleton County, May 8, 1796. The family was represented in the Valley of Virginia at the close of the Revolution by the Dietricks, which is the German form of the name Teter. They are said to have come from Pennsylvania to the Valley of Virginia, whence they entered Pendleton and crossed into Randolph, now Barbour. Jacob Teter was a son of Philip, and his children were, Jacob, Joseph, Isaac, James, Nancy, and probably Mary. At any rate, the records in Randolph show that in 1803 Mary "Tidricks" was married to Enoch Osborn, the ceremony being performed by Robert Maxwell. In 1809 Jacob Teter (son of Jacob, no doubt), was married to Nancy, daughter of Moses Cade. The ceremony was performed by Phineas Wells. In 1811 Solomon Yeager married Mary, daughter of Jacob Teter, the ceremony being performed by Simeon Harris. There is no mention in the Randolph County records of the marriage of any other of Jacob Teter's children; but three of them held office in Randolph: Jacob, who was Justice of the Peace in 1817 and Assessor in 1823; James, who was Constable in 1819, and Joseph, who was Justice of the Peace in 1832.

JOSEPH TETER, son of Jacob, was married to Mary McCann (Mitchell) who was born in 1786. They had two children, Joseph and Elizabeth. The latter married William P. Woodruff. Mr. Teter died February 17, 1881. He was Assessor in 1845, and was school commissioner in 1844.

JOSEPH TETER, son of Joseph and grandson of Jacob, was born 1828. On March 29, 1856, at Carrolton, Ohio, he was married to Dorrinda, daughter of Charles and Margary (Brooks) Fawcett. Their children were Charles Fawcett, Martha Virginia, John Mitchell, Gordon Battelle, Mary Margary, Daniel Patrick, William Steele, Joseph Henry, Letticia Grace and Addison Brooks. Mr. Teter died December 21, 1898. He was a member of the M. E. Church, and was a local preacher. He organized the first Sunday School in Valley District. He was a member of the Masonic Order; in politics he was a Republican, and by occupation a farmer, residing near Belington. He was educated in the public schools; and he filled the office of Colonel of the Militia. In 1864 he was elected Supervisor. He was a member of the first legislature of West Virginia, and his name was first on the roll. He was twice elected to the legislature. As a preacher, it is claimed that he married more couples than any other person in Barbour County, except Joshua S. Corder. He preached fifty years. He was an extensive owner of real estate, and was in all ways, an able and influential man.

GORDON BATTELLE TETER, born 1861, son of Joseph and Dorrinda Teter, was married June 6, 1894, to Flora, daughter of Watson and Elizabeth Tenney. He is a member of the M. E. Church; in politics is a Republican, and by occupation a farmer and stockman, living on the head of Simpson's Creek, where he owned 300 acres, recently sold for $12,000 to the Southern Coal and Export Company. Mr. Teter spent one year in Texas as a cowboy.

THOMAS BENTON TETER, born 1852, son of Jesse and Elizabeth (Phillips) Teter, was married March 5, 1874, to Mary, daughter of B. B. Durrett. Children, Minnie, Darwin, Ora Bessie and Bertzell. He is a Democrat, and is owner of the mill at Belington where he lives. In 1893 he was appointed United States Indian Agent over the Bannock and Shoshone Indians at Fort Hall Reservation, Idaho, and had control of the U. S. forces sent to Jackson Hole during the Indian trouble in 1896, which grew out of a dispute as to the right of the Indians to hunt in the Yellowstone Park. That right had been granted by treaty, but forbidden by the Wyoming game laws, and the Wyoming officers killed a few Indians, whereupon the tribes collected to avenge it. Mr. Teter's prompt action in getting troops on the scene prevented further trouble. Mr. Teter has traveled extensively, and he considers that West Virginia has resources and advantages possessed by few, if any States of the Union, and he has unbounded faith in the development of West Virginia.

CHARLES FAWCETT TETER, born August 4, 1858, son of Joseph and Dorrinda (Fawcett) Teter, was married at Philippi, December 17, 1890, to Lillian, daughter of James E. and Elizabeth (Wilson) Hall. Children, Dwight Hall, Charles Wilson and Elizabeth. He is a member of the M. E. Church; is a past master in Masonry; in politics he is a Republican, and by profession a lawyer. He was educated at Bethany College, and is a graduate of the University of Michigan. In 1882 he was elected on the Republican ticket District Attorney of Barbour County. In 1898 he made a trip to Europe. He is is secretary and treasurer of the Philippi Coal Mining Company. This company, in 1899, successfully placed upon the market large areas of coal in Barbour and Upshur Counties, and brought about the development of the section, and secured the building of the necessary plants. Mr. Teter takes an interest in politics and contributes largely to the success of the party.

NATHAN H. TAFT, a native of New England, located in Philippi about 1848, for the practice of law. Some years later he married Mary E., daughter of Rev. Solomon and Elizabeth Jarvis. In 1862 he moved to Buckhannon, having been elected Prosecuting Attorney of Upshur County. Later he became editor of the *Republican*, published in Buckhannon. It was the organ of the Conservative party, and opposed the conscriptive methods of the radicals. The paper incurred the enmity of those whom it opposed, and violence was threatened to prevent its publication. But it came out regularly with the assistance of James W. Woffindin, a young newspaper man. Mr. Taft died at Weston, January 3, 1867. He had taken a prominent part in politics during the war. In 1861 he was elected Prosecuting Attorney of Barbour; and the same year was chosen member of the second Wheeling Convention which re-organized the government of Virginia. Early in the same year, when Thomas A. Bradford and Sumuel Woods were candidates for the Richmond Convention, which passed the Ordinance of Secession, Mr. Taft supported Mr. Woods, believing that he was more friendly to a preservation of the Union. When Mr. Woods while a member of the Convention, introduced resolutions declaring the Federal Government ought to recognize the independence of the Seceded States, Mr. Taft upheld the position taken by Mr. Woods; and in a meeting held in Philippi March 7, 1861, was one of a committee which drafted resolutions sustaining Mr. Woods. When the war actually came, Mr. Taft supported the North. He was in Philippi on June 3 when the Federal artillery opened on the town; and from an attic window (present residence of C. P. Thompson, he watched the Confederates going up the pike, and was heard to exclaim, "Thank God!" He hated slavery, and although he did not wish for war, yet when the war came, he wanted it to stamp slavery out forever. He was instrumental in setting at liberty many persons who had been arrested because of their supposed sympathies with the South. He knew what arrest was, because he had been taken forcably from his own house by Confederates a short time before and had been confined in jail because of his sympathies with the North.

As a lawyer, Mr. Taft stood high in the profession, and as an orator, he was eloquent and successful, exercising much influence over a jury.

GRANVILLE ESKRIDGE TAFT, born July 19, 1862, in Taylor County, son of Nathan H. Taft,.was married January 10, 1889 to Emma L., daughter of John T. and Rachel B. (Critchfield) Alexander. Children, Cyril Daniel, Lottie Lee, John Hopkins and Rachel May. He is a Baptist, a Mason, an Odd Fellow, a K. of P., an Elk, and a Democrat. He is county clerk of Barbour, elected by a very large majority. He was educated in the public schools, and before he became clerk he was a printer and a railroad agent.

HUGH TURNER. This eccentric man, called "the Hermit" lived for the most of his life, and died in what is now Barbour County. The circumstances of his birth and early life are unknown. He was the first contractor to build the first court house in Randolph County, 1788; but he failed to fulfill his contract. He withdrew from the settlements and lived along Laurel Hill at several places in caves or in vaults made by building stone walls against the faces of cliffs. He was a Scotchman. He eked out a living by making millstones from the rock found along Laurel Hill suited to that purpose (Pottsville Conglomerate) and sold them to millers who built the first mills in Glade District. John G. Johnson says there are some of the unfinished millstone on Teter's Creek on Mrs. Catherine Poling's land. Some of his old camping places are nearby John Harris who died in 1882

Benjamin Holly Woodford.

John F. Woodford.

in his ninety-third year remembered him, and said that Turner seldom came into the settlements, and could never be induced to lie in bed, always lying on the floor before the fire. He was called a "woman hater." He had a camp on the top of Laurel Hill on the old road which led from Belington by way of Beaver Creek to Beverly. The camp was ten or twelve feet square, built of stones beside a cliff, and the ruins may still be seen. About 1860 Lewis Corley (who in 1898 hung himself at the Poor Farm in this county) found a copper rule one foot long, with inches and fractions marked on it, and some mason's tools, in a crevice of a cliff. The tools were probably his. The old man was found dead by some persons going from Glady Creek to court at Beverly. He had a fire near the roadside, and it was supposed that he had fainted and fallen into the fire. He had rolled into the road. Some of his millstones were near the place in recent years. Others had been rolled down the steep eastern face of Laurel Hill (toward Leading Creek) and they acquired such force that they knocked down trees

HENRY TRIMBLE, born 1872 in Highland County, Virginia, in politics is a Democrat, and belongs to the order of Good Templars. He is a harness maker at Belington where he located in 1899. He was educated in the public schools, and has followed his trade with success for eleven years.

JACOB SPOTSWOOD THACKER was born in Nelson County, Virginia, 1843, son of Jacob and Sarah (Demaster) Thacker; and on November 2, 1866 was married to Jerusha, daughter of Edward and granddaughter of Elisha Talbott; and as a second marriage, April 25, 1876, he married Isabel, daughter of Addison and Elizabeth Reed. Children, Dora Ellen, Henrietta, Theodosia Lee, Columbia Lily, Annie L., Cora V., Georgia, Gracie Cordelia, Estella, Jennings Bryan. Mr. Thacker is a member of the Christian Church, is an Odd Fellow, a Democrat and a farmer, residing near Mt. Zion Church where he owns 125 acres, mostly improved. His great grandfather came from Scotland and settled near Richmond; and his grandfather, Wyatt Thacker was born at Richmond, 1785; and his father was born in 1811 and lived to be 84 years old. His grandfather, Henry Demasters, served in the War of 1812. Mr. Thacker's children married as follows: Ellen married B. F. Vequesney at Elkins; Henrietta married Alman Poling; Columbia married Grant Williams at Junior; Annie married James Curtis of Harding; and Cora married Riley Poling. Mr. Thacker has travelled in seventeen States and has voyaged 4000 miles by sea. He has been a member of the Board of Education. During the Civil War he fought on the Confederate side.

JOHN P. THOMPSON, born 1826 in Barbour County, son of Henry and Mercy (Parrill) Thompson, was married April 7, 1864, in Philippi, to Helen, daughter of Daniel and Jerusha (Hart) Capito. Children, Flora, Eva, Claude H., John Paul, Edna and George P. Mr. Thompson is a member of the Old School Baptist Church, is a Democrat, and for many years was Jus-

486   FAMILY HISTORY.

tice of the Peace, and was Clerk of the Board of Supervisors. He was educated in private schools, and one of his instructors was William Ferguson, a pedagogue famous in his day for cruelty to his pupils. However, he made them learn. Mr. Thompson's brothers and sisters were, Hamilton G., William C., Hezekiah J. and Jane R., who married A. P. Wilson. The Thompsons were among the very first settlers in Barbour. The exact date of their coming is uncertain, but it is believed to have been near the time of the coming of the Talbotts; that is, 1780.

JAMES L. THOMPSON, born near Calhoun, 1864, son of James and Maria (Day) Thompson, was married May 5, 1889, to Lucy A., widow of Henry Dayton, who died in 1886. She is a daughter of Samuel and Catherine (Knapp) Delauder. Children, Ethel Catherine, Cornelia Edith, Benjamin Harold. He is a member of the M. E. Church, a Republican and a farmer, living near Calhoun. Mrs. Thompson's grandfather, Henry Knapp, came to West Virginia from New York, and her father was a soldier in the Union army. Catherine Knapp, mother of Mrs. Thompson, was born 1829 at Lost River, Hardy County. She was a daughter of Jacob and Barbara (Feather) Delauder, and came to Barbour when eighteen years of age, where she married Samuel Knapp. Their children were, John Williamson, Marietta, America, George W., Stephen Hezekiah, Edith Elizabeth, Cornelia Indiana, Lucy Adaline, Samuel Willie, David Festus. Mrs. Knapp has belonged to the M. E. Church 52 years. Mrs. Knapp's great grandfather, Lawrence Delauder, died in 1835 at the age of 103; her grandfather, Abram Delauder, lived to the age of 95, and her father to the age of 83. Her grandfather, George Feather, served in the Revolutionary War. Samuel Knapp was in the Union army.

HEZEKIAH THOMPSON, born 1845, son Henry and Mercy (Parrill) Thompson, was married December 20, 1883, to Augusta, daughter of John R. and Susan (Sinsel) Williamson. He is a Baptist, a Democrat and a farmer, living three miles east of Philippi, where he owns 200 acres of land, devoted to farming and grazing; it is underlaid with coal. Mr. Thompson was a deputy sheriff twelve years, and two years township treasurer, and is an energetic and progressive citizen.

U

MRS. AUGUSTA UMBACH was born in Germany, daughter of John Custer, and in 1879 was married in Pittsburg to Henry Umbach, who died in 1892. Children, Theodore, Marie, Hilda, Edna and Nelly. She is a member of the Lutheran Church, and is proprietress of the Luzerne Hotel at Belington. She received her education in Germany and came to America in 1873. Six years ago she came to Belington, previous to which time she had been living on a farm. Four years ago she took charge of the Hotel Luzerne, after having lost heavily by investing in West Virginia coal lands.

Her father was for twenty years overseer of a large estate in Germany, and she lost a brother in the Franco-Prussian War.

GEORGE WESLEY UTTERBACH, born 1842 in Fauquier County, Virginia, son of Wesley and Juliet (Bailey) Utterbach, was married March 4, 1866, to Florence, daughter of Miner and Matilda (Bolyard) Fleming. Children, Lloyd J., William S., Charles B., Elmona, James B., Lucy O., Floy D., Willie H., Grace P., Don G., Florence J. He is a member of the M. E. Church, a Republican and a farmer residing near the mouth of the Buckhannon River. He enlisted in the Federal army in 1861 and fought through the war, taking part in many battles. He was in the Lynchburg Raid with Hunter and Averell. In 1893 Mr. Utterbach was married to Jennie, daughter of John W. Ward, and has one daughter by this second marriage, Mary G.

JUDGE SAMUEL WOODS.* The true object of any one who attempts to write a sketch of the life of another should be to put on record the prominent traits of character of the subject of the sketch so all may know what manner of man he was, and gather from his life something which may inspire others in the journey.

Our greatest poet has said:

> "Lives of great men all remind us
> We can make our lives sublime,
> And, departing, leave behind us
> Footprints on the sands of time."

> "Footprints that perhaps another,
> Sailing o'er life's solemn main,
> A forelorn and shipwrecked brother,
> Seeing, may take heart again."

The life of Judge Woods was well-balanced and well-rounded, and from it may be gathered much by our young men to inspire them to greater effort and better living. Samuel Woods was born in Beauce County, Canada, East, on the 19th day of September, 1822. His birthplace, I have heard him say, was in the territory in dispute between England and the United States, and when the Maine boundary question was settled, his birthplace became a part of the territory of the United States, and so he became a citizen of this country.

His parents were Irish. He was born poor, and by experience knew what poverty meant. He knew, when a boy, if he were ever educated, he must do the greater part in furnishing his own opportunities. When a boy his father moved to Meadville, Pennsylvania, the seat of Allegheny Col-

---

*This sketch was written by Judge Okey Johnson, an associate with Judge Woods on the Supreme Bench of West Virginia, and now Professor of Law in the West Virginia University.

lege, where the boy, with his father, worked at the plasterer's trade. Fortunately for the boy the father took him to a college town. Seeing the college and the students did, no doubt, much to fire his young heart with the greatest desire for a college education. He did not give up this great desire of his heart, but toiled and studied, and entered the college, and graduated in the classical course in 1842, when he was twenty years old. He studied law with Fox Allen, a noted lawyer in Pittsburg. He also taught school. He was one of the teachers in the famous old Academy at Morgantown, where so many men, who afterwards gained distinction, commenced their education. In 1844 he married, at Meadville, Miss Isabella Neeson, sister of James Neeson, a prominent lawyer, afterwards at Fairmont, in this State, and afterwards in Richmond, Virginia. In 1849 young Woods moved to and located for the practice of the law at Philippi, Barbour County, Virginia. To this place the year after he brought his bride, and they then founded a home, which has as many pleasant memories surrounding it as any home in West Virginia; a home, the sweet influence of which has blessed the children reared therein, and from which benedictions have gone to bless the country all around it. Here in this town and at this home Mr. Woods commenced his professional career. Of splendid physique, of fine address, of great natural endowments, a classical education, a fine legal education under one of the leading lawyers in Pittsburg, in a comparatively new country, he commenced his career as a lawyer under most favorable circumstances. A man who despised falsehood, with no bad habits, strictly abstaining from all intoxicating liquor, and not even using tobacco, and being enthusiastic in religion, his fidelity to every trust reposed in him, his indomitable perseverance and great industry, his ability to take care of his client's interests in court, soon gave him a standing in the counties in which he practiced, that no other lawyer possessed. His zeal, honesty and ability gave him a clientage that placed him in the very front ranks of his profession, and until he retired from the practice in 1883, he was regarded as the Nestor of the bar in the counties of Barbour, Randolph, Taylor and Webster, where he practiced. He had so won the confidence of the people that with his learning and great legal ability, fine address and persuasive eloquence, he was well nigh irresistible before a jury. In more than one instance he successfully defended clients on indictment for murder on the ground of self-defense, when most people outside of the jury thought his client was the aggressor.

By his earnestness and tenacity to the interests of his clients, his influence was great, not only with juries but with the courts also. His great success in his profession did not come to him by extemporaneous efforts, but by a life of integrity, by his general education, by his legal learning, and by that without which his splendid talents would not have availed him, —his mastery of the facts and laws of his cases, and never going into an

important case without thorough preparation, unless forced in by the other side; then frequently the other side was sorry it brought on the battle, for few men were more ready for a sudden legal contest then he. He was a man of splendid physique, about six feet tall, with broad shoulders, with a grand personal presence; from his boyhood to old age he was what the world calls a handsome man. He was abstemious, using neither spirituous liquors nor tobacco, and in consequence through his long life enjoyed perfect health. He was erect, he was agile as a boy, and was fond of boyish sports; he fenced and boxed, and like a boy even in his manhood rollicked with the children. He was pure and earnest in speech and never used slang, was self-reliant, and with men bore himself with great dignity. Was skillful with mechanical tools, and understood surveying and could practice it. He was a man of great industry and indomitable will. He never worked without a purpose; and having formed the purpose he pursued it without change or flagging to its consummation. He did not wait for opportunities, but by his great will power made the opportunity.

He was blessed with an interesting family, three sons and three daughters. He educated his three sons at the University,—nice young men moral, Christian and upright like himself; endowed with bright minds, and all chose their father's profession. The eldest, Frank, has a good law practice in Baltimore. J. Hop. and Samuel V. are lawyers in good practice in Philippi, their native place. I had the privilege of examining all of them for admission to the bar, and the license of each bears my signature.

The three daughters were all sent to good female seminaries and all were finely educated. It was indeed a happy home, just such as might be expected with such a father and mother.

The judge had a fine law office in Philippi, in which was a good law library. On the wall of that office was placed the mortar-board and trowel, the tools with which he worked at the trade that enabled him to educate himself. He was not ashamed of them, but to his friends who called on him he exhibited them with pardonable pride.

He also had in his pleasant home a fine private library, in which could be found many valuable books, classical, scientific, philosophical, theological, poetical and many others. His books were not in his library for show, but for use, and no one used them so much as he. He found much of his recreation in reading and in solving difficult mathematical problems. He was a great mathematician. He was passionately fond of poetry. He could read poetry without his book for hours at a time. I have heard him repeat nearly all of Tam O'Shanter. He also kept up his French so that he could read it with facility.

He was very successful in business; accumulated quite a fortune, between 1848, when he located in Philippi, and the breaking out of the Civil War in 1861, thirteen years. He sympathized with the South. He was a candidate for a seat in the convention of 1861. He was elected. He went to the convention, and while the convention was in session the country was plunged into civil war. Sumpter had been fired on, and the vibration of the explosion was heard around the world. President Lincoln called for three hundred thousand troops for the purpose of suppressing the resistance to the government and apportioned Virginia's quota for her to raise. For what! as they viewed it, to fight against Virginia and Virginians. Brave old Jubal Early had stood up for the Union in that convention; even went so far as to indorse General Anderson's returning the fire from Fort Sumpter; said he had done nothing but his duty. But when Virginia was required to raise troops to fight against Virginia his love for the Union was destroyed. Mr. Woods, regarding the Civil War as actually begun and the dire alternative presented to fight for Virginia or the Union, he cast his fortune with Virginia, and a few days after Fort Sumter fell, and the call for troops was made; the ordinance of secession was passed by a large majority, although up to to that time a large majority of the convention was opposed to secession. But they regarded the die as cast, and they had no alternate but to stand by their State. How fixed they were in their opinions, and in their allegiance to Virginia, let the terrible struggle, the most gigantic in either modern or ancient history, attest. Poor Virginia bared her sacred bosom to the storm of war, and her soil drank up more fraternal blood in the Valley, at First and Second Bull Run, the Seven Days battles near Richmond, at Fredericksburg, Chancellorsville, First and Second Cold Harbor, the Wilderness, Spotsylvania Courthouse, Petersburg, Appomattox, and other places from Washington to Richmond, than was spilled in all other places, in that terrible four years of war and carnage. Mr. Woods was now an exile from his Philippi home for four years. He was in the South fighting for what he believed to be right. He was attached to the celebrated "Stonewall Brigade."

When the war closed and the angel of peace spread his white wings in benediction over the stricken land, and the South lay prostrate beneath a mighty load, singing the sad strain:—

> Around me blight, where all before was bloom,
>   And so much lost, alas, and nothing won
> Save this, that I can lean on wreck or tomb,
>   And weep, and weeping pray, "Thy will be done."
>
> And oh! 'tis hard to say, but said 'tis sweet:
>   The words are bitter, but they hold a balm,
> A balm that heals the wounds of my defeat,
>   And lulls my sorrows into holy calm.
>
> It is the prayer of prayers, and how it brings,
>   When heard in heaven, peace and hope to me;
> When Jesus prayed it, did not angels' wings
>   Gleam 'mid the darkness of Gethsemane?

Mr. Woods returned to his Philippi home. Not like a culprit, not like a traitor, but with head erect, realizing that God still reigned. "He was troubled on every side, yet not disturbed. He was perplexed, but not in despair; persecuted, but not forsaken; cast down, but not destroyed." Mr. Woods came home like a man and by his upright Christian conduct, won those who had looked askance upon him when he returned. When he left he was the class-leader in his little church in Philippi. He had not been long at home when he was invited by those who were "on the other side," to take his old place as class-leader. He took it, and at the alter of prayer he mingled his petitions with theirs, he visited their sick and dying, he spoke words of consolation to the bereaved ones, aye, he went with them to holy communion and partook with them of the emblems of the broken body and shed blood of their common Savior. He was good enough to do all this, they had the greatest confidence in his Christian character, but they would not let him vote. He was not good enough for that. But he waited, and but a few years of political persecution could endure, and he saw his political shackles fall to the ground.

In 1871 he was a candidate in the Sixth Senatorial District for a seat in the constitutional convention which was to meet in 1872. He was elected; and in that convention was Chairman of the Committee on Bill of Rights and Elections, a member of the Revisory Committee, composed of the Chairmen of the several committees. He was a very able, influential member of that convention and had much to do in forming a constitution that not only made test oaths odious and impossible, but a constitution that has stood the test of over a quarter of a century without very material change. He did much on the stump in his district to have the constitution ratified by the people. He was a fluent speaker and a clear logical reasoner, and his power with the people was great. He could say with truth, what but few justices could ever say, that he never was defeated for a public office by the people.

At the election in August, 1872, under the new constitution, all the officers of the State were elected. The candidates for circuit Judge in the Parkersburg Circuit, Geo. Loomis, the Republican candidate, and James M. Jackson, the Democratic, both claimed to be elected. Judge Jackson obtained the certificate, and Judge Loomis contested. In the special tribunal for the trial of the case, Mr. Woods was selected as one of the judges. He wrote the opinion in the case; a clear, concise and able opinion, deciding the contest in favor of Judge Jackson. For this opinion, see Loomis v. Jackson, 6 W. Va. Judge Haymond resigned his seat on the Supreme Bench of the State the last of December, 1882. Gov. J. B. Jackson, on the first of January, 1883, appointed Judge Woods to fill the vacancy until the next general election in November, 1884. He was a candidate for election to fill the unexpired term of Judge Haymond. He was elected by a good majority, after nearly a year's service on the bench. Of his qualifications for that high position, serving with him for the six years he was on the bench, I believe I am qualified to speak.

He brought with him to the bench fine native talents, his classical education, wide range of reading, his legal education, which was very much widened and deepened by his long and successful practice at the bar; these, with sound and mature judgment, practical good sense, great industry, with a profound sense of love of justice, and the obligation on him to find the justice and right of the case, fitted him in a high degree to discharge the duties of that most responsible position. He was a cautious, conscientious judge. He also studied and worked to keep himself in the line of the decisions. He did not believe he had any right, and he did not dare, to depart from the rule of settled law. For the strongest proof of this let me refer to this very able and exhaustive opinion in the case of Wilson v. Perry, 30 W. Va., where he was compelled to decide that of a testator's bequests, some were void because the settled law in this State and in Virginia said they were, because indefinite charities. A good and pious old man had left money in trust for churches and Sunday-schools, and Judge Woods would have been glad to have sustained the bequests if he could have done so. Authorities from many of the States would have upheld such bequests, but the decisions in Virginia and this State had pronounced such bequests void, and he did not dare to depart from those decisions. The Legislature had not overruled them, and he did not dare to usurp the law-making power. His duty was to decide what the law was, and not what he might think it ought to be. He and his associates would not, because they felt that they did not dare to do so, indulge at all in "judge-made law."

Another one of Judge Woods' decisions which I will cite displayed great ability of analysis, and all the other qualities of an able jurist. That is Flanagan's case in 26 W. Va. Flanagan had been indicted for the murder of a woman, who, with her child, had been burned to death in a log cabin in Randolph County. Flanagan was tried, convicted of the murder and sentenced to die on the gallows. In the opinion Judge Woods desplayed great ability. He came to the conclusion, in which all the judges concured, that there was absolutely no proof in the record, (and all evidence was certified) that the house was burned by an incendiary; that it did not take fire accidentally, and there was no proof of the *corpus delicti* and the court reversed the judgment, set aside the verdict, and remanded the case for a new trial. In that case the rules governing circumstantial evidence are well and forcibly laid down. Judge Woods wrote many strong opinions, covering a great number of subjects. His opinions will be found in eleven volumes of our Supreme Court reports from the twenty-first to the thirty-first, inclusive.

DAVID WILLIAM SHAW.

If our courts of last resort could have such judges as Samuel Woods there would be no room for complaint.

Judge Woods was a deeply religious man and for his religion he never apologized, and was careful not to put any strain upon it. He was ever ready to testify to the truth of religion. A scene occurred once at a skating rink in Wheeling that illustrates the faithfulness of Judge Woods to his religious principles. Miss Jennie Smith, the evangelist, was holding a series of meetings in the rink. One night a poor man in deep distress came to the anxious seat, to find comfort, that he sadly needed. Judge Woods and the president of the court were there, and Miss Smith called on both to pray for the poor penitent, which they did, and there on their knees wrestling with God for mercy for that poor distressed soul, was half the Supreme Court of Appeals of West Virginia. Did they lower their dignity? If there is anything in our holy religion, they did not. They were but doing their duty. Judge Woods was never ashamed of the profession he had made. For many long years he had been a consistent member of the Methodist Episcopal Church. The religion that he had exprienced in his youth was his solace though life and in death. Judge of the Supreme Court of Appeals of the State as he was, he felt he was but a poor mortal, and in daily need of forgiveness. He believed in prayer, as

> "The simplest form of speech
> That infant lips can try;
> Prayer, the sublimest strains that reach
> The Majesty on high."

and that

> "Prayer is the Christian's vital breath,
> The Christian's native air,
> His watchword at the gate of death,
> He enters heaven with prayer."

Judge Woods on the expiration of his term of office on the 31st day of December, 1888, retired from the bench and returned to private life, full of honor, and with a consciousness of having faithfully discharged the most sacred trust. He did not again go into active practice of the law as he might have done, but spent his time attending to his large private interests. In his retirement he enjoyed life; of his wife and family he was extremely fond, and his grandchildren were good company for him. A short time before his retirement from the bench in June, 1888, his *Alma Mater* conferred on him the degree of LL.D. He had a great sorrow in December, 1895, in the loss of his loving wife, with whom he had lived for forty-six years. It was a hard blow and he only survived it a year and a few months, for on the 17th day of February, 1897, he died very suddenly, after a few days illness, of heart disease; died so suddenly that he had no time to call his children about him and bid them good-bye. But what of that? Had he not talked to them many a time of the future? His whole life speaks to them now. He was trusted in the church, in the Masonic fraternity, of which he was a prominent member, in every station of life, in the home, at the bar, in the political service of the State, on the Supreme Bench. He was conscientious, able and upright, and left the world better for having lived in it.

JOHN HOPKINS WOODS, son of Judge Samuel and Elizabeth (Neeson) Woods, was born in Philippi, November 28, 1853; and on June 22, 1898, at West View, near Staunton, Virginia, he was married to Miss Jennie, daughter of John W. and Martha J. (Gammon) Canter. Mr. Woods is a member of the M. E. Church, is a Master Mason, in politics he is a Democrat, and by profession a lawyer, residing in Philippi, where his home, but recently completed, is a model of taste and elegance, both in architecture and furnishing. He is a gentleman of education and culture, of wide reading and correct appreciation, having received his training in the West Virginia University at Morgantown and at the United States Military Academy at West Point. He entered the University in 1872 and continued there till nearly the end of the sophomore year, 1875, when he entered West Point. His tastes were rather for law than for a military life, and he studied for that profession under the excellent guidance of his father, and in 1878 was admitted to practice after having been duly examined as to his qualifications by the Supreme Court of West Virginia; and he soon built up a large practice to which he has given his sole attention. He has always taken a deep interest in politics, and has contributed much to the support and success of the Democratic party. His ideas on political subjects are broad and liberal, and his principles are the result of sound thinking; and his party, in his county and in the State, has had no supporter more conscientious, more industrious or more hopeful of ultimate triumph of the doctrine which he upholds in defeat as well as in victory. He was a clerk in the Constitutional Convention, of which his father was a member, which met at Charleston in 1872 and framed the present constitution of the State. In 1883 he became the joint owner (in connection with Hon. D. W. Shaw) of the *Barbour Jeffersonian*, and his management of the paper was able and his editorial writings were vigorous. The paper was Democratic in politics. Subsequently Mr. Woods purchased the interest of Mr. Shaw, and for some time was sole editor and proprietor, finally selling the property to Hon. D. W. Gall, who consolidated it with the paper which he owned, making of the two the *Jeffersonian-Plaindealer*. After retiring from the newspaper field, Mr. Woods devoted his whole time to his profession, except that he neglected none of the calls of duty in matters social and political. In 1898 he received the Democratic nomination, in the Tenth Senatorial District, for the State Senate; and although the district was overwhelmingly Republican, yet he conducted an admirable campaign and merited and received the thanks of his party for the able fight he had made, having canvassed

FAMILY HISTORY.   499

and spoken in every county and nearly every magisterial district in the senatorial district, consisting of Barbour, Lewis, Randolph, Upshur and Webster Counties. In 1899 he was elected by the Philippi bar as special judge of the circuit court, and presided during the hearing of the result of the special election at Belington which divided that town.

SAMUEL VANHORN WOODS, son of Judge Samuel Woods, was born at Philippi, August 31, 1856, and was married March 9, 1893, at Philippi, to Mollie, daughter of Isaac H. and Margaret (Jarvis) Strickler. Their child, Ruth, is five years old. Mr. Woods is a member of the M. E. Church, is a Knight of Pythias, and in politics is a Democrat, and by profession a lawyer, living at Philippi. He was educated in the public schools and at the West Virginia University, where he was prevented from graduating because of sickness. He never permitted ambition for political preferment to interfere with his business as a lawyer, although he takes a strong interest in his party; and as a result he has attained to a degree of success in his profession which places him in the foremost ranks of the lawyers of West Virginia, while still a camparatively young man. His practice is now worth more than $5000 a year, and he is so situated that he can, to a large extent, select from what is offered him such business only as is agreeable and profitable. He was strongly urged in 1898, by influential members of his party, to permit his name to go before the convention as a candidate for Congress; but he persisted in declining the honor. He has been, at different times, chosen as a special judge of the circuit courts of the counties of Randolph, Upshur and Taylor. He has found time to take part in Sunday School work, and was president of the West Virginia Sunday School Convention which met in Fairmont July 26, 1894, and on that occasion he read a paper which attracted much attention. His residence at Philippi is one of the finest in the county and a handsome picture of it will be found in this book.

WILLIAM HENRY WENTZ was born 1863, son of James W. and Lucy Catherine (Harris) Wentz. His brothers and sisters are, John David, James Abner, Charles Columbus, George Wasnington, Virginia, Ellen, Martha, Emma and Allie. Mr. Wentz is a Baptist, an Odd Fellow, and K. of P., a Republican and a minister, now employed in the U. S. Fish Commission at Washington, D. C. He attended the Fairmont Normal School, the Mt. Pleasant Academy, Crozer Theological Seminary, and the University of New York City. He taught five years, was four years deputy clerk of the circuit court of Barbour; in 1895 was delegate to the National Convention of the League of Republican Clubs; in 1896 was alternate delegate to the Republican National Convention at St. Louis; U. S. Commissioner to International Fisheries Exposition held at Bergen, Norway, in 1898. He travelled through many parts of Norway, Denmark, Germany, Holland, Belgium, England, Ireland and Canada. James Wilson Wentz was born in Rockbridge County 1838, and was a son of John Wentz, who was born in the same county in 1812 and was a son of William Wentz, whose father was William and grandfather Warren Wentz, who came to this country from Germany in 1774. He had served seven years in the German army and served seven years in the American army. Lucy Catherine Harris was a daughter of David Harris and was born in 1840. The majority of her relatives live in and around Richmond, Virginia. John Wentz was a pronounced Abolitionist and five of his sons fought for the Union in the Civil War. They were William, Henry, James, David and John. Of these William was killed in battle during the Lynchburg Raid.

WILLIAM WOODFORD, son of General William Woodford, was the first of the name to settle in what is now Barbour County. He came from Rockingham County, Virginia, in 1804, and his family, some of whom were born before he came, consisted of five children. General Woodford, the father of the subject of this sketch, was an Englishman who married a daughter of Sir William, afterwards General Howe. The marriage was opposed by the lady's father, and Colonel Woodford left England with his wife and came to America, and made his home in Shenandoah Valley. He was one of the earliest to take up arms against the British in the cause of independence, and on December 9, 1776, he defeated the British under Captain Fordyce at Great Bridge. His father-in-law, General William Howe, was commander-in-chief of the British army in America from 1775 to 1778. William Woodford, the pioneer in Barbour, was an only son, but had seven sisters. He married Hannah Moss and settled on Bull Pasture River, now in Highland County, Virginia. He was the ancestor of all the Woodfords in Barbour and adjoining counties, and his descendants, both those by the name of Woodford and those who have intermarried with other families and bear other names, have always been distinguished for industry, perseverance and business ability. When William Woodford came to Barbour he made his home on Fox Grape Creek, near land owned by William Thompson, one of the earliest settlers. When Mr. Woodford came to Barbour, he carried all his household goods on a pack-horse. His children were, John Howe, Jacob, William, George and Mary.

JOHN HOWE WOODFORD, son of William and Hannah (Moss) Woodford, was born in Rockingham County, Virginia, in 1796, and when eight years old, emigrated with his father's family to what is now Barbour County. He was the oldest child, and very early in life he began to trade in cattle, buying calves, cutting brouse in the woods to winter them, supplementing it with a little corn, ranging them in the woods the next summer, until they were three or four years old, then selling them at a very low price, often from four to seven dollars per head. He hired himself for wages, among others to Jacob Lawrence, near Buckhannon, and to Samuel Wilson, on Sand Fork, of the West Fork, in Lewis County. He cleared heavily timbered land for Wilson at four dollars an acre, and made

STUART F. REED.

CHARLES I. ZIRKLE.

rails at twenty-five cents a hundred. But he did not always find it necessary to work for other people, and subsequently he became one of the largest landowners in Barbour County. He was for many years a magistrate, and was Judge of the county court part of the time, and was two terms Sheriff of the county. He was an old time Whig up to the close of the Civil War, and after that time he voted with the Democrats. He married Nancy Minear, daughter of Adam Minear. Nancy Minear was born in 1801, on the Valley River, near the Minear Ford, in Barbour County, near the Taylor line. The house in which she was born is still standing (1899.) Her grandfather, John Minear, was the pioneer settler of St. George, in Tucker County, and was killed by Indians in Barbour County in 1781. The children of John Howe Woodford numbered fourteen, as follows. Isaac, William, Adam M., John Harvey, Asa Wesley, James R., DeWitt Clinton, Phoebe, Mary, Emily, Elizabeth, Hannah, Cyntha, Phrena. All these children reached the age of maturity, and seven of them are yet living (1899.)

The children of George, son of William Woodford, were, Frank, William, John, Granville and Elmira.

The children of William, son of William Woodford, were, George, Robert, Emmett, Jackson, John Wesley, Mary Ann, Elizabeth and Josephine.

ASA WESLEY WOODFORD, son of John Howe Woodford, was born two miles west of Philippi, May 20, 1833. In 1855, near Flemington, Taylor County, he was married to Rebecca, daughter of Rev. Jasper Cather. To them were born six children, Iris Columbia, Phoebe Jane, Flora S. N., Clarkson J., Bruce S. and John Howe. Three of them are now dead. Rebecca Woodford died in 1885, and Colonel Woodford in 1895, married as his second wife, Sabra, daughter of Rev. Flavius J. Cather, a Baptist minister, a third cousin of Rebecca Woodford. The subject of this sketch has displayed, in a remarkable degree, the traits so common to the Woodford family—energy, pluck, business ability and stability of character. He began life with small educational advantages, his only schooling being in a log house on Pleasant Creek. He began life for himself by working at thirty-five cents a day, "and no dinner," as the saying was then; for he was in the employ of a cattle drover. In the winter of 1849, when he was seventeen years old, he helped take a drove of cattle to Pniladelphia, walking all the way there and back through snow and mud. The return trip from Philadelphia was made on foot in eleven days. The boy who, at the age of seventeen, was not ashamed to work for thirty-five cents a day, and not afraid to walk to Philadelphia and back, did not need to work long for wages, and in twelve years from that time, and over that same road to Philadelphia, he drove six hundred cattle of his own and sold them to the Government to feed the army. He was the first man who attempted to drive cattle from this part of West Virginia to the eastern market during the Civil War. He did a large business in supplying the Government with beef cattle. He was always successful in these transactions; but his fortune changed in 1863 when the great Confederate raid under Jones and Imboden swept across West Virginia. General Jones carried off two hundred and fifty cattle belonging to Colonel Woodford, and they went to gladden the stomachs of Confederate veterans on the march to Gettysburg. Colonel Woodford was paid in Confederate money for his cattle, but the money was worthless. General Jones took the cattle from the James Pickens farm, on Gnatty Creek, Barbour County.

Not discouraged by this heavy loss Colonel Woodford continued to ship cattle, horses and sheep to the eastern markets during the remainder of the war. He was a strong Union man, voted against the Ordinance of Secession, and when the war came he set to work, in Ritchie County, to raise a regiment for the Union army, and was to be colonel of the regiment, but he was superceded by Colonel Moses S. Hall, and for the rest of the war he devoted his energies to the cattle business. After the war he voted the Democrat ticket. In 1868 he was elected in Lewis County to the Legislature, and the next year helped to make the first code of West Virginia. He was twice elected Sheriff of Lewis County, and in 1882 received the Democratic nomination for Senator in the Tenth District, but was defeated at the polls by Captain Coburn, of Barbour County. In 1892 he was a candidate before the Democratic Convention for Governor of West Virginia. In April of that year he made a speech in Grafton before the Democratic Mass Convention, William J. Bryan, then a member of Congress, being present and commending the speech very highly. Colonel Woodford was then in advance of his party on the financial question, and the views held by him then were adopted and became the leading plank in the National Democratic platform of 1896.

Colonel Woodford has large land interests in Barbour, owning part of the old homestead where he was raised. His home is in Lewis County, where he owns a magnificent farm of more than one thousand acres, lying on the West Fork River between Janelew and Weston. This farm is stocked with Herford cattle, and he was the first man in West Virginia to ship cattle to the markets of London and Liverpool. He did not find that business profitable because of the sharp competition, and "because of the difficulty of bucking against the English bull and the cattle monopoly in the English trade." His farm in Lewis County is noted for its influence in improving the cattle of the country. A peculiarity of it is that a natural gas fire burns in his field, round which his Herford cattle gather to enjoy the warmth. In addition to other business enterprises to which he has given his attention, he built a large flour mill at Weston several years ago. Mrs. Woodford is an accomplished artist; her work has received the praise of competent critics. Colonel Woodford has traveled extensively, for business and pleasure, visiting all the principal portions of the United States and Europe.

Scenes on Col. A. W. Woodford's farm, from a painting by his daughter.

BENJAMIN HOLLY WOODFORD, son of Jacob and Mary (Robinson) Woodford, was born in 1843, five miles north of Philippi, where he now resides. On September 13, 1870, he was married at Winchester, Virginia, to Mary Elizabeth Scott Hodgson, daughter of Robert and Sally (Renner) Hodgson. Children, Robinson H., Benjamin Holly Scott, Blanche Maude,

Tom Brown, Scotia Pearl. Mr. Woodford belongs to the order of A. F. and A. M., and is a Democrat, a farmer and stockdealer, owning 196 acres of highly productive land, largely devoted to graizing. In 1896 he was elected a member of the County Court, and was president of that body one year; and he held the office of member of the Pleasant District Board of Education sixteen years, and he has also served as statistical correspondent of Barbour County for the Department of Agriculture. Mr. Woodford was in the Confederate army from 1862 till the close of the war. He surrendered at Staunton to General Duval at the close of the war, after taking part in more than thirty battles. He brought home with him many relics and trophies of his campaigns. After the war he entered actively upon the pursuits of civil life, and has met success in all his undertakings. He was four years a merchant at the "Burnt Store" on Taylor's Drain.

Mr. Woodford is a great grandson of Colonel Woodford who married Miss Howe, and a grandson of William Woodford, the first of the name in Barbour. The children of Jacob Woodford were, Hannah, Elizabeth, Robinson, William, James M., John and the subject of this sketch. Mrs. Woodford belongs to an old and respectable family of Virginia and Pennsylvania, the Hodgsons, English in origin, and now possessing many members in different States. Her ancestors can be traced in an unbroken line more than two hundred years to Robert Hodgson, an English Quaker who landed at New York in 1665, and who subsequently removed to Pennsylvania. It is believed that he finally lived in Maryland, and died in 1733 at the age of eighty-six, leaving a considerable fortune to his children. The line of descent from him to Mrs. Woodford is as follows: Robert had a son Phineas; Phineas had a son Robert, and Robert had a son Robert, who was Mrs. Woodford's father, she thus being of the fifth generation from the founder of the name in America. Through her mother's people she is of German descent, through the Renner family.

JOHN F. WOODFORD, born five miles north of Philippi, son of Isaac C. and James E. (Huffman) Woodford, was married on Pleasant Creek, April 22, 1869, to Eliza E., daughter of Jesse and Elizabeth (Knotts) Cole. Children, Rosaltha, Joseph M., Marie Belle, Elizabeth, Isaac C., John W., and Jessie E. Mr. Woodford is a member of the M. E. Church, an Odd Fellow, a farmer, stockdealer, merchant and manager of a telephone company. He is one of the extensive land-owners of Barbour County. His home farm at Cherry Hill, one of the finest in the county, contains 367 acres. It was formerly the Henson L. Hoff property, and Thomas Hite lived there during the Civil War. The house is of brick, and was built nearly a century ago. The farm is underlaid with valuable viens of coal. Mr. Woodford owns 201 acres three miles south of Philippi, and 141 acres surrounding Elk City, and he owns a general store at that place. He has always taken a lead in agricultural matters, and claims to have been the

FAMILY HISTORY. 507

first to introduce Polled Angus cattle into Barbour; also the first to introduce the Holstein-Friesian cattle. He also introduced the Clydesdale horses; and in 1870 he began the importation and use of commercial fertilizers into Barbour, claiming to be the first to use them.

Mr. Woodford has been identified with the Woodford Telephone Company since in 1897, and has been the moving spirit in that enterprise, being president of the company, which has lines in five counties.

His son, Joseph M. Woodford, born in 1871, began business at the age of eighteen as manager of his father's saw mill and timber interests. He is an Odd Fellow. After five years of profitable connection with saw mills, he turned his attention to buying and inspecting lumber for Eastern firms. In 1898 he moved his business headquarters to Elkins, and now is general manager of and the largest stockholder in the Woodford Telephone Company. Another son, Isaac C. Woodford, born 1878, graduated at Buckhannon in 1897, and immediately thereafter became a stockholder in the Woodford Telephone Company, and was chosen its secretary and electrician. He established a central office at Elkins. Another son, John W. Woodford, born 1881, was formerly treasurer of the telephone company, but early in 1899 he disposed of his interests to his brothers, and entered the West Virginia University as a student.

JAMES MADISON WOODFORD, born within five miles of Philippi, in 1866, son of Isaac and Jane (Huffman) Woodford, was married near Elk City, March 4, 1890, to Anna Lee, daughter of Jesse R. and Louisa (Smith) Green. His second marriage was to Isabel J., daughter of Joseph and Isabel Matlick, in 1895. Children, Walter Lee, Marion L., Ona Rosswell and an infant. He is a member of the M. E. Church, a farmer and merchant. He was educated at Flemington in the West Virginia College. His farm of 85 acres is nearly all improved and he handle fine grades of stock.

ISAAC C. WOODFORD, son of Isaac C. and Jane (Huffman) Woodford, was born 1860, and on May 9, 1889, at Philippi, he was married to Mary M., daughter of Elias and Catherine (McGee) Kelley. Children, Lottie, Katie, Harry, Camden, Ora and Ella. He is a member of the M. E. Church, a farmer and stockraiser, living five miles below Philippi. In 1886 he was elected Assessor of the west side of the county. He is a member of the firm of Zinn & Woodford, handling large numbers of sheep and cattle annually. His farm of 319 acres, highly improved, is underlaid with four veins of coal. The old Woodford homestead, known as the Hathaway land, is his property. His life has been an active one and his undertakings have been successful.

DAVID RILEY WOODFORD, born 1851, on Shook's Run, son of William and Mary Jane (Thompson) Woodford, was married in Randolph County in 1890 to Lily, daughter of Marshall and Elizabeth (Golden) Mullens. Children, Maude M., Asia Goodlaw, Baby. He is a member of the Missionary

Baptist Church, is a Democrat and a farmer, residing on the old Woodford homestead, two miles west of Philippi. He introduced the first full blooded Herford cattle into Barbour County.

MRS. COLUMBIA A. WOODFORD, born at Philippi, 1844, daughter of John R. and Lucinda (Sinsel) Williamson, was married June 9, 1864, at the Williamson homestead, to John Wesley, son of William and Sarah Woodford. Children, Charles E., Ira J., Robert T., Austin C., Zora E., Omar A. Mr. Woodford died October 20, 1887. Mrs. Woodford is a Baptist and contributed largely to the building of the Mt. Olive Baptist Church. The membership of the church is 55. The sons, Robert, Ira and Charles are married. She owns 100 acres, three-fourths improved, and raises stock. She has lived at the present place 35 years.

GEORGE C. WOODFORD, born 1854 at the old Woodford homestead on the head of Shook's Run, son of William and Mary Jane (Thompson) Woodford, was married November 9, 1882, at the David Shaw farm, to Madora, daughter of Samson and Mary (O'Neal) Zinn. Children, Ida Grace, Artie May, William Ray, Melvin Ray, David Wilson Mansfield, Delbert Riley, and two unnamed. He is a Democrat, a Missionary Baptist, a farmer, butcher and stock dealer, living on the headwaters of Shook's Run, where he owns 379 acres of land, mostly improved. He is of English descent, a grandson of John H. Woodford. His father was drafted in the Union army.

LEWIS WILSON, son of William F. Wilson, was born on Bill's Creek, then Randolph, now Barbour County, October 18, 1818. His marriage occurred May 20, 1844, and his wife was Ann M., daughter of Alexander and Rachel (Thompson) Keyes. The names of their children were, Elizabeth, Jane and Thomas Alman. When Mr. Wilson was about three years old he removed with his father's family to Ohio, and remained there two years, then returned to Bill's Creek, in Barbour. When he was twenty-one years of age he set out for the West and went to Wisconsin, which was then a territory, and remained there two years. The principal part taken by him was to cast his vote in a sod shanty for delegates to a convention to form a state constitution, preliminary to admission of Wisconsin into the Union as a State. He returned from Wisconsin in 1841, and two years later became half owner of a flour mill and carding machine at Philippi. This building stood on the site of the present mill owned by him; and in it the court met to organize Barbour County in April 1843. It was a snowy time, and when the weather was not too cold the court held its sessions under an apple tree in the lower end of town, and when a snowstorm threatened the court adjourned to the mill.

LEWIS WILSON'S MILL.

JOHN HOPKINS WOODS.

When the oil excitement took place in Wirt County, Mr. Wilson went to the region of Burning Spring in company with L. D. Morrall and J. W. Payne, and began boring for oil with every prospect of success. But it was an inauspicious time, for the war was at hand. Soon bands of Confederate guerrillas began to infest the country, and made it very unpleasant for Union sympathizers. They wore white bands round their hats, and would put in their appearance at unexpected places and at times entirely too frequent to suit Mr. Wilson. He abandoned his mill and left the country, not even bringing his tools with him. He sent back for them, but they were never recovered.

When he returned to Philippi the Confederate forces which had been stationed there under Colonel Porterfield had retreated; and the State Government was being reorganized. Nearly all the officers of the county had gone South, and the offices were vacant. On September 27 of that year, 1861, an election was held to fill the vacancies and Lewis Wilson was chosen County Clerk and filled the position eighteen years; and during a portion of that time was Circuit Clerk, also. He was the second County Surveyor of Barbour, serving ten years. He succeeded his father who was the first County Surveyor and who resigned on account of his age. Mr. Wilson served two terms in the West Virginia Legislature, delegate from Barbour. In 1863 he was appointed Notary Public, and has held the office thirty-six years. While Clerk, Mr. Wilson was also Commissioner in Chancery. He is now one of the directors of the Tygart's Valley Bank, and still takes a supervisory interest in his mill and carding machines.

Mr. Wilson belongs to a family which, during several generations, has been influential in business and politics. The family is Scotch, coming to America through Ireland, the founder of the name in America being William Wilson, great grandfather of the subject of this sketch. The father of Lewis Wilson was William F. Wilson, whose long and useful life left its impress upon Barbour County. He married Jane, daughter of Daniel Booth, who is buried near Belington, and lived for a time on Bill's Creek, then at Philippi. Their children were, Isaiah, Asher, Almond, Maria, Lewis, Albert, Daniel, Granger, Alpheus, Sarah Jane, Rezin B. and Eugenus. Of these children only two are now living, Lewis and Sarah Jane. She first married William M. Simpson, then Henson L. Yoke, and is now the wife of Sabeus Main. William F. Wilson owned the land on which Philippi was built, and he owned, at different times, property elsewhere. Like so many of the Wilson family, he was a mill owner. It is a fact worthy of note that the Wilsons were the pioneer mill builders in this part of the State. The second mill, within the limits of what is now Randolph County, was built by Colonel Benjamin Wilson, uncle of William F. Wilson. The first mill on Bill's Creek was built by Moses Wilson, and the second, on the same Creek, by William F. Wilson. John, brother of William F., built a mill, to run by horse power, six and a half miles southeast of Philippi. Some years later a mill was built near Belington by William F. The first mill, and also the first carding machine on the site of Philippi, was built about 1818 by William F. Wilson. He also built the first wagon road in what is now Barbour, east of the river. It extended from Philippi to Bill's Creek, and was seven miles long, and was built about 1800 by him for seventy-five cents a rod. It went up and down hills to avoid digging. William F. Wilson died in 1857.

The father of William F. Wilson was William Wilson. He was born in Hampshire, now Hardy County, February 8, 1754, and died January 1, 1851, thus lacking only five weeks of being ninety-seven years old. For many years he was chairman of the Randolph county court, and was the first representative from that county in the Virginia Legislature. He married a sister of Jonas Friend, the old Indian fighter and Revolutionary soldier who lived at the mouth of Leading Creek.*

The father of William Wilson was also William, and he married Elizabeth, daughter of Archibald Blackburn, about 1746. William Wilson was born in Ireland, November 16, 1722, and his wife was born in the same country, in Ulster Province, February 22, 1725. She came to America before she and Mr. Wilson were married. They took up their residence on a small stream called Trout Run, now in Hardy County, West Virginia, and became the parents of eleven children. He died January 12, 1801, and Elizabeth, his wife, May 2, 1806.

Of these children, John and Benjamin were delegates from Randolph County to the Virginia convention which met at Richmond in March, 1788, to ratify the Constitution of the United States. That was an important body, and twenty delegates were elected from what is now West Virginia. John Wilson was the first County Clerk of Randolph, 1787; first Circuit Clerk, 1809; first Justice of the Peace, 1787; Major of Virginia Militia, 1787; Assessor, 1788; Sheriff in 1798, and was a man of wide influence. Colonel Benjamin Wilson had command of the militia in this part of West Virginia during the Revolutionary War, and had charge of the defense of the frontiers against the Indians, and met them in many an encounter. He was the first Clerk of Harrison County, and held the office nearly forty

---

*Jonas Friend lived to be very old, and in his last years his mind was very weak, and his memory existed nearly altogether in the past. He fancied that he was still a soldier fighting the British in defense of his country; and with his knapsack on his back and his gun on his shoulder he would go from house to house, halting occasionally, as if on picket duty, when he would raise his gun and go through the act of firing, exclaiming in exultation that there was one Red Coat less.

Martin Poling married Mary ("Polly") daughter of William Wilson, 1810, and their children were, Phoebe, Absalom, Sarah, Wilson and Harvey. Mrs. Poling was born November 18, 1791. Mr. and Mrs. Poling were married by Simeon Harris. In 1794 Robert Clark was married to Mary Friend and sister of Mrs. William Wilson, and their children were, Elizabeth, Peggy, Sarah and Polly. Mr. and Mrs. Clark were married by Valentine Power.

years. He was remarkable also for his large family, his children numbering twenty-nine.

The Wilson family can be traced in Scotland two generations beyond William, the first who came to America. His father was David, and David's father was also David. Of the first David Wilson nothing is known except

First Wilson Homestead West of the Alleghanies—Near Beverly.

that he lived in Scotland and was born about 1650, and had a son David, born about 1685. This David Wilson, the second, took part in the Scotch rebellion of 1715, and being on the losing side, was compelled to leave his native country. He went to Ireland, and so far as there is any record he spent the remainder of his days there. At any rate he was still living in that country in 1722, in which year his son William was born, who settled in Hardy County. Thus the subject of this sketch, Lewis Wilson, traces his ancestry two and a half centuries unbroken, and the descent is thus summarized: Lewis Wilson was the son of William F., who was the son of William, who was the son of William, who was the son of David, who was the son of David Wilson the first. Five generations extend 250 years, which is fifty years to the generation. They are long-lived, for ordinarily a generation is only thirty-three years, and five generations would be 165 years. The descendants of William Wilson, who settled in Hardy County, counting both the dead and the living, probably number two thousand, although it is impossible now to take a full census of them. They are found all over West Virginia, and in many parts of the United States.

SOLOMON THOMAS WILSON, born in Maryland 1841, son of William P. and Eliza A. (Simmons) Wilson, was married in 1867 to Elizabeth, daughter of Benjamin O. and Matilda (Wooden) Ware. Children, Laura V., John W., Mattie B., Henry F., James S., Francis C., Benjamin K., Cora E., Eliza A. Harriet B., William H. and Blanch. He is a member of the German Baptist Church, a Republican and a farmer, living on Sugar Creek, where he owns 400 acres, nearly all improved and in sod, and on which he now grazes sixty-nine cattle. His daughter Mattie, married Ashford W. Stalnaker, a farmer of Glade District; his son James S., married Mertie, daughter of John C.

Right, a merchant at Huffman, Barbour County. His son Benjamin K., is a student at Buckhannon.

JOHN WILSON, born 1864, near Valley Furnace, is a son of Joseph and Loutta C. (Gainer) Wilson. In politics he is a Democrat, and by profession a teacher. He lives on Mill Run, a branch of Teter's Creek.

JOHN R. WILLIAMSON, born 1817, son of Archibald Williamson, was twice married, and following are the names of his children: Virginia, Edwin D., Columbia A., James A., Mary Florence, George F. Augusta and Laura. The grandfather of the subject of this sketch, came from Scotland and settled in Taylor County. Mr. Williamson was identified with almost every beneficent enterprise of a public nature which came before the people. He was the first Sheriff elected in Barbour County after the adoption of the Constitution of 1852 In all, Mr. Williamson was Sheriff of Barbour seventeen years. He accumulated property, which at his death, was considered worth eighty thousand dollars. His farming operations were on a large scale and usually successful. He died in 1876.

JAMES A. WILLIAMSON, born 1846 on Bonica Run, died 1895; son of John R. Williamson, was married in 1869 to Syrena, daughter of Minor and Abigail (Bartlett) Lake. Children, John Omar, Delta A., Thomas E., Guy A., Bessie O., Harold A. Mr. Williamson was an Odd Fellow, a Democrat, and a farmer, residing on Whitman Run where he owned 475 acres, mostly improved, and still in possession of his widow. He was Sheriff of Barbour County two terms. Mrs. Williamson's people are of Irish descent, the grandfather being raised in Taylor and his father in Barbour County.

ABRAHAM WARE, born 1822, at Valley Head, Randolph County, son of James Randolph and Dorothy (Mace) Ware, was married October 5, 1862, in Barbour County, to Diannah, daughter of Conrad and Elizabeth (Harper) Carpenter. Children of Mr. Ware are as follows: Eugenus, Marshall, Enoch, Dororthy, Joseph Worth, James K., Charles William Floyd, Rosa Belle, Daniel, Henrietta, Ida Ellen, Allie and Ada. He is a member of the U. B. Church, is a Republican, and a carpenter and a farmer, residing on Big Flat in Valley District. He has held the office of Constable. His father was born in 1822, and his grandfather was Richard Ware. Ware's Ridge in Randolph County was named from Richard Ware, the first of the family to cross the Alleghanies. Shortly after the Civil War Abraham Ware put up a shop and manufactured household articles, especially chairs, and nearly every home in Valley District has one or more of the Ware chairs. It was on Mr. Ware's farm that Daniel Carpenter found a rattlesnake den, killed thirteen of the reptiles in one fight and almost lost his sight, as was supposed from poison in the air. It was also on this farm that Mr. Carpenter, who was a noted hunter, killed his last buck, and lost his hunting knife. All seven of Mr. Ware's sons are carpenters. Eugenus and Enoch are jewelers, Joseph runs a carpenter shop, and James K. is a far-

RESIDENCE OF MRS. E. D. TALBOTT.

mer and teacher, having been born in 1872, and on November 5, 1893, he married Mary Emmaline, daughter of Haymond and Catherine, (Rinehart) Coberly. Their child, Alston Dayton, was born July 5, 1897. Mr. Ware is a member of the U. B. Church, is a Republican, and was educated at Buckhannon and at the American Correspondence Normal of Dansville, New York. Joseph Worth Ware married Samantha Jane, daughter of Simon and Louisa (Hewitt) Poling, and has four children, Simon Porter, Mertie Albert and George Dewey. In politics he is a Republican. In 1898 he lost his right leg by the accidental discharge of a gun.

J. BLACKBURN WARE, born near Belington in 1872, son of Elihu and Lucretia (Booth) Ware. He is a member of the United Brethern Church; in politics a Republican, by profession a lawyer, residing at Belington. He was educated in the public schools, the Normal and Classical Academy (1895) and in the Law Department of the West Virginia University (1897). He taught school six years, two years as principal of the Belington school.

DANIEL BURDETT WARD, born 1862, son of Abraham R. and Barbara E. (Cool) Ward, was married February 26, 1883, to Hattie U., daughter of John N. and Caroline (Hickman) Van Horn. Children, Otis A. and Emmett K. He is a member of the M. P. Church, is a Republican, a mechanic, and resides at Peel Tree, where he is post master and Notary Public, and was four years Justice of the Peace. He was educated in the public schools, and was four years secretary of the Board of Education of Union District. His great grandfather came from England and settled in Pennsylvania. Mr. Ward's father was born in Barbour, on Big Run, and at present resides in Lewis County.

SIMON WINANS, born near the Buckhannon River, in 1833, son of Benjamin and Catherine (Simons) Winans, was married to Elizabeth, daughter of Joseph Teets. Children, Louisa, Olive A., Benjamin, Margaret Catherine. He is a member of the M. E. Church, and of the G. A. R., is a Republican and a farmer. In 1862 he entered the Union army and fought until the close of the war, taking part in many hard battles. His ancestors were Virginians, and were of a hardy race.

ALBA WOLVERTON, born near Meadowville, 1870, son of Charles F. and Rebecca A. (Smith) Wolverton, was married at Philippi, March 25, 1892, to S. Clara, daughter of Alpheus P. and Jane R. (Thompson) Wilson. He is a member of the Missionary Baptist Church, a Democrat, a farmer and a civil engineer. He was elected County Surveyor of Barbour in 1892, and served four years. He lives on Bonica Run, and owns 36 acres, largely improved. After teaching eight years he began surveying, and has been following that for nine years, working not only for some of the leading companies and landowners of Barbour, but also in Randolph, Upshur, Tucker, Preston and Harrison Counties. Mr. Wolverton traces his ancestry back seven generations, through the Brown family. Beginning with himself, the line is as follows: His father, Charles F. Wolverton, married Rebecca Smith. The father of Charles was Benjamin M. Wolverton, who was born at Romney, West Virginia, 1828, and in 1847 married Ann Brown, who was born near Evansville, Preston County, 1823. She was a daughter of George Brown, who was born 1789, married Sarah F. Bartlett in 1819 and died 1862. George was a son of Thomas Brown, who was born 1760 in Prince William County, Virginia, and in 1785 married Anna Ash, and died 1844 in Preston County. Thomas was a son of William Brown, who was born in Prince William County about 1725, married Elizabeth Buckner in 1756, and died in 1807. He was a son of William Brown of the same county, who died before 1732, but the date of whose birth, or the facts of whose marriage, have not been ascertained.

JASPER WINCE, born 1848 in Monongalia County, son of Alexander and Hannah (Currence) Wince, was married May 19, 1872, to Loverna Catherine, daughter of Asberry P. and Mary (Hardesty) Sturm. He is a Southern Methodist, a Democrat and a farmer, being superintendent of the Barbour County Poor Farm, on Taylor's Drain. Six years he was a member of the Board of Education. His farm of 47 acres in Glade District is all under cultivation. The Poor Farm has been brought to a high state of cultivation under his management. His grandfather came from Germany to West Virginia, and his Grandmother Currence was born in the fort at Morgantown and lived to be 96 years old. Smith Wade Wince, his son, has taught school four years.

FRANCIS MARION WATRING, born 1844 in Barbour County, son of John and Catherine (Gainer) Watring, was married near his present home October 12, 1865, to Amanda Jane, daughter of Jacob and Lettis Ann (Poling) Sturm. Children, William Arthur, Victoria, Ida, married Andrew Miller; Victoria, married Oscar Kelley. Mr. Watring belongs to the United Brethren Church, is an Odd Fellow, a Democrat and a farmer, owning 125 acres, three miles east of Philippi, mostly improved, with a good orchard and underlaid with coal. He has been a member of the Board of Education. His great grandfather came from Germany and settled in Preston County.

JOHN C. WILLOUGHBY, born on French Creek, Upshur County, 1845, son of Alfred and Elizabeth (Carter) Willoughby, was married July 1, 1891, at Philippi, to Valeria, daughter of Mr. and Mrs. John C. and Elizabeth (Knapp) Bennett. He is a Missionary Baptist and a farmer, living two miles west of Philippi. On his father's side his people are Irish, his grandfather, Joshua Willoughby, came from Ireland and settled in Nelson County, Virginia, whence his son came to West Virginia about 1850. The Carters came into West Virginia from Virginia. Mrs. Willoughby was born 1848.

Y

FRANKLIN JEFFERSON YOWELL was born December 24, 1824, in Culpeper County, Virginia, son of William and Semphronia (Hawkins) Yowell. Mrs. Yowell's father's name was William Hawkins. Mr. Yowell was twice married, first, December 27, 1849, on Simpson's Creek, to Zepporah, daughter of John G. and Nancy (Goodwin) Bartlett; second, November 10, 1880, to Ruth Tyson. Mr. Yowell's children were, Marcellus, Vitellius, John Floyd, Semphronia, William Chester, Victoria. He is a Missionary Baptist, and was one of the charter members of the Point Pleasant Church at its organization in 1853, and for twenty years was Church Clerk. He is a Democrat and has held the office of Justice of the Peace sixteen years, and was six years a member of the county court. He owns a highly improved farm of 100 acres, underlaid with coal, on Simpson's Creek, and engages principally in grazing. His grandfather, William Yowell, emigrated from Scotland and settled in Culpeper County, Virginia. The subject of this sketch settled in Harrison County in 1847, and two years later his father, with his family, came, but after a sojourn of one year, moved to Iowa. The father served in the Mexican War, and the grandfather in the War of 1812. The youngest son of J. F. Yowell, William Chester, lives at the old homestead, where he has made his home after extensively traveling over the western country as far as the Rocky Mountains. He was born in 1866, and and on January 2, 1890, was married to Abbie, daughter of George G. and Mary Catherine (Lake) Cleavenger. Children, Walker, Russell, Ruby C. and Minnie L.

MARY CLARA YOUNG was born in Upshur County, and is a teacher in Union District, Barbour County, having by her perseverance gained a superior education, and having successfully taught four schools. The cause of education in the county has had an able advocate in her, and by her labor in the field of popular learning she has, both by precept and example, contributed to the upbuilding of the public schools.

Z

AGUSTUS J. ZINN, born in 1844, on the head of Shook's Run, son of Isaac and Elizabeth (Carlin) Zinn, was married September 12, 1867, at Bear's Run, to Mary Catherine, daughter of George and Louisa (Reed) Kerr. Children, Charlotte, Charles L., Asa G., Emory Otto, Oscar, E. Dowden, Herbert Goff. He is a member of the M. E. Church; a Republican and a farmer, living on the head of Shook's Run, where he owns 125 acres of highly improved land, including a sugar grove and strawberry garden. He had the first wheat reaped by machinery in Barbour. The Carlins came from Ireland, and the grandfather of the subject of this sketch settled near Wheeling on an island; and the grandfather on the other side, Peter Zinn, married Phoebe Chriss, and settled on the old Zinn homestead near Philippi. The Kerrs came from Highland County, Virginia. Charles Zinn married a daughter of David Smith, and Asa G. married Roberta J. Utz.

WILLIAM HARRISON ZINN, born 1846 near Philippi, son of David and Louisa Zinn, was married April 15, 1869, on Shook's Run, to Lucinda, daughter of John and Rebecca (Thompson) Corder. Their child's mane is Delbert W. Mr. Zinn is a Missionary Baptist and resides on Taylor's Drain, where he is engaged in farming and gardening. He owns 56 acres of highly improved land, on which he grows strawberries, raspberries and fruits. In educational matters he has always taken much interest, having given his son a good education and made of him a successful teacher.

SYLVANUS W. ZINN, born at the old Zinn homestead, one and a half miles west of Philippi, 1859; son of Alpheus and Lucinda (Gawthrop) Zinn, was married November 11, 1884, at the Adam Woodford homestead, to Lurina, daughter of Hensley and Caroline (Woodson) Harris. Children, Aubrey Lee, Ressa Ann, Rosetta, Lacy Glenn, Bertha Eoline, Gladys. He is a member of the Missionary Baptist Church, is a Democrat, a farmer and inventor. He owns 85 acres of improved land two miles west of Philippi, and handles fine grades of stock. He introduced, crossed and led up a new variety of wheat called the Zinn's Golden, which is a cross of the Fulse and Golden strains. It produces as high as 36 bushels to the acre and is preeminently suited to the soil of this country, and stands the winters well. He has also crossed and has introduced a valuable variety of corn and in addition has introduced a new wagon, and a new spike-tooth lever harrow. He invented and introduced a new land-roller. He introduced the first machine into Barbour for weaving wire fence.

JOHN AVIS ZINN, born in Barbour County 1848, son of David and Louisa Zinn, was married at Isaac Talbott's, on Hacker's Creek, March 20, 1872, to Mary Maneta, daughter of Isaac and Martha (Mitchell) Talbott. Children, Albert S. and Dora Belle. Mr. Zinn is a member of the Baptist Church, an Odd Fellow, a carpenter and painter, residing on the head of Hacker's Creek where he owns 50 acres of improved land. His ancestry was English, Irish and German. Mrs. Zinn was born April 17, 1855.

WILLIAM DAVIDSON ZINN, born at the old Zinn homestead west of Philippi, in 1857, son of Alpheus and Lucinda (Gawthrop) Zinn, was married at Grafton, West Virginia, October 23, 1879, to Florence, daughter of Festus Swearengen. Children, Dorrance Dana and Gay. He is a member of the Baptist Church and contributed largely to the construction of the house of worship at Mt. Olive in 1884. He is a Democrat and a farmer and stockdealer, residing on Shook's Run, where he owns 164 acres of highly improved land. He has also valuable land interests in Randolph, on which he grazes 100 cattle and 150 sheep. In his farming operations he has steadily improved on the methods formerly employed, and has become what may be called a man who farms with his head as well as with his hands. He was formerly an active worker along educational lines, and was twice elected Superintendent of the schools of Barbour County and

FAMILY HISTORY. 517

left the imprint of his labor upon them. He was, in the earlier part of his life, a teacher, who completed nineteen successful terms in Barbour and adjoining counties. In 1880 he conducted a summer normal at St. George, Tucker County; and later taught at Newburg, Preston County. He received his education in the public schools, in the West Virginia College at Flemington, and in the Fairmont Normal School. Mrs. Zinn, born in 1857, was formerly also a successful teacher in fifteen different schools. She was educated at the Presbyterian Institute at Charleston, West Virginia, and at Fairmont. Mrs. Lucinda Ann Zinn, mother of the subject of this sketch, was born near Pruntytown, Taylor County, in 1825, the daughter of James and Hulda (Waldo) Gawthrop. On January 4, 1854, she married, in Taylor County, Alpheus, son of Peter and Catherine (Chriss) Zinn. Their children were, William Davidson, Sylvanus Waldo, Luella and Claudius A. By a former marriage with a daughter of John H. Woodford, Alpheus Zinn had three children, Virginia C., Nancy E. and Rezin C. Mrs. Zinn belongs to the Baptist Church, and her father was one of the pioneers in that church in this State, preaching in Harrison, Preston, Randolph, Marion, Taylor, Ritchie and Wood counties. His great, great grandfather was Thomas Gawthrop, an Englishman who came to America and founded the family in this country.

CHARLES I. ZIRKLE, born in Barker's District in 1871, son of Jacob and Rebecca (Sluss) Zirkle, was married July 1, 1897, to Georgia, daughter of Albert G. and Rosanna J. (Jones) Wilson. Their child's name is J. Albert. He is a member of the M. E. Church, the Junior Order of United American Mechanics; in politics is Republican, and by occupation is editor of the Philippi *Republican* and commissioner in chancery of the circuit court of Barbour County. Mr. Zirkle graduated in 1894 from West Virginia Seminary at Buckhannon, and the same year was elected superintendent of the schools of Barbour and served four years. He has engaged earnestly in educational work, teaching both public and private schools in Barbour, among them being normal schools at Belington in 1895 and 1896, in connection with M. C. Lough. Mr. Zirkle became editor of the *Republican* in 1896 and has kept the paper fully up to the high standard of excellence which it has always borne. He owns a fine home in Philippi at the corner of Pike and High Streets. The first man wounded in the Civil War, in West Virginia was shot while in a stable, June 3, 1861, on the site where his residence now stands, a fuller account of which may be found elsewhere in this book.

JOHN H. ZIRKLE, born 1874 in Valley District, son of Jacob and Rebecca (Sluss) Zirkle, is junior editor of the Philippi *Republican*. He is a member of the M. E. Church, of the Junior Order of American Mechanics, and in politics is Republican. He was educated at the West Virginia Conference Seminary, at Buckhannon.

Index *to* Family Histories

ARNETT, William E. ...335
BOWMAN, Adam C. 335
    Leonard C. 339
    Stuart H. 338
BAEHM, Enoch W. 349
BARB, Stanberry 348
BARNES, George W. ...345
BARTLETT, Benjamin B. 342
    Gideon M. 342
    Hamilton C. 342
    John N. 340
    William 341
BENNETT, Charles S. .348
BIBEY, Robert M. 346
BOLYARD, Daniel 345
BOLTON, Napoleon B. .348
    William T. 348
BOOTH, Daniel 345
BOYLE, Barnett 350
    Charles W. 350
    David 350
    John I. 350
BRADFORD, Thomas A. .347
    Alexander S. ...347
BROOKS, Sylvester L. .349
BURGESS, James M. ...349
BURNER, R.B. 350
BYBER, David F. 350
CAMPBELL, George 362
CARDER, John M. 358
    Reuben B. 358
CARLIN, John G. 358
CHRISLIP, Albert G. .359
CLEAVENGER, Al 361
    Charles.........360
    James K. 360
    James W. 361

COFFMAN, James 365
COLE, John R. 359
COMPTON, E.H. 366
COONTS, Frederick M. .367
    Isaac J. 367
COONTZ, Philip 366
CORDER, Elmer J.S. ..351
    Willaim A. 356
    William B. 356
    Wilson P. 357
COX, William A. 365
CRIM, Joseph N.B. ...361
DADISMAN, Charles G. .379
    IraLee..........379
DAUGHERTY, Henry C. ..380
DAVIS, John A. 378
DAYTON, Alston G. 372
    Spencer.........367
DENNISSON, James M. ..377
DICKENSON, Georeg W. .379
DIGMAN, Jefferson D. .378
DURRETT, Francis B. ..378
DYER, Edmund R. 378
ELLIOTT, Guy C. 381
    Luther C. 381
    Truman T. 381
EKIS, Josiah 382
ELBON, William A. 382
FELTON, John C. 382
    Samuel D. 382
FOREMAN, Naylor 385
FRIDLEY, Isaac 385
GAINER, John W. 389
GALL, Andrew J. 387
    David W. 385
GAWTHROP, James W. ...387
GRAHAM, Grant 388

Index *to* Family Histories

GEORGE, William T. ...388	William K. 408
GOODE, John M. 388	**JENNINGS**, Mathis 410
GODWIN, Robert S. ...389	**JOHNSON**, I.V. 406
HALL, James E. 398	Joseh L. 407
Marion F. 398	Levi 408
HALLER, George E. 405	Mortimer C. 408
HAMILTON, Adolphus ...402	Richard M. 408
HAMRICK, David P. ...391	**JONES**, Albert W. 410
Graham H. 389	John L.B. 410
Joseph N. 391	**KELLEY**, Columbus 411
HARRIS, Georg A. 400	James L. 411
HASKINS, Ryland G. ...402	**KERR**, Adam 415
HATHAWAY, John P. 400	**KITTLE**, Warren B. 411
HAWKINS, A.F. 398	**KNAPP**, Jacob H. 415
Thomas 398	**KNIGHT**, Benjamin J. ..416
HEATHERLY, James E. .399	**KNOTTS**, James 415
HEWITT, John F. 402	**LANG**, David B. 416
HOFF, Hanson L. 392	William S. 420
Hartzell E. 392	**LANTZ**, William H. 425
Manzell, M. 392	Willis.........422
Orlando P. 395	**LAW**, Thomas A. 425
HOFFMAN, John I. 400	**LOUGH**, Myron C. 420
HOLDEN, Floyd T. 401	**MAIN**, Sabeus 429
HOLSEBERRY, Family ..396	**MANN**, John C. 429
James K. 397	**MARKS**, Orestes T. 431
John D. 397	**MARTIN**, Isaac D. 427
Leroy V. 397	**MASON**, John F. 431
HOVEY, James M. 399	Sanford.........430
HOWELL, Grant T. 395	Thomas B. 430
John 395	**McKINNEY**, George 428
R.B. Hayes 396	**McLEAN**, Jacob 427
HYMES, Gilbert S. ...401	**MEANS**, Jonathan E. ...428
ICE, Martin 406	**MILLER**, Andrew 426
William T. 405	Andrew K. 427
ISNER, James T. 406	John 426
JACKSON, Robrt E. 411	**MONTGOMERY**, Susan 429
JENKINS, Henry M. 408	**MOORE**, Samuel A. 430

Index *to* Family Histories

MORRALL, Lair D. 428
MURPHY, Benjamin F. .425
    Thomas J. 425
O'NEAL, Salathiel ...431
PARKS, Noah S. 440
PAYNE, Charles E. 442
PECK, Melville 431
PEPPER, Samuel D. 441
PHILLIPS, Granville ..436
    James M. 436
    John R. 435
    Samuel E. 436
    Washington 436
PITTS, William A. ...449
POLING, Family 437
    Aldine S. 438
    Columbus H. 440
    Cyrus 437
    James S. 439
    Ira C. 439
    Isaac 437
    Isaac M. 438
    Loman S. 439
    Rachel H. 439
    Riley D. 440
    Wade 438
PRICE, William G. ...441
PROUDFOOT, Alexander 445
    Delbert M. 445
    Elias..........445
    James 445
    James R. 442
    John 442,445
    John H. 445
    Mary 442
    Thomas.........445
    William........445

RACER, M.D. 455
REED, Ira L. 450
    Milton D. 448
    Stuart F. 449
RIGHT, George M. 455
RILEY, Mordecai D. ...455
ROBINSON, Family 446
    Elizabeth 446
    Jacob W. 448
    James..........447
    Jane 447
    Job 446
    John..........446
    Lloyd D. 448
    Mary..........447
    William.....446,447
ROHRBAUGH, Amos F. ...456
    Burton B. 456
    Clark L. 456
ROSENBERGER, Henry C. 456
RYAN, Henry H. 452
    John..........452
SEMMELMAN, Samuel L. .470
SHANK, Jacob 469
    John W. 469
SHAW, David W. 456
    John C. 457
SHOMO, Charles W. 473
SHROYER, John W. 470
SIMON, Andrew 469
SMITH, Bessheba M. ...473
SNODGRASS, Charles W. 468
STADER, Aaron 470
STALNAKER, Garretson 462
    Harrison........461
    Wade P. 462
    William.........461

Index *to* Family Histories

William W. 458
STEWART, Alexander . . . 464
    J.E. 462
STRAWDERMAN, Elizabeth
    464
    Samuel G. 464
STRICKLER, Arthur D. . 467
    Isaac H. 467
STRIPE, Charles R. . . . 464
STRUM, David 458
    Henry 458
    Isaac 458
    Jacob W. 458
SWITZER, Charles K. . . 462
    463
    Philip A. 463
TAFT, Granville E. . . . 482
    Nathan H. 481
TALBOTT, Columbus 479
    Isaac D. 475
    James W. 476
    Richard. 473
    Richard E. 476
    Robert M. 475
    Simon S. 475
    Sylvanus H. 476
    Willaim W. 475
TETER, Charles F. 481
    Gordon B. 480
    Jacob. 479
    Joseph. 480
    Thomas B 481
THACKER, Jacob S. 485
THOMPSON, Hezekiah . . . 486
    James L. 486
    John P. 485
TRIMBLE, Henry 485

TURNER, Hugh 482
UMBACH, Augusta 486
UTTERBACH, George . . . 487
WARD, Daniel B. 413
WARE, Abraham 512
    J. Blackburn . . . 513
WATRING, Fancis M. . . . 514
WENTZ, William H. . . . 499
WILLIAMSON, James A. . 512
    John R. 512
WILLOUGHBY, John C. . . 514
WILSON, John 512
    Lewis 508
    Solomon T. 511
WINANS, Simon 513
WINCE, Jasper 514
WOLVERTON, Alba 513
WOODFORD, Asa W. 503
    Benjamin H. 505
    Columbia A. 508
    David R. 507
    George C. 508
    Isaac C. 507
    James M. 507
    John F. 506
    John H. 500
    William. 500
WOODS, John H. 498
    Samuel. 487
    Samuel V. 499
YOUNG, Mary C. 515
YOWELL, Franklin J. . 514
ZINN, Agustus J. 515
    John A. 516
    William D. 516
    William H. 516
ZIRKLE, Charles I. . . 517
    John H. 517

www.ingramcontent.com/pod-product-compliance
Lightning Source LLC
Chambersburg PA
CBHW030224100526
44585CB00012BA/188